GH00724669

INTERNATIONAL CORRUPTION

CORKER BINNING SOLICITORS
12 DEVEREUX COURT
STRAND
LONDON
WC2R 3JJ

INTERNATIONAL CORRUPTION

PAUL COHEN

ARTHUR MARRIOTT QC

SWEET & MAXWELL

 THOMSON REUTERS

Published in 2010 by Thomson Reuters (Legal) Limited
(Registered in England & Wales, Company No 1679046.
Registered Office and address for trading: 100 Avenue Road,
London, NW3 3PF) trading as Sweet & Maxwell

For further information on our products and services, visit:
http://www.sweetandmaxwell.co.uk

Typeset by YHT Ltd, London
Printed and bound in Great Britain by CPI Antony Rowe,
Chippenham and Eastbourne.

No natural forests were destroyed to make this product;
only farmed timber was used and replanted

British Library Cataloguing in Publication Data

A CIP catalogue record for this book
is available from the British Library

ISBN 978-0-41404-172-1

GENERAL EDITORS

PAUL COHEN

ARTHUR MARRIOTT QC

CONTRIBUTORS

Chapter 1
Peter Burrell, Herbert Smith LLP
Susannah Cogman, Herbert Smith LLP
Paul Cohen

Chapter 2
Paul Cohen
Arthur Marriott QC

Chapter 3
Mark Radke, Arent Fox LLP
Angela Papalaskaris, Dewey & LeBoeuf LLP
Paul Cohen

Chapter 4
Barry O'Keefe QC

Chapter 5
Fabiano Robalinho Cavalcanti, Escritorio de Advocacia Sergio Bermudes

Chapter 6
Bertrand de Speville

Chapter 7
Pallavi Shroff, Amarchand & Mangaldas & Suresh A Shroff & Co
Nisha Harichandran
Nishant Joshi

Chapter 8
Angela Papalaskaris, Dewey & LeBoeuf LLP
Paul Cohen
Mark Radke, Arent Fox LLP

Chapter 9
Robert Wilson, PricewaterhouseCoopers LLP
Fred Miller, PricewaterhouseCoopers LLP
Will Kenyon, PricewaterhouseCoopers LLP

Chapter 10
Mark Radke, Arent Fox LLP
Paul Cohen
Angela Papalaskaris, Dewey & LeBoeuf LLP

Chapter 11
John Tracey, PricewaterhouseCoopers LLP
Tracey Groves, PricewaterhouseCoopers LLP

CONTENTS

Table of Cases   xv
Table of Legislation   xix

Introduction   xxvii

Chapter 1: UK Anti-Corruption Law

A. The current state of anti-corruption law in the UK   1–01
B. Pre-existing bribery law in the UK   1–03
    I.   Common law   1–04
    II.   Public Bodies Corrupt Practices Act 1889   1–06
    III. Prevention of Corruption Act 1906   1–12
    IV.   Prevention of Corruption Act 1916   1–18
    V.   Anti-Terrorism, Crime and Security Act 2001   1–20
C. Corporate criminal liability   1–26
D. Money laundering   1–27
E. Confiscation, civil recovery and procurement   1–30
    I.   Confiscation   1–31
    II.   Civil recovery   1–32
    III. Procurement   1–34
F. The UK's accession to the OECD Anti-bribery Convention   1–35
G. The Bribery Act   1–37
    I.   Liability of parent company for acts of subsidiary   1–39
    II.   Other provisions   1–40
H. The Serious Fraud Office   1–41
    I.   Aims and criteria for acceptance of cases   1–43
    II.   Section 2 powers   1–44
    III. City of London Police Overseas Anti-Corruption unit   1–46
    IV.   Mutual legal assistance   1–47
I. Noteworthy investigations and actions
    I.   Mabey & Johnson   1–49
    II.   BAE Systems & Al-Yamamah   1–51
J. The "Americanisation" of UK anti-corruption efforts
    I.   Increased use of plea agreements   1–72
    II.   Non-prosecution agreements & deferred prosecution
          agreements   1–73
    III. Increased resources and personnel for overseas corruption 1–74

Chapter 2: The OECD Anti-Bribery Convention

A. Introduction   2–01
B. History of the OECD   2–02
C. The OECD's purpose   2–03
D. The OECD's structure   2–04
E. Membership in the OECD   2–05
F. Functions of the OECD   2–07
G. History of the Anti-Bribery Convention   2–08
H. The Anti-Bribery Convention   2–13
     I. Applicability   2–18
     II. Jurisdiction   2–19
     III. Enforcement   2–20
     IV. Limitations   2–21
     V. International cooperation   2–22
I. The implementation process   2–24
J. The working group's mandate   2–25
     I. Phase I   2–26
     II. Phase II   2–27
K. Difficulties in implementation   2–28
     I. Argentina   2–31
     II. Chile   2–32
     III. Ireland   2–33
     IV. Japan   2–35
     V. Luxembourg   2–37
     VI. Spain   2–38
     VII. Turkey   2–39
     VIII. The United Kingdom   2–41

Chapter 3: The US Foreign Corrupt Practices Act

A. Introduction   3–01
     I. History of Legislation   3–05
B. Anti-bribery provisions
     I. Provisions   3–12
     II. Jurisdiction   3–13
     III. Interstate instrumentality   3–16
     IV. Corruptly   3–17
     V. Payment or anything of value   3–22
     VI. Foreign official   3–23
     VII. Knowledge standard   3–26
     VIII. Purpose—to obtain business or secure an improper advantage   3–27
     IX. Penalties   3–29
C. Exceptions and affirmative defences
     I. Exception: routine governmental action or facilitating
          payments   3–30

II. Affirmative defence: payments authorised by foreign country's
     written laws   3–33
III. Affirmative defence: reasonable or bona fide expenditure   3–35
D. Record-keeping and accounting provisions
     I.   Provisions   3–36
     II.   Jurisdiction   3–37
     III. Subsidiaries   3–38
     IV.   Payments   3–39
     V.   Books and records provision   3–40
     VI.   Falsification of books and records   3–41
     VII. Internal accounting controls provision   3–42
     VIII. Sanctions   3–43
E. Enforcement   3–44
     I.   DOJ   3–45
     II.   SEC   3–46
     III. General enforcement   3–47
     IV.   DOJ opinion procedure   3–49
     V.   Statute of limitations   3–52

Chapter 4: Dealing with International Corruption—Australia

A. The OECD Convention   4–01
B. The offence of bribing a foreign public official   4–02
C. Defences to the offence of bribing a foreign public official   4–05
     I.   Defence where the conduct is lawful in the foreign public
           official's country   4–06
     II.   Defence relating to facilitation payments   4–07
D. Territorial and nationality requirements   4–10
E. Prosecution   4–11
F. Penalties   4–12
G. Jurisdiction and international cooperation   4–15
H. Enforcement activities   4–16
     I.   Australian federal police   4–17
     II.   Other enforcing entities   4–19
     III. Whistleblowing   4–20
I. Noteworthy investigations   4–21
J. Australian wheat board oil-for-food programme
     I.   Background   4–22
     II.   Investigation and findings   4–24
K. Alkaloids of Australia Pty Limited   4–27
L. Rhine Ruhr Pty Limited   4–29
M. Rio Tinto Limited   4–30
N. United Nations Convention Against Corruption   4–32
O. Summary   4–34

Chapter 5: Brazil's Anti-Corruption Laws

A. Introduction   5–01
B. Current anti-corruption legislation
   I.   The 1988 Constitution   5–04
   II.   The 1992 Law of Administrative Probity   5–06
C. Negligence or willful misconduct   5–13
D. Burden of proof   5–14
E. Sanctions under law 8.492   5–15
F. Seizure, freezing of assets and other provisional remedies   5–18
G. Anti-corruption provisions under the penal code   5–22
H. Definition of public official by the Brazilian penal code   5–23
I. Embezzlement   5–25
J. Passive corruption   5–27
K. The furthering of private interests by a public official   5–30
L. Acts of corruption practiced by private parties
   I.   Active corruption   5–32
   II.   International Anti-Corruption Conventions adopted by Brazil   5–34
M. The enforcement of the conventions in Brazil   5–40
N. Bribery of foreign public officials in international commercial transactions
   I.   Definition of a foreign public official   5–41
   II.   Active corruption in international commercial transactions   5–42
   III.   Influence peddling in international commercial transactions   5–45
O. Deficiencies in the application in Brazil of anti-corruption conventions   5–48
P. The criminal liability of Brazilian companies   5–50
Q. Forthcoming legislation   5–53
R. Conclusion—Enforcement of the anti-corruption statutory provisions   5–55

Chapter 6: Hong Kong's Anti-Corruption Laws

A. Background   6–01
B. The statutory offences   6–05
C. The common law offence of misconduct in public office   6–10
D. Investigative powers enhanced   6–11
E. Interception of communications and surveillance   6–16
F. Procedural and evidential provisions enhanced to improve prospects of successful prosecution   6–17
G. Protection of informants and witnesses enhanced   6–22
H. Powers of sentencing and confiscation and consequences of conviction   6–26
I. Enforcement in practice   6–29
J. Investigating procedure (from report to disposal)   6–34
K. Relations with other agencies and the private sector   6–37

L. Investigative cooperation and mutual legal assistance   6–39
M. Results   6–40

Chapter 7: The Current State of Anti-Corruption Law in India

A. Introduction
    I.   Corruption in India   7–01
    II.   Legislative history & background   7–02
B. Anti-Corruption laws
    I.   The Prevention of Corruption Act 1988   7–05
    II.   Indian Penal Code 1860   7–13
C. Extra-territoriality reach
    I.   PCA   7–14
    II.   IPC   7–15
D. International conventions   7–16
    I.   Potential amendments to corruption laws pending ratification
        of the UN Convention Against Corruption ("UNCAC")   7–17
    II.   Prevention of Money Laundering Act 2002   7–18
    III.   Right to Information Act 2005   7–20
    IV.   The Representation of the People Act 1951   7–22
    V.   Subordinate legislation/Service rules   7–23
E. Public procurement   7–24
    I.   Liability of private individuals   7–25
    II.   Liability of foreign public officials   7–26
F. Institutional framework   7–27
    I.   Central Vigilance Commission   7–28
    II.   Central Bureau of Investigation   7–30
    III.   The office of the comptroller and auditor general   7–31
    IV.   Chief information commission   7–32
    V.   Serious fraud investigation office   7–33
    VI.   CVC   7–35
G. Corruption scandals
    I.   VK Krishna Menon scandal   7–38
    II.   1957 LIC-Mundra deals   7–39
    III.   Bofors scandal   7–40
    IV.   Jharkhand Mukti Morcha MP's   7–41
    V.   Judiciary scandals   7–42
    VI.   Other major sandals   7–43
H. Conclusion   7–44

Chapter 8: Conducting Internal Investigations in Connection With Allegations of Bribery

A. Introduction   8–01
B. The regulators
    I.   United States   8–02

II.	United Kingdom Serious Fraud Office	8–05
III.	Australian federal police	8–06
C.	Internal investigations	8–07
I.	Practical implications of the regulators powers	8–08
II.	Cooperation with regulatory investigations	8–10
III.	Impediments to the investigation of international corruption	8–16
D.	Internal investigations	
I.	Generally	8–34
II.	Employees and witnesses	8–43
III.	Documents and information	8–55
IV.	Coordinating responses to multi-jurisdictional investigations	8–64
V.	What may happen once the government obtains an ultimate finding	8–67

Chapter 9: Forensic and Accounting Issues Associated with International Corruption Enquiries

A.	Introduction	9–01
B.	Planning, scoping and orientation	9–04
I.	Who is at risk?	9–08
II.	Typical high risk activities	9–10
C.	Data collection and preservation	
I.	Context and focus	9–11
II.	Paper and documentary evidence	9–13
III.	Electronic data and media	9–15
VI.	Witness evidence	9–18
D.	Data protection and privacy law considerations	
I.	Data protection	9–21
II.	Further privacy considerations	9–22
E.	Field work—detecting corrupt payments in books and records	9–23
I.	Witnesses, whistleblowers, allegations	9–25
II.	Methods and techniques for detecting corrupt payments	9–27
III.	Data analytics	9–33
IV.	Corporate intelligence—Conflicts of interest	9–36
F.	Investigating agent and third party payments	9–38
G.	Follow-up and verification	9–39
H.	Reporting	9–40

Chapter 10: Anti-Corruption Considerations in International Mergers And Acquisitions

A.	Introduction	10–01
B.	Case studies	
I.	Titan	10–06
II.	Syncor	10–08

III. InVision 10–09
IV. Vetco Gray 10–10
V. Halliburton 10–12
VI. Monsanto 10–14
VII. El Paso 10–15
VIII. Opinion release 08-02 10–16
C. Best practices
I. Comprehensive due diligence/protective contractual
   provisions/FCPA compliance program integration 10–18
II. Comprehensive due diligence 10–20
III. Contractual protections 10–29
IV. Compliance programme integration 10–31
V. Conclusion 10–32

Chapter 11: Effective Anti-Corruption Programmes

A. Introduction 11–01
B. Why do organisations need an effective anti-corruption
   programme? 11–02
I. Ensuring the company, its directors and employees are
   compliant with the law in the jurisdictions that it operates in 11–03
II. Retaining market and stakeholder credibility around ethical
   business practices and protecting shareholder value 11–04
III. Providing a defence or mitigating evidence should it be
   determined that corruption has occurred 11–05
IV. Doing business globally 11–07
C. What does an effective anti-corruption compliance programme
   look like? 11–08
I. Existing guidance 11–09
II. An effective framework 11–10
D. How to design an effective anti-corruption compliance programme 11–13
I. Investigation 11–14
II. Framework/risk assessment 11–15
III. Gap analysis and reporting 11–16
IV. Design and development of framework 11–17
V. Remediation 11–28
E. Implementation of an effective anti-corruption compliance
   programme 11–29
I. Leadership 11–30
II. Adequate resource 11–31
III. Effective project planning 11–32
IV. Training and communications 11–33
F. Why do some anti-corruption programmes succeed while others
   fail? 11–38
G. Conclusion 11–39

Appendix A: Transparency International's Corruption Perceptions Index measures the perceived level of public sector corruption as seen by business people and country analysts; ranging between 10 (highly clean) and 0 (highly corrupt)

Appendix B: Bribery Act 2010

Appendix C: Convention on Combating Bribery of Foreign Public Officials in International Business Transactions

Appendix D: Anti-Bribery and Books & Records Provisions of The Foreign Corrupt Practices Act

Appendix E: Foreign Corrupt Practices Act Review Opinion Procedure Release 2004

Appendix F: Foreign Corrupt Practices Act Review Opinion Procedure Release 2008

Index   *p.421*

TABLE OF CASES

Australia
Macleod v Attorney General of New South Wales [1891] A.C. 455 PC (Aus) 4–08
R. v Tange, 1993, CA (Queensland) 4–04

Brazil
REsp 300184, November 3, 2003 5–16
REsp 505068/PR, November 29, 2003 5–16
REsp 507.574, February 2, 2006 5–16
REsp 626.034, June 5, 2006 5–13
REsp 880.662, March 1, 2007 5–14
REsp 842.428, May 21, 2007 5–13
REsp 885.836, June 26, 2007 5–16
REsp 751.364, August 2, 2007 5–13
REsp 401.437/SP, October 16, 2007 5–09
REsp 892818/RS, November 11, 2008 5–11
REsp 1038762/RJ, August 18, 2009 5–10
RMS 6.182, December 1, 1997 5–20
RMS 6.197, May 18, 1998 5–20

Hong Kong
Attorney General v Hui Kin Hong [1995] 1 HKCLR 227 6–07
R. v Ming Pao Newspapers Ltd [1995] 5 HKPLR 13 6–23
Shum Kwok Sher v HKSAR [2002] 5 HKCFAR 381 6–10

India
Andhra Pradesh, State of v C Uma Maheswara Rao (2004) 4 SCC 399 7–07,
 7–09, 7–10
Attorney General of India v Amratlal Prajivandas (1994) 5 SCC 54 7–04
B Hanumantha Rao v State of Andhra Pradesh, AIR 1992 SC 1201 7–09
CI Emden v State of Uttar Pradesh, AIR 1960 SC 548 7–09
Delhi Development Authority v Skipper Construction Co (P) Ltd, AIR 1996 SC
 2005 7–04
Dhanvantrai Balwantrai Desai v State of Maharashtra, AIR 1964 SC 575 7–09
Dinesh Trivedi v Union of India (1997) 4 SCC 306 7–04
Dr Subramanian Swamy v Director, CBI (2005) 2 SCC 317 7–36
Indra Sawhney v Union of India, AIR 1993 SC 477 7–02
Judicial Accountability v Union of India (1991) 4 SCC 699 7–42
Kartongen Kemi Och Forvaltning AB v State through CBI, 2004 (72) DRJ 693 .. 7–40
Kesavananda Bharati v State of Kerala, AIR 1973 SC 1461 7–03

Kumar Agrawal v State of Karnataka [1999] 1 Kar.L.J. 603 HC (Karnataka) 7–14
Kumari Shrilekha Vidyarthi v State of U.P. (1991) 1 SCC 212 7–24
Mohmoodkhan Mahboodkhan Pathan v State of Maharashtra (1997) 10 SCC 600   7–07
Pareena Swarup v Union of India (UOI), 2008 (13) SCALE 84 7–19
State of Madhya Pradesh v Shri Ram Singh (2000) 5 SCC 88 .... 7–05, 7–07
Union of India (UOI) v Prakash P. Hinduja (2003) 6 SCC 195 7–40
VD Jhangan v State of Uttar Pradesh, AIR 1966 SC 1762. 7–09
Vineet Narain v Union of India (1998) 1 SCC 226 SC 7–03, 7–28, 7–35

South Africa
S v Deal Enterprises (Pty) Ltd (South Africa) 1–04

United Kingdom
Air India v Wiggins [1980] 1 W.L.R. 815; [1980] 2 All E.R. 593; (1980) 71 Cr. App.
    R. 213; (1980) 124 S.J. 478 HL 1–21
Cooper v Slade, 10 E.R. 1488; (1858) 6 H.L. Cas. 746HL 1–10
DPP v Manners; R. v Holly; DPP v Holly (Michael Francis) [1978] A.C. 43; [1977]
    2 W.L.R. 178; [1977] 1 All E.R. 316; (1977) 64 Cr. App. R. 143; [1977] Crim.
    L.R. 289; (1977) 121 S.J. 103 HL 1–09
Fisher v Oldham Corp [1930] 2 K.B. 364 KBD 1–12
Graham v Hart, 1908 S.C. (J.) 26; (1908) 15 S.L.T. 749 HCJ 1–12
Hawkins v Powells Tillery Steam Coal Co Ltd [1911] 1 K.B. 988 CA 7–09
Mabey & Johnson Ltd 1–31
Neel Uberoi, December 10, 2009 1–31
R. v Barrett [1976] 1 W.L.R. 946; [1976] 3 All E.R. 895; (1976) 63 Cr. App. R. 174;
    [1976] Crim. L.R. 576; (1976) 120 S.J. 402 CA (Crim Div) 1–12
R. v Bodmin, (1869) 1 O'M. & H. 121 1–04
R. v Carr-Briant [1943] K.B. 607; (1944) 29 Cr. App. R. 76 CCA 1–18
R. v Gurney (1867) 10 Cox C.C. 550 1–04
R. v Harrison (1800) 1 East P.C. 382 1–04
R. v Innospec Ltd, March 26, 2010 .... 1–50, 1–64
R. v Natji [2002] EWCA Crim 271; [2002] 1 W.L.R. 2337; [2002] 2 Cr. App. R. 20;
    [2002] Crim. L.R. 580; (2002) 99(14) L.S.G. 25; (2002) 146 S.J.L.B. 63 1–09
R. v Pitt and Mead, (1762) 3 Burr. 1335, 97 E.R. 861 1–04
R. v Smith [1960] 2 Q.B. 423; [1960] 2 W.L.R. 164; [1960] 1 All E.R. 256; (1960) 44
    Cr. App. R. 55; (1960) 124 J.P. 137 CCA 1–10
R. v Tweedie [1984] Q.B. 729; [1984] 2 W.L.R. 608; [1984] 2 All E.R. 136; (1984) 79
    Cr. App. R. 168; (1984) 148 J.P. 716; [1984] Crim. L.R. 231; (1984) 81 L.S.G.
    657; (1984) 128 S.J. 262 CA (Crim Div) 1–15
R. v Vaughan 98 E.R. 308; (1769) 4 Burr. 2429 1–04
R. v Wellburn; R. v Nurdin; R. v Randel (1979) 69 Cr. App. R. 254; (1979) 1 Cr.
    App. R. (S.) 64 CA (Crim Div) 1–10, 1–12
R. v Whitaker, [1914] 3 K.B. 1283 1–04
R. v William Asseling, *The Times*, September 10, 1916 1–19
R. v Worrall (1890) 16 Cox C.C. 737 1–04
R. (on the application of Bermingham) v Director of the Serious Fraud Office;
    Bermingham v United States of America [2006] EWHC 200 (Admin); [2007]
    Q.B. 727; [2007] 2 W.L.R. 635; [2006] 3 All E.R. 239; [2006] U.K.H.R.R. 450;
    [2006] Extradition L.R. 52; [2006] A.C.D. 55 1–55
R. (on the application of Corner House Research) v Director of the Serious Fraud
    Office [2008] UKHL 60; [2009] 1 A.C. 756; [2008] 3 W.L.R. 568; [2008] 4 All
    E.R. 927; [2008] Lloyd's Rep. F.C. 537 .... 1–51, 1–52, 1–55, 1–56
Sage v Eicholz [1919] 2 K.B. 171 KBD 1–15

Sharma v Brown-Antoine [2006] UKPC 57; [2007] 1 W.L.R. 780 PC (Trin) 1–55
Treacy v DPP; sub nom. R. v Treacy (Eugene Anthony) [1971] A.C. 537; [1971] 2
  W.L.R. 112; [1971] 1 All E.R. 110; (1971) 55 Cr. App. R. 113; (1971) 115 S.J.
  12 HL 1–21

United States
Arthur Andersen LLP v US, 544 US 696 (2005) 8–70
Bryan v US, 524 U.S. 184 at 191–92 (1998) 3–19, 3–20
Columbia/HCA Healthcare, Re, 293 F.3d 289 (6th Cir. 2002) 8–63
Daniel Reeves, Dec. of, UBS AG, No.09-20423 (S.D. Fla.) 8–23, 8–24, 8–25
Dixson v United States, 465 U.S. 482 (1984) 3–24
Fujitsu Ltd v Federal Express Corp, 247 F.3d 423 at 436 (2d Cir. 2001) 8–56
Glazer Capital Management, LP v Sergio Magistri, 2008 LEXIS 24245 1 10–30
Grand Jury Subpoena: UNDER SEAL, Re, 415 F.3d 333 (4th Cir. 2005) 8–45,
                                                                        8–46, 8–54
Gregory v Helvering, 293 U.S. 465 (1935) 8–24
Kozeny, 493 F. Supp. 2d at 704 3–21
McKesson HBOC Inc v Superior Court, 9 Cal. Rptr. 3d 812 (Cal. App. 1 Dist.
  2004) 8–63
Miranda v Arizona, 384 U.S. 436 (1966) SC 8–45
Natural Gas Commodity Litig., 03 Civ 6186, 2005 U.S. Dist. LEXIS 11950, at *22-
  33 (S.D.N.Y. June 25, 2005) 8–63
Remington Products Inc v North American Philips Corp, 107 F.R.D. 642 (D. Conn.
  1985) 8–33
Richmark Corp v Timber Falling Consultants, 959 F.2d 1468 (9th Cir. 1992) 8–32,
                                                                                  8–33
Rio Algom, 480 F. Supp. 1138 .... 8–30, 8–32, 8–33
Royal Ahold NV Sec. & ERISA Litig., Re, 230 F.R.D. 433 (D. Md. 2005) 8–63
Saito v McKesson HBOC Inc Civ. A. No.18553, 2002 Del. Ch. LEXIS 125 (Del.
  Ch. October 25, 2002) 8–63
Schnitzer Steel Industries Inc, Re, Exchange Release No.54606 (October 16, 2006)   3–23
SEC v ABB Ltd, 1:04CV1141 (RBN), Litigation Rel. No.18775 (D.D.C. July 6,
  2004) 3–23
SEC v ABB Ltd, No.04-CV-01141 (DDC July 6, 2004) 10–10
SEC v Delta & Pine Land Co SEC Lit. Ref. No.20214 (July 26, 2007) 10–14
SEC v El Paso Corpm Lit. Ref. No.19991 (February 7, 2007) 10–15
SEC v Halliburton Co and KBR, Inc, No.4:09-CV-399, (S.D. Tex. (Houston)
  February 11, 2009) 10–12
SEC v Lucent Technology Inc No.1:07-CV-02301 (D.D.C. December 21, 2007) .   3–22,
                                                                                  3–35
SEC v Morgan Stanley Co Inc No.06 Civ. 0882 (D.D.C. May 10, 2006) 8–56
SEC v Syncor International Corp, 1:02CV02421, Litigation Rel. No.17887 (D.D.C.
  December 10, 2002) 3–23
SEC v Titan Corp, No.05–0411 (JR), 2005 WL 516541 (DDC March 30, 2005)   10–07,
                                                                                  10–30
Societe Internationale v Rogers, 357 U.S. 8–33
Societe Internationale Pour Participations Industrielles Et Commerciales v Rogers,
  357 U.S. 197 (1958) 8–30
Societe Nationale Industrielle Aerospatiale v District Court, 482 U.S. 522 (1987)   8–31
State v 7040 Colonial Rd Assocs. Co, 671 N.Y.S. 2d 938 8–08
Stichting Ter Behartiging Van De Belangen Van Oudaandeelhouders In Het
  Kapitaal Van Saybolt International BV v Schreiber, et al., 327 F.3d 173 (2d.
  Cir.2003) 3–18, 3–19

Strauss v Credit Lyonnais, 242 F.R.D. 199 (E.D.N.Y. 2007) 8–31
United Kingdom v United States, 238 F.3d 1312 (11th Cir. 2001) 8–20, 8–21
United States v Arthur Andersen, LLP, 374 F.3d 281 (5th Cir. 2004) SC 8–70
United States v Brewster, 506 F.2d 62 (DC Cir. 1974) 3–17
United States v Castle, 925 F.2d 831 (5th Cir. 1991) 3–25
United States v Evans, 572 F.2d 455 (5th Cir. 1978) 3–17
United States v Hang, 75 F.3d 1275 at 1280 (8th Cir.1996) 3–24
United States v Harry G. Carpenter and WS Kirkpatrick Inc. (Cr. No.85-353),
   D.N.J., 1985 3–16
United States v Kay, 359 F.3rd 738 (5th Cir. 2004) 3–27, 3–30
United States v Kay, 2007 WL 3088140 at *8 (5th Cir. 2007) (Kay 2007) 3–19, 3–20
United States v Kay, 2008 U.S. App. LEXIS 1047, at *7 (5th Cir. January 10, 2008)
   (Kay 2008) 3–18, 3–21
United States v Kenney, 185 F.3d 1217 (11th Cir. 1999) 3–24
United States v Kenny International Corp (Cr. No.79-372), D.D.C., 1979 3–16
United States v Kozeny, 493 F. Supp. 2d 693 (S.D.N.Y. 2007) 3–18
United States v Kozeny, 582 F. Supp. 2d 535 (S.D.N.Y. 2008) 3–33
United States v Liebo, 923 F.2d 1308 (8th Cir. 1991) 3–18, 3–20
United States v McLean, 738 F.2d 655 (5th Cir. 1984) 3–09
United States v Madeoy, 912 F.2d 1486 (D.C. Cir. 1990), cert. denied, 498 U.S.
   1105 (1991) 3–24
United States v Philip Morris USA Inc 327 F. Supp. 2d 21 (D.D.C. 2004) 8–56
United States v Sam P. Wallace Company Inc. (Cr. No.83-0034) (PG), D.P.R.,
   1983 3–16
United States v Scrushy, 366 F.Supp. 2d 1134 8–08
United States v Stein, 541 F.3d 130 at 155-156 (2d. Cir. 2008) 8–12
United States v Strand, 574 F.2d 993 (9th Cir. 1978) 3–17
United States v Stringer, 408 F.Supp. 2d 1083 8–08
United States v Stringer, 535 F.3d 929 (9th Cir. 2008) 8–08
United States v UBS AG, No.09-20423 (S.D. Fla. 2009) 8–23
United States v Vitusa Corp, 3 FCPA Rep. 699.155 (D.N.J. 1994) 3–31
Upjohn Co v US, 449 US 383 8–75
Upjohn v US, 449 U.S. 383 (1981) SC 8–45
Westinghouse Electric Corp Uranium Contracts Litig., Re 563 F.2d 992 at 996
   (10th Cir. 1977) 8–33
Westinghouse Electric Corp v Rio Algom Ltd, 480 F. Supp. 1138 at 1143 (N.D. Ill.
   1979) 8–30
Zubulake v UBS Warburg LLC, 220 F.R.D. 212 at 216 (S.D.N.Y. 2003) 8–56, 8–57

TABLE OF LEGISLATION

Australia

Commonwealth Constitution

s.109 4–09

1901 Acts Interpretation Act

§§ 22(1)(a)—(aa) 4–02

1918 Electoral Act 4–33

1936 Income Tax Assessment Act

§ 16 4–26

1958 Customs (Prohibited Exports)

Regulations 4–26

1959 Banking (Foreign Exchange)

Regulations 4–26

1982 Freedom of Information

Act 4–33

1986 Australia Act

§ 2 4–08

1987 Mutual Assistance in Crim-

inal Matters Act 4–15, 4–33

§ 8 4–15

§ 74 4–15

Proceeds of Crime Act 4–33

§ 4 4–14

§ 9A 4–14

(2)(a)—(e) 4–14

§ 10 4–14

§ 19 4–14

1988 Extradition Act 4–15

Independent Commission

Against Corruption Act . 4–19,
4–20

§ 8(2)(b) 4–18

§ 13(1)(a) 4–18

1999 Extradition (Bribery of For-

eign Public Official)

Regulations 4–15

1995 Criminal Code Act 4–01,
4–02, 4–03, 4–05—4–09,
4–12, 4–15, 4–24, 4–33

Pt 2.3 4–05

§§ 7.1—10.5 4–05

§§ 12.1—12.6 4–02

§§ 12.2—12.3(1) 4–02

§ 12.3(2) 4–02

§ 13.3(3) 4–06

(6) 4–06

Div 70 .... 4.01, 4–03, 4–04, 4–25

§ 70.2 .... 4–02, 4–06, 4–10,
4–11, 4–25, 4–30, 4–31

(1)(a) 4–02, 4–24

(a)—(c) 4–02

(b) 4–24

(c) 4–03, 4–25

(i) 4–02

(ii) 4–02

(1A) 4–03

(2) 4–03

(2)—(3) 4–24

(3) 4–03

(4) 4–12

(5) 4–13

§ 70.3 .... 4–05, 4–06, 4–25

§ 70.4 .... 4–05, 4–07, 4–08

(1)(a)—(b) 4–07

(c) 4–07

(d) 4–07

(2)(a)—(b) 4–07

(c)—(d) 4–07

(3) 4–07

§ 70.5 4–15

(1) 4–10

(2) 4–11

(3) 4–11

1997 Financial Management and

Accountability Act 4–33

Income Tax Assessment

Act 4–07

§ 26.52 4–07

1999 Mutual Assistance in Business

Regulation Act 4–15

Public Service Act 4–33
2001 Corporations Act 4–12, 4–19,
                         4–20, 4–26, 4–33
§ 206B 4–12
(1) 4–13
(2) 4–12
§ 915B 4–12
2007 International Trade Integrity
     Act 4–06, 4–21, 4–26
Sch.2 4–06

Azerbaijan
Criminal Code 3–33

Brazil
Civil Procedure Code
art.88 5–10
art.89 5–10
art.201 5–21
Code of Criminal Procedure 5–06
1824 Political Constitution of the
     Empire of Brazil 5–01
art.130 .... **5–01**
art.131 .... **5–01**
art.132 .... **5–01**
art.133 .... **5–01**
1890 Penal Code
art.214 5–01
1891 Constitution of the Republic
     of the United States of
     Brazil 5–01
art.54 .... **5–01**
1934 Constitution 5–01
art.57 5–01
1937 Constitution 5–01
art.85 5–01
1942 Decree-Law 4.657/42
art.12 5–10
Penal Code 5–06, 5–22, 5–25,
     5–35, 5–37, 5–40, 5–42, 5–49
Ch.II–A 5–41
art.91 5–37
art.155 5–26
art.312 .... **5–25**
§ 1 .... **5–25**
§ 2 .... **5–25**, 5–26
art.316 5–43
art.317 ... **5–27**, 5–29, 5–31, 5–43
§ 2 .... **5–28**
§ 3 .... **5–28**, 5–29
art.321 .... **5–30**, 5–32
art.327 .... **5–23**, 5–24
§ 1 .... **5–23**

§ 2 .... **5–24**
art.332 5–46
art.333 .... **5–32**, 5–42
art.337-B **5–42**, 5–45, 5–49
art.337-C **5–45**, 5–46, 5–47,
                               5–49
art.337-D **5–41**, 5–43
1946 Constitution
art.141 .... **5–02**
1957 Law 3164 (Pitombo-Godoy
     Ilha Law) 5–02
1958 Law 3502 (Bilac Pinto Law) 5–03
§ 1 5–03
1988 Constitution 5–04
art.4 5–15
art.14 § 9 5–04
art.37 5–04
§ 4 5–04
art.52 I 5–08
art.51 II 5–08
art.55 § 3 5–08
art.225 § 3 5–51
1992 Law 8.429 (Law of Adminis-
     trative Probity) **5–05**, 5–06,
         5–08—5–11, 5–14, 5–15,
         5–19, 5–22, 5–23, 5–35
art.1 .... 5–08, 5–09, 5–11
art.3 .... 5–09, 5–13, 5–15
art.7 .... **5–18**, **5–20**
art.9 .... 5–10, 5–11, 5–13,
                 5–16, 5–19, 5–20
art.10 .... 5–11—5–13
art.11 .... 5–11, 5–13
art.12 ..... 5–06, **5–15**, 5–16, 5–17
art.14(§ 2) 5–18
art.16 .... **5–18**
(§ 2) **5–20**
art.17(1) 5–07
art.18 5–18
art.21 5–12
art.37(4) 5–18
1998 Law 9.613 5–40
2002 Law 10.467 .... **5–41**, 5–42
2006 Legislative Decree 348 5–38

Cayman Islands
1996 Monetary Authority Law,
     Law 16 of 1996 (2004
     revision) (Cayman Islands)
§ 50(1)(d) 8–16

Chile
Penal Code 2–32

China
Criminal Code of the People's
Republic of China, revised
at the Twenty-Second
Meeting of the Standing
Committee of the Tenth
National People's Con-
gress of the People's
Republic of China on June
29, 2006
art.383 3–33
art.385 3–33
art.386 3–33
art.389 3–33
art.393 3–33
Measure Regarding the Stan-
dard of Placing a Case on
File on Directly Investi-
gated Cases (Proposed),
promulgated by the
Supreme People's Procur-
atorate on September 16,
1999
art.1 3–33
s.3 3–33
s.5 3–33
s.8 3–33

France
1980 Law No.80-538 8–30

Hong Kong
Basic Law of the Hong Kong
Special Administrative
Region of the People's
Republic of China 1990 . 6–04
Bill of Rights Ordinance 1991
(Cap 383) 6–04, 6–07,
6–23
Crimes Ordinance (Cap 200)
s.159A 6–19
Criminal Procedure Ordi-
nance (Cap 221) ....
s.102 6–27
Evidence Ordinance (Cap
8) 6–17
Interception of Communica-
tions and Surveillance
Ordinance 2006 (Cap
589) 6–11, 6–16
Magistrates Ordinance (Cap
227) ....
s.85 6–20

Organised and Serious
Crimes Ordinance (Cap
455) 6–27
Prevention of Bribery Ordinance 1971 (Cap 201 6–04,
6–05, 6–11, 6–19, 6–20, 6–22,
6–24, 6–27
Pt II 6–20, 6–24, 6–28
s.3 .... 6–05, **6–07**
s.4 .... **6–06**, 6–10
(2A) 6–06
(2B) 6–06
ss.4—9 6–27
s.5 6–26
s.6 6–26
s.9 .... 6–05, **6–09**, 6–26
(3) 6–05
s.10 .... 6–05, 6–07, **6–08**, 6–26
s.12 .... 6–26, **6–27**
s.12A **6–19**
s.12AA 6–27
s.12AB 6–27
s.12AC 6–27
s.13 .... 6–11, **6–12**
s.13A 6–12, **6–13**
s.13B 6–13
s.13C 6–13
s.14 .... 6–14, **6–15**, 6–17
s.20 .... **6–17**
s.21 .... **6–18**
(1) 6–17
(2) 6–17
s.21A **6–18**
s.22 .... 6–18, **6–19**
s.23 .... 6–19, **6–20**
s.24 .... **6–20**
s.30 .... 6–22, **6–23**, 6–30
(1) 6–23
(2) 6–23
s.30A **6–22**, 6–30
s.31 .... **6–25**
s.31A **6–24**
s.32 .... **6–21**
s.33 .... 6–26, **6–28**
s.33A 6–26, **6–28**
Prevention of Corruption
Ordinance (Cap 215) 6–05
Witness Protection Ordinance
(Cap 564) 6–31

India
Constitution ....
Pt III 7–03

art.14 ...... 7–35, 7–36
art.73 .... **7–02**
art.148 .... **7–31**
arts 148—151 .... **7–31**
art.226 7–24
art.243 7–03
art.368 7–03
Sch.7 7–03
  List II 7–03
  List III 7–03
1860 Penal Code 7–02, 7–13, 7–15,
        7–25
 Ch.IX 7–13
 s.1 .... **7–13**
 s.2 .... **7–13**
 s.3 .... **7–13**
 s.4 .... 7–13, 7–15
 art.120B 7–41
 ss.161—165A .. 7–02, 7–03, 7–13
 s.171B **7–13**
 s.171E **7–13**
1872 Evidence Act
 s.4 7–09
 s.114 7–09
1908 Code of Civil Procedure 7–32
1934 Reserve Bank of India Act
 s.45-I (c) 7–19
1946 Delhi Special Police Establishment Act 7–02
 Preamble **7–02**
 s.2 7–02
 s.5(1) 7–02
 s.6 7–02
 s.6A 7–35, 7–36
1947 Prevention of Corruption
 Act .... 7–02—7–05, 7–13, 7–14
 s.4(1) 7–07
1949 Banking Regulation Act 7–19
 s.51 7–19
1951 All India Services Act 7–23
 Representation of the People
 Act 7–22
 s.78 .... **7–22**
 s.123 .... **7–22**
1952 Criminal Law Amendment
 Act 7–02, 7–03
1956 Companies Act 7–33
 s.235 7–33
 s.237 7–33
 s.239 7–33
 s.240 7–33
 s.240(A) 7–33
 s.617 7–06

1964 Anti-Corruption   Laws
 (Amendment) Act 7–02
 Regulations for the Air
 Force 7–24
1968 All India Service (Conduct
 Rules) 7–23
1971 Duties, Powers and Conditions of Services Act 7–31
 s.10 .... **7–31**
 s.11 .... **7–31**
 s.12 .... **7–31**
 s.13 .... **7–31**
1973 Criminal Procedure Code
 s.154 7–30
 Foreign Exchange Regulation
 Act 7–18
 Preamble 7–18
1976 Smugglers and Foreign
 Exchange Manipulators
 (Forfeiture of Property)
 Act 7–04
1978 Delegation of Financial Powers Rules 7–24
 General Financial Rules 7–24
1984 Karnataka Lokayukta Act 7–03
1988 Prevention of Corruption
 Act ... 7–02, 7–03, 7–05—7–07,
  7–14, 7–25, 7–29, 7–37, 7–41
 Ch.III 7–06
 s.2(b) 7–05
  (c) 7–05
 s.7 7–07
 ss.7—16 7–06
 s.8 .... **7–10**, 7–12
 s.9 .... **7–10**, 7–12
 s.11 .... **7–08**
 s.12 .... 7–11, 7–12
 s.14 .... **7–12**
 s.16 7–12
 s.20 7–09
  (1) **7–09**
 s.31 .... **7–02**
1999 Foreign Exchange Regulation
 Act 7–18
 s.76 7–18
 Foreign Exchange Manage-
 ment Act 7–18, 7–19
 Preamble 7–19
2002 Prevention of Money Laundering Act 7–18, 7–19
 s.2(e) 7–19
  (l) 7–19
  (v) 7–19
 s.3 .... **7–19**

s.4 7–19
s.12 7–19
s.30 7–19
s.56 7–19
s.73(2) 7–19
2003 Central Vigilance Act 7–28,
7–35, 7–37
s.8(1)(b) 7–37
s.(8)(h) 7–35
s.26(4C)(2)(c) 7–35
2004 Protection of Informers
Resolution 7–04
2005 General Financial Rules 7–24
r.137 7–24
Prevention of Money-laun-
dering (Maintenance of
Records of the Nature and
Value of Transactions, the
Procedure and Manner of
Maintaining and Time for
Furnishing Information
and Verification and
Maintenance of Records of
the Identity of the Clients
of the Banking Compa-
nies, Financial Institutions
and Intermediaries) Rules,
2005
r.8 7–19
Right to Information Act 7–01,
7–20, 7–21, 7–32
Preamble 7–20
s.2(f) 7–20
(h) 7–20
s.6 7–21
s.8 .... 7–20, 7–21
s.18 .... 7–21, 7–32
(3) 7–32
s.19 7–21
(5) 7–21
(7) 7–21
2007 Prevention of Money Laundering (Appointment and
Conditions of Service of
Chairperson and Members
of Adjudicating Autho-
rities) Rules 7–19
Prevention of Money-Laun-
dering (Appointment and
Conditions of Service of
Chairperson and Members
of Appellate Tribunal)
Rules, 2007 7–19

Ireland
2001 Prevention of Corruption
(Amendment) Act (27) ... 2–34
Criminal Justice (Theft and
Fraud Offences) Act
(50) 2–34

Japan
Penal Code 2–36
2004 Whistleblower Protection
Act 2–35

Sweden
Criminal Code 3–06
Penal Code, SFS 1977: 102 ... 3–06

Switzerland
1934 Federal Act on Banks and
Savings Banks November
8, 1934, SR 952.0 (Loi
fédérale du 8 novembre
1934 sur les banques et les
caisses d'épargne [Loi sur
les banques, LB])
art.47 .... 8–16, 8–23, 8–25

United Kingdom
1889 Public Bodies Corrupt Practices Act (52 & 53 Vict.
c.69) 1–03, 1–06, 1–09,
1–10, 1–12—1–14, 1–18,
1–20, 1–21, 1–23, 1–24,
1–30, 1–37, 1–44
s.1 .... 1–11, 1–23, 1–44
(1) 1–06
(2) 1–03, 1–07
s.2 1–11
s.7 .... 1–06, 1–08
1906 Prevention of Corruption Act
(6 Edw.7 c.34) 1–03, 1–09,
1–10, 1–12—1–14, 1–17,
1–18, 1–20, 1–21, 1–23,
1–24, 1–30, 1–36, 1–37,
1–44, 1–69, 3–06
s.1 .... 1–13, 1–15, 1–16, 1–23
(1) 1–03, 1–12, 1–16
(2) 1–12, 1–13
(3) 1–12, 1–23
(4) 1–13, 1–23
1916 Prevention of Corruption Act
(6 & 7 Geo.5 c.64) 1–18,
1–20, 1–23,
1–24, 1–37

s.2 .... 1–18, 1–24
s.4(2) 1–08, 1–18
1946 United Nations Act (9 & 10
Geo.6 c.45) 1–49
1977 Criminal Law Act (c.45) 1–13
s.1 .... 1–21, 1–49
s.1A 1–22
1978 Theft Act (c.31)
s.17 1–15
1981 British Nationality Act
(c.61) 1–23
1984 Local Government and
Housing Act ....
Sch.11 para.3 1–08
1985 Companies Act (c.6) 1–33
s.221 .... 1–58, 1–62, 1–63
1987 Criminal Justice Act (c.38)
s.1(1) 1–42
(2) 1–42
(3) 1–42
s.2 .... 1–44, 1–45, 1–47,
8–05
(1) 1–44, 8–05
(2) 1–44, 8–05
(3) 8–05
(9) 1–44
(10) 1–44, 8–05
(13) 1–44
(14) 1–44
(16) 1–44, 8–05
(17) 8–05
s.2A 1–44
1988 Criminal Justice Act (c.33) ..
s.47 1–18
1989 Local Government and
Housing Act (c.42) 1–09
Pt V 1–08
s.11 1–08
1990 Criminal Justice International
Co-operation Act (c.5) ... 8–20
1996 Criminal Procedure and
Investigation Act (c.25) .. 1–72
s.3(1) 1–72
1998 Criminal Justice (Terrorism
and Conspiracy) Act (c.40)
s.5(1) 1–22
Human Rights Act (c.42) 1–18
Data Protection Act (c.29) .. 9–21
Public Interest Disclosure Act
(c.23) 9–25
2000 Financial Services and Markets Act (c.8) 1–70
Regulation of Investigatory
Powers Act (c.23) 9–22

Iraq (United Nations Sanctions) Order (SI 2000/
3241) 1–49
2001 Anti-Terrorism, Crime and
Security Act (c.24) 1–05,
1–08, 1–19—1–22,
1–25, 1–36, 1–69
Pt 12 .... 1–20, 1–24, 2–41
s.108 .... 1–24, 1–44
(2) 1–23
s.109 .... 1–23, 1–24
(1)—(3) 1–23
(4) 1–23
s.110 1–24
2002 Proceeds of Crime Act
(c.29) .... 1–27—1–29, 1–31,
1–32, 1–42, 1–61
Pt 2 1–31
s.327 1–27
s.328 1–27
s.329 1–27
s.338 1–28
2003 Crime (International Cooperation) Act (c.32) 1–47,
1–48
2005 Serious Organised Crime and
Police Act (c.15) 1–73
s.60 1–44
s.61 1–44
s.71 1–73
s.73 1–73
2006 Fraud Act (c.35)
s.1 1–15
Public Contracts Regulations
(SI 2006/5) 1–34
2007 Serious Crime Act (c.27) 1–42
Sch.8(2) para.91(2) ... 1–32, 1–37
2008 Criminal Justice and Immigration Act (c.4)
s.59(2) 1–44
2010 Bribery Act (c.23) 1–02, 1–03,
1–13, 1–19, 1–23, 1–26, 1–36,
1–38—1–40
s.7 1–38
s.9 1–38

United States
Bribery of Public Official and
Witnesses Act (18 U.S.C.
§ 201) 3–17, 3–24
Delaware Statute (8 Del. C.)
§ 145(a) 8–52
§ 145(f) 8–52

Exchange Act (17 C.F.R. §
240) 3–46
  s.13b2-1 3–41
  s.13b2-2 3–41
  s.21(a)(2) 8–66
Federal Rules of Civil
Procedure 8–30, 8–31
Fifth Amendment to the
United States
Constitution 8–44
Foreign Corrupt Practice's
Act 1977 (15 U.S.C.S. §§
78dd-1 et seq) 1–38,
      2–08—2–10, 3–01, 3–02,
      3–05, 3–06, 3–07, 3–08,
    3–09—3–11, 3–13, 3–14, 3–16,
      3–18, 3–19, 3–21—3–23,
      3–25—3–28, 3–32—3–37,
  3–39—3–42, 3–44, 3–45, 3–47,
      3–49, 3–50, 3–52, 6–33,
  8–02—8–04, 8–07, 8–08, 8–34,
  8–64, 8–65, 8–66, 8–77, 9–03,
  9–08, 9–09, 9–26, 9–31, 9–36,
      9–43, 10–03, 10–04,
  10–06—10–13, 10–18, 10–19,
      10–24, 10–30
  §§ 78dd-1 3–05
    (a) .. 3–05, 3–10, 3–12, 3–14
    (b) 3–07, 3–09, 3–30
    (c) 3–09, 3–33, 3–35
      (1) 3–05
      (2) 3–05
      (3) 3–05
      (4) 3–08
    (d)(2) 3–07
    (e) 3–49
      (1) 3–50
      (2) 3–50
      (3) 3–50
    (f) 3–23
      (1) .. 3–10, 3–23, 3–24
      (2)(A) 3–26
      (3) 3–30
        (b) 3–30
    (g) 3–14, 3–16
  §§ 78dd-2 3–05
    (a) .. 3–05, 3–10, 3–12, 3–14
    (b) 3–09, 3–30
    (c) 3–09, 3–33, 3–35
      (1) 3–05
        (B) 3–05
        (B)(2) 3–05
      (4) 3–08
    (d) 3–29

    (f) 3–49
      (1) 3–50
      (2) 3–50
        (A) 3–26
      (3) 3–50
    (g) 3–29
    (h) 3–14
      (2) 3–10, 3–23,
            3–24
        (A) 3–23
      (3)(A) 3–26
      (4) 3–30
        (b) 3–30
    (i) 3–14, 3–16
  §§ 78dd-3(3) 3–29
    (a) 3–12
    (c) 3–33, 3–35
    (d) 3–29
    (f)(2) 3–23, 3–24
      (3) 3–26
      (4)(b) 3–30
  §§ 78ff(c) 3–29
    (2)(A) 10–19
  §§ 78l 3–12
  §§ 78m 3–06
    (b) 3–37
      (2) 3–13
        (a) 3–40
        (b) 3–42
      (6) 3–38
      (7) 3–40, 3–42
  §§ 78o(d) 3–12
International Anti–Bribery
and Fair Competition Act
1998 3–10
International Organisations
Immunities Act (22
U.S.C. § 288)
s.1 3–24
International Securities
Enforcement Cooperation
Act 1990 8–66
New York General Business
Law (Martin Act) 8–08
Omnibus trade and Competi-
tiveness Act 1988 (15
U.S.C. § 78-dd-1
(1998)) 2–09, 3–09, 3–49
Restatement (Third) of For-
eign Relations Law
§ 442(1)(c) 8–32
Sarbanes-Oxley Act (15
U.S.C § 78j-1(1)) ... 8–34, 8–39

Securities Exchange Act 1934
    (15 U.S.C. §§ 78a) 3–05,
                3–37, 3–41, 10–30
    s.13(b) 3–05
          (2)(A) 3–41
    s.30A 3–05

INTRODUCTION

There is an old story that Alexander Graham Bell dialled the first wrong number the moment he created the third telephone. The story is of course apocryphal, but it makes a serious point: as soon as a system is open to mistake or misuse, the errors and abuses will swiftly follow.

So it has probably been, in reality, with corruption: once a class of public officials was in a position to direct the affairs of state, those people who might benefit from the officials' decisions—anyone with anything to gain or lose thereby—must have been tempted to influence the officials one way or another. Corruption, therefore, is probably as old as government itself.

The problem is ancient but persistent. It is not difficult to find evidence of corruption today across many of the world's jurisdictions. Rarely does a week go by without some mention in the press or the media of a corrupt, dysfunctional, or venal government. The phenomena often go together in mutually reinforcing fashion.

But we should resist being smug. Many functionaries, especially in developing countries, earn a pittance of what most of us would consider a living wage. The rot of corruption, moreover, is anything but limited to the developing world. The recent, well-published budgetary woes of the Greek government owe much, according to many experts, to the willingness of bureaucrats to accept personal bribes in lieu of due tax payments. And this is hardly an idiosyncrasy among the developed economies of the West and Far East.

The problem with corruption, therefore, is that it is personally beneficial (to the payer and the recipient of the bribe) but collectively detrimental to the health and integrity of the larger political system. It is anything but a victimless crime; to the contrary, the victim is the polity and its members as a whole. As former President Clinton said at a private gathering which one of the authors attended, "corruption makes governments incompetent."

The focus of this book, however, is a related but somewhat different phenomenon: what people (and corporations) do to influence public officials of governments not their own, and what their home jurisdictions try to do about it.

International corporations had long—and successfully—argued that what they did abroad was no great concern to their home government. If a foreign official controlled access to goods, services or resources, why not let the company ensure that the official was favourably disposed to it? A small payment, a first-class plane ticket for the official's spouse, tuition fees for their child; these were a trivial and—as far as the company was concerned—eminently worthwhile price to pay for access to substantial and often vastly lucrative markets.

Corporations could also convince themselves that local interests did not lose out as a result of their actions. These were not (always) bribes to keep the taxpayer away or to fix a fine; they were more like an ante in a high stakes game. The losers, moreover, were not the local government or its people but other, equally sophisticated and ruthless international entities.

And everybody did it. There was no point being holier-than-thou; if you were unwilling to pay to play, one of your competitors, from your country or a different one, would step into the breach.

Bribing officials to win and keep international contracts was therefore nothing more than the cost of doing business abroad. Companies treated it as an expense item much as they would a tax in the foreign jurisdiction (if they chose to pay it rather than bribe yet another functionary). Indeed, bribes to foreign officials were tax-deductible in major jurisdictions such as Germany and France until the turn of the millennium.

What changed? It would be gratifying to believe that evolving notions of good governance and transparency were solely responsible for the relatively rapid spread of anti-bribery laws across the globe. There is certainly truth to the assertion that international pressure groups did much to highlight the corrosive effects of corruption and shame international actors into ceasing to treat bribery as business-as-usual. For that these groups deserve great credit.

But it would be naïve to think that long-tolerated habits could become so undesired through the preaching of virtue and sound argument alone. Political pressure also played a central role.

That pressure came principally from the United States. Alone among the world's developed economies, the United States had enacted a foreign anti-bribery law back in the 1970s; these were the mists of antiquity by the standards of legislation against international corruption.

The impetus for change built up slowly over the next 20 years. Chafing at the restrictions of the US Foreign Corrupt Practices Act, American businesses urged successive US administrations and Congresses to do something about their freewheeling foreign competitors.

Eventually the US government took heed. It set about persuading its trading partners and competitors to do something about the global blight of corruption.

Years of US lobbying led to an international treaty: the Convention on Combating Bribery of Foreign Public Officials in International Business Transactions.

The signatory countries were those in the Organisation for Economic Cooperation and Development, the entity sometimes known as the Rich Men's Club. Its members were the countries from which the United States's principal industrial and commercial competitors hailed. The two-decade plea of America for a "level playing-field" on which to compete for international contracts had finally been answered.

The OECD Anti-Bribery Convention, discussed in detail in Ch.2, bound states parties to enact legislation criminalising the bribery of foreign officials and facilitating the exchange of information to prosecute offenders.

But it would be another decade or so before member states honoured the terms of the Convention they had signed. Up until 2008, not a single signatory of the OECD Convention other than the United States had successfully prosecuted a party for bribing a foreign official.

The tide began to turn with the massive Siemens corruption enquiry. Although American regulators initiated and did the lion's share of the work investigating the industrial titan, German authorities soon joined in. At around the same time, UK regulators beefed up their anti-bribery capabilities and secured the first guilty pleas and convictions for bribery of foreign officials.

Corruption investigations may have quietly marked a milestone in April 2010, when German and Russian authorities launched enquiries into alleged bribes in those countries by American software company Hewlett-Packard. American authorities soon followed suit. To the authors' knowledge, this was the first time in which non-American regulators beat their American counterparts to the punch in an anti-bribery investigation. It may be a sign of things to come.

The United Kingdom's recent record on combating foreign bribery was marred by the abandonment of part of a high-profile investigation into defence contractor BAE Systems.[1] But the UK's reputation as a bastion against corruption appears to have been burnished by the enactment in April 2010 of the Bribery Act. For the first time, the United Kingdom has a law specifically aimed at bribery by UK entities and individuals of foreign public officials.

The Bribery Act also takes a step beyond its counterparts by holding senior officials of companies criminally liable for bribery, unless the company has "adequate procedures" in place to prevent it. Much debate is likely to ensue over the coming years as to what exactly those "adequate procedures" should be.

So why does bribery of foreign officials remain prevalent, despite the emerging international consensus that it is both wrong and illegal? We can trace the problem to three interlocking phenomena: first, international companies are in fierce and constant competition for a finite set of markets and resources. The people who control those markets and resources know that they can command a premium for them. And that premium often can include a personal payment.

Secondly, by a quirk of geopolitical accident, the places where valuable industrial and commercial commodities abound tend also to be emerging markets with candidly poor histories of governance. Some commentators—notably American author and columnist Thomas Friedman—have hypothesised that abundant resources such as oil, natural gas and minerals actually retard good governance because their revenues allow governments to "buy off" the population. Whatever the reason, there is little doubting that the governments in whose

---

[1] Despite the disappointment felt at the BAE decision by supporters of robust anti-corruption prosecutions, the authors cannot find fault with the reasoning of the late Lord Bingham in the House of Lords' BAE Opinion. Indeed, we would go so far as to say that anti-corruption advocates owe a debt to Lord Bingham, perhaps the greatest common law jurist of his time, for his persistent and tireless efforts to advance the rule of law—a concept which of course goes hand in hand with efforts to combat corruption.

territories some of the world's most valuable resources can be found are among the more corruption-prone.

Thirdly, the still-recent legacy of communism has left a swath of countries a curious mixture of public and private entities. In those countries—China is a notable example—senior officials of nominally independent companies are also senior political figures. They therefore come within the ambit of the international corruption laws that this book examines.

We begin (along with our distinguished contributors) by examining the history and state of anti-bribery laws of a number of significant jurisdictions: the UK, the US, India, Brazil, Australia, and Hong Kong. We also look at the above-mentioned OECD Anti-Bribery Convention, since it provides the blueprint for virtually every domestic law against bribery of foreign officials.

The book continues in a practical vein: we examine what is involved in a corruption enquiry: what powers various regulators have and what steps companies can take to minimise liability. A chapter on forensic investigations explains the steps taken in a corruption enquiry from an accounting perspective.

We conclude with a chapter on effective anti-bribery compliance measures. These will be especially important in light of the UK Bribery Law's emphasis on "adequate procedures" described above.

Appendices will provide some of the key legal texts and references.

We hope that both lawyers and non-lawyers, experienced practitioners and those new to the field alike, find something useful in the pages that follow.

Paul H. Cohen
Arthur Marriott QC

New York and London,
September 2010

CHAPTER 1

UK ANTI-CORRUPTION LAW[1]

A. THE CURRENT STATE OF ANTI-CORRUPTION LAW IN THE UK

The United Kingdom boasts one of the oldest traditions in the world of anti-   1–01
bribery laws and has wide-ranging legislation criminalising bribery in both the
public and private sectors. Despite this heritage, however, the United Kingdom
was until very recently perceived as having fallen behind the leading members of
the international community in the promulgation, investigation and enforcement
of laws prohibiting the corruption of foreign officials.

This perception is based on two principal factors: first, until April 2010 the
United Kingdom[2] had not enacted legislation specifically addressing its responsibilities arising from the ratification of the OECD Anti-Bribery Convention. The
United Kingdom had argued—not entirely without justification—that existing
laws covered all aspects of its OECD obligations. The OECD, however, complained—also not without justification—that these existing laws were something
of a patchwork quilt that made investigation and prosecution difficult and
unpredictable.

The second factor was the United Kingdom's frankly unimpressive record
(until early 2010) in conducting anti-bribery investigations and prosecutions.
Indeed, this may be related to the complexity and lack of clarity in the law
referred to above. The perception that the government was unable, or reluctant,
to pursue UK companies suspected of having bribed foreign officials crystallized
in 2007 after the Serious Fraud Office dropped a key part of its investigation of
suspected bribery by BAE Systems Plc on national security grounds. Although
the House of Lords ultimately confirmed that the decision to do so had not been
unlawful, and the SFO later announced a settlement with BAE in relation to a

---

[1] The authors gratefully acknowledge the substantial assistance of Chris Howard in drafting this
chapter.
[2] The UK comprises three separate jurisdictions: England and Wales, Scotland and Northern
Ireland. There is no concept of "UK law" per se. This chapter therefore describes the position in
England and Wales. However, the statutory corruption offences referred to in this chapter (both under
the existing law, and under the Bribery Act) extend to Scotland and Northern Ireland, and to that
extent the substantive law is the same in all three UK jurisdictions; the criticisms levied by the OECD
also relate to the UK as a whole.

1

separate investigation, critics had already tarred the government with the brush of timidity.

1–02   In November 2009, after a number of false starts and more than a decade after the Law Commission's initial consultation on reform of the law of bribery, the government introduced a draft Bribery Bill into Parliament. The Bill became law on April 8, 2010, although many of the provisions have not yet been brought into force. The Bribery Act addresses the criticisms of the law in the United Kingdom levelled by the OECD. It replaces the current legislative "patchwork" with two new general offences of offering/giving a bribe and requesting/accepting a bribe, and introduces a free-standing offence specifically directed at the bribery of foreign officials. Most radically, it creates a new offence for corporate entities of failing to prevent those representing the company committing bribery, which will be coupled with an "adequate systems and controls" defence. Combined with what appears to be a more aggressive approach to prosecuting foreign corruption, the Bribery Act stands to put the United Kingdom back in good stead amongst the international anti-bribery community.

As of June 2010, the Bribery Act offences described below have not been brought into force. Until they are, the pre-Bribery Act common law and statutory regime will apply. The Bribery Act's transitional provisions provide that it will not affect any liability, investigation, legal prosecution or penalty for, or in respect of which, a common law bribery offence or an offence under the existing statutory corruption regime was committed, wholly or partly, before the Bribery Act comes into force. The pre-Bribery Act position, as well as the new law, is therefore considered below.

B. PRE-EXISTING BRIBERY LAW IN THE UK

1–03   Under English law prior to the Bribery Act's enactment, bribery was principally addressed by two statutory offences as well as by the common law.[3] The statutory offences were expanded and clarified by further legislation. Both offences criminalise both the offering/provision and the acceptance/receipt of a bribe. In summary, and focusing on the offences committed by the party paying the bribe:

- under the Public Bodies Corrupt Practices Act 1889 (1889 Act), it is a crime corruptly to give, promise or offer any gift, advantage etc. to officials of a public body, as an inducement to or reward for the official doing or forbearing to do anything in relation to a matter or transaction in which the public body is concerned[4]; and

---

[3] The patchwork of bribery offences has led to efforts for reform dating back many years. A 1998 Law Commission report described the bribery laws as "uncertain and inconsistent", although it was not until 2000 that the Government "accepted that there are difficulties in interpreting the language and concepts used in the statutes." Home Office, *Raising Standards and Upholding Integrity: The Prevention of Corruption*, (2000) Cm.4759 Ch.2.

[4] Public Bodies Corrupt Practices Act 1889 s.1(2).

- the Prevention of Corruption Act 1906 (1906 Act) creates an offence based on an agent/principal concept. Under the 1906 Act, it is an offence to corruptly offer or give any consideration to any *agent* as an inducement for doing any act to show favour or disfavour to any person, in relation to his/her *principal's* affairs or business.[5]

Both of these offences are considered in more detail below.

I. COMMON LAW

It is an offence at common law to bribe the holder of a public office, or for any such office holder to accept a bribe. The scope of the offence is, however, uncertain, and in practice prosecutions are generally brought (if at all) under the relevant statutory provisions. There is also considerable overlap with the common law offence of misconduct in public office.   1–04

Commentators debate whether bribery at common law was a general offence or a series of individual offences that were dependent on the offender's office or function.[6] In 1964, *Russell on Crime* defined bribery as: "the receiving or offering [of] *any undue reward* by or to any person whatsoever, *in a public office*, in order to influence his behaviour in office,[7] and incline him to act contrary to the known rules of honesty and integrity."[8]

It appears that the amount of the bribe, to be classified as an "undue reward," must be more than a trivial amount.[9] Further, case law suggests that those in "public office" extend beyond judicial or elected officials,[10] to anyone who "discharge[d] any duty . . . [in] which the public [is] interested, more clearly so if

---

[5] Prevention of Corruption Act 1906 s.1(1).

[6] Law Commission, *Reforming Bribery*, (HMSO 2008), Law Com. No.313, HC Paper No.928, p.5 (citing as examples: bribery of a privy councillor in *Vaughan* 98 E.R. 308; (1769) 4 Burr. 2429; bribery of a coroner in *Harrison* (1800) 1 East P.C. 382) [hereinafter Law Commission Report]. See also *Archbold on Criminal Pleading, Evidence and Practice*, edited by P.J. Richardson, 2008 edn (London: Sweet & Maxwell, 2008), para.31–129.

[7] In *Gurney*, the court found sufficient intent where the defendant, charged with attempting to bribe a justice of the peace, had intended to produce any effect at all on the justice's decision. (1867) 10 Cox C.C. 550.

[8] J.W. Cecil Turner, *Russell on Crime*, 12th edn (London: Stevens, 1964), p.381 (emphasis added).

[9] See *Bodmin*, (1869) 1 O'M. & H. 121 (mentioning how a Judge had to swear to not take any gift from a litigant with a case before him, unless it was "meat or drink, and that of small value"); see also David Lanham et al., Criminal Fraud (Australia: Thomson Reuters, 1987), p.204 (quoting South African case *S v Deal Enterprises (Pty) Ltd*):

"The difference between legitimate entertainment and bribery lies in the intention with which the entertainment is provided, and that is something to be inferred from all the circumstances, including the relationship between giver and recipient, their respective financial and social positions and the nature and value of the entertainment."

[10] *R. v Whitaker* [1914] 3 K.B. 1283 (rejecting the argument that an Army officer was not a public official because he did not serve as a judicial or ministerial official).

he is paid out of a fund provided by the public."[11] This definition also covers those exercising an ad hoc public duty, such as voting for local government[12] or Parliament.[13]

1–05   The common law offence was extended to encompass the bribery of foreign public officials by the Anti-Terrorism, Crime and Security Act 2001, which is considered further below. In practice, however, the case law in which the offence has been invoked is of a historic nature and there has been limited enforcement of the corruption offences generally as they apply to foreign officials. Thus, the common law bribery offence has not been used extra-territorially to date.

II. PUBLIC BODIES CORRUPT PRACTICES ACT 1889

1–06   Prior to the enactment of the Public Corrupt Practices Act 1889 (1889 Act) the government had prosecuted the crime of bribery under the common law for many centuries.[14] Bribery became a statutory crime when Lord Randolph Churchill introduced a Private Members' Bill that became the 1889 Act. The 1889 Act made it an offence to bribe public officials[15]; the bribery of people who are not public officials is outside its scope.

The Act makes the active or passive bribery of a member, officer or servant of a public body a criminal offence.[16] Section 1(1) of the 1889 Act provides:

> "Every person who shall by himself or by or in conjunction with any other person, corruptly solicit or receive, or agree to receive, for himself, or for any other person, any gift, loan, fee, reward,[17] or advantage[18] whatever as an inducement to, or reward for, or otherwise on account of any member, officer, or servant of a public body as in this Act defined, doing or forbearing to do anything in respect of any matter or transaction whatsoever, actual or proposed, in which the said public body is concerned, shall be guilty of an offence."

1–07   The offered bribe must act as an inducement or a reward for the receiver to do or not to do something in respect of a matter concerning his office.[19] Subsection 2 further provides that:

---

[11] *Whitaker* [1914] 3 K.B. 1283.

[12] *Worrall* (1890) 16 Cox C.C. 737.

[13] *R. v Pitt and Mead* (1762) 3 Burr. 1335; 97 E.R. 861.

[14] See OECD, *Steps taken to implement and enforce the OECD Convention on Combating Bribery of Foreign Public Officials in International Business Transactions*, September 12, 2008.

[15] See OECD, *Steps taken to implement and enforce the OECD Convention on Combating Bribery of Foreign Public Officials in International Business Transactions*, September 12, 2008.

[16] Public Bodies Corrupt Practices Act 1889 s.1(1).

[17] The terms "gift", "loan", "fee" and "reward" are not defined.

[18] "Advantage" includes any office or dignity, and any forbearance to demand any money or money's worth or valuable thing, and includes any aid, vote, consent, or influence, or pretended aid, vote, consent, or influence, and also includes any promise or procurement of or agreement or endeavour to procure, or the holding out of any expectation of any gift, loan, fee, reward, or advantage, as before defined. See 1889 Act s.7.

[19] Law Commission, *Reforming Bribery*, 2008, at 7.

"Every person who shall by himself or by or in conjunction with any other person corruptly give, promise, or offer any gift, loan, fee, reward, or advantage whatsoever to any person, whether for the benefit of that person or of another person, as an inducement to or reward for or otherwise on account of any member, officer, or servant of any public body as in this Act defined, doing or forbearing to do anything in respect of any matter or transaction whatsoever, actual or proposed, in which such public body as aforesaid is concerned, shall be guilty of an offence."

(a) Scope of the Act: Public Bodies

As amended by the Anti-terrorism, Crime and Security Act 2001 (see below), s.7 **1–08**
of the 1889 Act defines "public body" as:

"Any council of a county or county of a city or town, any council of a municipal borough, also any board, commissioners, select vestry, or other body which has power to act under and for the purposes of any Act relating to local government, or the public health, or to poor law or otherwise to administer money raised by rates in pursuance of any public general Act, and [this] includes any body which exists in a country or territory outside the United Kingdom and is equivalent to any body described above."

The expression "public office" means any office or employment of a person as a member, officer or servant of such public body.

Section 4(2) of the 1916 Act (see below) extended this definition to include "local and public authorities of all descriptions". Part V of the Local Government and Housing Act 1989 makes provision for including companies "under the control of one or more local authorities",[20] but this is not yet in force.[21]

The 1889 Act therefore covers, but is not limited to, corruption in local gov- **1–09**
ernment. It may extend to any body with public or statutory duties, other than one run for private profit.[22] There are two key limitations to its scope: firstly, it does not cover private sector corruption and, secondly, it does not cover crown servants. In relation to the former, the 1906 Act (considered further below) criminalises the bribery of "agents" regardless of whether they operate in the public or private sector. In relation to the latter, the Courts have found that the Crown is not a public body and therefore the corruption of Crown servants must also be prosecuted under the 1906 Act (*R. v Natji* [2002] EWCA Crim 271; [2002] 1 W.L.R. 2337).

The precise scope of the 1889 Act has given rise to some confusion and, as noted in the Law Commission's Report, the imperfect distinction between the scope of the 1889 Act and 1906 Act has led to some charging errors.[23]

---

[20] Local Government and Housing Act 1989 s.11.
[21] Local Government and Housing Act 1984 Sch.11, para.3.
[22] *DPP v Holly* [1978] A.C. 43.
[23] Law Commission, *Reforming Bribery*, 2008, at 10. In *Natji* [2002] EWCA Crim 271, the Court quashed the conviction of an employee of the Immigration and Nationality Department of the Home Office, who had been charged under the 1889 Act rather than the 1906 Act.

(b) Meaning of "corruptly"

1–10   Both the 1889 Act and the 1906 Act require the Defendant to have acted "corruptly", and this forms the key mens rea element of the statutory corruption offences. The word "corruptly" is not defined and one of the criticisms of the existing UK regime is that there is considerable uncertainty as to its meaning.

In *Cooper v Slade*,[24] the House of Lords stated that "corruptly" did not mean "dishonestly" (an expression which has been considered at length by the UK Courts in the context of other criminal offences, and the meaning of which is relatively clear), but rather "doing an act which the law forbids as tending to corrupt"—a largely circular definition. Although there have been some authorities which suggest that dishonesty must be proved, the current position seems to be that this is not necessary[25]; any improper and unauthorised gift, payment or inducement offered to a public official is likely to be corrupt, as long as it was given in connection with influencing or rewarding the public official for the performance of his public duties. Ultimately, whilst the Court has said that "corruptly" is an ordinary word, the meaning of which should cause a jury little difficulty, the need to prove this ill-defined concept in order to secure a conviction has continued to attract criticism.

In certain cases involving bidding for public contracts, a presumption of corruption applies. This is considered further below.

(c) Penalties

1–11   Those convicted of an offence under s.1 of the 1889 Act face a maximum of six months in prison and/or a fine if convicted on summary conviction, or a maximum of seven years and/or a fine for those convicted on indictment.[26]

III. Prevention of Corruption Act 1906

1–12   The 1906 Act is based on an agent/principal concept.[27] The Act makes it a crime to bribe any "agent."[28] Subsection 1(2) defines an agent as "include[ing] any person employed by or acting for another", whether in the public or private sector, and the expression "principal" includes an employer. An agent also

---

[24] (1858) 6 H.L. Cas. 746; 10 E. R. 488.

[25] *R. v Wellburn* [1979] 69 Cr. App. R. 254 and *R. v Smith* [1960] 2 Q.B. 423.

[26] Public Bodies Corrupt Practices Act 1889 s.2.

[27] In an October 2008 report, the OECD pointed to the 1906 Act and its lack of clarity as an example of the longstanding deficiencies in the existing UK laws that apply to foreign bribery. See Phase 2*bis* Report, OECD, *Combating Bribery of Foreign Public Officials*, 2008.

[28] Prevention of Corruption Act 1906 s.1(1).

includes "a person serving under the Crown or under any corporation or any borough, county or district council, or any board of guardians."[29]

Section 1(1) of the 1906 Act defines the bribery offence as follows:

"If any person corruptly[30] gives or agrees to give or offers any gift or consideration[31] to any agent as an inducement or reward for doing or forbearing to do, or for having after the passing of this Act done or forborne to do, any act in relation to his principal's affairs or business, or for showing or forbearing to show favour or disfavour to any person in relation to his principal's affairs or business ... he shall be guilty of [an offence] ..."

(a) Scope of the Act: Persons who can be bribed

The 1906 Act is extremely wide in scope. Other than local authority officials (who are covered by the 1889 Act) it appears to cover all employees within the public or private sector, any Crown servant, and other persons who act as agents for public bodies.   1–13

Prior to 2002, the Act did not make clear whether the term "agent" included any foreign public official. The Act now provides that:

"For the purpose of this Act it is immaterial if—(a) the principal's affairs or business have no connection with the United Kingdom and are conducted in a county or territory outside the United Kingdom; (b) the agent's functions have no connection with the United Kingdom and are carried out in a country or territory outside the United Kingdom".[32]

Nonetheless, the OECD continued to voice concern over the absence of an offence specifically targeted at the bribery of foreign public officials.[33]

---

[29] 1906 Act s.1(3). Serving under the Crown does not require employment by the Crown. See *Barrett* (1976) 1 W.L.R. 946 (finding a superintendent registrar of births, deaths and marriages to be serving under the Crown even though the Crown did not appoint, pay, or have the ability to fire him). It is unclear whether police officers, judicial officers and local councillors are "agents" for the purposes of the 1906 Act, although in such cases there may be recourse to the common law or the 1889 Act. See A.T.H. Smith, *Property Offenses* (1994), pp.792–793. For example, in the English case *Fisher v Oldham Corp* (1930) 2 K.B. 364, a police officer was held to be a servant of the State; but in the Scottish case *Graham v Hart* 1908 S.C. (J.) 26, a police officer was held to be an agent of the Chief Constable.

[30] Courts have interpreted "corruptly" as purposely doing an act that the law forbids as tending to corrupt. See *R. v Wellburn* (1979) 69 Cr.App.R. 254.

[31] Consideration is defined as including "valuable consideration of any kind," while "gift" is not defined. 1906 Act s.1(2).

[32] 1906 Act s.1(4).

[33] When the OECD expressed concern as to whether the 1906 Act applies to foreign public officials, the Government assured them it did. In support of its contention, the Government cited the 1998 Law Commission Report on the law on corruption (which stated at p.66 that "it is not entirely clear whether a public body existing outside the United Kingdom is a 'public body' within the meaning of the Acts" but that if an official were "employed by or acting for" a public body existing outside the UK, "he or she would be an agent within the original definition in section 1(2) of the 1906 Act." Id. at 173). The Government also relied on the Court of Appeal's decision in *R. v Raud* [1989] Crim. L.R. 809. In *Raud*, the Court of Appeal upheld a decision in which Raud was convicted of conspiring, contrary to the Criminal Law Act 1977, with an agent of the Government of Ireland and other persons in connection with a corrupt agreement to obtain money in exchange for providing Irish passports, contrary to s.1 of the 1906 Act.

Another concern in relation to the scope of the 1906 Act is that it does not expressly address bribes made through an intermediary. The UK authorities position was that a person who gives or offers a bribe to a foreign public official with the assistance of an intermediary would be guilty of an offence under the 1906 Act because the offence is aimed at any person who corruptly "gives or agrees to give or offers any gift or consideration to any agent...",[34] and it was argued that the "agreement to give" can be an agreement made with the intermediary, not with the agent (the intermediary would, of course, also be liable, subject to any jurisdictional issues). There is, however, an equally good, if not better, argument that the section should be construed so that it does not cover bribes which are to be paid via an intermediary where there is no direct agreement with the agent. The Law Commission's Report[35] notes that the law is probably sufficiently flexible to deal with "indirect" bribery through an intermediary, but that it may, at the least, be open to criticism for not being clear on these points. The new Bribery Act offences expressly address this issue; they have been drafted to include bribery which is effected through third parties.

(b) Meaning of "corruptly"

1–14 As discussed above, the key mens rea element for both the 1889 Act and 1906 Act corruption offences involves the Defendant acting "corruptly", an ill-defined term which has been the subject of considerable criticism.

(c) False Statements

1–15 Section 1 of the 1906 Act also creates an offence of knowingly giving to any agent (or an agent knowingly using with intent to deceive his principal) any receipt, account or other document in respect of which the principal is interested, and which contains any statement which is false, erroneous, or defective in any material particular, and which to his knowledge is intended to mislead the principal.

This offence does not require any bribery or corruption of the agent,[36] but the false document must originate from outside the agent/principal's organisation.[37]

In practice, there is a substantial overlap between this offence and other, more commonly charged, offences, such as false accounting under s.17 of the Theft Act 1978 or fraud under s.1 of the Fraud Act 2006.

---

[34] See Review of Implementation of the Convention and 1997 Recommendation, p.5.
[35] Law Commission, *Reforming Bribery*, 2008, at 67, para.4.23.
[36] *Sage v Eicholz* [1919] 2 K.B. 171.
[37] *R. v Tweedie* [1984] Q.B. 729.

(d) Penalties

Those convicted of an offence under s.1 of the 1906 Act face a minimum of six **1–16** months in prison and/or a fine if convicted on summary conviction, or a minimum of seven years and/or a fine for those convicted on indictment.[38]

(e) Modern Criticism of the agency/principal model

Under principles of (civil) agency law, a principal's informed consent to an **1–17** agent's actions will generally act as a defence to the agent's liability for any breach of his duties to the principal. In the context of the 1906 Act, the question which therefore arises is whether the principal's consent is a valid defence to a corruption offence under the Act. When this issue was raised in 2005, the UK was categorical in its submissions before the OECD that principal consent could not be a defence, but commentators have continued to raise concerns as to whether this is correct.[39]

Separately, the Law Commission notes concerns that the term "principal" may not be an accurate way to describe the victim of corruption, particularly where the person who suffered the loss and whose trust is betrayed is not the same person as the "principal."[40] Moreover, bribery can often occur where there is no personal victim or principal at all (e.g. if the person committing bribery is a worker in the public sector, he or she would not owe a duty to any identifiable individual principal).

IV. PREVENTION OF CORRUPTION ACT 1916

The Prevention of Corruption Act 1916 implemented three important changes. **1–18** First, it broadened the definition of "public body" to encompass "local and public authorities of all descriptions."[41] Secondly, it increased the maximum sentence for bribery in relation to contracts with the Government or public bodies.[42] Thirdly, and most importantly, s.2 of the 1916 Act introduced a presumption of corruption:

> "Where... it is proved that any money, gift, or other consideration has been paid or given to or received by a person in the employment of [Her] Majesty or any Govern-

---

[38] 1906 Act s.1(1).

[39] The government's position proved to be in sharp contrast to the views of the UK Attorney General (Att Gen) in the BAE Al Yamamah investigation when it was dropped in 2006. There, the Att Gen stated publicly that principal consent was the "principal obstacle" to the prosecution. See *Interview Transcript: Lord Goldsmith, Financial Times*, January 31, 2007 (cited in OECD Report at 13); Ashish Joshi, *Britain's Fight Against the 'Silver Lace'*, 33 Champion 36 at 39 (February 2009).

[40] Law Commission, *Reforming Bribery*, 2008 at 66. In its report, the Law Commission contends that the agency/principal model contained in the 1906 Act should be replaced, since it could lead to "interpretations that are not compliant with the OECD Convention".

[41] Prevention of Corruption Act 1916 s.4(2); see also fn.35 at para.2.13.

[42] From 2 years' hard labour to 7 years in cases to which the 1916 Act applied. The resulting disparity in sentencing between the 1889 and 1906 Acts was removed by s.47 of the Criminal Justice Act 1988.

ment Department or a public body by or from a person, or agent of a person, holding or seeking to obtain a contract from [Her] Majesty or any Government Department or public body, the money, gift, or consideration shall be deemed to have been paid or given and received corruptly as such inducement or reward as is mentioned in such Act unless the contrary is proved."

The presumption of corruption was originally thought to shift the burden of proof from the Prosecution to the Defence, meaning that, in cases where the presumption applies, the Defence must prove (on a balance of probabilities)[43] that a given payment was not corrupt.[44] There is a concern as to whether placing a burden of proof on the Defence in a criminal matter is consistent with the Defendant's right to a fair trial under the European Convention on Human Rights (art.6) and the Human Rights Act 1998. It may be that the burden of proof would now be interpreted as evidential only (i.e. that the Defendant must adduce some evidence that the payment was not corrupt, but that the burden of proof would then be on the Prosecution to prove corruption). Alternatively, the Prosecution could bring charges in relation to a conspiracy or attempt to commit a corruption offence, rather than the full offence, in order to avoid the application of the presumption and a challenge on human rights grounds.

1–19   The presumption applies only to payments made to employees of the Crown, Government departments or public bodies,[45] and only to cases involving contracts.[46] It does not apply where extra-territorial jurisdiction under the 2001 Act is relied upon (see further below).

Amongst its other changes, the Bribery Act abolishes the presumption of corruption "which is rendered unnecessary given that the distinction between the public and the private sectors is to be removed."[47] Instead, prosecuting authorities will be required to prove the elements of the Bribery Act offences beyond reasonable doubt (i.e. to the normal criminal standard).

V. Anti-Terrorism, Crime and Security Act 2001

1–20   With a view to demonstrating its compliance with the OECD Convention, the UK amended and strengthened the extra-territorial scope of the 1889 Act and 1906 Act through the enactment of Pt 12 of the Anti-Terrorism, Crime and Security Act 2001.[48] Part 12 of the 2001 Act, which came into force on February

---

[43] See *R. v Carr-Briant* [1943] K.B. 607.

[44] Law Commission, *Reforming Bribery*, 2008 at 9.

[45] It does not apply therefore to agents who are not so classified, such as employees of private companies engaged in contracted-out work, private sector secondees to Government departments or public officials who are not employees.

[46] William Asseling, *The Times*, September 10, 1916. Judge Low considered it impossible to prosecute a civil servant found in possession of banknotes traced to a contractor with whom he had had official dealings, because the prosecution was unable to prove why the money was paid. This case helps to explain the restricted application of the presumption of corruption.

[47] Ministry of Justice, Bribery Draft Legislation, s.2 (March 2009).

[48] Hereinafter 2001 Act.

14, 2002,[49] had the stated purpose of "strengthen[ing] the law on international corruption."[50]

(a) Existing jurisdictional position—Conspiracy

Prior to the 2001 Act coming into force, English courts faced difficulty in interpreting the substantive anti-corruption offences to include conduct committed outside England and Wales.[51] When interpreting a statute, the courts must start from a "strong presumption" that Parliament did not intend to enact an extraterritorial offence.[52] An Act must have clear words to displace this presumption. **1–21**

Separately, however, from the question of whether the 1889 Act or 1906 Act offences could be interpreted as applying to foreign public officials, there was some scope to charge defendants with criminal offences relating to (corrupt) oversees conduct, in particular under the laws of conspiracy. Pursuant to s.1 of the Criminal Law Act 1977, a conspiracy is committed if:

"A person agrees with any other person or persons that a course of conduct will be pursued which, if the agreement is carried out in accordance with their intentions, either—(a) will necessarily amount to or involve the commission of any offence or offences by one or more of the parties to the agreement..."

A conspiracy to commit an offence is itself a criminal offence, carrying the same penalties as the substantive offence.

The conspiracy offence is given extra-territorial scope by s.1A of the Criminal Law Act 1977[53] which was inserted by the Criminal Justice (Terrorism and Conspiracy) Act 1998 s.5(1). Under s.1A, where the parties agree to pursue a course of conduct which would involve acts or events taking place overseas, and those acts or events would be criminal under the relevant overseas law (but not **1–22**

---

[49] As the Law Commission's report points out, Pt 12 was intended to be a temporary measure to comply with the OECD Convention, pending the introduction of a comprehensive Corruption Bill. See Law Commission, *Reforming Bribery*, 2008, at 63. Since the Corruption Bill failed to proceed through Parliament, Pt 12 has continued to be the governing law, pending the enactment of the Bribery Bill.

[50] Paragraph 32 of the Explanatory Notes further states:

"The sections put beyond doubt that the law of bribery applies to acts involving officials of foreign public bodies, Ministers, MPs and judges; and to 'agents' (within the meaning of the 1906 Act) of foreign 'principals'. They give courts jurisdiction over crimes of bribery committed by UK nationals and UK incorporated bodies overseas. There is also a technical provision, to ensure that the existing presumption of corruption in the Prevention of Corruption Act 1916, which it is intended to abolish, does not apply any more widely as a result of these new provisions."

2001 Act para.32.

[51] Law Commission, *Reforming Bribery*, 2008, at 138.

[52] *Treacy v DPP* [1971] A.C. 537 at 551; *Air India v Wiggins* [1980] 1 W.L.R. 815. In the absence of an express stipulation, a court will infer that Parliament has chosen not to extend a statutory offence so that it can be committed by conduct occurring outside England and Wales. Law Commission, *Reforming Bribery*, 2008, at 138.

[53] Conspiracies to commit certain other types of offences have a broader extra-territorial reach by virtue of the Criminal Justice Act 1993 Pt 1 but these provisions do not apply to the statutory corruption offences.

under English law because of its jurisdictional scope), a conspiracy offence may be committed if, broadly speaking, there is some UK nexus, such as that a party to the agreement does anything in England and Wales in relation to the agreement before its formation, or a party becomes a party to the agreement in England and Wales, or a party does or omits anything in England and Wales in pursuance of the agreement.

As a result, there was some scope even prior to the 2001 Act to prosecute overseas corruption where there was some UK nexus to the agreement to pay the bribe. Nonetheless, the position was somewhat complex and unsatisfactory.

(b) Extending the jurisdictional reach of the corruption offences

1–23   Section 109 of the 2001 Act provides clarity as to the extraterritorial effect of the 1889 Act, 1906 Act and common law corruption offences. Its effect is to extend the jurisdictional reach of the UK courts to include acts of bribery committed abroad by UK nationals[54] or companies incorporated under UK law.[55] Section 109 makes it an offence for a national of the United Kingdom to do anything outside the United Kingdom which, if done in the United Kingdom, would constitute a corruption offence, irrespective of whether the act would be an offence in the territory in which it is perpetrated.[56]

The Act mandates that any references to public bodies in the 1889 and 1916 Acts now include "any body which exists in a country or territory outside the United Kingdom."[57] It further amends the 1906 Act by inserting language that makes it "immaterial" if the principal's or the agent's "affairs or business have no

---

[54] A UK "national" includes any individual who is "(a) a British citizen [or British overseas territories citizen or national] ... (b) a person who under the British Nationality Act 1981 (c.61) is a British subject, or (c) a British protected person within the meaning of that Act." 2001 Act s.109(4).

[55] Anti-terrorism, Crime and Security Act 2001 s.109(1)–109(3), in relevant part, states that:
(1) This section applies if:
    (a) a national of the United Kingdom or a body incorporated under the law of any part of the United Kingdom does anything in a country or territory outside the United Kingdom, and
    (b) the act would, if done in the United Kingdom, constitute a corruption offence (as defined below).
(2) In such a case:
    (a) the act constitutes the offence concerned, and
    (b) proceedings for the offence may be taken in the United Kingdom.
(3) These are corruption offences:
    (a) any common law offence of bribery;
    (b) the offences under s.1 of the Public Bodies Corrupt Practices Act 1889 (c.69) (corruption in office);
    (c) the first two offences under s.1 of the Prevention of Corruption Act 1906 (c.34) (bribes obtained by or given to agents).

[56] 2001 Act s.109. In this regard, s.109 actually goes beyond the OECD Convention requirements. As the Law Commission points out: "This is because paragraph 8 of the Commentaries on the Convention makes it clear that under the Convention a Party does not have to criminalise the giving of an advantage to a foreign public official if acceptance of the advantage was permitted or required by the law of the foreign public official's country, including case law." Law Commission, *Reforming Bribery*, 2008, at 142. In practice, it is likely that if the giving of the bribe law was permitted under local law, the defendant would seek to argue that he did not act "corruptly".

[57] 2001 Act s.109.

connection with the United Kingdom and are conducted in a country or territory outside the United Kingdom."[58]

The territorial extension does not apply, however, to foreign nationals who commit bribery offences whilst abroad, even if they reside or are domiciled in England and Wales.[59] Nor does it apply to bodies that are not incorporated. Unincorporated bodies, including many types of partnerships, unincorporated foundations, associations, and trusts, fall outside of the scope of s.109.[60]

(c) Presumption of Corruption

Section 110 of the 2001 Act states that a court should not apply the presumption **1–24** of corruption to any offences committed by virtue of the territorial extensions made by Pt 12.[61] In the Explanatory Notes, s.110 is described as a:

> "technical provision to ensure that the existing presumption of corruption in the Pre-vention of Corruption Act 1916, which it is intended to abolish, does not apply any more widely as a result of these new provisions."

(d) Remaining uncertainty with regard to definitions

Whilst it extended the jurisdictional reach of the 1889 Act and 1906 Act offences, **1–25** the 2001 Act retained in large part the definitions used in those Acts. In essence, the 2001 Act simply added the prefix "foreign" to the existing list of "public officers," "public bodies" and "agents" capable of being bribed. As the 2001 Act did not provide a clear definition of "foreign public official," the Law Commission warned that it remained theoretically possible to commit bribery in violation of the OECD Convention but outside the existing statutory definitions.[62]

C. CORPORATE CRIMINAL LIABILITY

Another feature of English law which regularly attracts criticism is the difficulty **1–26** of establishing corporate criminal liability. English law currently operates on the basis of the "identification principle". In broad terms, this means that a person who can be identified as the "directing mind and will" of a corporate entity must have the necessary mens rea for the offence, in order for that mens rea to be imparted to the corporate entity and for the entity itself to be found guilty.

---

[58] 2001 Act s.108(2) (amending Prevention of Corruption Act 1906 s.1(3)(4)).

[59] The position is different under the Bribery Act, which extends the jurisdictional reach of the proposed corruption offences to persons ordinarily resident in the UK.

[60] Individual persons such as trustees and partners who comprise the unincorporated bodies could still be prosecuted. Law Commission, *Reforming Bribery*, 2008, at 139.

[61] 2001 Act s.110 (s.2 of the Prevention of Corruption Act 1916 that deals with the presumption of corruption in certain cases is not to apply in relation to anything which would not be an offense apart from s.108 or s.109).

[62] Law Commission, *Reforming Bribery*, 2008, at 67 (citing Phase 1*bis* report, at 13–14; Phase 2 report, OCED, *Combating Bribery of Foreign Public Officials*, 2008, at para.183).

In practice, this means it can be very difficult to establish corporate criminal liability for corruption unless a senior official (i.e. generally an individual of board level or immediately below) can be proved to have some knowledge of the corrupt activity. Given that most bribes are paid on behalf of, and benefit, corporate entities, and are often effected via representatives, this can create serious difficulties in effectively addressing corrupt activity.

The whole area of corporate criminal liability was due to be reviewed by the Law Commission in 2009. This project has now evolved into, and been replaced by, a project on regulation, public interest and the liability of businesses, on which the Law Commission intend to publish a consultation paper in the summer of 2010. The issue of corporate criminal liability has therefore not been specifically addressed in the Bribery Act. The new corporate offence of failing to prevent bribery (discussed below) will, however, effectively cut across this problem because there is no requirement under the offence for any individual at the corporate entity to have any knowledge of the bribery.

D. MONEY LAUNDERING

1–27   Another important dynamic in corruption investigations is the UK anti-money laundering regime.

The Proceeds of Crime Act 2002 (Proceeds of Crime Act) creates three substantive money laundering offences relating to concealing or transferring the proceeds of crime (s.327), being involved in money laundering arrangements (s.328) or acquiring, using or possessing the proceeds of crime (s.329). These offences are widely defined and cover, in essence, any possession of or dealings with any benefit from any predicate criminal conduct, whether that predicate conduct took place in the UK or overseas.

The mens rea element of each offence is that the alleged offender knows or suspects that the property in question is criminal property (i.e. that it constitutes or represents, directly or indirectly, a person's benefit from criminal conduct).

1–28   The impact of this in the corruption sphere is that, where a bribe is paid to obtain a contract, not only the bribe monies but also the benefit of the contract may constitute criminal property, giving rise to additional criminal exposure for any company or individual on whose behalf a bribe has been paid.

The Proceeds of Crime Act has a mechanism for persons who could otherwise commit money laundering offences to report their suspicions to the UK Financial Intelligence Unit (FIU), the Serious Organised Crime Agency (SOCA) and obtain "consent" to what would otherwise be an offence under the Proceeds of Crime Act (e.g. the possession of criminal property).[63] Such consent provides

---

[63] Proceeds of Crime Act 2002 s.338.

protection against the commission of money laundering offences, but not in respect of any underlying corruption offences.[64]

Separately, the Proceeds of Crime Act imposes obligations on persons in the "regulated sector" (financial institutions, certain professional services firms and other defined categories of businesses) to report suspicions of money laundering which come to their attention in the course of their regulated work. Thus, for example, a firm of accountants, auditors or a financial broker or bank would, subject to certain limited exceptions, be required to report their client to SOCA if they became suspicious that it had paid bribes and received some benefit as a result.

The provisions of the Proceeds of Crime Act are in some respects complex and there is a dearth of case law on their interpretation. They do, however, play an important part, in practice, in determining whether and how suspicions of corruption are reported to law enforcement agencies.   **1–29**

E. CONFISCATION, CIVIL RECOVERY AND PROCUREMENT

As explained above, offences under the 1889 Act and 1906 Act are punishable by up to a maximum of two years imprisonment and/or an unlimited fine. Potentially more significant for corporate defendants, however, are the consequences that may follow from any conviction for corruption.   **1–30**

I. Confiscation

Part 2 of the Proceeds of Crime Act provides the current framework in England and Wales for the confiscation of the proceeds of crime following a conviction. Where a Defendant is convicted of an offence before the Crown Court, the Court must assess whether a Confiscation Order should be made if either the Prosecutor asks the Court to do so or the Court believes, on its own initiative, that it is appropriate for it to do so. The Court must assess, applying certain assumptions, what the "benefit" is from the Defendant's "criminal conduct" and make an order either to the value of that amount, or the value of all the defendant's assets at the time of the order, if less.   **1–31**

The issue, in the corruption context, is that where an organisation has paid a bribe in order to win a contract, the "benefit" of that criminal conduct may be taken to be the gross revenues from the contract rather than either the amount of the bribe or the net profit.[65] The result could be that the Court is compelled

---

[64] Which are then more likely to be investigated, having been drawn to the authorities' attention by virtue of the report.

[65] Such an approach has been taken in the context of insider dealing offences; on December 10, 2009, in the case of *Neel Uberoi*, an insider dealing prosecution brought by the FSA, H.H. Judge Testar certified that the benefit obtained by Mr Uberoi, who had been convicted of buying and selling shares on the basis of inside information, was the full worth of the shares purchased, not his profit from the transactions.

(because it has no discretion as to the amount of an order if the confiscation process is triggered) to make an order vastly in excess of the quantum of the bribe or, indeed, the net benefit to the defendant. There is little case law in this area given the scarcity of corruption prosecutions, and the case of *Mabey & Johnson*, the first conviction of a UK company for overseas corruption (described in more detail below), sheds little light on the issue as confiscation in that case was dealt with under the pre-Proceeds of Crime Act regime, because of the historical nature of the Defendant's conduct.[66]

There have been calls for this area of the UK confiscation regime, which is often described as draconian, to be reformed, as there are concerns that it acts as a deterrent to companies coming forward and self-reporting incidents of suspected bribery by their employees. These concerns are, for example, reflected in the Joint Committee on the Draft Bribery Bill's First Report[67] but to date there seems to have been little or no enthusiasm on the part of the government for reform.

II. CIVIL RECOVERY

1–32   The Proceeds of Crime Act also provides for a civil recovery regime, whereby an enforcement authority can recover, in civil proceedings before the High Court (or, in Scotland, the Court of Session), property which is, or represents, property which has been obtained through unlawful conduct. These powers were originally conferred on a statutory body called the Assets Recovery Agency, but that body has since been disbanded and, from April 2008,[68] these powers have been conferred on the Serious Fraud Office and others.[69]

The powers are not intended to be used where a criminal prosecution is more appropriate. The Attorney General's guidance to prosecuting bodies on their asset recovery powers under the Proceeds of Crime Act[70] explains that:

> "The reduction of crime is in general best secured by means of criminal ... proceedings. However, the non-conviction based asset recovery power ... can also make an important contribution ... where (i) it is not feasible to secure a conviction, (ii) a conviction is obtained but a confiscation order is not made, or (iii) a relevant authority is of the view that the public interest will be better served by using those powers rather than by seeking a criminal disposal".

The key feature of the civil recovery powers is that the Court may make a civil recovery order on the basis of the civil standard of proof (i.e. proof on the balance of probabilities) rather than to the criminal standard (i.e. proof "beyond a

---

[66] The confiscation regime under the Proceeds of Crime Act does not apply to convictions in respect of offences which took place prior to March 24, 2003, even if the conviction post-dates March 24, 2003.

[67] Paragraph 186.

[68] Pursuant to the Serious Crime Act 2007 Sch.8(2) para.91(2).

[69] In England and Wales, SOCA, the Director of Public Prosecutions and the Director of Revenue and Customs Prosecutions.

[70] Issued on November 5, 2009.

reasonable doubt"). The relevant authority will be required to show that there has been "unlawful conduct" (i.e. conduct which is criminal under UK law, or which takes place overseas, is unlawful there, and would be criminal if it had taken place in the United Kingdom) and that property has been obtained through that unlawful conduct. Such property may then be received via a civil recovery order, subject to various provisions protecting, for example, persons who acquire the property in good faith for value and without notice of its unlawful origin.

Two significant cases brought by the SFO to date have involved the use of these civil recovery powers rather than a criminal prosecution. In both the *Balfour Beatty* and *AMEC Plc* cases, described in more detail below, the SFO obtained civil recovery orders in relation to the "benefit" of unlawful conduct by the companies concerned, which was characterised as a criminal failure to comply with certain accounting requirements under the Companies Act 1985. Both cases were said to relate to "irregular payments" and in both cases the outcome was perceived to be a negotiated alternative to a criminal prosecution, given the companies' actions in coming forward to the SFO.   1–33

III. PROCUREMENT

Another significant aspect of the UK anti-corruption regime is the effect of the UK and EU procurement rules. The UK Public Contracts Regulations 2006 (which implement EU Directive 2004/18/EC on the Co-ordination of Procedures for the Award of Public Works Contracts, Public Supply Contracts and Public Services Contracts) provide for mandatory and perpetual debarment from certain types of public procurement for "economic operators" who are convicted (or whose directors are convicted) of a number of specified criminal offences, including bribery and the statutory corruption offences. A discretionary debarment regime also operates where economic operators have been convicted of other criminal offences relating to the conduct of their business.   1–34

As with the UK confiscation regime, there are concerns that these provisions are so draconian that they will discourage companies from self-reporting incidents of corruption, and calls for a more flexible regime have been made.[71]

F. THE UK'S ACCESSION TO THE OECD ANTI-BRIBERY CONVENTION

The United Kingdom signed the OECD Convention on Combatting Bribery of Foreign Public Officials in International Business Transactions ("the Convention") on December 17, 1997. It ratified the Convention on December 14, 1998.[72]   1–35

---

[71] Joint Committee Report on the Draft Bribery Bill First Report, paras 188–191.
[72] See OECD Report, *Combating Bribery of Foreign Public Officials*, 2008, 39, at 1.

The Convention's core concept is that its signatories pass domestic legislation forbidding acts of bribery committed by their nationals or within their territory and directed towards officials of another state.[73]

Many predicted that the impact of the OECD Convention would be significant in the United Kingdom because the United Kingdom had never passed legislation that explicitly addressed foreign bribes.[74] In 1999, the OECD released a survey that found the United Kingdom was behind almost every other country in explicitly criminalising the bribery of foreign officials.[75] The survey also found that British companies were among the worst offenders when it came to bribing foreign officials.[76]

1–36   Following ratification, the OECD's Working Group expressed concern that the United Kingdom's bribery offences only covered domestic bribery of public officials. The Working Group therefore suggested that the United Kingdom draft a statute that clearly and specifically prohibits bribing foreign public officials.[77]

Initially the United Kingdom rejected this view, maintaining that the 1906 Act did in fact prohibit foreign as well as domestic bribery.[78] The passage of the 2001 Act, with its explicit reference to extraterritorial activity, strengthened the United Kingdom's position. Nonetheless, in an apparent nod to the Working Group's concerns, the Bribery Act includes a specific offence of bribing foreign public officials.

G. THE BRIBERY ACT

1–37   For years, the OECD criticised the United Kingdom for its inadequate implementation and enforcement of anti-bribery laws.[79] In response, the UK Government published draft legislation on March 25, 2009 entitled the Bribery Bill.[80] The Bill received final royal assent—and therefore passed into law—on April 8, 2010, as the Bribery Act 2010.

The Act is modelled on and follows recommendations made by the Law

---

[73] OECD Report, *Combating Bribery of Foreign Public Officials*, 2008.

[74] See S. Ramage, Fraud and the Serious Fraud Office (2005) (hereafter "Ramage") at 40.

[75] *Corruption and OECD, Guardian*, December 13, 2000.

[76] *Corruption and OECD, Guardian* ("Some 37 of the 55 companies which the World Bank publicly blacklists and has disbarred from participating in its contracts because of evidence of corruption are domiciled in Britain.")

[77] OECD, United Kingdom: Phase 1 Report, at 24, December 2000.

[78] OECD, Phase 1 Report, 2000 ("It is the view of the UK government that the 1906 Act applies to foreign public officials.")

[79] See Jean Eaglesham, *Embarrassment for Blair as UK Faulted on Bribery*, *Financial Times*, March 18, 2005. A 2005 OECD report noted that the UK's effort to implement the treaty suffered from inadequate laws, poor enforcement, and lack of prosecutions. See OECD Phase 2 Report, at 4. Later, in October 2008, the OECD released a scathing 75-page report critical of Britain's decision to drop the BAE investigation at the Saudi's insistence and for failing to stop bribes being paid by British companies in foreign markets. In particular, the OECD felt that Britain's action in dropping the BAE investigation seriously undermined the Treaty. The OECD reiterated its previous recommendation, made in 2003, 2005, and 2007, that the UK enact new foreign bribery legislation as soon as possible. See OECD Phase 2 Report, at 4; Alex Spence, *UK Slammed 'Inaction' on Foreign Corruption*, *Times Online*, October 17, 2008.

[80] Bribery Draft Legislation, at para.8.

Commission in its November 2008 report, "Reforming Bribery."[81] After pre-legislative scrutiny by a Joint Committee of the House of Lords and House of Commons (Joint Committee) a revised Bribery Bill was introduced into the House of Lords on November 19, 2009 and the Government published its response to the Joint Committee's proposals. The Bill was passed into law, with some limited amendments, just prior to the UK Parliament dissolving for the 2010 elections. The Government has announced that it will be brought into force in April 2011.

The Act has two central goals. First, the draftsmen sought to modernise and simplify existing legislation. They aimed to achieve this by consolidating the existing legislation and replacing all current offences with two general offences of bribery and a new offence of bribing a public official. The Act's second aim, as expressed in the draft Bill, is to allow for more effective prosecution of bribery and related offences.[82]

The Bribery Act contains four principal categories of offences: 1–38

1. *Bribing Another Person (active bribery) (s.1)*

    This offence is concerned with the conduct of the payer of a bribe. The payer must be shown, either directly or through a third party, to have given, offered or promised an advantage to the recipient with the intention to induce the recipient to perform a function or activity improperly or to reward the recipient for such conduct or where the payer knows or believes that the receipt of the advantage is itself improper. An example of the latter would include where a civil servant asks for £1,000 in order to perform an official function, or, having done so, asks for £1,000 as a reward.[83] For the purposes of liability, it is immaterial whether the person who is offered the advantage is the same person who is intended to perform the function improperly, or whether the advantage is offered or given through a third party.

    The offence only applies where the function or activity which is to be performed improperly is of a public nature, connected with a business, performed in the course of a person's employment, or performed by or on behalf of a body of persons. In addition, it must be a function which the person is expected to perform in good faith, impartially, or where the person is in a position of trust by virtue of him performing it. The expectation is that of a reasonable person in the United Kingdom and is expressly stated not to have regard to any local custom or practice if the function in question is to be carried out overseas.[84] Performance of a function is "improper" if it is performed in breach of one of these expectations.

---

[81] The recommendations called for a drastic overhaul of the UK's current bribery and corruption laws. The Commission recommended repealing the common law offence of bribery and the whole of 1889, 1906, and 1916 Acts. See Law Commission, *Reforming Bribery*, 2008.

[82] Bribery Draft Legislation, at para.11.

[83] Examples taken from the November 2008 Law Commission Report; conduct of this sort would often be referred to as a facilitation payment.

[84] Unless it is permitted or required by the written law applicable to the country or territory concerned (s.5(2)).

2. *Offence Relating to Being Bribed (passive bribery) (s.2)*

Offence two is concerned with the conduct of the recipient of a bribe. The recipient must be shown to have requested, agreed to receive, or accepted an advantage, intending that, in consequence, a relevant function or activity should be performed improperly, or where the advantage is a reward for improper performance. An offence may also be committed where the request, agreement or acceptance itself constitutes the improper performance by the recipient of a relevant function or activity or where the function or activity is performed improperly in anticipation of the advantage. An example of this offence would be where an employee asks for £1,000 in return for providing a competitor with confidential information about his employer's company.[85] It does not matter whether the recipient receives or accepts the advantage directly or through a third party, or whether it is for the recipient's benefit or that of another. The functions and activities to which the offence relates, and the concept of "improper performance", are the same as in relation to the first offence.

Both the offence of bribing another person and the offence of being bribed apply, as with the current UK regime, to both the private and the public sector.

3. *Bribery of a Foreign Public Official (FPO) (s.6)*

The OECD Convention requires each Party to take measures to make it a criminal offence to bribe a foreign public official (FPO).[86] The Bribery Act does precisely that by adding a new, discrete offence of bribery of a foreign official to supplement the general offence of bribery. It closely tracks the language of the OECD Convention.

This new offence covers bribes to FPOs and advantages given to third parties at the FPO's request or with the FPO's assent or acquiescence. The Act defines an FPO as anyone holding a legislative, administrative or judicial position, or who exercises a public function for a foreign country or territory (or part thereof) or for one of its public agencies or enterprises.[87] It also includes officials and agents of public international organisations. It is thus an extremely broad definition.

The offence is committed if it can be proved that an advantage was

---

[85] Examples taken from the November 2008 Law Commission Report.

[86] OECD Convention on Combating Bribery of Foreign Public Officials in International Business Transactions. art.1, November 1997.

[87] Some have questioned why there is not a discrete offence for bribery of a foreign *private* person. In addressing the issue, the Law Commission stated that the most serious problems of bribery typically do not involve private persons, and where such bribery does occur, it can be dealt with under the general offences bribery outlined in category one above. See Law Commission, *Reforming Bribery*, 2008 at 103. Moreover, foreign governments are typically more willing to act in an allegation involving one of their private citizens than they are where a public official is concerned. At 104. Moreover, competition law or other trade regulation typically covers private individuals, whereas, with public officials, prosecutors must navigate thorny constitutional hurdles. Finally, the Bribery Bill singles out foreign public officials because they have been recognized by the international community as the most susceptible to bribery; OECD Convention, art.1.

offered, promised or given to an FPO with the intention of (i) influencing the FPO in his capacity as an official; and (ii) obtaining or retaining business or a business advantage. The offence will only be committed if the FPO is neither permitted nor required by applicable written law to be influenced in his capacity as an FPO by the offer, promise of gift. In practice, it is unlikely that an overseas jurisdiction would have specific legislation or case law permitting FPOs to be influenced by financial or other advantages in the course of their work, and accordingly this hurdle is likely to be easily overcome. The offence is, accordingly, extremely broadly drawn, and there are concerns that it could criminalise, for example, normal corporate hospitality provided to officials, as such hospitality will, arguably, often be extended with the intention of winning business and influencing FPOs.[88]

The more prosaic example given by the Law Commission was that of a representative from a construction company who asks a civil servant in country X to expedite their licence permitting them to engage in construction work in country X; the civil servant responds that this is only possible if the company helps the civil servant's relative by converting flats on the relative's land. If the construction company acquiesces to the demand, then they have committed the FPO offence.[89]

The Law Commission had proposed a defence that a bribe payer would not be liable if he could show he reasonably believed he had to, or was allowed to, pay the bribe under the law of the foreign jurisdiction. This is analogous to the US Foreign Corrupt Practice's Act affirmative defence that a bribe is legal under the written laws of the foreign country. The Government, however, rejected the Law Commission's proposal; the defence accordingly does not form part of the Bribery Act.

4. *The New Corporate Offence: Failure to Prevent Bribery (s.7)*
The fourth offence is the most controversial, and is interesting inasmuch as it has no equivalent in the anti-bribery laws of other major democracies: this offence creates a form of vicarious liability. It provides that a commercial organisation (a corporate or a partnership) whose registered office is in the United Kingdom, or an overseas entity or partnership which carries on a business, or part of a business, in the United Kingdom, will be guilty of an offence if a person ("A") associated with the commercial organisation bribes another person, intending to obtain or retain business, or a business advantage, for the organisation. The person ("A") is associated with the organisation if he is a person who performs services for or on behalf of the organisation.

---

[88] The Government's response to this concern, when it was expressed by the Joint Committee, was that "[w]e confirm that the Government does not intend that this legislation should be used to penalise the legitimate and proportionate use of corporate hospitality to establish or maintain good relations with prospective customers" (p.12). There is, however, no specific carve-out or defence to this effect.

[89] The offence will only apply to the payer, as the drafters wanted to focus on the supply side of bribery. See Law Commission, *Reforming Bribery*, 2008, at XV.

21

The draftsmen hope that the new offence will deter companies from creating or maintaining a culture where bribes are paid on the organisation's behalf.

The Bribery provides a defence for an organisation if it can show that it had "adequate procedures" in place designed to prevent persons associated with it from committing acts of bribery. Unhelpfully, however, the Bribery Act does not define the term "adequate procedures". The nature and extent of such procedures therefore remains a topic for future consideration and consultation.

A number of the submissions to the Joint Committee at the pre-legislative scrutiny stage suggested that there should be "safe harbour" guidance on adequate procedures published by professional bodies or trade associations and approved by an appropriate Government department, which, if complied with by an organisation, would be required to be taken into account by a Court in considering whether the corporate offence had been committed. The Joint Committee supported this approach, but the Government initially rejected it, instead proposing non-statutory guidance which "will be indicative by setting out broad principles and illustrative good practice examples of 'adequate procedures' rather than detailed and prescriptive standards" (see p.10 of the Government response).

As a result of further debate, s.9 of the Bribery Act was eventually introduced, which provides that the Secretary of State must publish guidance about procedures that commercial organisations can put in place to prevent associated persons committing acts of bribery. Although not a formal "safe harbour", one would expect compliance with such guidance to be taken into account by a prosecutor (and a Court) in determining whether an organisation's policies and procedures constitute adequate procedures for the purposes of the s.7 defence. The practical utility of such guidance is, however, heavily dependent on its content and, in particular, its level of granularity. The SFO has already provided some guidance on the procedures it would expect companies to have in place, but this is very high level. A consultation on the draft s.9 guidance was expected during 2010, but as of September 1, 2010, the guidance has not been published, and no date for the consultation has been set.

Given that "adequate procedures" will potentially be all that stand between a company and what is essentially an offence of strict liability for the acts of its agents, this will be an area of significant focus in the next six to twelve months. It is expected that the new corporate offence will not be brought into force before the associated guidance is finalised.

A final point to note concerns the breadth of the jurisdictional scope of the corporate offence. The offence applies not only to UK-incorporated bodies but also to bodies corporate (wherever incorporated) which carry on part of their business in the United Kingdom. There is no requirement for the bribe which the corporate fails to prevent to have any United

Kingdom nexus. Thus, for example, a company incorporated in country X, which pays a bribe in X for the benefit of its business in X, could, in theory, be subject to the Bribery Act merely by virtue of having an unrelated branch office in the United Kingdom. Whether there would be a public interest in pursuing an investigation or prosecution in such circumstances is, of course, a separate issue.

I. Liability of Parent Company for Acts of Subsidiary

The Bribery Act does not expressly provide that a parent company will be liable   **1–39** for bribery committed by a subsidiary on its own account.[90] Where, however, a subsidiary acts on behalf of its parent company, the parent might potentially be liable under offence four above, for its failure to prevent the bribery by the subsidiary. Whether the offence will apply in such circumstances will depend on whether the subsidiary is a person who "performs services for or on behalf of" the parent company.

The Bribery Act provides that the capacity in which 'A' performs services for the purposes of the corporate offence does not matter and that 'A' may be "(for example) ... [the organisation's] employee, agent or subsidiary" and that whether or not this is the case "is to be determined by reference to all the relevant circumstances and not merely be reference the nature of the relationship between 'A' and [the organisation]". Whether or not a subsidiary will fall within this test remains a key area of legal uncertainty. The Government Response does not specifically address this issue and does not, therefore, provide any further assistance.

With the increased risk of liability, companies will need to take more proactive steps to consider whether they should ensure their overseas subsidiaries understand and apply the parent company's ethics policies. If subsidiaries do fall within the scope of the offence, it is unlikely that a parent would be held to have "adequate procedures" merely by virtue of, for example, sending copies of its policies to the subsidiary. Rather, concrete steps would need to be taken to ensure that these policies were embedded and followed.

II. Other Provisions

The other main provisions of the Act include: **1–40**

- granting the Courts of England and Wales, Scotland and Northern Ireland extra-territorial jurisdiction over bribery committed abroad by a range of

---

[90] The Law Commission considered the extent to which the bribery offences should apply to subsidiaries. They concluded that the issue of a parent company's liability for negligently supervising the conduct of its subsidiaries should be left to a wider review. See Law Commission, *Reforming Bribery*, 2008, at 108; Ashurst London, *Reforming bribery*, December 2008, available at *http://www.ashurst.com* [Accessed July 15, 2010].

UK-connected persons including in particular persons ordinarily resident in the United Kingdom, British nationals, and UK corporate bodies;

- replacing the existing requirement for the Attorney General's consent to prosecute a bribery offence so that proceedings for the offences in the Act may only be instituted by, or with the consent of, the Director of the relevant prosecuting authority;

- providing for a maximum penalty of 10 years' imprisonment for all the new offences, except the corporate offence, which will carry an unlimited fine; and

- conferring authority on the Secretary of State to authorise conduct that would constitute a bribery offence by the intelligence agencies.

The extra-territorial extent of the main bribery offences and the FPO offence is significant, and goes beyond that of the current law. It also gives rise to a risk of double or even triple jeopardy. For example, a US national who is ordinarily resident in England and who pays a bribe overseas could be liable under the Bribery Act, the US FCPA, and the laws of the jurisdiction where the bribe is paid.

H. THE SERIOUS FRAUD OFFICE

1–41   To understand the current state of anti-corruption law in the United Kingdom, one must also understand the agencies which have a role in investigating and prosecuting corrupt conduct.

In relation to complex corruption cases, the most important of these is the Serious Fraud Office (SFO), whose responsibility it is to investigate and prosecute serious and complex fraud. For the purpose of bribery offences, the SFO's role is roughly equivalent to that of the US Department of Justice's Criminal Fraud Section.[91]

The SFO is a statutory body created in April 1988, and, unusually in the United Kingdom, has the power to both investigate and prosecute crime (by contrast, the police typically investigate cases and pass them to the Crown Prosecution Service for prosecution). The SFO also has a range of specific statutory powers, referred to below, which go beyond those available to the police.

1–42   The SFO is staffed by lawyers, accountants and other specialists as well as by staff with a law enforcement background.

The official in charge of the SFO, the Director, is statutorily granted the power to investigate any suspected offence which appears to him on reasonable grounds to involve serious or complex fraud.[92] Although the Director must execute his

---

[91] See Sue Reisinger, *Mission Critical*, Corporate Counsel, December 1, 2008.

[92] See Criminal Justice Act 1987 s.1(2) ("The Attorney General shall appoint a person to be the Director of the Serious Fraud Office, and he shall discharge his functions under the superintendence of the Attorney General") and s.1(3).

duties under the superintendence of the Attorney General, the Director retains sole discretion over decisions regarding investigations or prosecutions.[93] From April 2008, the Director has also, pursuant to the Serious Crime Act 2007, had powers[94] in relation to the civil recovery of the proceeds of unlawful conduct, civil recovery investigations and disclosure orders in relation to confiscation investigations. As noted above, these new civil powers (which were previously in the hands of the Assets Recovery Agency), have already been used in the corruption context in the Balfour Beatty and AMEC Plc cases.

The SFO is responsible for investigating and prosecuting foreign bribery in the United Kingdom.[95] Indeed, the SFO has recently significantly improved its resourcing in this area, having set up a separate work area in 2009 (the Anti-Corruption Domain), and having invested in relevant recruitment and training. In the last year, the SFO has been involved in encouraging companies to self-report corruption, and in 2009 published its "Approach of the Serious Fraud Office to Dealing with Overseas Corruption".[96]

I. AIMS AND CRITERIA FOR ACCEPTANCE OF CASES

The SFO's aim is to reduce the occurrence and cost of fraud, in order to maintain confidence in the United Kingdom's business and financial institutions.[97] When   1–43

---

[93] See OECD, United Kingdom: Phase 2*bis* Report on the Application of the Convention on Combating Bribery of Foreign Public Officials in International Business Transactions and the 1997 Recommendation on Combatting Bribery in International Business Transactions, October 16, 2008, at 7. The Director is appointed by the Attorney General, who is responsible to Parliament for: the Serious Fraud Office; the Crown Prosecution Service (CPS); the Treasury Solicitor's Department; the Department of the Director of Public Prosecutions for Northern Ireland; the CPS Inspectorate; the Revenue and Customs Prosecution Office. See What kind of organisation is the SFO?, Serious Fraud Office, available at *http://www.sfo.gov.uk/about/about.asp* [Accessed July 15, 2010].

[94] Under the Proceeds of Crime Act 2002.

[95] England, Wales, and Northern Ireland fall within the SFO's jurisdiction, but the Isle of Man and the Channel Islands do not. Criminal Justice Act s.1(1) (1987); see also *About the SFO*, Serious Fraud Office, *http://www.sfo.gov.uk/about/about.asp* [Accessed July 15, 2010]. The impetus for creating the SFO came from the Fraud Trials Committee Report, commonly known as the "Roskill Report," published in 1986. See *Creation of the SFO*, Serious Fraud Office, *http://www.sfo.gov.uk/about/creation.asp* [Accessed July 15, 2010]. The Report recommended the "formation of a single, unified organisation responsible for all the functions of detection, investigation and prosecution of serious fraud." Chaired by Lord Roskill, the Fraud Trials Committee believed that a unified organisation responsible for fraud would prevent serious frauds from slipping through the nets of independent agencies. At that time, several different organisations were separately responsible to police fraud, including the Fraud Investigation Group, the Department of Trade and Industry, the Inland Revenue, and HM Customs and Excise. See Sally Ramage, *Fraud and the Serious Fraud Office*, (2005), p.10.

[96] Available through *http://www.sfo.gov.uk* [Accessed July 15, 2010].

[97] *SFO Annual Report 2007/08*, Serious Fraud Office, at 4, July 17, 2008. To achieve this aim, the SFO "a) takes on appropriate cases, investigates them and brings them to a successful conclusion as quickly as individual circumstances allow; and, b) when a decision to prosecute is made, prosecutes fairly and in a way that enables the jury to understand the issues." The SFO also pledges to "a) work effectively and efficiently; b) co-operate with other agencies and overseas jurisdictions; c) ensure that its activities, and the way they are reported, contribute to deterring fraud; and, d) work with other law enforcement agencies to help reduce fraud through education."

the SFO considers whether to take on a case, it considers several key criteria.[98] First, it considers how much money is involved in the fraud. If less than £1 million is at stake, the SFO will typically not investigate or prosecute the case.[99] Secondly, the SFO will question whether the case is likely to give rise to "national publicity and widespread public concern."[100] Cases meeting the second criterion include both commercial cases of public interest and cases involving government departments, public bodies and the governments of other countries.[101] Thirdly, the case should be one that requires a highly specialised knowledge.[102] Fourthly, the SFO will consider whether the case has an international dimension. The fifth criterion examines whether legal, accountancy, and investigative skills need to be brought to bear. Finally, the SFO will consider whether the case is complex enough to justify the use of s.2 powers.

II. SECTION 2 POWERS

1–44   One of the important features of any SFO investigation is the SFO's ability to exercise the powers granted to it under s.2 of the Criminal Justice Act 1987[103] (commonly referred to as "section 2 powers"; exercised by way of a "section 2 notice"). A s.2 notice can be issued in cases where the Director[104] suspects serious or complex fraud,[105] to obtain information either through interviewing persons of interest or through the acquisition of documents, including electronically stored

---

[98] In its Annual Report, the SFO states that "[t]he key criterion ... is that the suspected fraud was such that the direction of the investigation should be in the hands of those who will be responsible for the prosecution." These criteria were developed following the DAVIE Report that considered, and ultimately rejected, the idea to merge the Fraud Divisions of the Crown Prosecution Service with the SFO. See Ramage, at 11.

[99] According to the SFO, the £1 million threshold should not be construed as the "main indicator of suitability," but rather, it provides "an objective and recognizable signpost of seriousness and likely public concern." *Criteria for acceptance of cases*, Serious Fraud Office, available through http://www.sfo.gov.uk [Accessed July 15, 2010].

[100] *Criteria for acceptance of cases*, Serious Fraud Office.

[101] *Criteria for acceptance of cases*, Serious Fraud Office.

[102] The SFO guidelines list "financial markets and their practices" as an example of a field that would require the level of expertise suitable for an SFO investigation.

[103] Section 2, in relevant part, provides that:
"The Director may by notice in writing require the person whose affairs are to be investigated or any other person whom he has reason to believe has relevant information to answer questions or otherwise furnish information with respect to any matter relevant to the investigation at a specified place and either at a specified time or forthwith.
Criminal Justice Act s.2(2) (1987). The Director is further authorized to 'require the person under investigation or any other person to produce ... any specified documents which appear to the Director to relate to any matter relevant to the investigation.' Criminal Justice Act s.2(3). If the requested documents are produced, 'the Director may (i) take copies or extracts from them; (ii) require the person producing them to provide an explanation of any of them.' "

[104] Or certain persons within the SFO exercising delegated authority.

[105] See *Dealing with Cases*, Serious Fraud Office, available through http://www.sfo.gov.uk [Accessed July 15, 2010]; Criminal Justice Act s.2(1) ("The powers of the Director under this section shall be exercisable, but only for the purposes of an investigation under section 1 above ... in any case in which it appears to him that there is good reason to do so for the purpose of investigating the affairs, or any aspect of the affairs, of any person.").

data.[106] The suspects or witnesses are given notice that they must respond to questions or produce documents in a specific time and place, or immediately.[107] The s.2 notice overrides any duties of confidentiality, and is therefore commonly used to obtain evidence from financial institutions or professional services firms.[108] It also overrides any privilege against self-incrimination, although there are statutory limitations on the use to which any evidence obtained from a suspect by compulsion can be put,[109] and the power is therefore generally only used to interview witnesses. Suspects, by contrast, are interviewed under caution.[110]

It is a criminal offence to fail, without reasonable excuse, to comply with a s.2 notice,[111] to knowingly or recklessly make statements which are materially false or misleading in purported compliance with a s.2 notice,[112] or to falsify, cancel or destroy documents which are suspected to be relevant to the investigation.[113]

Importantly, in the corruption context, the Director has from July 2008[114] had the power to exercise his s.2 powers to determine whether to start on an investigation into a corruption offence, as well as in connection with an existing investigation. The power is exercised if it appears to the Director to be expedient for the purpose of enabling him to determine whether to start an investigation into conduct which constitutes a corruption offence, whether under the 1889 Act, the 1906 Act or the common law offence of bribery, by virtue of s.108 of the 2001 Act.

In its first year of operation, the SFO issued 233 s.2 notices.[115] Between 2007-2008, that number rose to 863.[116] Banks and other financial institutions tend to be the most frequent recipient of s.2 notices.[117]   **1–45**

---

[106] *Dealing with Cases*, Serious Fraud Office.

[107] Criminal Justice Act s.2(2).

[108] A bank will not be forced to breach the confidentiality of a client unless "the person to whom the obligation of confidence is owed consents to the disclosure or production; or the Director has authorised the making of the requirement or, if it is impracticable for him to act personally, a member of the Serious Fraud Office designated by him for the purposes of this sub-section has done so" (Criminal Justice Act s.2(10)). A lawyer or client cannot be forced to disclose information which is subject to legal professional privilege, but a lawyer may be required to provide the name and address of his client (s.2(9)).

[109] A statement made in response to a s.2 requirement may only be used against its maker on a prosecution (a) for making a false or misleading statement in purported compliance with s.2, or (b) for some other offence if, in giving evidence, the Defendant makes the statement inconsistent with it, and evidence relating to it is induced, or a question relating to it is asked, by him or on his behalf.

[110] Similar powers to those under s.2 of the Criminal Justice Act 1987 are now available to the Director of Public Prosecutions and the Director of Revenue and Customs Prosecutions and their delegates under s.60 of the Serious Organised Crime and Police Act 2005, but only in respect of a list of offences specified in s.61 of that Act. The offences listed in s.61 are relatively extensive and include any common law offence of bribery, any offence under s.1 of the Public Bodies Corrupt Practices Act 1889 and the first two offences under s.1 of the Prevention of Corruption Act 1906.

[111] Section 2(13); punishable by a maximum of six months imprisonment and/or a fine.

[112] Section 2(14); punishable by a maximum of two years imprisonment and/or a fine.

[113] Section 2(16); punishable by a maximum of seven years imprisonment and/or a fine.

[114] Pursuant to s.2A of the 1987 Act, inserted by s.59(2) of the Criminal Justice and Immigration Act 2008.

[115] *SFO Annual Report 1990/91*, Serious Fraud Office, at para.21, July 15, 1991.

[116] *SFO Annual Report 2007/08*, Serious Fraud Office, at 36. Often, s.2 notices are used to assist foreign authorities by locating evidence in the UK. For instance, of the 863 total notices between 2007–2008, 281 of them went to support foreign investigations.

[117] *SFO Annual Report 2007/08*, Serious Fraud Office.

The SFO has other powers to obtain evidence, including in particular its ability to apply to Court for a Search Warrant where the conditions for doing so are met.

III. City of London Police Overseas Anti-Corruption Unit

1–46 Corruption cases which do not meet the SFO's criteria may be dealt with by the police, and in particular by the Overseas Anti Corruption Unit (OACU) of the City of London Police (COLP).

The OACU was established following a G8 summit in 2006, which had identified the need to tackle international corruption as a priority. The Government set up a new dedicated team for investigating international corruption, including money laundering in the United Kingdom by corrupt politicians from developing countries, and bribery by UK businesses overseas, drawing on officers from CoLP and the Metropolitan Police Service (see *http://www.cityoflondon. police.uk/CityPolice/Departments/ECD/anticorruptionunit/aboutus.htm* [Accessed July 15, 2010]). As of December 2008, the unit consisted of a Detective Superintendent, a Detective Inspector, two Detective Sergeants and eight Detective Constables.

The OACU is not a separate statutory body and does not have any special powers, but rather uses the "normal" powers of the police. It is not responsible for prosecutions, which are dealt with by the Crown Prosecution Service. The OACU also works closely with the SFO.

IV. Mutual Legal Assistance

1–47 Recently, the SFO has trended towards greater coordination with law enforcement agencies in other jurisdictions.[118] Mutual legal assistance arrangements are a central component to this increased coordination.[119] Foreign jurisdictions have traditionally viewed the SFO as a valuable and effective resource because it can use its powers under s.2 expeditiously to ask questions and obtain documents for

---

[118] Article 9.1 of the OECD Convention requires that each Party cooperate with each other to the fullest extent possible to provide "prompt and effective legal assistance" with respect to criminal investigations and proceedings within the scope of the Convention. The UK's trend towards greater cooperation is being replicated worldwide. Matthew Friedrich, the DOJ Acting Assistance Attorney General stated in a December 2008 speech: "We are now working with our foreign law enforcement colleagues in bribery investigations to a degree that we never have previously." See *FCPA Enforcement: The Paradigm Shift of 2008*, January 28, 2009, at 20. In the summer of 2008, anti-bribery officials from around the world met in Paris to discuss ongoing investigations and collaboration. Russell Gold & David Crawford, *U.S., Other Nations Step up Bribery Battle*, Wall St. J., September 12, 2008.

[119] See Ramage, at 14 ("Such a large part of [the SFO's] work in the assistance of other countries takes place that it has a Mutual Assistance Department. This department acts on behalf of foreign investigators who seek evidence of a fraud in the United Kingdom."). In 2007–2008, the SFO received 45 requests from 30 jurisdictions to obtain information in the UK to aid overseas investigation. See *SFO Annual Report 2007/08*, Serious Fraud Office, at 36 (listing participating jurisdictions as Italy, Switzerland, Germany, Ukraine, Sweden, Portugal, Belgium, Czech Republic, Bulgaria, Poland, Netherlands, Jersey, Spain, Russia, Monaco, Luxembourg, France, Argentina, Bahrain, Kazakhstan, Namibia, South Africa, Thailand, Iran, Kenya, Pakistan, Canada, Russia, Malaysia and Zambia).

overseas agencies. Before the SFO can use its s.2 powers, however, the foreign authority must first request assistance through the UK Central Authority at the Home Office.[120] The Home Office's Mutual Assistance unit then decides whether assistance is warranted and which agency should handle it.[121]

International mutual legal assistance in criminal matters is effected in the United Kingdom under the framework of the Crime (International Co-operation) Act 2003 (2003 Act), although many of the working arrangements with other countries are formalised under, or reflect, a Mutual Legal Assistance Treaty (MLAT) which permits signatory countries to benefit from each other's resources and powers.[122]

The provisions of the 2003 Act (for example as to the burden that must be discharged by a requesting state before a request will be actioned) vary depending on whether the requesting state is a "Category 1" or a "Category 2" country under the 2003 Act. There are also restrictions under the 2003 Act on the evidence that can be gathered—for example, a person's legal professional privilege, or privilege against self-incrimination, cannot be overridden, and there are rules against double-jeopardy. Subject to restrictions of these types, the UK's ability to assist overseas countries in the investigation of suspected corruption is generally very broad.

1-48

I. NOTEWORTHY INVESTIGATIONS AND ACTIONS

I. Mabey & Johnson

In what SFO Director Richard Alderman hailed as a "model for other companies who want to self report corruption," Mabey & Johnson pleaded guilty on July 10, 2009 to 10 counts of corruption and violating sanctions.[123] The British bridge-building company admitted to offering bribes to officials in Jamaica and Ghana when bidding for public contracts in the 1990s and to violating the terms of the UN oil-for-food scheme in Iraq.[124] Mabey admitted to making payments totalling €422,264 to the Iraqi government, then under the control of Saddam Hussein, in return for a 4.22 million bridge contract. Some are praising the conviction as an example that the SFO's investigations into the British firms participating in the

1-49

---

[120] *International Co-operation*, Serious Fraud Office, available at *http://www.sfo.gov.uk/international/international.asp* [Accessed July 15, 2010].

[121] Mutual Legal Assistance Guidelines for the United Kingdom 6th edn (2009).

[122] See fn.121 above.

[123] Press Release, *Mabey & Johnson prosecuted by the SFO*, Serious Fraud Office, July 10, 2009. Alderman also noted: "These are serious offences and it is significant that Mabey & Johnson has co-operated with us to get to this landmark point." Later, he added: "This has enabled this case to be dealt with in just over a year and is a model for other companies who want to self report corruption and have it dealt with quickly and fairly by the SFO."

[124] Mabey & Johnson prosecuted by the SFO, Serious Fraud Office, 2009; see also *Christopher Hale, Mabey & Johnson's corruption confession could lead to more SFO investigations, Telegraph*, July 10, 2009.

oil-for-food programme are beginning to pay dividends.[125] The corruption offences were prosecuted under s.1 of the Criminal Law Act 1977 (i.e. as a conspiracy offence), whilst the Iraq offences were prosecuted under the relevant sanctions regime.[126]

The company agreed to pay compensation and to submit its internal compliance programme to an SFO approved independent monitor. The company ordered to pay (i) fines of £1.5 million in respect of the charges relating to corruption in Ghana and Jamaica, (ii) fines of £2 million in respect of the Iraq sanctions offences, (ii) a confiscation order of £1.1 million, (iii) costs to the SFO of £350,000, and (iv) compensation of £658,000 to Ghana, £139,000 to Jamaica and £618,000 to Iraq.[127] The first year monitoring cost is capped at £250,000.

This case is a significant development for the SFO, as it represents the first time the SFO has successfully negotiated a US-type plea-bargain in relation to criminal charges with a company involved in foreign corruption.[128] The Attorney General published, in July 2009, the first UK "Guidelines on Plea Discussions in cases of Serious or Complex Fraud". The Mabey & Johnson investigation, whilst largely undertaken prior to the publication of the Guidelines, is the first case, in substance, to have followed these new procedures.

1–50   The Guidelines do not introduce a full plea bargaining system in the US-model. The SFO has no power to bind the Court in relation to the level of penalty or confiscation that should be imposed.[129] Rather, it can only agree a plea agreement (which will set out an agreed list of charges, statement of facts, and a declaration that the Defendant will plead guilty) and a joint submission on sentence and sentencing considerations. In the Mabey & Johnson case, the Court accepted the parties' submissions. The Attorney General's guidelines, however, make clear that the Court will retain an absolute discretion as to whether or not it sentences in accordance with the joint submission from the parties, which gives rise to an unwelcome element of uncertainty for defendants considering whether to use the procedure. This uncertainty has been reinforced by the *Innospec* case referred to below.

The Mabey & Johnson case is also an important example of the SFO's application of the principles set out in its (subsequently published) guidelines "The Approach of the SFO to Dealing with Overseas Corruption". These

---

[125] Christopher Hale, *Mabey & Johnson's corruption confession could lead to more SFO investigations, Telegraph*, July 10, 2009.

[126] The Iraq (United Nations Sanctions) Order 2000 and the United Nations Act 1946. It is notable that there are difficulties in framing any payments to the Saddam Hussein regime as "corrupt" payments, since these payments are understood (see the report of the Independent Inquiry Committee into the United Nations Oil-for-Food Programme, available at *http://www.iic-offp.org/story27-oct05.htm* [Accessed July 15, 2010]) to have been made to the regime itself (i.e. to the "principal") and not to any individual within the regime (i.e. to an "agent" as an inducement to do any act). This is therefore an example of the principal/agent distinction in the existing UK law operating to prevent this conduct being classed as bribery.

[127] Press Release, *Mabey & Johnson Ltd sentencing*, Serious Fraud Office, September 25, 2009.

[128] D. Leigh, *Mabey & Johnson agrees corruption plea bargain with Serious Fraud Office*, July 8, 2009.

[129] Courts in US jurisdictions are likewise not bound by plea bargains between prosecution and defence. In practice, however, a US court will usually accept the parties' plea bargain.

guidelines are part of a campaign by the SFO to encourage companies to come forward and admit historical offences. They highlight the benefit to a corporate entity of coming forward as being: "the prospect (in appropriate cases) of a civil rather than a criminal outcome as well as the opportunity to manage, with us, the issues and any publicity proactively. The corporate will be seen to have acted responsibly … a negotiated settlement rather than a criminal prosecution means that the mandatory debarment provisions under … [the EU Procurement Directive] … will not apply". The Guidelines also set out the considerations the SFO will apply in considering whether it will be pursuing a civil or criminal outcome and how it will approach the investigation, settlement discussions, and other matters such as publicity.

II. BAE SYSTEMS & AL-YAMAMAH

BAE Systems is the world's second largest defence company,[130] with major operations on five continents, annual sales of over £18.5 billion and approximately 105,000 employees worldwide.[131] Between 2004 and 2006, BAE was subject to an investigation by the UK's Serious Fraud Office into allegations of bribery in relation to a series of military aircraft contracts, known as Al-Yamamah ("the dove" in Arabic), which BAE had entered into with the Kingdom of Saudi Arabia.

1-51

On October 14, 2005, the SFO issued a statutory notice requiring BAE to disclose details of payments made to agents and consultants in connection with the Al-Yamamah contracts. In response, attorneys for BAE wrote a confidential memorandum to the UK's Attorney General, Lord Goldmith, urging him to halt the investigation because it would be "seriously contrary to the public interest" and would "seriously affect relations between the UK and Saudi Arabian Governments."

Following further correspondence, less than two months later, on December 6, 2005, the Director of the SFO and the Attorney General initiated a "Shawcross exercise,"[132] whereby the Attorney General seeks facts, including any consideration affecting public policy, from Government ministers before deciding whether it is in the public interest to pursue a prosecution. The ultimate decision, however, remains the Attorney General's.[133]

In this case the Cabinet Secretary warned that several factors must be considered before making any decision. While noting that the ultimate decision rested with the Attorney General, the Secretary pointed to the commercial considerations of the Al-Yamamah deal, the strategic importance of Saudi Arabia

1-52

---

[130] Based on 2008 revenues.

[131] BAE Systems, *Key Facts, http://www.baesystems.co.uk* [Accessed July 15, 2010].

[132] The phrase comes from a statement made by Sir Hartley Shawcross QC, then the Attorney General, in the UK's House of Commons in 1951. See Clare Dyer, *The importance of the Shawcross principle, Guardian,* February 27, 2004.

[133] *R. (on the application of Corner House Research) v Director of the Serious Fraud Office* [2008] UKHL 60; [2009] 1 A.C. 756 at 60.

as an ally in the fight against Islamic terrorism, and the damage to British security interests should the investigation continue.

The SFO continued its investigation through 2006. It did not believe that Britain's security or economic interests justified terminating the investigation, particularly since the UK had ratified the OECD Convention, art.5 which forbids economic considerations from influencing the investigation and prosecution of bribery.[134]

However, the claimants in "*Corner House*" alleged, citing a Sunday Times report of June 10, 2007,[135] that when the SFO was about to obtain access to certain bank accounts in Switzerland, an explicit "threat" was made with the intention of halting the investigation. It was alleged (although the UK Government has never made a specific admission of these facts) that a threat was made that the Al-Yamamah deal would be shut down and intelligence and diplomatic relations between Saudi Arabia and the UK would be severed if the investigation was not halted.

1-53   The evidence was that, on September 29, 2006, the Cabinet Secretary wrote to the Attorney General warning that severe damage to the UK's public interest "is now imminent". Similarly, the UK Ambassador to Saudi Arabia told the SFO Director that the threats to international security were very grave indeed and were as represented by the Cabinet Secretary in his letter dated September 29, 2006; that effectively "British lives on British streets were at risk."

On December 8, 2006, the Prime Minister stated in a personal minute to the Attorney General that the public interests at stake meant that continuation of the investigation would risk:

> "Seriously damaging Saudi confidence in the UK as a partner . . . [and] . . . such damage risks endangering UK national security, both directly in protecting citizens and service people, and indirectly through impeding our search for peace and stability in this critical part of the world."

On December 11, 2006 the Prime Minister and Attorney General met. The Attorney General cautioned that stopping the investigation would hurt the UK's credibility in the international community. However, the Prime Minister took the position[136] that "higher considerations" and "supervening national interest" were at stake.

1-54   On December 13, 2006 the Director told the Attorney General that he had concluded that to continue the investigation risked endangering the UK's security and the lives of UK citizens and service personnel. On December 14, 2006, the Director of the SFO issued a press release that confirmed his decision to end the investigation.

---

[134] OECD Convention, *Combating Bribery of Foreign Public Officials*, 2008, art.5.

[135] See *Sunday Times*, June 10, 2007 (cited in *Corner House* [2009] 1 A.C. 756).

[136] In a letter dated December 12, 2006 sent from the Prime Minister's Principal Private Secretary to the Legal Secretary recording the meeting.

(a) Judicial review of the decision to stop the investigation

In early 2007, Corner House Research[137-138] (Corner House), along with the   **1–55** Campaign Against Arms Trade, filed a lawsuit seeking a judicial review of the decision to stop the BAE/Al-Yamamah investigation.[139] The Claimants challenged the SFO Director's decision on six grounds,[140] including that it was "unlawful" for the Director of the SFO to accede to the "threat", and that such conduct was contrary to the UK's rule of law.[141] The Government's defence was essentially that it, not the courts, was best equipped to judge the proper course to adopt in response to the "threat".[142]

The SFO contended that the decision to terminate the investigation was not influenced by economic considerations, but rather was based solely on national security concerns. Dropping a prosecution on the basis of national security concerns, it argued, is permitted under international and English law.

The High Court realised that it was faced with a case where it felt "[s]o bleak a picture of the impotence of the law invites at least dismay, if not outrage."[143] In April 2008, the High Court released its judgment in favour of the Claimants. The Court ruled that "[s]ubmission to a threat is lawful only when it is demonstrated to a court that there was no alternative course open to the decision-maker."[144] Here, the SFO Director failed to satisfy the Court that he had done all that could reasonably be done to resist the threat.[145]

The SFO immediately appealed the decision to the House of Lords.[146] In July   **1–56** 2008, the House of Lords overturned the High Court's ruling and upheld the

---

[137-138] Corner House is a non-profit organisation that conducts research, education, and campaigns concerning overseas corruption and the UK's role in combating bribery. See *Corner House* [2001] 1 A.C. 756 at [45].

[139] Under UK law, prosecutorial decisions are subject to judicial review, but the courts have traditionally been reluctant to interfere. It is important to understand that a judicial review is not a review of the correctness of a decision, but rather of its legality on certain limited grounds (e.g. whether the decision was irrational, or reached contrary to the requirements of procedural fairness). See *Sharma v Brown-Antoine* [2007] 1 W.L.R. 780; *R. (on the application of Birmingham) v Director of the SFO* [2007] Q.B. 727.

[140] The six grounds were: (1) it was unlawful for the Director to accede to the threat made by Prince Bandar or his agent because such conduct was contrary to the constitutional principle of the rule of law; (2) the Director failed to take into account the threat posed to the UK's national security, the integrity of its system of criminal justice and the rule of law caused by surrender to the type of threats made in the case; (3) the Director misdirected himself and took into account irrelevant considerations by misinterpreting art.5 of the OECD Convention, which requires an independent role for law enforcement outside of economic or political considerations; (4) the Director failed to take into account as a relevant consideration that if the threats made by Saudi Arabia were carried out, it would commit an act in breach of its international law obligations; (5) the advice on the public interest given by ministers was tainted by irrelevant considerations, especially commercial interests of the UK and its diplomatic relations with Saudi Arabia; and (6) the Shawcross exercise was conducted improperly in that ministers expressed their opinions as to what the Director's decision should be. *Corner House* [2009] 1 A.C. 756 at [49].

[141] [2009] 1 A.C. 756 at [49].

[142] [2009] 1 A.C. 756 at [73].

[143] *Corner House* [2009] 1 A.C. 756 at [7].

[144] [2009] 1 A.C. 756 at [99].

[145] [2009] 1 A.C. 756 at [171].

[146] Now the Supreme Court.

SFO's decision to terminate the investigation.[147] The House of Lords stated that:

"The issue in these proceedings is not whether [the Director's] decision was right or wrong, nor whether the Divisional Court or the House agrees with it, but whether it was a decision that the Director was lawfully entitled to make."[148]

According to the House of Lords' unanimous opinion, the Director was within his legal rights when he chose to end the investigation based on national security concerns.[149] Lord Bingham of Cornhill, the senior law Lord on the panel, said the Director made a "courageous decision" to stop the investigation because "the public interest in saving British lives outweighed the public interest in pursuing BAE to conviction."[150] Lord Rodger added: "The Director concluded that he had no option ... British lives would be put at risk."[151]

The Court declined to answer the question of whether art.5 of the OECD Convention was intended to preclude member states from having regard to national security concerns.[152] Instead, the Court referred to the SFO Director's belief that art.5 "permitted him to take account of threats to human life as a public interest consideration" and the fact that the Director had given an assurance "that he would undoubtedly have made the same decision [to end the investigation] even if he had believed ... that it was incompatible with article 5 of the Convention."[153]

1–57   As to the High Court's finding that the Director failed to show there was no alternative course but to acquiesce to the Saudi "threats", the Lords determined that this was not the correct test for considering the legality of the decision to terminate the investigation—the question which the Court had to determine was not whether no alternative course had been open to the Director but whether, in deciding that the public interest in pursuing an important investigation into alleged bribery was outweighed by the public interest in protecting the lives of British citizens, he had made a decision outside the lawful bounds of the discretion entrusted to him by Parliament. Further, the Director was permitted to accord appropriate weight to the judgment of those with responsibility for national security who had direct access to sources of intelligence unavailable to him.[154]

---

[147] *R. (on the application of Corner House Research and Campaign Against Arms Trade) v Director of the Serious Fraud Office* [2008] UKHL 60 on appeal from [2008] EWHC 246 (Admin).
[148] [2009] 1 A.C. 756 at [41].
[149] [2009] 1 A.C. 756 at [41]–[42].
[150] [2009] 1 A.C. 756 at [35].
[151] [2009] 1 A.C. 756 at [51].
[152] [2009] 1 A.C. 756 at [47]. The Court noted that certain commentators had made a powerful case that there is no implicit exception for "national security" under the OECD Convention. Professor Susan Rose-Ackerman & Benjamin Billa, *Treaties and National Security*, 40 N.Y.U. J. I. L. & P. 437 (2008).
[153] [2009] 1 A.C. 756 at [47].
[154] [2009] 1 A.C. 756 at [54].

(b) The conclusion of other investigations into BAE's conduct

Whilst the SFO discontinued the investigation into the Al-Yamamah arms deal,   **1–58**
its investigation into some of BAE's non Saudi activities continued into early
2010. The US Department of Justice ("DOJ") also continued to pursue investigations relating to both the Al-Yamamah deal and BAE's conduct in other
jurisdictions.

On February 5, 2010, the SFO and the DOJ both announced settlements with
BAE, in what the SFO described as "a ground breaking global agreement". The
DOJ agreement involves BAE's business dealings in a number of countries, whilst
the SFO agreement concentrates on the company's operations in Tanzania.[155]

Under the SFO agreement, BAE will plead guilty to an offence under s.221 of
the Companies Act 1985 of failing to keep reasonably accurate accounting records
in relation to its activities in Tanzania in 1999. BAE has agreed to pay £30
million, comprising a financial order to be determined by a Crown Court judge
with the balance paid as an ex gratia payment for the benefit of the people of
Tanzania. The SFO stated that it had also taken into account the implementation
by BAE of substantial ethical and compliance reforms and BAE's agreement with
the DOJ. It has announced that no further prosecutions will be brought against
BAE or its employees in relation to the matters that have been under investigation
by the SFO.[156]

Under the agreement with the DOJ, which requires court approval, BAE will   **1–59**
plead guilty to one charge of conspiring to make false statements to the Defense
Department of the U.S. Government between 2000 and 2002 in connection with
statements and undertakings that BAE would create and implement policies and
procedures to ensure compliance with the FCPA and relevant provisions of the
OECD Convention. BAE is also alleged to have made certain false, inaccurate and
incomplete statements and failed to make required disclosures in connection with
applications for arms export licences. The allegations focus on the disclosure of
payments and commissions to "marketing advisers", and representations made in
relation to the adequacy of BAE's internal scrutiny and review of such payments.
BAE has issued a statement that:

> "In 2000, the Company gave a commitment to the US Government that it would
> establish and comply with defined US regulatory requirements within a certain period
> and it subsequently failed to honour this commitment or to disclose its shortcomings".

Under the DOJ agreement, BAE will pay a fine of $400 million and make
additional commitments concerning its ongoing compliance.

The fact that the UK agreement relates to "accounting" charges (rather than
corruption charges) is significant as regards BAE's ability to participate in future
public procurement exercises, as it will avoid the application of the mandatory
debarment regime referred to above. The SFO's agreement not to pursue charges

---

[155] SFO Press Release, available through *http://www.sfo.gov.uk* [Accessed July 15, 2010].
[156] SFO Press Release.

against individuals also assists BAE in finally drawing a line under the lengthy investigations to which it has been subject. As such, despite the high level of the agreed penalties, the settlement can be seen as a practical way forward for BAE; there has been some press comment expressing dismay that corruption charges have not been pursued. Richard Alderman, the Director of the SFO, has himself called this a "pragmatic end to a long-running and wide-ranging investigation".

1-60   In February 2010, Corner House and the Campaign Against Arms Trade made a fresh application to judicially review the SFO's decision to enter the plea agreement with BAE. The basis for the challenge was that the SFO failed properly to apply prosecution guidance (including its own guidance), and in particular that the plea agreement failed to reflect the seriousness and extent of BAE's alleged offending and to provide the court with adequate sentencing powers. The application was, however, unsuccessful.

The BAE agreement is significant not only in bringing to an end this substantial investigation, but also as being the first major coordinated transatlantic settlement involving the SFO and the DOJ.

Balfour Beatty

1-61   In October 2008, the SFO used a Civil Recovery Order (CRO) for the first time to recover £2.25 million from Balfour Beatty, a UK construction group.[157] The recovery stemmed from an SFO investigation into inaccurate accounting practices occurring within a subsidiary entity during the reconstruction of the Alexandria Library in Egypt. The project was undertaken by the Balfour Beatty subsidiary in a joint venture with an Egyptian company. The unlawful conduct on which the CRO was based relates to accounting inaccuracies, albeit that the SFO Press Release refers to "payment irregularities". Balfour Beatty also agreed to pay a contribution towards the costs of the CRO proceedings.[158]

In its Press Release, the SFO lauded its use of the CRO as "an important example of how the SFO will use the new tools at its disposal to enhance the criminal justice process." Historically, companies have had little incentive to "turn themselves in" because UK criminal law afforded prosecutors little discretion in charging offences or offering any alternative to a criminal prosecution. As explained above, a CRO, by contrast, permits the recovery of property obtained by unlawful conduct without a criminal prosecution, and does not require proof that a company or individual has committed any specific offence. Rather, the SFO needs only to prove (to the civil standard) that the money it seeks to recover represents the proceeds of certain types of unlawful conduct.

In a significant departure from past investigations, in particular in the corruption sphere, Balfour Beatty self-reported its conduct to the SFO; once Balfour

---

[157] The civil recovery powers were granted under the Proceeds of Crime Act 2002, under which the SFO can recover property obtained by unlawful conduct.

[158] Press Release, Balfour Beatty Plc, Serious Fraud Office successfully obtains first ever Civil Recovery Order involving major Plc, Serious Fraud Office, October 6, 2008.

Beatty discovered and investigated the payments, it immediately notified the SFO.

The SFO conducted its own investigation and found that the subsidiary's business records did not comply with the requirements of s.221 of the Companies Act 1985 (which require every company to keep accounting records which are, inter alia, sufficient to show and explain the company's transactions and, in particular, contain entries of all sums of money received and expended and the matters in respect of which the receipt and expenditure takes place). On October 6, 2008, the High Court entered a Consent Order whereby, in addition to the £2.25 million settlement, Balfour Beatty agreed to implement certain compliance systems and to allow external monitoring for an agreed period. The SFO agreed not to prosecute any individual or corporate entity related to Balfour Beatty. 1–62

The Balfour Beatty case may signal an important change in strategy by the SFO as it appears to move towards a US model of deferred and non-prosecution agreements.[159] By foregoing long, costly, and uncertain criminal prosecutions in favour of CROs, the SFO is able to secure a quicker victory against businesses. In turn, the SFO's strategy will likely lead to an increased willingness of businesses, like Balfour Beatty, to approach law enforcement agencies to admit wrongdoing.[160]

AMEC Plc

A further example of the use of a CRO was publicised in October 2009, when the SFO issued a press release confirming that it had obtained a CRO of almost £5 million against AMEC, an international engineering and project management firm.[161] 1–63

AMEC made a referral to the SFO in March 2008 following an internal investigation into the receipt of "irregular payments" between November 2005 and March 2007, which were associated with a project in which AMEC was a shareholder. Like Balfour Beatty, AMEC was said to have acted promptly and responsibly in self-reporting the case and co-operating with the SFO's investigation.

A Consent Order was agreed between AMEC and the SFO which involved AMEC admitting to unlawful conduct by virtue of inaccurately describing the payments in its books and records, contrary to the requirements of s.221 of the Companies Act 1985 (see above). As part of the settlement, AMEC also agreed to appoint an independent consultant to review improvements it was making in its ethics, compliance and accounting standards, and report on these to the SFO.

---

[159] The change also comes amid heavy criticism aimed at the SFO for its poor record in securing criminal convictions. See Michael Herman, *Balfour Beatty gives up £2.25m after SFO probe*, Times Online, October 6, 2008.

[160] The SFO said it "welcomed Balfour Beatty's transparent and responsible approach in self reporting the issue." The SFO "Approach to Dealing with Oversees Corruption" (see above) also emphasises the possibility of a civil 'deal' as a potential benefit of self reporting.

[161] Press Release, SFO obtains Civil Recovery Order against AMEC Plc, Serious Fraud Office, October 26, 2009.

Innospec Limited

1–64   Another recent case of interest in relation to settlements between prosecuting authorities and offenders is *Innospec*.[162] The case concerned a UK subsidiary (Innospec Ltd) of a US NASDAQ listed company (Innospec Inc). Innospec Ltd pleaded guilty to having engaged in systematic and large scale corruption of senior government officials of Indonesia to secure contracts for the supply of a fuel additive (TEL). Bribes totalling approximately $8 million were paid, and this was aggravated by the fact that Innospec Ltd's behaviour was aimed at blocking legislative moves to ban TEL, due to environmental and public health concerns.

   Following investigations by the DOJ and the SFO, those bodies considered that the level of fine and other penalties might in the circumstances have exceeded $400 million in the US and $150 million in the United Kingdom. Having investigated the financial health of the company, however, and given the co-operation of Innospec Ltd with the SFO's investigation, the US and UK authorities agreed to a global agreement resulting in the payment of approximately $40 million, of which Innospec Ltd agreed to pay some $12.7 million. This agreement was subject to approval by the US and English Courts.

   The settlement was approved, but not without some significant concerns being raised by the Judge. Thomas L.J., in his sentencing remarks, emphasised that the SFO has no authority to enter into agreements with offenders as to the penalty for an offence. He noted that sentencing is a matter for the judiciary, and whilst the SFO may discuss plea bargains with a Defendant, open and transparent justice requires Courts to scrutinise the basis of the plea, and any agreement, to determine whether it reflects the public interest.

1–65   Thomas L.J. considered the agreed $12.7 million fine to be inadequate, but "reluctantly" approved it in light of the unique circumstances of the case, including that:

- the US Courts had already approved the arrangement;

- Innospec had pleaded guilty to all charges and had co-operated fully with the SFO's investigation;

- Innospec Ltd was unable to pay the level of fine that would ordinarily be imposed without entering into immediate insolvency. Thomas L.J. considered that it would not be in the public interest for Innospec Ltd to cease trading, bearing in mind that the company had in place new systems and controls to prevent such corrupt activity in the future; and

- the details of the settlement had been announced to the markets. The Court was particularly critical of the SFO permitting Innospec Ltd to release a press announcement of the proposed settlement agreement.

---

[162] *R. v Innospec Ltd*, March 26, 2010.

The Judge emphasised that this decision sets no precedent for the future: "there will be no reason for any such limitation in any other case and the Court will not consider itself in any way restricted in its powers by any such agreement".

In terms of the level of the fine, the Judge indicated that the corruption of foreign government officials or ministers is at "the top end of serious corporate offending" and that, in his view, a fine comparable to that imposed in the US should have been the starting point, in addition to disgorgement by the company of any benefits obtained through its criminality. If that approach is followed in subsequent cases, it could signal a significant increase in penalties going forward; the Judge indicated that, but for the plea agreement and the factors referred to above, the fine would have been measured in "the tens of millions".

The Court also considered the use of civil recovery orders. The SFO had sought   **1–66** to allocate half of the amount Innospec Ltd was due to pay to a civil recovery order in relation to Innospec's conduct in connection with the Iraq oil for food programme. This had been dealt with as a criminal matter in the United States; the UK civil recovery route avoided issues of double jeopardy. Thomas L.J., whilst noting that civil penalties may be appropriate in addition to criminal penalties as a means of compensation, was concerned about their use more generally. He stated that it is of the greatest public interest that serious criminal behaviour is made "patent for all to see" through criminal penalties and not civil sanctions.

KBR & Nigeria LNG

The SFO has also been actively aiding foreign governments in their investigations   **1–67** of bribery and corruption offences, for example in relation to the KBR Nigerian corruption affair.

On February 17, 2009, Jeffrey Tesler and Wojchiech Chodan, two British residents, were indicted in the United States for allegedly conspiring to violate and violating the FCPA. On March 5, 2009, Tesler was arrested by the London Metropolitan Police at the request of the United States, who were seeking his extradition.

An indictment is, of course, merely a charge and defendants are presumed innocent until proven guilty. The US indictment alleges that Tesler was hired as an agent by a four-company joint venture consortium seeking engineering, procurement and construction (EPC) contracts to build liquefied natural gas (LNG) facilities on Bonny Island, Nigeria, valued at more than $6 billion. It is alleged that the joint venture entered into a series of consulting contracts with a Gibraltar corporation allegedly controlled by Tesler to which the joint venture paid approximately $132 million, allegedly to be used to bribe Nigerian government officials.

The DOJ stated that significant assistance was provided to its investigation by   **1–68** the authorities in France, Italy, Switzerland and the United Kingdom, including in particular the Serious Fraud Office's Anti-Corruption Unit, the London Metropolitan Police and the City of London Police.

The US government has asked for Tesler to be extradited and an extradition hearing was held in the United Kingdom in November and December 2009. Tesler is reported to have claimed before the hearing that he should not be extradited, inter alia, because he might also face prosecution in Britain where the SFO has been conducting its own investigation. Counsel for the US government is reported to have claimed that Tesler's conduct had clear links to the United States and that the SFO has ceded jurisdiction to the United States.[163] The Judge at first instance approved the extradition request on March 26, 2010, but it has been reported that Tesler intends to appeal this ruling. The final disposition of the case is unknown as at the date of writing.

Tumukunde & Tobiasen

1–69   As noted above, the SFO is not the only agency that has been taking enforcement action in relation to corporate bribery and corruption. On September 22, 2008, the Overseas Anti-Corruption Unit (OACU) of the City of London Police secured the first foreign bribery conviction in the United Kingdom since the changes to the territorial scope of the English laws brought about by the 2001 Act.[164]

Ananias Tumukunde was an adviser to the Ugandan government on science and technology. Danish national Niels Tobiasen was a director of a UK security consulting firm hired by the Ugandan government to supply services in relation to a forthcoming Commonwealth heads of state meeting. Tumukunde approached Tobiasen, claiming that he would need to make additional payments via Tumukunde to meet a "local tax" of 10 per cent. In fact, these payments were made directly into two bank accounts Tumukunde had opened in his own name in the United Kingdom.[165]

Tobiasen pleaded guilty to a charge under the Prevention of Corruption Act 1906 of paying more than £83,000 in bribes to two Ugandan officials, one of whom was Tumukunde, and was given a suspended sentence after cooperating fully with police enquiries. Tumukunde was charged with four counts of money laundering and sentenced to 12 months in prison (but is reported to have been released in October 7, 2008 on the basis of time spent on remand and good conduct[166]).

---

[163] David Leigh, *British lawyer laundered bribes to Nigeria, court told*, Guardian, November 23, 2009.
[164] The City of London Police press release is at *http://www.cityoflondon.police.uk/CityPolice/ECD/anticorruptionunit/guiltypleatobribery.htm* [Accessed July 15, 2010].
[165] UK Government "Self-assessment checklist on the implementation of the United Nations Convention against Corruption", September 2008, available at *http://www.dfid.gov.uk* [Accessed July 15, 2010].
[166] Anne Mugisa, *Britain returns bribe paid to Ugandan officials*, New Vision, December 9, 2008, available at *http://www.newvision.co.uk* [Accessed July 15, 2010].

Financial Services Authority—systems and controls enforcement

In addition to action taken by the SFO and OACU in relation to the actual **1–70**
payment of bribes, the Financial Services Authority (FSA)[167] has taken regulatory
enforcement action in relation to systems and controls issues in connection with
bribery and corruption related risks. In January 2009, the FSA announced a fine
of £5.25 million[168] against Aon Limited for failing to take reasonable care to
establish and maintain effective systems and controls to reduce the risk of bribery
and corruption in respect of payments to overseas firms and individuals.[169] This is
the first fine the FSA has imposed for anti-corruption controls issues,[170] and it was
the largest ever fine relating to financial crime risks imposed by the FSA.

The fine related to the company's failure to assess the risks involved in its **1–71**
dealings with overseas parties and its failure to implement effective controls to
mitigate those risks. As a result, Aon made a number of "suspicious payments" to
businesses and individuals in Bahrain, Bangladesh, Bulgaria, Burma, Indonesia
and Vietnam amounting to approximately $2.5 million and €3.4 million between
January 2005 and September 2007.[171] Although the payments were not found to
be corrupt (and the practice of paying referral fees is an accepted one in many
areas of insurance business) the FSA determined that "Aon failed adequately to
question the purpose and nature of these suspicious payments."[172]

The FSA fine was intended to send a warning to regulated businesses that "it is
completely unacceptable for firms to conduct business overseas without having in
place appropriate anti-bribery and corruption systems and controls."[173] The FSA
has since undertaken a thematic review of anti-corruption systems and controls in
commercial insurance intermediary firms, the results of which were published in
May 2010. It is anticipated that further enforcement actions in this area will flow
from the FSA's work during 2010.

---

[167] The FSA is an independent non-governmental body that regulates the financial services
industry in the UK. It has four objectives under the Financial Services and Markets Act 2000:
maintaining market confidence; promoting public understanding of the financial system; securing the
appropriate degree of protection for consumers; and fighting financial crime. It was created and given
broad statutory powers by the Financial Services and Markets Act 2000. See Financial Services
Authority, *What we do*, available *http://www.fsa.gov.uk* [Accessed July 15, 2010].
[168] This was after a 30% discount under the FSA's early settlement procedures; the fine would
otherwise have been £7.5 million.
[169] Press release, FSA fines Aon Limited £5.25 million for failings in its anti-bribery and corruption, Financial Services Authority, Jan. 8, 2009, available at *http://www.fsa.gov.uk*.
[170] Sara Arnott, FSA hits Aon with £5.25 million fine, *Independent*, January 9, 2009.
[171] FSA Final Notice to Aon Ltd, January 6, 2009.
[172] FSA Press release, fn.169 above.
[173] FSA Press release, fn.169 above (quoting Margaret Cole, FSA director of enforcement).

J. THE "AMERICANISATION" OF UK ANTI-CORRUPTION EFFORTS

I. INCREASED USE OF PLEA AGREEMENTS

1–72 The Mabey & Johnson case illustrates a new trend at the SFO: seeking plea bargain agreements rather than risking acquittals at trial.[174] Historically, the SFO has faced difficulty negotiating plea bargain deals with defendants because its conviction rate is so low[175] and because prosecutors had little power to vary the terms of their engagement with suspects.[176] A June 2008 government-commissioned review found that the SFO's five-year average conviction rate had dropped to 61 per cent, down from 82 per cent four years earlier, and well behind prosecutors in the United States whose conviction rates consistently rise above 90 per cent.[177] Among the reasons for the low conviction rate, the report pointed to a "complaint culture," "low morale," and "a skills shortage."[178] However, the chief reason, many commentators argue, for the low conviction rate is the burdensome pre-trial disclosure rules.[179]

Under the Criminal Procedure and Investigation Act 1996, prosecutors must disclose all relevant material to the defence.[180] Merely inviting opposing counsel to examine the material is not sufficient; instead, everything must be sifted, analysed and listed. This requires extensive funding and trained manpower, both of which are already in short supply.[181] It also has the effect of dragging out prosecutions and trials. A 2005 PricewaterhouseCoopers report found the average

---

[174] Currently, there are no provisions that permit a defendant in a fraud case to make admissions *without* these counting as evidence against him. A defendant who pleads guilty to a lesser offence could find that this is used to support the more serious charges. This greatly reduces any incentive to "come clean" on certain offences, or to give evidence against accomplices. See Fraud Advisory Panel, *Tackling the crisis in the investigation and prosecution of serious fraud*, May 2006, available through *http://www.fraudadvisorypanel.org* [Accessed July 15, 2010]. See also judicial comment in *R. v Innospec* March 26, 2010.

[175] See Simon Bowers, *SFO report looks at low conviction rate, Guardian*, June 11, 2008. The report was conducted by former New York prosecutor Jessica de Grazia.

[176] In March 2009, the Attorney General introduced a plea bargain framework for fraud cases that would offer limited scope for early-stage discussions between prosecutors and defendants. Unlike the US's system, however, the UK model is not concerned with offering discounts, immunity or incentives. See Christopher Hope, *Plea bargains to speed fraud cases, Telegraph*, March 18, 2009.

[177] S. Bowers, *SFO report looks at low conviction ratre, Guardian*, 2008. The SFO claims such snapshot statistics are misleading. More recently, the SFO's conviction rate is improving, jumping up to 68% from 2007–2008. See *SFO's conviction rate improving*, BBC News, July 17, 2008 (reporting that 17 of 25 individuals prosecuted led to convictions). However, the SFO's increase in conviction rate does not reflect an increased number of convictions overall. From 1998–2008, the number of defendants that stood trial following an SFO investigation fell from 42 to 25. Yet, during this period, the organization's costs rose from £16 million (roughly £42,000 a day) in 1998/99 to £42 million (£115,000 a day) in 2007/08. See Christopher Hope, *Serious Fraud Office under fire as conviction rate halves as budget doubles, Telegraph*, July 29, 2008. Some have complained that the increase in cost and decrease in prosecutions shows the incompetence of the SFO.

[178] S. Bowers *SFO report looks at low conviction rate, Guardian*, 2008.

[179] S. Bowers *SFO report looks at low conviction rate, Guardian*, 2008.

[180] Criminal Procedure and Investigations Act 1996 s.3(1).

[181] See Fraud Advisory Panel, *Tackling the crisis in the investigation and prosecution of serious fraud*, May 2006, available at *http://www.fraudadvisorypanel.org* [Accessed July 15, 2010].

SFO prosecution involved analysis of more than 5,000 e-mails and electronic documents.[182] Whilst several commentators have called for a change to the pre-trial disclosure rules,[183] no formal action has been taken.

II. NON-PROSECUTION AGREEMENTS & DEFERRED PROSECUTION AGREEMENTS

UK authorities are understood to be considering the possibility of non-prosecution agreements (NPAs) and deferred prosecution agreements (DPAs).[184] In an NPA, prosecutors agree not to file criminal charges at all after a sufficiently thorough investigation. In a deferred prosecution, prosecutors file charges but act no further for a period of time; as long as the defendant complies with the terms of the DPA, charges are dropped at the conclusion of the prescribed time period. Although not able to declare that they have secured a conviction, prosecutors are still able to achieve their aims of deterrence and punishment through financial penalties, remedial measures and/or the appointment of a compliance monitor.[185]

    1–73

At present, the only way in which the SFO can achieve a result of this nature is under the provisions of the Serious Organised Crime and Police Act 2005, which permits immunity agreements to be made in exchange for assistance by offenders,[186] or for a written agreement to be made whereby the defendant will provide assistance in exchange for the Court taking this into account in sentencing.[187] These provisions are, however, relatively inflexible, particularly by comparison to the position in the US. The SFO is understood to be seeking further powers in this area.

---

[182] Fraud Advisory Panel, *Tackling the crisis in the investigation and prosecution of serious fraud* (noting that in 2003–2004 fraud trials consumed nearly £100 million in legal aid alone and the average time between the SFO accepting a case for investigation and transferring it to the Crown Court was just over 33 months).

[183] See S. Bowers, *Guardian*, 2008 ("The criminal justice system of England and Wales is unlikely to obtain the full benefit of an early plea-negotiation framework unless the current system of disclosure is changed."); see also Fraud Advisory Panel, *Tackling the crisis in the investigation and prosecution of serious fraud* ("Relying on investigators to find evidence on the defendant's behalf is unnecessary and distracts them from their fundamental task.")

[184] See Eugene R. Erbstoesser, *The FCPA and analogous foreign anti-bribery laws—overview, recent developments, and acquisition due diligence*, C.M.L.J. (September 24, 2007). In the US, between 2002–2008, corporate defendants obtained deferred or non-prosecution agreements in 22 criminal FCPA cases, compared with seven corporate guilty pleas; Joseph Covington & Iris Bennett, *Signs of Life in International Anti-bribery Enforcement—Recent Enforcement of Anti-bribery Laws Outside the U.S. and Issues to Consider for a Multi-jurisdictional Defense Strategy*, Bloomburg Finance. Though the settlement means a company avoids a criminal conviction, it can also mean hefty fines and other burdensome remedies. For example, Chevron was fined $30 million in criminal and civil penalties even though the criminal case was resolved with a non-prosecution agreement. See DOJ, *Fact Sheet: the Department of Justice Public Corruption Efforts*, (March 27, 2008) available through *http://www.usdoj.gov* [Accessed July 15, 2010]. Willbros Group was fined $22 million in connection with an FCPA deferred prosecution agreement in 2008. See DOJ Press Release, *Willbros Group Inc. Enters Deferred Prosecution Agreement and Agrees to Pay $22 Million Penalty for FCPA Violations*.

[185] See generally *Crime Without Conviction: The rise of deferred and non prosecution agreements*, Corporate Crime Reporter, December 28, 2005.

[186] Serious Organised Crime and Police Act 2005 s.71.

[187] Serious Organised Crime and Police Act 2005 s.73.

III. Increased Resources and Personnel for Overseas Corruption

1–74   The SFO has recognised that international collaboration is vital in the fight against serious fraud.[188] In addition to its Mutual Legal Assistance programs, the SFO has also increased its resources for overseas anti-corruption investigations. According to its Director, the SFO is increasing by 50 per cent the number of investigators it has on anti-corruption work.[189] The influx in resources and personnel provides evidence that the UK is placing an increased focus on rooting out corruption at home and abroad.

---

[188] See International Co-operation, Serious Fraud Office, available at *http://www.sfo.gov.uk/international/international.asp* [Accessed July 15, 2010].

[189] Press Release, *More resources for anti-corruption work, Serious Fraud Office*, November 18, 2008 (increasing from 65 to around 100).

CHAPTER 2

THE OECD ANTI-BRIBERY CONVENTION[1]

A. INTRODUCTION

The Organisation for Economic Cooperation and Development has variously   2–01
been described as "a think tank, monitoring agency, a rich man's club, [and] an
unacademic university."[2] Judging by its origins and function, few would have
predicted that the OECD would become the single most important force in the
development of global anti-corruption standards. That it did so is largely testa-
ment to the vigorous efforts of the United States to secure a level playing field for
its multinational enterprises. The OECD's Anti-Bribery Convention has now
become the benchmark against which corruption legislation is measured.

It is difficult to conduct any meaningful analysis of the OECD's anti-
corruption regime without understanding the organisation's origins, structure,
and objectives.

The OECD is a highly influential multilateral organisation, boasting thirty
member countries, even more global partners and initiatives, and an annual
budget of €303 million.[3] The organisation provides a global resource for comparable statistics, economic and social forecasting, and public policy-related
publications.[4]

B. HISTORY OF THE OECD

The OECD developed out of the proverbial ashes of the Organisation for Eur-   2–02
opean Economic Co-operation (OEEC).[5] The OEEC was established in 1947 to
administer American and Canadian aid under the Marshall Plan for the post
Second World War reconstruction of a battered Europe.[6] In 1949, the organisa-

---

[1] The authors gratefully acknowledge the substantial assistance of Aditi Chatterjee and Josh Posner.
[2] Organisation for Economic Co-operation and Development [OECD], *About OECD*, available
through *http://www.oecd.org* [Accessed July 15, 2010].
[3] OECD, *About OECD*.
[4] OECD, *About OECD*.
[5] OECD, *History*, available through *http://www.oecd.org* [Accessed July 15, 2010].
[6] OECD, *History*.

tion made its home at the historic Château de la Muette in Paris, where the OECD maintains its headquarters today.[7] The OEEC was one of many international bodies (including GATT and the IMF) created in the post-war era in order to address common economic issues and formulate a unified European system of free trade.[8]

The OEEC declined after the unanticipated end of the Marshall Plan in 1952. Nearly a decade later the OECD succeeded it.[9] In 1961, the OECD consisted of the eighteen founding members of the OEEC, plus the United States and Canada.[10]

C. THE OECD'S PURPOSE

2–03   The goals set forth in the 1960 Convention on the Organisation for Economic Co-operation and Development encourage policies that adhere to the following core tenets:

> "(b) to achieve the highest sustainable economic growth and employment and a rising standard of living in Member countries, while maintaining financial stability, and thus to contribute to the development of the world economy;
>
> (c)   to contribute to sound economic expansion in Member as well as non-member countries in the process of economic development; and
>
> (d)   to contribute to the expansion of world trade on a multilateral, non-discriminatory basis in accordance with international obligations."[11]

As the words of the Convention clearly state, the OECD aspires to bring together countries committed to open markets and democratic institutions in order to compare their efforts to boost employment and living standards, as well as maintain sustainable economic growth and financial stability.[12]

D. THE OECD'S STRUCTURE

2–04   The OECD is composed of three main governing bodies. The highest of these is the Council.[13] The Council includes one representative from each Member

---

[7] OECD, *History*.

[8] Barbara C. George et al., *The 1998 OECD Convention: An Impetus for Worldwide Changes in Attitudes Toward Corruption in Business Transactions*, 37 Am. Bus. L.J. 485 at 487 (2000).

[9] OECD, *About OECD*.

[10] OECD, *About OECD*.

[11] Convention on Organisation for Economic Co-operation and Development, December 14, 1960 (hereinafter 1960 OECD Convention).

[12] OECD, *About OECD*.

[13] OECD, *Who Does What*, available through *http://www.oecd.org* [Accessed July 15, 2010].

country and one representative from the European Council. It is divided into the Ministerial level, which consists of a Chair and Vice Chairs, and the Permanent Representative Level, where the Secretary-General sits as Chair of the Council and directs the Secretariat. The Council meets at the Ministerial level to prioritise OECD work, and subsequently (and more frequently) at the Permanent Representative level to make decisions by consensus. The Council is the final source of all resolutions, agreements, and recommendations.[14]

Representatives divide themselves among some 200 specialised Committees devoted to specific policy areas. These Committees work with the Secretariat to request and review OECD work.[15]

The Secretariat is the third governing body, headed by the Secretary-General at the Permanent Representative level. With a staff of some 2500 lawyers, educators, economists, and other policy experts, the Secretariat carries out the daily work of the OECD.[16]

E. MEMBERSHIP IN THE OECD

Accession to the OECD is a multi-step process. Rather than making membership available to all applicants, Member countries decide whom to invite and under what conditions.[17] Typically, invited countries will have already maintained a significant relationship with the OECD by attending Committee meetings and participating in non-Member cooperation programs.[18] The OECD's approval in 2007 of a "road map" system places particular emphasis upon customising the accession process for individual invitees.[19] **2–05**

When accession negotiations begin, the appropriate Committees examine the policies of the prospective member country to determine whether or not there is a demonstrated commitment to "an open market economy, democratic pluralism and respect for human rights", which are the stated core values of the OECD.[20] Additionally, the potential invitee must state its position regarding the OECD's Decisions, Declarations, and Recommendations and to identify reservations to any OECD legal instruments which it does not wish fully to apply.[21]

The totality of the application will be reviewed in committee. The Committee on International Investment and Multinational Enterprises (or the Investment Committee), in particular, plays an essential role in examining how the Code of Liberalisation of Capital Movements and the Code of Liberalisation of Current

---

[14] OECD, *Who Does What.*
[15] OECD, *Who Does What.*
[16] OECD, *Who Does What.*
[17] OECD, *Members and Partners* available through *http://www.oecd.org* [Accessed July 15, 2010].
[18] OECD, *Becoming a Member of the OECD: The Accession Process* available through *http:// www.oecd.org* [Accessed July 15, 2010].
[19] OECD, *About OECD.*
[20] 1960 OECD Convention.
[21] 1960 OECD Convention.

Invisible Operations will be implemented. These binding Codes promote the non-discriminatory treatment of other Member countries' nationals, and their successful execution largely determines an invitee's readiness to join the OECD.[22]

2–06   When the review process is complete, the Committees present their evaluation to the Council. Should the Council find the results favorable, it will invite the country to accede to the OECD Convention. The Secretary-General and a representative from the country will sign the accession agreement. If (as is usually the case) the country does not view treaties as self-executing legal instruments, then the country's legislature will approve the treaty as a final step to membership.[23]

Although the OECD Convention focuses primarily upon the privileges and responsibilities of Member countries, the OECD itself enters into agreements with non-Member states and international organisations.[24] The Anti-Bribery Convention is a notable case in point. The OECD also maintains close relationships with global partners who work on regional initiatives designed to reach out to areas where the relevance of OECD work depends upon dialogue with non-Members. Also notable are the OECD's links with civil society and parliamentary bodies, exemplified in its long-standing association with the Council of Europe and its Parliamentary Assembly, among others.[25]

F. FUNCTIONS OF THE OECD

2–07   Much of the OECD's work consists of monitoring developments in Member countries.[26] To illustrate the workflow, the Secretariat gathers data from a Member country, the Committees analyse the data and suggest policy, the Council makes a recommendation, and the Member country implements it. At the heart of the OECD's monitoring system is the peer review process, in which Committees and working groups examine the implementation by signatories of the OECD legal instruments.[27]

These instruments may take many forms: formal multilateral agreements, such as the Anti-Bribery Convention, mandatory or voluntary standards to be applied in emissions-control agreements, and recommendations or guidelines on corporate governance, to name a few.[28] Additionally, the OECD frequently disseminates its findings through regular publications of outlooks and comparative statistics.

---

[22] 1960 OECD Convention.
[23] 1960 OECD Convention.
[24] OECD, *About OECD*.
[25] OECD, *About OECD*.
[26] OECD, *What We Do and How*, available through *http://www.oecd.org* [Accessed July 15, 2010].
[27] OECD, *What We Do and How*.
[28] OECD, *What We Do and How*.

G. HISTORY OF THE ANTI-BRIBERY CONVENTION

Before 1989 there had been little support in the OECD for initiatives to combat international corruption.[29] Many member states had laws in place that made it a crime to bribe domestic public officials, but they remained generally unconcerned about bribery on an international level. Considering the OECD's general apathy towards international corruption at the time, the United States deserves credit for pushing international corruption to the forefront of the OECD agenda.

2–08

The United States had a significant interest in seeing the international criminalisation of extraterritorial bribery. The Foreign Corrupt Practices Act of 1977 had made it illegal for United States business to offer bribes to foreign public officials.[30] The inability to offer bribes to foreign public officials to obtain contracts or benefits posed a significant constraint on United States business.

While the United States had hoped that other countries would follow suit and criminalise the bribery of foreign public officials, no other countries among its competitors had followed the US lead in the 1970s or 1980s. Accordingly, corporations located outside of the United States were free in many circumstances to bribe foreign public officials with impunity. Indeed, companies in some countries could even claim such bribes as a tax-deductible business expense.[31]

The freedom to bribe gave corporations located outside the United States a competitive advantage in bidding for international work. As a result, US business interests argued for substantial modification or repeal of the FCPA to create a "level playing field" in international markets.[32]

2–09

But rather than modifying or repealing the FCPA, Congress addressed this perceived competitive disadvantage in 1988 by amending the law to require the President to:

"Pursue the negotiation of an international agreement, among the members of the Organisation for Economic Cooperation and Development, to govern persons from those countries concerning acts prohibited with respect to issuers and domestic concerns by amendments made by this section."[33]

For Congress, the OECD was a logical starting point for the international proscription of bribery of foreign public officials. The 29 member states that comprised the OECD were the major business competitors of the United States and accounted for a substantial percentage of international contracting. Their

---

[29] Barbara Crutchfield George, Kathleen A. Lacey & Jutta Birmele, *The 1998 OECD Convention: An Impetus for Worldwide Changes in Attitudes Toward Corruption in Business Transaction*, 37 Am. Bus. L.J 485 at 490 (2000).

[30] See Ch.3 above.

[31] Implementation of the OECD Recommendation on The Tax Deductibility of Bribes to Foreign Public Officials, available through *http://www.oecd.org* [Accessed July 15, 2010].

[32] Tarullo, in Pieth, Low and Cullen, *The OECD Convention on Bribery: A Commentary*, at 674.

[33] Omnibus Trade and Competitiveness Act of 1988, P. .00-418, 1988 H.R. 48489 (1998) (codified as amended at 15 U.S.C. s.78-dd-1 (1998)).

submission to a binding international agreement, ratified and implemented by the OECD, would directly address what US businesses perceived as the anti-competitive restraints imposed on them by the FCPA.[34]

2–10   Following the 1988 Amendments to the FCPA, the United States brought the issue to the OECD in 1989. It was met with a lukewarm response by many countries, including Germany, France, Japan and Spain.[35] Whether these countries opposed international regulation out of legal principle, economic pragmatism, or mere inertia is unclear. But there is "little doubt that these other governments would gladly have allowed the issue to fade into obscurity, but for the persistence of the United States."[36]

The stated argument against criminalising bribery of foreign officials was that the crime was extraterritorial, and thus not easily punished. Given the insidious nature of bribery and the coordination and planning needed to prosecute an international crime, skeptics anticipated problems in the areas of discovery and proof.[37] To examine the issue further, the OECD created an exploratory ad hoc working group tasked with examining how different jurisdictions and legal systems might tackle towards corruption offenses committed abroad.

The creation of the ad hoc working group in 1989 was a first step towards the creation of a formal international agreement. But the real impetus to create the OECD Anti-Bribery Convention began in the early 1990s. Around this time, many developmental economists who measured the impact of bribery in developing countries began to change their views about its effects.[38] Previously, Western academics had argued that "bribery might be necessary to induce change in the ossified bureaucracies of developing countries."[39]

2–11   But, in the early 1990s, rather than regarding bribery as a path to progress in developing bureaucracies (a view that seems absurd today) or a necessary evil of conducting business in developing countries, economists began to analyse the deleterious impact that the corruption was having on these countries' economies. Corruption thus began to be seen as one of the major barriers to economic growth and political stability in the developing world.

The advent of the Clinton administration in 1993 also provided additional impetus. The passage of an international agreement that outlawed bribery of foreign public officials became a cornerstone of the new Administration's foreign policy.[40] The Clinton administration devoted significant resources and involved senior officials of the State Department, Treasury Department, Commerce Department, and Office of the US Trade Representative in meetings concerning the OECD's progress.[41]

American persistence helped lead to the adoption of the 1994 Recommendation

---

[34] Tarullo, *The OECD Convention on Bribery: A Commentary*, at 676-678.
[35] Crutchfield George, *The 1998 OECD Convention*, 37 Am. Bus. L.J. 485 at 496.
[36] Tarullo, *The OECD Convention on Bribery: A Commentary*, at 679.
[37] Crutchfield George, *The 1998 OECD Convention*, 37 Am. Bus. L.J. 485 at 496.
[38] Tarullo, *The OECD Convention on Bribery: A Commentary*, at 675.
[39] Tarullo, *The OECD Convention on Bribery*.
[40] Tarullo, *The OECD Convention on Bribery: A Commentary*, at 677.
[41] Tarullo, *The OECD Convention on Bribery*.

of the OECD Council on Bribery in International Business Transactions ("1994 Recommendation").[42] Though the 1994 Recommendation was not legally binding, it encouraged members to "take concrete and meaningful steps" that would "deter, prevent, and combat the bribery of foreign public officials in connection with international business transactions."[43] To combat bribery the states were encouraged to increase co-operation. It was recommended that each member take steps that include evaluating their own domestic criminal and civil bribery laws, tax legislation, business accounting requirements, banking and recordkeeping procedures, and laws and regulations relating to public subsidies.[44]

As a follow-up to the 1994 Recommendation, the OECD established the   2–12
Working Group on Bribery in International Business Transactions ("Working Group") to evaluate the progress made by the states in implementing anti-foreign bribery legislation and to determine the most effective way to criminalise the corruption of foreign public officials.[45]

Two years later, the OECD adopted the 1996 Recommendation of the Tax Deductibility of Bribes to Foreign Public Officials ("Tax Recommendation"). The Tax Recommendation took the first step towards eliminating tax deductions for bribe payments. The Tax Recommendation was aimed at member countries, such as France and Germany, which permitted corporate tax deductions of bribery payments made by businesses. While the OECD Convention did not incorporate the Tax Recommendation, both France and Germany eventually outlawed corporate tax deductions of bribery payments made by businesses.[46] This of course was a logical consequence of their intention to criminalise foreign bribery.

After the 1994 Recommendation and the Tax Recommendation, OECD efforts to find the most effective and coordinated way to criminalise the corruption of foreign public officials led to the adoption of the 1997 Revised Recommendation on Combating Bribery in International Business Transactions ("Revised Recommendation"). The Revised Recommendation concluded that bribery of foreign government officials in international business transactions was a serious threat to the development and preservation of democratic institutions.[47] The Revised Recommendation found that a ratified binding Convention implemented

---

[42] *Recommendation of the Council on Combating Bribery in International Business Transactions*, May 1994, available through *http://www.oecd.org* [Accessessed July 15, 2010]. [Hereinafter *Recommendation*].

[43] *Recommendation*, 1994.

[44] *Recommendation*, 1994.

[45] The Working Group is currently composed of government experts from the 38 countries participating in the Convention. It meets four or five times a year to monitor compliance with the Convention and to assess how effective a state's foreign anti-bribery laws are in practice.

[46] Tax deductions for bribery were resolved in Germany when bribery of foreign officials was criminalised. Once the bribes were illegal, the tax deductibility for the bribes paid will be automatically denied. In France, a 1997 revision of the tax code, denied the deductibility of bribes. See *Implementation of the OECD Recommendation on The Tax Deductibility of Bribes to Foreign Public Officials*, available through *http://www.oecd.org* [Accessed July 15, 2010].

[47] *Fighting Bribery and Corruption: Frequently Asked Questions*, available through *http://www.oecd.org* [Accessed July 15, 2010]. [hereinafter: *Frequently Asked Questions*].

by the OECD was the appropriate way to criminalise bribery of foreign public officials.[48]

H. THE ANTI-BRIBERY CONVENTION

2–13 After the Revised Recommendation had set the groundwork for a formal convention, the OECD officially adopted the Convention on Combating Bribery of Foreign Public Officials in International Business Transactions (herein after the "Convention") on November 21, 1997.[49] Twenty-nine OECD members and five non-members signed the Convention and committed to ratifying and implementing the Convention as part of their national legislation by December 31, 1998.[50] The Convention then entered into force in February 1999.[51]

The focus of the OECD Convention is the parties' obligation to make bribery of foreign public officials in international business transactions a criminal act.[52] Specifically, art.1, the heart of the Convention, obligates parties to:

> "Take such measures as may be necessary to establish that is a criminal offence under its law for any person intentionally to offer, promise, or give an undue pecuniary or other advantage whether directly or through intermediaries, to a foreign public official . . . in order that the official act or refrain from acting in relation to the performance of official duties in order to retain business or other improper advantage in the conduct of international business."[53]

Article 1 also requires that all parties take measures necessary to establish that complicity in, aiding and abetting, or authorisation of an act of bribery shall also be a criminal offence.[54] Taken together, the two offences described above outline the crime of bribery of a foreign official.

2–14 The offence of bribery can be committed by "any person." This is important for two reasons. First, as defined in the Convention bribery of a foreign official is not a special offense capable of being committed only be a certain category of persons such as a company's officers and directors. Rather, the pool of potential

---

[48] The Revised Recommendation also charged the Working Group with a mandate to carry out systematic country monitoring of the Convention. See *Recommendation*.

[49] *Convention on Combating Bribery of Foreign Public Officials in International Business Transactions*, December 17, 1997, 37 I.L.M. 1 (entered into force February 15, 1999) [hereinafter *OECD Convention*].

[50] There are currently 38 Parties to the OECD Convention. The parties include all 30 OECD countries (Australia, Austria, Belgium, Canada, Czech Republic, Denmark, Finland, France, Germany, Greece, Hungary, Iceland, Ireland, Israel, Italy, Japan, Korea, Luxembourg, Mexico, the Netherlands, New Zealand, Norway, Poland, Portugal, Slovak Republic, Spain, Sweden, Switzerland, Turkey, United Kingdom and the United States) as well as 8 non–OECD countries (Argentina, Brazil, Bulgaria, Chile, Estonia, Israel, Slovenia and South Africa). *Frequently Asked Questions*.

[51] The Convention entered into force in February 1999, sixty days after Canada deposited its instrument of ratification. The formal requirement for entry into force was ratification by five of the ten countries which have the largest export shares of the signatories and representing at least sixty percent of the combined total exports of those countries. *OECD Convention*, art.15.

[52] *OECD Convention*, art.1.

[53] *OECD Convention*, 1997.

[54] *OECD Convention*, 1997.

offenders is unlimited. Second, liability for acts of foreign bribery may also rest with legal persons, not only natural persons.

Arguably the most striking feature of art.1 is that while there are two sides to bribery, the Convention focuses exclusively on the "supply side" or the bribe-givers, and does not regulate the behavior of the "demand side" or bribe takers. This seems to let those who solicit bribes off the hook while disproportionally punishing those who provide the bribe.[55]

Given that many of the signatories are home to most of the world's multi-national enterprises, the OECD apparently felt that the supply side was a logical place to combat bribery.[56] Accordingly, the OECD's anti-corruption strategy is supply-side driven, attempting to cut the bribes off at the source to eliminate their impact on global trade. Implementing rules that regulate the demand side would also lack practical effect, because that demand side of bribery is disproportionly comprised of public officials from developing countries that are not signatories to the Convention.[57] Nonetheless, the OECD purports also to "work[ ] with partners from the private sector and civil society to investigate possible government actions to tackle the demand side of bribery."[58]

Note that art.1 only establishes a standard that parties must meet, but does not **2–15** require them to use precise terms in defining the offence under their domestic laws.[59] This approach allows the parties to use various methods to fulfill their obligations, provided that conviction of a person for the offense does not require proof of elements beyond those found in art.1.[60]

---

[55] Though it is not contemplated in art.1, one solution to this problem that has been implemented by some parties is to allow those accused of bribery to use the defence that solicitation had occurred. This defence would allow the adjudicator to take into account, at least to a certain degree, the act of the party soliciting the bribe. Consultation Paper: *Review of the OECD Instruments on Combating Bribery of Foreign Public Officials in International Business Transactions Ten Years after Adoption.*

One defence is known as "effective regret." It applies where the foreign public official solicits the bribe, and the briber voluntarily reports without delay to the law enforcement authorities that he or she bribed the official. Another defence applies when the foreign public official applies pressure or coercion to obtain the bribe. Regardless, neither of these defences is enough to push liability onto the party that receives the bribe, but it does help mitigate the seemingly disproportionate penalty.

[56] David E. Rovella, *Anti-Bribery Treaty Set for Signing*, Nat. L.J., December 22, 1997, at B1.

[57] Transparency International (TI), a leading non-governmental organisation in the fight against corruption, produces an annual measure of the perceived levels of public-sector corruption in a given country. The TI Corruption Perception Index (CPI) is a composite index, drawing on different expert and business surveys that scores 180 countries on a scale from zero (highly corrupt) to ten (highly clean). In the 2008 CPI, Denmark, Sweden, and New Zealand had the highest score of 9.3. While the lowest scoring countries were Somalia at 1.0, slightly trailing Iraq and Myanmar at 1.3 and Haiti at 1.4. available at *http://www.transparency.org/news_room/in_focus/2008/cpi2008* [Accessed July 15, 2010].

[58] See *Frequently Asked Questions.*

[59] *Commentaries on the OECD Convention on Combating Bribery*, para.3, Adopted November 21, 1997, available through *http://www.oecd.org* [Accessed July 15, 2010]. [Hereinafter: *OECD Commentaries*].

[60] *OECD Commentaries.* For example, a statute prohibiting the bribery of agents generally which does not specifically address bribery of a foreign public official, and a statute that specifically prohibits bribery of a foreign public official would both comply with art.1. Similarly, a statute which defined the offense in terms of payments "to induce a breach of the official's duty" could meet the standard provided that it was understood that ever public official had a duty to exercise judgment or discretion impartially and this was an autonomous definition that did not require outside proof of the law of the particular official's country.

While it was permissible—and sometimes necessary—to leave a few topics to be interpreted by the countries themselves, in some areas, it was equally necessary to provide autonomous definitions. Because art.1 imposes liability only on people who bribe foreign public officials, the Members felt that it was essential to define that term; but, each state had its own ideas about who was to be regarded as a foreign public official.[61]

The Convention prohibits bribing a person who has higher legal authority deriving from his status as a member of a public body. Accordingly, the Convention definition focuses on those public bodies which may exercise that higher legal authority. The Convention thus defines a "foreign public official" to include any person holding a legislative, administrative or judicial office of a foreign country, any person exercising a public function[62] for a foreign country, or any person in a public international organisation.[63] This definition, while broad, preserves the basic principle that a foreign public official is anyone who carries out a public function for another country or an international organisation. This means that a person's formal position in a branch of governmental organisation provides an indication, rather than conclusive proof, of his status. One may be a foreign public official without belonging to a branch of government and one who works for the government may not be performing a public function. As a result, determinations of a person's status will be fact-intensive in light of the activities in question.[64]

2–16   The term "public function" includes any "activity in the public interest, delegated by the foreign country."[65] This implies two elements: first, the act of delegation by a concerned foreign country and second, a connection between the delegated activity and the public interest.

The Convention also defines the phrase "act or refrain from acting in relation to the performance of official duties" to include any use of the public official's position, regardless of whether it is within the official's scope of authority.[66] This definition contemplates a situation where a person from a signatory state bribes an official of a foreign government, so that the official may use his power and influence to cause a different government official to procure something of value or other improper advantage for the person.

The phrase "improper advantage," is not specifically defined in the Conven-

---

[61] Mark Pieth et al., *The OECD Convention on Bribery A Commentary* 57 (2007) states domestic law will play a role in determining the actual field of activity of the official (thus domestic law will still determine whether a person is a Member of Parliament, a senator, or a judge within a national system). Whether that field of activity brings the person within the definition of "foreign public official" under the Convention's system is a matter to be determined exclusively in the light of art.1.

[62] In special circumstances, public authority may be held by persons (e.g. political party officials in single party states) not formally designated as public officials. *OECD Commentaries*, para.3.

[63] *OECD Commentaries* "Public international organisation" includes any international organisation formed by states, governments, or other public international organisations, regardless of the form of organisation. This includes a regional economic integration organisation such as the European Communities.

[64] Pieth, *OECD Convention on Bribery*, at 59.

[65] See *OECD Commentaries*, para.12.

[66] *OECD Commentaries*.

tion. The Commentaries on the Convention (the "Commentaries") define "improper advantage" as something to which the company concerned was not clearly entitled.[67] A concrete example would be granting an operating permit to a factory that fails to meet the statutory requirements. For the most part, it is up to the signatories to determine and define what activities constitute securing an improper advantage.

The Commentaries provide a number of noteworthy observations that are not   2–17 explicit in the Convention itself. First, the Commentaries draw a distinction between advantages permitted or required by written law or regulation of the foreign public official's country and advantages permitted or tolerated by local custom.[68] The former are not considered offenses under the Convention, while the latter are.[69]

Second, so called "facilitation" payments that do not constitute payments made "to obtain or retain business or other improper advantage" within the meaning of art.1 are not offenses.[70] For example, it is legal in Country A to make small payments to induce public officials to perform their functions, such as issuing licenses or permits. These same payments may be illegal in Country B. The Commentaries recommend that Country A address this through programs of good governance rather than having Country B criminalise the act.[71]

I. APPLICABILITY

Signatories to the Convention must take measures to establish the liability of both   2–18 companies and natural persons. Article 3 of the Convention requires that parties impose "effective, proportionate, and dissuasive criminal penalties" to those who bribe foreign public officials.[72] The Convention states that a party should make the range of penalties for bribing a foreign official comparable to the penalties applicable to the bribery of the party's domestic public officials.[73]

In the case of natural persons, criminal sanctions should be available. If a party's legal system does not permit criminal liability for corporate offenses, the party must provide for equivalent non-criminal sanctions, including monetary sanctions.[74] Further, parties should make all efforts to seize or confiscate[75] the bribe and proceeds[76] of the bribery of a foreign public official or property of

---

[67] See *OECD Commentaries*, para.21.
[68] *OECD Commentaries*, paras 6-7.
[69] *OECD Commentaries*, paras 6-7.
[70] *OECD Commentaries*, para.9.
[71] *OECD Commentaries*.
[72] *OECD Convention*, art.3.
[73] *OECD Convention*, art.3.
[74] *OECD Convention*, art.3.
[75] The term confiscate includes forfeiture where applicable and means the permanent deprivation of property by order of a court or other competent authority. See *OECD Commentaries*, para.22.
[76] Proceeds refers to the profits or other benefits derived by the briber from the transaction or other improper advantage obtained or retained through bribery.

similar value, or ensure that money sanctions of a comparable nature are in effect.[77]

II. JURISDICTION

2–19 Article 4 of the Convention provides two jurisdictional bases for parties to enforce the crime of bribery of a foreign public official: territorial jurisdiction and nationality jurisdiction.[78] Territorial jurisdiction is established when the offense of bribery is committed in whole or in part in a party's territory.[79] Territorial basis for jurisdiction should be interpreted broadly so that an extensive physical connection to the bribery act is not required.[80]

Article 4.2 creates nationality jurisdiction by providing that:

"Each Party which has jurisdiction to prosecute its nationals for offences committed abroad take such measures as may be necessary to establish its jurisdiction to do so in respect of the bribery of a foreign public official, according to the same principles."[81]

Given that the offense of bribing a foreign official will normally take place abroad, the application of s.4.2 can lead to multi-jurisdictional issues. Article 4.3 states that when multiple parties have jurisdiction, the parties shall consult to determine who has the most appropriate jurisdiction.[82] Neither the Convention nor the Commentaries elaborates.

III. ENFORCEMENT

2–20 Article 5 contains the general enforcement measures of the Convention. It obligates the Parties to take effective measures to deter, prevent, and combat bribery of foreign public officials. "Investigation and prosecution of the bribery of a foreign public official shall be subject to the applicable rules and principles of each Party."[83]

Article 5 places a great deal of confidence in the national systems of the parties by giving the broad discretion to decide to investigate or prosecute, with the only caveat being that the decisions not be "influenced by considerations of national economic interest, the potential effect upon relations with another State or the identity of the natural or legal persons involved."[84] The allegation that national economic interest derailed a corruption investigation played a significant role in

---

[77] *OECD Convention*, art.3.
[78] *OECD Commentaries*, art.4.1.
[79] *OECD Commentaries*, art.4.1.
[80] *OECD Commentaries*, para.25.
[81] *OECD Convention*, art.4.2. Nationality jurisdiction is established according to the general principles and conditions of the legal system of each party. See *OECD Commentaries*, para.26.
[82] *OECD Convention*, art.4.3.
[83] *OECD Convention*, art.5.
[84] *OECD Convention*, art.5.

legal proceedings against the UK's Serious Fraud Office when it dropped part of its investigation into the practices of BAE Systems.[85]

By excluding politics and economics from foreign bribery investigations and prosecutions, the Convention's enforcement section attempts to ensure that prosecution remains independent.[86] The issue of prosecutorial discretion was of great concern to the parties in the discussions leading to the adoption of the Convention.[87] On one hand, the parties wanted a degree of freedom to prosecute in accordance with their domestic laws. On the other hand, unchecked discretion could be used for political and non-professional reasons. In response to these concerns, art.5 attempts to limit only the abuse of prosecutorial discretion.[88] The parties are required to recognise the crime of bribery of a foreign public official as a serious offense; this section expresses confidence and trust that the parties will enforce it as such.

IV. LIMITATIONS

Parties may only enforce the offense of bribery of a foreign public official in accordance with the statute of limitations for the offense set forth in art.6:   **2–21**

> "[A]ny statute of limitations applicable to the offence of bribery of a foreign public official shall allow an adequate period of time for the investigation and prosecution of this offense."[89]

Given the diversity and specificity found in national rules, it would have been futile for the drafters of the Convention to insist on a single common statute of limitations.[90] Instead, art.6 operates in concert with the enforcement provisions contained in art.5, to ensure that Parties, by whatever means they choose, allow for adequate time to investigate and prosecute a potential offense.

V. INTERNATIONAL COOPERATION

Given that the offense of bribery of a foreign public official involves multiple nations, international cooperation will often be required to prosecute the offense. Articles 9, 10, and 11 address the role of mutual legal assistance and extradition in the battle against foreign corruption. Together, the sections create a framework for international cooperation in the fight against multinational bribery.   **2–22**

---

[85] See Ch.1.
[86] *OECD Commentaries*, para.27.
[87] Pieth, *OECD Convention on Bribery*, at 292.
[88] Pieth, *OECD Convention on Bribery*, at 292.
[89] *OECD Convention*, art.6.
[90] Pieth, at 346.

Mutual legal assistance in criminal matters can be defined as a:

> "Process by which the requested state executes on its territory an official act together evidence on a specific criminal case which is under investigation or is being prosecuted in the requesting state."[91]

This proves necessary for a wide array of matters related to foreign bribery including interviewing witnesses, transfer of evidence, coordinated searches of businesses and bank accounts, confiscation of assets, and service of summons.

Article 9 provides the basis for mutual legal assistance concerning the enforcement of the Convention. Parties are requested:

> "to the fullest extent possible under its laws and relevant treaties and arrangement, provide prompt and effective legal assistance to another Party for the purpose of criminal investigations and proceedings . . . within the scope of this Convention."[92]

Article 9 calls for the Party requesting assistance to act quickly and for the free and intensive exchange of assistance between the Parties in all investigations that pertain to the Convention.[93] In addition to cooperation after formal charges have been filed, each party is obligated to cooperate with other parties during the investigative stage of the criminal case.

2–23 Article 10 states that bribery of a foreign public official is an extraditable offense under the Convention, regardless of how it was previously classified under domestic law or other extradition treaties between the parties.[94] The parties are not obligated to extradite their own nationals. If a party does not wish to extradite a potential offender because that person is a national, the party must use its own judicial system to prosecute the offense.[95] Article 10 is silent on the actual process for extradition and leaves the process "subject to the conditions set out in the domestic law and applicable treaties and arrangements of each Party."[96]

Article 11 calls for the Parties to appoint officials responsible for receiving and sending communications relating to cooperation under the Convention.[97] Many countries have central authorities responsible has coordinating mutual legal assistance and extradition requests, but the responsibilities may also be shared among different agencies.[98] Article II attempts to avoid the confusion and delay that might otherwise occur when multiple agencies share these duties.

---

[91] Pieth, at 411.
[92] *OECD Convention*, art.9.
[93] *OECD Convention*, art.9.
[94] *OECD Convention*, art.10.
[95] *OECD Convention*, art.10.
[96] *OECD Convention*, art.10.
[97] *OECD Convention*, art.11.
[98] Pieth, *OECD Convention on Bribery*, at 425.

I. THE IMPLEMENTATION PROCESS

Recall that in 1994, the Investment Committee established the Working Group on   **2–24**
Bribery in International Business Transactions. In 1997, the Working Group's
mandate was amended to include systematic monitoring of each participating
country's implementation of the Convention.[99] Consisting of leading experts from
each of the 38 participating countries, the Working Group meets several times per
year to evaluate compliance with the Convention through a two-step peer monitoring process.[100] Phase I entails an analysis of the conformity of the country's
anti-corruption legislation with the Convention.[101] Phase II builds on that process
by interviewing government officials, as well as representatives from businesses
and unions, to assess the effectiveness of the country's anti-corruption legislation
in practice.[102]

J. THE WORKING GROUP'S MANDATE

The 1997 amendment to the Working Group's mandate authorises the following   **2–25**
procedures as essential to the peer review system:

(a)   receipt of notifications and other information submitted to it by the
      Member countries;

(b)   regular reviews of steps taken by Member countries to implement the
      Recommendation and to make proposals, as appropriate, to assist Member
      countries in its implementation; these reviews will be based on the fol-
      lowing complementary systems:

  (i)   a system of self-evaluation, where Member countries' responses on
        the basis of a questionnaire will provide a basis for assessing the
        implementation of the Recommendation;

  (ii) a system of mutual evaluation, where each Member country will
        be examined in turn by the Working Group on Bribery, on the
        basis of a report which will provide an objective assessment of the
        progress of the Member country in implementing the
        Recommendation.

  (iii) examination of specific issues relating to bribery in international
        business transactions;

  (iv) examination of the feasibility of broadening the scope of the work
        of the OECD to combat international bribery to include private

---

[99] OECD, *Country reports on the implementation of the OECD Anti-Bribery Convention*, available
through *http://www.oecd.org*.
[100] OECD, *Country reports on the implementation of the OECD Anti-Bribery Convention*.
[101] OECD, *Country reports on the implementation of the OECD Anti-Bribery Convention*.
[102] OECD, *Country reports on the implementation of the OECD Anti-Bribery Convention*.

sector bribery and bribery of foreign officials for reasons other than to obtain or retain business;

(v) provision of regular information to the public on its work and activities and on implementation of the Recommendation.[103]

The mandate also makes provisions for consulting and cooperating with non-member countries, as well as international governmental and non-governmental organisations:

XII. [The Council] INSTRUCTS the Committee on International Investment and Multinational Enterprises through its Working Group on Bribery, to provide a forum for consultations with countries which have not yet adhered, in order to promote wider participation in the Recommendation and its follow-up.

XIII. [The Council] INVITES the Committee on International Investment and Multinational Enterprises through its Working Group on Bribery, to consult and co-operate with the international organisations and international financial institutions active in the combat against bribery in international business transactions and consult regularly with the non-governmental organisations and representatives of the business community active in this field.[104]

I. PHASE I

2–26   The primary purpose of the Phase I analysis is to determine the extent to which each country's anti-corruption legislation meets the standard set by the Convention, as well as the standard of the 1997 Revised Recommendation that amended the Working Group's mandate.[105] The process begins when two countries are appointed as lead examiners to choose the experts who will help to prepare a preliminary report.[106] A questionnaire is sent to the country to be examined, soliciting detailed information on the legislature's implementation procedures to date.[107] The answers to the questionnaire are disseminated amongst all participants in the Working Group.[108] All parties to the Convention examine these reports before they come to any conclusions.[109]

Work on the preliminary report then begins, while consultation within the

---

[103] OECD, *1997 Revised Recommendation of the Council on Combating Bribery in International Business Transactions*, (1997), available through *http://www.oecd.org* [Accessed July 15, 2010].

[104] OECD, *1997 Revised Recommendation of the Council on Combating Bribery in International Business Transactions*.

[105] OECD, *Procedure of Self- and Mutual Evaluation—Phase 1*, available through *http://www.oecd.org* [Accessed July 15, 2010].

[106] OECD, *Procedure of Self- and Mutual Evaluation—Phase 1*.

[107] OECD, *Procedure of Self- and Mutual Evaluation—Phase 1*.

[108] OECD, *Procedure of Self- and Mutual Evaluation—Phase 1*.

[109] OECD, *Procedure of Self- and Mutual Evaluation—Phase 1*.

Working Group continues.[110] While other OECD bodies can and do provide information throughout the consultation process, business and civil society groups are not invited to participate in this primarily intergovernmental process, although they may present their views to the Working Group.[111] Additionally, the examined country has the opportunity to make an initial presentation of its legislative approach.[112] Meanwhile, the Working Group will ask questions and clarify answers until a Phase I report with conclusions on the examined country's performance is completed.[113]

II. PHASE II

Phase II differs from Phase I in that its goal is to examine the practical effec- 2–27
tiveness of the anti-corruption legislation put into place.[114] It analyses the extent to which the criteria of the Convention and the Revised Recommendation are applied.[115] Although many of the procedural elements are similar to those in Phase I, including the appointment of two lead examiner countries, the questionnaire, the consultation process, and the production of the Working Group's final report, there remain important differences.[116] In Phase II, the OECD Secretariat and lead examiners make an on-site visit to the examined country to interview law enforcement bodies, as well as to speak informally with key players from business and civil society.[117] The information gleaned from these interviews, combined with the examined country's replies to the questionnaire and the Secretariat's and lead examiners' independent research, form the basis of a preliminary report on which the examined country can then comment.[118]

The consultation process that produces the final report is a dialogue between the examined country and the Working Group. The examined country has the opportunity to present law enforcement experts and explain its legal system, and the Working Group makes recommendations for improvements.[119] As in Phase I, other OECD bodies may contribute relevant facts to this dialogue; while representatives from business and civil society groups have more input in the information-gathering process than in Phase I, they do not participate directly throughout the consultation.[120] Finally, the Working Group promulgates a Phase

---

[110] OECD, *Procedure of Self- and Mutual Evaluation—Phase 1.*
[111] OECD, *Procedure of Self- and Mutual Evaluation—Phase 1.*
[112] OECD, *Procedure of Self- and Mutual Evaluation—Phase 1.*
[113] OECD, *Procedure of Self- and Mutual Evaluation—Phase 1.*
[114] OECD, *Procedure of Self- and Mutual Evaluation—Phase 2,* available through *http://www.oecd.org* [Accessed July 15, 2010].
[115] OECD, *Procedure of Self- and Mutual Evaluation—Phase 2.*
[116] OECD, *Procedure of Self- and Mutual Evaluation—Phase 2.*
[117] OECD, *Procedure of Self- and Mutual Evaluation—Phase 2.*
[118] OECD, *Phase II Questionnaire (2001),* available through *http://www.oecd.org* [Accessed July 15, 2010] (listing questions asked of examined country, and quality and depth of answers expected).
[119] OECD, *Phase II Monitoring Information Resources,* at 9 (2006), available through *http://www.oecd.org* [Accessed July 15, 2010].
[120] OECD, *Who Does What.*

II report detailing its conclusions, which the examined country may not, but may have its views expressed fully therein.[121]

K. DIFFICULTIES IN IMPLEMENTATION

2–28   The Working Group's final report is adopted after Phase I and Phase II examinations and forwarded to the government of the examined country.[122] The evaluative commentary provided in these reports serves as a springboard for participating countries to take a more proactive role in fighting corruption.

The extent to which the Convention and the Revised Recommendation have been executed in both legislation and practice differs greatly from country to country.[123] These difficulties in implementation naturally vary depending upon the legal, economic, and social culture of the examined country.[124] The February 2009 Compilation of Recommendations made in the Phase II Reports neatly summarises several impediments common to many of the countries struggling to implement the OECD's anti-corruption instrumentation.

The problem is frequently rooted in the examined country's legislative implementation itself. The crime of bribery is often poorly defined, with varying degrees of imprecision as to what qualifies as a foreign public entity or a commercial enterprise, for example.[125] Liability and jurisdiction are often delineated in an equally amorphous manner, and the lack of certainty in interpreting these anti-corruption provisions further confounds the implementation process for example, the absence of nationality jurisdiction provision in some countries allows nationals to use non-nationals to bribe foreign public entities while out of their home country.[126] The inevitable result is that it is difficult to charge any potential offenders under the crime's loophole-riddled description. Further, the prescribed criminal sanctions for such offenders are frequently very limited in their application, too lenient to have significant deterrent value, and all but unknown to both the public and private sector, further reducing their power of dissuasion.[127] The lack of awareness of both the statutory crime and punishment of bribery matches a more broad-based ignorance of anti-corruption measures generally.

2–29   The failure to educate both the public and private sector about the importance of a muscular anti-corruption regime has had a discernible and widespread effect

---

[121] OECD, *Who Does What*.

[122] OECD, *Who Does What*.

[123] Tarullo, in Pieth, *The OECD Convention on Bribery: A Commentary*, at 683.

[124] Tarullo, in Pieth, *The OECD Convention on Bribery: A Commentary*, at 683.

[125] OECD, *Compilation of Recommendations made in the Phase 2 Reports*, at 6 (2009), available through *http://www.oecd.org* [Accessed July 15, 2010] (discussing implementation of a clearly definable foreign bribery offense in Argentina).

[126] OECD, *Compilation of Recommendations made in the Phase 2 Reports*, at 99 (discussing situation in which a Dutch legal person uses a non-Dutch national to bribe a foreign public official while outside the Netherlands).

[127] OECD, *Compilation of Recommendations made in the Phase 2 Reports*, at 15 (discussing need for increased criminal sanctions in Austria).

upon the quality of implementation from country to country.[128] Many Phase II reports note that there is very little awareness of the subject. Some tax officials in some jurisdictions remain unaware that bribes are no longer tax-deductible.[129] There are not enough training programs for judicial and executive officials at all levels of authority, or for commercial enterprises of all sizes.[130] Communication between the public and private sector regarding new reporting requirements is slender.[131] In particular, many governments have not adequately informed the auditing, accounting, and legal professions, the enterprises that operate largely internationally.[132] Without sufficient dissemination of information, it will be impossible properly to enforce even the best-drafted anti-corruption measures.

Probably the clearest indication that the implementation process has not had its desired effect is the conspicuous lack of new and ongoing prosecutions for crimes of bribery.[133] To date, there are still participating countries that have not formally prosecuted any offenders, perhaps lacking either the executive resolve or capacity to do so.[134] Frequently, the disparity between the number of suspicious activity reports and the number of official prosecutions is quite large.[135]

This disparity is emblematic of a larger problem, namely that many governments appear unable or unwilling to allocate the resources necessary to realize an effective anti-corruption regime, which would require formalising of regulatory bodies and more rigorously investigating bribery allegation.[136] Similarly, resources are also required to protect would-be whistleblowers from retaliation, to provide effective mutual legal assistance in foreign bribery cases, and to extradite nationals in furtherance of international comity; these have all posed challenges for countries that either cannot or will not give force to the above provisions in their individualised anti-corruption regimes.[137]

Indeed, some participating countries' implementation schemes, more than others, have forced the OECD's Working Group on Bribery to voice their concerns in a series of follow-up reports and repeated dialogues on progress. We discuss of the salient issues identified in some jurisdictions below.   **2–30**

---

[128] OECD, *Compilation of Recommendations made in the Phase 2 Reports*, (2009), available through *http://www.oecd.org* [Accessed July 15, 2010].

[129] OECD, *Compilation of Recommendations made in the Phase 2 Reports*, at 22 (discussing need to clarify prohibition on deductibility of bribes in Brazil, using 1996 Recommendation on the Tax Deductibility of Bribes to Foreign Public Officials).

[130] OECD, *Compilation of Recommendations made in the Phase 2 Reports*, at 44 (discussing need to train public and private sectors in Estonia on the Anti-Bribery Convention and 1997 Revised Recommendation, per art.I of the Revised Recommendation).

[131] OECD, *Compilation of Recommendations made in the Phase 2 Reports*, at 64 (discussing auditors' reporting requirements in Iceland).

[132] OECD, *Country reports on the implementation of the OECD Anti-Bribery Convention*.

[133] Tarullo, in Pieth, *The OECD Convention on Bribery: A Commentary*.

[134] Tarullo, in Pieth, *The OECD Convention on Bribery: A Commentary*.

[135] OECD, *Country reports on the implementation of the OECD Anti-Bribery Convention*, at 79 (discussing absence of formal investigations of foreign bribery offenses in Japan).

[136] Tarullo, in Pieth, *The OECD Convention on Bribery: A Commentary*.

[137] OECD, *Country reports on the implementation of the OECD Anti-Bribery Convention*.

I. ARGENTINA

2–31   As of June of 2008, the Working Group pointed to two overriding concerns, above and beyond the general implementation difficulties faced by many other countries.[138] The first was that Argentina had not adopted liability or legal persons for foreign bribery as required by arts 2 and 3 of the Anti-Bribery Convention, exemplifying the kind of legislative loophole that makes enforcement difficult.[139] As expected, the Working Group recommended that Argentina adopt legislation providing for liability and sanctions, concomitant with the Anti-Bribery Convention.[140]

Secondly, the Working Group noted that Argentina's government was "rarely able to effectively investigate and prosecute serious economic crimes to a resolution on the merits, in particular because of lengthy delays in getting to a decision due, inter alia, to the applicable rules of procedural law."[141] The example provided pointed to an allegation of foreign bribery from 2002 that was not investigated until 2006.[142] The Working Group did note that the Argentine Ministry of Justice had recently mandated publication of a new draft Criminal Procedure Code, based on an accusatorial system, and that this reform could potentially change the outlook on Argentine implementation of the Convention.[143]

II. CHILE

2–32   The Working Group noted (in October of 2007) with some alarm that Chile had failed fully to conform with arts 1, 2, 3, 4 and 9 of the Anti-Bribery Convention, despite governmental efforts to comply through a general overhaul of the Penal Code.[144] Given the "preliminary" and "uncertain" nature of the rehaul effort, however, the Working Group stated its intention to follow up with Chile with regards to its recommendations on the liability and sanctions for offenders, jurisdiction, bank secrecy, and the foreign bribery offense.[145]

III. IRELAND

2–33   The Working Group concluded that, as of March of 2007, Ireland had not met its Phase II obligations.[146] It pointed to the sparse attendance of Irish officials

---

[138] OECD, *Country reports on the implementation of the OECD Anti-Bribery Convention*, at 4.

[139] OECD, *Convention on Combating Bribery of Foreign Public Officials in International Business Transactions* (hereinafter: *Anti-Bribery Convention*) (art.2 discussing the responsibility of legal persons, and art.3 discussing sanctions).

[140] OECD, *Country reports on the implementation of the Anti-Bribery Convention*, at 6.

[141] OECD, *Country reports on the implementation of the Anti-Bribery Convention* at 4.

[142] OECD, *Country reports on the implementation of the Anti-Bribery Convention*.

[143] OECD, *Country reports on the implementation of the Anti-Bribery Convention*.

[144] OECD, *Country reports on the implementation of the Anti-Bribery Convention*, at 32.

[145] OECD, *Country reports on the implementation of the Anti-Bribery Convention*.

[146] OECD, *Country reports on the implementation of the Anti-Bribery Convention*, at 66.

throughout the Phase II on-site visit, indicating that the Irish government did not appreciate its crucial role in implementing the Convention.[147] At a panel concerning awareness-raising by the private sector, only the Office of the Director of Corporate Enforcement was present; additionally, the private sector was not consulted on the 2001 amendments to the relevant legislative framework, and so it was unsurprising that only one company attended the panel devoted to the private sector.[148]

Overall, the Working Group castigated what it characterised as Irish disinterest in the implementation process.[149] The Working Group also expressed concern that Ireland's legislative implementation of art.I of the Anti-Bribery Convention was "out of date" and "inconsistent", although a bill passing through the Irish parliament at the time could potentially fix that.[150]

When the lead examiners returned in December of 2008 for a Phase 2*bis* visit, they were pleased to witness a considerably higher level of participation amongst Irish officials at the relevant panels and events.[151] The Working Group also noted that Ireland had "initiated significant efforts to raise awareness of the foreign bribery offence among relevant officials in the Irish public sector, as well as within the business community."[152]

While the passage of the Prevention of Corruption (Amendment) Bill 2008 was certainly a step in the right direction, the Working Group expressed concern that it did not address a few of their Recommendations made a year before, namely the consolidation and harmonisation of "the two separate foreign bribery offences in the Prevention of Corruption (Amendment) Act 2001 and the Criminal Justice (Theft and Fraud Offences) Act 2001."[153] As a result, the Working Group recommended that this become a priority for the administration, and indicated that it would follow in due course.[154]   2–34

IV. JAPAN

In December 2004 the Working Group found itself unable to perform an objective assessment of the Japanese government's implementation scheme, as the authorities did not disclose the existence (or lack thereof) of any foreign bribery investigations on the basis of secrecy.[155] Pressed to submit limited non-identifying information about the nature and progress of foreign bribery investigations thus far in Japan, officials informed the Working Group of four such investigations that they had not pursued, mainly due to the absence of nationality jurisdiction   2–35

---

[147] OECD, *Country reports on the implementation of the Anti-Bribery Convention.*
[148] OECD, *Country reports on the implementation of the Anti-Bribery Convention.*
[149] OECD, *Country reports on the implementation of the Anti-Bribery Convention.*
[150] OECD, *Country reports on the implementation of the Anti-Bribery Convention.*
[151] OECD, *Country reports on the implementation of the Anti-Bribery Convention*, at 70.
[152] OECD, *Country reports on the implementation of the Anti-Bribery Convention.*
[153] OECD, *Country reports on the implementation of the Anti-Bribery Convention.*
[154] OECD, *Country reports on the implementation of the Anti-Bribery Convention*, at 71.
[155] OECD, *Country reports on the implementation of the Anti-Bribery Convention*, at 76.

and because of insufficient evidence.[156] The Working Group also noted in its report that "the Japanese authorities only canvassed three major District Public Prosecutors Offices and three major Police Prefectures about the existence of non-'filed' investigations."[157] As a result, the Working Group concluded that Japanese public officials needed to make a sincere effort to step up investigation (in the less formal non-"filed" stage) and prosecution (in the more formal filed stage) of foreign bribery offenses.[158] If there existed impediments to investigation and prosecution, the Working Group advised, the Japanese government should do its best to locate and remove them.[159] Additionally, the Working Group voiced its concern that then-current Japanese law might interfere with the disclosure requirements so necessary to maintaining the OECD's peer monitoring system.[160]

The Working Group made its reassessment after a return visit (Phase 2*bis*) a year later, in February of 2006, finding that Japanese authorities cooperated satisfactorily with their disclosure requirements, within the limits of Japanese law.[161] The Working Group also noted several positive developments in Japan's legal framework to date; for example: an "increase [in] the statute of limitations in respect of natural and legal persons for the foreign bribery offence", the establishment of an enhanced false accounting penalty under the Securities and Exchange Law, "the passage of the Bill to amend the Corporation Tax Law and Income Tax Law to expressly deny tax deductions for bribe payments to foreign public officials in all circumstances", and "the Cabinet Order specifying that the new Whistleblower Protection Act applies to offences under the UCPL. . . ."[162] The Working Group urged that the offense of bribing a foreign public official be placed in the Penal Code, rather than the UCPL, to strengthen it; they also stated unequivocally that Japan had still not fully complied with its Phase II recommendations.[163]

Furthermore, the Working Group noted that while Japan took a "passive" approach to investigation and prosecution of foreign bribery before the Phase II visit, the government's efforts were only marginally more forceful after the visit.[164] As the report states:

"Despite the continuing absence of formal investigations and prosecutions seven years after the foreign bribery offence came into force, Japan has not made a serious effort to act on the Phase 2 Recommendation of the Working Group. . . serious doubts continue

---

[156] Nationality jurisdiction is in force in Japan as of 2005; however, nationality jurisdiction does not expressly apply to legal persons for the offense. OECD, *Country reports on the implementation of the Anti-Bribery Convention*, at 81.

[157] OECD, *Country reports on the implementation of the Anti-Bribery Convention*, at 76.

[158] OECD, *Country reports on the implementation of the Anti-Bribery Convention*, at 77.

[159] OECD, *Country reports on the implementation of the Anti-Bribery Convention*.

[160] OECD, *Country reports on the implementation of the Anti-Bribery Convention*.

[161] OECD, *Country reports on the implementation of the Anti-Bribery Convention*, at 80.

[162] OECD, *Country reports on the implementation of the Anti-Bribery Convention*.

[163] OECD, *Country reports on the implementation of the Anti-Bribery Convention*, at 81.

[164] OECD, *Country reports on the implementation of the Anti-Bribery Convention*.

about the level of Japan's commitment to the effective implementation of the [Anti-Bribery] Convention."[165]

Yet another follow-up report came out in October of 2007. the report included a   2–36
including a self-assessment by Japanese authorities as well as an appraisal by the
Working Group. The latter concluded that the self-assessment, while sincerely
comprehensive in its effort, did not adequately consider all of the relevant issues,
and in of itself would not resolve the implementation problems in Japan.[166] The
self-assessment suggested that the primary impediments to the investigative
process were a lack of reliable leads, the result of language barriers, unfamiliarity
with foreign legal systems, and low awareness of anti-corruption measures in the
public and private sectors.[167] It went on to suggest solutions to these problems,
including a proactive approach to investigating in the early stages, raising public
and private awareness, and increasing coordination between police and
prosecutors.[168]

In its own appraisal, the Working Group reiterated that the Japanese needed to
be more proactive in investigating and prosecuting foreign bribery cases; the
government still needed to look into moving the foreign bribery offense from the
UCPL to the Penal Code and examine the adequacy of its territorial jurisdiction
for covering the acts of Japanese parent companies in relation to foreign bribery
by foreign subsidiaries.[169] The Working Group also suggested further improvements to the solutions contained within the Japanese self-assessment.[170]

The Working Group concluded by praising Japan for having "implemented the
majority of the Working Group's Recommendations", and made note of the
Recommendations to date that had only been partially implemented, or not
implemented at all.[171] As a result, the Working Group recommended a yearly
informal meeting between the lead examiners and Japanese authorities to discuss

---

[165] OECD, *Country reports on the implementation of the Anti-Bribery Convention.*
[166] OECD, *Japan: Phase 2* (2007), available through *http://www.oecd.org* [Accessed July 15, 2010].
[167] OECD, *Japan: Phase 2*, at 3.
[168] The Japanese self-evaluation report specifically recommended the following courses of action:
"(i) increase public awareness of the whistleblower law and the foreign bribery offence; (ii)
enhance information gathering at Japanese overseas missions; (iii) promote the conclusion of
bilateral MLA agreements, and utilise MLA at the earliest stage, where appropriate; (iv) actively
make use of voluntary investigative measures at the earliest stage, where appropriate; (v) enhance
the investigative authorities' foreign language abilities and knowledge of foreign legal systems; (vi)
promote coordination between police and prosecutors, where appropriate; and (vii) continue
exploring the use of immunity from prosecution and plea bargaining."
See *Japan: Phase 2*, at 4.
[169] OECD, *Japan: Phase 2*, at 4.
[170] "Moreover, the Working Group believes that the effectiveness of these recommendations could
be enhanced by including the following elements: (i) targeting the media, parliamentarians, and
lawyers in the awareness-raising campaign; (ii) addressing technical defects in the whistleblower law
regarding acts of whistle-blowing directly to the law enforcement authorities; (iii) including Japanese
overseas liaison officers in measures for enhancing information gathering abroad; and (iv) not over-
emphasising concerns about compromising the secrecy of investigations when considering whether to
apply for early MLA or non-compulsory investigative measures, given that there is a five year statute
of limitations for investigating cases of foreign bribery in Japan, and that, in any case, delays in
investigating could result in the disappearance of evidence." OECD, *Japan: Phase 2*, at 4.
[171] OECD, *Japan: Phase 2*, at 5.

the country's progress, specifically with regard to "whether Japan is proactively investigating and prosecuting foreign bribery cases."[172]

V. LUXEMBOURG

2–37 During their Phase 2*bis* visit to Luxembourg in March of 2008, the lead examiners pointed out that the country was still not in compliance with art.2 of the Anti-Bribery Convention, despite the fact that their Phase II evaluation had occurred four years before, in May of 2004.[173] They were particularly concerned "about the continuing absence of liability for legal persons that engage in bribery."[174] Taking into account "the seriousness of the situation", the Working Group decided that within the year, Luxembourg would make a written report of their progress in this matter, as well as other Recommendations; additionally, the Working Group reserved "the right, in the event of continued failure to implement the Convention, to take further steps."[175]

VI. SPAIN

2–38 In March of 2006 the Working Group noted with approval that Spain was working toward establishing liability and sanctions for legal persons, as well as accessorial sanctions, for the foreign bribery offense.[176] At the time of the report, however, no such administrative or criminal liability had been established, which was cause for some concern; the Working Group stated its intention to follow up once liability had been established and sufficient practice had commenced.[177]

VII. TURKEY

2–39 The lead examiners' Phase II on-site visit to Turkey in December of 2007 left them with some apprehension.[178] The Working Group noted the public and private sectors' low attendance rate and severe lack of awareness-raising activities.[179]

Liability of legal persons for the foreign bribery offense was in fact repealed in 2005 and replaced with severely limited measures.[180] Several representatives from Turkish enterprises articulated an attitude that "bribery in neighbouring countries where bribe solicitation seems to be common has to be accepted."[181]

---

[172] OECD, *Japan: Phase 2*, at 6.
[173] OECD, *Country reports on the implementation of the OECD Anti-Bribery Convention*, at 90.
[174] OECD, *Country reports on the implementation of the OECD Anti-Bribery Convention*, at 91.
[175] OECD, *Country reports on the implementation of the OECD Anti-Bribery Convention*.
[176] OECD, *Country reports on the implementation of the OECD Anti-Bribery Convention*, at 124.
[177] OECD, *Country reports on the implementation of the OECD Anti-Bribery Convention*, at 127.
[178] OECD, *Country reports on the implementation of the OECD Anti-Bribery Convention*, at 135.
[179] OECD, *Country reports on the implementation of the OECD Anti-Bribery Convention*.
[180] OECD, *Country reports on the implementation of the OECD Anti-Bribery Convention*.
[181] OECD, *Country reports on the implementation of the OECD Anti-Bribery Convention*.

Furthermore, a recent investigation of a foreign bribery allegation had been dropped on grounds that the Working Group hound suspicion: we had also been a two-year delay in response to the "allegations of illicit payments to the Iraqi government against 139 Turkish companies in the 2005 Final Report of the Independent Inquiry Committee into the United Nations Oil-for-Food Programme."[182]

Faced with these setbacks in the Turkish implementation process, the Working Group targeted three areas for improvement upon its return, namely: awareness-raising, more proactive investigation and prosecution (especially with regard to the Oil-for-Food Programme incident), and the reestablishment of liability of legal persons, per art.2 of the Convention.[183]

Since December of 2007, Turkey has made several strides in its anti-corruption **2–40** regime, most notably the following:

"Two foreign bribery cases are currently under investigation, and Turkish officials have recently increased their efforts to gather information about allegations against Turkish companies in the 2005 Final Report of the Independent Inquiry Committee in the UN Oil-for-Food Programme. A draft law re-introducing corporate liability for foreign bribery is currently under consideration by the Turkish Parliament. Turkey has implemented a wide range of awareness-raising efforts, which appear to have significantly raised awareness in the business community about the prohibition against bribing foreign public officials in the Turkish Penal Code."[184]

While commending the country for significant progress made, the Working Group stated that it would reevaluate after Turkey's government (re)enacted legislation establishing corporate liability for foreign bribery.[185]

VIII. THE UNITED KINGDOM

The United Kingdom has encountered no small amount of criticism from **2–41** the Working Group for its recalcitrance in implementing the appropriate anti-corruption measures, its Recommendations of 2003, 2005, and 2007.[186] In the Phase 1*bis* report, the Working Group noted that United Kingdom authorities had pledged that Pt 12 of the Anti-Terrorism, Crime and Security Act 2001 would be repealed to illustrate the government's commitment to fighting corruption.[187] At that time, the Working Group recommended that a more comprehensive anti-corruption statute replace it.[188] October 2008 OECD report not, the United Kingdom had not adopted any such measure, nor had the legislature

---

[182] OECD, *Country reports on the implementation of the OECD Anti-Bribery Convention*.
[183] OECD, *Country reports on the implementation of the OECD Anti-Bribery Convention*.
[184] OECD, *OECD acknowledges Turkey's progress in combating foreign bribery*, http://www.oecd.org [Accessed July 15, 2010].
[185] OECD, *OECD acknowledges Turkey's progress in combating foreign bribery*.
[186] OECD, *Country reports on the implementation of the OECD Anti-Bribery Convention*, at 143.
[187] OECD, *Country reports on the implementation of the OECD Anti-Bribery Convention*, at 140.
[188] OECD, *Country reports on the implementation of the OECD Anti-Bribery Convention*.

established "an effective corporate liability regime in accordance with the Convention, as recommended in 2005. . . ."[189]

Further, the report cited the need for a general overhaul of the United Kingdom's legal structures to "tackle foreign bribery".[190] In particular, the Working Group recommended that the United Kingdom ensure that its legislation did not permit principal consent as a defense to foreign bribery, and criminalised extraterritorial foreign bribery committed through a non-national intermediary.[191] The report also contained a strong Recommendation for the implementation of a broader territorial basis for jurisdiction that did not require an extensive physical connection to the bribery offense, as well as nationality jurisdiction over legal persons incorporated in the Crown Dependencies and Overseas Territories.[192]

The Working Group also strongly censured the United Kingdom for its failure at that time effectively to prosecute any offenders; a first conviction for foreign bribery in international transactions occurred September of 2008.[193] Consequently, the Working Group made several Recommendations commensurate to the United Kingdom's need for reform in the investigative and prosecutorial processes: art.5 of the Anti-Bribery Convention must apply to investigators and prosecutors at all stages of their respective undertakings, and relevant government officials must be aware of art.5's application herein.[194]

2–42 Furthermore, per the Recommendations, the Attorney General's role as superintendent must be limited, and the Serious Fraud Office should be able to access information relevant to a foreign bribery investigation from government agencies.[195] Reform efforts must include the foreign bribery offense to update the plea bargain system; steps should be taken to allow the Crown Dependencies and Overseas Territories to provide mutual legal assistance to the United Kingdom; finally, the Working Group concluded that the Al Yamamah investigation should be reopened if United Kingdom officials found that the reasons for discontinuing it had changed.[196]

These, amongst other Recommendations, addressed the Working Group's multitudinous concerns regarding the United Kingdom's implementation difficulties. A particularly stringent follow-up plan was also adopted, reflecting the gravity of those same concerns:

"In this context, the Working Group will seek to confer with the Law Commission about this Report and the concerns raised therein prior to the Commission's publication of its report. In addition, the Group welcomes the invitation of the UK government to

---

[189] OECD, *Country reports on the implementation of the OECD Anti-Bribery Convention*, at 143.
[190] OECD, *Country reports on the implementation of the OECD Anti-Bribery Convention*.
[191] OECD, *Country reports on the implementation of the OECD Anti-Bribery Convention*, at 144.
[192] OECD, *Country reports on the implementation of the OECD Anti-Bribery Convention*.
[193] OECD, *OECD Group demands rapid UK action to enact adequate anti-bribery laws*, available through *http://www.oecd.org* [Accessed July 15, 2010].
[194] *Id.*
[195] OECD, *Country reports on the implementation of the OECD Anti-Bribery Convention*, at 145.
[196] John Hatchard, *Recent Developments in Combating the Bribery of Foreign Public Officials: A Cause for Optimism?*, 85 U. Det. Mercy L. Rev. 1 at 4–6 (2007).

discuss the content of the Law Commission report soon after its publication in order to fully apprise the UK of the views of the Working Group before a draft bill is submitted for pre-legislative scrutiny."[197]

The United Kingdom was also requested to provide a written progress report at every meeting of the Working Group, "in light of the numerous issues of serious concern." The Working Group reserved the right to conduct on-site visits to the country and take further action as it deemed appropriate.[198] Indeed, the report went so far as to note that "failing to enact effective and comprehensive legislation undermines the credibility of the UK legal framework".[199] This uncertainty "may trigger a need for increased due diligence over UK companies by their commercial partners or multilateral development banks."[200]

The Bribery Act should go a long way to addressing the Working Group's concerns.

---

[197] OECD, *Country reports on the implementation of the OECD Anti-Bribery Convention*, at 144.
[198] OECD, *Country reports on the implementation of the OECD Anti-Bribery Convention*.
[199] OECD, *Country reports on the implementation of the OECD Anti-Bribery Convention*.
[200] OECD, *Country reports on the implementation of the OECD Anti-Bribery Convention*.

CHAPTER 3

THE US FOREIGN CORRUPT PRACTICES ACT[1]

A. INTRODUCTION

Virtually every other chapter in this book refers to the Foreign Corrupt Practices   **3–01**
Act. For good reason—it is impossible to understand global anti-corruption
efforts today without appreciating the FCPA's role in getting those efforts started.
It is impossible to discuss the development of international anti-corruption
instruments such as the OECD Anti-Bribery Convention without understanding
that the FCPA provided a spur to their enactment. And it is impossible—or at
least highly impractical—to consider anti-corruption compliance and best practices without drawing on the extensive examples offered by companies dealing
with the FCPA.

Those companies are not always American in the strictest sense. US authorities have not hesitated to reach out a long arm where they see a nexus with
American activity, even if other nations are unconvinced that any such nexus
exists. That is the other reason why it behoves companies and practitioners to
know about the FCPA: entities and individuals sometimes find themselves subject
to its provisions, even though they do not consider themselves American or
affiliated with the United States.

The purpose of this chapter is to familiarise the reader with the FCPA's history
and requirements. The chapter is not, however, intended to provide an exhaustive
interpretation of the FCPA. Whole books could be—and have been—written
about the statute. We refer the interested reader to those publications. Nonetheless, this chapter should provide companies and practitioners alike with a solid
grounding in the FCPA's principal provisions and defences.

The history of the FCPA begins, oddly enough, with the Watergate scandal.   **3–02**
The scandal began with the 1972 burglary of the headquarters of the Democratic
National Committee, in the Watergate building in Washington, DC. The burglars
were eventually identified as associates of people in President Richard Nixon's
administration. "Watergate" eventually became synonymous with a variety of
illegal and unethical practices by the Executive branch of the US government.

In 1973, the Watergate Office of the Special Prosecutor charged several cor-

---

[1] The authors acknowledge the assistance of Leslieann Cachola in preparing this chapter.

73

porations and executives with using corporate funds for illegal domestic campaign contributions. This led to an inquiry by the SEC for violations of federal securities laws in the interests of investors.[2]

This inquiry uncovered many instances of falsification of corporate records designed to disguise or conceal the source and illegal use of corporate funds, as well as the existence of hidden "slush funds" for illicit purposes. These included questionable payments to government officials of foreign countries.[3]

3–03   The SEC submitted an extensive report to Congress revealing that instances of undisclosed questionable or illegal corporate payments were both serious and widespread.[4]

Over 400 corporations admitted to making these payments totalling an excess of $300 million in corporate funds to foreign officials.[5]

The House Report summed up Congress' sentiment on the impact of foreign bribery:

"The payment of bribes to influence the acts or decisions of foreign officials, foreign political parties or candidates for foreign political office is unethical. It is counter to the moral expectations and values of the American public. But not only is it unethical, it is bad business as well."[6]

Corporate bribery was also seen as unnecessary.[7] Those seeking business in foreign destinations would substitute good price, quality, and service—the mainstays of good business—with corporate bribes, undermining the free market and interfering with healthy competition.

3–04   The results of the SEC investigations reverberated elsewhere, additionally causing severe foreign policy problems for the United States, notably in Japan, the Netherlands, and Italy.[8] Foreign companies would shy away from doing

---

[2] United States, Securities and Exchange Commission, *Report of the securities and exchange commission on questionable and illegal corporate payments and practices*, (May 12, 1976), at 2 [hereinafter "*SEC Report*"].

[3] *SEC Report*, at 2.

[4] *SEC Report*, at 56. Senate Report No. 93–114, at 1–2 (1977) [hereinafter "*Senate Report*"].

[5] House Report No. 95–640, at 4 (1977) [hereinafter "*House Report*"]. Over 117 of these companies ranked in the top Fortune 500 industries. The industry sectors that were typically involved included: drugs and healthcare; oil and gas production and services; food products; aerospace, airlines, and air services; and chemicals. The SEC Report analysed the public disclosures filed with the SEC of 89 corporations; six special reports resulting from SEC enforcement actions; and a description of the allegations made in eight additional cases in which the SEC obtained some form of judicial relief, but where reports have not been completed or were not required. The SEC commenced a "voluntary disclosure program" as it became apparent to the SEC through its enforcement actions that they needed to gather more information given the potential magnitude of the problem. *SEC Report*, at 1, 6.

[6] *House Report*, at 4–5.

[7] Secretary of the Treasury Michael Blumenthal also testified before the Subcommittee on Consumer Protection and Finance that "Paying bribes—apart from being morally repugnant and illegal in most countries—is simply not necessary for the successful conduct here or overseas." *House Report*, at 4. *Senate Report*, at 4.

[8] *House Report*, at 5. Prince Bernhard of the Netherlands was forced to resign from his official position as Inspector-General of the Dutch Armed Forces as a result of an inquiry into allegations that he received $1 million in pay-offs from US aircraft manufacturer Lockheed Corporation to influence the Dutch government's purchase of aircraft.

business with American companies for fear of being tainted with an aura of shady business dealings. In its report, the Commission also analysed the amount of disclosure of questionable foreign payments required under the existing Federal securities laws and recommended legislative and other responses, galvanising Congress to take action.[9]

Congress was faced with two different approaches in handling this newly-visible problem. One approach, supported by the Ford administration[10] and certain members of Congress,[11] was the "disclosure approach," which would require that the payments be publicly disclosed and criminal penalties imposed upon discovery of the failure to disclose. The other approach, supported by the Carter administration—which replaced the Ford administration in January 1977—was the "criminalisation approach." This approach would forthrightly prohibit payments with criminal penalties.[12]

Ultimately Congress chose the latter, with the backing of President Carter, due to a clear consensus that foreign bribery was a reprehensible activity better prohibited and punished than legalised through disclosure.[13] Congress believed that this approach would be more effective: it would act as a stronger deterrent; be less burdensome on business than disclosure, since it would require companies to report *all* foreign payments and not only questionable ones; and be no more difficult to enforce than disclosure.[14]

1. History of Legislation

(a) The Original 1977 Act

On December 19, 1977, Congress enacted the FCPA by amending the Securities Exchange Act of 1934 ("Exchange Act").[15] The FCPA was comprised of two components: i) the anti-bribery provisions and ii) the bookkeeping and internal accounting controls provisions.[16]   **3–05**

The anti-bribery provisions are generally enforced by the US Department of Justice (DOJ); the accounting provisions are generally enforced by the SEC. Specifically, the anti-bribery provisions contained in the 1977 Act stated that "it shall be unlawful" for any "issuer" that has a class of securities registered or is required to file reports, and any "domestic concern," as well as "any officer, director, employee, agent, of such issuer or any stockholder thereof" acting on

---

[9] *Senate Report*, at 2. On September 15, 1976, by a unanimous vote of 86–0, the Senate passed S. 3664, incorporating the SEC's recommendations.

[10] Don Zarin, *Doing Business Under the Foreign Corrupt Practices Act* (Practising Law Institute's Corporate and Securities Law Library 2008), at 1–2 [hereinafter *"Doing Business"*].

[11] *House Report*, at 19 ("Minority Views to H.R. 3815, Unlawful Corporate Payments Act").

[12] *House Report*, at 19 ("Minority Views to H.R. 3815, Unlawful Corporate Payments Act").

[13] *House Report*, at 6.

[14] *House Report*, at 6.

[15] Securities Exchange Act of 1934, 15 U.S.C. §§ 78a (June 6, 1934) [hereinafter *"SEC ACT"*].

[16] §§ 78dd–2 (anti-bribery provisions). These provisions were added to s.30A of the SEC Act. §§78dd–1 (accounting provisions). These provisions were added to s.13(b) of the SEC Act.

behalf of such issuer or domestic concern," to "make use of the mails or any means or instrumentality of interstate commerce corruptly in furtherance of an offer, payment, promise to pay, or authorisation of the payment of any money, or offer, gift, promise to give, or authorisation of the giving of anything of value" to "any foreign official, foreign political party or official thereof, or foreign political candidate," as well as "any person, while knowing or having reason to know that all or a portion of such money or thing of value will be offered, given, or promised, directly or indirectly" to such foreign officials for purposes of:

"i) influencing any act or decision of such person acting in his or her official capacity, including a decision to fail to perform official functions, or ii) inducing such person to his or her influence with a foreign government or instrumentality thereof to affect or influence any act or decision of such government or instrumentality in order to obtain or retain business, or direct business to such issuer or domestic concern."[17]

Violation of these provisions led to stiff penalties. An issuer or domestic concern convicted under the anti-bribery provisions was subject to a fine of $1 million.[18] Individuals found guilty of violating the provisions were subject to a fine of $10,000 or five years imprisonment, or both.[19]

3–06   The bookkeeping and internal accounting controls provisions of the 1977 Act applied to any "issuer" that had a class of securities registered or is required to file reports, and required them to "make and keep books, records, and accounts" that "in reasonable detail, accurately and fairly reflect the transactions and dispositions of the issuer," and to "devise and maintain a system of internal accounting controls sufficient to provide reasonable assurances that":

(i)   transactions are executed in accordance with management's general or specific authorisation;

(ii)   transactions are recorded as necessary (I) to permit preparation of financial statements in conformity with generally accepted accounting principles or any other criteria applicable to such statements, and (II) to maintain accountability for assets;

(iii) access to assets is permitted only in accordance with management's general or specific authorisation; and

(iv)   the recorded accountability for assets is compared with the existing assets at reasonable intervals and appropriate action is taken with respect to any differences.[20]

---

[17] §§ 78dd–1(a) (issuers); §§ 78dd–2 (a) (domestic concerns).
[18] §§ 78dd–1(c)(1) (issuers); §§ 78dd–2 (b)(1) (domestic concerns).
[19] §§ 78dd–1(c)(2) (officer or director of issuers); §§ 78dd–1(c)(3) (employee or agent of issuers); §§ 78dd–2 (b)(1)(B) (individuals who are domestic concerns); §§ 78dd–2 (b)(1)(B)(2) (officer, director, or stockholder acting on behalf of a domestic concern); §§ 78dd–2 (b)(1)(B)(2) (employee or agent of a domestic concern).
[20] §§ 78m.

With the passage of the Act, the United States enshrined the first prohibition explicitly against the bribery of foreign officials.[21] Laws criminalising bribery in other countries concerned those countries' own officials but not foreign officials. Companies doing business abroad simply followed the local laws of the foreign country and even the local customs accepting of the use bribery.[22] Bribery of foreign officials was a deeply embedded business practice in many countries.[23]

As a result, American businesses complained that they were falling behind their foreign competitors, who were not under the same restrictions. In the period from May 1994 through April 2000, the US Department of Commerce received reports that 353 contracts valued at $165 billion may have been influenced by bribery involving foreign firms.[24] Consequently, US firms were alleged to have lost 92 of these contracts, worth approximately $26 billion.[25]

The FCPA was criticised for the resulting impediment placed on American businesses abroad. Often US companies were discouraged from participating in business transactions because they knew that the outcomes are influenced by bribes.[26] Many also saw it as an imposition of American values abroad, albeit on American companies, that did business with foreign companies or possessed foreign subsidiaries. 3–07

The FCPA was also criticised for the lack of clear guidance for companies. Predominant concerns dealt with "facilitating payments," also known as "grease" payments. The bill's coverage was not to extend to "facilitating payments," which generally are payments made to expedite a bureaucratic or clerical activity that would otherwise be legal.[27] The Act expressly stated that the definition of "foreign official" did not include individual positions or companies whose duties are

---

[21] See D. Zarin, *Doing Business*. Sweden's criminal code arguably had a provision dealing with bribery of foreign officials, however there has not been any prosecution under that law. Swedish Penal Code, SFS 1977: 102 (entered into force January 1, 1978).

[22] See *Doing Business*, at 1–3. One Defence Security Assistance Agency memorandum written prior to the enactment of the FCPA suggested that firms pay large feels to local agents. Hearings on the Activities of American Multinational Corporations Abroad Before the Subcommittee on International Economic Policy of the House Committee on International Relations, 94th Cong., 1st Sess. (1975). Tamara Adler, COMMENT: Amending the Foreign Corrupt Practices Act of 1977: A Step Toward Clarification and Consolidation, 73 J. Crim. L. & Criminology 1740 at 1745 (1982) [hereinafter "*Amending the FCPA of 1977*"].

[23] *Addressing the Challenges of International Bribery and Fair Competition*: July 20 (Second Annual Report to Congress on the OECD Antibribery Convention), Executive Summary (2000), 5, available through http://tcc.export.gov [Accessed July 15, 2010] [hereinafter "*OECD Report*"]. For a discussion of corrupt practices in other countries, see *Doing Business*. See also *Amending the FCPA of 1977*, at 1745.

[24] *OECD Report*, at 5.

[25] *OECD Report*, at 5.

[26] In one study, a majority of exporting firms perceived an adverse impact of the FCPA on their export operations, and 30% reported no adverse impact. Jyoti N. Prasad, *Foreign Economic Policy of the United States: Impact of the Foreign Corrupt Practices Act of 1977 on US Import*, xv (1993). Some companies feared that prohibition of payments would affect their competitiveness. at 50.

[27] *House Report*, at 4. *Senate Report*, at 10. The Senate Report, however, gave a few examples of "facilitating payments," such as payments for expediting shipments through customs, placing a transatlantic telephone call, securing required permits, or obtaining adequate police protection, "transactions which may involve even the proper performance of duties."

"essentially ministerial or clerical."[28] However, the Act did not mention or define "facilitating payments," leaving standards uncertain for payments that could be made.

Another ambiguity in the act related to the scope of the word "corruptly," and whether or not gifts and business entertainment for foreign officials were included of the parameter of payments that would be seen as corrupt.[29] The term was not defined in the Act, leaving courts to glean its meaning from comments in the Senate and House reports.[30]

3–08   The Act did not allow a company to indemnify officers, directors, employees, agents, or shareholders upon conviction, consistent with the SEC's policy against corporate indemnification of fines imposed for wilful violation of the securities laws.[31] Confronted with the stark prospect of high fines and possible incarceration, American companies began to err on the side of caution, causing them to forego many business opportunities. Congress decided to amend the FCPA to provide certain clarifications.

(b) The Revisions of 1988

3–09   In 1988, Congress amended the FCPA by passing the Omnibus Trade and Competitiveness Act, leading to three major changes in the law.[32] The amendments created an exception for facilitating payments made towards the performance of "routine governmental actions."[33] The amendments also created two affirmative defences: 1) for payments lawful under the written laws of the foreign country, and 2) for "reasonable and bona fide expenditures."[34]

On the other side of the ledger, the 1988 amendments also removed the Eckhardt Amendment, which provided that an employee or agent of the company could not be held liable until the firm itself was found to have violated the anti-bribery provisions.[35] Now, company executives and employees could be sanctioned for their individual behaviour irrespective of whether or not the company was found guilty of violating the FCPA.

(c) The Revisions of 1998

3–10   On November 10, 1998, President Clinton signed into law the International Anti-Bribery and Fair Competition Act of 1998 in order to implement the Organisation for Economic Cooperation Development (OECD) Convention on Combating

---

[28] §§ 78dd–1(b) (issuers); §§ 78dd–2(d)(2) (domestic concerns).
[29] See John W. Duncan, COMMENT: Modifying the Foreign Corrupt Practices Act: The Search for a Practical Standard, 4 NW. J. INT. L. & Bus. 203 at 208 (1982).
[30] *Senate Report*, at 10; *House Report*, at 7–8.
[31] §§ 78dd–1(c)(4) (issuers); 78dd–2(b)(4) (domestic concerns).
[32] Lillian V. Blageff, *Guide to the Foreign Corrupt Practices Act*, FCPA Reporter (Thomson Reuters/West 2008) [hereinafter "*Guide to the FCPA*"].
[33] §§ 78dd–1(b) (issuers); §§ 78dd–2(b) (domestic concerns).
[34] §§ 78dd–1(c) (issuers); §§ 78dd–2(c) (domestic concerns).
[35] See *US v McLean* 738 F.2d 655 (5th Cir. 1984) (preventing the Government from prosecuting an individual where the firm had only been convicted for conspiracy to violate the FCPA, not for a substantive violation of the FCPA itself).

Bribery of Foreign Public Officials in International Business Transactions.[36] This revised the FCPA to bring it in accordance with the provisions of the OECD Anti-Bribery Convention. Several changes were made to expand the FCPA's jurisdiction. The FCPA now covered the actions of US nationals or corporations taken outside the United States, the actions of foreign persons or corporations inside the United States, and included "public international organisations" in the definition of "foreign official."[37]

The Act was also amended to cover corrupt payments made for purposes of securing "improper advantage" from foreign officials, and not only for purposes of obtaining or retaining business.[38]

The United State's efforts, as well as the passage of the OECD Convention, have spurred other activity on the international front to combat foreign bribery. On December 14, 2005, the United Nations Convention Against Corruption entered into force.[39]

As noted above, the FCPA has two distinct prongs: the more familiar prong   **3–11** consists of the anti-bribery provisions; the lesser-known prong deals with maintaining accurate books and records. The books-and-records provisions do not explicitly refer to the anti-bribery provisions. They could theoretically apply, therefore, to books and records in any context. As a matter of practice, however, US regulators generally consider the books-and-records provision only in cases where those books and records reflect (or fail to reflect) bribes to foreign officials.

B. ANTI-BRIBERY PROVISIONS

I. PROVISIONS

The anti-bribery provisions consist of five main elements that prohibit: **3–12**

1. "any issuer which has a class of securities registered pursuant to section 78l of this title or which is required to file reports under section 78o(d) of this title," or "any domestic concern," or "any officer, director, employee, or agent" or any stockholder thereof acting on behalf of such" issuer or domestic concern, or any person other than an issuer or domestic concern while in the territory of the United States;

---

[36] *Convention on Organisation for Economic Co-operation and Development*, December 14, 1960 [hereinafter "*OECD Convention*"] The Convention took effect in February 15, 1999 after ratification by the requisite number of countries.

[37] §§ 78dd–1(f)(1) (issuers); §§ 78dd–2(h)(2) (domestic concerns).

[38] §§ 78dd–1(a) (issuers); §§ 78dd–2(a) (domestic concerns).

[39] See *UN Convention Against Corruption*, G.A. Res. 58/4 (December 14, 2005), available through http://www.unodc.org [Accessed July 15, 2010] [hereinafter "*UN Convention*"]. The Convention entered into Force with the thirtieth ratification by Ecuador. As of July 25, 2009, there are 140 signatories to the UN Convention.

2. from "mak[ing] use of the mails or any means or instrumentality of interstate commerce";

3. "corruptly in furtherance of an offer, payment, promise to pay, or authorization of the payment of any money, or offer, gift, promise to give, or authorization of the giving of anything of value";

4. to any foreign official, any foreign political party or official thereof, any candidate for foreign political office, or any other person, knowing that all or a portion of such money or thing of value will be offered to any foreign official;

5. for purposes of "(A) influencing any act or decision of such foreign official in his official capacity, (ii) inducing such foreign official to do or omit to do any act in violation of the lawful duty of such official, or (iii) securing any improper advantage; or (B) inducing such foreign official to use his influence with a foreign government or instrumentality thereof to affect or influence any act or decision of such government or instrumentality;

6. in order to assist such issuer in obtaining or retaining business for or with, or directing business to, any person.[40]

II. Jurisdiction

(a) Issuers

3–13   Issuers under the FCPA are quite simply companies with a reporting obligation to the SEC.[41] Note that this includes non-US companies trading securities on a US exchange.

The books-and-records provision of the FCPA apply only to Issuers, not to domestic concerns.

(b) Domestic Concerns

3–14   A "domestic concern" under the FCPA is: (A) any individual who is a citizen, national, or resident of the United States; and (B) any corporation, partnership, association, joint-stock company, business trust, unincorporated organisation, or sole proprietorship which has its principal place of business in the United States, or which is organised under the laws of the United States or a territory, possession, or commonwealth of the United States).[42]

The provisions additionally apply to "any officer, director, employee, or agent" or "any stockholder thereof acting on behalf of such" issuer or domestic concern,

---

[40] §§ 78dd–1(a) (issuers); §§ 78dd–2(a) (domestic concerns); §§ 78dd–3(a) (persons other than issuers or domestic concerns).
[41] See 15 U.S.C. § 78m(b)(2).
[42] §§ 78dd–2(h) (domestic concerns).

regardless of that individual's nationality.[43] The above-mentioned actors have always been covered by the FCPA since the original 1977 Act; but, previously these actors could only be sanctioned under the FCPA if they made use of the mails or any means or instrumentality of interstate commerce.

The amendments of 1998 broadly expanded the FCPA's jurisdiction. One way in which the FCPA's jurisdiction was augmented was by making it unlawful for issuers[44] registered with the SEC or required to file with the SEC and organised under the laws of the United States, or a state, territory, possession, or commonwealth of the United States or a political subdivision thereof, or individuals acting on behalf of such issuers that were US nationals; or "any United States person,"[45] including any US national or any "corporation, partnership, association, joint-stock company, business trust, unincorporated organisation, or sole proprietorship which has its principal place of business in the US, or which is organised under the laws of the US or a territory, possession, or commonwealth of the US," to perform any act outside the US in furtherance of a foreign bribe. That is, it became illegal for all US companies and nationals to perform any act outside the United States in furtherance of a foreign bribe.

Another way in which the 1998 amendments augmented the FCPA's jurisdiction was in making it unlawful for any person to do any act within the territory of the United States in furtherance of a foreign bribe. Hence, the Act now captures foreign companies and individuals. These amendments impact the activities of foreign subsidiaries of US companies, whose risk of prosecution is higher if any acts took place in the US.[46]

3–15

The provisions also apply to companies that have certain categories of American Depository Receipts (ADRs).[47] ADRs are negotiable certificates issued by a US depositary bank representing ownership interest in a foreign stock traded on a US exchange. This mechanism allows many foreign companies to trade their stock on US stock exchanges. The underlying security of ADR is usually held by a financial institution overseas.

In sum, regarding acts within the United States, the anti-bribery provisions apply to all publicly-traded companies that have stocks, bonds, or ADRs registered with the SEC or that are required to file reports with the SEC (US or foreign) and associated individuals; all US companies; all US citizens, residents, or nationals; and all foreign persons. Regarding acts outside the United States, the anti-bribery provisions apply to all those mentioned above, as long as they made use of the mails or instrumentality of the United States *or* as long as they were a US company or national.

---

[43] §§ 78dd–1(a) (issuers); §§ 78dd–2(a) (domestic concerns).
[44] §§ 78dd–1(g) (issuers).
[45] §§ 78dd–2(i) (domestic concerns).
[46] *Guide to the FCPA*, at 1:13.
[47] Jay G. Martin, *Compliance with the Foreign Corrupt Practices Act and the Developing International Anti-Corruption Environment*, 9 (2008) [hereinafter "*Compliance with the FCPA*"], at 1.

III. Interstate Instrumentality.

3–16   The 1977 Act required the use of "the mails or any means or instrumentality of interstate commerce" in furtherance of the foreign bribe under the anti-bribery provisions, but following the 1998 amendments, the use of an interstate instrumentality was no longer required for any acts occurring within US territory. It is enough that any act in furtherance of the foreign bribe occurred in the United States. Therefore, the interstate instrumentality requirement is more pertinent to those companies and persons that are foreign, since the Act now captures any act by US companies and nationals through the 1998 "Alternative Jurisdiction" amendments.[48]

It is not very difficult to satisfy the interstate instrumentality requirement. This nexus to American jurisdiction can be satisfied for FCPA prosecution purposes through the use of a Western Union international telex,[49] a flight on a commercial aircraft,[50] and the mailing of checks.[51] Given the precedents, even an e-mail to a person on a US server would probably suffice.

IV. Corruptly

3–17   The term "corruptly" refers to the general intent required by the Act. Despite the amendments in 1988 and 1998 that provided for much–needed clarification of the Act, the word "corruptly" has been left undefined.

The legislative history of the Senate elaborates that the word "corruptly" is used in order to emphasise that "the offer, promise or gift, must be intended to induce the recipient to misuse his official position" for purposes of "wrongfully direct[ing] business to the payor or his client, or to obtain preferential legislation or a favourable regulation."[52] Moreover, the Senate Report states that the word "connotes an evil motive or purpose, an intent to wrongfully influence the recipient."[53]

The House Report puts forth a similar explanation and also states that the intent is similar to that which is required under the domestic bribery statute 18 U.S.C. 201(b).[54]

The domestic bribery statute has been interpreted by the courts as requiring an intentional violation motivated by evil. See, e.g. *US v Strand* 574 F.2d 993 (9th Cir. 1978); *US v Evans* 572 F.2d 455 at 480–81 (5th Cir. 1978); *US v Brewster* 506 F.2d 62 at 71 (DC Cir. 1974). This element does not require that the act be fully consummated or succeed in producing the desired outcome.[55]

---

[48] §§ 78dd–1(g) (issuers); §§ 78dd–2(i) (domestic concerns).
[49] See *US v Harry G. Carpenter and WS Kirkpatrick Inc.* (Cr. No. 85-353), D.N.J., 1985.
[50] *US v Kenny International Corp* (Cr. No. 79-372), D.D.C., 1979.
[51] *US v Sam P. Wallace Company Inc.* (Cr. No. 83-0034) (PG), D.P.R., 1983.
[52] *Senate Report*, at 10.
[53] *Senate Report*, at 10.
[54] *House Report*, at 7–8.
[55] *Senate Report*, at 10.

Within the context of the FCPA itself courts have found that: **3–18**

> "Corruptly mean[s] that the offer, promise to pay, payment or authorization of pay-
> ment, must be intended to induce the recipient to misuse his official position or to
> influence someone else to do so.... [A]n act is corruptly done if done voluntarily and
> intentionally, and with a bad purpose of accomplishing either an unlawful end or result,
> or a lawful end or result by some unlawful method or means."

US v Liebo 923 F.2d 1308 at 1312 (8th Cir. 1991) (internal citations omitted):

> "The word 'corruptly' in the Foreign Corrupt Practices Act (FCPA), 15 U.S.C.S. §§
> 78dd-1, et seq., signifies, in addition to the element of 'general intent' present in most
> criminal statutes, a bad or wrongful purpose and an intent to influence a foreign official
> to misuse his official position."

*Stichting Ter Behartiging Van De Belangen Van Oudaandeelhouders In Het Kapitaal
Van Saybolt International BV v Schreiber, et al.* 327 F.3d 173 at 182 (2d. Cir.
2003). The word "corruptly" signifies "a bad or wrongful purpose and an intent
to influence a foreign official to misuse his official position." *US v Kozeny* 493 F.
Supp. 2d 693 at 704 (S.D.N.Y. 2007).

Significantly, then, courts have held that corrupt payments require knowledge
that they were unlawful.

> "The requisite intent here only requires knowledge that one is doing something
> unlawful, and ... Defendants could [not] be convicted if there was a reasonable doubt of
> their knowledge of the "unlawfulness" of their conduct."

US v Kay 2008 U.S. App. LEXIS 1047, at *7 (5th Cir. January 10,
2008) (hereinafter *Kay 2008*).

In *Liebo*, the court determined that the accused acted corruptly where he gave
airline tickets to a Nigerian diplomat shortly before the Nigerian government
approved a third contract to buy military supplies from the accused's company.
923 F.2d at 1312. The evidence in *Liebo* further showed that the Nigerian diplomat who received the airline tickets had a close familial relationship with the
Nigerian Air Force Captain who recommended approval of the contracts. In *Kay
2008*, the court found that jury instructions sufficiently explained the meaning of
"corruptly" where the instructions asserted:

> "[A]n act is 'corruptly' done if done voluntarily and intentionally, and with a *bad purpose*
> or *evil motive* of accomplishing either an *unlawful* end or result, or a lawful end or result
> by some unlawful method or means."

2008 U.S. App. LEXIS 1047, at *2–3.

The legislative history of the FCPA further illuminates the meaning of the   **3–19**
term "corruptly" in the context of the statute:

"The word 'corruptly' is used in order to make clear that the offer, payment, promise, or gift, must be intended to induce the recipient to misuse his official position in order to wrongfully direct business to the payer or his client, or to obtain preferential legislation or a favorable regulation. The word 'corruptly' connotes an evil motive or purpose, and intent to wrongfully influence the recipient."

Sen. Rep. No. 114, 95th Cong., 1st Sess. 1, reprinted in 1977 U.S. Code Cong. & Admin. News 4098, 4108; H.R. Rep. No. 95–640 at 7–8 (1977); H.R. Rep. No. 95–640 at 7–8 (1977).

Any finding of intent in the criminal context requires a showing that the defendant acted willfully and deliberately to achieve the desired goal. An act cannot be willful, however, unless the accused has knowledge that his or her actions are illegal:

"As a general matter, when used in the criminal context, a 'willful' act is one undertaken with a 'bad purpose.' In other words, in order to establish a 'willful' violation of a statute, 'the Government must prove that the defendant acted with knowledge that his conduct was unlawful.'

Bryan v US 524 U.S. 184 at 191–92 (1998).

The accused need not intend to violate the particulars of a specific law, but must intend to act unlawfully. As explained further by the Fifth Circuit:

"[A] defendant must have acted intentionally—not by accident or mistake. The first and most basic interpretation of criminal willfulness is that committing an act, and having knowledge of that act, is criminal willfulness –provided that the actions fell within the category of actions defined as illegal under the applicable statute. In such cases, the defendant need not have known of the specific terms of the statute or even the existence of the statute. The defendant's knowledge that he or she committed the act is sufficient
. . .

Criminal willfulness requires only that criminal defendants have knowledge that they are acting unlawfully or knowledge of the facts that constitute the offense, depending on the definition followed, unless the statutory text provides an alternate definition of this element. The Foreign Corrupt Practices Act … does not define willfulness, so courts must rely upon the common law definition."

US v Kay 2007 WL 3088140 at *8 (5th Cir. 2007) (hereinafter *Kay 2007*); see also *Stichting* 327 F.3d at 181 ("Knowledge by a defendant that it is violating the FCPA— that it is committing all the elements of an FCPA violation—is not itself an element of the FCPA Crime").

3–20   In *Bryan*, the Supreme Court determined that jury instructions were proper where they explained that:

"A person acts willfully if he acts intentionally and purposely and with the intent to do something the law forbids, that is, with the bad purpose to disobey or to disregard the law. Now, the person need not be aware of the specific law or rule that his conduct may be violating. But he must act with the intent to do something that the law forbids."

524 U.S. at 190. In *Kay 2007*, the Fifth Circuit found that jury instructions adequately explained the element of willfulness where the instructions defined a knowing act as one "done voluntarily and intentionally, not because of accident or mistake." 2007 WL 3088140 at *8.

The case law and legislative history thus illustrate that a defendant could not be convicted unless the government could show beyond a reasonable doubt that he had the requisite corrupt intent willfully to break the law.

The case law and legislative history also suggest—though they do not con-clusively show—that the government may have an even steeper hurdle to clear. The legislative history states that the term "corruptly" refers to the intent that the recipient of a payment "misuse his *official* position." (emphasis added) The Eighth Circuit, whose law presumably would control in a prosecution against AGA, echoed this language in the *Liebo* case. 923 F.2d at 1312.

It is therefore possible that proof of corrupt intent under the FCPA requires   3–21
not only a showing of a bad motive, but also an implicit knowledge that the recipient of the payment had an official position to misuse. Proof of bad motive alone may be insufficient: it is not a crime to bribe a foreigner if he is not a public official.

Case law fails to clarify this point. As noted above, cases have stated that the government must prove that a defendant knew that his actions violated the law, but that it need not prove that the defendant was aware of the specific provisions of the FCPA. *Kay* 2008 at *11; *Kozeny* 493 F. Supp. 2d at 704; *Stichting* 327 F.3d at 181-83.

What exactly that means remains unclear. It does, however, appear to leave room for the argument that knowledge of a bribe recipient's government position is an essential element of the "corruptly" prong of the statute.

V. PAYMENT OR ANYTHING OF VALUE

In order to be found liable under the anti-bribery provisions, a person's actions   3–22
could be done in furtherance of a concrete payment, but could also simply be an offer or a promise to pay. The actions could also be the authorisation of the payment, offer, or promise to pay. The item being offered could be a payment, a gift or "anything of value." The term "anything of value" allows for a wide range of objects falling within the purview of the Act. The object could be money, but it could also be stock, a contractual right or interest, access to credit, free tickets to Disney World[56] or employment of a relative.[57] Significantly, in terms of the amount of money or the monetary value of the thing being offered, there is no prescribed statutory minimum. Any payment made for corrupt purposes will be treated with the utmost seriousness.

---

[56] See, e.g. *SEC v Lucent Technology Inc* No. 1:07-CV-02301.
[57] *Compliance with the FCPA*, at 9.

VI. FOREIGN OFFICIAL

3–23   The definition of "foreign official" is very inclusive. It covers senior officials belonging to the highest echelons of government, as well as any person working for a foreign government. It includes "any officer or employee of a foreign government or any department, agency, or instrumentality thereof."[58]

A foreign official for the purpose of the FCPA is:

> "Any officer or employee of a foreign government or any department, agency, or instrumentality thereof, or of a public international organization, or any person acting in an official capacity for or on behalf of any such government or department, agency, or instrumentality, or for or on behalf of any such public international organization."

15 U.S.C. §§ 78dd-1(f), 78dd-2(h)(2)(A).

"There is no limit to the definition of 'foreign official' by importance of the officer."[59] "Official" is defined broadly to include even low-level employees whose "official" status may not be readily apparent.[60]

Employees of state-owned enterprises may be considered covered officials.[61]

3–24   Courts have shed light on the scope of persons falling under the definition of a "public official" in the domestic context. In discussing the definition of a public official under the domestic anti-bribery statute, 18 U.S.C. § 201, courts have found that:

> "[T]his definition [of a public official] extends beyond merely government employees and contractors to include private individuals who "occupy a position of public trust with official federal responsibilities." Such an individual, however, "must possess some degree of official responsibility for carrying out a federal program or policy" to be considered a public official. . . .
>
> In order to be considered a public official a defendant need not be the final decision maker as to a federal program or policy. Rather, it appears to be sufficient that the defendant is in a position of providing information and making recommendations to decision makers as long as the defendant's input is given sufficient weight to influence the outcome of the decisions at issue."

---

[58]   §§78dd–1(f)(1) (issuers); §§78dd–2(h)(2) (domestic concerns); §§78dd–3(f)(2) (persons other than issuers or domestic concerns).

[59]   Barry A. Sanders, *Foreign Corrupt Practices Act—Antibribery Provisions*, 3 Transnational Business Transactions § 18:15 (2007).

[60]   Lucinda A. Low & John E. Davis, *The FCPA In Investment Transactions*, 1 Foreign Corrupt Practices Act Report 5:27 (2008) ("[T]he standard for being designated a 'foreign official' is relatively low.").

[61]   *Re Schnitzer Steel Industries Inc*, Exchange Release No. 54606 (October 16, 2006) (payments to managers of government-controlled steel mills in China; steel mill employees deemed foreign officials); Press Release, DPC (Tianjin) Ltd Charged with Violating the Foreign Corrupt Practices Act (May 20, 2005) (payments to physicians and laboratory personnel employed by government-owned hospitals in the People's Republic of China; hospital personnel deemed foreign officials), *SEC v ABB Ltd*, 1:04CV1141 (RBN), Litigation Rel. No. 18775 (D.D.C. July 6, 2004) (payments made to officials of a Nigerian state-owned agency responsible for overseeing the country's investment in petroleum exploration and production, and an Angolan state-owned oil company); *SECv Syncor International Corp*, 1:02CV02421, Litigation Rel. No. 17887 (D.D.C. December 10, 2002) (payments made to doctors at hospitals owned by foreign officials; doctors were deemed foreign officials).

United States v Kenney 185 F.3d 1217 at 1221–22 (11th Cir. 1999) (citing *Dixson v United States* 465 U.S. 482 at 496, 499 (1984)); see also *United States v Hang* 75 F.3d 1275 at 1280 (8th Cir.1996) (determining that an employee of a private corporation was a public official where the individual was responsible for screening applicants for a federal low-income housing program and was employed by a corporation specifically formed to administer federal programs and funds); *United States v Madeoy* 912 F.2d 1486 (D.C. Cir. 1990), cert. denied, 498 U.S. 1105 (1991) (upholding the conviction of an independent contractor for accepting bribes as a public official where government guaranteed loans based on the defendant's recommendation as a VA-approved fee appraiser).

In *Kenney*, the court found that an employee of a private company held a position of "public trust" because he advised the US military on decisions about the procurement of equipment, and the information and recommendations he provided served as the basis for many decisions. The court therefore found that the employee was a public official because "in the performance of his duties, Appellant had some official responsibility for the carrying out of a government program."[62]

In 1998, the definition was expanded to include "public international organisations," or "any person acting in an official capacity for or on behalf of any such government or department, agency, or instrumentality, or for or on behalf of any such public international organisation," in accordance with the OECD Convention.[63] The Act defines a "public international organisation" as an organisation that is designated by Executive Order pursuant to s.1 of the International Organisations Immunities Act (22 U.S.C. § 288), or any other international organisation that is designated by the President by Executive Order.[64]

Public international organisations were added to the list as they are increasingly serving as the gateway towards doing business abroad, especially in developing countries. Such organisations include the United Nations, the World Bank, the International Monetary Fund, the World Trade Organisation, the International Committee of the Red Cross, the Organisation of American States, and the African Union.[65]   3–25

The Act also prohibits the bribing of foreign political parties or officials thereof and foreign political candidates. These candidates could include current government officials seeking re-election or another position in a campaign. Additionally, the Act prohibits the bribing of "any person, while knowing or having reason to know that all or a portion of such money or thing of value will be

---

[62] *Kenney* 185 F.3d 1217 at 1222.

[63] For purposes of the Convention, "foreign public official" means "any person holding a legislative, administrative or judicial office of a foreign country, whether appointed or elected; any person exercising a public function for a foreign country, including for a public agency or public enterprise; and any official or agent of a public international organization." *OECD Convention*, art.1.

[64] §§78dd–1(f)(1) (issuers); §§78dd–2(h)(2) (domestic concerns); §§78dd–3(f)(2) (persons other than issuers or domestic concerns).

[65] There are over 70 entities designated as "public international organizations." For a list of public international organisations, see *http://www4.law.cornell.edu/uscode/html/uscode22/usc_sec_22_00000288——000-notes.html*.

offered, given, or promised, directly or indirectly" to such foreign officials. Such third parties can range from agents to family members or friends of officials.

The FCPA does not give authority for the prosecution of foreign officials as recipients of bribes, as the Act excludes foreign officials from prosecution under the FCPA itself, and also cannot be prosecuted as "conspirators" under the general conspiracy statute, 18 U.S.C. § 371, for conspiring to violate the FCPA. See *United States v Castle* 925 F.2d 831 (5th Cir. 1991).

VII. Knowledge Standard

3–26   The FCPA also prohibits issuers and domestic concerns from offering or authorising a bribe to "any person, while knowing that all or a portion of such money or thing of value" will be offered, directly or indirectly, to a foreign official. This knowledge requirement is at the core of matters dealing with third party agents and foreign subsidiaries. A company will be held liable for authorising the payment with the knowledge that that money will end up in the hands of a foreign official.

However, a "knowing" state of mind under the FCPA is said to exist if "such person is aware that such person is engaging in such conduct, that such circumstance exists, or that such result is substantially certain to occur," or "such person has a firm belief that such circumstance exists or that such result is substantially certain to occur."[66] If knowledge of a particular circumstance is required for an offense, that knowledge is established if a person is "aware of a high probability of the existence of such circumstance, unless the person actually believes that such circumstance does not exist."[67]

The knowledge standard therefore includes the concepts of "wilful ignorance," "conscious disregard," or "deliberate ignorance." Constructive knowledge will be imputed by courts where such circumstances exist that a person probably was aware that illegal conduct was occurring. This relaxed standard of knowledge makes it easier to reach senior executives at companies where it is difficult to find proof of authorisation of foreign bribes. Company officials may not simply feign ignorance and "bury their heads in the sand."

> "The knowing standard is ... intended to address actions characterized by courts in other contexts as conscious disregard, willful blindness, or deliberate ignorance. However, the knowledge requirement is not equivalent to recklessness. It requires an awareness of a high probability of the existence of the circumstance."[68]

---

[66] §§78dd–1(f)(2)(A) (issuers); §§78dd–2(h)(3)(A) (domestic concerns); §§78dd–3(f)(3) (persons other than issuers or domestic concerns).

[67] §§78dd–1(f)(2)(A) (issuers); §§78dd–2(h)(3)(A) (domestic concerns); §§78dd–3(f)(3) (persons other than issuers or domestic concerns).

[68] Otto G. Obermaier, Timothy E. Hoeffner & Amy S. Cline, *The Foreign Corrupt Practices Act, in* White Collar Crime: Business and Regulatory Offenses 16–9 (2007).

VIII. Purpose—To Obtain Business or Secure an Improper Advantage

According to the 1977 Act, the bribe had to be for purposes of "obtain[ing] or   3–27
retain[ing] business," so the bribe had to be made or offered in order to secure a
business contract, for example, or to continue doing business under a foreign
company. In order to conform to the OECD Convention, the 1998 amendments
expanded the objective of the bribe to include the purpose of "secur[ing] an
improper advantage."[69] Therefore, the Act includes purposes not confined to
simply obtaining business, but has been broadened to generally mean for purposes
of improving the business climate. The foreign official could, for example, use his
or her influence to lower customs or taxes, provide useful contact, or decline
investigation or prosecution of an alleged offense.[70]

This provision of the FCPA was the subject of an Appeals Court opinion in
United States v Kay 359 F.3rd 738 (5th Cir. 2004). The government had accused
the defendants in *Kay* of having bribed Haitian customs officials to under values
import taxes in grain that the defendants' company was supplying to Haiti. The
trial court granted the defendants' motion to dismiss on the ground that such
bribes were not directly for the purpose of obtaining or retaining business.

The Appeals Court neatly summarised the differing positions of the litigants:

> "The principal thrust of the defendants' argument is that the business nexus element,
> i.e., the 'assist... in obtaining or retaining business' element, narrowly limits the sta-
> tute's applicability to those payments that are intended to obtain a foreign official's
> approval of a bid for a new government contract or the renewal of an existing gov-
> ernment contract. In contrast, the government insists that, in addition to payments to
> officials that lead directly to getting or renewing business contracts, the statute covers
> payments that indirectly advance ('assist') the payer's goal of obtaining or retaining
> foreign business with or for some person. The government reasons that paying reduced
> customs duties and sales taxes on imports, as is purported to have occurred in this case,
> is the type of 'improper advantage' that *always* will assist in obtaining or retaining
> business in a foreign country, and thus is always covered by the FCPA."

359 F.3d 738 at 743.

After its own extensive review of the FCPA's legislative history, the Appeals   3–28
Court concluded:

> "Given the foregoing analysis of the statute's legislative history, we cannot hold as a
> matter of law that Congress mean to limit the FCPA's applicability to cover only bribes
> that lead directly to the award or renewal of contracts, Instead, we hold that Congress
> intended for the FCPA to apply broadly to payments intended to assist the payor, either

---

[69] Each Party shall take such measures as may be necessary to establish that it is a criminal offence
under its law for any person intentionally to offer, promise or give any undue pecuniary or other
advantage, whether directly or through intermediaries, to a foreign public official, for that official or for
a third party, in order that the official act or refrain from acting in relation to the performance of
official duties, in order to obtain or retain business or *other improper advantage* in the conduct of
international business. *OECD Convention*, art.1.

[70] *Compliance with the FCPA*, at 9.

directly or indirectly, in obtaining or retaining business for some person, and that bribes paid to foreign tax officials to secure illegally reduced customs and tax liability constitute a type of payment that can fall within this broad coverage.

. . .

Thus, in diametric opposition to the district court, we conclude that bribes paid to foreign officials in consideration fornlawful evasion of customs duties and sales taxes could fall within the purview of the FCPA's proscription. We hasten to add, however, that this conduct does not automatically constitute a violation of the FCPA: It still must be shown that the bribery was intended to produce an effect—here, through tax savings—that would "assist in obtaining or retaining business."

359 F.3d 739 at 755–756 (emphasis original)

IX. PENALTIES

3–29   Any company that violates the anti-bribery provisions is subject to a fine of $2,000,000.[71] Any individual who "wilfully violates" the anti-bribery provisions is subject to a fine of $100,000, imprisonment for five years, or both.[72] The Attorney General may bring a civil action against domestic concerns and companies other than issuers, as well as individuals acting on behalf of such entities may also seek injunctive relief if that person is engaged or about to engage in an act constituting a violation of the anti-bribery provisions.[73]

C. EXCEPTIONS AND AFFIRMATIVE DEFENCES

I. EXCEPTION: ROUTINE GOVERNMENTAL ACTION OR FACILITATING PAYMENTS

3–30   In 1988, Congress passed amendments to clarify some of the ambiguities in the original Act, creating one exception and two affirmative defences pertinent to the anti-bribery provisions. Congress created an exception for any "routine governmental action," which excludes from the Act's coverage "facilitating or expediting payment[s]" made for the purposes of expediting or securing the performance of a routine governmental action by a foreign official.[74] The 1988 Amendments defined "routine governmental actions" by outlining specific actions that the Act does not prohibit.[75] The term "routine governmental action" means only an action which is "ordinarily and commonly performed by a foreign official in":

> (i) obtaining permits, licenses, or other official documents to qualify a person to do business in a foreign country;

---

[71] §§ 78ff(c) (issuers); §§ 78dd–2(g) (domestic concerns); §§ 78dd–3(3) (persons other than issuers or domestic concerns).

[72] §§ 78ff(c) (issuers); §§ 78dd–2(g) (domestic concerns); §§ 78dd–3(3) (persons other than issuers or domestic concerns).

[73] §§ 78dd–3(d) (persons other than issuers or domestic concerns); §§ 78dd–2(d)(domestic concerns).

[74] §§ 78dd–1(b); §§ 78dd–2(b); §§ 78dd–3(b).

[75] §§ 78dd–1(f)(3); §§ 78dd–2(h)(4); §§ 78dd–3(f)(4).

(ii) processing governmental papers, such as visas and work orders;

(iii) providing police protection, mail pick-up and delivery, or scheduling inspections associated with contract performance or inspections related to transit of goods across country;

(iv) providing phone service, power and water supply, loading and unloading cargo, or protecting perishable products or commodities from deterioration; or

(v) actions of a similar nature.

Moreover, the definition explicitly excludes decisions or actions taken by a foreign official in the decision-making process to award new business or to continue doing business with a particular entity, or the terms for doing so.[76]

The statute states specific purposes for which payments could be made but does not actually define what a "facilitating payment" is.

Congress intended the "facilitating payments" exception to be a limited carve-out covering only payments made to hasten the process of reaching an outcome without influencing it. Payments "which merely move a particular matter toward an eventual act or decision or which do not involve any discretionary action" will fall under the exception. H.R. Rep. No. 95-640, at 8 (1977); see also *United States v Kay* 359 F.3d 738 at 747 (2004) ("Congress sought to prohibit the type of bribery that (1) prompts officials to misuse their discretionary authority and (2) disrupts market efficiency and United States foreign relations, [while] at the same time recognizing that smaller payments intended to expedite ministerial actions should remain outside of the scope of the statute").

There is no statutory minimum that the payment must exceed in order to be unacceptable. Generally, the greater the facilitating payment, the more suspect it will seem. However no court has interpreted the application of the facilitating payment exception; neither has the DOJ formally addressed the exception in an Opinion Procedure Release.[77]

3–31

Although the facilitating payments exception is premised only on the purpose of the payment and not the amount, in practice the government has considered larger payments to fall outside the exception.[78]

There is no set threshold above which a payment will be considered an illegal bribe. Commentators, however, have opined that even a $1,000 payment might be too large.[79]

---

[76] §§ 78dd–1(f)(3)(b); §§ 78dd–2(h)(4)(b); §§ 78dd–3(f)(4)(b)

[77] *Compliance with the FCPA*, at 6.

[78] See, e.g. *US v Vitusa Corp* 3 FCPA Rep. 699.155 (D.N.J. 1994) (indicting a company for paying a foreign official $50,000 in "service fees" to induce the foreign government to pay its $163,000 debt to the company).

[79] See, e.g. Arthur F. Mathews, *Defending SEC and DOJ FCPA Investigations and Conducting Related Corporate Internal Investigations: The Triton Energy/Indonesia SEC Consent Decree Settlements*, 18 Nw. J. Int. L. & Bus. 303 at 315 (1998) (arguing that payments above $1,000 would likely be considered too high); Stephen F. Black & Roger M. Witten, *Complying With the Foreign Corrupt Practices Act*, 4–9 to 4–10 (1995) (arguing that payments over $15,000 would likely be considered too high).

DOJ officials have even stated that a payment exceeding $200 will be viewed with suspicion.[80]

3–32   Some companies have instituted safeguards to prevent unacceptable facilitating payments, such as Baker Hughes, which revised its policy regarding facilitating payments by prohibiting company employees and representatives from make such payments to any foreign official unless the circumstances involve an imminent threat to the health, safety or welfare of any employee, family member, or co-worker.[81]

II. AFFIRMATIVE DEFENCE: PAYMENTS AUTHORISED BY FOREIGN COUNTRY'S WRITTEN LAWS

3–33   One affirmative defence that was added as part of the 1988 amendments is that the payment, gift, offer, or promise of anything of value was lawful under the written laws and regulations of the foreign country.[82] It does not matter whether or not the local "custom" or "tradition" is to offer bribes. The written laws of the foreign country must state specifically that that action was authorised.

No country of which the authors are aware explicitly permits bribing its official in its written laws. The laws of the People's Republic of China do provide that payments to government officials of more than RMB 200,000 (about US$30,000) by corporation are considered criminal.[83] It is tempting to reason that payments of smaller amounts are therefore not crimes under Chinese law. But this is an untested proposition.[84]

At least one US court, furthermore, has interpreted this affirmative defence very narrowly. One of the defendants in *US v Kozeny*[85] sought to claim that his payments to officials in Azerbaijan were legal under Azeri law. The defendant relied on a provision of the Azeri Criminal Code which stated that a person who bribed a government official would not be criminally liable if he voluntarily reported the bribe after the fact.[86] The defendant apparently had done this.

3–34   The court was unmoved:

---

[80] *Compliance with the FCPA*, at 6.
[81] *Compliance with the FCPA*, at 6.
[82] §§ 78dd–1(c); §§ 78dd–2(c); §§ 78dd–3(c).
[83] See *Criminal Code of the People's Republic of China*, revised at the Twenty-Second Meeting of the Standing Committee of the Tenth National People's Congress of the People's Republic of China on June 29, 2006, arts 383, 385, 386, 389, 393; Measure Regarding the Standard of Placing a Case on File on Directly Investigated Cases (Proposed), promulgated by the Supreme People's Procuratorate on September 16, 1999: art.1 s.3, s.5 and s.8.
[84] Moreover, the Chinese system allows the "Procuratorate" or a judge to consider other circumstances of wrongdoing to find a violation. See *Criminal Code of the People's Republic of China*, revised at the Twenty-Second Meeting of the Standing Committee of the Tenth National People's Congress of the People's Republic of China on June 29, 2006, arts 383, 385, 386, 389, 393; Measure Regarding the Standard of Placing a Case on File on Directly Investigated Cases (Proposed), promulgated by the Supreme People's Procuratorate on September 16, 1999: art.1 s.3, s.5 and s.8.
[85] 582 F. Supp. 2d 535 (S.D.N.Y. 2008).
[86] 582 F. Supp. 2d 535 at 538.

"[1][2] For purposes of the FCPA's affirmative defence, the focus is on the *payment*, not the payor. A person cannot be guilty of violating the FCPA id the payment was *lawful* under foreign law. But there is no immunity from prosecution under the FCPA if a person could not have been prosecuted in the foreign country due to a technicality (e.g., time-barred) or because a provision in the foreign law 'relieves' a person of criminal responsibility. An individual may be prosecuted under the FCPA for a payment that violates foreign law even if the individual is relieved of criminal responsibility for his actions by a provision o the foreign law."[87] (emphasis in original)

III. AFFIRMATIVE DEFENCE: REASONABLE OR BONA FIDE EXPENDITURE

The second, and last, affirmative defence that was added as part of the 1988   3–35
amendments is that the payment is a "reasonable or bona fide expenditure" made for purposes directly related to "the promotion, demonstration, or explanation of products or services," or "the execution or performance of a contract with a foreign government or agency thereof."[88]

Classic examples of such expenditures are those made for travel and lodging. Although it is permissible, for example, to fly government officials to tour manufacturing facilities, it is unlikely to be acceptable to pay for their families to come too. By the same token, US regulators will not look kindly on paid visits to tourist attractions—especially where such attractions are nowhere near the company's manufacturing sites.[89] There are several DOJ Opinion Releases that provide guidance, however no court has interpreted the application of this defence.[90]

D. RECORD-KEEPING AND ACCOUNTING PROVISIONS

I. PROVISIONS

Congress crafted the FCPA to include the accounting provisions as a complement   3–36
to the anti-bribery provisions combating foreign bribery. The accounting pro-
visions of the FCPA were intended to ensure the accuracy of books and records, and to ensure that management had a sufficient grasp over the use of company assets.

Congress wanted to stem the deliberate falsification of books and records, one of the core devices used by companies to disguise the source or disbursement of corporate funds, and hence cover up the trail of illegal campaign payments or foreign bribes. Congress also mandated that a robust internal controls system be in place to make sure that all transactions were authorised and to maintain

---

[87] 582 F. Supp. 2d 535 at 539.
[88] §§ 78dd–1(c); §§ 78dd–2(c); §§ 78dd–3(c).
[89] See, e.g. *SEC v Lucent Technology Inc* No. 1:07—CV-02301 (D.D.C. December 21, 2007).
[90] *Compliance with the FCPA*, at 11.

accountability for assets in the event of a lapse in compliance. Some illicit practices of companies included the establishment of unrecorded slush funds and the inaccurate recording of transactions to them appear legitimate.[91]

II. JURISDICTION

3-37 As with the anti-bribery provisions, the accounting provisions apply to all "issuers"—that is, all those that are registered with the SEC or that are required to file reports with the SEC, as well as "any officer, director, employee, or agent" or "any stockholder thereof acting on behalf of such issuer."[92] Unlike the anti-bribery provisions, however, the accounting provisions do not cover "domestic concerns." Thus, they generally apply to publicly-held companies in the United States and US citizens and resident aliens who work for them, as well as certain foreign companies and individuals.

Of noteworthy importance is that the accounting provisions apply to all issuers, regardless of whether or not they have any transnational business, since the provisions were incorporated in the 1934 Securities Exchange Act. Therefore all issuers must adhere to the high standards of the accounting provisions or otherwise risk prosecution under the FCPA.

III. SUBSIDIARIES

3-38 The issuer's responsibility under the accounting provisions extends to any entities that it owns, including foreign subsidiaries.[93] If an issuer possesses a majority stake in an entity, then the issuer must comply with the Act's accounting provisions with regard to that subsidiary. If, however, the issuer only "holds 50 percent or less of the voting power with respect to a domestic or foreign firm," then the provisions only require that:

> "the issuer proceed in good faith to use its influence, to the extent reasonable under the issuer's circumstances, to cause such domestic or foreign firm to devise and maintain a system of internal accounting controls . . ."[94]

Circumstances to consider include the relative degree of the issuer's ownership of the subsidiary and the laws and practices that govern the foreign country in which the subsidiary resides.[95] As long as the issuer demonstrates good faith

---

[91] *Guide to the FCPA*, at 1:19.

[92] §§ 78m (b).

[93] Stuart E. Deming, *The Foreign Corrupt Practices Act: The Accounting and Record-Keeping Provisions*, FCPA Reporter, 10:2 (Thomson Reuters/West 2008) [hereinafter "Accounting and Record-Keeping Provisions"].

[94] §§ 78m (b) (6).

[95] §§ 78m (b) (6).

efforts to influence the subsidiary, it will be "conclusively presumed" to have complied with the accounting provisions.[96]

IV. PAYMENTS

The accounting provisions of the FCPA apply to all payments, regardless of the amount. Traditionally, under US securities laws the only material payments required disclosure; after the FCPA, even small sums of money are subject to disclosure. Failure to do so could have potentially serious consequences.

3–39

Management and employees have to take special care in reporting facilitating payments, for mischaracterisation of a payment as a facilitating payment in order to obtain an exception to the FCPA has potentially serious ramifications. Regulators prefer that any facilitating payments be set out in a separate line item, as burying it among other payments would be improper.[97] Note that, the provisions apply to domestic as well as foreign payments. As stated above, the provisions apply to all issuers, irrespective of whether or not the company has foreign operations.

V. BOOKS AND RECORDS PROVISION

The books and records provision of the FCPA requires issuers to "make and keep books, records, and accounts, which, in reasonable detail, accurately and fairly reflect the transactions and dispositions of the assets of the issuer."[98] The statute elaborates that, the term "reasonable detail" means "such level of detail and degree of assurance as would satisfy prudent officials in the conduct of their own affairs."[99]

3–40

This is to make sure that what is written in the books matches the reality of the status of the company's assets. Companies have to conform to generally accepted accounting principles (GAAP).[100] Not only must the companies' records include the financial statistics of the transaction, they must also describe circumstances or information that make the transaction seemingly questionable and might alert the SEC to possible violations.[101] A failure to fully describe the transaction could constitute a violation of the record-keeping provisions.[102]

VI. FALSIFICATION OF BOOKS AND RECORDS

Following the passage of the FCPA in 1977, but prior to the 1988 Amendments, the SEC adopted two rules under the Securities Exchange Act to bolster the

3–41

---

[96] §§ 78m (b) (6).
[97] *Accounting and Record-Keeping Provisions*, at 10:7.
[98] §§ 78m (b)(2)(a).
[99] §§ 78m(b)(7).
[100] *Guide to the FCPA*, at 1:20.
[101] *Accounting and Record-Keeping Provisions*, at 10:5.
[102] *Accounting and Record-Keeping Provisions*, at 10:5.

FCPA.[103] The original Act did not explicitly cover the falsification of records and lying to auditors. Rule 13b2-1 of the Exchange Act (17 § C.F.R 240.13b2-1) provides that "no person shall, directly or indirectly, falsify or cause to be falsified, any book, record or account subject to Section 13(b)(2)(A) of the Securities Exchange Act."[104] This was to ensure that all "any person," not only directors and officers, were accurate and complete in filling out company financial records and in providing information to auditors.

In addition, r.13b2–2 (17 C.F.R. § 240.13b2–2) prohibits officers and directors of an issuer from making materially false, misleading or incomplete statements to an accountant in connection with any audit or examination of the financial statements of the issuer or the filing of required reports.[105] The rules were designed to promote compliance with the FCPA but also to address a broader range of abuses than just illegal payments, such as protecting the integrity of the independent examination of financial statements by auditors.[106]

VII. Internal Accounting Controls Provision

3–42   The internal accounting controls provisions were intended to ensure that management had a sufficient hold over the use of assets and to maintain accountability for assets. The internal accounting controls provisions require issuers to "devise and maintain a system of internal accounting controls sufficient to provide reasonable assurances that":

    (i)   transactions are executed in accordance with management's general or specific authorisation;

    (ii) transactions are recorded as necessary (I) to permit preparation of financial statements in conformity with generally accepted accounting principles or any other criteria applicable to such statements, and (II) to maintain accountability for assets;

    (iii) access to assets is permitted only in accordance with management's general or specific authorisation; and

    (iv) the recorded accountability for assets is compared with the existing assets at reasonable intervals and appropriate action is taken with respect to any differences.[107]

---

[103] SEC Release 34-15570 (February 15, 1979). The rules were initially published for comment in Securities Exchange Act Release No. 13185 (January 19, 1977).

[104] Rule 13b2-1 of the Exchange Act. Books are defined broadly to include accounts, correspondence, memoranda, tapes, discs, papers, books, and other documents or transcribed information of any type. *Accounting and Record-Keeping Provisions*, at 10:06.

[105] Rule 13b2-2 of the Exchange Act. This rule applies to statements made to internal and external auditors as well. *Accounting and Record-Keeping Provisions*, at 10:8.

[106] SEC Release 34-15570 (February 15, 1979).

[107] §§ 78m (b)(2)(b).

The FCPA does not mandate a particular structure or type of internal accounting controls system nor does it give guidelines, but the general test for determining whether or not the system is up to standards is to evaluate whether or not the system would provide to management with "reasonable assurances," or "such level of detail and degree of assurance as would satisfy prudent officials in the conduct of their own affairs," that a solid internal controls system is in place.[108] The statute requires "reasonable" assurance, but not absolute assurance, for the SEC recognises the impracticality of an overly expensive system, which would not be in the best interests of the company or investors.[109]

At the very least, there must be written policies and procedures. Management must be directly involved in the implementation, oversight, and enforcement of those policies. Tests should be routinely performed for management to evaluate, and there should be extensive documentation of these tests in the event that the SEC pursues an FCPA investigation.[110]

VIII. SANCTIONS

Under the accounting provisions, individuals are subject to criminal liability for "knowingly circumvent[ing] or knowingly fail[ing] to implement a system of internal accounting controls or knowingly falsify[ing] any book, record, or account." Companies have to be especially careful, as they would be more susceptible to civil enforcement for the accounting provisions, which of course do not require proof of criminal intent, as opposed to criminal intent.   3–43

E. ENFORCEMENT

Enforcement of the FCPA involves a complex sharing of responsibilities between the DOJ and SEC. As stated above, the anti-bribery provisions are generally enforced by the DOJ, and the accounting provisions are generally enforced by the SEC.   3–44

I. DOJ

The DOJ is responsible for all criminal enforcement of the FCPA; hence, the DOJ is responsible for prosecuting issuers, domestic concerns, and individuals for criminal violations under both the anti-bribery and accounting provisions. Specifically the Fraud Section of the DOJ's Criminal Division has sole control over   3–45

---

[108] §§ 78m(b)(7). This definition is used for both the terms "reasonable detail" and "reasonable details." The SEC has commented that decisions implementing these systems will be regarded as business decisions and will thus be afforded deference as long as they are reasonable. fn.3 West 10:09

[109] *Accounting and Record-Keeping Provisions*, at 10:14.

[110] *Accounting and Record-Keeping Provisions*, at 10:10.

the criminal enforcement of the FCPA.[111] The DOJ is also responsible for the civil enforcement of the anti-bribery provisions of the FCPA with respect to domestic concerns.

II. SEC

3–46   The SEC is responsible for civil enforcement with respect to issuers, since the accounting provisions were included in the Exchange Act, giving the SEC authority with respect to issuers. Thus, the SEC is responsible for bringing civil actions against issuers under both the anti-bribery and accounting provisions. The SEC has sought injunctions under the anti-bribery provisions of the act, which is fairly rare, but has been occurring with more frequency.[112] In fact, the majority of cases involving the accounting provisions do not involve bribery.[113]

III. GENERAL ENFORCEMENT

3–47   Possible violations come to the attention of the DOJ and SEC from a variety of sources, including competitors, former employees, foreign government officials, and journalists.[114] Many informants prefer to remain anonymous since there is no guarantee that their identity will not be disclosed in the course of an investigation or prosecution.[115]

Increasingly, companies are coming forth with information on possible infractions after launching internal investigations. From 2003 to 2004, the DOJ initiated the majority of investigations; however from 2005 to 2007, 44 of the 68 new FCPA investigations were voluntarily disclosed to the SEC or DOJ following internal investigations.[116] Cases have shown that cooperation with the SEC and DOJ will be seen as an alleviating factor in a court's determination of the outcome or sentencing.

Because of the severe consequences of an FCPA violation, many companies are incentivised to settle, resulting in few FCPA cases going to trial. Not only are companies faced with the prospect of heavy fines, but company executives and employees also face imprisonment if found guilty of a criminal violation.

3–48   Penalties can be harsh under the Federal Sentencing Guidelines. Although the guidelines are advisory, they provide potential for higher fines and incarceration. The Guidelines operate by a point system in which judges use a chart to guide them in calculating the penalty, adding points for aggravating factors, and decreasing the number of points for mitigating factors.[117]

---

[111] *Compliance with the FCPA*, at 21.
[112] *Guide to the FCPA*, at 1:18.
[113] *Guide to the FCPA*, at 1:22.
[114] *Compliance with the FCPA*, at 20.
[115] *Compliance with the FCPA*, at 20.
[116] Danforth Newcomb, *Recent Trends and Patterns in FCPA Enforcement*, 8 (2008), available through *http://www.shearman.com* [Accessed July 15, 2010].
[117] *Compliance with the FCPA*, at 3.

The stigma of a violation can damage the company's reputation at home and abroad, putting a company's business relationships at risk. Mere news of an investigation would also have a significant impact on a company's business and image. Many investigations lead to settlement, as the DOJ normally agrees to defer prosecution or not to prosecute at all if the corporation agrees to certain conditions. These conditions normally include a large fine and the involvement of an independent compliance monitor.

IV. DOJ OPINION PROCEDURE

In 1980, the DOJ instituted a Review Procedure in order to alleviate some of the concerns that arose out of the uncertainty and ambiguity of the 1977 Act.[118] The Review Procedure is similar to the Department's business review procedure. Under the procedure, companies could seek guidance from the DOJ, in which a company would submit a proposed, fact-specific transaction to verify whether or not it would comply with the anti-bribery provisions of the FCPA. The DOJ would then issue an opinion, in which it would state whether or not that proposed transaction would constitute a violation of the FCPA.   **3–49**

The amendments of 1988 contained in the Omnibus Trade and Competitiveness Act directed the Attorney General to establish the procedure.[119] On October 1, 1992, the new Opinion Procedure took effect.[120]

The Opinion Procedure requires that the request be submitted by an issuer or a domestic concern who is a party to the transaction being reviewed.[121] The request must accurately describe prospective, and not hypothetical, conduct.[122] It must be detailed and be accompanied by all relevant and material information bearing on the conduct.[123] It also must be submitted in writing to the Fraud Section, Criminal Division of the Department of Justice.[124] The proposal must be signed by a senior officer with operational responsibility for the proposed transaction.[125]

The new Opinion Procedure differs from the old Review Procedure in a few respects, although the basic procedure is similar. First, the DOJ no longer has the discretion to refuse to review a request.[126] Secondly, the Attorney General must issue the Opinion Release within thirty days after the request; however, the DOJ may request additional information, and the tolling period begins only when the DOJ deems the entirety of the information is complete and accurate.[127] Thirdly, any document or material provided to the DOJ shall be exempt from disclosure   **3–50**

---

[118] 45 Fed. Reg. 20800 (March 31, 1980).
[119] §§ 78dd–1(e); §§78dd–2(f).
[120] 57 Fed. Reg. 39600 (September 1, 1992).
[121] 28 C.F.R. §80.4.
[122] 28 C.F.R. §80.1.
[123] 28 C.F.R. §80.6.
[124] 28 C.F.R. §80.2.
[125] 28 C.F.R. §80.6.
[126] §§ 78dd–1(e)(1); §§78dd–2(f)(1).
[127] §§ 78dd–1(e)(1); §§78dd–2(f)(1); 28 C.F.R. §80.7.

under the Freedom of Information Act.[128] Fourthly, a withdrawal of a request must occur before an Opinion Release is issued.[129] The withdrawal would have no force or effect.[130] Lastly, a favourable opinion stating that the conduct is in conformity with the FCPA will create a rebuttable presumption of compliance.[131] Such a presumption may only be rebutted by a preponderance of evidence.

At first the review procedure was not used often. Between 1980 and 2004 only 42 opinions were released, averaging about two opinions per year.[132] Recent years have more or less maintained this average, with no opinions published in 2005, two in 2006, three in 2007, three in 2008, and one in 2009.[133]

There are several explanations for the few opinions. The Opinion Releases are not binding on other agencies, such as the SEC, rendering a rebuttable presumption a strong defence only against the DOJ.[134] Also, companies fear that the public Opinion Releases may reveal enough information that they would become identifiable, despite the fact that documents and materials submitted by the company are not subject to disclosure.[135]

3–51   Moreover, companies may desire to close a transaction hastily and thus do not wish to wait the thirty days or more for legitimisation under the DOJ. Lastly, if an unfavourable opinion is issued, this would discourage the company from pursuing the transaction in an effort to avoid investigation. Even if a company were to receive a favourable opinion, if the proceeding actions taken by the company differ substantially from those initially described to the DOJ, then the company could be found guilty of a violation.

V. STATUTE OF LIMITATIONS

3–52   There is no provision in the FCPA regarding a statute of limitations period; therefore, the general five-year limitation period for federal crimes applies for filing an indictment charging FCPA violations.[136] Upon request by a prosecutor, the limitations period may be extended for up to three years after a court order finding that additional time is needed to gather evidence abroad. This court order must be obtained before the statue of limitations period is exceeded.

---

[128] §§ 78dd–1(e)(2); §§78dd–2(f)(2).

[129] §§ 78dd–1(e)(3); §§78dd–2(f)(3).

[130] 28 C.F.R. §80.15.

[131] §§ 78dd–1(e)(1); §§78dd–2(f)(1). A court considering such presumption would look to the following factors, among others: whether the information submitted to the Attorney General was accurate and complete, and whether it was within the scope of the conduct specified in any request by the Attorney General.

[132] See *Doing Business*, at 12–1.

[133] See *http://www.justice.gov/criminal/fraud/fcpa/opinion/* [Accessed July 15, 2010].

[134] 28 C.F.R. §80.11.

[135] See *Doing Business*, at 12–5.

[136] 18 U.S.C. Sec. 3282.

CHAPTER 4

DEALING WITH INTERNATIONAL CORRUPTION— AUSTRALIA

A. THE OECD CONVENTION

The OECD Convention on Combating Bribery of Foreign Public Officials in International Business Transactions (the Convention) came into force on February 15, 1999 and was ratified by Australia on October 18, 1999.[1] Australia acted very quickly to implement the Convention. Even before the Convention had been ratified it amended its Criminal Code by introducing Division 70 of Ch.4 so as to add the crime of bribing a foreign public official to the existing law.[2] The amendments were assented to on June 17, 1999 but did not come into effect until December 18, 1999[3] after ratification of the Convention. The amendments were described by the Phase 2 examiners as "detailed and comprehensive," and because they were written in "plain language" were regarded as "accessible to the general public."[4]

4–01

B. THE OFFENCE OF BRIBING A FOREIGN PUBLIC OFFICIAL

Section 70.2 of the Criminal Code Act 1995 (the Code) creates the offence of bribing a foreign public official. The offence is committed if a person:

4–02

> "● Provides a benefit to another person; or
> ● causes a benefit to be provided to another person; or
> ● offers to provide, or promises to provide, a benefit to another person; or

---

[1] Organisation for Economic Co-Operation and Development, *Australia: Review of the Implementation of the Convention and 1997 Recommendation* 1(2000) [hereinafter referred to as *Australia Phase 1 Report*].

[2] *Australia Phase 1 Report.*

[3] *Australia Phase 1 Report.*

[4] Organisation for Economic Co-operation and Development Directorate for Financial and Enterprise Affairs, *Australia: Phase 2 Report on the Application of the Convention Combating Bribery of Foreign Public Officials in International Business Transactions and the 1997 Recommendation on Combating Bribery in International Business Transactions*, para.136 (2006) [hereinafter referred to as *Australia Phase 2 Report*].

- causes an offer of the provision of the benefit, or a promise of the provision of a benefit, to be made to another person; and
- the benefit is not legitimately due to the other person; and
- the first mentioned person does so with the intention of influencing a foreign public official in the exercise of the official's duty as a foreign public official in order to[5]:

  - obtain or retain business; or
  - obtain or retain a business advantage that is not legitimately due to the recipient, or intended recipient, of the business advantage."[6]

Various provisions in the Code specify who may be prosecuted for the offence of bribing a foreign public official.[7] Although the section which creates the offence does so in respect of a person, under Australian law "person" includes both legal and natural persons. As a consequence the offence is applicable to both corporations and individuals alike,[8] subject to one matter to which reference will be made later. Furthermore, a relatively recent provision in the Code, effective as of 2001, establishes an "ambitious and progressive"[9] model for determining the criminal liability of bodies corporate.[10] Under it a body corporate is liable for offences "committed by an employee, agent or officer of a body corporate acting within the actual or apparent scope of his or her employment, or within his or her actual or apparent authority" where the body corporate "expressly, tacitly or impliedly authorised or permitted the commission of the offence."[11] The Code then goes on to list quite expansively the ways in which authorisation by the body corporate may be established.[12]

4–03   Under Division 70 of the Code, the prosecution does not have to prove that the business, or a business advantage, was actually obtained or retained,[13] i.e. it is irrelevant that the purpose or intention of influencing a foreign public official was not achieved. What is important in this regard is the intention of the person who provides the benefit,[14] not the outcome of the action which such person takes.

The Code states that when determining whether a benefit is "not legitimately due", a court is required to disregard:

"•   The fact that the benefit may be, or be perceived to be, customary, necessary or required in the situation;
- the value of the benefit; and
- any official tolerance of the benefit."[15]

---

[5] *Australia Phase 2 Report.* § 70.2(1) (a)–(c).
[6] § 70.2 (1)(c)(i),(ii).
[7] Criminal Code Act 1995 § 70.2(1)(a).
[8] Acts Interpretation Act 1901 § 22(1)(a)–(aa).
[9] Australia Phase 2 Report, para.148.
[10] Criminal Code Act 1995 §§ 12.1-12.6.
[11] Criminal Code Act 1995 §§ 12–2-12.3(1).
[12] Criminal Code Act 1995 § 12.3(2).
[13] § 70.2(1A).
[14] § 70.2(1)(c).
[15] Criminal Code Act 1995 § 70.2(2).

The fact that the business advantage may be or be perceived to be customary must also be disregarded.[16]

As a result of these provisions, the fact that offering bribes is common, or even **4–04** necessary, in order to conduct business in a particular country is irrelevant to the determination of criminal liability under Australian law.

While s.70 of the Code does not explicitly address the issue, bribes to a foreign public official to induce him or her to refrain from carrying out one of his or her duties are also proscribed under Australian law.[17] In 1993 the Court of Appeal of the Supreme Court of Queensland held that the provision of a benefit to cause an omission to perform a duty can amount to a bribe. In that case, the defendant was alleged to have given a large sum of money to a detective to take no action against him or to deal with charges against him on a summary basis rather than on indictment. This was held to amount to a bribe.[18] Thus, it would appear that under Australian law, if an individual or company bribes a foreign public official so that he will not, for instance, carry out a required inspection of a business operation or of items being imported, that individual or company can be prosecuted for the crime of bribing a foreign public official.

C. DEFENCES TO THE OFFENCE OF BRIBING A FOREIGN PUBLIC OFFICIAL

The Code provides a number of defences both general and specific, in respect of **4–05** the offence of bribing a foreign public official. General defences, which apply to most crimes and are contained in Pt 2.3 of the Code, include mental impairment, intoxication, mistake of fact and duress.[19] In addition, ss.70.3 and 70.4 of the Code provide for defences that are specific to the offence of bribing a foreign public official.

I. DEFENCE WHERE THE CONDUCT IS LAWFUL IN THE FOREIGN PUBLIC OFFICIAL'S COUNTRY

Section 70.3 provides a defence where the conduct is lawful in the foreign public **4–06** official's country.[20] The section consists of a table which outlines the situations in which a person is not guilty of the offence created by s.70.2. Eleven situations are identified in which such a defence may be invoked. They all concern a variety foreign public officials but, as the law in Australia presently stands, all require a *written law* of the country of such official under which the provision of the benefit is required or permitted. That was not the situation when s.70.3 was first enacted.

---

[16] § 70.2(3).
[17] *Australia Phase 2 Report*, 2006, para.138.
[18] *R v. Tange* (Supreme Court of Queensland, Court of Appeal, 1993).
[19] Criminal Code Act 1995 2.3; § 7.1–10.5.
[20] Criminal Code Act 1995 § 70.3.

At that time it was sufficient for the availability of the defence if there was "a law in force" in the foreign country or place. That law could have been customary or as a result of a decided case or cases. That situation was tightened by an amendment that was effected in 2007.[21]

A defendant who relies on such a defence to deny criminal responsibility "bears an evidential burden in relation to that matter."[22] That evidential burden requires the defendant to adduce or point to evidence that suggests a reasonable possibility that the matter exists or does not exist.[23]

A person is not guilty of an offence against s.70.2 in the cases set out in the table in s.70.3.[24]

Defence of lawful conduct

Item	In a case where the person's conduct occurred in relation to this kind of foreign public official...	and if it were assumed that the person's conduct had occurred wholly..,	this written law requires or permits the provision of the benefit...
1	an employee or official of a foreign government body	in the place where the central administration of the body is located	a written law in force in that place
2	an individual who performs work for a foreign government body under a contract	in the place where the central administration of the body is located	a written law in force in that place
3	an individual who holds or performs the duties of an appointment, office or position under a law of a foreign country or of part of a foreign country	in the foreign country or in the part of the foreign country, as the case may be	a written law in force in the foreign country or in the part of the foreign country, as the case may be

---

[21] International Trade Integrity Act 2007; Act No. 147 of 2007, Sch.2.
[22] Criminal Code Act 1995 § 13.3(3).
[23] Criminal Code Act 1995 § 13.3(6).
[24] Criminal Code Act 1995 § 70.3. The table is reproduced here in full directly from the Code as the most effective way of showing the different situations in which the defence may be envoked.

Defence of lawful conduct

Item	In a case where the person's conduct occurred in relation to this kind of foreign public official...	and if it were assumed that the person's conduct had occurred wholly..,	this written law requires or permits the provision of the benefit...
4	an individual who holds or performs the duties of an appointment, office or position created by custom or convention of a foreign country or of part of a foreign country	in the foreign country or in the part of the foreign country, as the case may be	a written law in force in the foreign country or in the part of the foreign country, as the case may be
5	an individual who is otherwise in the service of a foreign government body (including service as a member of a military force or police force)	in the place where the central administration of the body is located	a written law in force in that place
6	a member of the executive, judiciary or magistracy of a foreign country or of part of a foreign country	in the foreign country or in the part of the foreign country, as the case may be	a written law in force in the foreign country or in the part of the foreign country, as the case may be
7	an employee of a public international organization	in the place where the headquarters of the organization is located	a written law in force in that place
8	an individual who performs work for a public international organization under a contract	in the place where the headquarters of the organization is located	a written law in force in that place

Defence of lawful conduct

Item	In a case where the person's conduct occurred in relation to this kind of foreign public official...	and if it were assumed that the person's conduct had occurred wholly..,	this written law requires or permits the provision of the benefit...
9	an individual who holds or performs the duties of a public office or position in a public international organization	in the place where the headquarters of the organization is located	a written law in force in that place
10	an individual who is otherwise in the service of a public international organization	in the place where the headquarters of the organization is located	a written law in force in that place
11	a member or officer of the legislature of a foreign country or of part of a foreign country	in the foreign country or in the part of the foreign country, as the case may be	a written law in force in the foreign country or in the part of the foreign country, as the case may be

The Phase 2 examiners were critical of the defences as first enacted on the basis that they exceeded the limits of the defences permitted by the Convention.[25] The section as then in force provided for the defence to apply where there was simply no law in place in the foreign public official's country that criminalised the conduct, rather than where a written law of that country explicitly permitted or required the relevant conduct.[26] To remedy this situation, the International Trade Integrity Act 2007 included an amending provision requiring that the written law of the country explicitly permit or require the conduct in question before the defence was able to be invoked. The defences set out above incorporate such amendment.

---

[25] *Australia Phase 2 Report*, 2006, paras 139–141.
[26] *Australia Phase 2 Report*, 2006, para.140.

II. Defence relating to Facilitation Payments

Section 70.4 provides for a defence (which the defendant has the evidentiary **4–07** burden of proving), in respect of "facilitation payments."[27] Facilitation payments are those made for "the sole or dominant purpose of expediting or securing the performance of a routine government action of a minor nature" where the value of the benefit received is also "of a minor nature".[28] In addition, in order to be able to rely on this defence, the defendant must, "as soon as practicable after the conduct occurred," make a record of the conduct that includes the value of the benefit, the date on which the conduct occurred, the identity of the foreign public officials involved and the particular nature of the routine government action.[29] This record must be retained "at all relevant times," unless it is lost or destroyed for reasons beyond the defendant's control or where the prosecution is instituted more than seven years after the conduct occurred.[30]

The Code provides that the "routine government action" must be one that is "ordinarily and commonly performed by the official". It can include such activities as granting a permit or licence; processing government papers such as a visa or work permit, providing police protection or mail collection and delivery, scheduling inspections, providing telecommunication services or water, or power; loading and unloading cargo and protecting products or commodities from deterioration.[31] Routine government actions do not, however, include making or encouraging decisions about whether to award new business or continue existing business with a particular person nor do they include the terms on which a new business or existing business is conducted.[32]

Under the Australian Income Tax Assessment Act, facilitation payments are tax-deductible; bribes are not.[33]

While the Code outlines with some specificity the circumstances in which **4–08** facilitation payments may be available as a defence, in practice the application of these provisions is somewhat problematic. The Australian legal system does not provide for individuals or companies to obtain judicial advisory opinions regarding contemplated payments to foreign public officials, nor is there any administrative mechanism to do so.[34] As a result, individuals and companies cannot know in advance whether a proposed payment will be prohibited, i.e. whether the payment will amount to a bribe or be merely a facilitation payment. Because of this situation, individuals and companies may be less likely to record even legitimate facilitation payments out of fear that they will be creating a paper trail for what may turn out to be a bribe. An Australian Chamber of Commerce and Industry representative stated that the likelihood of individuals and com-

[27] Criminal Code Act 1995 § 70.4.
[28] Criminal Code Act 1995 § 70.4(1)(a)-(b).
[29] Criminal Code Act 1995 § 70.4(1)(c) & (3).
[30] Criminal Code Act 1995 § 70.4(1)(d).
[31] Criminal Code Act 1995 § 70.4(2)(a)-(b).
[32] Criminal Code Act 1995 § 70.4(2)(c)-(d).
[33] Income Tax Assessment Act 1997 § 26.52.
[34] *Australia Phase 2 Report*, 2006, para.142.

panies keeping records of facilitation payments is quite small, as they will be likely to view them as "an admission of guilt."[35]

Finally, the criminal codes of the individual Australian States need to be adverted to. The Phase 2 examiners considered that nearly all acts that would be considered to be facilitation payments under s.70.4 of the Code are outlawed under state law.[36] However, at the time those laws came into force this would not have been a problem, since at that time there was a presumption that when the parliament of a State legislated so as to control or proscribe activities, it did so only in relation to activities under the direct territorial authority of that particular parliament. Indeed it was held by the Judicial Committee of the Privy Council[37] that state law had no competence extra territorially. The court held that the jurisdiction of the respective States was "confined to their own territories".[38]

In 1986 the legislative powers of the parliaments of each of the States were extended by Act of the Australian Parliament so as to include full power to make laws for the peace, order and good government of each State "that have extra-territorial operation".[39] So the defences under the Code may be argued not to be effective because of the provisions of the various state acts that will now apply to offences that occur both within a particular State and as well as outside of that State, including outside Australia.[40]

4–09   This possibility is, however, likely to be overcome by s.109 of the Commonwealth Constitution if, as seems probable, the provisions of the Code are to be construed as covering the relevant field. In that case the law of the Commonwealth would prevail and to the extent of any inconsistency the law of the State would be invalid.

D. TERRITORIAL AND NATIONALITY REQUIREMENTS

4–10   A person does not commit an offence against s.70.2 unless:

"•   The conduct in question occurs wholly or partly in Australia; or
•   the conduct in question occurs wholly or partly on board an Australian aircraft or an Australian ship; or
•   where the conduct constituting the alleged offence occurs wholly outside Australia:

   •   the person is an Australian citizen; or
   •   the person is a resident of Australia; or
   •   the person is a body corporate incorporated by or under a law of the Commonwealth or of a State or Territory".[41]

---

[35] *Australia Phase 2 Report*, 2006, para.146.
[36] *Australia Phase 2 Report*, 2006, para.147.
[37] *MacLeod v Attorney General (NSW)* (1891) A.C. 455.
[38] (1891) A.C. 455 at 458.
[39] Australia Act 1986 s.2.
[40] Australia Act 1986 s.2.
[41] § 70.5(1).

These provisions make it clear that there must be a nationality, residential or other territorial nexus between the alleged offence or offender and Australia. No doubt this provision is designed to ensure that acts done outside Australia by non Australians or non Australian residents will have to be dealt with by other jurisdictions.

E. PROSECUTION

Commencement of proceedings for the offence of bribing a foreign public official **4–11**
requires the written consent of the Commonwealth Attorney-General if the alleged offence occurred wholly outside Australia and the person alleged to have committed the offence is a resident of Australia and not an Australia citizen.[42] However, a person may be arrested for and charged with an offence under s.70.2 even before the necessary consent has been given by the Attorney-General. Furthermore, even though such consent has not yet been given a person may not only be arrested but may also be remanded in custody or given bail in connection with the alleged offence.[43]

F. PENALTIES

For a natural person, the Code specifies that the maximum penalty for the offence **4–12**
of bribing a foreign public official is imprisonment for ten years or a fine of 10,000 penalty units (AUD $66,000) or both.[44] However, if the individual is tried summarily (as opposed to being tried on indictment), the maximum sentence that may be imposed is reduced to two years imprisonment or a fine of 300 penalty units (AUD $13,200) or both.[45] Furthermore, a conviction for bribing a foreign public official will result in automatic disqualification of the individual from managing corporations and could result in loss of the individual's financial services licence.[46]

Under the Corporations Act the disqualification is dependent not on the penalty that is in fact imposed but on the maximum penalty that may be imposed. Where the offence also involves a breach of the Corporations Act and the maximum sentence that may be imposed is greater than twelve months imprisonment, or, in a case involving dishonesty at least three months imprisonment, then the disqualification applies.

The commencement of the period of the disqualification depends on whether the person convicted is sentenced to a term of imprisonment or not. Where such

---

[42] Criminal Code Act 1995 § 70.5(2).
[43] § 70.5(3).
[44] § 70.2(4).
[45] *Australia Phase 2 Report*, 2006, para.156.
[46] *Corporations Act 2001* §§ 206B, 915B.

person is not sentenced to a term of imprisonment, the period of disqualification extends for five years after the day on which such person was convicted. If, however, the person is sentenced to a term of imprisonment then the disqualification is for a period of five years after the day on which such person is released from prison.[47]

4–13   It should be noted that under the law of Australia the disqualification also applies to offences against the law of a foreign country provided that the offence is punishable by imprisonment for a term greater than twelve months.[48]

The penalty for a body corporate is more severe than that for an individual. Under s.70.2 (5) as initially enacted, a body corporate could be liable for a fine of up to AUD $330,000 for the offence of bribing a foreign public official.[49] The Phase 2 examiners expressed the view that this was likely to be an inadequate penalty, given the operating budgets of many multi-national corporations.[50] In the light of these comments the Australian government agreed to review the penalties.[51] It has now done so and has increased the maximum penalty. For a body corporate it is now the greater of a fine AUD $660,000 or three times the value of the benefit received or, where the court cannot determine the value of the benefit, 10 per cent of the annual turnover of the body corporate for the twelve months ending at the end of the month in which the conduct constituting the offence occurred.

The Phase 2 examiners also recommended that Australia impose administrative sanctions on legal entities convicted of bribing a foreign public official.[52] For instance, they could be made ineligible for public procurement contracts, export credits, and public subsidies.[53] The legislation has not been amended to provide for this, but in many public sector tender documents, tenderers are required to agree to adhere to a specified code of conduct and to reveal any antecedent breaches of such code, which would include a conviction for bribing a public official. This is then had regard to in the process of making a decision in relation to the tenders.[54] In the Commonwealth Procurement Guidelines, there is a requirement concerning the ethical use of resources when awarding contracts.[55] Under such provision it would be open to the contracting agency to take into account a conviction for or evidence of bribing a foreign public official in deciding to refuse to award a public procurement contract. It should be noted, however, that the Commonwealth does not maintain a "black list" of entities convicted of criminal offences, including the bribing of a foreign public official.[56]

---

[47] Corporations Act 2001 §§ 206B(2).
[48] Corporations Act 2001 §§ 206B(1).
[49] *Australia Phase 2 Report*, 2006, para.154.
[50] *Australia Phase 2 Report*, 2006, paras 154–155.
[51] *Australia Phase 2 Report*, 2006, para.155.
[52] *Australia Phase 2 Report*, 2006, paras 162–168.
[53] *Australia Phase 2 Report*, 2006, paras 162–168.
[54] e.g. contracting agencies such as the Department of Finance and Administration, Export and Credit Insurance Corporation, Australian Agency for International Development, etc.
[55] Part 6 of the Commonwealth Procurement Guidelines, January 2005.
[56] *Australia Phase 2 Report*, 2006, para.164.

In addition to imprisonment and fines, a court may order that "tainted **4–14** property" be forfeited where the person is convicted of an indictable offence.[57] "Tainted property" is defined as "property used in, or in connection with, the commission of the offence," or the "proceeds of the offence."[58] The property that is used in or in connection with the offence of bribing a foreign public official is normally money, goods in kind or something tangible that has a value. Such property is invariably given to the foreign public official. Orders of forfeiture by an Australian court in respect of such property are unlikely to be effective, even if the money or goods have not been mingled with other monies or goods or converted to other property. It is an open question whether the concept of "proceeds of the offence" has application to the subject matter of the bribe. If, for example, an amount of money is paid to a foreign public official to exercise his discretion favourably to an applicant for a permit, can it be said that the profits that flow from the activities that are undertaken pursuant to the permit are "proceeds of the offence"? This example can be extended into many fields. There is no case law in Australia concerning this matter.

Merely transferring tainted property to a subsidiary or related entity will not adversely affect the court's power. This is because such power extends to property which is subject to the effective control of the offender. This concept of effective control of property extends beyond legal or equitable estates and in determining the question of effective control the court may have regard to a variety of matters that include family, domestic and business relationships, trusts and direct or indirect interests in any company that has an interest in the property.[59]

The court may thus order forfeiture of property that is in the hands of a third party where the value of the benefit can be determined and the third party is under the effective control of the defendant.[60]

G. JURISDICTION AND INTERNATIONAL COOPERATION

As indicated above, the Code provides that Australia has jurisdiction to prosecute **4–15** the offence of bribing a foreign public official:

- where the person or body corporate commits the offence wholly or partly in Australia or wholly or partly on board an Australian aircraft or Australian ship;

- where the person is an Australian citizen, or is a resident of Australia and commits the offence wholly outside Australia;

---

[57] Proceeds of Crime Act 1987 § 10 and § 19.
[58] Proceeds of Crime Act 1987 § 4.
[59] § 9A(2)(a)-(c).
[60] Proceeds of Crime Act 1987 § 9A.

- where the offender is a body corporate incorporated in Australia and commits the offence wholly outside Australia.[61]

Pursuant to two acts governing mutual assistance with foreign countries, Australian authorities may provide legal assistance to a foreign country seeking to prosecute the crime of bribing a foreign public official.[62] For example, Australian authorities may assist in taking evidence and producing documents, undertaking searches and seizures and in the confiscation of the proceeds of crime.[63] There are grounds on which the Attorney-General may refuse such assistance, such as when the crime is a political offence, where the death penalty may be imposed, or where the sovereignty, security, or the national interest of Australia is implicated.[64] However, such refusals are quite rare: between 1999 and 2004, only three mutual legal assistance requests were refused.[65]

The Extradition Act, as well as a number of treaties, permits extradition for various offences, even where the defendant is an Australian national.[66] In 1999, regulations were gazetted in relation to the extradition of foreign public officials. Under these regulations, all parties to the Convention are "extraditable countries," and offences that meet the dual criminality requirement are "extraditable offences."[67]

H. ENFORCEMENT ACTIVITIES

4–16   Whilst Australia was listed as number 8, with a score of 8.7 out of a possible of 10, in the 2009 Corruption Perception Index published by Transparency International Australia, i.e. the perception was that Australia was *not* a country in which corruption was a serious problem, Transparency International none-the-less designated Australia as a country that has "little or no enforcement" of the OECD Convention.[68] Notwithstanding this designation, twelve of the twenty-two recommendations made by the Phase 2 examiners have been implemented, while ten have been either partially implemented or not implemented at all.[69]

Until 2009 no person or entity had been prosecuted in Australia for bribing a foreign public official.[70] However, extensive investigations were undertaken regarding payments made by the Australian Wheat Board under the Oil-for-Food

---

[61] § 70.5.

[62] Mutual Assistance in Criminal Matters Act 1987; Mutual Assistance in Business Regulation Act 1999.

[63] Mutual Assistance in Criminal Matters Act 1987 § 74.

[64] Mutual Assistance in Criminal Matters Act 1987 § 8.

[65] *Australia Phase 2 Report*, 2006, para.172.

[66] Extradition Act 1988.

[67] Extradition (Bribery of Foreign Public Official) Regulations 1999.

[68] Transparency International, Progress Report 2009, *Enforcement of the OECD Convention on Combating Bribery of Foreign Public Officials in International Business Transactions*.

[69] *Australia Phase 2 Follow-Up Report*.

[70] *Australia Phase 2 Follow-Up Report*.

Programme contrary to the resolutions of the United Nations. At the conclusion of the investigation and after a Royal Commission into the Australian Wheat Board had been held, a prosecution was initiated but those proceedings did not lead to a conviction. Since that time the Commonwealth authorities have announced that further prosecutions against the Australian Wheat Board and its officers in respect of the Oil-for-Food Programme would not be undertaken. The probable reasons for this decision are dealt with below.

Investigations are also said to be currently underway by Indian and Portuguese officials regarding possible bribery activities by Australian companies.[71] No independent information is available regarding bribery of Australian officials by foreign entities.[72]

I. Australian Federal Police

The Australian Federal Police (AFP) is the primary federal law investigative and enforcement entity in Australia. Its activities include investigating allegations of bribery of foreign officials.[73] However, there is no entity that specialises in investigating or prosecuting bribery of foreign officials in Australia.[74] Instead, all law enforcement agencies, under a "whole of government" approach,[75] work together in one coordinated effort to stop crime.[76] The Phase 2 examiners expressed some reservations about this approach. However Australian officials pointed out that the "whole system is looking at foreign bribery" and that it would be very costly, due to the size of Australia, to establish specialised bribery investigation offices in each of the States and Territories.[77]

4–17

Whilst as a general rule the AFP only opens an investigation based on complaints rather than actively seeking out instances of bribery of foreign public officials,[78] investigations into the offence of bribery of a foreign public official may be triggered where there is:

"(a) A formal referral of allegations to the AFP; (b) pro-active intelligence gathering by the AFP; (c) identification of a foreign bribery offence during the investigation of another criminal offence; or (d) proactive investigation of persons or organisations where foreign bribery is suspected."[79]

---

[71] *Australia Phase 2 Follow-Up Report.*
[72] *Transparency International*, 2009, at 18.
[73] *Australia Phase 2 Report*, 2006, para.46,
[74] *Australia Phase 2 Report*, 2006, para.48.
[75] For an examination of the whole of government approach, see Peter Homel, *The Whole of Government Approach to Crime Prevention*, Trends & Issues in Crime & Crim. Just., November 2004.
[76] *Australia Phase 2 Report*, 2006, para.48.
[77] *Australia Phase 2 Report.*
[78] *Australia Phase 2 Report*, para.53.
[79] *Australia Phase 2 Report*, para.54.

The AFP does not follow up on media reports alone. An example of this is that after a news entity reported[80] possible bribery of a foreign public officials by an Australian company, the AFP indicated that it would not be opening an investigation in respect of that matter unless a formal referral was made, primarily because it felt that media reports are "not consistently credible."[81] Media reports will, however, be considered when combined with "independent supporting information."[82]

Cooperation between other government entities and the AFP is essential for the successful detection of bribery. Guidelines are in place that encourage government entities to report possible bribery to the AFP.[83] Concerns about matters of a politically sensitive nature, such as those involving "the national economic interest or any potential effects upon relations with another State," are to be referred to the relevant Minister, who then forwards the information on to the AFP.[84] This is to ensure that such matters are properly investigated.

4–18   The Phase 2 examiners believed that there were some indications that cooperation between the AFP and other government entities was not ideal. In one instance, allegations were made to the Australian Securities and Investment Commission (ASIC) regarding possible bribery of foreign officials by a corporation.[85] After a review of the corporation's documents, ASIC determined that there was "no evidence supporting the complaints." It therefore ceased its investigation. It did not contact the AFP, even informally.[86] Additionally, one state agency, the New South Wales Independent Commission against Corruption (ICAC) declined to "participate in the [Phase 2] on-site visit (in June 2005) on the ground that its functions and roles do not cover investigations of the Commonwealth offence of foreign bribery."[87] However, the writer believes that the current Commissioner, the Hon David Ipp, would be unlikely to adopt such a negative approach. In this regard it should be noted that the ICAC has as one of its principal functions the investigation of any allegation or complaint that in its opinion implies that corrupt conduct may have occurred.[88] Corrupt conduct is defined as including bribery.[89] Furthermore, the ambit of corrupt conduct, which is limited by s.9 of its Act, refers to a criminal offence. Such an offence may arise under the common law or under a law of the State or of the Commonwealth. Provided that the corrupt conduct involved a public official of the State of New South Wales, the ICAC would have authority to investigate.

Because of the foregoing the Phase 2 examiners encouraged the implementation of measures "to ensure the continued referral of cases . . . to the AFP even where

---

[80] A report that was "credible" according to an officer of the Attorney General's Department.
[81] *Australia Phase 2 Report*, 2006, para.53.
[82] *Australia Phase 2 Follow-Up Report*, at 12.
[83] *Australia Phase 2 Report*, 2006, para.60.
[84] *Australia Phase 2 Report*, 2006, para.63.
[85] *Australia Phase 2 Report*, 2006, para.61.
[86] *Australia Phase 2 Report*, 2006.
[87] *Australia Phase 2 Report*, 2006, para.75.
[88] Independent Commission Against Corruption Act 1988, § 13(1)(a).
[89] Independent Commission Against Corruption Act 1988, § 8(2)(b).

the State or Territorial law establishes a bribery offence that is sufficiently broad to cover the specific act of bribing a foreign public official."[90]

II. OTHER ENFORCING ENTITIES

The Australian Transaction Reports and Analysis Centre (AUSTRAC), is Aus-   **4–19**
tralia's anti-money laundering regulator and specialist financial intelligence unit.[91]
Cash dealers[92] must report transactions to AUSTRAC where they involve AUD
$10,000 or more or the foreign currency equivalent, suspicious transactions, and
international funds transfer instructions.[93] AUSTRAC receives roughly 11 million reports per year, of which 11,500 concern suspicious activities.[94]

Under the Corporations Act, companies with financial reporting obligations must have their annual financial report audited.[95] While auditors must report possible violations of the Corporations Act to ASIC, there is no requirement that possible bribery of a foreign official be reported, unless such a payment "made the accounts 'materially' inexact."[96] Furthermore, auditors commented that they dislike legal requirements to report certain findings to the government.[97] They believe that their first obligation is to shareholders and therefore they feel that frauds and kindred matters should be reported to the company itself rather than to the government.[98]

III. WHISTLEBLOWING

Whistleblowing is an area of particular concern. The Corporations Act provides   **4–20**
protection to individuals who report certain information to ASIC or to certain
company officials.[99] However, under that legislation a whistleblower must provide
his or her name and must have "reasonable grounds to suspect violation of the

---

[90] Independent Commission Against Corruption Act 1988.
[91] Independent Commission Against Corruption Act 1988, para.120.
[92] "Cash dealers ... include banks, building societies and credit unions referred to as 'financial institutions'; financial corporations; insurance companies and insurance intermediaries; securities dealers and futures brokers; cash carriers; managers and trustees of unit trusts; firms that deal in travelers cheques, money orders and the like; persons who collect, hold, exchange or remit currency on behalf of other persons; currency and bullion dealers; and casinos and gambling houses." Independent Commission Against Corruption Act 1988, para.121.
[93] Independent Commission Against Corruption Act 1988, para.120.
[94] Independent Commission Against Corruption Act 1988, para.123.
[95] Independent Commission Against Corruption Act 1988, para.130.
[96] Independent Commission Against Corruption Act 1988, para.131. According to representatives of the Institute of Chartered Accountants in Australia (ICAA), any amount below five per cent of the total of the specific expense account audited would not "generally" be considered "material", while any amount over ten per cent would definitely be considered material. Amounts between five and ten per cent constitute a "grey area", where the materiality would have to be determined by the auditor based on other relevant information.
[97] Independent Commission Against Corruption Act 1988.
[98] Independent Commission Against Corruption Act 1988.
[99] Independent Commission Against Corruption Act 1988, para.133.

Corporations Act."[100] When such a disclosure is made, the person is immune from civil or criminal penalties for making the disclosure and could be reinstated by a court to his or her job if it were terminated because of the disclosure.[101] Various of the States in Australia have their own whistleblower legislation. Each piece of legislation provides protection for whistleblowers, but this varies according to the particular State.

There are five dissimilar whistleblower statutes in place at the State level.[102] Two Australian non-governmental organisations[103] have expressed the view that whistleblower protection in Australia is inadequate.[104] The statutes generally provide for compensation to be paid to the victim after the event, but they also provide various levels of protection in the interim. As in most countries, the levels of protection tend to be rudimentary and less than adequate.[105] It has been reported that a slim majority of Australia's 100 top companies have whistleblower protection rules in place to encourage reporting to the proper entities[106]. However, whistleblower protection is a usual feature of codes of conduct that operate in respect of government departments and agencies. Griffith University completed a study on public sector whistleblowing in 2008, which provided recommendations for changes to Australia's whistleblowing system.[107]

I. NOTEWORTHY INVESTIGATIONS

4–21 A number of cases in Australia are commonly referred to in connection with allegations of bribery of public officials in other countries. The four cases most commonly referred to are those involving the Australian Wheat Board, Alkaloids of Australia Pty Ltd, Rhine Ruhr Pty Ltd and Rio Tinto. In no case was there a finding that the company involved had breached the provisions of the Code.

Each case is a salutary reminder that, at least in common law countries, treaties and international conventions do not form part of domestic law unless ratified by the local legislature and furthermore that the provisions of such treaties and conventions do not, even then, constitute domestic offences unless there is legislation to that effect.

---

[100] Independent Commission Against Corruption Act 1988.
[101] Independent Commission Against Corruption Act 1988.
[102] Independent Commission Against Corruption Act 1988.
[103] Whistleblowers Australia and the Australian Chapter of Transparency International.
[104] *Australia Phase 2 Report*, 2006, para.134.
[105] *Australia Phase 2 Report*, 2006 para.134.
[106] *Australia Phase 2 Report*, 2006, para.135.
[107] See *Whistleblowing in the Australian Public Sector*, edited by A.J. Brown (ANU E Press, 2008), 289–312.

Each of the cases also highlights that a resolution by the United Nations does not form part of domestic law and that, absent particular domestic legislation, an action by an individual or corporation which is in breach of such a resolution does not make the action in question a breach of the criminal law within a particular jurisdiction—whatever may be the moral sanction involved in a breach of such a resolution.[108]

J. AUSTRALIAN WHEAT BOARD OIL-FOR-FOOD PROGRAMME

I. Background

Australia's most publicised bribery scandal since the implementation of the Convention is that relating to the Australian Wheat Board (AWB).   **4–22**

In response to Iraq's invasion of Kuwait in August 1990, the United Nations implemented economic sanctions against Iraq in an attempt to bring pressure on it to withdraw from Kuwait.[109] Due to the ongoing existence of the sanctions following the conclusion of the Gulf War, humanitarian concerns for the Iraqi people prompted the creation of the Oil-for-Food Programme.[110] Under that programme, Iraq could sell oil under UN approved contracts and the proceeds of those sales were to be deposited into a UN controlled escrow account.[111] With UN approval, and using the money from such escrow account, Iraq could then purchase certain humanitarian goods, most notably food and medicine.[112] Under this regime the United Nations could monitor and approve the goods being exported and imported by Iraq and thereby deny Iraq military goods and foreign hard currency.

In an endeavour to circumvent these UN policies, Iraq instituted "inland transport fees" and "after-sales-service fees" on imports.[113] The inland transportation fee eventually reached US $25 per metric ton, while the after-service fee

---

[108] The International Trade Integrity Act 2007 (No. 147 of 2007) makes provision for an offence of conduct that contravenes a UN sanction enforcement law, whether such conduct be by an individual or a body corporate. A UN sanction enforcement law requires a specific legislative instrument to be made by the relevant Minister. Such instrument may only be made to the extent that it gives effect to a decision of the Security Council made under Chapter VII of the Charter of the United Nations and art.25 of the Charter requires Australia to carry out such decision.

[109] Terence R.H. Cole, *Report of the Inquiry into certain Australian Companies in relation to the UN Oil-For-Food Programme* (2006).

[110] Terence R.H. Cole, *Report of the Inquiry into certain Australian Companies in relation to the UN Oil-For-Food Programme* (2006), at 4.

[111] Terence R.H. Cole, *Report of the Inquiry into certain Australian Companies in relation to the UN Oil-For-Food Programme* (2006), at xiii.

[112] Terence R.H. Cole, *Report of the Inquiry into certain Australian Companies in relation to the UN Oil-For-Food Programme* (2006).

[113] Terence R.H. Cole, *Report of the Inquiry into certain Australian Companies in relation to the UN Oil-For-Food Programme* (2006), at 83.

on food was 10 per cent of the contract value.[114] Iraq required that these fees be paid in foreign currency and that they be paid directly to the government of Iraq, an Iraqi embassy, or certain Iraqi "front" companies.[115] Iraq would deal only with companies that paid such fees.[116] The companies that paid these fees did not, however, actually lose the money; instead, contract prices were inflated to include the fees.[117] Since the fees had to be paid in advance, companies would be without the money spent on fees for a period of time, but would ultimately recoup them out of the UN escrow account.[118] Consequently, relative to the ideal execution of the programme as envisaged by the United Nations, the United Nations had less money in its escrow account to buy humanitarian goods, the Iraqi government had a corresponding increase in its foreign currency reserves and the companies selling goods to Iraq were about as well off as they would have been had there been no scheme in place. Coupled with illicit surcharges on oil shipments, the Iraqi government ultimately received US $1.8 billion in income through the Oil-for-Food Programme.[119]

4–23   AWB and its predecessor, the Australian Wheat Board,[120] began selling wheat to Iraq in 1948.[121] It is one of the world's largest wheat exporters.[122] Over the course of its participation in the Oil-for-Food Programme from 1996 to 2003, AWB shipped 6.8 million metric tons of wheat to Iraq, for which it received US $2.3 billion in payments from the UN.[123]

Prior to June 1999, the contract prices agreed to by the Australian Wheat Board and AWB included the costs of transport from Australia to Iraq, insurance on the shipment, as well as the value of the wheat itself.[124] The Iraqi Grain Board was responsible for moving the wheat from the Iraqi port, storing it, and distributing it.[125] In June 1999, the Iraqi Grain Board informed the Australian Wheat Board that an inland transport fee had to be paid in order to ship the wheat from the

[114] Terence R.H. Cole, *Report of the Inquiry into certain Australian Companies in relation to the UN Oil-For-Food Programme* (2006).

[115] Terence R.H. Cole, *Report of the Inquiry into certain Australian Companies in relation to the UN Oil-For-Food Programme* (2006).

[116] Terence R.H. Cole, *Report of the Inquiry into certain Australian Companies in relation to the UN Oil-For-Food Programme* (2006).

[117] Terence R.H. Cole, *Report of the Inquiry into certain Australian Companies in relation to the UN Oil-For-Food Programme* (2006) at 84.

[118] Terence R.H. Cole, *Report of the Inquiry into certain Australian Companies in relation to the UN Oil-For-Food Programme* (2006).

[119] Independent Inquiry Committee into the United Nations Oil-For-Food Programme, Report on Programme Manipulation 1 (2005) [hereinafter IIC Report].

[120] T. Cole, *Report of the Inquiry into Certain Australian Companies in relation to the UN Oil-For-Food Programme*, 2006, at Vol.2, para.9.1.

[121] The Australian Wheat Board was created by the Australian government in 1939 "to control the domestic and export marketing of wheat in Australia." at para.9.4. In 1997 and 1998, the law was amended to transfer a significant number of the Australian Wheat Board's powers to a company structure, which AWB Limited heads. *Id.* at para 9.9. On 1 July 1999, "AWB was fully privatized and became an unlisted public company." On 21 August 2001, AWB "was floated and listed on the Australian Stock Exchange".

[122] T. Cole, 2006, at 31.

[123] T. Cole, 2006, at 37.

[124] T. Cole, 2006, at 95.

[125] T. Cole, 2006.

port of importation to the rest of Iraq.[126] This fee had to be paid directly to the shipping company.[127] AWB realised that the fee was a subterfuge to circumvent UN sanctions.[128] It was reported that the shipping company, Alia, did not even have any trucks in Iraq.[129] After-sales service fees were introduced in November 2000.[130] AWB paid US $224 million in such fees.[131]

II. INVESTIGATION AND FINDINGS

AWB's payments were ultimately discovered. In April 2004, the UN Security Counsel passed a resolution approving of UN Secretary-General Kofi Annan's decision to form a committee to investigate Oil-for-Food Programme corruption.[132] In October 2005 the Independent Inquiry Committee produced a report, commonly known as the "Volcker Report," implicating almost 2,500 companies worldwide in wrongdoing.[133] Three of these were Australian. One was AWB; another was Alkaloids of Australia Pty Ltd; a third was Rhine Ruhr Pty Ltd.   **4–24**

In November 2005, the Australian government issued Letters Patent for a Royal Commission (the Terms of Reference in which were subsequently expanded on a number of occasions), directing the Hon Terence Cole QC (Commissioner Cole, a retired Judge of the Supreme Court of New South Wales) to investigate, among other things, whether the actions of any of the three Australian companies mentioned in the Volcker Report, or individuals associated with them, had violated Australian law.[134] However, investigation into any government official wrongdoing, either intentional or negligent, was not included in the ambit of the Letters Patent.[135] This was a point of some contention in Australia.[136]

Commissioner Cole made findings regarding whether any relevant entities may have committed criminal acts.[137] He found that no crimes had been committed

---

[126] T. Cole, 2006, at 96.

[127] T. Cole, 2006.

[128] T. Cole, 2006, 95–138.

[129] David Marr & Marian Wilkinson, Editorial, *Deceit by the Truckload*, Sydney Morning Herald, April 15, 2006, available through *http://www.smh.com.au* [Accessed July 15, 2010].

[130] See T. Cole, *Report of the Inquiry into Certain Australian Companies in relation to the Oil-For-Food Programme*, at 42.

[131] See T. Cole, *Report of the Inquiry into Certain Australian Companies in relation to the Oil-For-Food Programme*, para.11.27.

[132] See S.C. Res. 1538, U.N. Doc. S/RES/1538 (April. 21, 2004).

[133] *IIC Report*, 2005, at 1.

[134] T. Cole, *Report of the Inquiry into Certain Australian Companies in relation to the Oil-For-Food Programme*, at 13.

[135] T. Cole, *Report of the Inquiry into Certain Australian Companies in relation to the Oil-For-Food Programme*.

[136] See, e.g. Richard Ackland, Editorial, *This Inquiry is Only Half the Job*, Sydney Morning Herald, April 14, 2006, available through *http://www.smh.com.au* [Accessed July 15, 2010]; *Call for Expanded AWB Probe*, news.com.au, November 23, 2006, available through *http://www.news.corn.au* [Accessed July 15, 2010].

[137] See T. Cole, 2006, Vol.4.

involving anti-bribery legislation.[138] For the purposes of his analysis, Commissioner Cole assumed that AWB was the bribing entity and that the Iraqi Grain Board was the recipient of the bribes.[139]

Under s.70.2(1)(a), the payments undoubtedly constituted a benefit.[140] Therefore, that element of the offence was satisfied. However, there are significant concerns as to whether the benefits "were not legitimately due"[141] as required by s.70.2(1)(b). Under Iraqi law, the payments were almost certainly legal. Commissioner Cole held that they were "akin to a tariff."[142] He considered whether the payments might not have been legitimately due because of UN sanctions but he did not make a finding on this issue.[143] He did note, however, that UN resolutions alone do not have the force of law in Australia, in the absence of implementing legislation, of which there was none at that time.[144]

The definition of "not legitimately due" is fairly vague, both within the Convention itself and under Australian law. In line with the Convention, the Code specifies that the value of the benefit, the customary nature of the benefit and official tolerance of the benefit cannot be used to determine whether a benefit is not legitimately due.[145] However, there is no explanation beyond these exclusions that defines the phrase. The accompanying explanatory memorandum from the Australian Senate is not helpful. It states that "not legitimately due" should have "its ordinary meaning—the prosecution must establish that the benefit was not legitimately due to the person who received it."[146] The Commentaries on the OECD Convention Combating Bribery are not of real assistance either. They provide that:

> "[I]t is also an offence irrespective of, inter alia, the value of the advantage, its results, perceptions, local custom, the tolerance of such payments by local authorities, the alleged necessity of the payment in order to obtain or retain business or other improper advantage."[147]

It is thus unclear whether the payments made by AWB should be considered as "not legitimately due".

4-25   The money paid by AWB was to the shipping company, Alia. It was not paid to an individual. Accepting that the whole or some part of the monies so paid was then paid to the Iraqi Grain Board, there is a question as to whether the Iraqi

---

[138] T. Cole, 2006, at 109.

[139] T. Cole, 2006, Vol.5 at 346–347.

[140] T. Cole, 2006, Vol.5 at 347.

[141] T. Cole, 2006.

[142] T. Cole, 2006.

[143] T. Cole, 2006, Vol.1 at 61–62.

[144] T. Cole, 2006, at 61-62.

[145] Criminal Code Act 1995 § 70.2(2)-(3).

[146] Explanatory Memorandum, Parliament of the Commonwealth of Aust, Senate, Criminal Code Amendment (Bribery of Foreign Public Officials) Bill 1999, at 17, available through *http://www.oecd.org* [Accessed July 15, 2010].

[147] *http://www.oecd.org* [Accessed July 15, 2010] 132 OECD Negotiating Conference, Commentary, *Commentaries on the OECD Convention on Combating Bribery*, para.7, (1997) available through *http://www.oecd.org* [Accessed July 15, 2010].

Grain Board falls within the definition of "foreign public official". The definition of that term is limited in subparas (b) to (j) and (l) to "an individual". From the context of Division 70 of Ch.4 of the Code it is clear that the concept of "an individual" is different from the concept of "a person" and "a body corporate". As a consequence it would seem that none of the subparagraphs just referred to would apply to the Iraqi Grain Board.

Subparagraphs (a) and (k) of the definition refer to "an employee or official" of a government body and "a member or officer" of the legislature of a foreign country. They do not refer to the government body itself or to the relevant legislature as such. Again it would seem that in these subparagraphs of the definition, an individual is being referred to rather than a body corporate or like entity. As a consequence it is at least an open question, and probably adverse to a successful prosecution, whether the payments that were made were payments to a foreign public official; yet this is an essential element of the offence, as is clear from s.70.2(1)(c) of the Code.

Even if, as is unlikely, the various elements of the offence were satisfied, it seems clear that AWB's actions would fall within one of the categories of defence specified in s.70.3 of the Code. One of the defences in s.70.3, as in place at the time the payments were made, provides that if the actions were assumed to have occurred in the country of the foreign official and those actions were not against the law of that country, then the person who did such actions is not guilty of an offence against s.70.2.[148] As discussed above, the payments in question were not illegal in Iraq; in fact, they were legally required.[149] Therefore AWB would very likely be able to invoke this defence successfully and avoid criminal prosecution, despite the fact that the actions were in violation of UN sanctions.[150]

Commissioner Cole considered the possibility of other criminal offences having been committed.[151] He found no possibility that offences involving money laundering[152] had been committed or that the laws of Australia against terrorism, had been breached[153] or that the Customs (Prohibited Exports) Regulations had been contravened.[154] No finding of tax violations was made[155]. However, he did find that offences could have been committed relating to corporate responsibility,[156] the Banking (Foreign Exchange) Regulations,[157] and the Corporations Act.[158]

4–26

---

[148] T. Cole, *Report of the Inquiry into Certain Australian Companies in relation to the Oil-For-Food Programme*, at 349.

[149] T. Cole, *Report of the Inquiry into Certain Australian Companies in relation to the Oil-For-Food Programme*.

[150] T. Cole, *Report of the Inquiry into Certain Australian Companies in relation to the Oil-For-Food Programme*.

[151] T. Cole, Vol. 4, at 1-324.

[152] T. Cole, at 109-110.

[153] T. Cole, at 110-113.

[154] T. Cole, at 113.

[155] T. Cole, at 324.

[156] T. Cole, at 114-18.

[157] T. Cole, at 113.

[158] T. Cole, at 113.

Twelve individuals were implicated in all.[159] Even though it was perhaps outside his mandate, Commissioner Cole stated that there were no indications that any Australian government officials did anything illegal.[160]

Commissioner Cole made recommendations in his report in relation to legislative changes.[161] These were largely implemented through the introduction of the International Trade Integrity Act 2007.[162] That Act dealt primarily with violations of UN sanctions by Australian entities, however, it also amended[163] the law regarding bribery, so as to provide that in order to raise a defence of legality, the giving of a benefit must either be required or permitted by the *written law* of the foreign country. As indicated above, this was a change from the former law, which allowed for the defence to be raised if the conduct was merely not illegal in the foreign country.

Commissioner Cole also investigated two other companies in connection with the Oil-for-Food Programme, namely Alkaloids of Australia Pty Ltd and Rhine Ruhr Pty Ltd. In both cases he concluded that the companies, their officers, and their employees had not breached Australian law.[164]

K. ALKALOIDS OF AUSTRALIA PTY LIMITED

4–27   Alkaloids of Australia Pty Ltd (Alkaloids) is primarily involved in the business of producing a pharmaceutical product called hyoscin-N-butyl bromide (hyoscine). It is an antispasmodic used to relieve the symptoms of muscle spasm caused by food poisoning and stomach upsets.[165] From 2000 to 2001, marketing for the company was handled by Australian Pioneer Pistachio Company Pty Ltd.[166]

Christopher Joyce of Pioneer Pistachio discovered that the previous marketing agent for Alkaloids had contacted Albert Shimoon, a Canada-based Iraqi national, concerning the possibility of selling hyoscine to Iraq under the Oil-for-Food programme.[167] Shimoon explained that he had significant Iraqi connections and could help Alkaloids with sales for a commission of 16 per cent, a figure significantly higher than the five per cent Alkaloids had normally paid.[168] Joyce

---

[159] T. Cole, Vol.4 at lxxxi–lxxxii.

[160] T. Cole, Vol.4 at 100–101.

[161] T. Cole, at lxxxiii–lxxxv.

[162] Organisation for Economic Co-operation and Development, Steps Taken to Implement and Enforce The OECD Convention on Combating Bribery of Foreign Public Officials in International Business Transactions—Australia (2008), available through *http://www.oecd.org* [Accessed July 15, 2010].

[163] See International Trade Integrity Act 2007.

[164] T. Cole, *Report of the Inquiry into Certain Australian Companies in relation to the Oil-For-Food Programme*, Vol.4 at 347, 386.

[165] T. Cole, at 331.

[166] T. Cole, *Report of the Inquiry into Certain Australian Companies in relation to the Oil-For-Food Programme*.

[167] T. Cole, at 332.

[168] T. Cole, *Report of the Inquiry into Certain Australian Companies in relation to the Oil-For-Food Programme*.

inquired about the possibility of reducing the commission, but Shimoon explained that it could not be reduced because Shimoon had to "pay the people" about eight per cent.[169] It was not made clear who "the people" were.[170] Shimoon would later say he needed money up front to pay "the director," which probably referred to the Director General of Health of Iraq.[171] Joyce denied he was shutting his eyes to whether bribery was involved.[172] Shimoon's commission, after being set initially at 15 per cent, was later increased to 17.5 per cent, along with an "overprice" commission to be paid when the tender price exceeded a certain threshold.[173] Although Shimoon typically had other commission arrangements recorded in writing, the overprice provision was not written down.[174]

Shimoon indicated to the Iraqi State Company for Manufacturing of Drugs and Medical Appliances that Alkaloid was willing to sell hyoscine at a particular price per kilogram.[175] The State Company agreed to purchase the hyoscine for a price that was 10 per cent above that offered by Alkaloid.[176] Joyce said that he "assumed it was because Shimoon had gained himself an overprice".[177] Later, there was an incident at the Jordanian-Iraqi border where a "guarantee extension" to a bank in an amount slightly more than 10 per cent of the original tender offer price had to be issued in order to keep the shipment moving.[178] A later contract was also "enhanced" by 10 per cent above the price Shimoon initially discussed.[179]

Commissioner Cole concluded that there was insufficient evidence to find that   4–28
Joyce knew the 10 per cent payments were going to the Iraqi government, saying instead that it was likely Shimoon was primarily to blame.[180] However, since Shimoon committed no acts in Australia, he was outside the country's jurisdiction.[181] The Commissioner concluded that no laws of Australia had been broken by Alkaloids, its directors, or Joyce.[182]

---

[169] T. Cole, at 333.
[170] T. Cole, *Report of the Inquiry into Certain Australian Companies in relation to the Oil-For-Food Programme*.
[171] T. Cole, at 334.
[172] T. Cole, at 335.
[173] T. Cole, at 333, 336.
[174] T. Cole, *Report of the Inquiry into Certain Australian Companies in relation to the Oil-For-Food Programme*.
[175] T. Cole, at 337.
[176] T. Cole, *Report of the Inquiry into Certain Australian Companies in relation to the Oil-For-Food Programme*.
[177] T. Cole, *Report of the Inquiry into Certain Australian Companies in relation to the Oil-For-Food Programme*.
[178] T. Cole, at 339-41.
[179] T. Cole, at 342.
[180] T. Cole, at 346.
[181] T. Cole, *Report of the Inquiry into Certain Australian Companies in relation to the Oil-For-Food Programme*.
[182] T. Cole, at 347.

L. RHINE RUHR PTY LIMITED

4–29   Rhine Ruhr Pty Ltd (Rhine Ruhr) is an Australian company, the principal business of which is the design and supply of removable vessel internals used in oil refineries, chemical plants, water treatment plants and gas processing facilities.[183] From 2001 to 2002, Rhine Ruhr had a business turnover of $3 million to $5 million annually.[184] In 2000, Rhine Ruhr was contacted by a Mr Davies of Eastoft Hall, a UK corporation.[185] Davies said that he had expertise in the Iraqi market and inquired as to whether Rhine Ruhr would be interested in shipping goods to Iraq.[186] Rhine Ruhr indicated that it was interested and agreed to pay a 10 per cent commission to Davies for his assistance.[187]

Rhine Ruhr tendered an offer under which it would provide valve trays, along with transportation for the valve trays, to an Iraqi company called North Gas Company.[188] A draft contract was prepared that included a ten percent "Engineering Services Fee" relating to installation, which had to be paid to an Iraqi entity.[189] This contract was never performed, although it set the stage for future contracts.[190] Over the course of later discussions, the fee was referred to in a number of ways, such as the "10% Iraqi government fee," a "10% surcharge," or had quotation marks around it in order to indicate that its meaning was euphemistic.[191]

Commissioner Cole concluded that while some of Rhine Ruhr's employees knew that the fee did not relate to installation, they did not know that the fee was being used for an illicit purpose, primarily because the company relied on Mr Davies' representations.[192] Commissioner Cole concluded that Rhine Ruhr had not breached Australian law.[193]

M. RIO TINTO LIMITED

4–30   Rio Tinto Ltd (Rio Tinto) is one of the world's leading mining and exploration companies. Its products include iron ore and other minerals, a good deal of which is exported to the People's Republic of China. It is a major business enterprise in Australia and it controls a large part of the mineral deposits in Australia.

---

[183] T. Cole, at 353.
[184] T. Cole, *Report of the Inquiry into Certain Australian Companies in relation to the Oil-For-Food Programme*.
[185] T. Cole, at 354.
[186] T. Cole, *Report of the Inquiry into Certain Australian Companies in relation to the Oil-For-Food Programme*.
[187] T. Cole, at 355.
[188] T. Cole, at 356.
[189] T. Cole, at 357, 359.
[190] T. Cole, at 362.
[191] T. Cole, at 378-379.
[192] T. Cole, at 380.
[193] T. Cole, at 386.

On July 5, 2009, four employees of Rio Tinto were arrested by the government of the People's Republic of China (PRC) on allegations of "espionage and stealing state secrets",[194] in addition to harming China's "economic security and interests."[195] In the PRC, steel makers must receive government permission to enter into "long-term iron ore supply contracts with foreign suppliers such as Rio Tinto."[196] One of the detainees was Stern Hu, an Australian citizen.[197] According to an unnamed industry insider, Rio Tinto employees had bribed executives of all 16 Chinese steel mills which were "participating in iron ore price talks."[198] There was nothing to suggest that any of the executives was a foreign public official and there is no suggestion that there had been an breach of s.70.2 of the Code. The Foreign Ministry of the PRC stated that sufficient evidence existed to prove the allegations,[199] while Rio Tinto believed that the claims were unfounded.[200] Some Australian officials suggested that the detention of Hu was a retaliation for Rio Tinto's decision to call off a $19.5 billion deal in June 2009 that would have given a company owned by the government of the PRC called Chinalco a "large stake" in Rio Tinto.[201] Additionally, despite a report from the *China Daily*[202] indicating that five steel makers were under investigation,[203] those companies denied being under investigation, with one calling the report "fake news."[204]

Subsequently Stern Hu pleaded guilty to having bribed certain steel company executives and was sentenced to a term of imprisonment.

It is difficult to ascertain the full facts in relation to this matter since Hu was **4–31** held in custody and incommunicado for a considerable period, his lawyer was either disinclined or not permitted to discuss the matter either before or after the trial and a good deal of the evidence was taken in camera. As a consequence knowledge of the actual facts is limited and reliance has had to be placed on statements and press reports.

From the material available in the public domain no question of a breach of the Convention or of s.70.2 of the Code was involved in the case.

---

[194] Wan Zhihong & Qian Yanfeng, *Rio Employees 'Held for Espionage,'* China Daily, July 7, 2009, http://www.chinadaily.com. [Accessed July 15, 2010]

[195] David Barboza, *Rio Tinto Gave Bribes to Many, China Says*, N.Y. Times, July 5, 2009, http://www.nytimes.com. [Accessed July 15, 2010]

[196] Tong Hao & Wang Linyan, *Govt: Proof Against Rio Spies Sticks*, China Daily, July 10, 2009, http://www.chinadaily.com.

[197] Wan Zhiliong & Qian Yanfeng, *Rio Employees 'Held for Espionage'*, 2009.

[198] Zhang Qi & Tong Hao, *'Bribery is widespread' in Rio Case*, China Daily, July 15, 2009, http://www.chinadaily.com.

[199] Zhang Qi & Tong Hao, *'Bribery is widespread' in Rio Case*, 2009.

[200] *Rio Tinto Says china Steel Bribe Claims Unfounded*, CNBC, July 17, 2009, http://www.cnbc.com [Accessed July 15, 2010].

[201] Barboza, *Rio Tinto Gave Bribes to Mary*, 2009.

[202] The *China Daily* is China's official English language newspaper.

[203] Zhang Qi & Tong Hao, *'Bribery is widespread in Rio Case*, 2009.

[204] Barboza, *Rio Tinto Gave Bribes to Mary*, 2009.

N. UNITED NATIONS CONVENTION AGAINST CORRUPTION

4–32   The United Nations Convention against Corruption (UNCAC) was adopted by the United Nations General Assembly by Resolution 58/4 in October 2003. Australia signed the treaty on December 9, 2003 and ratified it on December 7, 2005. The treaty came into force on December 14, 2005 in accordance with art.68, namely on the nineteenth day after the date of deposit of the thirtieth instrument of ratification, acceptance, approval or accession.

The Convention provides that in order to prevent and combat corruption more efficiently and effectively, to promote international cooperation and technical assistance in the prevention of and fight against corruption and to promote integrity, accountability and proper management of public affairs and public property,[205] the States Parties are required to take specific actions in relation to, amongst other matters:

- preventative anti-corruption policies and practices[206];

- ensuring the existence of bodies that prevent corruption[207];

- making provision in relation to the strengthening of systems of public sector recruitment[208];

- establishing codes or standards of conduct for the public sector[209];

- establishing appropriate systems of procurement based on transparency, competition and objective criteria[210];

- adopting procedures for allowing members of the general public to obtain information[211];

- taking measures to strengthen integrity and prevent opportunities for corruption amongst the judiciary[212];

- involving the private sector and civil society in the prevention of and fight against corruption[213];

- instituting a domestic regulatory and supervisory regime in relation to the transmission of money[214];

---

[205] UNCAC art.1.
[206] UNCAC art.5.
[207] UNCAC art.6.
[208] UNCAC art.7.
[209] UNCAC art.8.
[210] UNCAC art.9.
[211] UNCAC art.10.
[212] UNCAC art.11.
[213] UNCAC arts 12 and 13.
[214] UNCAC art.14.

- adopting legislative and other measures to criminalise bribery of national public officials and foreign public officials and officials of public international organisations[215];

- taking measures to provide effective protection for witnesses and whistleblowers[216];

- providing for cooperation between national authorities of different States parties[217];

- making provision for international cooperation[218], extradition[219] and mutual legal assistance[220];

- making provision for asset recovery[221];

- developing training programs for personnel responsible for preventing and combating corruption.[222]

As can be seen from the foregoing summary a number of the provisions of the UNCAC require the state's parties to take action in relation to several of the matters that are covered, albeit not in identical terms, by the Convention. For example the provisions in arts 15, 16, 38, 43, 44 and 46 parallel provisions in the Convention in so far as international anti-corruption initiatives are concerned.

Australia meets its obligations under the UNCAC through a combination of **4–33** legislation,[223] the work of various government bodies,[224] procedural safeguards such as auditing of government agencies by the Australian National Audit Office, by Public Budget Statements and by cooperation with regional and international authorities.

The UNCAC Treaty requires each of the States Parties to take specific actions. The legislative situation in Australia is as already dealt with above in relation to the Convention.

---

[215] UNCAC arts 15 and 16.
[216] UNCAC arts 32 and 33.
[217] UNCAC art.38.
[218] UNCAC art.43.
[219] UNCAC art.44.
[220] UNCAC art.46.
[221] Ch.5.
[222] UNCAC art.60.
[223] Criminal Code Act 1995; Public Service Act 1999; Electoral Act 1918; Financial Management and Accountability Act 1997; Freedom of Information Act 1982; Corporations Act 2001; Proceeds of Crime Act 1987; the Mutual Assistance in Criminal Matters Act 1987.
[224] The Attorney General's Department; Australian Federal Police; Australian Crime Commission; Australian Securities and Investment Commission; Australian Public Service Commission; Australian Transaction Reports and Analysis Centre.

O. SUMMARY

4–34 Australia regards dealing with corruption of foreign public officials as an important matter. It has investigated a number of allegations that have been made in respect of actions said to breach the intent of the Convention. To date, the major matters investigated have not revealed a breach of the law of Australia in relation to the bribery of foreign public officials by Australian citizens or companies.

Furthermore, since 2003 the Australian government has embarked on a campaign to raise public awareness in relation to the offence of bribery of a foreign public official and has encouraged support for anti-bribery efforts in Australia's public and private sectors.[225]

---

[225] Attorney General's Department Release, June 2010.

CHAPTER 5

BRAZIL'S ANTI-CORRUPTION LAWS[1]

A. INTRODUCTION

The first law in Brazil to address bribery was the 1824 Political Constitution of   **5–01** the Empire of Brazil introduced by the emperor D. Pedro I. Under this Constitution, it was an offence for Ministers of State to accept any kind of bribe in return for influence in favour of an individual. Article 133 stipulated:

"Art. 133—Ministers of State will be held liable:

(. . .)

II. For gifts, bribes or extortion.

(. . .)

VI. For any wasteful misuse of public goods."[2]

In turn, the Empire Penal Code provided that it was an offence to:

"Art. 130. Receive money or some other gift; or accept a direct or indirect promise in return of the performance of or refraining from of a given official act [whether said act was contrary to] or in accordance with the law:

Penalty—loss of job and unfitness for any other; fine of two times the undue reward; and prison from one to nine months.

The penalty of prison will not apply when the act was not realized

Art. 131. The same penalties will apply, to a judge who makes an order in return for an undue reward, [even when] said order is fair.

If the order was unfair, the penalty of prison shall be from six months to two years; if it was a criminal sentence, the same penalty shall be applied [to the judge], unless it was a sentence of death, in which case the penalty [for the judge] shall be life imprisonment.

In any event, the order made will be null and void.

---

[1] This article has been written with the intense cooperation of Fernando Pessoa Novis, whom I thank for the great effort dedicated to this work.

[2] "Art. 133—Os Ministros de Estado serão responsáveis: (. . .) II. Por peita, suborno ou concussão. (. . .) VI. Por qualquer dissipação dos bens públicos.", available through *http://www.planalto.gov.br* [Accessed July 15, 2010].

Art. 132. The same penalties, save for the penalty of loss of position, shall be applied to those who give or promise an undue reward, as per the previous provisions, when applicable, and any act in which corruption was involved will be null."[3]

The 1891 Constitution of the Republic of the United States of Brazil (as the country was then known), in addition to introducing provisions as to the criminal liability of Ministers of State who accepted bribes, also provided that the President could be prosecuted for violating the integrity of the administration or for not safekeeping public money:

"Art. 54—The President shall be deemed to be liable under criminal law for any acts ("crimes of responsibility") that violate:

6⁰) the integrity of the administration;

7⁰) the safekeeping and use of public money in accordance with the constitution;"[4]

In turn, the 1890 Penal Code defined passive and active corruption in arts 214 to 219.

The Constitutions introduced in 1934 and 1937 made little headway, merely repeating art.54 of the 1891 Constitution.[5]

5–02   In 1946, legislation for the first time stated that acts of administrative misconduct were a legal offence that could lead to the assets of the perpetrator being liable to forfeiture. To wit:

"Art. 141 The Constitution guarantees to Brazilians and foreigners residing in the country the inviolability of life, liberty, personal safety and property, as follows:

(...)

§ 31—(...) The law will provide for the seizure and confiscation of assets, in the event of unlawful enrichment gained by the trafficking of influence or the abuse of public office or function or position in an autonomous government entity."[6]

---

[3] Available through *http://www.planalto.gov.br* [Accessed July 15, 2010].

[4] "Art 54—São crimes de responsabilidade os atos do Presidente que atentarem contra: 6⁰) a probidade da administração; 7⁰) a guarda e emprego constitucional dos dinheiros públicos;" available through *http://www.planalto.gov.br* [Accessed July 15, 2010].

[5] Article 57 of the 1934 Constitution provided that "It is crime of responsibility the acts of the President that violates: (...) f) the integrity of the administration. g) the legal safekeeping and usage of public money, available through *http://www.planalto.gov.br* [Accessed July 15, 2010]. In turn, art.85 of the 1937 Constitution provided that "Art . 85—It is crime of responsibility the acts of the President that violates: (...) d) the integrity of the administration and the safekeeping and usage of public money", available through *http://www.planalto.gov.br* [Accessed July 15, 2010].

[6] "Art. 141—A Constituição assegura aos brasileiros e aos estrangeiros residentes no País a inviolabilidade dos direitos concernentes à vida, à liberdade, à segurança individual e à propriedade, nos termos seguintes: (...) § 31—Não haverá pena de morte, de banimento, de confisco nem de caráter perpétuo. São ressalvadas, quanto à pena de morte, as disposições da legislação militar em tempo de guerra com país estrangeiro. A lei disporá sobre o seqüestro e o perdimento de bens, no caso de enriquecimento ilícito, por influência ou com abuso de cargo ou função pública, ou de emprego em entidade autárquica", available through *http://www.planalto.gov.br* [Accessed July 15, 2010].

This constitutional provision was a significant development in the fight against corruption, covering a much larger range of offences and individuals who could be held liable for them. It was a step towards the current "Law of Administrative Probity".

As required, legislation then has came into force to regulate the application of the constitutional anti-corruption provisions. The so-called Pitombo-Godoy Ilha Law[7] established procedures for the confiscation and freezing of assets unduly acquired by a public officer by means of influence or abuse of public office, function or position in an autonomous government entity. Moreover, the law drew a clear distinction between criminal liability and liability for this (civil) wrong, so that an offender's assets could be forfeited under this law even if said offender were to be acquitted under criminal law in proceedings arising out of the same facts. Any individual (in addition to the Public Prosecution Service) was entitled to commence proceedings under the Pitombo-Godoy Ilha Law.

The Bilac Pinto Law[8] also regulated the confiscation and seizure of the assets of   5–03
public officers in the event of embezzlement of public assets by the misuse of influence or abuse of public office or function. For the purposes of said Law the term "public officer" included:

"All persons who hold any position, function or post, in the Union, States, Territories, Federal District or municipalities, whether civil or military, elected or by appointment or contract, in the executive, legislative or judicial powers."[9]

Both those laws, however, were deficient in terms of the practical definition of procedures and definitions that courts could use to enforce the sanctions established. The Pitombo-Godoy Ilha Law, for instance, had only four articles regulating this very complex matter.

B. CURRENT ANTI-CORRUPTION LEGISLATION

I. THE 1988 CONSTITUTION

The current Brazilian Constitution sets out a series of principles that must be   5–04
observed by all public bodies and their officials as well as by autonomous entities (quasi governmental organisations) and public companies. Article 37 establishes that:

---

[7] Law 3164, which came into force on June 1, 1957, available through *http://www6.senado.gov.br* [Accessed July 15, 2010].

[8] Law 3502, which came into force on December 21, 1958, available through *http://www6.senado.gov.br* [Accessed July 15, 2010].

[9] "§ 1º A expressão servidor público compreende todas as pessoas que exercem na União, nos Estados, nos Territórios, no Distrito Federal e nos municípios, quaisquer cargos funções ou empregos, civis ou militares, quer sejam eletivos quer de nomeação ou contrato, nos órgãos dos Poderes Executivo, Legislativo ou Judiciário", available through *http://www6.senado.gov.br*.

"The direct and indirect public administration of any of the bodies of the Union, States, Federal District and municipalities are to abide by the principles of legality, impersonality, morality, publicity and efficiency,: (...)".[10]

With a view to ensuring that these principles are respected, the Constitution provides that administrative misconduct is to be subject to suspension of political rights (prohibition on standing for office), dismissal from office, freezing of assets and the imposition of a duty to make redress to public funds.[11] The Constitution sets out general principles and stipulates that infra-constitutional legislation is to provide specific regulation of the sanctions.

The 1988 Constitution also provides that infra constitutional legislation is to govern the application of the sanction of ineligibility for political office and the duration of such penalty in order to uphold administrative probity, morality, legitimacy of the elections in direct or indirect administration.[12]

5–05   In order to regulate these provisions, Law 8.429, the so-called "Law of Administrative Probity" came into force on June 2, 1992. The law was introduced at a time of deep political scandal in Brazil that culminated in the impeachment of then President Fernando Collor, accused of misfeasance in office.

II. THE 1992 LAW OF ADMINISTRATIVE PROBITY[13]

(a) The public interest civil lawsuit

5–06   First, it is important to define the legal nature of the sanctions provided by the Law of Administrative Probity and the proceedings leading to their imposition. There has been considerable debate amongst commentators as to whether the Public Interest Civil Lawsuit for administrative misconduct, when filed by the Public Prosecutor's Office, is, as its name suggests, a civil prosecution, or whether it falls within the ambit of criminal law.[14] This is a significant issue in that the classification of the proceedings affects the range and types of defenses and other legal challenges open to defendants—there being fewer such defenses available if the proceedings are deemed civil in nature than would be the case if they were to be considered criminal proceedings.

---

[10] "Art. 37. A administração pública direta e indireta de qualquer dos Poderes da União, dos Estados, do Distrito Federal e dos Municípios obedecerá aos princípios de legalidade, impessoalidade, moralidade, publicidade e eficiência e, também, ao seguinte: (...)", available through *http:// www.planalto.gov.br* [Accessed July 15, 2010].

[11] "§ 4º—Os atos de improbidade administrativa importarão a suspensão dos direitos políticos, a perda da função pública, a indisponibilidade dos bens e o ressarcimento ao erário, na forma e gradação previstas em lei, sem prejuízo da ação penal cabível.", available through *http://www.planalto.gov.br*.

[12] "Art. 14. § 9º Lei complementar estabelecerá outros casos de inelegibilidade e os prazos de sua cessação, a fim de proteger a probidade administrativa, a moralidade para exercício de mandato considerada vida pregressa do candidato, e a normalidade e legitimidade das eleições contra a influência do poder econômico ou o abuso do exercício de função, cargo ou emprego na administração direta ou indireta.", available through *http://www.planalto.gov.br*.

[13] Law 8.429, which came into force on June 2, 1992, available through *http://www.planalto.gov.br*.

[14] See Zavascki, Teori Albino, *"Processo Coletivo"*, 3rd edn (Revista dos Tribunais, São Paulo, 2008), p.124.

The predominant view in legal doctrine and case law is that this lawsuit is in fact a civil action, albeit that the sanctions imposed are more severe than those usually applied in the civil area.[15]

The fact that the proceedings are considered to be civil in nature means that the defendant may additionally be subject to a separate criminal prosecution arising out of the same events.[16] In fact the majority view amongst legal scholars is that it is possible for said defendant to be held liable in three separate proceedings—administrative, civil and criminal—arising out of the same act of administrative misconduct. Administrative proceedings may be commenced in accordance with the provisions of the relevant Civil Service Regulations or Statute. The civil proceedings will apply the provisions of Law 8.429/92 (Law of Administrative Probity) whilst the criminal proceedings will apply the relevant provisions of the Penal Code and Code of Criminal Procedure.[17]

Once the Public Interest Civil Lawsuit has been filed, it cannot, according to art.17(1) of Law 8.429,[18] be withdrawn by means of settlement between claimant and defendant. Furthermore, said civil action, which may be commenced by an individual, requires the participation of the Public Prosecution Service. The proceedings may be deemed to be null and void in the absence of such participation.[19]   5–07

(b) Offenders that may be held liable under the law of administrative probity

Brazilian public officials

Law 8.429 of June 2, 1992, sets forth in its art.1 that: 5–08

"Misconduct perpetrated by any public agent, whether or not s/he is a civil servant, against the direct or indirect administration or public foundation of any of the powers [executive, legislature, judiciary] of the Union, the States, the Federal District, the Municipalities and the Territories, or of a state owned company, or an entity to the

[15] For Teori Albino Zavascki, Minister of the Superior Court of Justice, "the Public Interest Civil Lawsuit pursued under administrative misconduct addresses sanctions; and the sanctions provided for the said offences vary, some of typically civil legal nature and others of punitive nature. Observing this aspect is essential for the adequate comprehension of Law 8.429/92 and to solve its several issues, including procedural matters, that arise in its application", see original at Zavascki, 113 and 114 (2008).

[16] Article 12 of Law 8.429 that sets forth the penalties for administrative misconduct provides that they will be applied regardless of other criminal, civil and administrative sanctions: "Art. 12. Independentemente das sanções penais, civis e administrativas previstas na legislação específica, está o responsável pelo ato de improbidade sujeito às seguintes cominações, que podem ser aplicadas isolada ou cumulativamente, de acordo com a gravidade do fato", available through *http://www.planalto.gov.br.*

[17] See Di Pietro, Maria Sylvia Zanella, Curso de Direito Administrativo, 23rd edn (Editora Atlas, São Paulo, 2010), pp.825 and 826.

[18] "Art. 17. A ação principal, que terá o rito ordinário, será proposta pelo Ministério Público ou pela pessoa jurídica interessada, dentro de trinta dias da efetivação da medida cautelar. §1º É vedada a transação, acordo ou conciliação nas ações de que trata o caput.", available through *http://www.planalto.gov.br.*

[19] "Art. 17. (. . .) §4 O Ministério Público, se não intervir no processo como parte, atuará obrigatoriamente, como fiscal da lei, sob pena de nulidade."

establishment or maintenance of which the state has contributed (or continues to contribute) over 50% of the assets or annual revenue shall be punished in accordance with the provisions of this Law"[20]

Furthermore, misconduct in entities in which the contribution of the state [or equivalent public authority] is less than 50 per cent is also subject to the same penalties, albeit that in such cases the personal liability of the perpetrator is limited to the actual loss incurred of public funds invested in said entity.[21]

There is broad agreement amongst commentators that these provisions cover a very wide range of individuals related to the government, enabling the punishment of virtually all and any public officer. There are however some limitations regarding certain politicians, in that according to art.52, I and II, and 55, §3, of the Constitution,[22] members of congress and the president cannot be deprived of their mandates without the prior approval of congress. Furthermore, the Supreme Court has held that Ministers of State and the Commanders in Chief of the Navy, Army and Air Force, members of the Superior Courts and Public Finance Court and members of diplomatic missions are not subject to prosecution for administrative misconduct under Law 8429, as they are subject to special rules of responsibility.[23]

Liability of companies and other individuals

5–09 Law 8.429 of June 2, 1992, sets forth in art.3 that:

"The provisions of this law shall apply, where relevant, to persons who, despite not being public agents, induce or contribute to the perpetration of the act of impropriety or directly or indirectly benefit from such act."[24]

According to most Brazilian commentators, administrative misconduct is characterized by the conduct which is detrimental to a public body (public body for

---

[20] "Art. 1º Os atos de improbidade praticados por qualquer agente público, servidor ou não, contra a administração direta, indireta ou fundacional de qualquer dos Poderes da União, dos Estados, do Distrito Federal, dos Municípios, de Território, de empresa incorporada ao patrimônio público ou de entidade para cuja criação ou custeio o erário haja concorrido ou concorra com mais de cinqüenta por cento do patrimônio ou da receita anual, serão punidos na forma desta lei.", available through *http://www.planalto.gov.br.*

[21] "Parágrafo único. Estão também sujeitos às penalidades desta lei os atos de improbidade praticados contra o patrimônio de entidade que receba subvenção, benefício ou incentivo, fiscal ou creditício, de órgão público bem como daquelas para cuja criação ou custeio o erário haja concorrido ou concorra com menos de cinqüenta por cento do patrimônio ou da receita anual, limitando-se, nestes casos, a sanção patrimonial à repercussão do ilícito sobre a contribuição dos cofres públicos.", available through *http://www.planalto.gov.br.*

[22] See Di Pietro, Maria Sylvia Zanella, Curso de Direito Administrativo, 23rd edn, Editora Atlas, pp.825 and 826, São Paulo, 2010.

[23] Rcl 2138/DF, June 20, 2007, available at *http://www.stf.jus.br* [Accessed July 15, 2010].

[24] "Art. 3. As disposições desta lei são aplicáveis, no que couber, àquele que, mesmo não sendo agente público, induza ou concorra para a prática do ato de improbidade ou dele se beneficie sob qualquer forma direta ou indireta.", available through *http://www.planalto.gov.br.*

these purposes being broadly defined) perpetrated by people in some way connected or responsible for its management, administration or upkeep.[25]

Third parties who are not otherwise related to a public body for the purposes of Law 8.429 can only be subject to a lawsuit under said law if a public official, listed in art.1, is also a defendant. The Superior Court of Justice has held that a third party and the public official accused of malfeasance are to be tried together as co-defendants[26] via compulsory joinder.[27]

Said individuals may face criminal and other civil charges in addition to the **5–10** Public Interest Civil Lawsuit continuation. The Superior Court of Justice has further held that the provisions of the Law of Administrative Probity apply to legal entities as well as to individuals.[28]

The possibility of filing suit against a company in Brazil under the Law of Administrative Probity for bribing an international official has not been addressed by the courts or legal commentators. However, it can be logically deduced that such proceedings would be legally impossible. Brazilian courts have no jurisdiction to prosecute foreign officials for acts performed in their native country. A Public Interest Civil Lawsuit for administrative misconduct against a private party requires a compulsory joinder (i.e. the public official needs to be a defendant). Companies and foreign officials could never be codefendants and, therefore, neither could be prosecuted under the said Law.

Law of Administrative Probity may be applied to international companies operating in Brazil, as well as to their officers and directors, since their activities are subject to the jurisdiction of Brazilian courts' in accordance with art.12 of Decree-Law 4.657/42 and arts 88 and 89 of the Civil Procedure Code.[29]

(c) Administrative misconduct under the law of administrative probity

Law 8.429 describes three different types of acts of administrative misconduct. **5–11** Article 9 deals with acts that result in unlawful enrichment; art.10 with acts that cause loss to public finances and art.11 with acts that violate constitutional principles.

These provisions list in their respective subsections a series of acts that constitute administrative misconduct. Other acts not set forth in said lists may also be

---

[25] See Zavascki, Teori Albino, "*Processo Coletivo*", 3rd edn (Revista dos Tribunais, São Paulo, 2008), pp.113 and 114.

[26] See Lucon, Paulo Henrique dos Santos, Litisconsórcio Necessário e Eficácia da Sentença na Lei de Improbidade Administrativa, pp.322 and 323, *in* Improbidade Administrativa, Questões Polêmicas (2001). According to the author, charging only one of the individuals that profited from the misconduct act, when there are other participants, would represent an unlawful enrichment of the party that remained out of the procedure. Also, it could paradoxically make null and void an act for a convicted party whilst the act would persist being valid for the other offender that was not included in the lawsuit.

[27] REsp 401.437/SP, October 16, 2007, available at *http://www.stj.jus.br*.

[28] REsp 1038762/RJ, August 18, 2009, available at *http://www.stj.jus.br*.

[29] "Art. 9o Para qualificar e reger as obrigações, aplicar-se-á a lei do país em que se constituirem."; "Art. 12. É competente a autoridade judiciária brasileira, quando for o réu domiciliado no Brasil ou aqui tiver de ser cumprida a obrigação." available through *http://www.planalto.gov.br*.

subject to sanction on the basis that said lists are of examples only, and are not exhaustive.[30] This issue has in fact been the subject of considerable debate before the courts and in legal doctrine, due to the well established constitutional principle, the courts cannot impose a penalty in the absence of prior and clear definition in law of the type of conduct which is to be subject to sanction. The prevailing view in relation to Law 8249 is that its provisions are to be applied notwithstanding the fact that they may lead to the imposition of penalties for misconduct which has not been specifically defined.[31]

Under art.9, deriving any type of undue material benefit from the exercise of a function, position, mandate or activity in the entities referred to in art.1 of the law constitutes administrative improbity: (. . .)[32]; the proscribed conduct under art.10, is:

"An act or omission, willful or culpable, that leads to the loss, misapplication, misappropriation or squandering of property or assets of the entities mentioned in art. 1 of the Law, (. . .)".[33]

Finally, under art.11, conduct that:

"Violates the principles of public administration, by any act or omission that breaches the obligations of honesty, fairness, legality, and loyalty to institutions, (. . .) amounts to misconduct."[34]

Article 9 is particularly relevant in the fight against corruption in that it clearly forbids any kind of undue material benefit that the individuals referred to in art.1 might derive by virtue of their being in a privileged public position. Applying this provision, the Superior Court of Justice has held that the amount received is irrelevant. The mere fact of accepting any such benefit constitutes an offence. Clearly, however, the amount involved may be relevant to the severity of the penalty.[35]

5–12   Another important aspect of this law is set out in art.21, which states that it is not necessary, for the purposes of the lawsuit, for actual damage to public assets/finances be incurred. It further states that approval of a transaction by the Public

---

[30] See Di Pietro, 834 (2010) and Zavascki, 121 (2008).

[31] See Zavascki, 121 (2008).

[32] "Art. 9° Constitui ato de improbidade administrativa importando enriquecimento ilícito auferir qualquer tipo de vantagem patrimonial indevida em razão do exercício de cargo, mandato, função, emprego ou atividade nas entidades mencionadas no art. 1° desta lei, e notadamente: (. . .)", available through *http://www.planalto.gov.br.*

[33] "Art. 10. Constitui ato de improbidade administrativa que causa lesão ao erário qualquer ação ou omissão, dolosa ou culposa, que enseje perda patrimonial, desvio, apropriação, malbaratamento ou dilapidação dos bens ou haveres das entidades referidas no art. 1° desta lei, e notadamente: (. . .)", available through *http://www.planalto.gov.br.*

[34] "Art. 11. Constitui ato de improbidade administrativa que atenta contra os princípios da administração pública qualquer ação ou omissão que viole os deveres de honestidade, imparcialidade, legalidade, e lealdade às instituições, e notadamente: (. . .)", available through *http://www.planalto.gov.br.*

[35] REsp 892818/RS, November 11, 2008, available at *http://www.stj.jus.br.*

Finance Court is not a defense.[36] According to legal doctrine, the effect of this article is limited to economic damage so that whilst proof of said damage is not necessary in order for a penalty to be imposed there does need to be evidence of some form of damage (e.g. "moral").[37] Furthermore, art.10 is an exception to this provision, since it deals specifically with economic damage to public funds, so that, obviously, there must have been economic damage in order to incur in the offence stipulated in that provision.

C. NEGLIGENCE OR WILLFUL MISCONDUCT

In order to be considered an offence under Law 8.249, the act must normally be   5–13
the result of willful misconduct. There must be evidence of bad faith demonstrating dishonest behaviour. Although the legal nature of the sanctions is mostly civil, the standard of liability for such misconduct is considered to be similar to the standard required in criminal proceedings.[38] This, in Brazil, according to the majority view, excludes strict liability. The only provision that expressly allows a lawsuit to be filed for negligent conduct is that arising under art.10, which forbids acts that cause damage to public funds.

This is the prevailing view amongst commentators[39] and the Superior Court of Justice,[40] notwithstanding some dissenting views in the case law of said court to the effect that there may be strict liability in relation to art.11,[41] which classifies as misconduct violations of constitutional principles.

In relation to art.9, which covers most situations of bribery, there may be a presumption of misconduct when the occurrence of certain events is demonstrated. According to Zavascki, however:

"Given that willful misconduct is required for the public servant to be considered liable, said requirement is even more significant in relation to the participation of third parties in article 3 of Law 8.429".[42]

---

[36] "Art.21. A aplicação das sanções previstas nesta lei independe:
I—da efetiva ocorrência de dano ao patrimônio público, salvo quanto à pena de ressarcimento;
II—da aprovação ou rejeição das contas pelo órgão de controle interno ou pelo Tribunal ou Conselho de Contas."

[37] See Di Pietro, 834 (2010).

[38] See Zavascki, 120 (2008); Di Pietro, 837 (2010).

[39] See Mello, Claudio Ari. Improbidade Administrativa: considerações sobre a Lei 8.492/92, pp.49/62; Zavascki, 118 (2008); Di Pietro, 836 (2010).

[40] REsp 626.034, June 5, 2006; REsp 842.428, May 21, 2007; REsp 751.364, August 2, 2007; available at *http://www.stj.jus.br*.

[41] REsp 880.662, March 1, 2007, available at *http://www.stj.jus.br*.

[42] See Zavascki, 120 (2008).

D. BURDEN OF PROOF

5–14   The principle, applicable in Brazilian criminal procedure, that a person cannot be required to prove his innocence (in other words that, in accordance with the presumption of innocence, it falls to the accuser to prove guilt) applies to proceedings brought under Law 8.492.

This means that the accuser is required to provide all the evidence necessary to demonstrate that the defendant perpetrated the relevant misconduct. Furthermore, the defendant cannot be subject to judgment in default, which would be tantamount to a presumption of the veracity of the charges laid against him

E. SANCTIONS UNDER LAW 8.492

5–15   Article 4 of 1988 Brazilian Constitution makes provision for the introduction of further infra-constitutional legislation regulating penalties for administrative misconduct, said penalties being the suspension of political rights, dismissal from office, freezing of assets and a duty to pay compensation for damage to public funds.[43]

These constitutional provisions are not exhaustive and do not represent a final and definitive list of penalties to which offenders may be subject under Brazilian legislation. The overall aim, in addition to the provision of sanctions such as suspension of political rights and that other penalties, is to ensure that the damage caused to public finances is redressed and that unjust enrichment of any kind is avoided.[44] The Constitution makes provision for the freezing of assets of the individuals involved, thereby ensuring that said assets will be available in the event of a later court decision requiring them to be transferred/returned to the exchequer.[45]

Law 8.492 does in fact go further than the constitutional mechanisms set out in art.4 of the Constitution.[46] Article 12 of the statute sets out a series of penalties that can be applied to individuals for administrative misconduct, over and beyond those provided for in art.3. Article 12 of law 8.492 provides:

> "Article 12. Independently of criminal, civil and administrative penalties imposed in specific legislation, the person liable for the act of administrative improbity shall be subject to the following penalties, which may be applied in isolation or cumulatively, in accordance with the gravity of the occurrence:

---

[43]   "§ 4⁰—Os atos de improbidade administrativa importarão a suspensão dos direitos políticos, a perda da função pública, a indisponibilidade dos bens e o ressarcimento ao erário, na forma e gradação previstas em lei, sem prejuízo da ação penal cabível.", available through *http://www.planalto.gov.br*.

[44]   See Di Pietro, 838 (2010).

[45]   See Velloso Filho, Carlos Mario. A Indisponibilidade de Bens na Lei 8.429, de 1992, p.102 in Improbidade Administrativa, Questões Polêmicas e Atuais (2001); Zavascki, 132 (2008).

[46]   See Zavascki, 114 (2008).

I—in the event of a breach of art. 9°, forfeiture of the goods or assets unlawfully acquired, full reparation of the damage caused to public funds, if any, loss of public office/position, suspension of political rights for a period of eight to ten years, payment of a penalty of up to three times the amount of the material benefit gained plus prohibition on entering into an agreement with a Public Authority or receiving benefits or tax incentives or credits, directly or indirectly even via the intermediation of a legal entity in which said individual is a majority shareholder, for a period of ten years;

II—in the case of a breach of art. 10, full reparation of the damage caused, forfeiture of the goods or assets unlawfully acquired, when applicable, loss of public office/position, suspension of political rights for a period of eight to ten years, payment of a penalty of up to twice the amount of the damage caused plus prohibition on entering into an agreement with a Public Authority or receiving benefits or tax incentives or credits, directly or indirectly even via the intermediation of a legal entity in which said individual is a majority shareholder, for a period of five years;

III—in the case of a breach of art. 11, full reparation of the damage caused to public funds, if any, loss of public office/position, suspension of political rights for a period of three to five years, payment of a penalty of up to one hundred times the agent's remuneration and prohibition on entering into an agreement with a Public Authority or receiving benefits or tax incentives or credits, directly or indirectly even via the intermediation of a legal entity in which said individual is a majority shareholder, for a period of three years;

Sole paragraph: When applying the penalties provided by this law the judge will take into consideration the extent of the damage, as well as the gain obtained by the agent."[47]

First, it is important to note that those sanctions may be combined or applied separately, depending on the extent of the damage, as provided in the sole paragraph.[48] There are no fixed criteria upon which a judge is to apply these   **5–16**

[47] "Art. 12. Independentemente das sanções penais, civis e administrativas previstas na legislação específica, está o responsável pelo ato de improbidade sujeito às seguintes cominações, que podem ser aplicadas isolada ou cumulativamente, de acordo com a gravidade do fato:
I—na hipótese do art. 9°, perda dos bens ou valores acrescidos ilicitamente ao patrimônio, ressarcimento integral do dano, quando houver, perda da função pública, suspensão dos direitos políticos de oito a dez anos, pagamento de multa civil de até três vezes o valor do acréscimo patrimonial e proibição de contratar com o Poder Público ou receber benefícios ou incentivos fiscais ou creditícios, direta ou indiretamente, ainda que por intermédio de pessoa jurídica da qual seja sócio majoritário, pelo prazo de dez anos;
II—na hipótese do art. 10, ressarcimento integral do dano, perda dos bens ou valores acrescidos ilicitamente ao patrimônio, se concorrer esta circunstância, perda da função pública, suspensão dos direitos políticos de cinco a oito anos, pagamento de multa civil de até duas vezes o valor do dano e proibição de contratar com o Poder Público ou receber benefícios ou incentivos fiscais ou creditícios, direta ou indiretamente, ainda que por intermédio de pessoa jurídica da qual seja sócio majoritário, pelo prazo de cinco anos;
III—na hipótese do art. 11, ressarcimento integral do dano, se houver, perda da função pública, suspensão dos direitos políticos de três a cinco anos, pagamento de multa civil de até cem vezes o valor da remuneração percebida pelo agente e proibição de contratar com o Poder Público ou receber benefícios ou incentivos fiscais ou creditícios, direta ou indiretamente, ainda que por intermédio de pessoa jurídica da qual seja sócio majoritário, pelo prazo de três anos.
Parágrafo único. Na fixação das penas previstas nesta lei o juiz levará em conta a extensão do dano causado, assim como o proveito patrimonial obtido pelo agente.", available through *http://www.planalto.gov.br.*
[48] See Di Pietro, 839 (2010); Zavascki, 130 (2008).

penalties, which means that the order made is to be based on reasonableness and proportionality following analysis of the offences.[49]

The Superior Court of Justice has held that it is essential that an order which applies the penalties indicate the grounds for every sanction imposed on each of the offenders involved in the act of misconduct, otherwise said order will be null and void.[50] For instance, a company cannot be ordered to pay a civil fine of three times the increase in its assets and be prohibited from contracting with the government on the sole argument that the public official bribed by the legal entity was acting in bad faith. The precise reasoning for each specific penalty, and for the severity of said penalty, must, of necessity, be set out.

Furthermore, it is clear from the subsections to art.12 that violations related to the acceptance of offer of an undue reward (bribe), as set forth on art.9, are considered the most serious offenses, subject to the severest sanctions.[51] By their nature, the effect of such offences is rarely limited to unlawful enrichment, and usually results in (direct or indirect) loss of public funds as well as violation of the fundamental principles governing public authorities, so that such misconduct merits a harsher response from the judiciary.[52]

5–17   The loss of assets unlawfully obtained by the offender is not a penalty in the strict sense of the word, but rather amounts to an order for payment of damages to the exchequer (public funds). It is to be ordered whenever the court finds that there has been unjust enrichment.[53] This redress[54] may in fact be sought by the public body that suffered the loss without the need for a Public Interest Civil Lawsuit filed by the Public Prosecutor's Office.[55] The only reason for this provision in art.12 is to expedite judicial proceedings on misconduct, in that it enables within a single order both the imposition of sanctions and the ordering of measures aimed at redress.

Companies involved in bribery, besides returning assets unlawfully obtained, may be ordered to pay a civil fine of up to three times the value of the corresponding increase in their assets and face prohibition on contracting with the Government or receiving benefits, fiscal or credit incentives for a period of ten years. The effects of this penalty may be extended to cover subsidiaries and partners of the violator, in which said violator is the majority shareholder, in order to avoid attempts to frustrate the effectiveness of the sanctions applied.

There are no restrictions on the application of the sanctions to said third party

---

[49] Superior Court of Justice precedents: REsp 300184, November 3, 2003; REsp 505068/PR, November 29, 2003, available at *http://www.stj.jus.br.*

[50] "Havendo, na Lei 8.429/92 (Lei de Improbidade Administrativa), a previsão de sanções que podem ser aplicadas alternativa ou cumulativamente e em dosagens variadas, é indispensável, sob pena de nulidade, que a sentença indique as razões para a aplicação de cada uma delas, levando em consideração o princípio da razoabilidade e tendo em conta a extensão do dano causado, assim como o proveito econômico obtido pelo agente (art. 12, parágrafo único)." REsp 507.574, February 2, 2006; also: REsp 885.836.

[51] See Di Pietro, 838 (2010).

[52] See Zavascki, 130 (2008); Di Pietro, 839 (2010).

[53] See Velloso Filho, 101 (2001).

[54] See Zavascki, 124 (2010).

[55] See Di Pietro, 837 (2010).

legal entities. The only provisions that cannot be applied are those related to the loss or suspension of political rights and removal from office, for the obvious reason that said rights are exercisable by individuals only.

F. SEIZURE, FREEZING OF ASSETS AND OTHER PROVISIONAL REMEDIES

In accordance with the constitutional provisions established in art.37(4), Law **5–18** 8.429 provides for the seizure and freezing of assets involved in or arising out of an act of misconduct, and for other precautionary measures.[56]

Article 7 of Law 8.429 provides that:

"Article 7. When the misconduct causes damage to public assets or results in unjust (unlawful) enrichment the administrative authority responsible for the inquiry [into the misconduct] shall contact the Public Prosecutor's Office seeking an order for the freezing of the assets of the suspected offender."[57]

Law 8.492 further provides that:

"Article 16. When there are reasonable grounds indicating liability, the commission will request that the Public Prosecutor's Office or the legal representative of the relevant body apply to the competent court for an order for seizure of the assets of the agent or third party who derived unjust enrichment or caused damage to public assets."[58]

In fact it is open to any individual to require that the Public Prosecutor take the appropriate measures in accordance with art.14 (§2).[59]

The freezing and seizure of the assets are not a sanction per se, but rather a measure aimed at safeguarding the enforcement of a possible final order in the proceedings,[60] requiring that such assets be returned to the relevant public authority legal entity that suffered the act of misconduct.[61]

Due to their legal nature, these provisional measures are rarely applied to cases **5–19**

---

[56] See Zavascki, 134 (2008).

[57] "Art. 7º Quando o ato de improbidade causar lesão ao patrimônio público ou ensejar enriquecimento ilícito, caberá a autoridade administrativa responsável pelo inquérito representar ao Ministério Público, para a indisponibilidade dos bens do indiciado.", available through *http://www.planalto.gov.br.*

[58] "Art. 16. Havendo fundados indícios de responsabilidade, a comissão representará ao Ministério Público ou à procuradoria do órgão para que requeira ao juízo competente a decretação do seqüestro dos bens do agente ou terceiro que tenha enriquecido ilicitamente ou causado dano ao patrimônio público.", available through *http://www.planalto.gov.br.*

[59] "Art. 14. §2º A autoridade administrativa rejeitará a representação, em despacho fundamentado, se esta não contiver as formalidades estabelecidas no § 1º deste artigo. A rejeição não impede a representação ao Ministério Público, nos termos do art. 22 desta lei.", available through *http://www.planalto.gov.br.*

[60] See Di Pietro, 838 (2010); Velloso Filho, 107 (2001).

[61] "Art. 18. A sentença que julgar procedente ação civil de reparação de dano ou decretar a perda dos bens havidos ilicitamente determinará o pagamento ou a reversão dos bens, conforme o caso, em favor da pessoa jurídica prejudicada pelo ilícito." available through *http://www.planalto.gov.br.*

other than those arising under art.9 of Law 8.492, which deals with unjust enrichment.[62] Most commonly, assets frozen or seized will be in the hands of a company that participated in an act of bribery so as to receive some privilege or in the hands of a public official who unlawfully acquired said assets.

Other precautionary measures necessary to safeguard a future order may also be applied, even if they are not provided for in Law 8.492.[63] In all cases, it will be necessary to demonstrate to the court that the measure sought is essential to avoid any final order being undermined or rendered ineffective.[64]

If the precautionary measure is aimed at assets that were unlawfully acquired by an individual or a company or the public official involved in the act of misconduct, the applicable order will be for seizure, the relevant assets being placed on judicial deposit.[65] Even assets which are otherwise considered to be "inalienable" under Brazilian law may be seized in accordance with these provisions.[66]

5–20   Only the judiciary can order such conservatory measures, any other public body which may have commenced or be dealing with the inquiry into misconduct has no similar powers.[67]

Article 7 of the Law 8.492 further provides that:

"Sole paragraph. The freezing [of assets] to which the head note to this article refers shall apply to assets [capable of] guaranteeing full reparation of the damage or to the increase in assets that resulted from the unjust enrichment."[68]

Accordingly, in relation to offences arising under art.9, assets that were not unlawfully acquired by the defendants are not subject to seizure.[69] For instance, company assets that were owned by said company prior to the alleged misconduct cannot be the subject of an order for seizure.[70] Furthermore, said assets cannot be seized if they represent the natural development of property previously acquired by the company.[71] The defendant, however, cannot invoke these arguments if it unlawfully acquired such assets from public bodies.[72] Seizure cannot be ordered merely to guarantee future payment of civil fines.[73]

Finally, Law 8.492 provides that:

---

[62] See Zavascki, 130 (2008); Di Pietro, 839 (2010).

[63] See Zavascki, 132 (2008).

[64] See Velloso Filho, 103 (2001); Zavascki, 133 (2008).

[65] See Zavascki, 134 (2008).

[66] See Zavascki, 133 (2008).

[67] See Di Pietro, 841 (2010).

[68] "Parágrafo único. A indisponibilidade a que se refere o caput deste artigo recairá sobre bens que assegurem o integral ressarcimento do dano, ou sobre o acréscimo patrimonial resultante do enriquecimento ilícito.", available through *http://www.planalto.gov.br*.

[69] See Tolosa Filho, Benedicto. Comentários à Lei de Improbidade Administrativa, Forense, p.146, Rio de Janeiro (2003); Velloso Filho, 106 (2008).

[70] See Superior Court of Justice precedent: RMS 6.182, December 1, 1997; RMS 6.197, May 18, 1998.

[71] See Velloso Filho, 106 (2001).

[72] See Velloso Filho, 108 (2001).

[73] See Velloso Filho, 106 (2001).

"Art. 16. (...)§2. When appropriate, the application shall include a request for investigation, examination and freezing of assets, bank accounts and investments held by the suspect in foreign countries, in accordance with the provisions of the law and international treaties."[74]

When necessary to ensure the enforcement of the final order an application may be made within the Public Interest Civil Lawsuit for the freezing of assets in foreign countries, as provided for in applicable international treaties. Said application may also be made in free-standing conservatory measure proceedings. Under art.201 of the Code of Civil Procedure,[75] the request for freezing must be forwarded to the relevant foreign authorities by means of letter rogatory, since Brazilian courts have no jurisdiction to freeze assets outside the country. This is an important tool in avoiding the frustration of any final order which may otherwise occur if the foreign companies in question transfer assets out of the country.

5–21

G. ANTI-CORRUPTION PROVISIONS UNDER THE PENAL CODE[76]

As mentioned earlier in this paper, Law 8.492 is not a criminal statute as such, even though some of its provisions contain severe sanctions that are similar to those applied in criminal prosecutions.[77]

5–22

A criminal prosecution for acts of corruption may occur independently of the filing of a Public Interest Civil Lawsuit, when the administrative misconduct in question falls within the ambit of the Penal Code.[78]

The anti-corruption provisions of the Penal Code may be applied to a public official and to private parties, but never to legal entities which, generally speaking, are not subject to criminal liability under Brazilian law. Furthermore, there is no presumption under Brazilian Law that those in charge of companies' in which employees committed acts of bribery are also to be held liable. Both these aspects will be addressed in further detail in this paper.

---

[74] "Art. 16. §2° Quando for o caso, o pedido incluirá a investigação, o exame e o bloqueio de bens, contas bancárias e aplicações financeiras mantidas pelo indiciado no exterior, nos termos da lei e dos tratados internacionais.", available through *http://www.planalto.gov.br.*

[75] "Art. 201. Expedir-se-á carta de ordem se o juiz for subordinado ao tribunal de que ela emanar; carta rogatória, quando dirigida à autoridade judiciária estrangeira; e carta precatória nos demais casos.", available through *http://www.planalto.gov.br.*

[76] The Brazilian Penal Code came into force on January 1, 1942, available through *http://www.planalto.gov.br.*

[77] See Zavascki, 124 (2008).

[78] See Di Pietro, 825/826 (2010).

H. DEFINITION OF PUBLIC OFFICIAL BY THE BRAZILIAN PENAL CODE

5–23 The Brazilian Penal Code defines a public official as follows:

"Article 327—Anyone who holds a post, position or public function, even on a transitory or unpaid basis, is to be considered a public servant."[79]

Firstly, it is important to note that, as in Law 8.492, the Penal Code adopts a broad definition of public servant,[80] including even those individuals who are performing a public function on a temporary or unpaid basis.

The Penal Code further provides that:

"§1—A person who holds a post, position or function in a quasi-governmental organization or who works for a service providing company contracted or hired for the performance of activities which are typically those of the Public Administration are to be considered equivalent to a public servant."[81]

Under this provision, individuals that work for autonomous government entities, public foundations, public companies, public-private joint stock companies as well as other entities contracted by the government to perform typical public administration activities may also be held criminally liable as though they were public officials.[82] The reason for this extension is to ensure that the constitutional principles of public administration will be observed regardless of the increasing decentralization of public activities.[83]

5–24 Therefore, even employees of a private company, contracted by the government, may be subject to the penalties established for public officials, since the activity they perform are typically governmental. For instance, employees of a private hospital who treat and assist non-fee paying public health care patients may be deemed subject to criminal sanctions[84]; the employees of a contractor building public premises, however, are not liable under such provisions.[85]

Article 327 also establishes higher penalties for some individuals in privileged public positions, as follows:

"§ 2—The penalty will be increased by one-third when the perpetrators of the crimes mentioned in this chapter occupy positions in committees or boards or advisory organs

---

[79] "Art. 327—Considera-se funcionário público, para os efeitos penais, quem, embora transitoriamente ou sem remuneração, exerce cargo, emprego ou função pública.", available through *http:// www.planalto.gov.br*.

[80] Cretella Júnior, José. Curso de Direito Administrativo, Forense, p.421, Rio de Janeiro (2002).

[81] "§ 1º—Equipara-se a funcionário público quem exerce cargo, emprego ou função em entidade paraestatal, e quem trabalha para empresa prestadora de serviço contratada ou conveniada para a execução de atividade típica da Administração Pública.", available through *http://www.planalto.gov.br*.

[82] Mirabete, Julio Fabbrini. Manual de Direito Penal, Editora Atlas, p.294, São Paulo (1999).

[83] Prado, Luiz Regis. Curso de Direito Penal Brasileiro, Vol.3, Forense, p.534, São Paulo (2008).

[84] See Prado, 534 (2008).

[85] See de Jesus, Damásio. Direito Penal, Vol. 4, Saraiva, p.121, São Paulo (2005).

of the direct administration, public-private joint stock company, state owned companies or foundations established by the public administration."[86]

This penalty increase is justified by the position of trust of those occupying higher functions or positions in committees and advisory organs which have wide powers over public property and significant influence on the acts performed by the respective public bodies or legal entities. Moreover, said individuals are subject to less supervision, considering their higher position in the hierarchy.[87]

I. EMBEZZLEMENT

The first corruption related crime referred to in the Penal Code is embezzlement. **5–25** Said crime is defined as follows:

> "Article 312—Appropriation by a public official of money, a valuable asset or any other movable property (chattel), public or private, which is in his possession by virtue of his position, or the misappropriation of said asset for his own benefit or the benefit of another: Penalty—imprisonment, from two to twelve years plus a fine.
>
> §1⁰— The same penalty is to be imposed if the public official, despite not being in possession of the money, asset or property removes it, or participates in its removal, for his own benefit or the benefit of a third party, taking advantage of the opportunity afforded to him by virtue of his being a civil servant. "[88]

This provision normally applies to crimes which, by their nature, do not involve the participation of private (i.e. non-public employee) third parties.[89] However situations may arise in which a public official may misappropriate a given asset for his own benefit or for the benefit of others not related to the entity he works for, but who nevertheless induced or aided and abetted him in the commission of the offence. In that case, if the third party who derives benefit from the crime is aware of the public official's occupation, said third party may be prosecuted as a co-offender.[90]

Article 312 further provides that:

> "§ 2—If the public official contributes with his negligence to the crime of others:
>
> Penalty—detention from three months to one year."[91]

---

[86] "§ 2⁰—A pena será aumentada da terça parte quando os autores dos crimes previstos neste Capítulo forem ocupantes de cargos em comissão ou de função de direção ou assessoramento de órgão da administração direta, sociedade de economia mista, empresa pública ou fundação instituída pelo poder público.", available through *http://www.planalto.gov.br*.

[87] See Prado, 432 (2008).

[88] "Art. 312—Apropriar-se o funcionário público de dinheiro, valor ou qualquer outro bem móvel, público ou particular, de que tem a posse em razão do cargo, ou desviá-lo, em proveito próprio ou alheio: Pena—reclusão, de dois a doze anos, e multa. §1⁰—Aplica-se a mesma pena, se o funcionário público, embora não tendo a posse do dinheiro, valor ou bem, o subtrai, ou concorre para que seja subtraído, em proveito próprio ou alheio, valendo-se de facilidade que lhe proporciona a qualidade de funcionário".

[89] See de Jesus, 128 (2005).

[90] See Mirabete, 299 (1999); de Jesus, 128 (2005).

[91] "2⁰—Se o funcionário concorre culposamente para o crime de outrem: Pena—detenção, de três meses a um ano.", available through *http://www.planalto.gov.br*.

5–26   There is debate amongst commentators as to whether the negligence referred to in subs.2 occurs when a public official willfully seizes an opportunity created by the negligence of another official,[92] or if the crime defined by this provision can also occur when a private party takes the opportunity to steal public property, said opportunity arising out of a negligent failure by the official to perform his duty.[93] In this last case, the private party could be charged with straightforward theft, without the aggravating circumstance of aiding and abetting (or being aided and abetted by) a public official,[94] according to art.155 of the Penal Code.

J. PASSIVE CORRUPTION

5–27   Article 317 of the Penal Code defines the crime of passive corruption as follows:

> "Article 317—Soliciting or receiving, for oneself or on behalf of another, undue advantage or accepting a promise of such advantage, even if such conduct takes place away from the place of work or prior to taking up the post, but nevertheless due to said post:
>
> Penalty—imprisonment from two to twelve years and fine."[95]

First, it is important to note that, although this provision was issued under the name of passive corruption, it may involve active conduct by the public official when s/he solicits the undue advantage.[96] This solicitation may be express or a mere insinuation.[97] Receiving is the act of obtaining the undue reward, while the active conduct is practiced by the corruptor, who offers such reward.[98] Acceptance is the consent of the official to the corruptor's offer.[99] The crime is committed by the mere fact of soliciting, accepting or receiving the undue reward, therefore it is not necessary for the public official to perform the act expected by the corruptor.[100] It is irrelevant if the offer or the promise is made directly or by an intermediary.[101]

The act sought does not have to be illegal or unjust. A crime is committed whenever an advantage is solicited or received, or the promise accepted whether

---

[92] See Mirabete, 305 (1999).

[93] See Prado, 433 (2008).

[94] See Prado, 433 (2008).

[95] "Art. 317—Solicitar ou receber, para si ou para outrem, direta ou indiretamente, ainda que fora da função ou antes de assumi-la, mas em razão dela, vantagem indevida, ou aceitar promessa de tal vantagem: Pena—reclusão, de 2 (dois) a 12 (doze) anos, e multa", available through *http://www.planalto.gov.br*.

[96] See Prado, 475 (2008).

[97] See Mirabete, 320 (1999).

[98] See Mirabete, 320 (1999); Prado, 475 (2008).

[99] Mirabete, 320 (1999); Prado, 475 (2008).

[100] See Hungria, Nelson. Comentários ao Código Penal, Forense, p.369, Rio de Janeiro (1959); Prado, 477 (2008); Mirabete, 321 (1999).

[101] See Prado, 477 (2008).

or not the actual act itself is lawful.[102] It is also irrelevant whether or not the act precedes the reward.[103]

There are dissenting opinions about the necessity for economic value[104] of said   **5–28** undue reward. For those that defend a broader interpretation of the term, the reward may be a political privilege, a promotion and so on.[105] Nevertheless, commentators state that the existence of personal interest by the public official in receiving that specific retribution for his misconduct act is necessary,[106] and this therefore excludes trivial goods such as beverages or food offered to guests at a celebration.[107]

For the crime defined under this provision, it is essential that the act that the public official is willing to perform be related to his administrative attributes[108]; otherwise the applicable criminal charge may be one of aiding and abetting or influence peddling.[109]

Article 317 further provides that:

> "§ 2—The penalty is increased by one third, if, in consequence of the advantage or promise thereof the official delays or ceases the performance of any mandatory act or performs it in violation of his official duty.
>
> § 3—If the official performs, fails to perform or delays any mandatory act, in violation of official duties, acceding to the request or influence of others:
>
> Penalty—detention from three months to one year or a fine."[110]

As stated, the performance of the act sought is not necessary for a prosecution   **5–29** under art.317, but in the event of the public official in fact performing said act, the penalty may be increased in accordance with the provisions set out above.[111]

Subsection § 3 describes a mitigated form of corruption, where the public official breaches his duty of probity in order to comply with an illicit request made by a third party.[112] In that case, no undue reward is offered or promised to the public official; the act is practiced under pressure or desire to please such individual.[113]

---

[102] See Mirabete, 320 (1999).
[103] See Mirabete, 321 (1999).
[104] See Hungria, 370 (1959).
[105] See Prado, 475 (2008).
[106] See Mirabete.
[107] See Hungria, 370 (1959); Prado, 476 (2008).
[108] See Mirabete, 320 (1999); Prado, 477 (2008).
[109] See Mirabete, 320 (1999).
[110] "§ 2º A pena é aumentada de um terço, se, em conseqüência da vantagem ou promessa, o funcionário retarda ou deixa de praticar qualquer ato de ofício ou o pratica infringindo dever funcional. § 3º Se o funcionário pratica, deixa de praticar ou retarda ato de ofício, com infração de dever funcional, cedendo a pedido ou influência de outrem:
Pena—detenção, de três meses a um ano, ou multa.", available through *http://www.planalto.gov.br*.
[111] See Prado, 479 (2008).
[112] See Prado, 479 (2008).
[113] See Mirabete, 323 (1999).

K. THE FURTHERING OF PRIVATE INTERESTS BY A PUBLIC OFFICIAL

5–30 "Article 321—Fostering, directly or indirectly, private interest before the public administration, taking advantage of the status of employee:

Penalty—detention, from one to three months, or fine.

§—If the interest is unlawful:

Penalty—detention from three months to one year plus fine."[114]

The misconduct defined by art.321 consists of the fostering of private interests by a public official,[115] who uses his privileged access to public departments and influence over his colleagues to promote the interests of a specific party,[116] failing to deliver fair and equal treatment to other citizens. The fact that the person who furthers the interests is a public official is not enough for the characterization of this crime, it is also necessary that he uses the prerogatives of his function to carry out such misconduct.[117]

It is irrelevant whether the act is committed directly by the public official (i.e. presenting motions) or through an intermediary, secretly coordinated by the offender.[118] The performance of the act is enough to characterize the crime, regardless of its result.[119] Even if the act is legal, the fostering will be unlawful.[120] If the offender is aware that a certain act of fostering is illegal and performs it to promote a private interest, the increased penalty provided for under the subsection applies.[121]

5–31 It is also irrelevant whether or not the official receives a reward for such misconduct.[122] Note that in this case the public official uses the prerogatives of his function in order to secure the performance of an act he cannot consummate by himself. Otherwise the applicable provision is that of passive corruption defined by art.317.[123]

The party that benefits from this offence (e.g. a company officer who requests

---

[114] "Art. 321—Patrocinar, direta ou indiretamente, interesse privado perante a administração pública, valendo-se da qualidade de funcionário

Pena—detenção, de um a três meses, ou multa.

Parágrafo único—Se o interesse é ilegítimo

Pena—detenção, de três meses a um ano, além da multa", available through *http://www.planalto.gov.br*.

[115] Hungria, 382 (1959).
[116] Prado, 501 (2008).
[117] Mirabete, 333 (1999).
[118] Prado, 501 (2008).
[119] Prado, 501 (2008).
[120] Prado, 501 (2008).
[121] Prado, 501 (2008).
[122] Hungria, 383 (1959).
[123] Prado, 502 (2008).

privileged treatment in a public bid) may be prosecuted for aiding and abetting the crime.[124]

L. ACTS OF CORRUPTION PRACTICED BY PRIVATE PARTIES

I. ACTIVE CORRUPTION

"Art. 333—Offering or promising an inducement to a public official in return for his performing, refraining from or delaying a given official act: **5–32**

Penalty—imprisonment from two to twelve years plus fine.

Sole paragraph—the penalty is increased by a third if the official delays of fails to perform an official act or performs such act in breach of his official duties"[125]

For the purposes of this article, any means used to offer or promise the bribe or undue reward constitute an offence: words, gestures, writing and so on.[126] The offer, however, must be explicit; a mere request for unlawful assistance does not fall within the ambit of the article.[127] Note that the provision forbids any undue reward offered or promised, regardless of its economic value.[128] Legal scholars are of the view that the bribe may take the form of moral, political or sexual favors.[129]

The act expected by the corruptor charged under this provision must be one which is within the public official's powers to perform; otherwise the conduct in question will be the crime of furthering private interests as defined by art.321.[130] The crime is committed even if the offer or promise was solicited or suggested by the public official himself.[131] In any event, the criminal conduct is characterized regardless of acceptance by the official.[132]

The offer or promise can be made directly or through an intermediary who, in this case, may be charged as a co-offender.[133] The corruptor and the intermediary may be any private party or even a public official (not using his powers or   **5–33**

---

[124] See Mirabete, 333 (1999).

[125] "Art. 333—Oferecer ou prometer vantagem indevida a funcionário público, para determiná-lo a praticar, omitir ou retardar ato de ofício:
Pena—reclusão, de 2 (dois) a 12 (doze) anos, e multa.
Parágrafo único—A pena é aumentada de um terço, se, em razão da vantagem ou promessa, o funcionário retarda ou omite ato de ofício, ou o pratica infringindo dever funcional.", available through *http://www.planalto.gov.br.*

[126] See Noronha, E. Magalhães. Direito Penal, Vol. 4, Saraiva, p.430, São Paulo (1978); Mirabete, 375 (1999); Hungria, 431 (1959); de Jesus, 234 (2005); Prado, 564 (2008).

[127] See de Jesus, 234 (2005); Mirabete, 375 (1999).

[128] See Prado, 565 (2008); Mirabete, 375 (1999). Defending the reward must have economic value, see Hungria, 370 (1959).

[129] Prado, 565 (2008); Mirabete, 375 (1999).

[130] Prado, 565 (2008); Mirabete, 375 (1999).

[131] See Delmanto, Celso. Código Penal Comentado, Renovar, p.596, São Paulo (2000); Mirabete, 376 (1999).

[132] See Hungria, 429 (1959); de Jesus, 235 (2005); Mirabete, 377 (1999).

[133] See de Jesus, 234 (2005); Prado, 565 (2008); Hungria, 430 (1999).

influence—as this conduct would fall within another legal definition), and the individual who has been offered or promised the undue reward may be any of those covered by art.327.[134]

If a reward is offered to prevent or delay an illegal act (e.g. an unjustified administrative punishment against a company that is legally performing its activities), there is no crime of corruption.[135] However, there is corruption when the offer or promise is aimed at influencing the public official to perform an act, even if said act is legal[136] (e.g. punishing a competitor that is violating environmental legislation).

In order to be considered a bribe, the reward cannot be frivolous, such as food and beverages offered at celebrations.[137]

The penalty increase provided for in the subsection to the article will apply whenever a legitimate act is delayed or not performed, or an illegitimate act is performed as a result of the offer or promise.[138]

II. INTERNATIONAL ANTI-CORRUPTION CONVENTIONS ADOPTED BY BRAZIL

5–34   Brazil is a signatory to three international conventions setting out commitments to combating domestic and transnational corruption. The first such treaty was the Inter-American Convention against Corruption drawn up by the Organization of American States (OAS), adopted on March 29, 1996, in Venezuela, and which came into force on March 7, 1997.[139] On December 17, 1997, Brazil signed in Paris the Organization for Economic Co-operation and Development (OECD) Convention on Combating Bribery of Foreign Public Officials in International Business Transactions. Said treaty came into force on February 15, 1999.[140] Finally, the last convention of this nature adopted by Brazil was the United Nations Convention against Corruption, signed on October 31, 2003, in Mexico and which came into force on December 14, 2005.[141]

The Inter-American Convention against Corruption (IACC) was the first of its kind to be widely adopted. It called for the implementation of effective legislation against corruption by the signatory states. Domestic and transnational bribery as well as active and passive corruption are covered by the convention, which is broader in scope than the analogous OECD convention.

There are two major parts to the IACC: the first dedicated to preventive measures which signatory states commit themselves to adopting with a view to avoiding corruption and pursuing greater transparency in administration (e.g. denying access to favorable tax treatment (tax incentives) to corporations that

---

[134]   See Mirabete, 375 (1999).
[135]   See Delmanto, 596 (2000); de Jesus, 235 (2005).
[136]   See Mirabete, 376 (1999).
[137]   See Prado, 565 (2008).
[138]   See Noronha, 336 (1978); Prado, 566 (2008).
[139]   Available at *http://www.oea.org* [Accessed July 15, 2010].
[140]   Available at *http://www.oecd.org* [Accessed July 15, 2010].
[141]   Available at http://www.unodc.org [Accessed July 15, 2010].

violate anti-corruption laws and establishing systems for the protection of whistle-blowing public servants and private citizens, instructing government personnel about responsibilities, ethical rules and so on).

The second major part is almost exclusively dedicated to criminal provisions 5–35 that signatory states undertake to introduce and the required commitment to cooperation and mutual assistance among signatories. It is important to note that Brazilian criminal legislation already covered many of the crimes defined by the IACC (e.g. embezzlement, misconduct in office). Illicit (unjust) enrichment is an exception, not being provided for by the Brazilian Penal Code although it is covered by civil legislation (the Law of Administrative Probity).

The IACC adopts a broad definition of public function,[142] public official, government official, public servant[143] and property,[144] and requires that they, as well as private individuals, be held criminally liable for any acts of corruption they commit. It also calls for the prohibition of illicit (unjust) enrichment, improper use of state property and for all perpetrators, instigators and accomplices to acts of corruption to be brought to account.

The OECD Convention, ratified in Brazil on June 15, 2000 and promulgated on November, 30, 2000, also adopts a broad definition of foreign public official,[145] and sets out more detailed provisions on transnational public activities. It also clearly defines the terms "foreign country"[146] and "act or refrain from acting in relation to the performance of official duties",[147] since its overriding aim is to restrain international acts of active corruption.

In fact the earlier IACC contains an even broader definition of public official, 5–36 which includes officials of public bodies that are not related to the legislature, executive or judicial powers as well as individuals appointed or elected to perform public functions or activities but who have yet to take office. On the other hand, the OECD Convention contains a wider definition of agents of international public organisations, who are not covered by the IACC.

The OECD Convention establishes that a signatory state:

---

[142] "Public function" means any temporary or permanent, paid or honorary activity, performed by a natural person in the name of the State or in the service of the State or its institutions, at any level of its hierarchy.

[143] "Public official", "government official", or "public servant" means any official or employee of the State or its agencies, including those who have been selected, appointed, or elected to perform activities or functions in the name of the State or in the service of the State, at any level of its hierarchy.

[144] "Property" means assets of any kind, whether movable or immovable, tangible or intangible, and any document or legal instrument demonstrating, purporting to demonstrate, or relating to ownership or other rights pertaining to such assets.

[145] "a) 'foreign public official' means any person holding a legislative, administrative or judicial office of a foreign country, whether appointed or elected; any person exercising a public function for a foreign country, including for a public agency or public enterprise; and any official or agent of a public international organisation."

[146] "b) 'foreign country' includes all levels and subdivisions of government, from national to local"

[147] "c) 'act or refrain from acting in relation to the performance of official duties' includes any use of the public official's position, whether or not within the official's authorised competence."

"Shall take such measures as may be necessary to establish that it is a criminal offence under its law for any person intentionally to offer, promise or give any undue pecuniary or other advantage, whether directly or through intermediaries, to a foreign public official, for that official or for a third party, in order that the official act or refrain from acting in relation to the performance of official duties, in order to obtain or retain business or other improper advantage in the conduct of international business" (article 1,1).

It provides that signatory states are to introduce legislation criminalising complicity in and incitement of said acts of corruption.

5–37 The OECD Convention sets out that signatory states are to adopt measures to hold corporations and other legal entities criminally liable for acts of corruption of foreign public officials. In practice, however, the Brazilian legal system rarely makes provision for the criminal liability of legal entities, as will be explained further in this article.

The OECD Convention further stipulates that each signatory state is to adopt the measures necessary to ensure that a bribe and the proceeds of bribery of a foreign public official are subject to confiscation. In this respect, the Brazilian Penal Code provides (in provisions introduced prior to the OECD Convention) that, as one of the effects of a criminal conviction, the proceeds of crime or any other goods or assets acquired as a result of criminal conduct may be confiscated by the government, without prejudice to the rights of the victim and third parties acting in good faith.[148]

Money laundering is other main concern addressed in the OECD Convention. Article 7 sets forth that signatory states, which have made bribery of a national public official a predicate offence for the purpose of the application of money laundering legislation, are to do likewise in relation to the bribery of a foreign public official.

5–38 The United Nations Convention against Corruption (UNCC) was promulgated in Brazil on January 31, 2006, through Legislative Decree 348. Of the three anti-corruption conventions adopted by Brazil it is by far the most detailed and the broadest in scope, although in practice the application of its 71 articles has led to fewer effective changes than might have been originally envisaged.

The UNCC definitions of public official[149] and foreign public official[150] are

---

[148] "art. 91—São efeitos da condenação: (...)
II—a perda em favor da União, ressalvado o direito do lesado ou de terceiro de boa-fé:
b) do produto do crime ou de qualquer bem ou valor que constitua proveito auferido pelo agente com a prática do fato criminoso.", available through *http://www.planalto.gov.br*.

[149] "(a) 'Public official' shall mean: (i) any person holding a legislative, executive, administrative or judicial office of a State Party, whether appointed or elected, whether permanent or temporary, whether paid or unpaid, irrespective of that person's seniority; (ii) any other person who performs a public function, including for a public agency or public enterprise, or provides a public service, as defined in the domestic law of the State Party and as applied in the pertinent area of law of that State Party; (iii) any other person defined as a 'public official' in the domestic law of a State Party. However, for the purpose of some specific measures contained in chapter II of this Convention, 'public official' may mean any person who performs a public function or provides a public service as defined in the domestic law of the State Party and as applied in the pertinent area of law of that State Party."

[150] " 'Foreign public official' shall mean any person holding a legislative, executive, administrative or judicial office of a foreign country, whether appointed or elected; and any person exercising a public function for a foreign country, including for a public agency or public enterprise."

similar to those set out in the IACC and the OECD convention, respectively. As in the IACC, preventive measures against acts of corruption are established, but with a broader description of the initiatives signatory states are expected to take. Most notably, the UNCC requires the introduction of measures to tackle bribery in the private sector and embezzlement of private sector property, issues that were not addressed in previous anti-bribery conventions.

The other main objective of the UNCC is to promote mutual cooperation **5–39** between signatory states, including legal assistance, joint investigations, extradition and cooperation on law enforcement. It is drafted in such a way as to encourage signatory states to reach further agreement on specific issues, with the overall aim of the treaty being to establish general principles in the fight against corruption and a move towards transparency in government.

M. THE ENFORCEMENT OF THE CONVENTIONS IN BRAZIL

The main legislation passed by Brazil to enforce the conventions was Law **5–40** 10.467/02, which introduced into the Brazilian Penal Code provisions prohibiting acts of corruption by private parties in international commercial transactions. This law also extended the provisions of Law 9.613/98, which governs money laundering crimes, classifying as a criminal offence the concealment of the nature, source or ownership of property, rights or values derived directly or indirectly from acts of bribery of foreign public officials.

N. BRIBERY OF FOREIGN PUBLIC OFFICIALS IN INTERNATIONAL COMMERCIAL TRANSACTIONS

I. DEFINITION OF A FOREIGN PUBLIC OFFICIAL

Chapter II-A, introduced into the Penal Code by Law 10.467/02 defines a foreign **5–41** public official in its art.337–D as follows:

> "Article 337–D. Anyone who holds a post, position or public function in public bodies or in diplomatic representations abroad, even on a transitory or unpaid basis, is to be considered a public official."

The definition of foreign public official in art.337–D covers all public law legal entities (public authorities), which are part of the constitutional structure of the State and have political and administrative powers.[151] Diplomatic representations are the consular, ambassadorial and related staff that seek to promote and uphold the country's interests abroad.[152] Technical and administrative personnel working

---

[151] See Meirelles, H. L. Direito Administrativo Brasileiro, p.66.
[152] See Mello, C. D. Direito Internacional Público, II, pp.1299–1300.

at or with the diplomatic missions are also considered public officials under this provision.[153] The term "foreign country", according to the OECD Convention, covers all levels of government, from federal to municipal.

"A person who holds a post, position or function in companies controlled, directly or indirectly, by the Public Administration of a foreign country, or in international public organizations is to be considered equivalent to a foreign public official."[154]

Under this provision, individuals who work for autonomous government entities (quasi governmental organisations), public foundations, public (state owned) companies, public-private joint stock companies controlled by the government, as well as international public organisations, are subject to the same criminal liability as public officials.[155] The international public organisations referred to are associations between states that are established under treaties and possess a legal personality which is distinct from that of its members (e.g. UN, OECD, OAS).[156]

II. Active Corruption in International Commercial Transactions

5–42   The crime of active corruption in international commercial transactions in the Brazilian Penal Code, which resulted from OECD provisions,[157] is defined as follows:

"Art. 337–B—Offering, promising or giving undue inducement to a foreign public official, or to a third party, in return for his performing, refraining from or delaying a given official act related to an international commercial transaction:

Penalty—imprisonment from one to eight years plus fine.

§—the penalty is increased by a third if the official delays or fails to perform an official act or performs such act in breach of his official duties."[158]

As with the analogous crime of domestic corruption defined by art.333, the offence provided for under art.337–B is autonomous, and does not require the

---

[153] See Prado, 613 (2008).
[154] "Art. 337-D. Considera-se funcionário público estrangeiro, para os efeitos penais, quem, ainda que transitoriamente ou sem remuneração, exerce cargo, emprego ou função pública em entidades estatais ou em representações diplomáticas de país estrangeiro.
Parágrafo Único. Equipara-se a funcionário público estrangeiro quem exerce cargo, emprego ou função em empresas controladas, diretamente ou indiretamente, pelo Poder Público de país estrangeiro ou em organizações públicas internacionais", available through *http://www.planalto.gov.br*.
[155] See Prado, 613 (2008).
[156] See Prado, 614 (2008).
[157] Also introduced by Law 10.467/02.
[158] "Art. 337-B. Prometer, oferecer ou dar, direta ou indiretamente, vantagem indevida a funcionário público estrangeiro, ou a terceira pessoa, para determiná-lo a praticar, omitir ou retardar ato de ofício relacionado à transação comercial internacional.
Pena—reclusão, de 1 (um) a 8 (oito) anos, e multa.
Parágrafo único. A pena é aumentada de 1/3 (um terço), se, em razão da vantagem ou promessa, o funcionário público estrangeiro retarda ou omite o ato de ofício, ou o pratica infringindo dever funcional.", available through *http://www.planalto.gov.br*.

prosecution of the foreign public official.[159] Each legal system can therefore punish the individuals involved in the offence independently of any action being taken by the corresponding legal system of the other state.

Moreover, the offender may be charged under Brazilian law regardless of his nationality, provided he offered, promised or gave the reward on Brazilian soil.[160] The act which the accused corruptor expected the official to perform (or refrain from or delay), must be one which is within said public official's powers to perform.[161] Therefore, in order to constitute a crime the inducement must be given, promised or offered to a foreign public official whose duty it is to perform (or refrain from performing) a given act pertaining to an international commercial transaction.[162]

The offer or promise may be made directly, when the corruptor himself **5–43** expresses his willingness to bribe, or through an intermediary who transmits the corruptor's willingness to promise, offer or give.[163] In this case, the intermediary may never be charged for passive corruption under art.317, but as a co-offender.[164] It is important to note that the corruptor and the intermediary may be private parties or even public officials (note however that if the official uses influence he holds by virtue of his office, his conduct constitutes a separate crime), and the individual who has been offered or promised the undue reward may be any of those covered by art.337–D.[165]

For the purposes of this article, any means used to offer or promise the bribe or undue reward constitute an offence: words, gestures, writing and so on.[166] Note that the provision forbids any undue reward offered or promised, regardless of its economic value or whether it is to be given immediately or in the future.[167] Also, such a bribe may be intended as a benefit to the foreign public official himself or a third party.[168] The offer or promise, however, has to be made to such official, directly or indirectly, otherwise there is no crime under this provision.[169]

The crime is committed even if the offer or promise was solicited or suggested

---

[159] de Jesus, 269 (2005).

[160] de Jesus, 269 (2005).

[161] de Jesus, 270 (2005); Prado, 614 (2008), who precisely states that "in a dissenting definition, the OECD Convention considers that 'act or refrain from acting in relation to the performance of official duties' includes any use of the public official's position, whether or not within the official's authorized competence (article 1, 4, c). This definition is better than that provided for Brazilian legislation, because, although one can assume that corruption intends the act or omission of any act that does not pertain to governmental activities, it may occur that the public official uses his influence or authority out of the ambit of his powers to perform or exceeding its limits to obtain what the corruptor expects with the bribe."

[162] See de Jesus, 269 (2005).

[163] See Prado, 613 (2008); de Jesus, 269 (2005).

[164] See de Jesus, 269 (2005); Prado, 614 (2008).

[165] See de Jesus, 269 (2005).

[166] See Prado, 612 (2008).

[167] See Prado, 613 (2008).

[168] See de Jesus, 270 (2005).

[169] See de Jesus, 270 (2005).

by the public official himself.[170] In any event, the criminal conduct is characterised by the mere offer or promise of the bribe and it is immaterial whether the foreign public official accepts or refuses the reward.[171]

5-44 If a reward is offered to prevent or delay an illegal act, there is no crime of corruption.[172] However, there is corruption when the offer or promise is aimed at influencing the public official to perform an act, even if said act is legal.[173]

Customary gratuities, without the purpose of corrupting the foreign public official, are not to be considered bribes.[174]

The penalty increase provided for in the article's subsection will apply whenever a legitimate act is delayed or not performed, or an illegitimate act is performed as a result of the offer or promise.[175]

III. INFLUENCE PEDDLING IN INTERNATIONAL COMMERCIAL TRANSACTIONS

5-45 As a consequence of the OECD provisions, the Penal Code further criminalises:

> "Article 337-C. Soliciting, demanding, charging or obtaining, for oneself or for others, directly or indirectly, an advantage or promise of advantage sought on the pretext of influencing an act to be performed by a foreign public official in the exercise of his functions relating to an international business transaction:
>
> Penalty—imprisonment from two to five years plus fine.
>
> §—the penalty is increased by half if the perpetrator alleges or insinuates that the undue reward is also aimed at (to be offered to) a foreign public official."[176]

The crime provided for under this article covers the fraud perpetrated by an individual who states to another that he has influence over a foreign public official. The offender claims that he will use alleged prestige to secure the performance, non-performance or delay of a certain act that is supposedly within the powers of a given official, related to an international commercial transaction.

Hence, for the purposes of this legal provision, the person from whom the undue inducement is solicited or demanded is, in effect, misled into believing that the offender will effectively influence the act of a foreign public official act.[177] If in

---

[170] See de Jesus, 269 (2005), who is of the opinion that there is no crime under this article if the public official imposed such an offer, what would be characterized as the offence of concussion defined by Penal Code's article 316.

[171] See Prado, 615 (2008); de Jesus, 270 (2005).

[172] See Prado, 615 (2008); de Jesus, 235 (2005).

[173] See de Jesus, 270 (2005).

[174] See Prado, 613 (2008).

[175] See Prado, 616 (2008); de Jesus, 270 (2005).

[176] "Art. 337-C. Solicitar, exigir, cobrar ou obter, para si ou para outrem, direta ou indiretamente, vantagem ou promessa de vantagem a pretexto de influir em ato praticado por funcionário público estrangeiro no exercício de suas funções, relacionado a transação comercial internacional.
Pena—reclusão, de 2 (dois) a 5 (cinco) anos, e multa.
Parágrafo único. A pena é aumentada da metade, se o agente alega ou insinua que a vantagem é também destinada a funcionário estrangeiro."

[177] Prado, 619 (2008).

fact the offender does fulfill the promised maneuver (e.g. by trying to convince the official to perform or unlawfully refrain from an act related to an international commercial transaction) the crime in question will not fall within art.337–C, but will be covered by another legal provision, such as art.337–B, in the event of an offer of undue reward being made to the official.

Even though the fraud referred to in art.337–C presupposes the existence of a foreign public official, it is immaterial whether the offender specifically indicates the relevant official or mentions his name.[178] **5–46**

Furthermore, this crime may occur even if such official does not have the expected powers, or even if he does not in fact exist.[179] However, if said official is identified by the offender, it is necessary for the purposes of this provision that he is a foreign public official, otherwise the conduct will not be the crime provided for under art.337–C[180] (i.e. if he is a Brazilian public official, the crime will be one of domestic influence peddling, defined by art.332).

The conduct of the individual who offers or delivers the reward to the person who requested it (but then failed to carry out the promised act of influence) is not punishable as a crime, in that whilst said individual assumes he will participate in an act of transnational corruption, he does not in fact do so.[181]

The undue reward or promise of such a reward may be intended to benefit the offender or a third party.[182] It is irrelevant whether the reward is material or moral.[183] **5–47**

Furthermore, the influence alleged by the offender must be related to an international commercial transaction, otherwise art.337–C will not apply.[184] Note however that the mere act of requesting, demanding or charging is enough to constitute the offence.[185]

If the offender, who claims to have influence over the practice of any official act by a foreign public official also claims or implies that the benefit (inducement) sought is to be given to said official the penalty will be increased by half.[186]

O. DEFICIENCIES IN THE APPLICATION IN BRAZIL OF ANTI-CORRUPTION CONVENTIONS

The OECD Working Group on Bribery in its Phase 2 Report, published in 2007, identified several deficiencies in Brazil's implementation of the Convention on Combating Bribery of Foreign Public Officials.[187] **5–48**

---

[178] Gusmão, S. C. Exploração de Prestígio, p.21.
[179] de Jesus, 276 (2005).
[180] Prado, 619 (2008); de Jesus, 276 (2005).
[181] de Jesus, 277 (2005).
[182] de Jesus, 277 (2005).
[183] Prado, 620 (2008).
[184] Prado, 620 (2008).
[185] Prado, 620 (2008).
[186] de Jesus, 277 (2005).
[187] Available through *http://www.oecd.org*.

The report referred to the fact that the 2006 Transparency International Bribe Payers Index, which measures perceptions of the propensity of companies in a given country to offer or pay bribes when operating abroad, ranked the perception of the propensity for such bribery by Brazilian companies as very high. In terms of transparency (i.e. absence of bribery) Brazil was ranked 23rd out of the 30 countries included in the survey, with a score of 5.65 out of a possible 10 (10 being the perfect score, indicating complete absence of propensity to bribe).[188]

Furthermore, the OECD report makes a series of recommendations for the enforcement of the Convention on Combating Bribery of Foreign Public Officials in International Business Transactions, such as[189]:

(a) That the Brazilian authorities remind the Federal Police Department and the Federal Public Prosecutor's Office of the importance of actively investigating possible sources of foreign bribery. Also, that Brazilian authorities remind the Working Group on the Convention to assess whether the limitation period on investigations under Brazilian law provides adequate time for investigation of foreign bribery offences, in particular, where information is required from abroad.

(b) That the Working Group take steps to ensure that Brazil provides prompt and effective mutual legal assistance for the purpose of investigation of offences within the scope of the Convention.

(c) That Brazil adopt comprehensive measures to protect whistleblowers in order to encourage such employees to report suspected cases of foreign bribery without fear of retaliation.

(d) That Brazil ensure that the liability of legal entities ("juridical persons") for the bribery of a foreign public official is covered under legislation and effective, proportionate and dissuasive sanctions are provided.

5–49   In addition to pointing out the deficiencies in the enforcement of the OECD Convention in Brazil, the report draws attention to the fact that up until 2007 there were no reported cases in which Brazilian courts had applied the provisions of arts 337–B and 337–C, which had been incorporated into the Penal Code as a result of the ratification of the Convention. This continues to be the case.[190]

The absence of judicial examination of issues arising under the Convention precludes full and proper analysis of the existing deficiencies in the enforcement of its provisions in Brazil. However, the failure of the competent Brazilian

---

[188] The TI 2006 Bribe Payers Index is based on the responses of 11 232 business executives from companies in 125 countries. The executives were asked about the propensity of foreign firms that do business in their country to pay bribes or to make undocumented extra payments.

[189] For full content of report's recommendations and follow-ups consult: *http://www.oecd.org*.

[190] The investigations mentioned on the report did not result in criminal prosecutions, such as the oil for food case. Considering that these investigations are confidential, no case law is available on that matter.

authorities to detect violations and prosecute offenders is a major concern, as pointed out by the report, and should be a priority in the fight against corruption.

P. THE CRIMINAL LIABILITY OF BRAZILIAN COMPANIES

One of the main issues raised by the 2007 OECD report is that there are scant **5–50** possibilities under Brazilian legislation for holding legal entities (corporate bodies) liable for acts of corruption in international commercial transactions. According to the report:

> "As of December 2007, Brazil had not taken the necessary measures to establish the liability of legal persons for the bribery of a foreign public official, in accordance with its legal principles. Accordingly, the lead examiners have concluded that the current statutory regime for liability of legal persons under Brazilian law is inconsistent with Article 2 of the Convention. The lead examiners regard this situation as a serious gap in the law that needs to be urgently addressed.
>
> In relation to sanctions, and under the current legislation, the lead examiners consider that bribery of a foreign public official by legal persons is not punishable in Brazil by effective, proportionate and dissuasive sanctions as required by Article 3 of the Convention principally because of the considerations set forth above relating to the regime for the liability of legal persons."[191]

In fact the implementation of effective legislation providing for the liability of legal persons involved in acts of corruption faces major obstacles in the Brazilian legal system. There are currently no legal grounds that might enable the commencement of a criminal prosecution against a company in Brazil or the application of civil sanctions arising out of the bribery by said company of a foreign public official.

The prevailing view among Brazilian lawmakers and legal scholars is that the intangible and "artificial" nature of companies precludes the moral effect that criminal penalties should have over these and other potential offenders.[192] Criminal sanctions could therefore only be applied to those in charge of the administration of the companies.[193]

Moreover, the main principles that govern Brazilian criminal law are incon- **5–51** sistent with the extension of criminal liability to cover offences committed by legal persons, since criminal law should be applied to a minimum.[194] The widely held view is that the liability of corporate and other legal entities is best addressed by the provisions of civil law, generally considered to be more equitable, swift and effective in terms of discouraging unlawful conduct by legal entities.[195]

---

[191] See item 3, a, of the said report, available through *http://www.oecd.org*.
[192] Machado, H. de B. Responsabilidade Penal no Âmbito das Empresas in Direito Penal Empresarial, Dialética, p.116, São Paulo (2001).
[193] Prado, 608 (2008).
[194] Prado, 608 (2008).
[195] Machado, 116 (2001).

Furthermore, under Brazilian legislation a criminal conviction of legal entities is for the most part unnecessary, since the sanctions that can be applied to those entities are, in any event, asset based.[196] There is clear legal prohibition on holding individual administrators, managers or directors strictly liable for the acts of companies.[197]

There are, however, some exceptions to this general view, particularly in relation to environmental crimes for which, according to the 1988 Constitution, corporate entities may be held (criminally) liable.[198]

5-52 In relation to the application of civil sanctions to companies involved in foreign bribery, the OECD report accurately summarises the current situation of Brazilian legislation:

> "The lead examiners have concluded that Brazil has failed to implement Article 2 of the Convention. Indeed of the three statutes submitted by Brazil as having relevance to the liability of legal persons for the bribery of foreign public officials, none is directly relevant to such bribery. The first (Law 8 666) relates to domestic public procurement-related activities, and does not provide for monetary sanctions. The second (Law 6 385) is entirely domestic in scope, only provides penalties for individuals with a certain relationship to the company, and only applies in relation to publicly held companies. The third (Law 8 884) applies specifically to anti-competitive behavior which could indirectly involve foreign bribery, but only if it affects the Brazilian market. Moreover, a recommendation by the Working Group in Phase 1 to amend this statute to refer specifically to foreign bribery in the list of acts deemed a violation of the economic order has not been acted on."[199]

Furthermore, as previously demonstrated in this paper, companies cannot be prosecuted under the Administrative Probity Law for acts involving foreign public officials.

Q. FORTHCOMING LEGISLATION

5-53 The Brazilian Congress is currently analysing a Bill that sets out civil and administrative sanctions for legal entities that commit corruption offences.

Under said Bill (6826/2010),[200] any national or foreign legal person is liable for acts perpetrated against national or foreign public assets, for acts that contravene

---

[196] Machado, 116 (2001).

[197] Noronha, Vol.I, 144 (1991).

[198] "Art. 225 (...) § 3⁰—As condutas e atividades consideradas lesivas ao meio ambiente sujeitarão os infratores, pessoas físicas ou jurídicas, a sanções penais e administrativas, independentemente da obrigação de reparar os danos causados.", available through *http://www.planalto.gov.br*.

[199] Available through *http://www.oecd.org*.

[200] Available through *http://www.camara.gov.br* [Accessed July 15, 2010].

the principles of public administration or that contravene international commitments agreed to by Brazil.[201] The offences covered by its art.6 include the bribery of any public official (including foreigners), fraud in public tenders, fraudulent setting up of legal persons and failure to pay payroll taxes or social security related to the execution of contracts with the government.

The sanctions provided for under such Bill are: a civil fine of one to thirty per cent of annual gross revenues, excluding taxes; a declaration of unfitness; full redress of the loss caused; publication of the court's order (i.e. negative publicity); prohibition on contracting, receiving incentives, subsidies, donations or loans from public bodies and financial institutions controlled by the government; revocation of delegated powers, concessions, authorisations or permits, license revocation or termination of contracts with the government.

The Bill defines foreign public official as follows: 5–54

"§3 Anyone who holds a post, position or public function in public bodies or in diplomatic representations abroad, as well as companies controlled, directly or indirectly, by the government of a foreign country or in public international organizations even on a temporary or unpaid basis, is to be considered a foreign public official for the purposes of this Law."[202]

The Bill also provides that the Public Prosecutor's office and public bodies are entitled to file lawsuits seeking the forfeiture of assets, rights or an amount equivalent to the proceeds of the offences, without prejudice to the right of third parties acting in good faith; and to apply for orders that that the business activities of the offender be suspended or partially paralysed; or for the compulsory dissolution of the legal person.[203]

This Bill, if passed is likely to engender further progress in the fight against corruption and the application in practice of the provisions of the three Conventions signed by Brazil, ensuring that legal persons are held liable for acts of corruption in relation to foreign officials.

---

[201] "Art. 6⁰ Constituem atos lesivos à administração pública, nacional ou estrangeira, para os fins desta Lei, todos aqueles, praticados pelas pessoas jurídicas mencionadas no parágrafo único do art. 2⁰, que atentem contra o patrimônio público nacional ou estrangeiro, contra princípios da administração pública ou contra os compromissos internacionais assumidos pelo Brasil, assim definidos: (. . .)", available through *http://www.camara.gov.br.*

[202] "§ 3⁰ Considera-se agente público estrangeiro, para os fins desta Lei, quem, ainda que transitoriamente ou sem remuneração, exerça cargo, emprego ou função pública em órgãos, entidades estatais ou em representações diplomáticas de país estrangeiro, assim como em empresas controladas, direta ou indiretamente, pelo poder público de país estrangeiro ou em organizações públicas internacionais.", available through *http://www.camara.gov.br.*

[203] "Art. 19. Em razão da prática de atos previstos no art. 6o desta Lei, o Ministério Público e as pessoas jurídicas de direito público interessadas poderão ajuizar ação com vistas à aplicação das seguintes sanções às pessoas jurídicas infratoras:
I—perdimento dos bens, direitos ou valores que representem vantagem ou proveito direta ou indiretamente obtidos da infração, ressalvado o direito do lesado ou de terceiro de boa-fé;
II—suspensão ou interdição parcial de suas atividades;
III—dissolução compulsória da pessoa jurídica.", available through *http://www.camara.gov.br.*

R. CONCLUSION—ENFORCEMENT OF THE ANTI-CORRUPTION STATUTORY PROVISIONS

5–55 This brief description of the existing statutory provisions in force in Brazilian legal system shows that Brazil may not be in a leading position with respect to the adoption of anti-corruption statutory provisions, but it seems to be in the correct path.

However, passing bills and increasing the number of anti-corruption statutory provisions in force in the Brazilian legal system is not enough. It is needless to say that the adoption of such provisions will only produce the expected result in the fight against corruption if they are duly applied. And, this might be the material issue that one needs to pay attention to in Brazil.

In the last decade, Brazilian authorities have launched a crusade against corruption and white-collar crimes. There has been a significant increase of the number of cases under investigation and prosecution, with an intense coverage by the media.

Despite the effort applied by the authorities throughout this period, it is still difficult to assess what will be the concrete result of the application of the legal provisions described in this article, because most of the legal proceedings involving these matters have not yet come to an end, due to the slow pace implied by Brazilian courts, which have an insufficient number of judges, who are drowned by the overloaded court dockets.

CHAPTER 6

HONG KONG'S ANTI-CORRUPTION LAWS

A. BACKGROUND

From the end of the Second World War corruption grew rapidly in Hong Kong **6–01** and by the 1970s it was rampant. Hong Kong was generally regarded as one of the most corrupt places in the world. In every sector of the community bribery and extortion had become norms of daily life.

Over the years the reaction of the Hong Kong authorities to the growing problem was the orthodox reaction of authorities the world over: more corruption offences and severer penalties. As elsewhere, the problem only grew worse.

Gradually the realisation dawned that corruption had to be addressed differently from other forms of criminality. A three part strategy was required. Of course, the values on corruption set out in the laws had to be upheld by enforcement of those laws. In addition, however, two other elements were needed. First, the systems and procedures which provided the opportunities for corruption had to be adjusted to eliminate those opportunities. Secondly, people in all sectors of the community had to be educated about "the evils of corruption" and their support for the fight against corruption had to be enlisted. This chapter deals with the first part of that strategy—enforcement of the laws by investigation and prosecution.

A vociferous minority of the public made the government realise that the **6–02** investigation of corruption could no longer be left to the police which had itself become one of the most corrupt institutions of the administration. Overriding police objections, the government decided that a specialised body, separate from and independent of the police was needed. Its role would be to lead the coordinated implementation of a three-part strategy against corruption comprising enforcement, prevention and public education and support.

Things began to improve only after the Independent Commission Against Corruption was established. It began operations in February 1974 and some three years later the Commissioner was able to report that the ICAC had been able to "break the back" of syndicated corruption; by July 1977 "no major corruption syndicates were known to exist at that time." Progress was rapid, even if the longer term objective of bringing about a change of community attitude to corruption took a good few years. The struggle was only just beginning.

The mandate of the ICAC as set out in the Independent Commission Against Corruption Ordinance 1974 required the Commission to address corruption in all sectors of the community, not merely the public sector. Initially it was the corruption of public servants that most angered the community. For the first several years reports from members of the public consisted almost entirely of complaints against public servants, a high proportion of which concerned police officers and other disciplined services. But the ICAC mandate also embraced the business sector. A few reports concerned corruption in the private sector where both parties to the alleged corrupt transaction were employed in the business world.

6–03　　As the business community gradually realised that the new initiative against corruption meant that the age-old way of doing business was under scrutiny, its resentment of the ICAC and the strategy is was pursuing grew. Hostility developed to the point where leading businesses and chambers of commerce formally petitioned the governor to "keep the ICAC out of business". All the arguments were advanced: business was unaffected by corruption; interfering with the way it had always been conducted would adversely affect business and, inevitably, the economy of Hong Kong and government revenues; while it was right that corruption in the public service should be addressed, businessmen were the best judges of what was good for business.

The government rejected these pleas and the ICAC continued its work in all sectors of the community. Over time the business sector became reconciled to the aims of the ICAC and gradually the same chambers of commerce that had petitioned the governor became some of the strongest supporters of the ICAC. The reason for this change of attitude was not hard to find. As businessmen realised that it was in their interest not to have their business undermined behind their backs by their own employees, that clean business was better for profits, they gave their active support to the ICAC and took a leading role in the fight. It took a decade or more for that change to occur but it resulted in significant progress in bringing the problem under control.

Over the years since the ICAC was established, the profile of the corruption reports received has changes. Initially, almost 90 per cent of reports concerned the public sector and some 10 per cent concerned the private sector. Currently public sector reports amount to less than 35 per cent of the total while private sector reports make up about 65 per cent

6–04　　The law setting out the corruption offences, the Prevention of Bribery Ordinance 1971, has been amended several times since its enactment. A major review of the law was undertaken in 1994 and a number of amendments made to ensure that the Ordinance was consistent with the recently enacted Bill of Rights Ordinance, which incorporated into Hong Kong's domestic law the provisions of the International Covenant on Civil and Political Rights, and with the constitutional provisions of the Basic Law enacted by mainland China and coming into force on July 1, 1997.

B. THE STATUTORY OFFENCES

The Prevention of Bribery Ordinance 1971 repealed the Prevention of Corruption **6–05** Ordinance (Cap 215, 1964 edn). It simplified the offence of bribery in both the public and private sectors by doing away with the requirement of proving that the actus reus had been done "corruptly". It introduced two offences that more closely reflected the view's of the community. The first was s.3 (soliciting or accepting an advantage) which makes it an offence for a civil servant to solicit or accept a broadly defined "advantage" whether or not the advantage is solicited or accepted as an inducement or reward. The second was s.10 (possession of unexplained property)[1] which makes it an offence for a civil servant to possess assets in excess of his official emoluments or to have a standard of living out of keeping with his official emoluments unless he gives the court a satisfactory explanation therefor.

Bribery in the non-public sector was addressed by a separate provision dealing with "corrupt transactions with agents". Section 9 of the POBO was so framed as to be applicable also to public sector employees but from the outset was used only in respect of the principal/agent relationship in the private sector.

The offence contained in s.9(3) of the POBO is committed by an agent who deceives his principal by using a false or erroneous document in which the principal is interested with intent to deceive him. It was simplified: 'corruptly' and 'dishonestly' form no part of the mens rea and the offence applies only to the agent and not to a third party who may have provided the document.

The main offence of bribery contained in s.4 of the Ordinance was given **6–06** extraterritorial application by providing that the offence is committed whether the soliciting, accepting or offering occurs "in Hong Kong or elsewhere".

Section 4 now reads:

"(1) Any person who, whether in Hong Kong or elsewhere, without lawful authority or reasonable excuse, offers any advantage to a public servant as an inducement to or reward for or otherwise on account of that public servant's—

    (a)   performing or abstaining from performing, or having performed or abstained from performing, any act in his capacity as a public servant;

    (b)   expediting, delaying, hindering or preventing, or having expedited, delayed, hindered or prevented, the performance of an act, whether by that public servant or by any other public servant in his or that other public servant's capacity as a public servant; or

    (c)   assisting, favouring, hindering or delaying, or having assisted, favoured, hindered or delayed, any person in the transaction of any business with a public body,

shall be guilty of an offence.

---

[1] Referred to as "illicit enrichment" in the UN Convention Against Corruption, art.20.

(2) Any public servant who, whether in Hong Kong or elsewhere, without lawful authority or reasonable excuse, solicits or accepts any advantage as an inducement to or reward for or otherwise on account of his—

    (a)   performing or abstaining from performing, or having performed or abstained from performing, any act in his capacity as a public servant;

    (b)   expediting, delaying, hindering or preventing, or having expedited, delayed, hindered or prevented, the performance of an act, whether by himself or by any other public servant in his or that other public servant's capacity as a public servant; or

    (c)   assisting, favouring, hindering or delaying, or having assisted, favoured, hindered or delayed, any person in the transaction of any business with a public body,

shall be guilty of an offence.

[Subsections (2A) and (2B) make clear that the offences of 'active' and 'passive' bribery apply also in relation to the Chief Executive of Hong Kong.]

(3) If a public servant other than a prescribed officer solicits or accepts an advantage with the permission of the public body of which he is an employee being permission which complies with subsection (4), neither he nor the person who offered the advantage shall be guilty of an offence under this section.

(4) For the purposes of subsection (3) permission shall be in writing and—

    (a)   be given before the advantage is offered, solicited or accepted; or

    (b)   in any case where an advantage has been offered or accepted without prior permission, be applied for and given as soon as reasonably possible after such offer or acceptance,

and for such permission to be effective for the purposes of subsection (3), the public body shall, before giving such permission, have regard to the circumstances in which it is sought."

6–07   By contrast the lesser offence of soliciting or accepting an advantage set out in s.3 of the POBO applies only to a public servant and not to the other party to the transaction, and does not require the advantage to have been given as an inducement or reward.

    Section 3 reads:

"Any prescribed officer who, without the general or special permission of the Chief Executive, solicits or accepts any advantage shall be guilty of an offence."

For the purpose of this section the general permission of the Chief Executive is given in the Acceptance of Advantages (Chief Executive's Permission) Notice 2007. Advantages not covered by the Notice require his special prior permission.

    As regards the offence of possession of unexplained property, the Hong Kong Bill of Rights Ordinance (Cap 383), which, as previously mentioned, incorporated into Hong Kong domestic law the provisions of the International Covenant on Civil and Political Rights, provided the opportunity for a defendant to challenge the validity of the offence. The Hong Kong Court of Appeal concluded that the offence contained in s.10 of the POBO was "dictated by necessity and goes no further than necessary. The balance is right."[2]

Section 10 reads:

6–08

"(1) Any person who, being or having been the Chief Executive or a prescribed officer—

(a) maintains a standard of living above that which is commensurate with his present or past official emoluments; or

(b) is in control of pecuniary resources or property disproportionate to his present or past official emoluments,

shall, unless he gives a satisfactory explanation to the court as to how he was able to maintain such a standard of living or how such pecuniary resources or property came under his control, be guilty of an offence.

(1A) If the accused in any proceedings for an offence under subsection (1) is or has been the Chief Executive, the court, in determining whether the accused has given a satisfactory explanation as provided in that subsection, shall take into account assets that he declared to the Chief Justice pursuant to Paragraph 2, Article 47 of the Basic Law.

(1B) The Chief Justice shall disclose to a court information about assets declared to him pursuant to Paragraph 2, Article 47 of the Basic Law if the disclosure is required by an order made by the court for the purposes of subsection (1A).

(2) Where a court is satisfied in proceedings for an offence under subsection (1)(b) that, having regard to the closeness of his relationship to the accused and to other circumstances, there is reason to believe that any person was holding pecuniary resources or property in trust for or otherwise on behalf of the accused or acquired such resources or property as a gift from the accused, such resources or property shall, in the absence of evidence to the contrary, be presumed to have been in the control of the accused.

(5) In this section, 'official emoluments' includes a pension or gratuity payable under the Pensions Ordinance (Cap 89), the Pension Benefits Ordinance (Cap 99) or the Pension Benefits (Judicial Officers) Ordinance (Cap 401)."

The offence of possessing unexplained property contained in s.10 has been part of Hong Kong's anticorruption armoury for almost 40 years. In that time it has been seldom used, but it has proved effective against those who are clever at concealing their soliciting or accepting of a bribe. It is an offence that usually requires a wide-ranging investigation of the extent and acquisition value of the property held by, or on behalf of, the suspect.

As regards bribery in the private sector, s.9 of the POBO provides:

6–09

"(1) Any agent who, without lawful authority or reasonable excuse, solicits or accepts any advantage as an inducement to or reward for or otherwise on account of his—

(a) doing or forbearing to do, or having done or forborne to do, any act in relation to his principal's affairs or business; or

(b) showing or forbearing to show, or having shown or forborne to show, favour or disfavour to any person in relation to his principal's affairs or business,

shall be guilty of an offence.

---

[2] *Attorney General v Hui Kin-hong* [1995] 1 HKCLR 227 at 236.

(2) Any person who, without lawful authority or reasonable excuse, offers any advantage to any agent as an inducement to or reward for or otherwise on account of the agent's—

(a)   doing or forbearing to do, or having done or forborne to do, any act in relation to his principal's affairs or business; or
(b)   showing or forbearing to show, or having shown or forborne to show, favour or disfavour to any person in relation to his principal's affairs or business,

shall be guilty of an offence.

(3) Any agent who, with intent to deceive his principal, uses any receipt, account or other document—

(a)   in respect of which the principal is interested; and
(b)   which contains any statement which is false or erroneous or defective in any material particular; and
(c)   which to his knowledge is intended to mislead the principal,

shall be guilty of an offence.

(4) If an agent solicits or accepts an advantage with the permission of his principal, being permission which complies with subsection (5), neither he nor the person who offered the advantage shall be guilty of an offence under subsection (1) or (2).

(5) For the purposes of subsection (4) permission shall—

(a)   be given before the advantage is offered, solicited or accepted; or
(b)   in any case where an advantage has been offered or accepted without prior permission, be applied for and given as soon as reasonably possible after such offer or acceptance,

and for such permission to be effective for the purposes of subsection (4), the principal shall, before giving such permission, have regard to the circumstances in which it is sought."

C. THE COMMON LAW OFFENCE OF MISCONDUCT IN PUBLIC OFFICE

6–10   More recently a number of prosecutions have been successfully brought for the common law offence of misconduct in public office. The following examples of the misconduct of public officers[3] illustrate the scope of the offence: civil servants who awarded government contracts to firms with which they were associated in some way; those who by their actions prevented open competition in the government tendering process; an officer who unlawfully awarded his staff pay increases and fraudulently concealed his actions; a Legislative Councillor who compromised his position in the course of carrying out consultancy work for an organisation which was to be affected by new legislation being debated in the Council; civil servants who committed fraud in relation to their housing renting allowances; officers of the Correctional Services Department in their dealings

[3] The examples are cited in Ian McWalters, *Bribery and Corruption Law in Hong Kong*, (Asia: LexisNexis, 2003), p.99.

with prisoners and their relatives; and civil officers who falsified records about their attendance at work and the performance of their duties.

A decision of the Court of Final Appeal in 2002[4] clarified the elements and scope of the offence. It is committed by a public official who in the course of or in relation to his public office wilfully, intentionally and culpably misconducts himself. The court made clear that the gravity of the misconduct is an important requirement of the offence and emphasized that it was not every breach of discipline that would amount to the criminal offence. It was described by the trial judge as "analogous to corruption" and is punishable by a maximum of seven years' imprisonment, the same maximum as for bribery under s.4 of the POBO.

D. INVESTIGATIVE POWERS ENHANCED

One of the main changes made by the POBO was the strengthening of the powers   6–11
of investigation granted to the ICAC. In the second reading speech on the Prevention of Bribery Bill the Attorney General said:

> "I believe that, if any real progress is to be made in the reduction of bribery, those responsible for the detection of these offences must be given the enhanced powers of investigation contained in Part III, unpalatable as some of them may seem. If some infringement of traditional liberties and privacy is involved, then I believe it is a price which te community ought to be prepared to pay, if it really wishes to see corruption ousted from our public life."[5]

The combined effect of the POBO and the Independent Commission Against Corruption Ordinance (enacted in February 1974) was to grant the Commissioner Against Corruption strong powers of investigation. The Commissioner was given powers of arrest, detention, search and seizure, plus the power to obtain information, including information from banks and the tax authorities, and the power to obtain a court order to detain a suspect's travel documents. Surveillance and the interception of Communications was finally regulated in primary law by the Interception of communications and Surveillance Ordinance (Cap 589) in 2006.

Under s.13 of the POBO as amended, the Commissioner, if satisfied that there is reasonable cause to believe that an offence under the Ordinance has been committed and any account, banker's or company books, documents or other article are likely to be relevant to an investigation of such offence, may authorise an officer to inspect and take copies of any of them. Where the requirement to produce documents for inspection is intended to be addressed to a suspect, the prior authorisation of a court is necessary. In 1980 the definitions of "banker's books" and "company books" were amended to allow access to a range of records that went beyond only accounting records.

---

[4] *Shum Kwok Sher v HKSAR* [2002] 5 HKCFAR 381.
[5] Hong Kong Hansard October 21, 1970, p.137, cited at p.22.

6–12   Section 13 provides:

"(1) Where the Commissioner is satisfied that there is reasonable cause to believe—

(a) that an offence under this Ordinance may have been committed by any person; and

(b) that any share account, purchase account, club account, subscription account, investment account, trust account, mutual or trust fund account, expense account, bank account or other account of whatsoever kind or description, and any banker's books, company books, documents or other article of or relating to any person named or otherwise identified in writing by the Commissioner are likely to be relevant for the purposes of an investigation of such offence, he may for those purposes authorize in writing any investigating officer on production by him of the authorization if so required—

    (i) to investigate and inspect such accounts, books or documents or other article of or relating to the person named or otherwise identified by the Commissioner;

    (ii) to require from any person the production of such accounts, books, documents, or other article of or relating to the person named or otherwise identified by the Commissioner which may be required for the purposes of such investigation and the disclosure of all or any information relating thereto, and to take copies of such accounts, books or documents or of any relevant entry therein and photographs of any other article.

(1A) The Commissioner shall not, without the leave of the Court of First Instance obtained on ex parte application in chambers, issue an authorization under or by virtue of which any particular person who is alleged or suspected to have committed an offence under this Ordinance can be required to comply with any requirement of the description mentioned in subsection (1)(i) and (ii).

(1B) The Court of First Instance shall not grant leave for the issue of an authorization under subsection (1)(i) and (ii) unless, on consideration of an application under subsection (1A), it is satisfied as to the matters that the Commissioner is required to be satisfied under subsection (1).

(2)(a) Every authorization given under subsection (1) shall be deemed also to authorize the investigating officer to require from any person information as to whether or not at any bank, company or other place there is any account, book, document or other article liable to investigation, inspection or production under such authorization.

(b) A requirement under paragraph (a) shall be made in writing and any statement therein as to the existence of the appropriate authorization under subsection (1) shall be accepted as true without further proof of the fact.

(3) Any person who, having been lawfully required under this section to disclose any information or to produce any accounts, books, documents or other article to an investigating officer authorized under subsection (1), shall, notwithstanding the provisions of other Ordinance or rule of law to the contrary save only the provisions of section 4 of the Inland Revenue Ordinance (Cap 112), comply with such requirement, and any such person who fails or neglects, without reasonable excuse, so to do, and any person who obstructs any such investigating officer in the execution of the authorization given under subsection (1), shall be guilty of an offence and shall be liable on conviction to a fine of $20000 and to imprisonment for 1 year.

(4) Any person who falsely represents that an appropriate authorization has been given under subsection (1) shall be guilty of an offence and shall be liable on conviction to a fine of $20000 and to imprisonment for 1 year."

Section 13A of the POBO, added in 1998, allows the Commissioner to apply to a court for an order requiring the Commissioner of Inland Revenue to produce specific material held by him. Reflecting the balance legislators felt should be struck between the secrecy of tax matters and the public interest in the effective investigation of corruption, the law requires the court to be satisfied of certain matters before it can make an order.

Section 13A provides: 6–13

"(1) The Commissioner or an investigating officer with the approval of the Commissioner or the Deputy Commissioner may, for the purpose of an investigation into, or proceedings relating to, an offence suspected to have been committed under this Ordinance, make an ex parte application to the Court of First Instance in chambers for an order under subsection (2) in relation to particular material or material of a particular description held by the Commissioner of Inland Revenue or by any officer of the Inland Revenue Department.

(2) Subject to subsection (6), the Court of First Instance may, if on such an application it is satisfied that—

(a) there are reasonable grounds for suspecting that an offence under this Ordinance has been committed;

(b) there are reasonable grounds for believing that the material to which the application relates is likely to be relevant to the investigation or proceedings for the purpose of which the application is made; and

(c) there are reasonable grounds for believing that it is in the public interest, having regard to—

(i) the seriousness of the offence suspected to have been committed;

(ii) whether or not the suspected offence could be effectively investigated if an order under this subsection is not made;

(iii) the benefit likely to accrue to the investigation or proceedings if the material is so produced or if access to it is given; and

(iv) the public interest in preserving secrecy with regard to matters relating to the affairs of persons that may come to the knowledge of the Commissioner of Inland Revenue or to any officer of the Inland Revenue Department in the performance of their duties under the Inland Revenue Ordinance (Cap 112),

make an order that the Commissioner of Inland Revenue or any officer of the Inland Revenue Department—

(i) shall—

(A) produce the material for the Commissioner or an investigating officer to take away; or

(B) give them access to it,

within such period as the order may specify;

(ii) shall, in relation to that material, render to the Commissioner or an investigating officer in the exercise of the powers of the Commissioner or an investigating officer or the discharge of the duties of the Commissioner or an investigating officer under this Ordinance such assistance as the Commissioner or an investigating officer, as the case may be, may reasonably require.

(3) The period to be specified in an order under subsection (2) shall be 7 days unless it appears to the Court of First Instance that a longer or shorter period would be appropriate in the particular circumstances of the application.

(4) Where an order is made under subsection (2) the Commissioner of Inland Revenue or any officer of the Inland Revenue Department shall, notwithstanding the provisions of any other law to the contrary including the provisions of section 4 of the Inland Revenue Ordinance (Cap 112) and sections 13 and 14 of this Ordinance, comply with the terms of that order within such period as the order may specify.

(5) For the purposes of the prosecution of an offence under this Ordinance where an order is made under subsection (2), the giving of evidence by the Commissioner of Inland Revenue or any officer of the Inland Revenue Department in relation to particular material or material of a particular description with respect to which the order is made shall not be subject to any obligation as to secrecy or other restriction as to disclosure imposed by section 4 of the Inland Revenue Ordinance (Cap 112) or otherwise.

(6) Where an application under subsection (1) relates to material of a particular description, an order under subsection (2) shall only be made where an application in relation to particular material is not reasonably practicable.

(7) Where material to which an application under this section relates consists of information recorded otherwise than in legible form—

    (a)   an order under subsection (2)(i)(A) shall have effect as an order to produce the material in a form in which it can be taken away; and

    (b)   an order under subsection (2)(i)(B) shall have effect as an order to give access to the material in a form in which it is visible and legible.

(8) Where an order made under subsection (2)(i) relates to information recorded otherwise than in legible form, the Commissioner or an investigating officer may by notice in writing require the Commissioner of Inland Revenue or an officer of the Inland Revenue Department to produce the material in a form in which it is visible and legible and can be taken away.

(9) The Commissioner or an investigating officer may by notice in writing—

    (a)   extend the period specified in an order under subsection (2) (and any such extension
shall be deemed to be an order made by the Court of First Instance under that subsection);

    (b)   release the Commissioner of Inland Revenue or an officer of the Inland Revenue Department from any obligation under an order of the description mentioned in subsection (8) to produce material in the form in which it was recorded.

(10) The Commissioner or an investigating officer may photograph or make copies of any material produced under this section."

Section 13B allows the disclosure of information obtained from the Commissioner of Inland Revenue under s.13A to the Secretary for Justice for the purpose of any proceedings under the Ordinance but may not ortherwise be disclosed.

Section 13C restricts the disclosure of information obtained from the Commissioner of Inland Revenue relating to a named person where the Secretary for Justice has decided to institute proceedings for an offence under the Ordinance but not against that person.

The power to obtain information is also contained in s.14 of the POBO. That **6–14** provision allows the Commissioner to apply to a court for an order requiring the person named to provide to the ICAC information by statutory declaration or statement in writing.

In the case of a suspect the information may relate to all property acquired or disposed of in the previous three years, all expenditure incurred in living expenses and private expenditure in the previous three years, all liabilities incurred in the previous three years and all money or other property sent out of Hong Kong in any specified period.

In the case of any other person the Commissioner may require the enumeration of property in specified categories and the particulars of when and from whom the property was acquired.

Any person other than the suspect may also be required to appear before an officer to answer on oath or affirmation any question relevant to the investigation and to produce any document under his control.

The person in charge of any public body is placed under a similar duty to **6–15** provide any requested document. The manager of any bank can be required to produce copies of the bank accounts of any person, his spouse, parents or children named in the notice of request.

Failure to comply with the notice is an offence, as is the making of a false statement.

Section 14 provides:

"(1A) The Commissioner or an investigating officer may, for the purpose of an investigation into, or proceedings relating to, an offence suspected to have been committed by any person under this Ordinance, make an ex parte application to the Court of First Instance in chambers for an order under subsection (1).

(1B) The Court of First Instance shall not make an order under subsection (1) unless on an ex parte application made to it under subsection (1A) it is satisfied that there are reasonable grounds for suspecting that—

(a) in the case of an application relating to subsection (1)(c), that the information to be required from the person being the subject of the application is likely to be relevant to the investigation or the proceedings;

(b) in the case of an application relating to subsection (1)(d) or (e), that the person being the subject of the application has or may reasonably have access to information likely to be relevant to the investigation or the proceedings.

(1) Where on an application under subsection (1A) the Court of First Instance is satisfied that there are reasonable grounds for suspecting that an offence under this Ordinance has been committed it may make an order authorizing the Commissioner by a notice in writing to require—

(a) such person to furnish to the investigating officer specified in such notice a statutory declaration or, as the Commissioner sees fit, a statement in writing, enumerating—

(i) the property, being property in such categories or classes of property, movable or immovable, as may be specified in such notice, belonging to or possessed by, or which at any time during the 3 years immediately preceding the date of such notice or during such shorter period as may be specified in such notice belonged to or was possessed by, such person, his agents or trustees, specifying in respect of each property enumerated whether it is or was possessed jointly (and, if so, with whom) or severally; and specifying the date upon which, and the person from whom, each such property was acquired and whether by purchase, gift, bequest, inheritance or otherwise, and, where it was acquired by purchase, specifying the consideration paid therefor; and in respect of any property enumerated which has been disposed of, whether by sale, gift or otherwise, at any time during the 3 years immediately preceding the date of the notice or such shorter period as aforesaid, specifying how and to whom the same was disposed of and, where it was disposed of by sale, specifying the consideration given therefor;

(ii) all expenditure incurred by such person in respect of himself, his spouse, parents or children with regard to living expenses and other private expenditure during any period specified in such notice (not, however, being a period commencing earlier than 3 years from the date of the notice);

(iii) all liabilities incurred by such person, his agents or trustees, at such time or during such period as may be specified in such notice (not, however, being a time or a period commencing earlier than 3 years from the date of the notice), and specifying in respect of each such liability whether it was incurred jointly (and, if so, with whom) or severally;

(b) such person to furnish to the investigating officer specified in such notice a statutory declaration or, as the Commissioner sees fit, a statement in writing of any money or other property sent out of Hong Kong by him or on his behalf during such period as may be specified in the notice;

(c) any other person to furnish to the investigating officer specified in such notice a statutory declaration or, as the Commissioner sees fit, a statement in writing enumerating the property, being property in such categories or classes of property, movable or immovable, as may be specified in such notice, belonging to or possessed by him and further stating, in respect of each such property, the date upon which and the person from whom it was acquired, if the Commissioner believes that such information may assist the investigation or proceedings;

(d) any other person whom the Commissioner believes to be acquainted with any facts relevant to such investigation or proceedings to furnish to the investigating officer specified in such notice all information in his possession or to which he may reasonably have access (not being information readily available to the public) respecting such matters as are specified in the notice or, as the Commissioner sees fit, to appear before the investigating officer specified in such notice or such other person specified in the notice and to answer orally on oath or affirmation any questions relevant thereto; and, on demand by the investigating officer specified in such notice or such other person, to produce or deliver or otherwise furnish to him the original or a copy of any document in his possession or under his control or to which he may reasonably have access (not being a document readily available to the public) which, in the opinion of the investigating officer specified in such notice or such other person, may be relevant to such investigation or proceedings; for the purposes of this paragraph the investigating officer specified in such notice or such other person shall have authority to administer any oath or take any affirmation;

(e)   the person in charge of any public body or any department, office or establishment of any public body to produce or furnish to the investigating officer specified in such notice any document or a copy, certified by the person in charge, of any document which is in his possession or under his control or to which he may reasonably have access (not being a document readily available to the public);

(f)   the manager of any bank to give to the investigating officer specified in such notice copies of the accounts of such person or of his spouse, parents or children at the bank as shall be named in the notice.

(2) Without prejudice to the generality thereof, the powers conferred by subsection (1)(d) include the power to require information from, and to require the attendance for the purpose of answering questions of—

(a)   any person, or any employee of any person, who has acted for or is acting for any party to any particular land or property transaction; and

(b)   any person, or any employee of any person, who was concerned in the passing of any consideration, brokerage, commission or fee, or in the clearing or collection of any cheque or other instrument of exchange, respecting any particular land or property transaction, as to any of the following matters, that is to say—

(i)   the full names (including aliases) and addresses of any of the persons referred to in paragraphs (a) and (b) and any other information in his possession which may be helpful in identifying or locating any such person;

(ii)   any consideration, brokerage, commission or fee paid or received in respect of or in connection with any such land or property transaction; and

(iii)   the terms and conditions of any such land or property transaction.

(3) A notice under subsection (1) shall be served on the person to whom it is addressed either personally or by registered post addressed to his last known place of business or residence.

(4) Every person on whom a notice under subsection (1) is served shall, notwithstanding the provisions of other Ordinance or rule of law to the contrary save only the provisions of section 4 of the Inland Revenue Ordinance (Cap 112), comply with the terms of that notice within such time as may be specified therein or within such further time as the Commissioner may, in his discretion, authorize, and any person on whom such a notice has been served, who, without reasonable excuse, neglects or fails so to comply shall be guilty of an offence and shall be liable on conviction to a fine of $20000 and to imprisonment for 1 year.

(5) A person who wilfully makes any false statement in answer to a notice under subsection (1) shall be guilty of an offence and shall be liable to a fine of $20000 and to imprisonment for 1 year."

E. INTERCEPTION OF COMMUNICATIONS AND SURVEILLANCE

6–16   Until 2006 interception of communications and surveillance was controlled by executive authorisations given by the Governor in accordance with the Telecommunications Ordinance in the case of interceptions or, as regards surveillance undertaken by the ICAC, by the Commissioner. From 2006 these matters have been regulated by statute. The long title of the Interception of Communications and Surveillance Ordinance (Cap. 589) states its purpose: "to regulate the conduct of interception of communications and the use of surveillance devices by or on behalf of public officers and to provide for related matters." In essence the Ordinance subjects the interception of communications and the more intrusive forms of surveillance to judicial control.

F. PROCEDURAL AND EVIDENTIAL PROVISIONS ENHANCED TO IMPROVE PROSPECTS OF SUCCESSFUL PROSECUTION

6–17   Section 20 of the POBO regulates the evidentiary use that may be made of a statement made under s.14 by an accused who tenders himself as a witness in the proceedings against him for an offence under the Ordinance. Section 20 also allows any failure by the accused to comply with a s.14 notice to be adduced in evidence and to be commented on by the court and the prosecution.

Section 20 reads:

> "In any proceedings against a person for an offence under this Ordinance—
>
> (a)   if such person tenders himself as a witness then any statutory declaration or statement in writing furnished by him in compliance or purported compliance with the terms of a notice served on him under section 14 shall be regarded as a former statement made by him relative to the subject-matter of the proceedings and sections 13 and 14 of the Evidence Ordinance (Cap 8) shall apply with respect to that witness;
>
> (b)   the fact of the person's failure in any respect to comply with the terms of a notice served on him under section 14 may be adduced in evidence and made the subject of comment by the court and the prosecution."

The provisions of the Evidence Ordinance referred to in s.20 regulate the procedure for cross-examining a witness on a statement made by him on a previous occasion.

The prosecution is also assisted by s.21(1) of the POBO. The assistance is given only if the prosecution first proves either that the accused is in possession, for which he cannot satisfactorily account, of property disproportionate to his known sources of income or that at or after the date of the offence he acquired an increase in his property for which he cannot satisfactorily explain. Upon proof of either of those matters the court may make use of it in two ways: first, as corroboration of testimony that the defendant solicited or accepted an advantage, and second, that the advantage was solicited or accepted as an inducement or reward.

Section 21(2) provides further assistance by allowing a court to presume that **6–18** property held by another is actually in the possession of the defendant or was a gift from him, having regard to the closeness of the relationship between the two or to any other circumstances.

Section 21 provides:

"(1) In any proceedings against a person for an offence under Part II (other than section 10), the fact that the accused was, at or about the date of or at any time since the date of the alleged offence, or is in possession, for which he cannot satisfactorily account, of pecuniary resources or property disproportionate to his known sources of income, or that he had, at or about the date of or at any time since the date of the alleged offence, obtained an accretion to his pecuniary resources or property for which he cannot satisfactorily account, may be proved and may be taken by the court—

(a) as corroborating the testimony of any witness giving evidence in such proceedings that the accused accepted or solicited any advantage; and

(b) as showing that such advantage was accepted or solicited as an inducement or reward.

(2) For the purposes of subsection (1) a person accused of an offence under Part II (other than section 10) shall be presumed to be or to have been in possession of pecuniary resources or property, or to have obtained an accretion thereto, where such resources or property are or were held, or such accretion was obtained, by any other person whom, having regard to his relationship to the accused or to any other circumstances, there is reason to believe is or was holding such resources or property or obtained such accretion in trust for or otherwise on behalf of the accused or as a gift from the accused."

Section 21A allows a public servant's official emoluments (and related matters as to his status and position as a public servant) to be proved by certificate. The section provides:

"(1) In any proceedings against a person for an offence under this Ordinance, a certificate purporting—

(a) to certify—

(i) the rate of, and the total amount of, official emoluments and the allowances, other than such emoluments, paid to any prescribed officer in relation to the discharge by him of his duties as a prescribed officer;

(ii) that any person was or was not serving at any specified time or during any specified period as a prescribed officer or ceased to be a prescribed officer at or before any specified time; or

(iii) that a prescribed officer held or did not hold at any specified time any specified office; and

(b) to be signed by the Chief Secretary for Administration,

shall be admitted in such proceedings by any court on its production without further proof.

(2) On the production of a certificate under subsection (1) the court before which it is produced shall, until the contrary is proved, presume—

(a)   that the facts stated therein are true; and

(b)   that the certificate was signed by the Chief Secretary for Administration.

(3) In this section, 'official emoluments' includes a pension or gratuity payable under the Pensions Ordinance (Cap 89), the Pension Benefits Ordinance (Cap 99) or the Pension Benefits (Judicial Officers) Ordinance (Cap 401)."

The law regarding the testimony of an accomplice having to be corroborated is modified by s.22 of the POBO by stating that a witness is not to be regarded as an accomplice only because he gave or received a bribe.

6–19   Section 22 provides:

"Notwithstanding any Ordinance, rule of law or practice to the contrary, no witness shall, in any proceedings for an offence under Part II, be regarded as an accomplice by reason only of any payment or delivery by him or on his behalf of any advantage to the person accused or, as the case may be, by reason only of any payment or delivery of any advantage by or on behalf of the person accused to him."

Conspiracy to commit a substantive offence became an offence separate and distinct from the substantive offence when the offence of conspiracy was codified by s.159A of the Crimes Ordinance (Cap 200). In consequence it became necessary to ensure that the investigative powers and the evidentiary and sentencing provisions contained in the POBO applied to the offence of conspiracy to commit an offence under the POBO.

Section 12A provides:

"(1) Any person convicted of conspiracy to commit an offence under this Part shall be dealt with and punished in like manner as if convicted of such offence and any rules of evidence which apply with respect to the proof of any such offence shall apply in like manner to the proof of conspiracy to commit such offence.

(2) The powers of investigation conferred by Part III of this Ordinance shall apply with respect to a conspiracy to commit an offence under this Ordinance in like manner as they apply to the investigation of any such offence."

Given the secret and complicitous nature of bribery, usually the only witnesses to the corrupt transaction are the parties themselves. It is therefore often necessary for the prosecutor to rely on the evidence of one of the parties. He is unlikely to testify unless given immunity from prosecution. Section 23 of the POBO recognises that reality and allows a court to inform a person involved in the offence that he will not be prosecuted if he gives "full and true evidence".

6–20   Section 23 provides:

"In or for the purpose of any proceedings for an offence under Part II, the court may, at the request in writing of the Secretary for Justice, inform any person accused or suspected of such offence or of any other offence under Part II that, if he gives full and true evidence in such proceedings and, where such proceedings are proceedings held with a view to committal for trial under section 85 of the Magistrates Ordinance (Cap 227), in the trial before the High Court of all things as to which he is lawfully examined, he will not be prosecuted for any offence disclosed by his evidence; and upon such person giving evidence in any such proceedings no prosecution against him for any offence disclosed by his evidence therein shall be instituted or carried on unless the court before which he gives evidence considers that he has wilfully withheld evidence or given false testimony and so certifies to the Secretary for Justice in writing."

A further provision assists the prosecution of corruption offences under the POBO. The legal burden, as opposed to merely the evidential burden, of proving the defence that the suspect act was done with lawful authority or reasonable excuse is placed squarely on the defendant.

Section 24 provides:

"In any proceedings against a person for an offence under this Ordinance, the burden of proving a defence of lawful authority or reasonable excuse shall lie upon the accused."

The prosecution of corruption offences receives valuable assistance where the evidence develops in unexpected directions during the course of the trial. First, the defendant may be convicted of some other offence under the POBO revealed by the evidence. Secondly, the court may allow an amendment to the particulars of the charge where the evidence is at variance with the original particulars.

Section 32 provides: 6–21

"(1) If, on the trial of any person for any offence under Part II, it is not proved that the accused is guilty of the offence charged but it is proved that the accused is guilty of some other offence under Part II, the accused may, notwithstanding the absence of consent under section 31 in respect of such other offence, be convicted of such other offence, and be liable to be dealt with accordingly.

(2) If on the trial of any person for any offence under Part II there is any material variance between the particulars of the offence charged and the evidence adduced in support thereof, such variance shall not, of itself, entitle the accused to an acquittal of the offence charged if, in the opinion of the court, there is prima facie evidence of the commission of that offence, and in such a case the court may, notwithstanding the absence of consent under section 31 in respect of the particulars supported by the evidence adduced, make the necessary amendment to the particulars, and shall thereupon read and explain the same to the accused and the parties shall be allowed to recall and examine on matters relevant to such amendment any witness who may have been examined and, subject to the provisions of subsection (3), to call any further witness.

(3) If an amendment is made under subsection (2) after the case for the prosecution is closed no further witness may be called by the prosecution other than such and on such matters only as it would, apart from the provisions of this subsection, be permissible to call and put in evidence in rebuttal.

(4) Nothing in this section shall exclude the application of any other law whereby a person may be found guilty of an offence other than that with which he is charged."

G. PROTECTION OF INFORMANTS AND WITNESSES ENHANCED

6-22   The identity of informants was given legal protection from disclosure by a provision introduced in 1980. First, no information for an offence under the POBO can be admitted in evidence in any civil or criminal proceedings. Secondly, where an informant or a person who has assisted the Commissioner in respect of an offence under the Ordinance is not to be called as a witness, no witness can be obliged to disclose the name or address of the informant or to answer any question that might lead to his identification. Furthermore, the court is required to cause any document that is to be put in evidence or liable to inspection and that could identify the informant to be edited so far as necessary to prevent the discovery of the informant's identity or address.

Section 30A provides:

"(1) Save as provided in subsection (2)—

(a)   no information for an offence under this Ordinance shall be admitted in evidence in any civil or criminal proceeding; and

(b)   no witness in any civil or criminal proceeding shall be obliged—

(i)   to disclose the name or address of any informer who has given information to the Commissioner with respect to an offence under this Ordinance or of any person who has assisted the Commissioner in any way with respect to such an offence; or

(ii)   to answer any question if the answer thereto would lead, or would tend to lead, to discovery of the name or address of such informer or person,

if, in either case, such informer or person is not himself a witness in such proceeding,

and, if any books, documents or papers which are in evidence or liable to inspection in any civil or criminal proceeding contain an entry in which any such informer or person is named or described or which might lead to his discovery, the court shall cause all such passages to be concealed from view or to be obliterated so far as may be necessary to protect the informer or such person from discovery.

(2) If in any proceeding before a court for an offence under this Ordinance the court, after full inquiry into the case, is satisfied that an informer wilfully made a material statement which he knew or believed to be false or did not believe to be true, or if in any other proceeding a court is of opinion that justice cannot be fully done between the parties thereto without disclosure of the name of an informer or a person who has assisted the Commissioner, the court may permit inquiry and require full disclosure concerning the informer or such person."

The law provides another form of protection for the person who provides information to the ICAC. Section 30 of the POBO is usually regarded as protecting the integrity of an investigation and the reputation of a suspect. It does so by making it an offence to disclose the identity of a suspect or the fact that an investigation is underway or any detail of that investigation. An often overlooked aspect of the prohibition is that it also protects the source of the information and the identity of the informant.

Section 30 provides: 6–23

"(1) Any person who knowing or suspecting that an investigation in respect of an offence alleged or suspected to have been committed under Part II is taking place, without lawful authority or reasonable excuse, discloses to—

(a)   the person who is the subject of the investigation (the "subject person") the fact that he is so subject or any details of such investigation; or

(b)   the public, a section of the public or any particular person the identity of the subject person or the fact that the subject person is so subject or any details of such investigation,

shall be guilty of an offence and shall be liable on conviction to a fine of $20000 and to imprisonment for 1 year.

(2) Subsection (1) shall not apply as regards disclosure of any of the descriptions mentioned in that subsection where, in connection with such investigation—

(a)   a warrant has been issued for the arrest of the subject person;
(b)   the subject person has been arrested whether with or without warrant;
(c)   the subject person has been required to furnish a statutory declaration or a statement in writing by a notice served on him under section 14(1)(a) or (b);
(d)   a restraining order has been served on any person under section 14C(3);
(e)   the residence of the subject person has been searched under a warrant issued under section 17; or
(f)   the subject person has been required to surrender to the Commissioner any travel document in his possession by a notice served on him under section 17A.

(3) Without affecting the generality of the expression 'reasonable excuse' in subsection (1) a person has a reasonable excuse as regards disclosure of any of the descriptions mentioned in that subsection if, but only to the extent that, the disclosure reveals—

(a)   any unlawful activity, abuse of power, serious neglect of duty, or other serious misconduct by the Commissioner, the Deputy Commissioner or any officer of the Commission; or

(b)   a serious threat to public order or to the security of Hong Kong or to the health or safety of the public."

The section is resented by the media who call it "the press gag law" and its validity has been challenged on the ground of incompatibility with the Bill of Rights Ordinance referred to earlier, particularly art.16 which ensures the right to freedom of expression. The Court of Appeal held that "section 30(1), in its full amplitude, is necessary both for the respect of the rights and reputations of others and for the protection of public order."[6]

It is clear from s.30(2) that the prohibition on disclosure is limited in time. It ceases to apply when a public act occurs, for example the arrest of the suspect or where he has been required to surrender his travel documents. Furthermore the subsection specifically adds to the meaning of "reasonable excuse" the disclosure of wrongdoing by the ICAC itself or of serious threat to public order, security, health or safety.

As regards time limits for the prosecution of offences, it should be noted that   6–24

---

[6] *R. v Ming Pao Newspapers Ltd* [1995] 5 HKPLR 13 at 21.

limits of one year and two years apply for the lesser offences contained in the POBO, but no time limit applies for the more serious offences of bribery and possession of unexplained property.

Section 31A provides:

"(1) Notwithstanding section 26 of the Magistrates Ordinance (Cap 227), a complaint may be made or an information laid in respect of an offence under section 3, 14(5), 14A(5), 14C(6) or 33A within 2 years from the time when the matter of such complaint or information respectively arose.

(2) Notwithstanding section 26 of the Magistrates Ordinance (Cap 227), a complaint may be made or an information laid in respect of an offence under section 13(3), 13(4), 29 or 30(1) within 1 year from the time when the matter of such complaint or information respectively arose.

(3) *[this subsection preserves the time limit that applied to offences committed before 1980]*"

The consent of the Secretary for Justice is required for every prosecution for an offence under Pt II of the POBO. The absence of consent does not, however, prevent the arrest or detention of a suspect nor his release on bail. He can also be brought before a court for the charge to be put to him but cannot be called on to plead if the consent has not yet been given.

6–25   Section 31 provides:

"(1) No prosecution for an offence under Part II shall be instituted except with the consent of the Secretary for Justice.

(2) Notwithstanding subsection (1) of this section a person may be charged with an offence under Part II and may be arrested therefor, or a warrant for his arrest may be issued and executed, and any such person may be remanded in custody or on bail notwithstanding that the consent of the Secretary for Justice to the institution of a prosecution for the offence has not been obtained, but no such person shall be remanded in custody or on bail for longer than 3 days on such charge unless in the meantime the consent of the Secretary for Justice aforesaid has been obtained.

(3) When a person is brought before a magistrate before the Secretary for Justice has consented to the prosecution, the charge shall be explained to the person accused but he shall not be called upon to plead and the provision of the law for the time being in force relating to criminal procedure shall be modified accordingly.

(4) Neither section 7 of the Legal Officers Ordinance (Cap 87) nor section 43 of the Interpretation and General Clauses Ordinance (Cap 1) shall apply to or in respect of the giving by the Secretary for Justice of his consent to the institution of a prosecution for an offence against section 10."

H. POWERS OF SENTENCING AND CONFISCATION AND CONSEQUENCES OF CONVICTION

On conviction for an offence under the POBO, the sentencing options available to   **6–26**
the court and the consequences of conviction are contained in ss.12, 33 and 33A of
the POBO.

The offences of possession of unexplained property under s.10, bribery for
giving assistance in regard to contracts under s.5 and bribery for procuring
withdrawal of tenders under s.6 attract maximum sentences of 10 years imprisonment and a fine of HKD 1 million (HKD 500,000 in the case of ss.5 and 6). In
the case of a conviction under s.10 for possessing excessive wealth, the defendant
may, in addition to any fine and imprisonment, be ordered to pay to the government a sum up to the value of the excess.

The other bribery offences, including the more usual bribery involving a public
servant under s.4 and bribery in the private sector under s.9 attract a maximum of
seven years' imprisonment and a fine of HKD 500,000.

On conviction of any of the bribery offences (ss.4–9 of the POBO) the   **6–27**
defendant may in addition be ordered to pay to any person or public body the
amount or value of any advantage he received.

The offence committed by a public servant of soliciting or accepting an
advantage is punishable by a maximum of one year's imprisonment and a fine of
HKD 100,000 and must be ordered by the court to pay to the government the
whole or any part of the value of the advantage.

Section 12 of the POBO provides:

"(1) Any person guilty of an offence under this Part, other than an offence under section
3, shall be liable—

(a)   on conviction on indictment—

    (i)   for an offence under section 10, to a fine of $1000000 and to imprisonment
for10 years;

    (ii)   for an offence under section 5 or 6, to a fine of $500000 and to impri-
sonment for 10 years; and

    (iii)   for any other offence under this Part, to a fine of $500000 and to
imprisonment for 7 years; and

(b)   on summary conviction—

    (i)   for an offence under section 10, to a fine of $500000 and to imprisonment
for 3 years; and

    (ii)   for any other offence under this Part, to a fine of $100000 and to
imprisonment for 3 years,

and shall be ordered to pay to such person or public body and in such manner as the
court directs, the amount or value of any advantage received by him, or such part
thereof as the court may specify.

(2) Any person guilty of an offence under section 3 shall be liable on conviction to a fine
of $100000 and to imprisonment for 1 year, and shall be ordered to pay to the Gov-

ernment in such manner as the court directs the amount or value of the advantage received by him or such part thereof as the court may specify.

(3) In addition to any penalty imposed under subsection (1), the court may order a person convicted of an offence under section 10(1)(b) to pay to the Government

(a)   a sum not exceeding the amount of the pecuniary resources; or
(b)   a sum not exceeding the value of the property, the acquisition of which by him was not explained to the satisfaction of the court.

(4) An order under subsection (3) may be enforced in the same manner as a judgment of the High Court in its civil jurisdiction.

(5) An order may be made under subsection (3) in respect of an offence under section 10(1)(b) where the facts that gave rise to that offence arose before 15 February 1974."

A comprehensive confiscation regime of the proceeds of offences under the POBO is provided by ss.12AA, 12AB and 12AC of the POBO, s.102 of the Criminal Procedure Ordinance (Cap 221) and the Organized and Serious Crimes Ordinance (Cap 455). This regime includes the power of a court to dispose of property that is in the possession of the authorities in connection with any offence, whether or not a conviction has resulted and whether or not the offence was committed or appears to have been committed in Hong Kong.

6–28   The consequence of a conviction for an offence under Pt II of the POBO is disqualification for a period of five years from the date of conviction from being elected to the Legislative Council or from being or being elected or appointed to the Executive Council and certain other public bodies.

Section 33 of the POBO provides:

"Any person convicted of an offence under Part II of this Ordinance shall, by reason of such conviction, be disqualified for a period of 5 years from the date of such conviction from—

(a)   being elected as a Member of the Legislative Council; or
(b)   being or being elected or appointed as a member of the Executive Council and any other public body, other than a public body specified in Schedule 1."

In connection with employment the court has power to prohibit a person convicted of an offence under Pt II of the POBO from taking or continuing employment in a directing or managerial role in a corporation or public body, in his profession or as a partner in a firm for a period of up to seven years.

Section 33A of the POBO reads:

"(1) Where a person has been convicted of an offence under Part II, a court may, on the application of the prosecution or on its own motion, where it considers it to be in the public interest so to do, order that the convicted person be prohibited from taking or continuing employment, whether temporary or permanent and whether paid or unpaid—

(a)   in the case where the convicted person was employed by a corporation or a public body at the time of or prior to his conviction, as a director or manager or in such other capacity concerned with, whether directly or indirectly, the

184

management of that corporation or any public body or any corporation that is a subsidiary of that corporation or any public body within the meaning of section 2 of the Companies Ordinance (Cap 32); or

(b) in the case where the convicted person was practising any profession or was otherwise self-employed at the time of or prior to his conviction, in the practice of his profession or in the business, or class of business, in which he was so employed, as the case may be;

(c) in other cases, as a partner or as a manager of or in such other capacity concerned with, whether directly or indirectly, the management of such partnership, firm or person or such class of partnership, firm or person; and

(d) for such period not exceeding 7 years, as the court may determine.

(2) A person in respect of whom an order under subsection (1) has been made may at any time during the continuance in force of the order apply to the court for the order to be varied or cancelled.

(3) On an application under subsection (2) the court shall consider all the circumstances including any changes in the applicant's circumstances since the making of the order and whether it would be in the public interest for the order to be varied or cancelled.

(4) Not less than 7 days before the hearing of an application under subsection (2) the person applying shall give written notice to the Secretary for Justice of his intentions and on any hearing of an application the Secretary for Justice shall have the right to appear and be heard.

(5) Any person in respect of whom an order under subsection (1) has been made who contravenes the order commits an offence and is liable to a fine of $50000 and to imprisonment for 12 months."

I. ENFORCEMENT IN PRACTICE

One of the elements of the strategy mentioned earlier was educating the public **6–29** and enlisting its support. That element has two objectives: one is the long-term aim of changing people's personal attitude to corruption; the other more immediate aim was, and is, to persuade people to come forward with information. The nature of a corrupt bargain is such that information from one of the parties is unlikely. To uncover this secret and complicitous crime investigators must receive information from third parties who know or suspect what is going on.

However Hong Kong people, like people everywhere, were reluctant to go to the authorities to report corruption. Everything possible was and is done to overcome that reluctance and assuage people's fears.

First, the ICAC makes sure it is itself readily accessible. At any time of the day or night every day of the year anyone can speak to an officer by telephone and have his report recorded. He can walk into the ICAC's main office at any time and see an officer or into any of the ICAC's eight regional offices during office hours. He will be seen promptly and discreetly. He can provide his information by letter or email. He does not have to identify himself or make any written or oral statement, nor is his signature required.

Secondly, everything is done to protect the identity of the informant and the **6–30** confidentiality of his information. At the outset he is assured that what he has to say is confidential. The law prohibiting the disclosure of any detail of an investigation (s.30 of the Prevention of Bribery Ordinance) applies equally to officers of the ICAC. Within the ICAC the law is reinforced by a requirement of confidentiality in the disciplinary code of conduct; the "need to know" principle is strictly observed.

The information from an anonymous informant is treated no differently from any other. However informants are encouraged to identify themselves because the prospects of a successful investigation are higher when the identity of the informant is known.

Where an informant is not himself a witness in any civil or criminal proceedings, protection is further afforded by the provision in the law (s.30A of the POBO) that prohibits the admission in evidence of any information that was provided to the ICAC about the commission of a corruption offence or the identity of the informant.

6–31   Thirdly, everyone, whether witness or informant, is protected in his person by the law. The general criminal law makes it an offence to threaten with violence or otherwise intimidate a witness in any legal proceedings.

Fourthly, witnesses can be further protected in witness protection programmes. These programmes are now regulated by the Witness Protection Ordinance (Cap. 564).

Fifthly, action on reports received by the ICAC is taken quickly, at most within 48 hours if the report comes in on a Saturday, normally within 24 hours. As will be seen below, if the information is capable of being investigated, the report is assigned to an investigating officer within the periods just mentioned. The sooner investigative action is taken and the quicker the matter is disposed of, the less time the informant or witness is kept in suspense.

6–32   The ICAC makes a point of keeping the complainant informed of the progress of his report. If it is operationally possible to do so without risking the integrity of the investigation, he is told that the matter is being investigated. In a lengthy investigation he is periodically informed of progress. In due course he is informed of the outcome.

The ICAC's public relations information unit keeps the public informed on all these aspects of the way the Commission operates. In particular the public is constantly told that no report is too trivial, that people have nothing to fear in reporting if they have a genuine belief in their suspicion and that, provided they believe their report is true, their motive for reporting is irrelevant.

In order that the public can see that their reporting of corruption results in effective action being taken, the ICAC ensures that court proceedings of their cases are regularly carried by the news media and that the statistics of investigations and prosecutions are fully set out in the Commissioner's annual report.

6–33   A fundamental aspect of the enforcement element of the anticorruption strategy is the ICAC's investigating policy. From the outset the policy has been, and continues to be, that the ICAC will investigate with a view to prosecution every report of corruption it receives if the report is capable of being investigated. The reasons for adopting this policy are these:

- What appears to be a minor matter quite often unravels into a much more serious case.

- For the citizen who has brought himself to make a complaint, the matter will be important. If it is dismissed as unimportant, he is unlikely ever to return to the authorities, perhaps with a crucial piece of information. If community support is to be won, the minor complaint must be taken seriously.

- Picking and choosing which reports to investigate and which to ignore gives rise to suspicion of improper influence having affected the decision or, worse, of corruption in the investigating unit.

- Ignoring some complaints gives the impression that some corruption is tolerated, that double standards apply.

- The fact is that widespread small scale corruption can do serious damage to the well-being of a community. Furthermore, a single small act of corruption can have catastrophic consequences.

If a report of a non-corruption offence nevertheless raises the suspicion that bribery has facilitated that offence, the report is accepted and investigated in order to uncover the underlying corruption. If, as often is the case, there is insufficient evidence for a prosecution but the investigation has revealed evidence of a possible breach of discipline, the matter is referred to the suspect's disciplinary authority for that authority to consider taking disciplinary action.

Two related consequences followed from the investigation policy adopted in Hong Kong. The first was that an investigation was never initiated from the anticorruption body's own intelligence sources. The second was that the anticorruption body showed itself to be responsive to the public's wishes—it reacted by investigating what the public complained about; it did not barge into what the public was not ready to complain about. In recent years, with public confidence in the ICAC being consistently strong, the Commission has occasionally undertaken investigations initiated from its internal intelligence resources.

It would be prudent for foreign entities doing business in Hong Kong to note that, whatever the USA Foreign Corrupt Practices Act and the OECD's Convention on Combating Bribery of Foreign Public Officials in International Business Transactions may say about exempting facilitating payments from the ambit of those instruments, Hong Kong's policy is clear. Any attempted bribery of a Hong Kong official, whether done in Hong Kong or abroad, will be an offence in Hong Kong. When it comes to the notice of the ICAC, the allegation will be investigated with a view to prosecution.

J. INVESTIGATING PROCEDURE (FROM REPORT TO DISPOSAL)

6–34 The process by which reports of corruption are dealt with by the ICAC is one of the reasons for the high level of public confidence in the Commission. All the reports received in a 24 hour period (48 hours at weekends) are logged and put before the senior management of the investigation department early the following morning.

Each report is considered and classified either as a corruption report falling within the ICAC's mandate or as a non-corruption report to be referred to another agency, such as the police or the social welfare department. Corruption reports are further classified into those capable of investigation and those that are not pursuable. Pursuable reports are immediately assigned to an investigating team which investigates the matter with a view to prosecution.

The role of the investigation department is to investigate. It does not prosecute; that function is the responsibility of the Director of Public Prosecutions. It is he who decides whether or not the matter is to be prosecuted.

6–35 When the management of the investigation department decides that the investigation has resulted in sufficient evidence, the matter is sent for consideration of prosecution by a public prosecutor of the Director of Public Prosecutions Office. If the investigation department's management considers that the evidence is insufficient, it will recommend to the Commissioner that the investigation proceed no further.

The great majority of investigations do not result in prosecution, either because the reported suspicion is unfounded or the evidence is insufficient or the legal advice from the public prosecutor precludes prosecution. The community needs to be reassured, nevertheless, that the reports it made to the ICAC have been properly investigated and that the investigations can properly be closed. Since these investigations cannot be opened to public scrutiny, a method of reassuring the community was devised that has proved successful for over 30 years.

A committee of trustworthy citizens is given the role of looking at investigations that investigators propose should be closed and of advising whether or not the investigation should be closed. These citizens meet about once a month for half a day and consider the cases that are to be closed. They can question the investigating officers. If they agree with the proposed closure, they advise accordingly. If they do not, they can advise that further investigation should be done or that the legal advice should be reconsidered. Their work is, of course, confidential.

6–36 In that way the community is reassured that ordinary citizens, acting in the public interest and on behalf of the public, have satisfied themselves that investigations have been thoroughly done and can properly be closed. If that committee is satisfied, so can the public.

Where the consent of the Secretary for Justice for prosecution has been obtained, the matter will be taken before, and dealt with in, the criminal court in accordance with the procedures applicable to all other forms of criminality.

K. RELATIONS WITH OTHER AGENCIES AND THE PRIVATE SECTOR

The ICAC's relations with other agencies of the administration affect the effec-   6–37
tiveness of the fight against corruption. The relationships are as important in the
prevention and education aspects of its work as in the enforcement arm.

As regards enforcement, operational liaison with the police is a matter of daily
routine. Investigations of criminality where the corruption aspects fall away leave
the related fraud or trafficking or other criminality still to be pursued. On a case
by case basis the decision of whether the investigation should be taken over by the
police or remain with the ICAC is jointly taken by ICAC and police management.
Search and arrest operations where the ICAC anticipate the need for security
protection is as often as not provided by the police.

As regards prevention and education, the willingness and active cooperation of
the police in the examination of police systems and procedures and in providing
time for officers to be made aware of corruption problems in their official duties
have been an essential ingredient in the transformation of the police service. The
same observation is as true of the other disciplined services as of the public service
in general.

In the business sector the change from hostility to active support was men-   6–38
tioned earlier. That active support continues, and is exemplified by the participation of business men and women in the ICAC's advisory committees and by the
Business Ethics Resource Centre managed by a board of business people and
serviced by ICAC personnel.

The ICAC has played a prominent role in the development of the international
anticorruption knowledge-sharing and networking institutions, such as the
International Anti-Corruption Conference. It continues to participate in these
activities and regularly hosts expert gatherings in Hong Kong.

L. INVESTIGATIVE COOPERATION AND MUTUAL LEGAL ASSISTANCE

Over the years the ICAC has developed an extensive network of operational   6–39
cooperative arrangements with investigative agencies abroad. Given Hong Kong's
constitutional position as a special administrative region of China, these
arrangements were based on knowledge and trust rather than on formal treaty
obligations. As fugitives from Hong Kong have discovered, these arrangements
have proved effective.

The UN Convention Against Corruption now applies to Hong Kong as part of
China, which ratified the convention in 2006. Hong Kong created a central
authority to manage a large number of cases involving requests for mutual legal
assistance. The Mutual Legal Assistance Unit in Hong Kong's Department of
Justice manages the entire process of cooperation in criminal matters, assisting

foreign authorities in drafting MLA requests, overseeing communication between local and foreign officials, and receiving and processing foreign court orders and other MLA requests.[7]

M. RESULTS

6–40   It is generally accepted that Hong Kong has transformed itself from one of the most corrupt cities in the world to one of the world's least corrupt. On Transparency International's Corruption Perception Index for 2009 it ranked 12th out of the 180 jurisdictions measured and scored 8.2 on a 10 point scale. The community attitude has changed from one of tolerance and resignation to one that consistently demonstrates its intolerance of corruption.

Corruption reports continue to be received by the ICAC at the rate of between 3,000–3,500 a year. About 65 per cent of these reports concern private sector corruption (where both sides of the transaction involve the private sector). In 74 per cent of all reports the complainants are prepared to identify themselves, a proportion that stood at around only 30 per cent in the early years of the ICAC.

The annual public opinion survey commissioned by the ICAC shows that public support for the Commission has for the past few years run at 98-99 per cent. It seems clear that that level of public support is a key element of Hong Kong's success against corruption.

As mentioned earlier, the great majority of investigations do not result in prosecution. That has proved to be the reality of investigating corruption over many years, not only in Hong Kong but also in other jurisdictions. Of those that do go to court, about 85 per cent result in conviction.

Hong Kong is widely acknowledged to have succeeded, and to continue to succeed, in its struggle against corruption. Its three-part strategy is universally recognised and is now reflected in the UN Convention Against Corruption. The ICAC, which leads the implementation of the strategy, enjoys a level of public support that does much credit to the community itself.

---

[7] World Bank and UNODC report, *Articles of the United Nations Convention against Corruption on asset recovery: analysis of reported compliance and policy recommendations*, November 2009.

CHAPTER 7

THE CURRENT STATE OF ANTI-CORRUPTION LAW IN INDIA

A. INTRODUCTION

1. CORRUPTION IN INDIA

There has been a wave of developments in India to create a transparent,   7–01
accountable and corruption-free environment. The aforementioned have been in
the form of enactment of legislations such as the Right to Information Act 2005
and The Public Interest Disclosure (Protection of Informers Bill) 2009, presently
pending, establishment of various enforcement mechanisms notably, the Central
Vigilance Commission and the Central Bureau of Investigation and participation
in international efforts to tackle corruption. Despite the above, India ranks 84 out
of the 180 countries surveyed[1] in the recent Corruption Perception Index 2009
("CPI") published by Transparency International,[2] a global anti-graft watchdog.
This phenomenon can be attributed to several factors such as the continued
exploitation of the Indian custom of giving and receiving of gifts,[3] the nexus
between parties and those in power and the lack of deterrence in the penalty
measures.

The chapter attempts to take the reader through the evolution of anti-
corruption laws in India, the position today, the challenges faced and the potential
amendments to India's anti-corruption laws pending ratification of the UN
Convention against Corruption.

---

[1] Available at *http://www.transparency.org/policy_research/surveys_indices/cpi/2009/cpi_2009_
table* [Accessed July 15, 2010].
[2] Transparency International, is an international non-governmental organization which was set up
in 1993 and consists of more than 90 locally established national chapters and chapters information.
Available at *http://www.transparency.org/about_us* [Accessed July 15, 2010].
[3] C. Raj Kumar, *Corruption and Human Rights: Promoting Transparency in Governance and the
Fundamental Right to Corruption-Free Service in India*, 17 Colum. J. Asian L. 31 at 41.

II. LEGISLATIVE HISTORY & BACKGROUND

7–02   History traces the battle against corruption to the Rig Veda, a sacred Hindu text described as "the oldest literary monument of the Indo-European races" which discusses measures for the prevention of corruption and extortion.[4] The Indian Penal Code 1860 ("IPC"), the primary instrument for controlling crime and administering criminal justice, was the earliest piece of legislation to contain a codification of general anti-corruption laws in its earlier ss.161–165A.[5] The limited provisions under the IPC were not adequate to control the floodgates of corruption that were pervasive during the Second World War. Hence, the government set up the Special Police Establishment ("SPE") in 1941 through an executive order[6] to deal with cases of bribery and corruption within the War and Supply department of the government.[7]

In 1946, the Parliament passed the Delhi Special Police Establishment Act ("DSPE") to make provision for the constitution, superintendence and administration of a special police force in Delhi for the investigation of certain offences in the Union.[8] It is observed that this special force, now known as the Central

---

[4] Jessica Jones, *India Versus the United Nations: The Central Vigilance Commission Act Does Not Satisfy the U.N. Convention Against Corruption*, 22 Emory Int'l L. Rev. 799 at 820.

[5] The Indian Penal Code 1860 ss.161–165A have been repealed by The Prevention of Corruption Act 1988 s.31, which reads as follows:

"Omission of certain sections of Act 45 of 1860–Sections 161 to 165A (both inclusive of the Indian Penal Code, 1860 (45 of 1860) shall be omitted, and section 6 of the General Clauses Act, 1897 (10 of 1897), shall apply to such omission as if the said sections had been repealed by a Central Act."

[6] An Executive Order is an Order passed by the Government having similar force as an enactment for the smooth functioning of the Government and have efficacy as an Act of the parliament or the rules made by the President. It as further observed by the Supreme Court in *Indra Sawhney v Union of India* AIR 1993 SC 477 at [610] that an "'Executive order' is no less a law under Article 13(3) which defines law to include, among other things, order, by-laws and notifications."

See also, Article 73 of the Constitution of India which reads as follows:

"(1) Subject to the provisions of this Constitution, the executive power of the Union shall extend—

    (a) to the matters with respect to which Parliament has power to make laws; and
    (b) to the exercise of such rights, authority and jurisdiction as are exercisable by the Government of India by virtue of any treaty on agreement:
        Provided that the executive power referred to in sub-clause (a) shall not, save as expressly provided in this Constitution or in any law made by Parliament, extend in any State1[***] to matters with respect to which the Legislature of the State has also power to make laws.

(1) Until otherwise provided by Parliament, a State, and any officer or authority of a State may, notwithstanding anything in this article, continue to exercise in matters with respect to which Parliament has power to make laws for that State such executive power or functions as the State or officer or authority thereof could exercise immediately before the commencement of this Constitution."

[7] Jessica Jones, *India Versus the United Nations: The Central Vigilance Commission Act Does Not Satisfy the U.N. Convention Against Corruption*, 22 Emory Int'l L. Rev. 799 at 824. At the end of 1942, the activities of the SPE were extended to include cases of corruption in Railways. See Annual Report 2008, *Central Bureau of Investigation, CBI–An Overview*, at para.1.1.

[8] The Preamble to the DSPE reads as follows:

"An Act to make provision for the constitution of a special police force in Delhi for the investigation of certain offences in the Union territories for the superintendence and administration of the said force and for the extension to other areas of the power and jurisdiction of the members of the said force in regards to the investigation of the said offences. Whereas it is necessary to

Bureau of Investigation ("CBI"), was set up much later by the government, in 1963[9] and derives its powers to investigate from the DSPE.[10]

Along with establishing the enforcement agencies to fight corruption, efforts were made to put in place a comprehensive legislation with respect to the prevention of corruption as it was realised that the existing provisions under the IPC were not adequate to meet exigencies of the time.[11] In 1947, the Parliament enacted The Prevention of Corruption Act 1947 a social legislation defined to curb illegal activities of the public servants. It was intended that the provisions of the legislation be liberally construed to advance the object of the legislation.[12] This Act was amended twice; once by the Criminal Law Amendment Act 1952 and later in 1964 by the Anti-Corruption Laws (Amendment) Act, 1964 based on the recommendations of the Santhanam Committee Report.

The Santhanam Committee, constituted by the Central Government, was headed by Sri K. Santhanam, an Indian Politician[13] with the task of reviewing existing corruption laws and bodies.[14] The committee emphasised four major causes of corruption: administrative delays; unnecessary regulations; scope of personal discretion; cumbersome procedures[15] and outlined the preventive measures with regard to each of these causes.[16] For example, with respect to administrative delays, the Santhanam Committee prescribed the following steps: 7–03

constitute a special police force in Delhi for the investigation of certain offences in the Union territories and to make provisions of for the superintendence and administration of the said force and for the extension to other areas of the powers and jurisdiction of the members of the said force in regard to the investigation of the said offences".

[9] The Government of India set up the Central Bureau of Investigation vide Resolution dated April 1, 1963. Annual Report 2008, *Central Bureau of Investigation, CBI–An Overview*, at para.1.6.

[10] DSPE s.2 gives the CBI jurisdiction to investigate offences in the Union Territories only, which can be extended by the Central Government to other areas including Railways and States under s.5(1) of the DSPE with the consent of the State Government under s.6 of the DSPE.

[11] Prevention of Corruption Act 1988, Introduction at p.1.

[12] D.R. Kaarthikeyan, *Commentary on Anti-Corruption Laws*, (India, New Delhi: Ashoka Law House, 2006), p.6.

[13] *http://en.wikipedia.org/wiki/K_Santhanam* [Accessed July 15, 2010] and *http://en.wikipedia.org/wiki/Lal_Bahadur_Sastri* [Accessed July 15, 2010]. Shri Kasturiranga Santhanam, an Indian Politician, was appointed by Lal Bahadur Sastri, the then Prime Minister of India to preside over the corruption committee. Due to its thorough investigative work and important recommendations, the Committee earned a reputation as the Santhanam Committee on Corruption.

[14] Jessica Jones, *India Versus the United Nations: The Central Vigilance Commission Act Does Not Satisfy the U.N. Convention Against Corruption*, 22 Emory Int'l L. Rev. 799 at 824.

[15] Chapter XVIII of Vigilance Manual, *The Role of Chief Vigilance Officers*, p.290, available at *http://cvc.nic.in/vigman/chapterxviii.pdf* [Accessed July 15, 2010] at p.290. Deepa Mehta, *Tackling Corruption: An Indian Perspective*, 126th International Senior Seminar Visiting Experts' Papers.

[16] Chapter XVIII of Vigilance Manual, *The Role of Chief Vigilance Officers*, p.290, available at *http://cvc.nic.in/vigman/chapterxviii.pdf*. With regard to the second cause, i.e. government overburdening itself with regulatory functions, the Santhanam Committee recommended that: each Ministry/Department should undertake a review of the regulatory functions which are its responsibility, with a view to see whether all of them are strictly necessary and whether the manner of discharge of these functions and of the exercise of powers of control are capable of improvement. As for the third cause, i.e. scope for personal discretion, the Santhanam Committee recommended that adequate methods of control should be devised over exercise of discretion. The Committee also advised to look into the fairness of the method by which the discretionary decision was arrived at may certainly be looked into. In respect of the fourth cause, i.e. cumbersome procedures, the Committee saw education as the way forward to tackle the problem. In view of this, the Committee recommended

- undertake a review of existing procedures and practices to find out the cause of delay, the stage(s) at which it occurs and device suitable steps to minimise delay at the said stages;

- set down definite time-limits for dealing with receipts, files, etc. which should be strictly enforced;

- limit the number of people involved in the administrative trail and fix levels at which substantive decisions can be taken.[17]

The Santhanam Committee also found that the DSPE was inadequate to attack the menace of corruption and suggested the "creation of an independent high level watchdog body."[18] The government took cognisance of the advice and this resulted in the establishment of the Central Vigilance Commission ("CVC") in 1964, the apex anti-corruption body, dedicated to fight against corruption.[19]

The Prevention of Corruption Act 1947 was subsequently repealed by The Prevention of Corruption Act 1988 ("PCA") which came into force on September 9, 1988.[20] The PCA incorporated the Prevention of Corruption Act, 1947 the Criminal Law Amendment Act 1952, and ss.161 to 165A of the IPC with modifications. The PCA enlarged the scope of the definition of the expression "Public Servant" thereby widening the coverage and strengthening the provisions to make them more effective.

The government, with helpful recommendations from the judiciary continued

that citizens should be educated as regard the procedures of dealing with various matters and they should also be provided with an easy access to administration at various levels without the need for the intervention of touts and intermediaries. Some of the other important preventive measures recommended by the Committee are:
  (a) only those whose integrity is above board should be appointed to high administrative positions;
  (b) in making selections from non-gazetted to gazetted rank for the first time, all those whose integrity is doubtful should be eliminated;
  (c) every officer who sponsors a name for promotion should be required to record a certificate that he is satisfied that the government servant recommended by him is a man of integrity;
  (d) an essential condition for grant of extension/re-employment should be that the person concerned has a good reputation for integrity;
  (e) in every Ministry/Department, there should be a proper agency which a person with a genuine complaint can approach for redress. Bona fide complainants should be protected from harassment or victimisation;
  (f) all visitors to offices dealing with licences/permits should enter their names and purpose of their visits in a register to be kept at the Reception Office; and
  (g) steps should be taken to prevent sale of information. Information not treated as secret should be made freely available to the public.

[17] Chapter XVIII of Vigilance Manual, *The Role of Chief Vigilance Officers*, at p.291.
[18] Jessica Jones, *India Versus the United Nations: The Central Vigilance Commission Act Does Not Satisfy the U.N. Convention Against Corruption*, 22 Emory Int'l L. Rev. 799 at 824.
[19] 161st Law Commission Report (1998) on 'Central Vigilance Commission': The report revolves around the issue of conferral of statutory status on the Central Vigilance Commission. The report also looked at the *Vineet Narain v UOI*, wherein the Supreme Court ordered the government to confer statutory status on the Commission. The commission restricted itself to examining the ramifications of the many directions given by the Supreme Court in this case. The law commission brought out its recommendations in the form of a bill titled "*the Central Vigilance Commission Bill, 1998*". It also looks into the allegations and recommendation made by the Vohra Report.
[20] The PCA is discussed in detail in the following segment entitled "Anti-Corruption Laws".

to take efforts to fortify the legislation.[21] In 1967 the Administrative Reforms Commission[22] recommended a two-tier machinery, akin to a Ombudsman, namely, Lokpal and Lokayukta at the Central and State levels for redressal of grievances. The Lokpal and Lokayuktas were assigned the task of investigating into administrative actions taken by, or on behalf of, Central Government or State Government or any public authorities. These institutions were intended to serve as institutions independent of the government and to supplement the judicial institutions. The Karnataka State for example, has heeded to this recommendation and enacted the Karnataka Lokayukta Act 1984 for investigating into allegations or grievances in respect of matters specified in List II or List III of the 7th Schedule[23] to the Constitution of India.[24]

Based on the observations made by the Supreme Court in the case of *Delhi*   7–04
Development Authority v Skipper Construction Co (P) Ltd[25] the Law Commission in its 166th Report[26] submitted a draft Bill entitled "The Corrupt Public Servants (Forfeiture of Property) Bill". The Bill was intended to "provide for the forfeiture of illegally acquired properties of corrupt public servants and for matters connected therewith or incidental thereto".[27] It is highlighted that the forfeiture envisaged under this draft Bill was not limited to the assets of the corrupt public servant but extended to the relative(s) or associate(s) who acquired the said assets from the corrupt deals. The concept of forfeiture as a penalty was previously laid in the Smugglers and Foreign Exchange Manipulators (Forfeiture of Property) Act 1976 ("SAFEMA"). The Law Commission included this concept in its report given that the constitutionality of the same was upheld by the Supreme Court in the case of *Attorney General of India v Amratlal Prajivandas*[28] on the basis

---

[21] The Government established commissions to investigate into the acts of corruption in various industries and suggest preventive measures, which recommendations were documented in reports. For example, Hota Committee Report (2004) recommended the following: (1) that all civil servants found guilty of corruption should be punished; (2) the use of secret ballot in their general body meeting to identify corrupt officials in their department. Available through *http://www.indianofficer.coml* [Accessed July 15, 2010].

[22] Problems of Redressal of Citizens Grievances is the subject on which the Administrative Reforms Commission headed by Late Shri. Morarji Desai, who later became the Prime Minister of India gave its first report. Available at *http://lokayukta.kar.nic.in/index.asp* [Accessed July 15, 2010].

[23] The 7th Schedule of the Indian Constitution lays down three lists, namely, the Union List; the State List; and the Concurrent List, which define the scope of the law-making power each legislature. The State Legislatures may authorise the Union to legislate on a matter falling under the State List under art.243 of the Indian Constitution. Both the Union and State can legislate on subjects falling under the Concurrent List; and in case they overlap, the law made by the Union shall prevail. The Union Legislature, additionally, has the power to amend the Constitution under art.368 of the Indian Constitution, without altering the "basic structure" of the Constitution, such as Pt III of the Indian Constitution. See generally, *Kesavananda Bharati v State of Kerala* AIR 1973 SC 1461 (on basic structure).

[24] Available at *http://lokayukta.kar.nic.in/index.asp* [Accessed July 15, 2010].

[25] AIR 1996 SC 2005 at para.31.

[26] Government of India, Law Commission of India, 166th Report on *The Corrupt Public Servants (Forfeiture of Property) Bill*, February 1999.

[27] Government of India, Law Commission of India, 166th Report on *The Corrupt Public Servants (Forfeiture of Property) Bill*, February 1999, at p.23.

[28] (1994) 5 SCC 54.

that the law had to be made strict given the seriousness of the evil sought to be curbed.[29] Despite the above, the Bill remains pending.

In 1997, the Supreme Court in the case of *Dinesh Trivedi v Union of India*[30] discussed how to deal with the broader issue identified by the "Vohra Committee",[31] being the hindrance to effective prosecution resulting from amongst others, the nexus between criminal syndicates and bureaucrats, politicians and members of the judiciary. The Supreme Court observed that the Nodal Committee which was set up following recommendations from the Vohra Committee was ineffective given its supervisory nature.[32] The Supreme Court recommended the creation of "a body which can function with the highest degree of independence, being completely free from every conceivable influence and pressure."[33]

[29] Government of India, Law Commission of India, 166th Report on *The Corrupt Public Servants (Forfeiture of Property) Bill*, February 1999, at para.62.

[30] (1997) 4 SCC 306 [hereinafter the *"Dinesh Trivedi Case"*]. The petitioners averred that the people at large had a right to know about the full investigatory details of the Report and that such disclosure was stated to be essential for the maintenance of democracy and for ensuring that transparency in government is secured and preserved. Towards this end, the petitioners also urged the Supreme Court to direct the Union Government to make public the annexures, memorials and the written evidence that were placed before the Committee. A direction to the Union Government to reveal the names of all bureaucrats, police officials, Parliamentarians and judicial personnel against whom there is tangible evidence, to enable action to be taken in accordance with law, was also being sought. (para.3).

[31] The Vohra Committee was established by the Union of India on July 9, 1993, by its Order No. S/7937/SS (ISP)/93.

[32] The Supreme Court at para.29 in the *Dinesh Trivedi Case* held as follows: "However, as we have already noted, the Nodal Agency suffers from certain limitations. Being only a supervisory body, without having clearly delineated powers, it cannot effectively control the pace and thrust of investigative efforts."

[33] *Dinesh Trivedi Case* at paras 30 and 31. The observations of the Supreme Court at the said paras read as follows:

"We are of the view that the grave nature of the issue demands deft handling by an all-powerful body which will have the means and the power to fully secure its foundational ends."

"...In view of the seriousness of the charges involved and the clout wielded by those who are likely to become the focus of investigation, it is necessary that the body which is entrusted with the task of following the investigation through to the stage of prosecution, be such that it is capable of enjoying the complete trust and confidence of the people. Moreover in view of the suspicion that those involved may well be individuals who occupy, or have occupied, high positions in Government, it is necessary that the body be able to obtain the sanctions which are necessarily required before any prosecution can be launched. In the case of public servants, sanctions are required, for instance, under Section 197 of the CrPC and under Section 6 of the Prevention of Corruption Act, 1947. The Nodal Agency, in its present form, may not command the confidence of the people in this regard; this is a serious handicap for, in such matters, people's confidence is of the essence. An institution like the Ombudsman or a Lokpal, properly set-up, could command such confidence and respect."

"We are, therefore, of the view that the matter needs to be addressed by a body which can function with the highest degree of independence, being completely free from every conceivable influence and pressure."

"Such a body must possess the necessary powers to be able to direct investigation of all charge thoroughly before it decides, if at all, to launch prosecutions. To this end the facilities and services of trained investigators with distinguished records and impeccable credentials must be made available to it. The Report, the supporting material upon which it is based and the unequivocal assistance of all existing intelligence agencies must be forwarded to this body. In time if the need is so felt, the body may even consider the feasibility of designating Special Courts to

In August 1999, the then Commissioner of the CVC, Shri N. Vittal submitted a request to the Law Commission of India requesting the Commission to draft a Bill "encouraging and protecting honest persons to expose corrupt practices on the part of public functionaries."[34] The then Commissioner found support for such a law in the United Kingdom, the United States and Australia where whistle blowing legislations were already implemented. The Government faced increased pressure to ensure whistleblower protection following the murder of Sri Satyendra Dubey who exposed corruption in the National Highway Authority, in 2003 and in this regard, issued a resolution known as the Public Interest Disclosure Resolution. The Law Commission took cognizance of this request and drafted The Public Interest Disclosure (Protection-of Informers) Bill 2002. Given the pending status of the Bill, the government, receiving further pressure from courts issued an order entitled Protection of Informers Resolution 2004, designating the CVC as the chief agency to handle complaints on corruption.[35] The government reexamined the previously drafted Public Interest Disclosure Bill of 2002 in light of the system prevalent in other countries and formed a consensus (which was concurred by the specially constituted Committee of Secretaries) that the Resolution was insufficient.[36] Accordingly, both the Bill and Resolution were discarded. In the latter half of 2009, the Department of Personnel and Training prepared and submitted the Public Interest Disclosure (Protection of Informers) Bill 2009.[37] The same remains pending.

Having reviewed the legislative history and background, it is pertinent to have regard to the anti-corruption laws in India.

B. ANTI-CORRUPTION LAWS

I. THE PREVENTION OF CORRUPTION ACT 1988

The Prevention of Corruption Act 1988 ("PCA") is the pre-eminent anti-corruption legislation in India and contains both anti-corruption and bribery provisions. It extends to the whole of India except the State of Jammu and   7–05

---

try those who are identified by it, which proposal may then be considered by the Union Government. To this end, and in the absence of any existing suitable institution or till its creation, we recommend that a high level committee be appointed by the President of India on the advice or the Prime Minister, and after consultation with the Speaker of the Lok Sabha. The Committee shall monitor investigations involving the kind of nexus referred to in the Vohra Committee Report and carry out the objectives described earlier."

[34] Government of India, Law Commission of India, 179th Report on *The Public Interest Disclosure and Protection of Informers*, December 2001, at pp.4 and 5.

[35] Maneesh Chhibber, *Govt ready with whistleblower draft law, but exempts ministers from its ambit*, Indian Express.Com, posted online Thursday, August 27, 2009 available through *http://www.india-nexpress.com* [Accessed July 15, 2010].

[36] Maneesh Chhibber, *Govt ready with whistleblower draft law, but exempts ministers from its ambit*, Indian Express.Com, posted online Thursday, 27 August 2009.

[37] Maneesh Chhibber, *Govt ready with whistleblower draft law, but exempts ministers from its ambit*, Indian Express.Com, posted online Thursday, 27 August 2009.

Kashmir. The PCA was passed with the intention of making the existing anti-corruption laws more effective by widening their coverage and strengthening the provisions. The Supreme Court, in the case of *State of Madhya Pradesh v Shri Ram Singh*,[38] observed as follows:

> "In order to consolidate and amend the laws relating to prevention of corruption and matters connected thereto, the Prevention of Corruption Act, 1947 was enacted which was amended from time to time. In the year 1988 a new Act on the subject being Act No. 49 of 1988 was enacted with the object of dealing with the circumstances, contingencies and shortcomings which were noticed in the working and implementation of 1947 Act. The law relating to prevention of corruption was essentially made to deal with the public servants, as understood in the common parlance but specifically defined in the Act."

The definition of public servant under the PCA is very wide. The Statement of Objects and Reasons of the PCA reveals that the legislators wanted to extend the scope and ambit of the definition "public servant" to bring within its sweep each and every person who held an office by virtue of which he was required to perform any public duty.[39] Apart from public servants, the PCA also takes within its ambit private citizens who "act as a tout or intermediary" in the offence of corruption.[40]

Broadly, a public servant means any person who is remunerated out of public money and/or government funds or who performs a public duty. For the purposes of PCA, the term "Public Servant" under s.2(c)[41] of the Act includes:

---

[38] (2000) 5 SCC 88 at [8].

[39] D.R. Kaarthikeyan, *Commentary on Anti-Corruption Laws*, (India, New Delhi: Ashoka Law House, 2006), pp.72–73.

[40] Hemant K Batra, *Part 1 Anti-Corruption Compliance and Enforcement Issues in India*, The Free Library by Farlex, available through *http://www.thefreelibrary.com* [Accessed July 15, 2010].

[41] Section 2(c) defines public servant as:

> "(i) any person in the service or pay of the Government or remunerated by the Government by fees or commission for the performance of any public duty;
>
> (ii) any person in the service or pay of a local authority;
>
> (iii) any person in the service or pay of a corporation established by or under a Central, Provincial or State Act, or an authority or a body owned or controlled or aided by the Government or a Government company as defined in section 617 of the Companies Act, 1956;
>
> (iv) any Judge, including any person empowered by law to discharge, whether by himself or as a member of any body of persons, any adjudicatory functions;
>
> (v) any person authorised by a court of justice to perform any duty, in connection with the administration of justice, including a liquidator, receiver or commissioner appointed by such court;
>
> (vi) any arbitrator or other person to whom any cause or matter has been referred for decision or report by a court of justice or by a competent public authority;
>
> (vii) any person who holds an office by virtue of which he is empowered to prepare, publish, maintain or revise an electoral roll or to conduct an election or part of an election;
>
> (viii) any person who holds an office by virtue of which he is authorised or required to perform any public duty;
>
> (ix) any person who is the president, secretary or other office-bearer of a registered co-operative society engaged in agriculture, industry, trade or banking, receiving or having received any financial aid from the Central Government or a State Government or from any corporation established by or under a Central, Provincial or State Act, or any authority or body owned

(i) any person in the service of the government, local authority, a corporation established by, or under, a Central, Provincial or State Act;

(ii) any judge, or person authorised by a court to perform any duty including an arbitrator, liquidator, receiver;

(iii) any person who conducts an election;

(iv) an officer of a registered cooperative society;

(v) any person who holds an office by virtue of which they are authorised or required to perform any public duty.

The term "public duty" is defined under s.2(b) of the PCA to mean "a duty in the discharge of which the State, the public or the community at large has an interest". Public Sector includes a local authority; a corporation established by or under the Central, Provincial or State Act and a body controlled, owned or aided by government or a government company.

The PCA defines a Government Company in terms of s.617 of the Companies   7-06 Act 1956, i.e. any company in which not less than 51 per cent of the paid up share capital is held by the Central Government/State Government or jointly by the Central Government and one or more State Governments and also includes a company which is a subsidiary of a Government Company.

Chapter III of the PCA (ss.7 to 16 respectively) outlines the provisions regarding offences and penalties. It can be observed that these provisions are wide in scope and do not restrict the offence of corruption, in conventional terms, that is, the direct receipt of pecuniary advantage and includes taking gratification in respect of an official act or to influence and accepting/obtaining a valuable thing without consideration (favours and gifts). The salient provisions are now discussed below.

(a) Public Servant Taking Gratification other than Legal Remuneration in Respect of an Official Act

The PCA makes it a crime for a public servant to take gratification other than   7-07 legal remuneration in respect of an official act. Section 7 of the PCA in

or controlled or aided by the Government or a Government company as defined in section 617 of the Companies Act, 1956;

(x) any person who is a chairman, member or employee of any Service Commission or Board, by whatever name called, or a member of any selection committee appointed by such Commission or Board for the conduct of any examination or making any selection on behalf of such Commission or Board;

(xi) any person who is a Vice-Chancellor or member of any governing body, professor, reader, lecturer or any other teacher or employee, by whatever designation called, of any University and any person whose services have been availed of by a University or any other public authority in connection with holding or conducting examinations;

(xii) any person who is an office-bearer or an employee of an educational, scientific, social, cultural or other institution, in whatever manner established, receiving or having received any financial assistance from the Central Government or any State Government, or local or other public authority."

unequivocal terms explains that "gratification is not restricted to pecuniary gratifications or to gratifications estimable in money." The legislative intent of widening the definition has been supported in the following judgments of the Supreme Court.[42] In *Mohmoodkhan Mahboodkhan Pathan v State of Maharashtra*[43] the Supreme Court has taken the same meaning for the word "gratification", as appearing in s.4(1) of the Prevention of Corruption Act 1947 and observed as follows:

> "... The word 'gratification' is not defined in the Act. Hence, it must be understood in its literal meaning. In the Oxford Advanced Learner's Dictionary of Current English, the word 'gratification' is shown to have the meaning 'to give pleasure or satisfaction to'. The word 'gratification' is used in Section 4(1) to denote acceptance of something to the pleasure or satisfaction of the recipient."

The Supreme Court in the case *State of Andhra Pradesh v C Uma Maheswara Rao*,[44] prevailed with a similar view where it held as follows:

> "In Black's Law Dictionary, 'gratification' is defined as 'a recompense or reward for services or benefits, given voluntarily, without solicitation or pomise'. But in Oxford Advance Learner's Dictionary of Current English the said word is given the meaning 'to give pleasure or satisfaction to'. Among the above two descriptions for the word 'gratification' with slightly differing nuances as between the two, what is more appropriate for the context has to be found out..."

The offence under s.7 of PCA is punishable with imprisonment for a period not less than six months extendable to five years, with an additional liability of fines.

(b) Public Servant obtaining Valuable Thing Without Consideration from Person Concerned in Proceeding or Business Transacted by such Public Servant

7–08   Apart from gratification, s.11 of PCA prohibits the acceptance of a valuable thing without consideration or consideration which is inadequate from a person known or likely to be concerned in any proceeding/business transacted by the public servant. The offence under s.11 of PCA is punishable with imprisonment for a period not less than six months extendable to five years, with an additional liability of fines. The said s.11 reads as follows:

> "Whoever, being a public servant, accepts or obtains or agrees to accept or attempts to obtain for himself, or for any other person, any valuable thing without consideration, or for a consideration which he knows to be inadequate, from any person whom he knows to have been, or to be, or to be likely to be concerned in any proceeding or business

---

[42] Quoting the Supreme Court in *State of MP v Shri Ram Singh* (2000) 5 SCC 88, at [10], "Procedural delays and technicalities of law should not be permitted to defeat the object sought to be achieved by the Act. The overall public interest and the social object is required to be kept in mind while interpreting various provisions of the Act and decided cases under it."
[43] (1997) 10 SCC 600 at [7].
[44] (2004) 4 SCC 399 at [20].

transacted or about to be transacted by such public servant, or having any connection with the official functions of himself or of any public servant to whom he is subordinate, or from any person whom he knows to be interested in or related to the person so concerned, shall be punishable with imprisonment for a term which shall be not less than six months but which may extend to five years and shall also be liable to fine."

(c) Presumption: Public Servant Accepts Gratification other than Legal Remuneration

Section 20(1) of the PCA outlines the position with respect to the burden of proof and reads as follows: 7–09

"Presumption where public servant accepts gratification other than legal remuneration:

'Where, in any trial of an offence punishable under section 7 or section 11 or clause (a) or clause (b) or sub-section (1) of section 13 it is proved that an accused person has accepted or obtained or has agreed to accept or attempted to obtain for himself, or for any other person, any gratification (other than legal remuneration) or any valuable thing from any person, it shall be presumed, unless the contrary is proved, that he accepted or obtained or agreed to accept or attempted to obtain that gratification or that valuable thing, as the case may be, as a motive or reward such as is mentioned in section 7 or, as the case may be, without consideration or for a consideration which he knows to be inadequate.'"

A reading of the above provision shows that once the offence of corruption is made against an accused, the burden shifts on the accused "to explain the circumstances to prove his innocence."[45] A failure to discharge this burden would only go to show that the said person is guilty of the offence. It is pertinent to note that s.20 makes reference to the words "shall be presumed", "shall" being a mandatory reference as opposed to "may", which is discretionary. In this regard, reference may be made to s.4 of the Indian Evidence Act 1872 ("Evidence Act") which defines the expressions "may presume" and "shall presume". The presumptions under "may presume" are known as "factual or discretionary presumptions" whilst the presumptions under "shall presume" are known as "legal or compulsory presumption".[46] Thus, it appears that the only requirement for drawing such a legal presumption under s.20 of the PCA is that during trial it must be proved that the accused has accepted or agreed to accept gratification. Nonetheless, the phrase "it shall be presumed" used in s.20(1) of the PCA makes it incumbent on the Court to proceed, once the existence of illegal gratification is proved, on the presumption as the burden stands transferred to the accused to prove the contrary.[47] It has been observed by the Supreme Court in *CI Emden v State of Uttar Pradesh*[48] and *VD Jhangan v State of Uttar Pradesh*[49] that if any money is received and no convincing or credible proof is offered by the accused as

---

[45] *B. Hanumantha Rao v State of Andhra Pradesh* AIR 1992 SC 1201.
[46] *Andhra Pradesh v C. Uma Maheswara Rao* (2004) 4 SCC 399 at [11].
[47] See generally the case of *Dhanvantrai Balwantrai Desai v State of Maharashtra* AIR 1964 SC 575.
[48] AIR 1960 SC 548.
[49] AIR 1966 SC 1762.

to how it came to be received by him, the presumption would be made available and it would be for the accused to prove as to how the presumption is not available. Thus, the burden shifts on the accused to prove that he had not obtained any gratification.

As for the mode of proof, the same can be by oral or documentary evidence. Proof or evidence in such cases depends upon the standard of probability of its existence and the standard required for reaching the supposition is that of a prudent man acting in any important matter concerning him.[50]

(d) Taking Gratification & the Means of Influence

7–10   Sections 8 and 9 of the PCA deal with the offence of improperly influencing a public servant in return for consideration paid or promised by a third person. The said sections read as follows:

> "Section 8—Taking gratification, in order, by corrupt or illegal means, to influence public servant
> Whoever accepts or obtains, or agrees to accept, or attempts to obtain, from any person, for himself or for any other person, any gratification whatever as a motive or reward for inducing, by corrupt or illegal means, any public servant, whether named or otherwise, to do or to forbear to do any official act, or in the exercise of the official functions of such public servant to show favour or disfavour to any person, or to render or attempt to render any service or disservice to any person with the Central Government or any State Government or Parliament or the Legislature of any State or with any local authority, corporation or Government company referred to in clause (c) of section 2, or with any public servant, whether named or otherwise, shall be punishable with imprisonment for a term which shall be not less than six months but which may extend to five years and shall also be liable to fine.

> Section 9—Taking gratification, for exercise of personal influence with public servant
> Whoever accepts or obtains or agrees to accept or attempts to obtain, from any person, for himself or for any other person, any gratification whatever, as a motive or reward for inducing, by the exercise of personal influence, any public servant whether named or otherwise to do or to forbear to do any official act, or in the exercise of the official functions of such public servant to show favour or disfavour to any person, or to render or attempt to render any service or disservice to any person with the Central Government or any State Government or Parliament or the Legislature of any State or with any local authority, corporation or Government company referred to in clause (c) of section 2, or with any public servant, whether named or otherwise, shall be

---

[50] *Hawkins v Powells Tillery Steam Coal Co Ltd* [1911] 1 K.B. 988 at 995 quoted with approval by the Supreme Court in *State of Andhra Pradesh v Uma Maheswara Rao* (2004) 4 SCC 399 at [13] and [14].

> "Proof does not mean proof to rigid mathematical demonstration, because that is impossible; it must mean such evidence as would induce a reasonable man to come to a particular conclusion".

Furthermore, Courts have also been vested with the discretion to presume the existence of any fact which it thinks likely to have happened. The discretion is clearly envisaged in s.114 of the Evidence Act, which reads as follows:

> "The Court may presume the existence of any fact which it thinks likely to have happened, regard being had to the common course of natural events, human conduct and public and private business, in their relation to the facts of the particular case."

punishable with imprisonment for a term which shall be not less than six months but which may extend to five years and shall also be liable to a fine."

Upon a bare reading of the provisions, it is noticeable that both provisions are identical, the only difference being the means by which the public servant is influenced. Section 8 deals with influence by corrupt or illegal means, whilst the inducement under s.9 is the exercise of personal influence. An offence under both ss.8 and 9 are punishable with imprisonment for a term not less than six months but which may extend to five years, and shall also be liable to fine.

(e) Abetment

The offence of abetment is dealt with under s.12 of the PCA, which specifically states that: **7–11**

"Whoever abets any offence punishable under Section 7 (public servant taking gratification other than any legal remuneration in respect of an official act) or Section 11 (public servant obtaining valuable thing, without consideration from person concerned in proceeding or business transacted by such public servant) whether or not that offence is committed in consequence of that abetment, shall be punishable with imprisonment for a term which shall be not less than six months but which may extend to five years and shall also be liable to fine."

(f) Habitual Commission of Offence

Section 14 of PCA[51] deals with habitual commission of offences punishable under ss.8, 9 or 12 of PCA. An offence under s.14 is punishable with imprisonment for a minimum term of two years, extendable up to seven years and possible liability of a fine. Where a sentence of fine is imposed, s.16 of PCA provides that the court should "take into consideration the amount or the value of the property, if any, which the accused person has obtained by committing the offence."   **7–12**

II. INDIAN PENAL CODE 1860

The Indian Penal Code ("IPC") is the substantive code that enlists all situations and circumstances that may lead to a person being charged with a criminal offence and the corresponding punishments for the same. It covers Indian citizens, residing in India or abroad, every person within India and any person on any ship   **7–13**

---

[51] PCA s.14 reads as follows:
"Habitual committing of offence under sections 8, 9 and 12:
Whoever habitually commits—
    (a) an offence punishable under section 8 or section 9; or
    (b) an offence punishable under section 12,
shall be punishable with imprisonment for a term which shall be not less than two years but which may extend to seven years and shall also be liable to fine."

or aircraft registered in India.[52] The IPC extends to the whole of India (except to the State of Jammu and Kashmir).[53] The IPC is wide in its application and the punishment extends to every person who may have committed an offence outside India but, by Indian law, are to be tried in India.[54]

As mentioned earlier, the IPC was one of the initial legislations which laid the foundation for anti-corruption laws in India. The IPC provided for offences by or relating to public servants under Ch.IX which included ss.161 to 165A, which were later repealed and incorporated into the PCA. Only a limited provision concerning corruption and bribery is retained and this is s.171B[55] which seeks to criminalise the offence of bribery during elections. Section 171E[56] of the IPC makes this offence is punishable by imprisonment for one year or fine or both.

---

[52] IPC ss.2 and 4 reads as follows:
"Section 2—Punishment of offences committed within India.–Every person shall be liable to punishment under this Code and not otherwise for every act or omission contrary to the provisions thereof, of which he shall be guilty within [India][***]"
"Section 4—Extension of Code to extra-territorial offences.—The provisions of this Code apply also to any offence committed by—
[(1) any citizen of India in any place without any beyond India;
(2) any person on any ship or aircraft registered in India wherever it may be.]"

[53] IPC s.1 reads as follows:
"Section 1—Title and extent of operation of the Code.—This Act shall be called the Indian Penal Code, and shall [extend to the whole of India [except the State of Jammu and Kashmir]]."

[54] IPC s.3 reads as follows:
"Section 3—Punishment of offences committed beyond, but which by law may be tried within, India.–Any person liable, by any [Indian law] to be tried for an offence committed beyond [India] shall be dealt with according to the provisions of this Code or any act committed beyond [India] in the same manner as if such act had been committed within [India]."

[55] IPC s.17B reads as follows:
"Bribery—(1) Whoever—
   (i) gives a gratification to any person with the object of inducing him or any other person to exercise any electoral right or of rewarding any person for having exercised any such right; or
   (ii) accepts either for himself or for any other person any gratification as a reward for exercising any such right or for inducing or attempting to induce any other person to exercise any such right; commit the offence of bribery:
Provided that a declaration of public policy or a promise of public action shall not be an offence under this section.
(2) A person who offers, or agrees to give, or offers or attempts to procure, a gratification shall be deemed to give a gratification.
(3) A person who obtains or agrees to accept or attempts to obtain a gratification shall be deemed to accept a gratification, and a person who accepts a gratification as a motive for doing what he does not intend to do, or as a reward for doing what he has not done, shall be deemed to have accepted the gratification as a reward."

[56] IPC s.171E reads as follows:
"Whoever commits the offence of bribery shall be punished with imprisonment of either description for a term which may extend to one year, or with a fine, or with both:
Provided that bribery by treating shall be punished with fine only.
Explanation—"Treating" means that form of bribery where the gratification consists in food, drink, entertainment, or provision."

C. EXTRA-TERRITORIALITY REACH

I. PCA

The PCA applies to all Indian citizens residing in India or abroad.[57] In *Arun*   **7–14**
Kumar Agrawal v State of Karnataka,[58] the Karnataka High Court, opining on the
scope of the PCA on foreign nationals in India who engage in bribery and corruption and its applicability to them, observed as follows:

> "The Legislators and the people had at that time not envisaged the inflow of corruption
> in the political arena. Corruption amongst politicians was unheard of in the Indian
> society. Such a corruption is generally related to the inflow of foreign capital investment
> in the Indian economy. The foreign investors being generally not amenable to the
> jurisdiction of the Indian Courts, are alleged to be finding it easy to resort to corruption
> amongst the politicians with the sole object of amassing wealth and earning profits. The
> latest phenomenon is attributed to the so called liberalisation policy permitting the
> foreign investors for the proclaimed object of strengthening the Indian economy for the
> alleged betterment of the people. Corruption amongst politicians is related to various
> scandals such as relating to Bofors, the Hawala, the Fodder Scam, Import of Sugar,
> Telecommunications, etc. etc. connected with or related to the foreign investors in their
> specified fields of activities."

II. IPC

The IPC extends to all citizens of India and to any person on Indian Territory   **7–15**
which includes any ship/aircraft registered in India.[59]

D. INTERNATIONAL CONVENTIONS

In terms of international norms, India endorsed the ADB-OECD Anti-Corrup-   **7–16**
tion Action Plan in 2001, and has signed but not yet ratified the UN Convention
against Corruption and the UN Convention against Transnational Organised
Crime.

I. POTENTIAL AMENDMENTS TO CORRUPTION LAWS PENDING RATIFICATION OF THE UN CONVENTION AGAINST CORRUPTION ("UNCAC")

In spite of the fact that the Union Cabinet has given its approval for initiating the   **7–17**
process of enacting necessary enabling legislation before approval for ratification

---

[57] PCA s.1(2).
[58] [1999] 1 Kar.L.J. 603 at [2].
[59] IPC s.4.

of the Convention,[60] no concrete steps have been taken to ensue the same. Consequently, there have been continuous calls by international organizations such as Transparency International,[61] the global corruption watchdog to ratify UNCAC which is an international agreement to tackle corruption. The UNCAC introduces a comprehensive set of standards, measures and rules that countries can apply in order to strengthen their legal and regulatory regime to fight corruption. It calls for preventive measures and the criminalisation of the most prevalent forms of corruption both in the public and private sectors.

India should study the implications of UNCAC more closely and proceed to ratify the same as it would also be demonstrative of its efforts to fight corruption on an international platform. Pending ratification of UNCAC, the potential amendment to the present corruption laws would be the inclusion of provisions enabling freezing, seizure and confiscation of assets obtained/gained through commission of the offence. This provision could be brought into effect either through an amendment to the existing corruption laws or by enactment of a separate legislation.[62]

Whilst India is deliberating with its efforts on the international front, on the domestic side, it has taken forward steps to address the issue of corruption. India has not left the issue to be dealt with by corruption laws alone but has devised mechanisms in related laws, which is reviewed below.

II. Prevention of Money Laundering Act 2002

7–18   The Prevention of Money Laundering Act 2002 ("PMLA") was not enacted as an anti-corruption legislation but as an off-shoot to regulations intended to regulate and manage foreign exchange within India. In view of the above, it is beneficial to first have a brief background of the march of law respecting foreign exchange in the Indian Economy.

The first legislation that was enacted in India to regulate and standardise foreign exchange was the Foreign Exchange Regulation Act 1973 ("FERA"). FERA was enacted at a time when foreign exchange reserves in the country were low and consequently, the government proceeded with the assumption that all foreign exchange earned by the Indian residents belonged to the government. Thus, the objectives of FERA were to consolidate the laws relating to dealings in foreign exchange and securities, payments and transactions affecting foreign exchange[63] with a view to help the Reserve Bank of India (the central bank in

---

[60] *Cabinet nod for UN Convention against Corruption* published December 9, 2005 available through *http://www.hindu.com* [Accessed July 15, 2010].

[61] *Transparency International Urges India To Ratify United Nations Convention Against Corruption*, published November 4, 2009, available through *http://www.india-server.com* [Accessed July 15, 2010].

[62] For example, The Corrupt Public Servants (Forfeiture of Property) Bill proposed by the Law Commission of India in its 166th Report in 1999, envisaged a similar tracing and confiscation of property, which was however, limited to corrupt public servants.

[63] Refer to the Preamble of the FERA.

India constituted for the purposes of taking over the management of the currency from the central government), maintain the stability of the exchange rate and conserve the previous foreign exchange earned.[64]

However, with the onset of liberalisation in 1991 and the change in the economic policy (move towards opening up of international trade and investment and deregulation), it was observed that FERA, under its existing structure, was ill-equipped to regulate and manage the foreign exchange that was pouring into India. The Indian economy called for a shift from "regulation" of foreign exchange to "management" of foreign exchange. Pursuant to the same, the legislature enacted the Foreign Exchange Management Act 1999 ("FEMA") which had a different mandate and an "objective of facilitating external trade and payments and for promoting the orderly development and maintenance of foreign exchange market in India".[65]

The enactment of FEMA also brought with it the enactment of PMLA to put   7–19 in place a legislative framework to combat money laundering and provide preventive measures. PMLA achieves this objective through provisional attachment of the proceeds of crime, which are likely to be concealed, transferred or dealt with in any manner. Section 3 of PMLA defines the offence of "money laundering" as under:

"Whosoever directly or indirectly attempts to indulge or knowingly assists or knowingly is a party or is actually involved in any process or activity connected with the proceeds of crime and projecting it as untainted property shall be guilty of offence of money laundering."

The term "property" has been defined under s.2(v) very widely to include any property or asset of every description, whether movable or immovable, tangible or intangible. It also includes within its ambit deeds and instruments evidencing title. Section 4 of PMLA makes the offence of money laundering punishable with imprisonment for a term not less than three years, extendable to seven years and may include liability to a fine of upto five lakhs rupees.[66]

The PMLA casts obligations on all banking companies, financial institutions

---

[64] Refer to s.76 of the Act which lays down the factors which are to be taken into consideration by the Central Government and the Reserve Bank of India while granting permission.

[65] Preamble to the FEMA.

[66] PMLA s.4 reads as follows:
"4. Whoever commits the offence of money-laundering shall be punishable with rigorous imprisonment for a term which shall not be less than three years but which may extend to seven years and shall also be liable to fine which may extend to five lakh rupees:
Provided that where the proceeds of crime involved in money-laundering relates to any offence specified under paragraph 2 of Part A of the Schedule, the provisions of this section shall have effect as if for the words 'which may extend to seven years', the words 'which may extend to ten years' had been substituted."

and intermediaries to maintain records of transactions[67] and to furnish information of such transactions within the time prescribed under the Rules.[68] However, both "banking company" as well as "financial institution" have been given a restrictive interpretation with the former being defined to mean a "banking company or a co-operative bank to which the Banking Regulation Act, 1949 (10 of 1949) applies and includes any bank or banking institution referred to in section 51 of that Act"[69]; and the latter "a financial institution as defined in clause (c) of section 45-I of the Reserve Bank of India Act, 1934 (2 of 1934) and includes a chit fund company, a co-operative bank, a housing finance institution and a non-banking financial company".[70]

However, the extra-territorial applicability of the Act is limited as it extends only to the territory of India. Furthermore, s.56 of the PMLA clearly vests the authority with the Central Government to enter into agreements with the government of any other country for enforcing the Act in that country; and for exchanging information for the prevention of any offence under the Act.[71]

In exercise of powers conferred by Clause(s) of subs.(2) of s.73 read with s.30 of PMLA, the Central Government has framed various Rules regulating, amongst others, the appointment and conditions of service of persons appointed as

---

[67] The relevant parts of s.12 reads as follows:

"12. (1) Every banking company, financial institution and intermediary shall—
  (a) maintain a record of all transactions, the nature and value of which may be prescribed, whether such transactions comprise of a single transaction or a series of transactions integrally connected to each other, and where such series of transactions take place within a month;
  (b) furnish information of transactions referred to in clause (a) to the Director within such time as may be prescribed;
  (c) verify and maintain the records of the identity of all its clients, in such a manner as may be prescribed."

[68] Rule 8 of the Prevention of Money-laundering (Maintenance of Records of the Nature and Value of Transactions, the Procedure and Manner of Maintaining and Time for Furnishing Information and Verification and Maintenance of Records of the Identity of the Clients of the Banking Companies, Financial Institutions and Intermediaries) Rules, 2005 reads as follows:

"8. Furnishing of information to the Director—
  (1) The Principal Officer of a banking company, a financial institution and an intermediary, as the case may be, shall furnish the information in respect of transactions referred to in clauses (A), (B) and (BA) of sub-rule (1) of rule 3 every month to the Director by the 15th day of the succeeding month.
  (2) The Principal Officer of a banking company, a financial institution and an intermediary, as the case may be, shall furnish the information promptly in writing or by fax or by electronic mail to the Director in respect of transactions referred to in clause (C) of sub-rule (1) of rule 3 not later than seven working days from the date of occurrence of such transaction.
  The Principal Officer of a banking company, a financial institution and an intermediary, as the case may be, shall furnish the information promptly in writing or by fax or by electronic mail to the Director in respect of transactions referred to in clause (D) of sub-rule (1) of rule 3 not later than seven working days on being satisfied that the transaction is suspicious."
Available at *http://fiuindia.gov.in/notifications-overview.htm* [Accessed July 15, 2010].

[69] PMLA s.2(e).
[70] PMLA s.2(1).
[71] PMLA s.56.

Chairperson and Members of the Appellate Tribunal, procedure and manner of furnishing information, verification and maintenance of records, etc.[72]

III. RIGHT TO INFORMATION ACT 2005

The Right to Information Act ("RTI Act") was enacted with a view "to promote **7–20** transparency and accountability in the working of every public authority".[73] The statement encapsulating the objective and purpose behind the enactment of the RTI Act can be summarized as follows: "Citizens must have access to information about what their government is doing and how decisions have been reached".[74] Whilst this is the clear intent of the legislation, the government has also infused within this legislation, its determination to tackle corruption and this is evident from the statement of the Indian Prime Minister, Dr. Manmohan Singh at the time of presenting the Bill in Parliament on May 11, 2005, when he remarked, "I believe that the passage of this bill will see the dawn of a new era in our processes of government... an era which will eliminate the scourge of corruption."[75]

The RTI Act provides a gateway for quick search of information from various public authorities under the Central Government as well as the State Governments and provides a mechanism for ensuring timely response to a citizen's request for government information.[76] Under the provisions of the RTI Act any Indian citizen may request information[77] from a "public authority".[78] RTI Act

---

[72] Prevention of Money-Laundering (Appointment and Conditions of Service of Chairperson and Members of Appellate Tribunal) Rules, 2007, Prevention of Money Laundering (Appointment and Conditions of Service of Chairperson and Members of Adjudicating Authorities) Rules, 2007, etc. See generally, *Pareena Swarup v Union of India (UOI)*, 2008 (13) SCALE 84 at [2].

[73] Refer to the Preamble of the RTI Act.

[74] Lotte E. Feinberg, Open Government and Freedom of Information: Fishbowl Accountability?, in Handbook of Public Law and Administration (Philip J. Cooper & Chester A. Newland, eds., Jossey-Bass Publishers, 1997).

[75] Wajahat Habibullaha, *Corruption and the Right to Information,* available through http://www.india-seminar.com [Accessed July 15, 2010].

[76] Available at *http://www.rightoinformation.gov.in* [Accessed July 15, 2010].

[77] Section 2(f) defines "information" as follows:
" 'information' means any material in any form, including records, documents, memos, e-mails, opinions, advices, press releases, circulars, orders, logbooks, contracts, reports, papers, samples, models, data material held in any electronic form and information relating to any private body which can be accessed by a public authority under any other law for the time being in force."
However, under s.8, certain information, categories of which have been listed in the Section itself, can be denied to the applicant. This includes information which would affect the sovereignty and integrity of India, information which has been expressly forbidden by a court to be published, information including a commercial confidence, trade secret or intellectual property, etc.

[78] Section 2(h) of the RTI Act defines "public authority" as follows:
"(h) 'public authority' means any authority or body or institution of self-government established or constituted—
    (a) by or under the Constitution;
    (b) by any other law made by Parliament;
    (c) by any other law made by State Legislature;
    (d) by notification issued or order made by the appropriate Government,
        and includes any—
        (i) body owned, controlled or substantially financed;
        (ii) non-Government organisation substantially financed,
    directly or indirectly by funds provided by the appropriate Government;"

recognises that information held in any form should be made available to citizens as long as the same is made in public interest thereby empowering every citizen to act as whistle-blowers and watchdogs against corruption.[79]

The RTI Act requires every public authority to computerise their records for wide dissemination and to proactively publish certain categories of information for easy citizen access.

7–21   The request for information has to be made in writing accompanied with the prescribed fee (INR 10/-) to the Central or State Public Information Officer of the concerned public authority.[80] Such Information Officer is required to reply within 30 days. However, the officer may refuse to provide the information requested if they fall within any of the grounds set out in s.8 of the RTI Act as follows: information which would affect the sovereignty and integrity of India, information which has been expressly forbidden by a Court to be published, information including a commercial confidence, trade secret or intellectual property.

In the event the information is refused on unjust or frivolous grounds, an Appeal may be preferred to the Departmental Appellate Authority which acts as the First Appellate Authority. The second Appeal, from the Departmental Appellate Authority, may be made to the Central Information Commission ("CIC") or the State Information Commission under ss.18 and 19 of the RTI Act. The CIC decides the appeals and complaints and conveys its decision to the appellant/complainant and first appellate authority/Public Information Officer. In such a case, the onus to prove that a denial of information was justified (with reference to the aforementioned s.8) rests upon the respective Information Officer.[81] The decision of the CIC or State Information Commission, as the case may be, is binding upon the Applicant.[82]

The RTI Act poses as "an important democratic privilege"[83] in addition to representing one of the country's most critical achievements in the fight against corruption in recent years. A very recent example of the same can be seen wherein, pursuant to an RTI Application, the CIC directed the concerned authorities to display the information pertaining to entitlement of essential commodities for all type of Ration Cards, opening and closing stock of essential commodities, working hours of fair price shops, samples of food grains online and outside 70 ration shops/circles of Delhi, before January 31, 2010. A compliance report was also demanded by the CIC,[84] a march towards curbing the rampant

---

[79] See also *About Right to Information*, available at *http://fightcorruption.wikidot.com/knowrti* [Accessed July 15, 2010] and Wajahat Habibullaha, *Corruption and the Right to Information*, available through *http://www.india-seminar.com* [Accessed July 15, 2010].

[80] Refer to s.6 of the RTI Act.

[81] Refer to s.19(5) of the RTI Act.

[82] Refer to s.19(7) of the RTI Act.

[83] Hemant K Batra, *Part 1 Anti-Corruption Compliance and Enforcement Issues in India*, The Free Library by Farlex, available through *http://www.thefreelibrary.com* [Accessed July 15, 2010].

[84] Shaweta Anand, *CIC Orders Publication of PDS Details*, available through *http://www.indiato-gether.org* [Accessed July 15, 2010].

corruption existing in the public distribution system in India. The accessibility to information has afforded citizens a mechanism to control public spending, besides also to be aware on how the funds for public spending are being utilised. In the first year of National RTI, 42,876 (not yet official) applications for information were filed to Central (i.e. Federal) public authorities. According to the CIC, RTI applications have annually increased by 8 to 10 times annually. Less than 5 per cent of the million applications for information have been denied information under various exemption categories.[85]

IV. THE REPRESENTATION OF THE PEOPLE ACT 1951

The Representation of the People Act 1951 ("RPA") is an act to provide for the conduct of elections, the corrupt practices and other offences in connection with elections. Section 123 of the RPA[86] deems the following as constituting corrupt practices:

7–22

(a) bribery, that is to say by giving any gift, offer or promise by a candidate or his agent or by any other person with the consent of a candidate or his election agent of any gratification, to any person whomsoever, with the object, directly or indirectly of inducing; the receipt of, or agreement to receive, any gratification, whether as a motive or a reward;

(b) the exercise of undue influence, that is to say, any direct or indirect interference or attempt to interfere on the part of the candidate or his agent, or of any other person [with the consent of the candidate or his election agent], with the free exercise of any electoral right.

---

[85] Transparency International, CMI, U4 Expert Answers, *Overview of Corruption and Anti-Corruption Efforts in India*, available at *http://www.u4.no* [Accessed July 15, 2010].

[86] Section 123 of the RPA reads as follows:
"123. Corrupt practices—The following shall be deemed to be corrupt practices for the purposes of this Act:
[(1) 'Bribery', that is to say—
(A) any gift, offer or promise by a candidate or his agent or by any other person with the consent of a candidate or his election agent of any gratification, to any person whomsoever, with the object, directly or indirectly of inducing—
    (a) a person to stand or not to stand as, or [to withdraw or not to withdraw] from being a candidate at an election, or
    (b) . . .
(B) the receipt of, or agreement to receive, any gratification, whether as a motive or a reward—
    (a) by a person for standing or not standing as, or for 6 [withdrawing or not withdrawing] from being a candidate; or
    (b) by any person whomsoever for himself or any other person for voting or refraining from voting, or inducing or attempting to induce any elector to vote or refrain from voting, or any candidate [to withdraw or not to withdraw] his candidature.
Explanation—For the purposes of this clause the term 'gratification' is not restricted to pecuniary gratifications or gratifications estimable in money and it includes all forms of entertainment and all forms of employment for reward but it does not include the payment of any expenses bona fide incurred at, or for the purpose of, any election and duly entered in the account of election expenses referred to in section 78.]"

For the purpose of this section, "gratification" is not restricted to pecuniary gratifications or gratifications estimable in money and it includes all forms of entertainment and all forms of employment for reward. However, it does not include the payment of any expenses bona fide incurred at, or for the purpose of, any election and duly entered in the account of election expenses referred to in s.78.[87]

V. SUBORDINATE LEGISLATION/SERVICE RULES

7–23   Apart from the primary legislations set out above, there is a vast body of subordinate legislation formulated/issued by the Central and State Government in the form of service rules which are applicable to various categories of public servants. These rules prescribe the code of conduct to be observed by public servants and also lay down the rules relating to acceptance of gifts, hospitality, etc. These internal rules of conduct are issued for different categories of public servants such as civil servants,[88] defence and air force personnel.[89] Some of these rules are publicly available. In essence, these rules relate to:

(a)   conduct of public servants in public;

(b)   matters relating to acceptance of gifts from members of public;

(c)   matters relating to activities of the family members of the public servants;

(d)   matters related to acquisition of movable and immovable property by the public servants;

(e)   matters related to employment of near relatives of the public servants in private companies or firms;

(f)   matters related to carrying on private trade or business by the public servants.

---

[87] Section 78 of the RPA reads as follows:
"Lodging of account with the district election officer—4[(1)] Every contesting candidate at an election shall, within thirty days from the date of election of the returned candidate or, if there are more than one returned candidate at the election and the dates of their election are different, the later of those two dates, lodge with the 5 [district election officer] an account of his election expenses which shall be a true copy of the account kept by him or by his election agent under section 77."

[88] The All-India Service (Conduct Rules), 1968 made pursuant to the All India Services Act, 1951 which is an Act to regulate the recruitment, and the conditions of services of persons appointed, to the All-India Services common to the Union and the States.

[89] Directorate of Personal Services, Discipline and Welfare, 2006 (Regulations for the Air Force, 1964). These are a set of Regulations which deals with the discipline and welfare in defence organizations and is applicable to the whole of India. The Defence Procurement Procedure provides comprehensive policy guidelines for capital acquisition process for the armed forces in India.

E. PUBLIC PROCUREMENT

Public procurement is a matter of grave importance given the large numbers **7–24** involved in the said projects. Consequently, the government has framed important guidelines and regulations to regulate, amongst others, the management, procedures in respect of the procurement as well as the establishment of vigilance commission to supervise the same. The primary rules and mechanisms are the General Financial Rules and the Delegation of Financial Powers Rules 1978, framed by the Government of India, Ministry of Finance. Further, the Directorate General of Supplies & Disposals (DGS&D) Manual on Procurement and the Central Vigilance Commission ("CVC").

The General Financial Rules 2005 establishes the principles for general financial management and procedures for Government procurement and purchases. Rule 137 of the same articulates the fundamental principles of public purchasing and requires that the Government Ministries and Departments provide:

- adequate information and announcement;

- non-discriminatory practices to provide equality of opportunity, transparency in bidding, as well as in the evaluation process;

- accountability; and

- non-restrictive bidding conditions to unlock the particular market.

With regard to the tender process in public procurement, the Office Memorandum issued by CVC dated June 8, 2004 clearly mandates that the bids be opened in the presence of the bidders. Further, the Office Memorandum issued by CVC dated July 9, 2003, provides that the acceptance/rejection should not be arbitrary but on justified grounds as per specifications/evaluation criteria. Government agencies must also follow certain guiding principles and code of conduct, in the process of evaluation and award of tenders and contracts. These are highlighted in CVC Circular No. 4/3/07 dated March 3, 2007 and are as follows:

- the lowest bidder (L1) must be awarded the contract;

- due diligence must be exercised by the competent authority while accepting a tender or ordering negotiations or calling for a re-tender;

- post-tender negotiations will only be allowed in exceptional cases;

- any clarifications must be uniformly issued to all bidders;

- no new condition should be brought in while evaluating the tenders. Similarly, no tender enquiry condition (specially the significant/essential ones) should be over looked while evaluating the tenders;

- "transparency, fairness and maintenance of competition" as the corner stones while bids are being evaluated.[90]

Violation or breach of the CVC guidelines could entail proceedings against the State in a Court of law. A tenderer has a right to be heard if that the proper tendering process has not been followed or if bid has been wrongly rejected. In such an event, a tenderer has to make a representation to the specified authority to whom such a representation is to be made.[91] However, the decision of such an authority would be final unless challenged before a High Court in its "writ jurisdiction" under art.226 of the Constitution of India.[92] It would be pertinent here to note that while exercising power of judicial review under art.226, the Court does not sit as a court of appeal over the government's decision but seeks to examine the decision making-process on the grounds of arbitrariness,[93] irrationality, bias, violation of principles of natural justice, etc.

It appears that the anti-corruption laws in India are primarily targeted towards curbing this ailment of corruption in the public sectors. The position on private individuals and foreign public officials are discussed below.

I. LIABILITY OF PRIVATE INDIVIDUALS

7–25   The conduct of private entities is primarily regulated by their internal code of conduct and ethics. Private parties/entities may find themselves liable under the PCA and IPC if they are found to have taken gratification to influence public servants or have abetted the commission of an offence of bribery/corruption. This would include a person making a payment to a public servant to perform or refrain from performing an act.

II. LIABILITY OF FOREIGN PUBLIC OFFICIALS

7–26   Indian law does not create an offence of bribery of a foreign public official. However, UNCAC has envisaged for specific provisions which govern the conduct of foreign public officials. Whilst India has signed the UNCAC in December, 2005 it is yet to ratify the same.

---

[90] See CVC Circular No. 4/3/07 dated March 3, 2007.

[91] Public procurement in India, Sumeet Kachwaha, Kachwaha & Partners, Source: Mondaq dated May 25, 2009.

[92] Under art.226, a High Court can be moved for enforcement of any right including fundamental right. It has to be noted that these provisions can only be invoked against the sovereign actions of the "State" and not against private individuals.

[93] *Kumari Shrilekha Vidyarthi v State of UP* (1991) 1 SCC 212.

F. INSTITUTIONAL FRAMEWORK

There are various bodies in place for implementing anticorruption policies and   7–27
raising awareness on corruption issues. At the federal level, key institutions
include the Supreme Court, the Central Vigilance Commission, the Central
Bureau of Investigation, the Office of the Comptroller & Auditor General, and the
Chief Information Commission. At the state level, the key institutions include the
CB-CID, Anti-Corruption Bureau, State Vigilance Departments and the forthcoming Lokpal and Lokayukta.

I. CENTRAL VIGILANCE COMMISSION

The Central Vigilance Commission ("CVC/Commission") was set up by the   7–28
government on the recommendations of the Santhanam Committee in 1964 It is
the apex vigilance institution in India, free of control from any executive
authority, and monitors vigilance activity under the Central Government with
regard to the planning, executing, reviewing and reforming their vigilance work.[94]

The Supreme Court in *Vineet Narain v Union of India*[95] had directed the
Central Government to confer statutory status to the CVC and make it responsible for effective supervision of the functioning of the CBI.[96] In view of the same,
an Ordinance was passed by the President, through which the CVC was granted
"statutory status" and made a multi member Commission with effect from
August 25, 1998.[97] The CVC Bill was passed by both the houses of Parliament in
2003 and the Central Vigilance Commission Act 2003 ("CVC Act") came into
effect on September 11, 2003 following receipt of assent from the President.

The CVC Act vested the Commission with superintendence over vigilance
matters, anti-corruption measures, and at times, CBI practices. The Commission
consists of a Central Vigilance Commissioner i.e. the Chairperson and not more
than two Vigilance Commissioners, i.e. the Members.

The CVC does not come under any Ministry or department. It is an inde-   7–29
pendent watchdog which is only responsible to the Parliament. The CVC's primary role is vigilance superintendence. The CVC is empowered to enquire or
cause inquiries to be conducted in to offences alleged to have been committed
under the PCA by certain categories of public servants.[98] After the GOI Resolution on "Public Interest Disclosure and Protection of Informer" dated April
2004, the Government of India has authorised the Commission as the "Designated Agency" to receive written complaints for disclosure on any allegation of
corruption or misuse of office and recommend appropriate action. The CVC can
receive complaints against officials including those working for the Central

---

[94] Available at *http://cvc.nic.in/cvc_back.htm* [Accessed July 15, 2010].
[95] (1998) 1 SCC 226.
[96] Available at *www.cvc.nic.in/faqs.htm* [Accessed July 15, 2010].
[97] Available at *http://cvc.nic.in/cvc_back.htm* [Accessed July 15, 2010].
[98] See above.

Government ministries and departments, Central Government public sector undertakings, nationalised banks, insurance companies, and other centrally administered territories.[99]

Furthermore, the Commission has its own Secretariat, Chief Technical Examiners' Wing and a wing of Commissioners for Departmental Inquiries. The Chief Technical Examiner's Wing constitutes the technical wing of the CVC. Its main functions are:

- technical audit of construction works of Governmental organisations from a vigilance angle;

- investigation of specific cases of complaints relating to construction works;

- extension of assistance to CBI in their investigations involving technical matters and for evaluation of properties in Delhi.

It also provides assistance and advice on the tendering processes to the Commission in vigilance cases involving technical matters.[100]

The Commissioners for Departmental Inquiries functions as Inquiry Officers to conduct Oral inquiries in departmental proceeding initiated against public servants.[101]

II. CENTRAL BUREAU OF INVESTIGATION

7–30 The Central Bureau of Investigation ("CBI") is the prime investigating agency of the Central Government and derives power to investigate from the DSPE.[102] The CBI is placed under the Ministry of Personnel, Pensions & Grievances and consists of three divisions: the Investigation and Anti-Corruption Division, which deals with cases of corruption and fraud committed by public servants of all Central Government Departments, Central Public Sector Undertakings and Central Financial Institutions, the Special Crimes Division, which deal with cases of terrorism, bomb blasts, sensational homicides, kidnapping for ransom and crimes committed by the mafia/underworld, and the Economic Offences Division, which deals with bank frauds, financial frauds, Import Export & Foreign Exchange Violations, large scale smuggling of narcotics, antiques, cultural property and smuggling of other contraband items, etc. These units have the power to investigate cases of alleged corruption in all branches of the Central Government, but need the permission of state governments to investigate cases at the state level. The Supreme and High Courts can instruct the CBI to conduct investigations.

---

[99] Jessica Jones, *India Versus the United Nations: The Central Vigilance Commission Act Does Not Satisfy the U.N. Convention Against Corruption*, 22 Emory Int'l L. Rev. 799 at p.835.
[100] Available at *http://cvc.nic.in/cvc_org.htm*.
[101] See above.
[102] Available at *http://cbi.nic.in/aboutus/aboutus.php*.

The CBI also has a complaint mechanism similar to the CVC, which is set out on its website.[103] Each complaint is, however, scrutinised as to whether the same would fall within the purview of the CBI and would merit its attention. That not being the case, the matter is then forwarded to the department concerned.[104] The general procedure which is followed is as set out below. Issues which fall within the ambit of CBI and needs further verification, require permission of the Competent Authority to verify the same.[105] After such approval, the complaint would be assigned a regular complaint number.[106] If the complaint indicates serious misconduct on the part of a public servant, a Preliminary Enquiry may be registered after obtaining approval of the Competent Authority.[107] Once sufficient material/information is gathered, a Regular Case is registered.[108] Thereafter, a First Information Report ("FIR") is recorded under s.154 of the Criminal Procedure Code 1973 ("CrPC") and an investigation taken is taken up.

The CBI's 2008 Annual Report reports that out of the 991 cases registered with the CBI, the largest number, being 752 were registered with the anti-corruption division.[109] Out of the said number, "279 cases were registered for demand of bribe by public servants for showing official favours and 93 were registered for possession of assets disproportionate to known sources of income."[110]

III. The Office of the Comptroller and Auditor General

The objective behind setting up the Office of the Comptroller and Auditor   7–31
General ("The Office of C&AG") was: "to enhance the accountability of the executive, i.e., the Government, to the Parliament and State Legislatures by carrying out audits in the public sector and providing accounting services to the States in accordance with the Constitution of India and laws as well as best international practices".[111] Articles 148 to 151 of the Constitution of India establish The Office of C&AG[112] while also giving their duties and powers. It reads as follows:

---

[103] Available at *http://cbi.nic.in/contactus/contact.php* [Accessed July 15, 2010].

[104] Chapter 8: *Complaints & Source Information, Crime Manual*, 2005 available through *http://cbi.nic.in*.

[105] The Competent Authority is one who could order registration of a Regular Case for the particular rank of officer against whom the complaint has been made.

[106] Chapter 8: Complaints & Source Information, Crime Manual, 2005 available through *http://cbi.nic.in*.

[107] Chapter 9: Preliminary Enquires, Crime Manual, 2005 available through *http://cbi.nic*.

[108] Chapter 10: Regular Cases, Crime Manual, 2005 available through *http://cbi.nic.in*.

[109] Annual Report 2008, Central Bureau of Investigation Government of India at para.2.2.1.

[110] Annual Report 2008, Central Bureau of Investigation Government of India at para.2.2.1.

[111] Available at *http://www.cag.gov.in/* [Accessed July 15, 2010].

[112] "148. Comptroller and Auditor-General of India—

a. There shall be a Comptroller and Auditor-General of India who shall be appointed by the President by warrant under his hand and seal and shall only be removed from office in like manner and on like grounds as a Judge of the Supreme Court.

b. Every person appointed to be the Comptroller and Auditor-General of India shall, before he enters upon his office, make and subscribe before the President or some person appointed in that behalf by him, an oath or affirmation according to the form set out for the purpose in the Third Schedule.

"Duties and Powers of the Comptroller and Auditor-General—

The Comptroller and Auditor-General shall perform such duties and exercise such powers in relation to the accounts of the Union and of the States and of any other authority or body as may be prescribed by or under any law made by Parliament and, until provision in that behalf is so made, shall perform such duties and exercise such powers in relation to the accounts of the Union and of the States as were conferred on or exercisable by the Auditor-General of India immediately before the commencement of this Constitution in relation to the accounts of the Dominion of India and of the provinces respectively."

The powers and duties of the Office of C&AG, however, are dealt with under the Comptroller and Auditor-General's (Duties, Powers and Conditions of Service) Act 1971. Primarily, it is the duty of the Office of C&AG's to compile accounts of the Union and States. The relevant statutory provisions have been highlighted below:

"10. (1) The Comptroller and Auditor-General shall be responsible—

(a)   for compiling the accounts of the Union and of each State from the initial and subsidiary account rendered to the audit and accounts offices under his control by treasuries, offices or departments responsible for the keeping of such accounts; and

(b)   for keeping such accounts in relation to any of the matters specified in clause (a) as may be necessary:
       . . .

(2) Where, under any arrangement, a person other than the Comptroller and Auditor-General has, before the commencement of this Act, been responsible—

(i)   for compiling the accounts of any particular service or department of the Union or of a State, or

(ii)   for keeping the accounts of any particular class or character,

. . . "

The Office of the C&AG also has to prepare and submit accounts to the President, Governors of States and Administrators of Union Territories having

c. The salary and other conditions of service of the Comptroller and Auditor-General shall be such as may be determined by Parliament by law and, until they are so determined, shall be as specified in the Second Schedule:
    Provided that neither the salary of a Comptroller and Auditor-General nor his rights in respect of leave of absence, pension or age of retirement shall be varied to his disadvantage after his appointment.

d. The Comptroller and Auditor-General shall not be eligible for further office either under the Government of India or under the Government of any State after he has ceased to hold his office.

e. Subject to the provisions of this Constitution and of any law made by parliament, the conditions of service of persons serving in the Indian Audit and Accounts Department and the administrative powers of the Comptroller and Auditor-General shall be such as may be prescribed by rules made by the President after consultation with the Comptroller and Auditor-General.

f. The administrative expenses of the office of the Comptroller and Auditor-General including all salaries, allowances and pensions payable to or in respect of persons serving in that office, shall be charged upon the Consolidated Fund of India."

Legislative Assemblies and has general powers of auditing and rendering assistance to the States and the Union.[113]

The auditing and accounting work of The Office of C&AG was praised by the 2007 Global Integrity Report for being independent and well-staffed in all the states. The Office of C&AG has produced several reports on state departments such as railways, telecommunications, public sector enterprise, and tax administration. These reports have revealed many financial irregularities, suggesting a lack of monitoring of public expenses, poor targeting and corrupt practices in many branches of the government.

However, the statutory authority of The Office of C&AG are restricted to auditing, compiling, preparing and submitting reports, it does not have the authority to ensure compliance with its recommendations or any have any concrete mechanism to get its proposals implemented.[114] Despite this limitation, the recommendations made by The Office of C&AG are considered seriously as on the whole, its institution "is well respected for its independence and even feared, curbing initiative and encouraging avoidance of decisions."[115]

---

[113] The relevant statutory provisions read as follows:

"11. The Comptroller and Auditor-General shall from the accounts compiled by him or by the Government or any other person responsible in that behalf prepare in each year accounts (including, in the case of accounts compiled by him, appropriation accounts) showing under the respective heads the annual receipts and disbursements for the purpose of the Union, of each State and of each Union territory having a Legislative Assembly, and shall submit those accounts to the President or the Governor of a State or Administrator of the Union territory having a Legislative Assembly, as the case may be on or before such dates as he may, with the concurrence of the Government concerned, determine:

...

12. The Comptroller and Auditor-General shall, in so far as the accounts, for the compilation or keeping of which he is responsible, enable him so to do, give to the Union government, to the State Governments or to the Governments of Union Territories having Legislative Assemblies, as the case may be, such information as they may, from time to time, require, and render such assistance in the preparation of their annual financial statements as they may reasonably ask for.
General Provisions Relating to Audit
13. It shall be the duty of the Comptroller and Auditor-General—

   (a) to audit all expenditure from the Consolidated Fund of India and of each State and of each Union territory having a Legislative Assembly and to ascertain whether the moneys shown in the accounts as having been disbursed were legally available for and applicable to the service or purpose to which they have been applied or charged and whether the expenditure conforms to the authority which governs it;

   (b) to audit all transactions of the Union and of the States relating to Contingency Funds and Public Accounts;

   (c) to audit all trading, manufacturing, profit and loss accounts and balance-sheets and other subsidiary accounts kept in any department of the Union or of a State;

and in each case to report on the expenditure, transactions or accounts so audited by him."

[114] Transparency International, CMI, U4 Expert Answers, *Overview of Corruption and Anti-Corruption Efforts in India*, available at *http://www.u4.no* [Accessed July 15, 2010].

[115] Report No. 27859-IN, *India Country Procurement Assessment Report*, December 10 2003, Procurement Services South Asia Region, Document of the World Bank, para.7.0 at p.17

IV. Chief Information Commission

7–32   The Chief Information Commission ("CIC"), as pointed out earlier, was established in 2005 with the enactment of the RTI Act and came into operation in 2006. While enquiring into any matter it has the same powers as are vested in a civil court while trying a suit under the Code of Civil Procedure, 1908.[116] The scope of the CIC has been detailed in s.18 of the RTI Act and includes the power to receive and inquire into any complaint received involving:

- Non-appointment of an Information Officer;

- refused access to any particular information;

- not given a response within the time frame;

- where incomplete, misleading or false information was provided;

- or any other issue pertaining to access of records.

It has delivered decisions instructing the government, courts, universities, police, and ministries on how to share information of public interest. The CIC has recently held that the disclosure of information regarding the assets of a public servant, routinely collected by the public authority, should be made available to the public under the RTI Act. Thus, public officers have been put on par with politicians and Supreme Court judges who recently, bowing to pressure, agreed to open up their assets to public scrutiny.[117]

V. Serious Fraud Investigation Office

7–33   The Serious Fraud Investigation Office ("SFIO") was set up by the Ministry of Corporate Affairs (MCA) and started functioning on October 1, 2003.[118] It was set up in the backdrop of stock market scams, failure of non financial banking companies, phenomena of vanishing companies and plantation companies on the basis of the recommendations made by the Naresh Chandra Committee[119] (set up

---

[116] Refer to s.18(3) of the RTI Act.

[117] See http://timesofindia.indiatimes.com [Accessed July 15, 2010].

[118] Standing Committee on Finance (2004-2005), Ministry of Company Affairs, Fourteenth Lok Sabha, Demand for grants, Fifth Report.

[119] The Committee inter alia made following recommendations on setting up of "Serious Fraud Office":
- A Corporate Serious Fraud Office (CSFO) should be set up in the department of Company Affairs with specialists inducted on the basis of transfer/deputation and on special term contracts.
- This should be in the form of a multi-disciplinary team that not only uncovers the fraud, but is able to direct and supervise prosecutions under various economic legislations through appropriate agencies.
- There should be a Task Force constituted for each case under a designated team leader.
- In the interest of adequate control and efficiency, a Committee each, headed by the Cabinet

220

by the government on August 21, 2002 on corporate governance).[120]

The SIFO has been given a limited mandate to investigate corporate frauds,[121] referred to it by the governmental authorities under s.235 or 237 of the Companies Act 1956[122] and to forward its investigation reports to the concerned agencies, for prosecution and appropriate action.[123] The powers of the Inspector for carrying out the investigation are contained in ss.239, 240 and 240(A) of the Companies Act 1956[124] and consequently, the Officer of SFIO appointed as Investigating Officer by the government has the final say in the matter related to investigation.[125] The subject specific groups of officers which render necessary assistance to the Investigating Officer have to examine the issues involved in the case within a given time frame, as given by the Central Government, and give requisite inputs to the Investigating Officer.[126] The SFIO normally takes up for investigation only such cases, which are characterised by:

- complexity and having inter-departmental and multi-disciplinary ramifications;

- substantial involvement of public interest to be judged by size, either in terms of monetary misappropriation or in terms of persons affected, and;

- the possibility of investigation leading to or contributing towards a clear improvement in systems, laws or procedures.[127]

It is only in 2009 that the Ministry decided to recognise the role and powers of SFIO in the revised Companies Bill, making it an important arm of the MCA.[128] Currently, SFIO does not find any mention in the Companies Act 1956.

Secretary should directly oversee the appointments to, and functioning of this office, and coordinates the work of concerned departments and agencies.
- Later, a legislative framework, along the lines of the SFO in the UK, should be set up to enable the CSFO to investigate all aspects of the fraud, and direct the prosecution in appropriate courts.

[120] Available at http://www.sfio.nic.in [Accessed July 15, 2010].

[121] Available at http://www.sfio.nic.in [Accessed July 15, 2010].

[122] "Both these provisions enable the Central government to appoint one or more competent persons as inspectors to investigate and submit a report on the affairs of a company if, in its opinion, or in the opinion of the RoC or the Company Law Board, there are circumstances suggesting that the business of a company is being conducted with the intention to defraud its creditors or members, or for a fraudulent or unlawful purpose." as available on http://www.hinduonnet.com [Accessed July 15, 2010].

[123] See above.

[124] Sections 239, 240 and 240A deals with the powers of investigation and seizure of documents by the Inspector. Section 239 lays down the power of the Investigator to carry out investigation into the affairs of related companies including the managing agent associate of the same. Section 240 deals with production of documents and evidence by the officers, employees or agents of the company which is being investigated upon under Section 239. Section 240A deals with the power of seizure of documents by an Inspector.

[125] Available at http://www.sfio.nic.in.

[126] Ibid.

[127] Available at http://www.sfio.nic.in.

[128] Available at http://www.financialexpress.com [Accessed July 15, 2010].

(a) Limitations/Inadequate Enforcement Agencies

7–34 It is observed that despite creation of several enforcement agencies, the same are not autonomous and have limited powers.

VI. CVC

7–35 The CVC, for example, whilst being the apex vigilance institution and having statutory status, can only inquire or instigate an inquiry against a public servant of a certain designation.[129] Section (8)(h) of the CVC Act stipulates that "the CVC cannot act in a way not consistent with the directions relating to vigilance matters issued by the Government." It is observed that the Central Government has hardly established the "apex" anti-corruption body envisioned by the Santhanam Committee, i.e. (i) the establishment of a Director of Central Complaints and Redress under the Central Vigilance Commission to look into grievances of citizens against the administration; and (ii) the centralisation of all powers and responsibilities in disciplinary matters in the Commission. Instead, the government has set up an institution limited in its vigilance practices.

The other limitations of the CVC include: (i) inability to effectively implement anti-corruption policies; (ii) absence of independent investigatory department, instead, it instructs the CBI to initiate investigations; (iii) inability to commence prosecution against offenders.[130]

Apart from limitation in its powers, the provisions of the CVC are in conflict with, amongst others, recommendations by the judiciary and fundamental principles. The CVC Act clashes greatly with the Supreme Court's recommendations in the Vineet Narain Case and re-codifies the once maligned Single Directive shielding the highly placed public servants. The Single Directive refers to a set of instructions restricting the CBI from opening an investigation against any official holding the rank of Joint Secretary or higher, without the permission of the Central Government.[131] Section 26(4C)(2)(c) of the CVC Act has gone beyond Vineet Narayan Case resurrecting the Single Directive by inserting into the DSPE Act a new s.6A, which reads as follows:

"(1) The Delhi Police Special Establishment shall not conduct any inquiry or investigation into any offence alleged to have been committed under the Prevention of Corruption Act, 1988 except with the previous approval of the Central Government where such allegation relates to—

(a) the employees of the Central Government of the level of Joint Secretary and above; and

(b) such officers as are appointed by the Central Government in corporations

---

[129] Jessica Jones, *India Versus the United Nations: The Central Vigilance Commission Act Does Not Satisfy the U.N. Convention Against Corruption*, 22 Emory Int'l L. Rev. 799 at p.835.

[130] Jessica Jones, *India Versus the United Nations: The Central Vigilance Commission Act Does Not Satisfy the U.N. Convention Against Corruption*, 22 Emory Int'l L. Rev. 799 at p.836.

[131] Jessica Jones, *India Versus the United Nations: The Central Vigilance Commission Act Does Not Satisfy the U.N. Convention Against Corruption*, 22 Emory Int'l L. Rev. 799 at p.829.

established by or under any Central Act, Government companies, societies and local authorities owned or controlled by that Government."

It is evident that the CVC Act also ignores the spirit of equality found in the Supreme Court's judgment and art.14 of the Indian Constitution as the return of the Single Directive restores differential treatment among certain classes of people for the same alleged offenses.

(a) Why was the Single Directive brought back despite decision of the Supreme Court to the contrary?

To nullify the court ruling in Vineet Narain, the parliament, as mentioned above, passed the necessary amendment and revived it on the recommendations of a Joint Parliamentary Committee. This amendment, it was contended by the government, was to protect the bureaucrats from vexatious litigations by disgruntled elements.[132] The return of the Single Directive has been justified on the grounds that the officials needed this protection in order to halt harassment[133] and that "no protection was available to persons at the decision-making level".[134]

7–36

This amendment was subsequently challenged in the Supreme Court in the case of *Dr Subramanian Swamy v Director, CBI*.[135] on a footing different than that of Vineet Narain, i.e. the touchstone of art.14 of the Constitution of India.[136] Section 6A creates two classes of people, namely, high public officials that are protected from investigations and others who are not granted such privileges. It was contended by the Petitioner's counsel that it was wholly irrational and arbitrary to protect highly placed public servants from inquiry or investigation in the light of the conditions prevailing in the country and the corruption at high places.[137] However, the Supreme Court did not determine the constitutionality of

---

[132] Available through *http://www.business-standard.com* [Accessed July 15, 2010].

[133] Jessica Jones, *India Versus the United Nations: The Central Vigilance Commission Act Does Not Satisfy the U.N. Convention Against Corruption*, 22 Emory Int'l L. Rev. 799 at p.829.

[134] Available through *http://timesofindia.indiatimes.com* [Accessed July 15, 2010].

[135] (2005) 2 SCC 317.

[136] Article 14—Equality before law
"The State shall not deny to any person equality before the law or the equal protection of the laws within the territory of India."

[137] (2005) 2 SCC 317, para.3, quoting:
"The contention is that Vineet Narain's decision frames structure by which honest officers could fearlessly enforce the criminal law and detect corruption uninfluenced by extraneous political, bureaucratic or other influences and the result of the impugned legislation is that the very group of persons, namely, high ranking bureaucrats whose misdeeds and illegalities may have to be inquired into, would decide whether the CBI should even start an inquiry or investigation against them or not. There will be no confidentiality and insulation of the investigating agency from political and bureaucratic control and influence because the approval is to be taken from the Central Government which would involve leaks and disclosures at every stage. The very nexus of the criminal-bureaucrat-politician which is subverting the whole polity would be involved in granting or refusing prior approval before an inquiry or investigation can take place. Pointing out that the essence of a police investigation is skilful inquiry and collection of material and evidence in a manner by which the potential culpable individuals are not forewarned, the submission made is that the prior sanction of same department would result in indirectly putting to notice the officers to be investigated before commencement of investigation. Learned senior counsel con-

the Single Directive and decided to refer the case to a larger bench.[138] However, there have been no further developments on this front.

(b) Is the Jurisdiction of the CVC Limited?

7-37   The CVC Act also has put into motion a mechanism which creates the reverse effect of that initially intended. For example, the Supreme Court having the view that the work done by CBI was inadequate suggested the switching of super-intendence from the Central Government to the CVC. However, the CVC Act gives the CVC supervisory power only over cases falling under the PCA, vesting the authority with the Central Government regarding all other cases.[139] In this regard reference may be made to s.(8)(1)(b) of the CVC Act which states that the Commission is not allowed to "investigate or dispose of any case in a particular manner."

It can be contended that the aforementioned limitations have prevented the CVC from discharging its functions to the fullest. Having reviewed the enforcement agencies and the limitations, we now seek to highlight some of the major corruption scandals which India has witnessed.

G. CORRUPTION SCANDALS

I. VK Krishna Menon Scandal

7-38   Post independence, the first major corruption scandal related to VK Krishna Menon, the then Indian High Commissioner UK. The Indian army had placed orders for procurement of 155 Jeeps worth INR 8 million. They were to be used in the then troubled Hyderabad and Kashmir regions. The Indian army had sought to use the services of a Brigadier, which Krishna Menon bypassed and instead outsourced through an agent, Cleminsan.[140]

II. 1957 LIC-Mundra deals

7-39   It was the first financial scandal of independent India. With his connections, Haridas Mundhra, a Kolkata based industrialist and stock speculator, got Life Insurance Corporation (LIC) to invest INR 1.24 crores in the shares of his six troubled companies such as Richardson Cruddas, Jessops & Company, Smith

---

tends that it is wholly irrational and arbitrary to protect highly placed public servants from inquiry or investigation in the light of the conditions prevailing in the country and the corruption at high places as reflected in several judgments of this Court including that of Vineet Narain's.
[138] (2005) 2 SCC 317 at [8].
[139] Jessica Jones, *India Versus the United Nations: The Central Vigilance Commission Act Does Not Satisfy the U.N. Convention Against Corruption*, 22 Emory Int'l L. Rev. 799 at 838.
[140] See generally, *http://www.southasiaanalysis.org* [Accessed July 15, 2010].

Stanistreet, Osler Lamps, Agnelo Brothers and British India Corporation. The investment was done under governmental pressure and bypassed the LIC's investment committee, which was informed of this decision only after the deal had gone through. In the event, LIC lost most of the money. The irregularity was brought to the notice of the Lok Sabha by the ruling party member Feroze Gandhi, the son-in-law of the then Prime Minister. The matter was disposed in record 24 day inquiry by one-man Committee of Justice MC Chagla. Haridas Mundhra was sentenced to imprisonment. The Committee found the Finance Minister T.T. Krishnamachari constitutionally responsible. He subsequently resigned. The Committee recommended trial of Finance Secretary, H. M. Patel, along with two LIC officials, L.S. Vaidyanathan for suspected collusion. The incident turned to be the harbinger for the coming up of statutory CVC to play a pivotal role looking into the phenomenon.[141]

III. BOFORS SCANDAL

The Bofors scandal was a major corruption scandal in the 1980s when the then **7–40** Prime Minister Rajiv Gandhi and several others were accused of receiving payments from M/s AB Bofors for winning them a bid to supply India's 155 mm field howitzer. A contract was entered between Government of India and M/s AB Bofors on March 24, 1986 for supply of 400 FH 77-B gun systems along with vehicles, ammunition and other accessories at a total cost of SEK 8,410,660,984 (equivalent to about INR 1437.72 crores as per exchange rate on March 21, 1986) and on May 2, 1986 advance payment equivalent to 20 per cent of the contract value was paid to M/s AB Bofors. On April 16, 1987 Swedish Radio came out with a story that Bofors had managed to obtain the contract from Government of India after payment of large amounts as bribe. On April 21, 1987 the Government of India made a formal request to Government of Sweden for an investigation into the allegations. The CBI registered a case being RC 1A/90-ACU.IV on January 22, 1990 and proceeded to investigate the matter.[142]

Interestingly, Prakash Hinduja, one of the key accused, moved an application before the Special Judge praying that "the charge sheets submitted by the CBI be dismissed and the cognizance taken and the process issued against the accused be revoked."[143] The application was moved on the ground that the cases were never reported to CVC and the CVC has neither reviewed the cases nor had considered them fit for continuance of the prosecution and as such there was a non-compliance of the directions issued by this Court in the case of Vineet Narain.[144] However, the said Application was dismissed by the Supreme Court. The scale of the corruption was far worse than any that India had seen before, and directly led

---

[141] See generally, *http://www.iif.edu* [Accessed July 15, 2010].
[142] *Union of India (UOI) v Prakash P. Hinduja* (2003) 6 SCC 195 at [2] [Hereinafter *Hinduja Case*].
[143] *Hinduja Case*, at [3].
[144] *Hinduja Case*, at [3].

to the defeat of Gandhi's ruling Indian National Congress party in the November 1989 general elections.[145] However, in 2004, Rajiv Gandhi was cleared of all charges by the Delhi High Court. The High Court held that there was no evidence on record to suggest that Rajiv Gandhi had used any direct or indirect influence on anybody, including the Technical or Negotiating Committee, or as to the price.[146] The other accused, however, were being tried on other charges.

IV. JHARKHAND MUKTI MORCHA MP'S

7–41   Another major scandal was the "vote for money" scandal in 1993 involving the Jharkhand Mukti Morcha Members of Parliament. Former Prime Minister, P.V. Narasimha Rao, was accused and later convicted in a trial court on charges of bribing a few MPs of the Jharkhand Mukti Morcha in a bid to convert his minority government into a majority government in the no-confidence motion he faced in 1993.[147] All the accused were charged under s.120B for Criminal Con-

---

[145]   See *http://www.rediff.com* [Accessed July 15, 2010] for an analysis.

[146]   *Kartongen Kemi Och Forvaltning AB v State through CBI* 2004 (72) DRJ 693, quoting the relevant paras as follows:

"77. Aforesaid conspectus of facts itself shows that so far as Public Servants viz late Sh. Rajiv Gandhi and Late Sh. S.K. Bhatnagar are concerned sixteen long years of investigation by a premier agency of the country viz CBI could not unearth a scintilla of evidence against them for having accepted bribe/illegal gratification, in awarding the contract in favor of Bofors. All efforts of CBI ended in fiasco as they could not lay hand upon any secret or known account of these public servants where the alleged money might have found its abode either in Swiss Banks or any other Bank or vault. However, their efforts, particularly due to the cooperation of Swiss authorities and Swiss Banks fructified in tracing the money received as "commission" by middlemen/agents employed by Bofors for negotiating the contract.

78. Again not an iota of evidence has surfaced that may even remotely suggest or suspect that the money received as "commission" by them was held by them as a money for the public servants for such a long period. On the other hand, the evidence is that Hindujas used the money for their own business by way of withdrawing from the main account and transferring it to other accounts of theirs.

79. Had there been any such arrangement or conspiracy that as many as three agents would be paid "commission in the garb of illegal gratification for public servants for awarding contract there was no difficulty because of the "confidentiality clause" for the recipients and the givers to give indication in the accounts as nominee or joint-holder or any other kind of arrangement or indication that any amount was subsequently withdrawn and transferred to any secret account of public servants."

However, the Court further observed:

"87. If decision making authorities be in any field are prosecuted like this, no authority, no person would take decision nor would dare to take decision. However, it does not mean that the element of illegal gratification cannot exist in deserving cases. Possibility of procuring award of even of well deserving contract through illegal gratification to the persons involved for taking decision cannot be ruled out. Offence of giving or taking illegal gratification is independent of all such considerations. But the condition is that like any other offence, offence of "illegal gratification" has to be proved by way of evidence even if it gives rise to "strong suspicion" because of available material in trying a person for this offence..."

[147]   Available at *http://www.indianexpress.com* [Accessed July 15, 2010]. A similar cash-for-votes scam also came into the public limelight in 2008. Three BJP MPs displayed inside the House bundles of currency notes, allegedly paid to them for abstaining from the trust vote. A parliamentary committee has been tasked to probe the matter but no concrete conclusions have been reached so far. See generally, *http://www.thaindian.com* [Accessed July 15, 2010]; and *http://timesofindia.indiatimes.com* [Accessed July 15, 2010].

spiracy and the PCA for either giving or receiving the alleged bribes.[148] In this regard, Supreme Court had held that MPs were covered by the PCA but noted that the Act did not specify the authority which was to give the sanction. It was suggested that sanction be given by the chairperson of the Rajya Sabha[149] or the Speaker of the Lok Sabha[150], till a law specifying the authority was enacted.[151] However, no further action has been taken in this regard.

V. JUDICIARY SCANDALS

More recently it has been the judiciary that is bearing the close scrutiny of the public in connection with bribery and corruption. A string of judicial scandals have erupted in the recent past, starting with Chief Justice Sabharwal's case, the most recent involving the Chairman of the Company Law Board. The former Chief Justice had allegedly passed judgments that gave business advantage to his sons by calling for and dealing with the sealing of commercial property cases in March 2005, though they were not assigned to him. In this case, instead of taking an affirmative action in ordering an enquiry, the Court sentenced the four journalists who brought the news to light to four months' imprisonment for contempt of court for writing and publishing news reports critical of the former Chief Justice.[152]

7–42

The Supreme Court had observed in Sub-Committee of *Judicial Accountability v Union of India*[153] that:

> "It is true that society is entitled to expect the highest and most exacting standards of propriety in judicial conduct. Any conduct which tends to impair public confidence in the efficiency integrity and impartiality of the court is indeed forbidden."

This observation brings into sharp focus the recent controversy surrounding the disclosure of assets by the judges where the Delhi High Court stayed the order of the CIC, asking the Supreme Court Registry to provide information on declaration of assets by judges of the apex court and High Courts.[154] However, following the disclosure by some of the acting Supreme Court judges it was

---

[148] Available at *http://www.rediff.com* [Accessed July 15, 2010]
[149] It is the Upper House of the Parliament of India. The Council of States elected by the states' assemblies.
[150] Lok Sabha consists of representatives of the people chosen by direct election. It constitutes the Lower House of the Parliament of India.
[151] Available at *http://www.telegraphindia.com* [Accessed July 15, 2010].
[152] See generally, *http://www.merinews.com* [Accessed July 15, 2010]; *http://www.outlookindia.com* [Accessed July 15, 2010]. See also, *http://www.indianexpress.com* [Accessed July 15, 2010].
[153] (1991) 4 SCC 699 at [59].
[154] Available through *http://www.thehindu.com* [Accessed July 15, 2010].

decided to make the assets of Supreme Court judges' public.[155] This has to be seen as a radical, yet welcome, move as an internal mechanism, would not only ensure that perception of corruption in the judiciary is obliterated but also would encourage others occupying high posts of responsibility to come forward. It is important to dispel the general public's notion rather than let it fester and result in unwanted controversies.

It has been recently reported that the CBI is currently carrying out an operation at the Company Law Board in respect of a senior member who has been caught red-handed while accepting a bribe of INR 6 lakh to settle a case in favour of the company.[156] The investigation is ongoing.

VI. OTHER MAJOR SANDALS

7–43   Other major corruption scandals includes the release by an Indian news website of a videotape showing 31 politicians in March 2001 showing high level officials, bureaucrats and army officials taking bribes. The Defence Minister and leaders of the ruling BJP party were forced to resign.[157] Four defence ministry officials were also suspended. In September 2005 Laloo Prasad Yadav, the then Railway Minister, was charged with misappropriating state funds in the long running "fodder scam", embezzling over US \$40 million in state funds intended for the purchase of animal fodder.[158] In total, 170 persons were charged in connection with this scandal, including the then, Railway Minister.

H. CONCLUSION

7–44   The above is aimed at providing an overview of corruption in India, the legislative framework and the institutions put in place to combat this illness. It is evident from the above that there are sufficient laws and enforcement mechanisms in India to deal with the issue of corruption. The enactment of a further law would not seek to advance the steps or efforts that have already been taken. Essentially, it appears that what is required is stricter implementation and enforcement of the laws presently in place. Additionally, there is a strong and urgent need to change the cultural mindset of the people. For example, that one needs to go through the proper channels, instead of relying on other means to achieve the same. Education, awareness and increased in-house compliance could be some of the efforts that can be undertaken as a stepping stone towards changing this mindset.

---

[155] Available through *http://ibnlive.in.com* [Accessed July 15, 2010].
[156] *CBI catches top CLB official accepting bribe* published on Tuesday, November 24, 2009. Source: CNBC-TV18.
[157] See generally, *http://timesofindia.indiatimes.com* [Accessed July 15, 2010].
[158] Available through *http://www.u4.no*. See generally, *http://www.financialexpress.com* [Accessed July 15, 2010].

CHAPTER 8

CONDUCTING INTERNAL INVESTIGATIONS IN CONNECTION WITH ALLEGATIONS OF BRIBERY[1]

A. INTRODUCTION

In the preceding chapters, we examined the substantive anti-bribery laws of a **8–01** specific jurisdiction. For each jurisdiction, there are one or more regulatory authorities responsible for enforcing those laws. This chapter discusses certain regulatory authorities that enforce the anti-bribery laws and explores the practical steps involved in responding to an inquiry from regulators in any jurisdiction. Such a response typically involves conducting an internal investigation, especially when responding to an anti-bribery inquiry from US regulators.

Internal investigations come in all shapes and sizes. There is no "one size fits all" approach. The nature and scope of an internal investigation may depend on numerous practical considerations. In general, these considerations may include the nature of the alleged bribery offense, the nature of the company involved—as well as the role of the alleged wrongdoers within the company—and, to the extent a regulatory inquiry precedes or accompanies the start of the investigation, the nature of that inquiry.

Nevertheless, there are certain "best practices" to keep in mind for any organisation looking to conduct an efficient and thorough internal investigation. We will identify and expand upon those practices below in terms of commencing, conducting, and concluding an internal investigation of bribery allegations.

B. THE REGULATORS

I. UNITED STATES

Responsibility for enforcement of the FCPA is shared among two US govern- **8–02** mental agencies: the US Department of Justice (the "DOJ") and the US Securities and Exchange Commission (the "SEC").

---

[1] The authors gratefully acknowledge the substantial assistance of Jena Tiernan and Mark Rizik in drafting this chapter.

"The DOJ is responsible for all criminal enforcement and for civil enforcement of the anti-bribery provisions with respect to 'domestic concerns' and foreign companies and nationals. The SEC is responsible for civil enforcement of the anti-bribery provisions with respect to 'issuers.' "[2]

(a) DOJ Enforcement Authority

8–03   The DOJ is "an executive department of the government of the United States," headed by the Attorney General, with control over all criminal prosecutions and civil suits in which the United States has an interest, as well as federal law enforcement.[3] Within the DOJ are a number of agencies and divisions with specific activities and missions relating to the DOJ's overall federal law enforcement authority. Two of these divisions, the US Attorneys ("USAO")[4] and the Criminal Division,[5] share primary responsibility for enforcement of the FCPA. More specifically, within the Criminal Division, enforcement of the FCPA is handled by the Fraud Section.[6]

The United States Attorneys' Manual sets forth the DOJ's policy concerning criminal investigations and prosecutions of the FCPA.[7] According to that policy:

"[N]o investigation or prosecution of cases involving alleged violations of the antibribery provisions of [FCPA] . . . or of related violations of the FCPA's record keeping provi-

---

[2] Lay-Person's Guide—Foreign Corrupt Practices Act, available through *http://www.justice.gov/criminal/fraud/fcpa/docs/lay-persons-guide.pdf*.

[3] US DOJ Mission Statement and Statutory Authority, available through *http://www.usdoj.gov* [Accessed July 15, 2010]. The DOJ's mission is:
   "To enforce the law and defend the interests of the United States according to the law; to ensure public safety against threats foreign and domestic; to provide federal leadership in preventing and controlling crime; to seek just punishment for those guilty of unlawful behavior; and to ensure fair and impartial administration of justice for all Americans."

[4] The USAOs represent the federal government in the United States District Court, which is the federal court's trial level; 28 USC § 547; see also *US Attorneys' Manual (USAM)*, § 1–2.500 (November 2003) ("The United States Attorneys serve as the nation's principal litigators under the direction of the Attorney General. As such, the United States Attorneys conduct most of the trial work in which the United States is a party").

[5] "The mission of the Criminal Division is to serve the public interest through the enforcement of criminal statutes in a vigorous, fair, and effective manner; and to exercise general supervision over the enforcement of all federal criminal laws, with the exception of those statutes specifically assigned to the Antitrust, Civil Rights, Environment and Natural Resources, or Tax Divisions." DOJ Website, *http://www.justice.gov* [Accessed July 15, 2010].

[6] The Fraud Section investigates and prosecutes "complex white collar crime cases throughout the country . . . . The Section frequently coordinates interagency and multi-district investigations and international enforcement efforts." DOJ Website, *http://www.justice.gov/criminal/fraud/* [Accessed July 15, 2010].

[7] "The United States Attorneys' Manual is designed as a quick and ready reference for United States Attorneys, Assistant United States Attorneys, and Department attorneys responsible for the prosecution of violations of federal law. It contains general policies and some procedures relevant to the work of the United States Attorneys' offices and to their relations with the legal divisions, investigative agencies, and other components within the Department of Justice." USAM, § 1-1.100.

sions ... shall be instituted without the express authorization of the Criminal Division."[8]

The Manual provides that all information relating to a potential FCPA violation should be immediately brought to the attention of the Fraud Section of the Criminal Division:

"Unless otherwise agreed upon by the [Assistant Attorney General ("AAG")], Criminal Division, investigations and prosecutions of alleged violations of the antibribery provisions of the FCPA will be conducted by Trial Attorneys of the Fraud Section. Prosecutions of alleged violations of the record keeping provisions, when such violations are related to an antibribery violation, will also be conducted by Fraud Section Trial Attorneys, unless otherwise directed by the AAG, Criminal Division."[9]

The need for centralised supervision of investigations and prosecutions under the FCPA is deemed "compelling" because such investigations and prosecutions "raise complex enforcement problems abroad as well as difficult issues of jurisdiction and statutory construction."[10]

The Manual also addresses civil injunctive actions against violations of the antibribery provisions by domestic concerns and foreign nationals. Such proceedings "shall be instituted by Trial Attorneys of the Fraud Section in cooperation with the appropriate United States Attorney, unless otherwise directed by the AAG, Criminal Division."[11]

(b) SEC Enforcement Authority

The SEC is the primary federal government agency responsible for enforcing the federal securities laws and for regulating the securities industry. Its mission is "to protect investors, maintain fair, orderly, and efficient markets, and facilitate capital formation."[12]   **8–04**

Like the DOJ, the SEC is organised by certain divisions relevant to the agency's overall mission.[13] Of those divisions, the Enforcement Division is charged with investigating possible violations of, and enforcing, the federal

---

[8] USAM, § 9-47.110.
[9] USAM, § 9-47.110.
[10] USAM, § 9-47.110.
[11] USAM, § 9-47.130.
[12] US SEC, *The Investor's Advocate: How the SEC Protects Investors, Maintains Market Integrity, and Facilitates Capital Formation* [hereinafter *Investor's Advocate*], *http://www.sec.gov/about/whatwedo.html* [Accessed July 15, 2010].
[13] See P. Cohen and A. Papalaskaris, *Corporate Internal Investigations: An International Guide* (OUP, 2008). Each division has its own director, whose responsibilities and duties are set forth by federal regulations promulgated pursuant to the federal securities laws. See 17 CFR § 200.18 (Director of the Division of Corporate Finance); 17 CFR § 200.19a (Director of the Division of Market Regulation); 17 CFR § 200.19b (Director of the Division of Enforcement); 17 CFR § 200.20b (Director of the Division of Investment Management).

securities laws.[14] Due to a recent internal reorganisation within the SEC, there is now a Foreign Corrupt Practices unit, which focuses solely on violations of the FCPA.[15]

The reason why the SEC has a role in investigating violations of the anti-bribery provisions of the FCPA in connection with "issuers" is because these companies were already under the SEC's jurisdiction when the FCPA was enacted. At the time, the SEC was "the principal agency of the Government taking the lead in the investigation of foreign bribery."[16] Congress concluded that the "SEC has thus developed considerable expertise in investigation [sic] corrupt overseas payments. This same expertise can be put to work in investigating potential violations of the antibribery provisions" of the FCPA.[17]

Nevertheless, as stated above, the SEC's regulatory authority is only civil in nature. The SEC has no authority to bring criminal charges against individuals or corporations, but must instead refer such cases to the DOJ.[18]

II. United Kingdom Serious Fraud Office

8–05 The Serious Fraud Office (the "SFO") is "the lead agency in England, Wales and Northern Ireland for investigating and prosecuting cases of overseas corruption."[19] According to guidance released by the SFO on July 21, 2009, this agency "is responsible for enforcing the current law."[20] This now includes the Bribery Law.

Recent efforts to step up enforcement efforts with respect to overseas corruption have included the establishment of a separate work area (the Anti-Corruption Domain) under the leadership of "a very experienced Head of Domain."[21]

Generally speaking, when the SFO considers whether to take on a case, it

---

[14] 17 CFR § 200.19b provides, in relevant part, that:
"The Director of the Division of Enforcement is Responsible to the Commission for supervising and conducting all enforcement activities under the acts administered by the Commission. The Director recommends the institution of administrative and injunctive actions arising out of such enforcement activities and determines the sufficiency of the evidence to support the allegations in any proposed complaint."

[15] The creation of this unit, among four others, was meant to "help provide the additional structure, resources, and expertise necessary for enforcement staff to keep pace with ever-changing markets and more comprehensively investigate cases involving complex products, markets, regulatory regimes, practices and transactions." SEC Press Release, *SEC Names New Specialized Unit Chiefs and Head of New Office of Market Intelligence*, (January 13, 2010), available through *http://www.sec.gov*.

[16] *Senate Report.*

[17] *Senate Report.*

[18] See 17 CFR § 200.19b ("The Director supervises the Regional Directors and, in collaboration with the General Counsel, reviews cases to be recommended to the Department of Justice for criminal prosecution"); 17 CFR § 202.5(b) (granting the SEC discretion to refer willful violations of fraud to the DOJ for criminal prosecution but not allowing the SEC to prosecute directly).

[19] *Approach of the Serious Fraud Office to Dealing with Overseas Corruption*, (July 21, 2009) [hereinafter "*SFO Guidance*"], available through *http://www.sfo.gov.uk* [Accessed July 15, 2010].

[20] *SFO Guidance.*

[21] *SFO Guidance.*

considers several criteria.[22] First, it considers how much money is involved in the fraud. If less than £1 million is at stake, the SFO will typically not investigate or prosecute the case.[23] Secondly, the SFO will question whether the case is likely to give rise to "national publicity and widespread public concern."[24] Cases meeting the second criterion include both commercial cases of public interest and cases involving government departments, public bodies and the governments of other countries.[25] Thirdly, the case should be one that requires a highly specialised knowledge.[26] Fourthly, the SFO will consider whether the case has an international dimension. The fifth criterion examines if legal, accountancy, and investigative skills need to be brought together. Finally, the SFO will consider whether the case is complex enough to justify the use of s.2 powers.[27] A s.2 notice is a power available to the SFO, in cases only where the Director suspects serious or complex fraud,[28] to obtain information either through interviewing persons of interest or through the acquisition of documents, including electronically stored data.[29] In practice, this means lawyers and accountants, not police, question suspects. The suspects are given notice that they must respond to questions in a specific time and place, or immediately.[30]

In its first year of operation, the SFO issued 233 s.2 notices.[31] Between 2007-

---

[22] In its Annual Report, the SFO states that "[t]he key criterion ... is that the suspected fraud was such that the direction of the investigation should be in the hands of those who will be responsible for the prosecution." These criteria were developed following the DAVIE Report that considered, and ultimately rejected, the idea to merge the Fraud Divisions of the Crown Prosecution Service with the SFO. See Rampage, at 11.

[23] According to the SFO, the £1 million threshold should not be construed as the "main indicator of suitability," but rather, it provides "an objective and recognizable signpost of seriousness and likely public concern." *Criteria for acceptance of cases*, Serious Fraud Office, available through *http://www.sfo.gov.uk*.

[24] *Criteria for acceptance of cases*, Serious Fraud Office.

[25] *Criteria for acceptance of cases*, Serious Fraud Office.

[26] The SFO guidelines list "financial markets and their practices" as an example of a field that would require the level of expertise suitable for an SFO investigation.

[27] Section 2 powers refer to s.2 of the Criminal Justice Act 1987. S.2, in relevant part, provides that: "The Director may by notice in writing require the person whose affairs are to be investigated or any other person whom he has reason to believe has relevant information to answer questions or otherwise furnish information with respect to any matter relevant to the investigation at a specified place and either at a specified time or forthwith."
Criminal Justice Act 1987 s.2(2). The Director is further authorised to "require the person under investigation or any other person to produce ... any specified documents which appear to the Director to relate to any matter relevant to the investigation." S.2(3). If the requested documents are produced, "the Director may (i) take copies or extracts from them; (ii) require the person producing them to provide an explanation of any of them."

[28] See *Dealing with Cases*, Serious Fraud Office, available through *http://www.sfo.gov.uk*; Criminal Justice Act 1987 s.2(1) ("The powers of the Director under this section shall be exercisable, but only for the purposes of an investigation under section 1 above ... in any case in which it appears to him that there is good reason to do so for the purpose of investigating the affairs, or any aspect of the affairs, of any person.").

[29] Criminal Justice Act 1987 s.2.

[30] Criminal Justice Act 1987 s.2(2).

[31] *SFO Annual Report 1990/91*, Serious Fraud Office, para.21.

2008, that number rose to 863.[32] The SFO can obtain information through a s.2 notice that would otherwise be protected under duties of confidentiality.[33] Failing to comply with a notice, either by destroying, falsifying or concealing evidence, can lead to criminal prosecution.[34]

III. AUSTRALIAN FEDERAL POLICE

8–06   The Australian Federal Police (AFP) is the primary law enforcement entity of Australia and its activities include investigating bribery of foreign officials.[35] There is no entity, however, that specialises in investigating or prosecuting bribery of foreign officials in Australia.[36] Instead, all law enforcement agencies, under the "whole of government" approach,[37] work together in one coordinated effort to stop crime.[38] In the OECD's Phase 2 Report on Australia, the examiners expressed concern with this approach, though the Australian officials "point[ed] out that . . . the 'whole system is looking at foreign bribery'" and that it would be very costly, due to the size of Australia, to have regional bribery investigation offices.[39]

The AFP generally only investigates alleged bribery based upon formal referrals rather than actively seeking out bribery activities.[40] When a news entity reported possible bribery of a foreign official by an Australian company, AFP officials indicated that they would not be opening an investigation unless a formal referral was made, primarily because they felt that media reports are "not consistently credible."[41] Instead, investigations are undertaken by the AFP in the presence of:

---

[32] *Annual Report from 5 April 2007 to 4 April 2008*, Serious Fraud Office, at 36. Often, s.2 notices are used to assist foreign authorities by locating evidence in the UK. For instance, of the 863 total notice between 2007-2008, 281 of them went to support foreign investigations.

[33] A bank will not be forced to breach the confidentiality of a client unless "the person to whom the obligation of confidence is owed consents to the disclosure or production; or the Director has authorised the making of the requirement or, if it is impracticable for him to act personally, a member of the Serious Fraud Office designated by him for the purposes of this subsection has done so." Criminal Justice Act 1987 s.2(10). Similarly, a lawyer will not be forced to breach his duty to his client, but will be required to provide the name and address of his client. s.2(9).

[34] Criminal Justice Act 1987 s.2(16). A person found guilty of an offence can face a maximum of seven years in prison and a fine, and on summary conviction, be liable to imprisonment for a term not exceeding 6 months or to a fine not exceeding the statutory maximum or to both." s.2(17). However, a party can refuse to answer questions or provide documents provided that they have a "reasonable excuse for not doing so. A person's answers to questions required under section 2 may not be used in evidence against them at their trial unless the trial is in relation to an offence of providing misleading information during the section 2 interview itself." See *Dealing with Cases*, Serious Fraud Office, available through *http://www.sfo.gov.uk*.

[35] Organisation for Economic Cooperation and Development, Australia Phase 2 Report, para.46, available through *http://www.oecd.org* [Accessed July 15, 2010].

[36] OECD, *Australia Phase 2 Report*, para.48.

[37] For an examination of the whole of government approach, see Peter Homel, *The Whole of Government Approach to Crime Prevention*, Trends & Issues in Crime & Crim. Just., November 2004.

[38] OECD, *Australia Phase 2 Report*, para.48.

[39] OECD, *Australia Phase 2 Report*, para.48.

[40] OECD, *Australia Phase 2 Report*, para.53.

[41] OECD, *Australia Phase 2 Report*, para.53.

"(a) a formal referral of allegations to the AFP;
(b) pro-active intelligence gathering by the AFP;
(c) identification of the foreign bribery offence during the investigation of another criminal offence; or
(d) proactive investigation of persons or organisations where foreign bribery is suspected."[42]

Media reports are only considered when combined with "independent supporting information."[43]

Cooperation by other government entities with the AFP is essential to the successful detection of bribery. Guidelines are in place encouraging government entities to report possible bribery to the AFP.[44] Concerns about matters of a politically sensitive nature, such as those involving "the national economic interest or any potential effects upon relations with another State," are to be referred to the Minister for Justice and Customs, who then forwards the information on to the AFP.[45] This is to ensure that such matters are properly investigated.

C. INTERNAL INVESTIGATIONS

An internal investigation typically begins when a company discovers circum- 8–07
stances that raise a serious concern that a potential bribery offense may have occurred. The source of concern may be external, via the receipt of an auditor or regulatory inquiry. Regulators may be prompted to make an inquiry based on various grounds, including tips from the public, allegations in publicly filed court documents, stories in the news media, or leads from other cases.

As for leads from other cases, indeed, it is not uncommon for a bribery offense—and corresponding regulatory inquiry—to involve more than one potential target of regulatory inquiry. For example, assume that the company paying the bribe was a contractor to several other companies that used its services. A regulator may choose to make inquiries not only of the company that paid the bribe, but also the other companies that employed that company as a contractor. This is especially common in the United States where, under the FCPA, both direct and indirect improper payments to foreign officials are prohibited. If the other companies knew that its contractor was paying bribes in connection with rendering services, they too could be liable under the FCPA. At the very least, it could easily prompt an inquiry.

Alternatively, the concern may be prompted by an internal source—for example, from a "whistleblower" or concerned employee who notices and reports of irregularities in the company's books and records.

---

[42] OECD, *Australia Phase 2 Report*, para.54.
[43] OECD, *Australia Phase 2 Follow-up Report 12*, available through *http://www.oecd.org* [Accessed July 15, 2010].
[44] See OECD, *Australia Phase 2 Report*, para.60.
[45] OECD, *Australia Phase 2 Report*, para.63.

In either case, there are several reasons why a company may decide to conduct an internal investigation. For one, the company may have a legal duty to investigate. Even when a company does not have an affirmative obligation to investigate, it may be in the company's best interest to do so.

I. PRACTICAL IMPLICATIONS OF THE REGULATORS POWERS

(a) Government Actions

8–08   In the United States the DOJ, but not the SEC, has power to prosecute criminal violations of US securities laws such as the FCPA.[46] The SEC is authorised only to refer cases to the DOJ if it suspects that criminal activity has occurred.[47] The SEC and DOJ regularly conduct simultaneous, or parallel, investigations.[48] The DOJ may be willing to defer or decline prosecution if the company comes forward on its own accord, conducts an investigation and agrees to cooperate with the SEC and DOJ.[49]

Recently, courts have enforced limits on how regulators may conduct parallel investigations. For example, courts have ruled that the DOJ cannot use the SEC to gather evidence for a criminal proceeding. One US District Judge dismissed an indictment against defendants who cooperated with an SEC investigation without having been told that the USAO was closely monitoring the SEC investigation, or that the SEC was transmitting information gathered in its investigation to federal prosecutors.[50] The court's rationale was that "[t]he strategy used [by the regulators] to conceal the criminal investigation from [the] defendants was an abuse of the investigative process" and that "[t]he government's tactic to move forward under the guise of a civil investigation, [sic] violated defendants' due process rights."[51] Although the District Court's holding was overturned by the Ninth

---

[46] Cohen and Papalaskaris, *Corporate Internal Investigations* 2008.

[47] Cohen and Papalaskaris, *Corporate Internal Investigations*, 2008; see also SEC, E. Tafara, Director, Office of International Affairs, *Speech by SEC Staff: Remarks Presented at the IMF Conference on Cross-Border Cooperation and Information Exchange* (July 7-8, 2004), available through *http://www.sec.gov* [Accessed July 15, 2010] ("SEC staff may refer a matter to DOJ for investigation, and DOJ may conduct its criminal investigations parallel to SEC investigations").

[48] See Cohen and Papalaskaris, *Corporate Internal Investigations: An International Guide*, 2008, para.61-64. Hence, companies often find themselves facing both regulators. See L. Rohde, *Time Warner Cuts DOJ Deal on AOL Case, SEC May Follow*, The Industry Standard (April 4, 2005), available through *http://www.thestandard.com* [Accessed July 15, 2010] (regarding certain accounting practices); DOJ News Release, *Diagnostic Products Corporation Announces Settlements with the SEC and DOJ* (May 20, 2005), available through *http://allbusiness.com* [Accessed July 15, 2010] (concerning compliance with the US FCPA).

[49] See A. W. H. Gourley and C. F. Fletcher, *Combating Corruption: Lessons and Trends From 2008 FCPA Enforcement*, 6 No. 1 International Government Contractor 2 (2009).

[50] *US v Stringer* 408 F.Supp. 2d 1083 (D Ore. 2006).

[51] 408 F.Supp. 2d 1083 at 1088-1089.; cf *US v Scrushy*, 366 F.Supp. 2d 1134 (ND Ala 2005). In *Scrushy*, the court found that the DOJ prosecutors and the SEC regulators acted improperly because the parallel investigations were "inescapably intertwined," which "negated the existence of parallel investigations." 366 F.Supp. 2d 1134 at 1140. To be parallel, the investigations should never intersect. Thus, upon the defendant's motion, his statements made during an SEC deposition were ordered to be suppressed and could not be used to criminally prosecute him.

Circuit, the Court of Appeals affirmed that regulators can not make affirmatively misleading statements during an investigation.[52]

Parallel investigations are not limited to federal authorities.[53] For example, New York State has used its authority to investigate and prosecute corporate misconduct through former Attorney General Eliot Spitzer.[54] In one case, several different regulators, including the New York Attorney General, the SEC and the DOJ, led an investigation into alleged conflicts of interest between the research analysis and investment banking divisions of various financial intuitions, which led to an industry-wide global settlement.[55]

Self-Regulatory Organisations (SROs) also have the power to conduct parallel investigations. Although SROs do not have formal compulsory powers for use during an investigation,[56] SROs possess considerable authority to obtain cooperation from their members through the threat of sanctions.[57] Failure to abide by

8–09

---

[52] *US v Stringer* 535 F.3d 929 (9th Cir. 2008). The Ninth Circuit held that the SEC's behavior was not affirmatively misleading.

[53] Indeed, state authorities may also conduct parallel investigations. The American doctrine of dual sovereignty provides that the filing of federal charges does not preclude a subsequent filing of state charges based on the same facts. States are separate sovereigns with respect to the federal government and to each other.

Additionally, most states have laws regulating the offering and sale of securities. See G. P. Lander, *US securities law for international financial transactions and capital markets*, 2nd edn (Thomson/West: 2005), para.1.10 ("Except where state law is specifically preempted, the various statutes under which the SEC operates all contain provisions generally preserving the jurisdiction of the state securities commissions. As a result, the federal and state governments have separate, independent securities laws"). The state laws date largely from the era prior to federal legislation on securities and are commonly known as "blue sky" laws. P. G. Mahoney, *The Origins of the Blue-Sky Laws: A Test of Competing Hypotheses* (2003), 46 Journal of Law & Economics 229 at 231. Thus, it is possible for a company to face both federal and state charges of securities fraud.

[54] For instance, during joint investigations of the mutual fund industry, a bank employee accused of alleged wrongdoing faced New York state criminal charges as well as a federal civil enforcement action for his role in a scheme that involved the unlawful trading of mutual funds. See Press Release, Office of NYS Attorney General Eliot Spitzer, *Attorney General Spitzer and Securities and Exchange Commission File Charges Against Bank of America Broker* (September 16, 2003), *http://www.ag.ny.gov* [Accessed July 15, 2010] (noting SEC Director of Enforcement Stephen M. Cutler's remark: "I am pleased that the staff of the Commission and Attorney General Spitzer were able to work closely and cooperatively in bringing today's important actions"). Spitzer relied upon New York's blue sky law, New York General Business Law, paras 352-359h, also known as the Martin Act, which provides the Attorney General with the broadest investigative and prosecutorial powers among any securities regulator, whether federal or state. See *State v 7040 Colonial Rd Assocs. Co*, 671 N.Y.S. 2d 938 at 941-942 (1998). With the addition of criminal penalties in 1955, the Martin Act became a formidable weapon in the hands of a prosecutor willing to use it. See B. A. Masters, *Eliot Spitzer Spoils for a Fight: Opponents Blast Unusual Tactics of NY Attorney General, Washington Post* (May 31, 2004), at A1 ("[Eliot Spitzer's] office has a history of picking cases that make imaginative, but legally supportable, use of New York's unusually strong anti-fraud laws").

[55] For information about the Global Settlement, see SEC, *Spotlight on Global Research Analyst Settlement*, available through *http://www.sec.gov*.

[56] See M. I. Steinberg and R. C. Ferrara, *Securities Practice: Federal and State Enforcement*, 2nd edn (2001), § 14.5.

[57] Pursuant to its NYSE r.476, for example, the NYSE can impose the following types of sanctions: "Expulsion; suspension; limitation as to activities, functions, and operates, including the suspension or cancellation of a registration in, or assignment of, one or more stocks; fine; suspension or bar from being associated with any member or member organization; or any other fitting sanction."

NYSE, NYSE Rules, *http://www.nyse.com* [Accessed July 15, 2010].

SROs' rules or to cooperate with their inquiries may result in a fine and/or censure, suspension, or possible delisting, which may have devastating consequences akin to those of governmental sanctions.[58]

II. COOPERATION WITH REGULATORY INVESTIGATIONS

(a) In General

8–10   When a company has reason to believe that bribery or related misconduct has occurred that may subject it to investigation by the SEC or DOJ, the company may pre-emptively conduct an internal investigation.[59] Such investigations vary in form and scope, and their various procedures cannot be summarised briefly.[60] Various legal advantages may accrue to a company that conducts internal investigations, if government authorities determine that the company has effectively cooperated with them.[61]

(b) Triggers for Internal Investigations

8–11   A variety of incidents may call for internal investigations. For instance, a company may learn of irregularities or errors in its financial statements.[62] The SEC or DOJ may notify it of imminent investigation.[63] Accusations of misconduct may surface in the press.[64] A whistle-blower may allege misconduct by company executives.[65] A private plaintiff may serve the company with a civil complaint, triggering further criminal investigation.[66] Generally speaking, a company calls for an internal investigation when it faces the threat of legal penalties, and cooperation with authorities offers the chance to mitigate those penalties.[67]

---

[58] See NYSE News Release, *NYSE Regulation Fines Deutsche Bank Securities, Inc. $1.275 Million in Two Disciplinary Actions*, (February 8, 2007), http://www.nyse.com; NYSE News Release, *NYSE Regulation Announces Decision to Suspend, Apply to Delist, Navistar International Corp.*, (February 6, 2007).

[59] See Cohen and Papalaskaris, *Corporate Internal Investigations: An International Guide*, 2008, para.3.97 at 98; Dustin Ruta & Laura I. Bushnell, *Cooperation with Caution: Considerations for Corporate Officers in an Internal Corporate Investigation*, available through http://www.boardmember.com [Accessed July 15, 2010].

[60] Cohen and Papalaskaris, *Corporate Internal Investigations*, 2008, § 3.97, at 98.

[61] See Cohen and Papalaskaris, *Corporate Internal Investigations*, 2008, § 3.101, at 99; Ruta & Bushnell, *Cooperation with Caution*.

[62] Cohen and Papalaskaris, *Corporate Internal Investigations*, 2008, § 3.105, at 101.

[63] Cohen and Papalaskaris, *Corporate Internal Investigations*, 2008, § 3.105, at 101.

[64] Cohen and Papalaskaris, *Corporate Internal Investigations*, 2008, § 3.105, at 101.

[65] Cohen and Papalaskaris, *Corporate Internal Investigations*, 2008, § 3.105, at 101.

[66] Cohen and Papalaskaris, *Corporate Internal Investigations*, 2008, § 3.105, at 101.

[67] See Ruta & Bushnell, *Cooperation with Caution*.

(c) DOJ Guidelines on Cooperation: Filip Memorandum

In the Filip Memorandum, named after Deputy Attorney General Mark Filip,[68] **8–12**
the DOJ has laid out a list of factors that prosecutors should consider in determining whether to charge a corporation and with what offenses.[69] The Memorandum suggests that factor number one, the "nature and seriousness of the
offense, including the risk of harm to the public," may sometimes weigh more
than the other eight factors put together.[70] Factors four through six seek to weigh
how effectively the corporation has cooperated with authorities.[71]

Factor four asks whether the corporation has made a "timely and voluntary
disclosure of wrongdoing," and measures its "willingness to cooperate in the
investigation of its agents."[72] The Second Circuit recently held that the government may not induce a company not to pay for the legal defence of its
personnel, by rewarding this practice as "cooperation."[73] For this reason, unlike
the old McNulty Memorandum,[74] the new Filip Memorandum stresses that in
measuring cooperation:

> "Prosecutors should not take into account whether a corporation is advancing or
> reimbursing attorneys' fees or providing counsel to employees, officers, or directors
> under investigation or indictment" or "request that a corporation refrain from taking
> such action."[75]

This addition serves to protect the constitutional rights of defendant employees.[76]

The Filip Memorandum also makes clear that "[e]ligibility for cooperation
credit is not predicated upon the waiver of attorney-client privilege or work
product protection," but rather depends mainly on the "disclosure of the relevant
facts concerning such misconduct."[77] This clarification or alteration to the
McNulty Memorandum addresses the heavy criticism the government had
received in previous years, for inducing companies to waive their attorney-client
privilege in exchange for more moderate penalties.[78]

Factor five in the Filip Memorandum considers whether the corporation had **8–13**

---

[68] Allison D. Burroughs and Maya L. Sethi, *The McNulty Memo Changes Represent A Minor Victory For Corporate Rights*, available through *http://www.mondaq.com* [Accessed July 15, 2010].

[69] Deputy Att Gen Mark Filip, The Department of Justice, *Principles of Federal Prosecution of Business Organizations*, available through *http://www.usdoj.gov* [Accessed July 15, 2010], § 9-28.300.A.1-9, at 3-4.

[70] Deputy Att Gen Mark Filip, *Principles of Federal Prosecution of Business Organizations*, § 9-28.300.A.-B., at 3-4.

[71] Deputy Att Gen Mark Filip, *Principles of Federal Prosecution of Business Organizations*, § 9-28.300.A.4.-6., at 4.

[72] Deputy Att Gen Mark Filip, *Principles of Federal Prosecution of Business Organizations*, § 9-28.300.A.4., at 4.

[73] *US v Stein* 541 F.3d 130 at 155-156 (2d. Cir. 2008).

[74] See Deputy Att Gen Paul J. McNulty, *Memorandum to Heads of Dep't Components & U.S. Attorneys*, available through *http://www.usdoj.gov* (December 12, 2006).

[75] M. Filip, *Principles of Federal Prosecution of Business Organizations*, § 9-28.730, at 13.

[76] See generally *Stein* 541 F.3d 130.

[77] M. Filip, *Principles of Federal Prosecution of Business Organizations*, § 9-28.720, at 9.

[78] Cohen and Papalaskaris, *Corporate Internal Investigations*, § 3.103, at 100.

already set up a compliance program.[79] A compliance program seeks to ensure that the practices of a corporation are in line with the requirements of the most recent laws and regulations.[80] The Filip Memorandum states that the:

"Critical factors in evaluating any program are whether the program is adequately designed for maximum effectiveness in preventing and detecting wrongdoing by employees and whether corporate management is enforcing the program or is tacitly encouraging or pressuring employees to engage in misconduct to achieve business objectives."[81]

While the "existence of a compliance program is not sufficient, in and of itself, to justify not charging a corporation for criminal misconduct," the DOJ "encourages such corporate self-policing," and it weighs in favour of the corporation in the DOJ's determination of whether to bring charges.[82]

The sixth factor weighs the "remedial actions" of the corporation:

"Including any efforts to implement an effective corporate compliance program or to improve an existing one, to replace responsible management, to discipline or terminate wrongdoers, to pay restitution, and to cooperate with the relevant government agencies."[83]

Again, while a corporation cannot "avoid prosecution merely by paying a sum of money," the willingness of a corporation to make restitution and its progress in doing so weigh in favour of some leniency.[84] This factor also accounts for any improvements made to existing compliance programs and any discipline administered to wrongdoers in the company.[85] The Filip Memorandum notes the difficulty of effectively disciplining employees, especially those with seniority or positions of power, and counsels that prosecutors "should be satisfied that the corporation's focus is on the integrity and credibility of its remedial and disciplinary measures rather than on the protection of the wrongdoers."[86]

(d) SEC Guidelines for Cooperation: The Seaboard Report

8–14 The SEC Seaboard Report dictates similar guidelines for "whether, and how much, to credit self-policing, self-reporting, remediation and cooperation."[87] The Report states that the "paramount" consideration is always "what best protects

---

[79] Filip, *Principles of Federal Prosecution of Business Organizations*, § 9-28.300, § 9-28.800, at 4, 15.
[80] M. Filip, *Principles of Federal Prosecution of Business Organizations*.
[81] M. Filip, *Principles of Federal Prosecution of Business Organizations*.
[82] M. Filip, *Principles of Federal Prosecution of Business Organizations*.
[83] M. Filip, *Principles of Federal Prosecution of Business Organizations*, § 9-28.300, § 9-28.900, at 4, 16.
[84] M. Filip, *Principles of Federal Prosecution of Business Organizations*.
[85] M. Filip, *Principles of Federal Prosecution of Business Organizations*.
[86] M. Filip, *Principles of Federal Prosecution of Business Organizations*.
[87] Report of Investigation Pursuant to s.21(a) of the Securities Exchange Act of 1934 and Commission Statement on the Relationship of cooperation to Agency Enforcement Decisions, Exchange Act Release No. 44969, Enforcement Release No. 1470, 2001 SEC LEXIS 2210 (October 23, 2001) [Seaboard Report], available at *http://www.sec.gov* [Accessed July 15, 2010].

investors."[88] It warns that "there may be circumstances where conduct is so egregious, and harm so great, that no amount of cooperation or other mitigating conduct can justify a decision not to bring any enforcement action at all."[89] The Report lists thirteen factors to consider in deciding whether or how to charge a corporation that may be cooperating with the SEC investigation.[90] The Report stresses that the SEC does not intend to confine itself to these factors, or to allow its case-by-case weighting of the facts to be gainsaid by invoking a supposed majority of the thirteen factors.[91]

In brief, the factors are as follows:

(1) the nature of the misconduct, including the intentions of the offenders;

(2) the process by which the misconduct arose, whether through pressure to achieve results, an atmosphere of lawlessness, or an absence of compliance procedures;

(3) the location in the organisation that the misconduct arose, and how far up in the chain of command;

(4) the length of time the misconduct lasted, and whether it facilitated the company going public;

(5) the amount of harm the misconduct inflicted on investors and other corporate constituencies, and whether the discovery of such misconduct led to a drop in stock price for the company;

(6) the process by which the misconduct was detected, including the question of who detected and uncovered it;

(7) the length of time between the discovery of the misconduct and effective response;

(8) the steps the company took upon learning of the misconduct, including whether it immediately stopped the misconduct, terminated or disciplined the parties responsible, disclosed all relevant information to the authorities, and in general cooperated thoroughly with the investigation;

(9) the process the company followed to resolve these issues and ferret out the necessary information;

(10) the commitment of the company to learn the truth fully and expeditiously, including the nature and efficacy of any review it conducted;

(11) the prompt disclosure of the results of the review to the SEC with all disclosure necessary for clarification;

---

[88] Report of Investigation Pursuant to s.21(a) of the Securities Exchange Act of 1934.
[89] Report of Investigation Pursuant to s.21(a) of the Securities Exchange Act of 1934.
[90] Report of Investigation Pursuant to s.21(a) of the Securities Exchange Act of 1934.
[91] Report of Investigation Pursuant to s.21(a) of the Securities Exchange Act of 1934.

(12) any assurances that the conduct will not recur, including the presence of new and more effective internal controls and procedures;

(13) any merger or bankruptcy that has affected the company since the misconduct occurred.[92]

The SEC urges anyone with potential contributions to this list to direct them to its Division of Enforcement.[93]

(e) Summary of Cooperation

8–15   Cooperation with authorities offers an appealing alternative to criminal fines and possibly imprisonment. As a general rule, cooperation does not weigh as heavily in the minds of authorities as the nature of an offense. Cooperation generally cannot erase the misconduct that gave rise to an investigation. However, cooperation can help to mitigate the potentially severe penalties inflicted for misconduct, and may persuade authorities that they can safely direct their legal attention elsewhere.

III. Impediments to the Investigation of International Corruption

(a) Bank Secrecy In General

8–16   Bank secrecy laws prevent bank employees from divulging information about bank customers and their money.[94] In most countries with bank secrecy laws, offending bank employees are subject to criminal fines, and often jail time and civil liability.[95] In Switzerland, a country famous for its strict bank secrecy, first-time offenders face fines of up to 250,000 francs or up to three years imprisonment.[96] The bank secrecy laws of the Cayman Islands subject violators to up to $50,000 in fines and three years imprisonment.[97]

Most countries with strong bank secrecy laws are relatively small, with limited tax bases.[98] These countries pass bank secrecy laws because they attract money from other countries.[99] Persons who legitimately take advantage of such laws may

---

[92] Report of Investigation Pursuant to s.21(a) of the Securities Exchange Act of 1934.

[93] Report of Investigation Pursuant to s.21(a) of the Securities Exchange Act of 1934.

[94] See, e.g. Loi fédérale du 8 novembre 1934 sur les banques et les caisses d'épargne [Loi sur les banques, LB] [Federal Act on Banks and Savings Banks] November 8, 1934, SR 952.0, art.47 (Switz.) (unofficial translation), available through KPMG Web Site, *http://www.kpmg.ch* [Accessed July 15, 2010] [hereinafter "Swiss Bank Secrecy Act"]; Monetary Authority Law, Law 16 of 1996 (2004 revision) § 50(1)(d) (Cayman Islands) [hereinafter "Cayman Islands Monetary Authority Law"].

[95] See fn.94 above and fn.102 below.

[96] Swiss Bank Secrecy Act, art.47.

[97] Cayman Islands Monetary Authority Law, § 50(1)(d).

[98] For instance, Switzerland, the Cayman Islands, Liechtenstein, Jersey and Panama. See fn.94 above and fn.102 below.

[99] See Timothy V. Addison, *Shooting Blanks: The War on Tax Havens*, 16 Ind. J. Global Legal Stud. 703 at 710-711 (2009); Bryan S. Arce, *Taken to the Cleaners: Panama's Financial Secrecy Laws Facilitate the Laundering of Evaded U.S. Taxes*, 34 Brook. J. Int'l L. 465 at 465 (2009).

be protecting the sensitive information of their clients or their own private assets.[100] The same countries frequently have low taxes, and thus serve as havens for business.[101]

(b) Bank Secrecy, Money Laundering and Non-Transparency

Bank secrecy laws also attract money that was unlawfully obtained or has not been reported to tax authorities in other countries.[102] In particular, bank secrecy makes money laundering convenient.[103] Money laundering tends to involve three steps: placement, layering and integration.[104] In the first step, placement, the owner of the "dirty money" moves it to the financial system.[105] The next step, layering, involves transferring the money to foreign bank accounts.[106] A series of wire transfers through offshore banks obscures the trail leading back to the owner.[107] This is particularly effective when those offshore banks are subject to bank secrecy laws, and thus cannot legally disclose information about their customers.[108] This effectively creates a gap in the money trail. In the third step, placement, the owner uses his cleansed money for apparently legitimate purposes, like investment or political campaign donations.[109] An archetypal money-laundering scheme might have the proceeds of drug trafficking or bribery being wired through countries with bank secrecy laws and then deposited in a tax haven, before being withdrawn for personal and business use.[110]

8–17

Money laundering is a popular enterprise. One source estimates that $1.5 trillion is laundered yearly,[111] or two to five per cent of the world GDP.[112] Partly as a result, it is estimated that half of the world's trade passes through small tax havens that represent only three percent of the world GDP.[113] Money laundering

---

[100] See Patrick J. Kish, *Is Bank Secrecy Disappearing?*, available through *http://ezinearticles.com* [Accessed July 15, 2010].

[101] T. Addison, *Shooting Blanks*, 2009, at 706.

[102] T. Addison, *Shooting Blanks*, 2009, at 704 ("[T]ax evasion is facilitated by the bank secrecy laws of tax havens"); B. Arce, *Taken to the cleaners*, 2009, at 467 ("[F]inancial havens and bank secrecy are a 'tool kit' for money launderers") (quoting U.N. Office on Drugs & Crime [UNODC], Report on Financial Havens, Bank Secrecy and Money-Laundering, U.N. Doc. UNIS/NAR/641 (June 8, 1998)).

[103] See Ndiva Kofele-Kale, *Change or the Illusion of Change: The War against Official Corruption in Africa*, 38 Geo. Wash. Int'l L. Rev. 697 at 726 (2006).

[104] Comptroller of the Currency Administrator of National Banks, Bank Secrecy Act/Anti-Money Laundering Comptroller's Handbook 2 (2000); Frank E. Hagan, Crime Types and Criminals 313 (2009); Heinz Duthel, The Professionals, Politic and Crime, International Moneylaundering 18 (2008).

[105] Comptroller of the Currency Administrator of National Banks, at 2; Hagan, at 313; Duthel, at 10.

[106] Comptroller of the Currency Administrator of National Banks, at 2; Hagan, *Crime Types and Criminals* at 313; Duthel, *The Professional, Politic and Crime*, at 10.

[107] Comptroller of the Currency Administrator of National Banks, at 2; Hagan, *Crime Types and Criminals* at 313; Duthel, *The Professional, Politic and Crime*, at 10.

[108] See Duthel, *The Professional, Politic and Crime*, at 18.

[109] Hagan, *Crime Types and Criminals*, at 313.

[110] See Addison, *Shooting Blanks*, 2009, at 710.

[111] Arce, *Taken to the Cleaners*, 2009, at 465.

[112] Arce, *Taken to the Cleaners*, 2009, at 465.

[113] Addison, *Shooting Blanks*, 2009, at 711.

has disastrous effects. It can thwart a nation's economic policies, disturb its financial system, and facilitate governmental corruption.[114]

When a government official improperly receives money, for instance through bribery, and then launders it for personal use, the offense is commonly termed "illicit enrichment."[115] Illicit enrichment is "the significant increase in the assets of a public official or any other person which he or she cannot reasonably explain in relation to his or her income."[116] The "cancerous effects"[117] of such corruption on public administration and society are well-documented.[117] Corruption is a symptom of undemocratic institutions, lack of accountability, national markets that fail to adhere to international standards, the nonexistence of the rule of law, and generally a lack of transparency.[118]

8–18   Bank secrecy laws exemplify that non-transparency. They make it difficult to investigate financial crime,[119] and often even more difficult to investigate offenses such as tax evasion.[120] Bank officials in countries with bank secrecy laws are legally prevented from cooperating in foreign investigations, because they cannot divulge information belonging to bank customers.[121]

(c) Bank Secrecy and Mutual Legal Assistance Treaties

MLATs in the United States

8–19   In recent years, countries like the United States have sought increasingly to break through barriers to investigation like bank secrecy using Mutual Legal Assistance Treaties, or MLATs.[122] MLATs place unambiguous obligations on signatory nations to assist one another with criminal investigations.[123] They allow prosecutors to obtain financial and banking information, examine and take statements from witnesses, serve subpoenas and other documents, obtain government records, execute requests for searches and seizures, and recover the proceeds of illegal activity.[124] The United States has negotiated MLATs with over sixty

---

[114] Arce, *Taken to the Cleaners*, 2009, at 465–466.

[115] See Kofele-Kale, *Change or the Illusion of Change*, 2006, at 719.

[116] Kofele-Kale, *Change or the Illusion of Change*, 2006, at 719–720.

[117] Kofele-Kale, *Change or the Illusion of Change*, 2006, at 697–698.

[118] Kofele-Kale, *Change or the Illusion of Change*, 2006, at 697–698.

[119] Lewis D. Solomon & Lewis J. Saret, Asset Protection Strategies, § 9.05, at 561.

[120] Arce, *Taken to the Cleaners*, 2009, at 468; Business Week, *Bank Secrecy Gives Way in Switzerland*, available through *http://www.businessweek.com* [Accessed July 15, 2010] (March 3, 2009).

[121] See fn.94. See also Arce, *Taken to the Cleaners*, at 468.

[122] See Solomon & Saret, *Asset Protection Strategies*, § 9.04[C], at 556.

[123] U4 Anti-Corruption Resource Centre, *Mutual Legal Assistance Treaties and Money Laundering*, *http://www.u4.no* [Accessed July 15, 2010], at 7; Paul H. Cohen, *Mutual Legal Assistance Treaties*, *http://www.deweyleboeuf.com* [Accessed July 15, 2010] (on file with author).

[124] Solomon & Saret, *Asset Protection Strategies*, § 9.04[C], at 556; U4 Anti-Corruption Resource Centre, *Mutual Legal Assistance Treaties and Money Laundering*, at 7; Cohen, *Mutual Legal Assistance Treaties*, at 1. See also Arce, *Taken to the Cleaners*, 2009, at 485.

foreign countries.[125] These include Switzerland, the United Kingdom, France, Hong Kong, the Cayman Islands, Liechtenstein and Panama.[126]

Many countries interfere with foreign investigations by requiring that the acts in question be crimes in both the "requesting" and "requested" countries before cooperating in the investigation.[127] These nations follow what is called the "dual criminality" principle.[128] Certain MLATs create exceptions to the dual criminality requirement.[129] These treaties help with complex investigations of money laundering and tax evasion,[130] particularly by allowing foreign investigators to pierce through bank secrecy laws.[131]

MLATs in the United Kingdom

The United Kingdom has developed a legal structure to enable mutual legal   **8–20** assistance as well. In 1990, it passed the Criminal Justice International Co-operation Act, which lists the procedures involved in making requests for mutual legal assistance.[132] The United Kingdom has at least 38 bilateral MLATs with various countries, including the United States, Panama, Hong Kong, Germany and Italy.[133]

The United Kingdom's MLAT with the United States gives it access to US bank accounts in serious crime investigations, and is designed to reduce delays.[134] Nevertheless, the United Kingdom has run into difficulties obtaining evidence from the United States.

In one case, UK authorities were prosecuting several individuals for participation in a credit card fraud scheme.[135] They sought evidence from the United States including "wiretap applications, supporting affidavits, court orders authorizing wiretaps, and Secret Service interviews of persons arrested" on

---

[125] IRS Master List *Mutual Legal Assistance Treaties*, available through *http://www.irs.gov* [Accessed July 15, 2010].

[126] IRS Master List.

[127] Arce, *Taken to the Cleaners*, 2009, at 4; U4 Anti-Corruption Resource Centre, *Mutual Legal Assistance Treaties and Money Laundering*, at 7.

[128] Arce, *Taken to the Cleaners*, 2009, at 4; U4 Anti-Corruption Resource Centre, *Mutual Legal Assistance Treaties and Money Laundering*, at 7; Cohen, *Mutual Legal Assistance Treaties*, at 2.

[129] U4 Anti-Corruption Resource Centre, *Mutual Legal Assistance Treaties and Money Laundering*, at 7; Cohen, *Mutual Legal Assistance Treaties*, at 2.

[130] U4 Anti-Corruption Resource Centre, *Mutual Legal Assistance Treaties and Money Laundering*, at 7.

[131] Cohen, *Mutual Legal Assistance Treaties*, at 1; Business Week, *Bank Secrecy Gives Way in Switzerland, http://www.businessweek.com* [Accessed July 15, 2010] (March 3, 2009); Panama Legal, S.A., *Panama Bank Secrecy Laws*, available through *http://www.panamalaw.org* [Accessed July 15, 2010].

[132] Criminal Justice (International Co-operation) Act 1990, c.5 (Eng.), available through *http://www.opsi.gov.uk* [Accessed July 15, 2010].

[133] UK Foreign & Commonwealth Office, *Bilateral Agreements on Mutual Legal Assistance in Criminal Matters*, available through *http://www.fco.gov.uk* [Accessed July 15, 2010].

[134] Monty Raphael, Joint Head of the Fraud and Regulatory Department, *United Kingdom: Investigating and Prosecuting Fraud & Corruption in the International Business Environment*, available through *http://www.mondaq.com* [Accessed July 15, 2010].

[135] *UK v US*, 238 F.3d 1312 (11th Cir. 2001).

related matters, all of which the US government disclosed.[136] However, the United States refused to produce other materials, including grand jury materials and attorney work product protected by privilege, intercepted conversations and certain proprietary and personal credit card customer information.[137]

8–21   The Eleventh Circuit refused to order US authorities to disclose this information, despite the existence of an MLAT between the United States and Britain.[138] The court first pointed to the breadth of the treaty, which allowed:

(1)   the taking of testimony or statements of witnesses;

(2)   the provision of documents, records, and evidence;

(3)   the service of legal documents;

(4)   the location or identification of persons;

(5)   the execution of requests for searches and seizures; and

(6)   the provision of assistance in proceedings relating to the forfeiture of the proceeds of crime and the collection of fines imposed as a sentence in a criminal prosecution.[139]

However, the court continued, none of these broad provisions applied, because requests for information under the MLAT must be made to the US Attorney General.[140] This request had been made directly to the court,[141] perhaps seeking to circumvent the delays and political problems of dealing with the Executive branch. The fact that a valid MLAT request had been made recently on a related matter was held irrelevant.[142]

Summary of MLATs

8–22   Despite the progress toward financial transparency since the late twentieth century, to which MLATs have contributed, obtaining information from foreign nations remains a major hurdle in fighting international crime. Political concerns continue to interfere with criminal investigations even between the most avid proponents of MLATs.

The Case of UBS

8–23   Bank secrecy will not necessarily prevent a regulator from investigation suspected bribery. Recent investigations have a set precedent for putting pressure on

---

[136]   *UK v US*, 238 F.3d 1312.
[137]   *UK v US*, 238 F.3d 1312.
[138]   *UK v US*, 238 F.3d 1312.
[139]   *UK v US*, 238 F.3d 1312.
[140]   *UK v US*, 238 F.3d 1312.
[141]   *UK v US*, 238 F.3d 1312.
[142]   *UK v US*, 238 F.3d 1312.

"uncooperative" jurisdictions to divulge requested information despite their bank secrecy laws.

In 2008, the Permanent Subcommittee on Investigations of the Senate Committee on Homeland Security, or PSI, issued its report on "Tax Havens and US Tax Compliance."[143] The Tax Haven Report indicated that UBS sought to attract US clients by assuring them that US authorities would not discover their undeclared Swiss accounts.[144] UBS informed clients that they were not required to disclose their clients' accounts and that UBS procedures made disclosure unlikely.[145] Moreover, the information was "shielded by Swiss bank secrecy laws,"[146] rendering it unlawful for any UBS agent to divulge information about bank customers.[147]

According to the Declaration of IRS Agent Daniel Reeves,[148] UBS made great efforts to obtain US clients by offering to obscure their account activity from US authorities.[149] It also sold banking and securities products in the United States without a valid license to do so.[150] From 2000 to 2007, UBS opened thousands of Swiss accounts, containing billions of dollars, which taxpayers did not report to the IRS with Forms W-9.[151] Furthermore, UBS failed to file Forms 1099 to report any earnings on what UBS itself called "undeclared accounts."[152] In 2008, UBS admitted to the PSI that about 19,000 of its 20,000 Swiss accounts for US clients remained undeclared to the IRS.[153] These accounts hold assets worth roughly $18 billion.[154]

In a Qualified Intermediary Agreement with the IRS, or QI Agreement, UBS   8–24 had promised the IRS to obtain Forms W-9 from US clients.[155] This would provide UBS the information it needed to report income paid on offshore accounts.[156]

Rather than report this income, UBS devised sophisticated methods to help its

---

[143] Dec. of Daniel Reeves para.22, *US v UBS AG*, No. 09-20423 (S.D. Fla. 2009).

[144] *US v UBS AG*, No. 09-20423.

[145] *US v UBS AG*, No. 09-20423.

[146] *US v UBS AG*, No. 09-20423.

[147] Swiss Bank Secrecy Act, art.47.

[148] Dec. of Daniel Reeves, *UBS AG*, No. 09-20423 (S.D. Fla.), para.22.a–b. Because this case did not proceed to verdict, it cannot be said with certainty that every detail of Reeves' Declaration was true. UBS did, however, acknowledge in general terms that the accusations were true when it reached a Deferred Prosecution Agreement with the United States, paying $780 million to defer prosecution for 18 months and to seek dismissal with prejudice thereafter. Deferred Prosecution Agreement para.2–3, 14, *UBS AG*, No. 09-20423 (S.D. Fla.) ("UBS acknowledges and accepts that . . . [it] participated in a scheme to defraud the United States and its agency, the IRS, by actively assisting or otherwise facilitating a number of United States individual taxpayers in establishing accounts at UBS in a manner designed to conceal the United States taxpayers' ownership or beneficial interest in these accounts").

[149] Dec. of Daniel Reeves, *UBS AG*, No. 09–20423 (S.D. Fla.), para.22.a–b.

[150] Dec. of Daniel Reeves, *UBS AG*, No. 09–20423, para.22.b.

[151] Dec. of Daniel Reeves, *UBS AG*, No. 09–20423, para.22.c.

[152] Dec. of Daniel Reeves, *UBS AG*, No. 09–20423.

[153] Dec. of Daniel Reeves, *UBS AG*, No. 09–20423, para.22.d.

[154] Dec. of Daniel Reeves, *UBS AG*, No. 09–20423.

[155] Dec. of Daniel Reeves, *UBS AG*, No. 09–20423, para.25.

[156] Dec. of Daniel Reeves, *UBS AG*, No. 09–20423.

US clients avoid reporting and thereby evade taxes.[157] While the "legal right of a taxpayer to decrease the amount of what otherwise would be his taxes . . . cannot be doubted,"[158] UBS explicitly warned its clients that this particular evasion may carry "legal ramifications."[159] UBS required its clients to sign a declaration stating, "I would like to avoid disclosure of my identity to the U.S. Internal Revenue Service."[160] Many clients declined to sign because it would "fully incriminate[] a U.S. person of criminal wrongdoing should this document fall into the wrong hands."[161] UBS did not change its activities in response to these complaints.[162] UBS knew that reporting offshore account income would entirely "defeat the purpose" of many such accounts,[163] and that the account holders may just take their money elsewhere. To avoid this, UBS merely altered the text on its form so the client must indicate his "consent to the new tax regulations."[164]

UBS offered its clients two main approaches by which to avoid reporting their offshore income. First, UBS suggested that its clients liquidate their US securities from Swiss accounts.[165] These clients could thereafter trade non-US securities in such accounts, while UBS formally, if not substantially, avoided the reporting requirements of the QI Agreement.[166] Secondly, UBS helped its clients hide their ownership and control of their own offshore assets by placing them in sham foreign corporations.[167] UBS helped clients prepare Forms W-8BEN, or Certificates of Foreign Status of Beneficial Owner for United States Tax Withholding, indicating that the sham corporations controlled the Swiss accounts.[168] Substantially, of course, the US taxpayer retained full control of his offshore assets.[169]

8–25   UBS was aware that helping its clients to create sham corporations may itself be criminal. In a memorandum, one UBS official stated that:

> "Recommendations [to create offshore corporations] could infringe upon our Qualified Intermediary status, if . . . it is determined that we have systematically helped U.S. person[s] to avoid the QI rules."[170]

To avoid advising clients directly on how to break the law, UBS sought out "service providers" who would recommend various "structures" or "vehicles" to

[157] Dec. of Daniel Reeves, *UBS AG*, No. 09–20423, para.31-32.
[158] *Gregory v Helvering* 293 U.S. 465 (1935) ("The legal right of a taxpayer to decrease the amount of what otherwise would be his taxes, or altogether avoid them, by means which the law permits, cannot be doubted."
[159] Dec. of Daniel Reeves, *UBS AG*, No. 09–20423 (S.D. Fla.), para.26.
[160] Dec. of Daniel Reeves, *UBS AG*, No. 09–20423, para.27.
[161] Dec. of Daniel Reeves, *UBS AG*, No. 09–20423.
[162] Dec. of Daniel Reeves, *UBS AG*, No. 09–20423.
[163] Dec. of Daniel Reeves, *UBS AG*, No. 09–20423, para.28.
[164] Dec. of Daniel Reeves, *UBS AG*, No. 09–20423, para.27.
[165] Dec. of Daniel Reeves, *UBS AG*, No. 09–20423, para.31.
[166] Dec. of Daniel Reeves, *UBS AG*, No. 09–20423.
[167] Dec. of Daniel Reeves, *UBS AG*, No. 09–20423, para.32.
[168] Dec. of Daniel Reeves, *UBS AG*, No. 09–20423.
[169] Dec. of Daniel Reeves, *UBS AG*, No. 09–20423.
[170] Dec. of Daniel Reeves, *UBS AG*, No. 09–20423, para.33.

US customers who failed to declare offshore income.[171] UBS recommended to its clients those service providers who appeared most reliable and effective in relocating clients' assets to foreign sham corporations.[172]

An illustration of exactly how this process worked for any given client will be helpful. It begins with a US client who opened a "predecessor account" at UBS sometime in the 1980s or 1990s.[173] Not long before the effective date of the QI Agreement in 2000, the US client would create a foreign sham corporation.[174] This corporation would formally open its own account with UBS.[175] The US client would fill out a form entitled "Verification of the Beneficial Owner's Identity" to confirm for UBS that the taxpayer actually controlled the corporation's account.[176] Meanwhile, the taxpayer indicated on his Form W-8BEN that the *sham corporation* controlled the foreign account.[177] Even though UBS recognised that the taxpayer controlled the account, as confirmed by its "Verification of the Beneficial Owner's Identity," UBS would report to the IRS that the foreign corporation was the true owner.[178]

Thus, UBS helped its clients to evade taxation of their offshore income.[179] UBS went to impressive lengths for its clients: one UBS banker even bought diamonds for a US client using the client's undeclared Swiss account and "smuggled the diamonds into the United States in a toothpaste tube."[180] Bank secrecy laws made this tax evasion scheme possible, first by making Swiss banks enormously attractive to wealthy US citizens,[181] and second by legally preventing Swiss bankers from divulging any information about such clients.[182] Swiss bankers had to reject requests for information from US authorities, due to the threat of jail time and large fines.[183]

(d) Bank Secrecy, Tax Havens and Corruption

In General

Bank secrecy laws and tax havens are closely tied to international corruption. The 8–26 money used to bribe foreign officials frequently comes from accounts protected by

---

[171] Dec. of Daniel Reeves, *UBS AG*, No. 09-20423, para.34.
[172] Dec. of Daniel Reeves, *UBS AG*, No. 09-20423.
[173] Dec. of Daniel Reeves, *UBS AG*, No. 09-20423, para.38.a.
[174] Dec. of Daniel Reeves, *UBS AG*, No. 09-20423, para.38.b.
[175] Dec. of Daniel Reeves, *UBS AG*, No. 09-20423, para.38.c.
[176] Dec. of Daniel Reeves, *UBS AG*, No. 09-20423, para.38.d.
[177] Dec. of Daniel Reeves, *UBS AG*, No. 09-20423, para.38.e.
[178] Dec. of Daniel Reeves, *UBS AG*, No. 09-20423, para.38.f.
[179] See Deferred Prosecution Agreement para.2, *US v UBS AG*, No. 09-20423 (S.D. Fla. 2009).
[180] *US v UBS AG*, No. 09-20423 para.58.c.
[181] See Addison, *Shooting Blanks*, 2009, at 710-11; Arce, *Taken to the Cleaners*, at 465.
[182] Swiss Bank Secrecy Act, art.47.
[183] Swiss Bank Secrecy Act, art.47.

bank secrecy laws.[184] This is partly because criminal enterprises tend to keep their money in tax havens with bank secrecy laws anyway, to minimise their tax burdens.[185] Moreover, bank secrecy laws make it more difficult for authorities to identify the accounts from which bribes are coming, and who owns them.[186]

Efforts to Oppose the Use of Bank Secrecy for International Corruption

8–27   The Organisation for Economic Cooperation and Development has taken steps to combat the exploitation of bank secrecy laws for international corruption, urging nations such as Chile to lift bank secrecy and accept mutual legal assistance requests in cases of foreign bribery.[187] Failure to follow the OECD's recommendations may place a nation on the OECD "black list" of non-compliant tax havens.[188] This is not an empty threat: all nations that have been placed on the black list have scrambled to comply or promise future compliance. As a result, as of May 2009, the last remaining non-compliant tax havens were removed from the OECD list.[189] At least 42 nations have made "commitments to transparency and exchange of information" as required by the OECD.[190]

The United Nations has also fought the use of bank secrecy laws for international corruption. The General Assembly issued a *Declaration against Corruption and Bribery*, stressing the negative effects of international corruption on competition and society:

> "[E]ffective efforts at all levels to combat and avoid corruption and bribery in all countries are essential elements of an improved international business environment, ... enhance fairness and competitiveness in international commercial transactions and form a critical part of promoting transparent and accountable governance, economic and social development and environmental protection in all countries, and ... such efforts

---

[184] See Mark Pieth, Lucinda A. Low, et al., *The OECD Convention on Bribery* 429 (2007) ("In states with bank secrecy laws, ... bank account details [are] often crucial evidence in international bribery cases"); General Assembly of the United Nations, *Declaration against Corruption and Bribery in International Commercial Transactions*, A/RES/51/191 (December 16, 1996), available through *http://www.un.org* [Accessed July 15, 2010] (member states commit "[t]o ensure that bank secrecy provisions do not impede or hinder criminal investigations or other legal proceedings relating to corruption, bribery or related illicit practices in international commercial transactions, and that full cooperation is extended to Governments that seek information on such transactions").

[185] Addison, *Shooting Blanks*, 2009, at 704 ("[T]ax evasion is facilitated by the bank secrecy laws of tax havens"); Arce, *Taken to the Cleaners*, at 467 ("[F]inancial havens and bank secrecy are a 'tool kit' for money launderers") (quoting U.N. Office on Drugs & Crime [UNODC], *Report on Financial Havens, Bank Secrecy and Money-Laundering*, U.N. Doc. UNIS/NAR/641 (June 8, 1998)).

[186] Pieth, Low, et al., *The OECD Convention on Bribery*, at 429; General Assembly of the United Nations, *Declaration against Corruption*.

[187] OECD, Working Group on Bribery, *Report on the Application of the Convention on Combating Bribery of Foreign Public Officials in International Business Transactions*, paras 220–227, at 52–54, available athrough *http://www.oecd.org*; OECD, *OECD Working Group on Bribery Expresses Serious Concerns about Chile's Compliance, http://www.oecd.org*.

[188] M&C, *OECD Releases List on Compliance with Tax Haven Guidelines*, available through *http://www.monstersandcritics.com* [Accessed July 15, 2010] (April 9, 2009).

[189] OECD, *List of Uncooperative Tax Havens, http://www.oecd.org*.

[190] OECD, *List of Uncooperative Tax Havens*.

are especially pressing in the increasingly competitive globalized international economy."[191]

Therefore, the United Nations required member states to commit to:

"ensure that bank secrecy provisions do not impede or hinder criminal investigations or other legal proceedings relating to corruption, bribery or related illicit practices in international commercial transactions, and that full cooperation is extended to Governments that seek information on such transactions."[192]

Nevertheless, bank secrecy laws continue to hinder the investigation of international corruption. The process of requesting and obtaining foreign bank information under mutual legal assistance treaties is long and tedious, and often results in denial.[193] Even valid requests may be denied on grounds of dubious merit, if the foreign government objects to the release for its own reasons.[194]

The Case of Siemens

A recent example is the case of Siemens. According to Uwe Dolata of Germany's association of federal criminal investigators, "[b]ribery was Siemen's business model. Siemens had institutionalized corruption."[195] Company officials referred to bribes as "useful money."[196] This culture of corruption had been present for some time. In the Second World War, Allied forces heavily bombed Siemens' German factories and seized its patents.[197] During the war's aftermath, Siemens was desperate to obtain contracts and rejuvenate its business.[198] It sought business in less developed countries, exploiting their less transparent governments by offering bribes to win business contracts.[199]

8–28

This practice flourished until 2006, when German and American investigators cracked down on Siemens.[200] When one Siemens employee was cornered by six police officers, he commented, "I know what this is about. I have been expecting you."[201] This employee had supervised an annual bribery budget of up to $50 million, paying bribes of at least $12.7 million for government contracts in Nigeria and $5 million for a cellular phone contract in Bangladesh.[202]

---

[191] General Assembly of the United Nations, *Declaration against Corruption*.
[192] General Assembly of the United Nations, *Declaration against Corruption*.
[193] See, e.g. Panama Offshore Legal Law Firm, fn.131.
[194] See, e.g. Panama Legal, S.A., fn.131.
[195] Siri Schubert & T. Christian Miller, *At Siemens Bribery Was Just a Line Item*, New York Times, at BU1 (December 20, 2008), available through *http://www.nytimes.com* [Accessed July 15, 2010].
[196] S. Schubert & T. Miller, *At Siemens Bribery Was Just a Line Item*, New York Times.
[197] S. Schubert & T. Miller, *At Siemens Bribery Was Just a Line Item*, New York Times.
[198] S. Schubert & T. Miller, *At Siemens Bribery Was Just a Line Item*, New York Times.
[199] S. Schubert & T. Miller, *At Siemens Bribery Was Just a Line Item*, New York Times.
[200] S. Schubert & T. Miller, *At Siemens Bribery Was Just a Line Item*, New York Times; David Crawford & Mike Esterl, *Siemens Pays Record Fine in Probe*, Wall St. J., at B2 (December 16, 2008), available through *http://online.wsj.com* [Accessed July 15, 2010].
[201] S. Schubert & T. Miller, *At Siemens Bribery Was Just a Line Item*.
[202] S. Schubert & T. Miller, *At Siemens Bribery Was Just a Line Item*.

Siemens was active elsewhere in the world. It bribed Argentinean officials $40 million for a $1 billion contract to make national identity cards.[203] It bribed Saddam Hussein and his officials $1.7 million for contracting work.[204] In Israel, Siemens paid off officials with $20 million for a power plant job.[205] It paid Venezuelan officials $20 million for contracts to build rail lines, and gave Chinese officials $14 million for a job producing medical equipment.[206] Allegedly, over the course of a decade, Siemens paid out over $1 billion in bribes for government contracts.[207]

8–29 A critical element of Siemens' "institutionalized corruption" lay in its use of foreign bank accounts protected by bank secrecy laws. Siemens relocated money from its Austrian accounts to tax havens Switzerland and Liechtenstein.[208] A Swiss trustee devised front companies to obscure the money trail from Siemens to offshore accounts in the British Virgin Islands and Dubai.[209] This "web of secret bank accounts and shadowy consultants" was a central feature in Siemens' massive bribery enterprise.[210]

Siemens' corrupt practices did not go without punishment. The DOJ sought and obtained fines against Siemens of $800 million.[211] It declined to seek the other $1.9 billion in fines the law would permit, citing Siemens' "extraordinary" cooperation with the investigation.[212] Toward this end, Siemens paid over $850 million to law firm Debevoise & Plimpton LLP and accounting firm Deloitte & Touche to privately investigate Siemens and report their findings to American and German authorities.[213] Furthermore, Siemens paid $528 million in fines to settle criminal charges in Germany.[214] Such fines, totalling over $2 billion dollars, will likely deter bribery for contracts in developing nations, where citizens have historically paid far too much for the basic infrastructure such as roads, hospitals and power plants.[215]

(e) Blocking Statutes

In General

8–30 Various nations have passed blocking statutes specifically tailored to discourage discovery requests. These statutes impose criminal penalties and other sanctions on citizens who comply with foreign discovery requests by providing valuable

---

[203] S. Schubert & T. Miller, *At Siemens Bribery Was Just a Line Item.*
[204] S. Schubert & T. Miller, *At Siemens Bribery Was Just a Line Item.*
[205] S. Schubert & T. Miller, *At Siemens Bribery Was Just a Line Item.*
[206] S. Schubert & T. Miller, *At Siemens Bribery Was Just a Line Item.*
[207] Crawford & Esterl, *Siemens Pays Record Fines in Probe.*
[208] S. Schubert & T. Miller, *At Siemens Bribery was Just a Line Item.*
[209] S. Schubert & T. Miller, *At Siemens Bribery was Just a Line Item.*
[210] S. Schubert & T. Miller, *At Siemens Bribery was Just a Line Item.*
[211] Crawford & Esterl, *Siemens Pays Record Fines in Probe.*
[212] Crawford & Esterl, *Siemens Pays Record Fines in Probe.*
[213] Crawford & Esterl, *Siemens Pays Record Fines in Probe.*
[214] Crawford & Esterl, *Siemens Pays Record Fines in Probe.*
[215] Schubert & Miller, *At Siemens Bribery was Just a Line Item.*

documentation or information.[216] France has passed a particularly robust blocking statute, forbidding any French citizen or employee of a French company from divulging any information "of an economic, commercial, industrial, financial or technical nature" if it may bear on France's "fundamental economic interests," security or sovereignty.[217] Other nations with blocking statutes of varying strength include Australia, Canada, Japan, the Netherlands, South Africa and the United Kingdom.[218]

There is evidence that Australia, Canada and South Africa, for instance, passed blocking statutes specifically to frustrate US jurisdiction over an alleged international uranium cartel.[219] This is not true for all blocking statutes, many of which were enacted with an eye toward excessive foreign discovery in general.[220]

US courts may order a party to discover documents or information even if it subjects that party to civil or criminal liability in a foreign jurisdiction.[221] That party is still considered to be "in control" of a document under the Federal Rules of Civil Procedure, even if the party faces criminal penalties in another nation for producing information.[222]

US Discovery Rules and International Discovery: Aerospatiale

In the 1987 case *Aerospatiale*, the Supreme Court ruled that American federal courts need not adhere to the Hague Evidence Convention, and may instead simply allow discovery of foreign materials as permitted by the Federal Rules of Civil Procedure.[223] This means federal-court litigants need only serve discovery requests on foreign parties in the same way they would serve domestic parties.[224] The court noted that resort to the Hague evidentiary procedures would be exceedingly clumsy, forcing American courts to attempt to follow multiple conflicting sets of law whenever foreign parties were involved.[225] Justice Stevens reasoned that the Hague Evidence Convention would "amount to a major regulation of the overall conduct of litigation between nationals of different signatory states, raising a significant possibility of very serious interference with the jurisdiction of United States courts."[226]

8–31

---

[216] Paul H. Cohen, *Blocking Statutes*, available through *http://deweyleboeuf.com* [Accessed July 15, 2010].

[217] Law No. 80-538 of July 16, 1980, Journal Officiel de la Republique Francaise, July 17, 1980, at 1799.

[218] Marc J. Gottridge & Thomas Rouhette, *Blocking Statutes Bring Discovery Woes*, available through *http://www.law.com*; [Accessed July 15, 2010] *Westinghouse Electric Corp v Rio Algom Ltd* 480 F. Supp. 1138 at 1143, 1148 (N.D. Ill. 1979).

[219] *Rio Algom* 480 F. Supp. at 1143.

[220] See Restatement (Third) of Foreign Relations Law § 442, Reporter's Notes 4 (1987).

[221] *Rio Algom* 480 F. Supp. 1138 at 1144–45 & n.4.

[222] *Societe Internationale Pour Participations Industrielles Et Commerciales v Rogers* 357 U.S. 197 at 204 (1958). See also Fed. R. Civ. P. 26.

[223] *Societe Nationale Industrielle Aerospatiale v District Court* 482 U.S. 522 at 546–47 (1987).

[224] Gottridge & Rouhette, *Blocking Statutes*. See also *Strauss v Credit Lyonnais* 242 F.R.D. 199 (E.D.N.Y. 2007) (permitting discovery from foreign bank despite its prohibition by French blocking statute and bank secrecy laws).

[225] *Aerospatiale* 482 U.S. at 539.

[226] *Aerospatiale* 482 U.S.

The court also noted the difficulties that American-style discovery may create for foreign entities, and cautioned against subjecting foreign parties to excessive production.[227] US courts should "exercise special vigilance" to protect foreign litigants from "unnecessary" or "unduly burdensome" discovery.[228] An American court should seek to minimise costs for foreign parties and supervise discovery for abuses and improper motives.[229] This danger, present in domestic cases, escalates significantly in international matters that require the "additional cost of transportation of documents or witnesses" over long distances.[230] Litigants may seek to impose excessive costs on foreign parties to induce settlement.[231]

For all these reasons, the court concluded, objections by foreign parties to "abusive discovery" must receive the "most careful consideration."[232] American courts should "demonstrate due respect" for the difficulties foreign parties face in attempting to satisfy the demands of both US courts and foreign law.[233] Besides the above words of caution, the Supreme Court declined to "articulate specific rules to guide this delicate task of adjudication."[234]

US Discovery Rules and International Discovery: The State of the Law

8–32   Courts have developed discretionary factors in considering whether to impose discovery orders on foreign parties, and what penalties are appropriate for violators.[235] Courts should examine foremost the strength of Congressional policies that successful discovery would further, versus the strength of the foreign government's interest.[236] Judges should pay particular attention to whether the foreign sovereign objected to revealing the information involved before the litigation at hand.[237] A country with a genuine interest in keeping information private would likely have already announced as much and acted accordingly, while a country that suddenly develops an interest in protecting information on commencement of a US suit may seek merely to harass US jurisdiction.[238]

Courts may also evaluate whether the information is "crucial" to resolving a "key issue" in the dispute.[239] This stands in sharp contrast to the ordinary lenient

---

[227] *Aerospatiale* 482 U.S. at 546.
[228] *Aerospatiale* 482 U.S.
[229] *Aerospatiale* 482 U.S.
[230] *Aerospatiale* 482 U.S.
[231] *Aerospatiale* 482 U.S.
[232] *Aerospatiale* 482 U.S.
[233] *Aerospatiale* 482 U.S.
[234] *Aerospatiale* 482 U.S.
[235] See Cohen, *Blocking Statutes*, at 1.
[236] *Richmark Corp v Timber Falling Consultants* 959 F.2d 1468 at 1476 (9th Cir. 1992) (citing Restatement (Third) of Foreign Relations Law § 442(1)(c) (1987)) (noting the relevancy of both American and foreign interests).
[237] See Cohen, *Blocking Statutes*, at 1.
[238] Cohen, *Blocking Statutes*, at 1.
[239] *Rio Algom* 480 F. Supp. 1138 at 1146 (holding that, while information ordinarily need only be "relevant" to permit discovery, information on foreign shores must be "crucial" to a "key issue").

standard for discovery, under which information need only be "relevant" to warrant production.[240]

Thirdly, courts may examine the flexibility of the foreign law prohibiting discovery, and whether the requested party could obtain a waiver from the foreign government.[241] The blocking statute in France, for example, has generally proven to be a "paper tiger."[242] It has rarely if ever been enforced.[243] This apparently "hollow French threat of criminal prosecution" of its own citizens now plays a diminished role in American courts' analysis of whether to permit discovery of information and documents on French soil.[244]

Finally, courts also consider the good faith of the foreign party and any   8–33 hardship it faces due to compliance.[245] The foreign party should rapidly inform the court of any applicable blocking statutes and seek relevant waivers from its home government.[246] It should not, for instance, request that its government bolster its non-disclosure laws to generate an excuse not to reveal the information to American courts.[247] Hardship to the foreign party weighs against permitting discovery, but not if that hardship was self-imposed.[248]

D. INTERNAL INVESTIGATIONS

I. GENERALLY

US regulators not only welcome internal corporate investigations but fully expect   8–34 them to occur. This has been the case for some time, but is all the more so in the past decade that seen the enactment of the Sarbanes-Oxley Act, aggressive anti-bribery enforcement, and other phenomena associated with an atmosphere of enhanced corporate governance.

UK regulators have increasingly taken the same tack. Internal corporate investigations are now the norm in UK anti-bribery inquiries. This is likely to become all the more so in the wake of the Bribery Law's requirement that companies have "adequate procedures" in place to prevent bribery.

The age of internal corporate investigations in the United States is generally

---

[240] *Rio Algom* 480 F. Supp. 1138.

[241] *Rio Algom* 480 F. Supp. 1138.

[242] Gottridge & Rouhette, *Blocking Statutes.*

[243] Gottridge & Rouhette, *Blocking Statutes.*

[244] Gottridge & Rouhette, *Blocking Statutes.*

[245] See, e.g. *Societe Internationale v Rogers* 357 U.S. at 212; Cohen, *Blocking Statutes*, at 2.

[246] See e.g. *Societe Internationale v Rogers* 357 U.S. at 205; *Richmark Corp v Timber Falling Consultants* 959 F.2d 1468 at 1479 (9th Cir. 1992); *Re Westinghouse Electric Corp Uranium Contracts Litig.* 563 F.2d 992 at 996 (10th Cir. 1977). See also Cohen, *Blocking Statutes*, at 2.

[247] See *Rio Algom* 480 F. Supp. 1138 at 1147; *Remington Products Inc v North American Philips Corp* 107 F.R.D. 642 at 643-645 (D. Conn. 1985); Cohen, *Blocking Statutes*, at 2.

[248] *Timber Falling Consultants* 959 F.2d 1468 at 1477.

thought to date back to the 1970s.[249] Spurred by the Watergate scandal, which uncovered evidence of illicit corporate campaign contributions, the SEC began a series of inquiries into these and other corporate practices, including those of paying foreign government officials.[250] The SEC provided a report to Congress on the subject, which culminated in the enactment of the FCPA, discussed in Ch.2.

8–35   In the course of its investigation, however, the SEC quickly determined that instances of payments to foreign officials were so widespread that it would not have the capacity to look into each and every example of such practice. Accordingly, the SEC instituted a voluntary disclosure program that permitted self-reporting corporations to avoid enforcement action. More than 650 companies subsequently admitted wrongdoing after having undertaken internal investigations to determine the extent of their payments to foreign officials and other questionable payment practices.[251]

Following the success of this self-policing and self-reporting exercise, internal investigations expanded and flourished as a mechanism of corporate governance. Thus, "by the 1990s, the internal investigation had evolved into '[t]he primary method for corporations to address past and present misconduct.'"[252]

(a) Internal Investigations in Conjunction with Regulatory Investigations

8–36   Because of the longstanding existence and widespread acceptance of internal investigations in the United States, regulators have allowed such investigations to occur in conjunction with a regulatory inquiry, and will give evidence to their findings provided they are deemed sufficiently thorough, wide-ranging and independent. The United Kingdom and other jurisdictions may be headed in the same direction.

But there is a downside for the company when regulators credit the findings of internal investigations. It is simply this: acceptance reflects not so much a willingness to trust the bona fides of regulated companies as it does the reality that those conducting the internal investigation are increasingly independent of the company itself.

The regulatory enticements to cooperation reinforce this dynamic. The more a company cedes control of the internal investigation, by making the government privy to its attorney-client communications and the work product of investigators and otherwise, the more the government will be inclined to view the investigation favourably and to credit the company accordingly.

---

[249] See William R. Baker III & Joel H. Trotter, *Corporate Internal Investigations after Sarbanes-Oxley, in* 2 The Practitioner's Guide to the Sarbanes-Oxley Act VII–4–1 (John J. Huber, Stanley Keller, Vasiliki B. Tsaganos & Jonathan Wolfman eds., 2005).

[250] See Andrew Longstreth, *Double Agent; In the New Era of Internal Investigation, Defense Lawyers Have Become Deputy Prosecutors*, 27 Am. Law. 2 (2005).

[251] See Longstreth, *Double Agent*.

[252] Baker & Trotter, *Corporate Internal Investigations*, at VII–4–3 (quoting Anton R. Valukas & Robert R. Stauffer, *Internal Investigations of Corporate Misconduct*, Insights Vol. 6, No. 2, at 17 (February 1992)).

Thus, the term "independent internal investigation" has become something of   8–37
a misnomer; to be sure, investigations are increasingly independent of *the com-pany*. But investigations tend at the same time to be correspondingly less inde-pendent of the regulator(s) under whose scrutiny the company ultimately falls. Perhaps, a more accurate term to describe the phenomena of inquiries being led by outside counsel, paid for by the company, and shared with regulators would be "cooperative internal investigation."

This trend has led some commentators to express frustration and concern at the erosion of the attorney-client relationship that used to be thought to under-gird an internal investigation[253]:

> "lawmakers' zeal in rooting out corporate fraud, combined with lazier prosecutors, effectively forces companies to do the government's job for them by investigating themselves and surrendering their findings to the authorities;"[254]

> "[t]oday, the investigating lawyer essentially acts as a fact-finder with a badge—the newest [and highest-paid] government agent. He [or she] conducts hundreds of inter-views, scans company computers for damaging e-mails, rummages through the CFO's wastebasket, and then hands potential evidence over to the government;"[255]

> "lawyers conducting these probes have been transformed from trusted counsellors, who in the past were all too willing to lend their credibility to whitewashes, into inquisitorial cops."[256]

(b) Hiring Outside Counsel to Conduct an Internal Investigation

There is nothing in theory to prevent a company from using in-house counsel to   8–38
conduct an internal investigation. Indeed, there is no specific requirement that an internal investigation be conducted by lawyers. As a practical matter, however, considerations of independence, or perceived independence, usually militate against using in-house counsel to conduct an internal investigation.[257]

The notion that lawyers conduct the internal investigation has its roots in the principle of the attorney-client privilege and attorney work-product protection and it English cousin, the litigation privilege. The value of those protections has been eroded in recent years, not so much by the quality of the protections themselves but by the knowledge that waiver will be seen by regulators in a positive light. Why, then, continue to hire lawyers to conduct internal corporate investigations?

[253] The indictment of US law firm Milberg Weiss, which allegedly occurred only after the firm refused to waive attorney-client privilege at the request of the DOJ, has raised the level of frustration and concern regarding both erosion of the privilege and the DOJ's controversial policy on waiver. See, e.g. Marcia Coyle, *Battle on Waivers Expanding; Attorney-Client Privilege is at Stake*, Nat'l L.J. (May 15, 2006).

[254] John Gibeaut, *Junior G-MEN: Corporate Lawyers Worry That They're Doing the Government's Bidding While Doing Internal Investigations*, 89 A.B.A. J. 46 (2003).

[255] Longstreth, *Double Agent*.

[256] David Henry, Mike France & Louis Lavelle, *The Boss on the Sidelines; How Auditors, Directors, and Lawyers are Asserting Their Power*, Bus. Wk., April 25, 2005, at 86.

[257] Indeed, in asking whether "company employees or outside persons" conducted the investiga-tion, the Seaboard guidelines speak to this very issue. See *Seaboard Report* at *8.

The answer is three-fold: first, a company is well-advised to evaluate the findings of an investigation before making a decision as to whether an investigation report, and concomitant work product, should be handed over to regulators. There may well be cases in which the company concludes that the detriments of producing the report and/or waiving privilege and work product protection outweigh the benefits. This the company cannot do if it does not have an investigation conducted by lawyers in the first place.

8–39   Secondly, lawyers, especially large law firms, have over the years developed considerable experience conducting internal investigations. Law firms therefore tend to have both the expertise and the manpower to undertake these kinds of probing investigations.

Thirdly, and relatedly, there are few if any other people to turn to who are equipped to conduct internal investigations. The other logical candidates, auditors and audit firms, may be constrained by conflicts of interest: an accounting firm providing accounting advice and services to a public company is prohibited in several jurisdictions from also auditing the company and its books.[258] The same conflict of interest considerations could make it inappropriate for a firm that either renders accounting services to, or audits a company, also to conduct an internal investigation. In conducting an internal investigation it is often of great assistance to have access to the skills and expertise of forensic accountants, particularly where detailed financial transactions and high volumes of data are involved (see Ch.9). Some of the larger forensic accounting practices sit within audit firms and it is therefore important to consider these conflict issues carefully when selecting an appropriate firm, as it would be for a law firm which works for or typically provides advice to the company.

Thus, internal investigations in which there is potentially significant exposure to risk for the company are usually undertaken by outside legal counsel. But who at the company decides whether to undertake an investigation in the first place, and if so, whom to retain? Until recently, the answer would have been that such decisions rested with the company's senior management, and were the particular province of its general counsel. Today, however, it is the firm's audit committee that has usually the principal responsibility for gauging the necessity of an internal investigation, and for selecting a firm to conduct such investigation.

(c) Audit Committee Criteria for Hiring Outside Counsel

8–40   Since there is nothing to prevent company management from retaining counsel to conduct an internal investigation, management may decide to do so. If it sees fit—in other words, if it perceives no conflict—an audit committee may well endorse management's choice of counsel.

Management will typically opt to retain a firm with which it is familiar based on previous work. There is undoubtedly a certain advantage to having a known quantity as counsel in an internal investigation. Such counsel will be pre-

---

[258] See, e.g. 15 U.S.C. § 78j-1(l) (Sarbanes Oxley).

sumptively competent and equipped in the eyes of management to handle the logistics of the inquiry. (In this respect, however, companies should obviously resist the temptation to retain a law firm as investigative counsel merely because it gives the company unrelated legal advice.) There is something to be said, furthermore, for hiring counsel with both an understanding of the industry and an appreciation of the company's work culture and idiosyncrasies.

These very same considerations, however, can also work to a company's disadvantage as it considers the potential regulatory reaction to an internal investigation. Outside counsel deemed overly familiar with the company may also be deemed insufficiently independent from it. If, for example, a law firm derives a substantial portion of revenue from its representation of the company in other matters, and/or one or more partners in the law firm has a close working relationship with senior management, regulators may be inclined to view an internal investigation conducted by that law firm with a certain scepticism. An audit committee thus faced with the selection of such outside counsel would be less likely to ratify management's choice, and more likely to select alternative counsel to conduct a separate investigation.

The audit committee criteria for selecting outside counsel therefore may **8–41** conflict with what previously prevailed as conventional wisdom when the selection of counsel was still primarily the province of management. The audit committee, in anticipation of giving regulators the requisite assurance that any internal investigation was sufficiently fair-minded and independent, will gravitate toward outside counsel with little or no other connection to the company. Unlike with audit firms, this process is not complicated by a dearth of choices.

The audit committee's search for outside counsel that can be deemed independent is impelled in no small part by regulatory opinion on the subject. One commentator has observed that the SEC's pronouncements in its Seaboard Report and elsewhere provide de facto instruction that otherwise disinterested outside counsel should conduct an investigation, and that the audit committee should supervise it:

> "[The Seaboard] factors speak generally to the importance of an internal investigation, but also provide specific guidance about the kind of investigation that the Commission believes should be undertaken—including who should direct the investigation, who should conduct the investigation, what should be the scope of the investigation, the appropriate form of the report of the investigation and the appropriate audience(s) for that report."[259]

Other considerations will of course factor in the audit committee's decision. Once it has determined that an internal investigation is warranted and that such an investigation should be conducted by outside counsel with little or no other connection to the company, the audit committee will need to decide which law

---

[259] See William R. Baker III & Joel H. Trotter, *Corporate Internal Investigations after Sarbanes-Oxley,* in 2 The Practitioner's Guide to the Sarbanes-Oxley Act VII–4–1 (John J. Huber, Stanley Keller, Vasiliki B. Tsaganos & Jonathan Wolfman eds., 2005), at VII–4–25 to VII–4–26.

firm(s) to select. For even the very largest companies that use myriad law firms for various matters, many law firms will remain that can legitimately be deemed disinterested and independent.

8–42   The first and foremost criterion that the audit committee must take into account will be outside counsel's ability to conduct the investigation competently and thoroughly. This will implicate the law firm's size and reputation. Depending upon the scope and scale of the investigation, a larger law firm is sometimes warranted. One with several offices nationally or internationally may be better-positioned to conduct an inquiry to the extent that relevant documents and witnesses are located in disparate parts of the country or the world.

Another factor to consider will be the reputation of the law firm and/or the lead partner. Regulators will tend to give greater deference to an internal investigation conducted by a firm that has a high-profile investigations practice, or a well-known partner with a reputation for probity and zeal. It is for this reason that the investigations practices of many law firms are staffed with former regulators and ex-prosecutors.

None of this is to say that smaller law firms with less well-established reputations in the field cannot serve as outside counsel in an internal corporate investigation. The demands of internal investigations in the current regulatory climate, however, tend to favour outside counsel with enough personnel and resources to conduct extensive document review (including review of e-mails and electronic documents) and dozens or hundreds of employee interviews, and with enough clout in the legal world to lend credibility to the premise that their findings will be full, fair and unvarnished by a desire to pull their punches.

II. EMPLOYEES AND WITNESSES

(a) Inducing or compelling employees to cooperate with an internal investigation

8–43   At the risk of stating the obvious, an internal investigation cannot occur without the investigators' speaking with company employees.[260] At the same time, their doing so raises a host of troublesome issues: will the employees agree to speak with them? What if they do not? Do they need counsel of their own? What assurances, if any, can the investigators give them about the confidentiality of their discussions? Should certain employees be suspended while the investigation is underway?

Prior to all these considerations, the investigators must decide which employees

---

[260]   In the words of one commentator:

"The employee interview is the heart of the internal investigation. Documents, accounting ledgers, and other corporate records are important, but words and numbers come to life through the stories related by real people. Talking with those who have knowledge of key developments facilitates understanding of what happened and why better than any other investigative tool."

Sarah Helene Duggin, *Internal Corporate Investigations: Legal Ethics, Professionalism and the Employee Interview*, 2003 Colum. Bus. L. Rev. 859 at 864 (2003).

they ought to interview. The initial list need not be exhaustive. Indeed, it is virtually inevitable that the first several employee interviews will generate names of additional employees with relevant information. The investigators are unlikely to be able to compile even an initial list without input from management (several members of whom might themselves be interviewees). Such input obviously should not constrain the investigators from going beyond the names given to the extent that the investigators believe other employees may have useful information.

Even when investigations are conducted by outside counsel (and even in the era of audit committees selecting such counsel), the traditional liaison between the investigator and employees is still a member of the in-house counsel staff. The typical procedure is for a member of that staff to contact the employee and advise him or her that lawyers for the company wish to conduct an interview. The in-house counsel will usually apprise the employee in general terms of the nature of the investigation (if he or she is not already aware of it), and may also inquire as to whether the employee wishes to secure independent legal representation.

Companies in the United States are able to bring significant pressure to bear   **8–44** upon their employees in order to secure their cooperation with an internal investigation. An employee cannot, of course, be physically compelled to submit to an interview with an investigator. The company nonetheless is within its rights for disciplining or even firing the employee for refusing to do so.

Some employees, anticipating the risk of criminal exposure, may decline to be interviewed on the ground that what they say might end up incriminating them. The Fifth Amendment to the US Constitution contains a provision against self-incrimination,[261] but, again, employees' invocation of the Constitution will not prevent a company from firing the employee.[262] The right against self-incrimination, like other constitutional protections for individuals, is a right against government, not private, action. Thus, while the US (and state local) government cannot abridge an individual's freedom of speech, a private company's restrictions upon employees' freedom of speech is relatively routine. By the same token, an employee cannot count on the constitutional protection against self-incrimination to protect his job.

In an international corruption investigation, however, employees subject to interview may be scattered across the world. The local law governing their employment engagement will determine the extent to which they must cooperate with an internal investigation, and to which the company may sanction them for refusing to do so.

Employees who do agree to speak to an investigator about alleged or potential   **8–45** wrongdoing at the company may have concerns about the confidentiality of their statements. Employees may have knowledge that will incriminate their colleagues

---

[261] "No person . . . shall be compelled in any criminal case to be a witness against himself." U.S. Const. amend. V.
[262] For Maurice R. "Hank" Greenberg, head of insurance giant AIG, invoking the Fifth Amendment right against self-incrimination during a regulatory investigation ultimately forced his resignation. See Dean Starkman, *Greenberg Opens Attack on Spitzer, Allegations, Washington Post,* December 16, 2005, at D1.

and superiors, or otherwise shed them in unflattering light. Employees may fear that the relevance of their knowledge will result in their being interviewed at a later date by regulators and prosecutors.

Any assurances of confidentiality, however, will necessarily be limited in scope. The investigator needs to preserve the ability to disclose what the employee says to the client (the audit committee and/or management of the company), to regulators, and potentially to other employees. It is important for the investigator to make clear to the employee that he or she (the investigator) represents the company, not the employee. Because the client is the company, the employee should have no expectation that the investigator will withhold information learned in the interview from the company, even though the conversation is within the scope of the attorney-client privilege. The privilege belongs to the company and the company, in turn, may choose to share the information with regulators or otherwise disclose it.

Counsel conducting an employee interview therefore begin by making a brief statement to this effect. The statement is usually a rote repetition of the above-noted principles, and variously known in the US as an "Upjohn" warning,[263] a civil "Miranda,"[264] or an "Adnarim"[265] warning.[266]

8–46   Many employees, especially those with knowledge of questionable conduct that occurred, will want assurances that their cooperation with the investigation will immunise them from sanction or dismissal. The investigating attorney is in no

---

[263] In *Upjohn v US* 449 U.S. 383 (1981), the US Supreme Court clarified the scope of the attorney-client privilege in the context of communications with company employees. The Court held that even communications with lower-level employees could be privileged, provided that those communications were made in the course of counsel's seeking to give legal advice to the company. An internal investigation clearly fits that mold. The appellation nonetheless fails to capture the spirit of the investigator's caution to the employee that, although their conversation will be privileged, it is the company's privilege to waive.

[264] In *Miranda v Arizona* 384 U.S. 436 (1966), the US Supreme Court established that an arrestee or detainee must be advised by police of certain constitutional rights, including the right against self-incrimination. Hence, the statement given by all police when arresting suspects (and known to all who watch American police dramas and movies) that the suspect has a "right to remain silent. . . ."

[265] Adnarim is Miranda spelled backward. See, e.g. Robert G. Morvillo & Robert J. Anello, *White Collar Crime; Beyond "Upjohn": Necessary Warnings in Internal Investigations*, 234 N.Y.L.J. 3 (2005).

[266] Investigating attorneys ought to keep in mind that the provision and quality of such warnings have been the subject of recent judicial scrutiny in the US. See *Re Grand Jury Subpoena: UNDER SEAL*, 415 F.3d 333 (4th Cir. 2005), for a recent example where three former employees of AOL Time Warner ("AOL") moved to quash, on the basis of attorney-client privilege, a grand jury subpoena for documents relating to an internal investigation. The salient facts are that, in March 2001, AOL began an internal investigation into one of its business relationships. In November 2001, the SEC began to investigate the same relationship and sought information previously provided by the employees to AOL's investigating attorneys during interviews that took place during the course of AOL's internal investigation. AOL agreed to waive the privilege and produce the documents. The employees attempted to prevent production claiming that the information was privileged. The court found in favor of the company, concluding that the employees "could not have reasonably believed that the investigating attorneys represented them personally during the [relevant] time frame." At 339. Hence, there was never any attorney-client relationship between the investigating attorneys and the employees. The court noted that, at the time of their interviews, each employee was advised (to some extent) that the investigating attorneys represented AOL and that, although their conversations were privileged, the privilege belonged to AOL.

position to give any such assurances.[267] The company's treatment of the employee will depend upon the nature and scope of his or her disclosures. Revelations that the employee participated in illegal activity will necessitate that the employee be terminated. Disclosure of less serious behaviour may warrant lesser action or no action at all. The employee, for his or her part, faces a Hobson's Choice: cooperate and risk censure, or worse, for what you reveal, or do not cooperate and risk the same penalties as a consequence.

Companies under investigation will sometimes draft consulting agreements with departing employees, which specify that the ex-employee will be paid a consulting fee for his or her time spent submitting to interview by investigators and/or assisting with their inquiries.

(b) Employee protections against company action for non-cooperation

Despite employees' being largely obligated to cooperate with internal investiga-   8–47
tions, they are not entirely without recourse if they choose not to do so and subsequently are sanctioned or dismissed. The rights of employees who have a contract with their employer will be determined by the terms of that contract. Such a contract, however, is unlikely to make mention of cooperation in an internal investigation.[268] There may nonetheless be an implied duty to cooperate as part of the employee's exercise of his contractual functions.

Employees without a contract are understood to be "at-will" employees. This means that they or the company can terminate their relationship at any time. The company need not terminate the relationship for cause; any reason will do, provided that it is not capricious or discriminatory.

Termination for failure to cooperate with an internal investigation would not be viewed as capricious. The company must take care, however, to treat similarly situated employees the same way. If it were to suspend or dismiss a female employee who declined to be interviewed but took no action against a similarly situated male colleague who also failed to cooperate, the female employee might have a case that her non-cooperation was a pretext for discriminatory action.

---

[267] In a similar vein, the investigating attorney should refrain from even stating that he or she "could" represent the employee "as long as no conflict appeared." At 335. The court in *Re Grand Jury Subpoena: UNDER SEAL* commented upon these "watered-down" warnings provided by AOL's investigating attorneys to the employees under investigation, stating:

"It is a potential legal and ethical mine field. Had the investigating attorneys, in fact, entered into an attorney-client relationship with [the employees], as their statements to the [employees] professed they could, they would not have been free to waive the [employees'] privilege when a conflict arose. It should have seemed obvious that they could not have jettisoned one client in favor of another. Rather, they would have had to withdraw from all representation and to maintain all confidences. *Indeed, the court would be hard pressed to identify how investigating counsel could robustly investigate and report to management or the board of directors of a publicly-traded corporation with the necessary candor if counsel were constrained by ethical obligations to individual employees.*"

415 F.3d 333 at 340 (emphasis added).

[268] Note that unionized employees, however, may have rights appurtenant to interviews in internal investigations as a result of collective bargaining agreements. See Coyne & Barker, *Internal Corporate Investigations*, at 172.

8–48   Once again, however, local law will determine the rights and responsibilities of employees in connection with internal investigations. Some jurisdictions have much stronger protections for employees than others; in those jurisdictions, it will simply be difficult to convince a recalcitrant employee to cooperate.

The company should also take great care with whistleblowers.[269] It might at first blush seem unlikely that a whistleblower would refuse to cooperate with an investigation for which he or she in some way was responsible. But the whistleblower may have lost faith in the company and distrust lawyers who represent it. He or she may be counting upon regulators to uncover the full scope of alleged wrongdoing, and have no interest in speaking about it with the internal investigation team.

(c) Providing counsel for employees

8–49   One way in which the company can address the concerns of nervous employees facing the prospect of interviews is by providing them with counsel of their own. Because, as discussed above, counsel conducting the internal investigation represents the company, he or she is ethically conflicted from providing legal advice to interviewed employees. Moreover, employees involved or implicated in misconduct will thereby find their interests to be at odds with those of the company, making the conflict all the starker.

Therefore, it is common for the company to offer any and all employees interviewed in an investigation the option of having their own lawyer to advise them. Typically, this offer will come from in-house counsel, or whoever at the company is coordinating the investigation, in advance of a request by investigating counsel for an interview.[270] If the employee accepts the offer to be separately represented, ethical guidelines in several jurisdictions—including the US—mandate that any further communication with the employee concerning the investigation occur through his or her lawyer.[271]

The representing lawyer will meet with the employee prior to the interview and will attend of course the interview itself. Having spoken initially with the employee, however, the lawyer may conclude that an interview is not in the

---

[269] See, e.g. Joseph F. Coyne, Jr. & Charles F. Barker, *Employees' Rights and Duties During an Internal Investigation*, Internal Corporate Investigations 173 at 189-190 (Brad D. Brian & Barry F. McNeil eds., 2d edn, 2003), p.173.

[270] If an employee is not offered separate representation before the initial interview:

"Investigating counsel should be prepared to answer the question: "Do I need my own lawyer?" by advising the constituent that it is in his best interest to obtain individual representation if counsel has enough information to make a judgment and reasonably believes that this is so. Otherwise, counsel should inform the constituent either that counsel does not have enough information to make such a judgment, or that only the employee can make this decision."

Duggin, *Internal Corporate Investigations*, at 960 (proposing "new ethical ground rules for investigative employee interviews").

[271] See Model Rules of Professional Conduct R. 4.2 ("In representing a client, a lawyer shall not communicate about the subject of the representation with a person the lawyer knows to be represented by another lawyer in the matter, unless the lawyer has the consent of the other lawyer or is authorized to do so by law or a court order.").

client's best interests and advise the employee not to be interviewed. This is a risk that the company must take in the course of the investigation.

The vast majority of employees are unlikely to know a lawyer who can **8–50** adequately represent them in an internal investigation. It therefore usually falls to the company to provide them with one. Often the company opts to choose one lawyer (or, if the number of employees to be interviewed is large, one law firm) to represent all the employees.

Outside counsel conducting the investigation often have a pre-existing working relationship with counsel for the employees. Indeed, it may fall to investigating counsel to recommend to the company a lawyer or law firm that can represent the employees. To the extent that such relationship may be perceived as overly cozy, employees must count on the ethical and professional obligation of their lawyers to represent the employees' interests first and foremost. As a practical matter, the interests of the employee and the company in many cases will not diverge. It therefore makes sense for those representing the employees to be professionally familiar with investigating counsel.

It will also be common, nonetheless, for employees to have interests that substantially diverge from the interests of fellow employees. Under those circumstances, not all employees can be represented by the same lawyer or law firm. Thus, the company must be prepared to have more than one lawyer or law firm available for individual representation.

(d) Indemnification for and advancement of legal fees

At the risk of again stating the obvious, lawyers are expensive. The overwhelming **8–51** majority of employees, including senior officers and directors, will be unable to afford their own legal services. If the company means to offer its employees a realistic possibility of separate representation, it must be prepared to do so in a way that would not be ruinous to those who take up the offer.

Companies in the United States therefore routinely guarantee and advance the employee's legal fees in connection with the investigation.[272] This is a not insignificant addition to the already high legal costs associated with an internal investigation. But it is a price that the company nonetheless must pay to secure the cooperation of its employees and to ensure the thoroughness of the internal review.

Under certain circumstances, companies have the power to indemnify employees for the cost of their legal representation. Local law will determine the extent of this ability. It typically arises in the context of regulatory or law enforcement inquiries and private civil litigation. Laws in many jurisdictions

---

[272] Note that the SEC traditionally opposes indemnification of directors and officers against liability in connection with securities violations. See Jesse A. Finkelstein & Mark J. Gentile, *Relationship to State Law*, in 2 The Practitioner's Guide to the Sarbanes-Oxley Act, at V–4–26, n.116. One commentator, however, in proposing that companies should not be hindered from treating employees fairly in internal investigations, notes that the "advancement of legal fees to individuals under investigation or charged with crimes related to their responsibilities as officers, directors or employees of the entity should not be considered as an adverse factor against the organization . . . ." Duggin at 963.

provide that a company can indemnify its officers and directors who are being sued or who are under threat of suit in connection with actions they took or failed to take in the course of their professional duties. The purpose of such legislation is to attract talented and capable executives and board members to companies without their fearing that they will be bankrupted by defending charges arising out of their work with the company.[273]

8–52   The archetypal statute providing for indemnification of directors and officers comes from the state of Delaware. Attractive to companies because of its favourable laws on incorporation and corporate governance, and with courts that are unusually sophisticated in matters of corporate affairs, Delaware is disproportionately important as a locus for American corporate activity. Thus, despite its small size, fully half of all public companies in the US are incorporated in Delaware.[274]

Delaware's relevant statute allows for the indemnification of any director, officer, or employee "who was or is a party or is threatened to be made a party to any threatened, pending or completed action, suit or proceeding, whether civil, criminal, administrative or investigative . . . ."[275] An internal investigation would probably fall within this rubric if it occurred in connection with a regulatory inquiry. If the investigation preceded any such inquiry, however, the statutory indemnification likely would not apply. Nonetheless, a separate statutory provision states that the indemnification criteria set forth above are not exhaustive, and that the company may expand them.[276] The charters and bylaws of many corporations do so expand them and thereby provide for indemnification of employees in all internal investigations.

The company will nonetheless want the ability to claim back legal fees it has paid on behalf of employees who prove to have been engaged in the misconduct under investigation. Again, Delaware law (and other states following suit) provides a statutory mechanism to do so. The provision on indemnification states that such fees will be paid to the director or officer:

> "If the person acted in good faith and in a manner the person reasonably believed to be in or not opposed to the best interest of the corporation, and, with respect to any criminal action or proceeding, had no reasonable cause to believe the person's conduct was unlawful."[277]

The company bylaws will generally set forth the mechanism whereby the company determines whether the employee has fulfilled this criterion. Such a

---

[273] Many US public companies provide indemnification for and advancement of legal fees in their corporate charters or by-laws or by virtue of indemnification agreements with certain employees. See Finkelstein & Gentile, *Relationship to State Law*, in 2 The Practitioner's Guide to the Sarbanes-Oxley Act, at V-4-25.

[274] "More than half a million business entities have their legal home in Delaware including more than 50% of all U.S. publicly-traded companies and 60% of the Fortune 500." State of Delaware, Department of State: Division of Corporations, *http://www.state.de.us/corp/* [Accessed July 15, 2010].

[275] 8 Del. C. § 145(a).

[276] 8 Del. C. § 145(f).

[277] 8 Del. C. § 145(a).

mechanism usually consists of a vote by the Board or a special committee of Board members.

(e) Joint defence agreements

Even with separate representation paid for by the company, and even with the threat of sanction for non-cooperation, employees may still be uncomfortable divulging sensitive and potentially damaging information to investigators. One further step that the company can take in order to assuage employees' concerns is to enter into a joint defence agreement.[278]   **8–53**

Joint defence agreements are a mechanism whereby different parties, having concluded that they share a common interest in the conduct and outcome of an investigation or litigation, undertake to share information and collaborate strategically with each other. Joint defence agreements are common among and between similarly situated defendants in private US lawsuits, who may be able to benefit from the exchange strategic ideas and drafts of legal papers. The crux of the joint defence agreement is that it permits such exchange without waiving the attorney–client privilege and other protections from disclosure. Privileged information shared with a party pursuant to a joint defence agreement therefore remains protected from disclosure.[279]

The corollary to this situation is that all parties to the joint defence agreement must concur before any one party is permitted voluntarily to waive the privilege. In the context of an internal investigation, this raises a serious problem: given regulators' well-established preference for a free flow of information from the company, up to and including waiver of privilege, can the company afford to condition its communication with regulators upon the consent to the disclosure of information by employees?

For those companies that enter into joint defence agreements with employees, it should be borne in mind that most joint defence agreements allow any party to withdraw from the arrangement at any time, and in particular when it becomes apparent that the interests of parties have diverged. There is therefore no impediment to a company's withdrawal from a joint defence agreement with an employee who turns out to have engaged in misconduct. For purposes of dis-   **8–54**

---

[278] See Robert A. Creamer, *Criminal Law Concerns for Civil Lawyers*, 52 Fed. Law. 34 at 41 (2005), for provisions to consider upon entering into a joint defense agreement.

[279] "The joint defense privilege, an extension of the attorney-client privilege, protects communications between parties who share a common interest in litigation. The purpose of the privilege is to allow persons with a common interest to communicate with their respective attorneys and with each other to more effectively prosecute or defend their claims. For the privilege to apply, the proponent must establish that the parties had some common interest about a legal matter. An employee's cooperation in an internal investigation alone is not sufficient to establish a common interest; rather some form of joint strategy is necessary."
Re Grand Jury Subpoena: UNDER SEAL 415 F.3d 333 at 341 (citations and quotations omitted) (finding no evidence of a common interest where there was neither agreement nor common legal strategy).

closure, however, the joint defence privilege remains intact for all documents and information shared while the joint defence agreement remained in effect.

III. DOCUMENTS AND INFORMATION

(a) Document Preservation

8–55   Few, if any, things are more important in an internal investigation than acquiring, preserving, and understanding relevant documents.[280] Documents provide clues to, or evidence of, the misconduct at issue; confirm or contradict the accounts of key witnesses; and set forth the story that will need to be told to regulators in a form that may not require the testimony of dozens of employees.

So it should come as no surprise that regulators, as well as outside counsel conducting internal investigations, feel strongly about maintaining the integrity of relevant documents. Because many companies have standing document retention policies in place, however, preserving documents for an investigation will likely mean overriding those policies.

Document retention policies are somewhat misnamed. Generally they advise employees about the importance of *not* retaining certain kinds of documents— such as draft versions of final products—and instruct employees to be vigilant in discarding such materials. The phrase "document destruction policy," however, sounds sinister and evokes precisely the kind of cover-up mentality that a document retention policy is designed to avoid. The point, after all, is that companies cannot reasonably be held to account for not preserving documents that their employees are instructed in the ordinary course of business to discard.

8–56   Certain types of companies nonetheless have affirmative document preservation obligations. Broker-dealers registered with the SEC, for example, must preserve certain records for a three-year period.[281] The failure by several to do so has resulted in steep fines by the SEC.[282] Aside from these and other regulatory obligations, document retention policies frequently (and permissibly) mandate that certain classes of documents be periodically and systematically destroyed.

---

[280] Equally important to any investigation therefore is document control. *See* Larry A. Gaydos, *Gathering and Organizing Relevant Documents: An Essential Task in Any Investigation*, in Internal Corporate Investigations at 141, for a good discussion on how to process documents once they are collected so that they can be further reviewed by investigating counsel for evidence of misconduct or possible wrongdoing.

[281] See Records to be Made by Certain Exchange Members, Brokers and Dealers, 17 C.F.R. § 240.17a-3; Records to be Preserved by Certain Exchange Members, Brokers and Dealers, § 240.17a-4.

[282] In December 2002, five major broker-dealers were each fined $1.65 million for violating SEC record-keeping requirements concerning e-mail communications. See Cutler, Bar Association Remarks, (discussing various cases involving failure to preserve or produce documents). See also *SEC v Morgan Stanley Co Inc* No. 06 Civ. 0882 (D.D.C. May 10, 2006) (alleging that Morgan Stanley violated Rule 17a-4 by failing to produce e-mails less than three years old that were requested by subpoenas and requests in connection with the Commission's IPO and Research Analyst investigations; the Company agreed to pay a $15 million penalty and undertake reforms to settle the charges).

Such policies are spurred by the ever-present possibility of private civil litigation. Although it would be improper to destroy any documents potentially relevant to a private civil action when such action is underway or realistically threatened,[283] it is acceptable to apply an across-the-board policy for the company that will have the net result of reducing the range of relevant documents when litigation occurs.

A regulatory inquiry or internal investigation requires a prompt suspension of any procedures that mandate or permit the destruction of documents.[284] In the regulatory context, document destruction, if seen as wilful, can constitute obstruction of justice, and can expose the company to criminal liability. While failing to suspend an existing policy would not be viewed as seriously as affirmatively destroying relevant documents that otherwise would have been preserved, it might nonetheless qualify as obstruction of justice,[285] and there is no question that regulators would at the very least take a dim view of it.

Although it is far less likely to have criminal ramifications, failure to suspend document retention practices for internal investigations is equally inadvisable. Internal investigators need to be confident that all relevant documents will remain undisturbed, lest their investigation be compromised. Practically speaking, moreover, that investigation will either accompany or immediately precede a regulatory inquiry. Regulators would rightly question the sense and utility of an internal investigation in which no steps were taken to preserve all applicable and relevant documents.

The question of exactly which documents may be relevant, and therefore need   8–57
to be preserved notwithstanding corporate document retention policies, is a difficult one. The company cannot know in advance which documents bear upon any alleged misconduct; that, after all, is part of the point of conducting an internal investigation. Nor is suspending the company's document retention policy system-wide necessarily the answer. This will be burdensome and infeasible for large companies, and would involve notifying the entire firm, to ensure that all employees comply with the suspension, of potential wrongdoing at a nascent phase of an investigation.

---

[283] "The obligation to preserve evidence arises when the party has notice that the evidence is relevant to litigation or when a party should have known that the evidence may be relevant to future litigation." *Zubulake v UBS Warburg LLC* 220 F.R.D. 212 at 216 (S.D.N.Y. 2003) (quoting *Fujitsu Ltd v Federal Express Corp* 247 F.3d 423 at 436 (2d Cir. 2001)).

[284] Failure to do so could be costly. In July 2004, Philip Morris USA was required to pay a monetary sanction of $2.75 million after a federal court found that several high-ranking employees of the company failed to retain documents pursuant to an order to preserve "all documents and other records containing information which could be potentially relevant to the subject matter of this litigation." Rather, the company continued for two years after receiving the document preservation order to keep in place its internal document retention policies that permitted the deletion of e-mail over sixty days old, on a monthly system-wide basis. See *US v Philip Morris USA Inc* 327 F. Supp. 2d 21 (D.D.C. 2004).

[285] Stephen M. Cutler, Dir., Div. of Enforcement, U.S. Sec. & Exch. Comm'n, Speech by SEC Staff: Remarks Before the National Regulatory Services Investment Adviser and Broker-Dealer Compliance/Risk Management Conference (September 9, 2003) ("Commission is bringing more cases for failures to preserve or produce required documents and records, and . . . encouraging criminal authorities to back [SEC] up in appropriate situations with obstruction of justice prosecutions.").

The advent of e-mail has posed particular problems for document preservation.[286] Because companies routinely archive employee e-mails on back-up servers, an immense volume of materials is available for review by regulators and outside counsel conducting an internal investigation. A demand by regulators or a request by investigators to retrieve and review these e-mails often necessitates Herculean efforts by a company's information technology department. Such efforts can be avoided by hiring outside consultants who specialise in the retrieval and sorting of electronic information for litigation and investigation purposes. These consultants unsurprisingly have proliferated in recent years. Their services, however, generally come at considerable cost.

(b) Securing documents from employees

8–58   Counsel conducting an investigation must initially choose how to retrieve documents from employees. The choice is either to ask the employees themselves to gather relevant documents, or send lawyers and paralegals from investigating counsel's firm to do so.

The principal advantage of having a company's employees search for documents is economy: it can be expensive to send attorneys and paralegals to the offices of every employee, and in the direction of every file cabinet, with potentially relevant and/or responsive materials. This is especially so with international companies that may have relevant documents in far-flung corners of the world. Moreover, the attorneys and paralegals will have far less familiarity with the location of documents and the company's filing system, thus prolonging their visits.

Employees, by contrast, will (or ought to) be intimately familiar with the location and content both of their own documents and of the company's filing and archiving procedures. They therefore should be able to locate documents more expeditiously. Furthermore, the presence, often in large numbers, of investigators, attorneys, and paralegals, gathering documents and materials throughout offices, is likely to be disruptive to the daily functioning of the company, and will almost certainly raise awkward questions among employees in the case of an investigation intended to be low-profile and somewhat confidential.

8–59   Against all these considerations must be weighed the following factors: first, as disruptive as it may be to have lawyers and paralegals searching offices and files for documents, it may prove even more distracting for employees to ask them to set aside time to search their own files and their office files. Many employees may prefer to set aside a smaller period of time in which to be interviewed briefly by an investigating lawyer about their files, and in which to point lawyers and paralegals in the direction of relevant documents and materials.

---

[286] For one of the earliest but most comprehensive discussions of document preservation and disclosure in the electronic era, see *Zubulake v UBS Warburg LLC*, 220 F.R.D. 212 at 214 (S.D.N.Y. 2003) ("As documents are increasingly maintained electronically, it has become easier to delete or tamper with evidence (both intentionally and inadvertently) and more difficult for litigants to craft policies that ensure all relevant documents are preserved.").

Secondly, despite employees' greater familiarity with the documents, it is ultimately lawyers who understand the legal issues associated with the investigation, and who can best determine whether certain kinds of documents will be relevant or responsive in the context of that investigation. As such, it may be preferable to have lawyers mediate the document search process in conjunction with the employees. Often, employees will take a narrow and literal understanding of the documents requested of them, missing swathes of materials that would be relevant and useful in an investigation. Employees are also often not as thorough as lawyers in the investigation, opting to save themselves the trouble of searching certain drawers and file cabinets.

In situations where employees are suspected of wrongdoing, they obviously ought not to be given the discretion to search their own files. The potential for evidence-tampering and destruction, already no doubt a temptation, becomes too great.

Deciding between employees and lawyers is less of an issue with electronic documents. First, their sheer volume often makes sifting through all but the very best-organised sub-files impracticable; instead, whole hard drives and servers are copied in their entirety. Secondly, the technical nature of the medium on which these documents are stored generally means that neither an employee nor a lawyer has the means to gather them effectively. That task will be performed instead by the company's information technology department or by an outside consultant. **8–60**

(c) Limitations on the types of documents that the company or investigating counsel can collect

Employees may be concerned that some documents in their possession contain personal or private information. It is understood and generally accepted, for instance, that employees will use e-mail for messages unrelated to their work. In some jurisdictions, notably several in continental Europe, employees can preserve the privacy of such communications by placing them within a private sub-folder and designating them as such. **8–61**

This is generally not so in the United States. The assumption is that materials kept at work, including e-mails on a company server, are property of the company, not the employee. Companies thus generally retain the right to search and inspect all documents in the employee's custody without exception.

Employees should not feel confident that personal communications will necessarily escape the eye of regulators and investigators. First, investigators must review substantially all of an employee's documents in order to ascertain which are relevant to the investigation. Secondly, regulators are increasingly demanding that companies produce entire, unfiltered files from the desks, e-mails and hard drives of employees. When such production proves impracticable for electronic documents, regulators and companies generate an agreed-upon list of search terms to apply across, or filter, the employees' e-mails and other electronic documents. Such searches invariably end up yielding documents that are manifestly irrelevant to the investigation, but that the company must nonetheless turn over as the part of the results of its search.

(d) Consequences of waiver of privileges and protections from disclosure

8–62   One of the more vexing issues that companies undergoing internal investigations confront is that of privilege waiver. On one hand, as has been discussed above, regulators looking for signs of cooperation and good corporate citizenship may ask for or expect a waiver of the company's privilege.[287] On the other hand, such waiver may later play into the hands of private civil litigants—especially in the United States.

Internal investigations virtually always become known to regulators because the company chooses to inform them that they are occurring (indeed, often the internal investigation is itself triggered by a regulatory inquiry). When the existence of a regulatory inquiry becomes publicly known, the risk of attendant private civil litigation is considerable. Knowing that the company is or has been embroiled in a regulatory investigation, private plaintiffs are likely (and are entitled) to ask for all materials that the company has produced to regulators. If the company has waived privilege, private plaintiffs therefore will ask the company to provide privileged as well as non-privileged materials.

Regulators are not insensitive to this dilemma. They have tried to give companies an assurance that they do not consider privileged materials produced to them to be available to private litigants. In other words, the regulators contend that the waiver of privilege as to documents provided to them does not constitute a waiver by the company as to all other potential litigants, especially private civil plaintiffs.

8–63   US Regulators therefore have been increasingly willing to enter into non-waiver or limited waiver agreements, whereby the privilege is ostensibly waived only as to the regulators.[288] The SEC appears to support limiting the waiver of the work product protection when parties disclose to it confidential documents prepared by counsel. In *McKesson HBOC Inc v Superior Court*,[289] the SEC filed a brief in support of the corporation's efforts to maintain the work product privilege over an audit committee report and interview memorandum prepared by outside counsel during an internal investigation. The SEC argued that allowing parties to provide protected documents to it without waiving the work product protection served the public interest by enhancing the SEC's ability to conduct investigations more effectively and expeditiously. The court, however, determined that the corporation's disclosure to the government resulted in a waiver of the attorney-client privilege and work product protection.[290]

---

[287] See Judah Best & Bruce E. Yannett, *"I'm from the Government and I'm Here to Help You": Cooperation, Waiver of Attorney-Client Privilege, Disclosure & the Consequences* (Twenty-second Annual Corporate Counsel Institute, March 23-24 & April 13-14, 2000).

[288] A similar privilege issue exists as to auditors. Many outside auditors demand access to attorney work product from the internal investigation as a precondition to signing off on outstanding audits and continuing to work with the client. A client is often torn between the likelihood that attorney work product, including interview memos, will be fully discoverable by future civil litigants and the auditor firm's demand that it satisfy itself with respect to the scope and results of the internal investigation before it will issue a report on the company's financial statements.

[289] 9 Cal. Rptr. 3d 812 (Cal. App. 1 Dist. 2004).

[290] 9 Cal. Rptr. 3d 812 at 821.

But saying it does not make it so. Courts have frequently and increasingly disagreed with regulators on this issue, and have held that a company's waiver of privilege in connection with a regulatory inquiry also operates as a waiver as to current and future civil litigants suing on the same claim.[291]

A company therefore faces the unpleasant but unavoidable prospect of risking the displeasure of regulators by declining to turn over privileged materials in connection with its internal investigation, or in the alternative facing private civil litigation without the shield of privilege that normally would provide a measure of protection from disclosure of key documents and materials.

IV. COORDINATING RESPONSES TO MULTI-JURISDICTIONAL INVESTIGATIONS

A company acting internationally "should ensure their [anti-corruption] com-   8–64
pliance programs are robust and adequately protect against the risk of employees taking the expedient but improper course in the pursuit of new opportunities and business."[292] With the globalisation of businesses and the corresponding internationalisation of the anti-corruption market, a company may face multiple inquiries resulting from any violation.[293] In the past year, a trend in the internationalisation of foreign anti-corruption enforcement has developed.[294] Affected

---

[291] See, e.g. *Re Royal Ahold NV Sec. & ERISA Litig.* 230 F.R.D. 433 (D. Md. 2005) (holding that limited confidentiality agreement under which interview memos were disclosed to the government was not sufficient to preserve confidentiality of interview memos from class action plaintiffs); see also *Re Columbia/HCA Healthcare* 293 F.3d 289 (6th Cir. 2002) (rejecting concept of selective waiver); *Re Natural Gas Commodity Litig.* 03 Civ 6186, 2005 U.S. Dist. LEXIS 11950, at *22-33 (S.D.N.Y. June 25, 2005) (collecting cites—good discussion of case law in the area of non-waiver agreements). But see *Saito v McKesson HBOC Inc* Civ. A. No. 18553, 2002 Del. Ch. LEXIS 125 (Del. Ch. October 25, 2002) (holding that "the corporation did not waive the work product privilege when it gave documents to the SEC and the USAO under [a] confidentiality agreement").

[292] See A. W. H. Gourley & C. F. Fletcher, *Combating Corruption: Lessons and Trends From 2008 FCPA Enforcement*, 6 No. 1 Int'l Government Contractor 2 (2009).

[293] This is especially pertinent in light of Organisation for Economic Cooperation and Development's Convention on Combating Bribery of Foreign Public Officials and International Business Transaction (OECD Convention). This agreement took place in 1997 and members "agreed to criminalize bribery of foreign public officials and officials of public agencies and public international organizations, to cooperate with each other in this effort by providing mutual assistance in investigations and proceedings, and to make bribery of foreign officials an extraditable offense." F. C. Razzano & T. P. Nelson, *The Expanding Criminalization of Transnational Bribery: Global Prosecution Necessitates Global Compliance*, 42 Int'l Lawyer 1259 at 1260 (2008). Over thirty seven countries are members of this agreement. Also, in 2003, the United Nations Convention Against Corruption became effective and required that each member to the agreement criminalize transnational bribery of foreign officials. At 1261.

[294] Indeed:
"Anti-bribery compliance has for several years now attracted increasing attention from companies in Europe, as well as the United States, in the wake of a burgeoning number of bribery-related investigations and prosecutions (in the United States, anti-bribery prosecutions of both U.S. and overseas companies have increased by nearly 400 percent since 2000). Among the affected European companies are AB Volvo, BAE Systems plc, Daimler, Innospec, Norsk Hydro, Novo Nordisk, Panalpina, and Siemens."
R. M. Witten, et. al., *Navigating the Increased Anti-Corruption Environment in the United States and Abroad*, 1737 PLI/Corp. 527 at 532 (2009).

companies include AB Volvo, Halliburton Co. and Norsk Hydro.[295] The investigation of engineering giant, Siemens AG ("Siemens") shows how the rise of cross-border investigations raises additional problems for companies facing investigations under the FCPA.

The US DOJ, SEC and Munich Public Prosecutor's Office charged Siemens with pervasive violation of the FCPA, which began in the mid-1990s and continued for nearly a decade. The company, a German conglomerate, was reported to regularly bribe German officials to receive contracts with favourable terms.[296] In 2006, Siemens came under intense regulatory scrutiny in a number of jurisdictions, including the United States, amid revelations of bribery and corruption.[297] Siemens was charged with making approximately $1.4 billion in corrupt payments to foreign officials in over ten countries.[298] The SEC and DOJ said that Siemens falsified its books and records to circumvent Siemens' internal controls and evade detection.[299] The SEC and DOJ said that Siemens' corporate culture tolerated and rewarded bribery.[300]

---

[295] R. M. Witten, et. al., at 532 (stating that, recently, "Kellog[g] Brown & Root LLC and Halliburton Co. agreed to pay $579million in total fines to the SEC and DOJ, the largest fine ever assessed against a U.S. company."); B. Zagaris, 25 No. 2 Int'l Enforcement L. Rep. 75 (2009) ("The combined U.S. penalties is the largest monetary sanction ever imposed in an FCPA case"); see also B. C. George & K. A. Lacey, *Investigation of Halliburton Co./TSKJ's Nigerian Business Practices: Model for Analysis of the Current Anti-Corruption Environment on Foreign Corrupt Practices Act Enforcement*, 96 J. Crim. L. & Criminology 503 (2006) (detailing the factual background of the alleged misconduct and the French, US and Nigerian investigations).

[296] T. W. Schmidt, *Sweetening the Deal: Strengthening Transnational Bribery Laws Through Standard International Corporate Auditing Guidelines*, 93 Minn. L. Rev. 1120 (2009).

[297] Although Siemens is a German company, it lists its shares on the NYSE and has extensive operations in the US and is, therefore, subject to the provisions of the FCPA. See J. Ewing, *Siemens Braces for a Slap from Uncle Sam*, Business Week (November 26, 2007).

[298] D. Newcomb, et al., FCPA Digest of Cases and Review Releases Relating to Bribes to Foreign Officials Under the Foreign Corrupt Practices Act of 1977 (As of February 13, 2008), 1665 PLI/Corp 367 at 377 (2008).

[299] More specifically, "Siemens allegedly created elaborate payment schemes to conceal the nature of its corrupt payments, and the company's inadequate controls allowed the conduct to flourish." C. P. Mahoney, International Enforcement of U.S. Securities Laws, 1743 PLI/Corp 861, 17 (2009). For instance:

> "Employees allegedly obtained large amounts of cash from cash desks, which were sometimes transported in suitcases across international borders for bribery. Authorizations for payments were placed on post-it notes and later removed to eradicate any permanent record. The [SEC] also alleged that Siemens used numerous slush funds, off-books accounts maintained at unconsolidated entities, and a system of business consultants and intermediaries to facilitate the corrupt payments."

Even more:

> "False invoices and payment documentation were allegedly created to make payments to business consultants under false business consultant agreements that identified services that were never intended to be rendered. The SEC alleged that illicit payments were falsely recorded as expenses for management fees, consulting fees, supply contracts, room preparation fees, and commissions."

See also B. Zagaris, 25 No. 2 Int'l Enforcement L. Rep. 75 (2009). This warranted a criminal FCPA internal controls charge by the DOJ, in addition to the other charges filed against Siemens. Archibald Preuschat, *UPDATE: Siemens Reaches Further Pact To Settle Investigations*, The Wall Street Journal, July 2, 2009, available through *http://online.wsj.com/* [Accessed July 15, 2010].

[300] C. P. Mahoney, International Enforcement of U.S. Securities Laws at 918 ("the company's tone at the top was inconsistent with an effective FCPA compliance program and created a corporate culture in which bribery was tolerated and even rewarded at the highest levels of the company").

Siemens incurred high costs during its own investigation, apart from involvement of regulatory authorities. It spent over $500 million on its internal investigation,[301] which was hampered by the "absence of subpoena powers, wary Siemens employees and its lawyers' own missteps."[302] Initially, the company announced that it had unearthed $1.9 billion in bribes and questionable payments made by Siemens to third parties around the world from 2000-2006.[303]

Despite Siemens' cooperation, disclosure and reform, the formal investigation was costly. American and German authorities worked closely together in the investigation of Siemens along with other foreign regulatory authorities, including the UK and Chinese authorities. After the investigations were complete, Siemens and the involved regulatory authorities had expended more than $1 billion in investigation efforts.[304]   **8–65**

As a result of these investigations, Siemens "pleaded guilty to FCPA charges and consented to the SEC's filing of a civil complaint charging Siemens with FCPA violations."[305] The SEC also charged a few of Siemens' regional operating companies with FCPA charges.[306]

On December 15, 2008, Siemens reached an agreement to pay $1.6 billion in penalties, after pleading guilty to violations of the FCPA.[307] This amount represents the largest monetary sanction imposed in an anti-corruption case.[308] The case shows that the costs of participating in a government investigation may be quite high as a company responds to parallel inquiries from the United States and from international regulatory powers.[309] For instance, Alstom, BAE Systems Plc, DaimlerChrysler, Halliburton and other companies, have been subject to

---

[301] J. Ewing, *Siemens Braces for a Slap from Uncle Sam*.

[302] See M. Esterl, et. al., *Siemens Internal Review Hits Hurdles*, Wall St J, A18 (January 23, 2008).

[303] M. Esterl, *Siemens Internal Review Hits Hurdles*, Wall St J, A18; see also T. W. Schmidt, *Sweetening the Deal*, at 1120.

[304] 2008 Year-End FCPA Update, available at *http://www.gibsondunn.com/publications/pages/2008year-endfcpaupdate.aspx*. The report lists that of the money expended there were:

"1.6 million billable hours logged by Siemens Audit Committee counsel and the company's forensic auditor at a cost of over $840 million; 1,750 interviews and 800 informational meetings concerning the company's operations in 34 countries; ... over 100 million documents preserved and 80 million documents stored in an electronic database at a cost to Siemens of more than $100 million; ... [and] more than $5.2 million in document translation costs."

Lastly, the costs incurred by Siemens included "more than $150 million spent on the creation of an anti-corruption kit for 162 district operating entities, including six weeks of auditors 'on the ground' at each of the fifty-six entities determined to be a 'high risk.'"

[305] See fn.305 above.

[306] B. Zagaris, 25 No.2 Int'l Enforcement L. Rep. 75 (2009). The Argentinean company pleaded guilty to conspiring for violate the FCPA books-and-records provisions and agreed to pay a $500,000 fine. B. Zagaris, 25 No.2 Int'l Enforcement L. Rep. 75 (2009). The Bangladeshi and Venezuelan companies both pleaded guilty to violating the same provisions and agreed to both pay a $500,000 fine. Siemens agreed to pay a $448.5 million fine in addition to the three individual fines paid by Siemens Argentina, Bangladesh and Venezuela.

[307] C. P. Mahoney, *International Enforcement of U.S. Securities Laws*, at 916-917 (2009).

[308] B. Zagaris, 25 No.2 Int'l Enforcement L. Rep. 75 (2009).

[309] E. Richardson, et. al., *Understanding Risks and Obligations in the Foreign Corrupt Practices Act*, 45 APR Tenn. Bar J. 14 at 18 (2009) ("The costs of responding to a government investigation—much less being found liable—are often staggering. Siemens paid more than $850 million in fees and costs to its U.S. law firm and accounting firm—or $50 million more than it agreed to pay to the U.S. government").

investigation and prosecution in more than one country.[310] The number of parallel international investigations may increase as the United States and other countries increase anti-corruption efforts.

8–66   American regulatory powers are not hesitant to enforce the FCPA against foreign companies with jurisdictional ties to the United States.[311] In the United States:

> "[i]n recent years, the SEC [has] hired hundreds of employees to enforce all corporate compliance claims, the DOJ hired two attorneys to focus only on FCPA cases, and the FBI created a new four-person unit that handles only FCPA investigations."[312]

The penalties for violating the FCPA are high and the investigation process may be lengthy.[313] Additionally, companies facing investigation may experience an increased focus on individual prosecution charges in addition to FCPA charges, multiple inquiries from the SEC, DOJ or SROs and potential transnational investigations.

    European and other foreign regulatory authorities, including Italy, France and the Netherlands,[314] have also increased anti-bribery enforcement efforts.[315] With

---

[310] R. Grime, et. al., *FCPA Jurisdiction Over Foreign Entities & Individuals: The Trend of Increasingly Aggressive Enforcement*, 1696 PLI/Corp 163 at 189 (writing that companies subject to parallel international investigations include "Alstom (Switzerland, France, Brazil, and Mexico), BAE Systems Plc (United Kingdom, Austria, Chile, Czech Republic, Hungary, Romania, South Africa, Sweden, Switzerland, Tanzania, and the United States), CBK Power Company (Argentina, Philippines), and Halliburton (France, Nigeria, Switzerland, United States, United Kingdom)").

[311] R. M. Witten, et. al., *Navigating the Increased Anti-Corruption Environment in the United States and Abroad*, at 534-535. Witten goes on to provide examples, that:
  "U.S. authorities charged the U.K. subsidiary of ABB with violations based on e-mails sent to the United States. Similarly, in 2002, U.S. authorities charged a Taiwanese company for actions in Taiwan on the basis that the chairman of the Taiwanese company authorized improper payments while he was in the United States. More recently, in October 2007, U.S. authorities asserted jurisdiction over a Korean company on the basis that bank transfers originated from the United States and accounting information had been transmitted to South Korea."
The SEC's authority to assist foreign regulatory authorities derives from s.21(a)(2) of the Exchange Act and from the International Securities Enforcement Cooperation Act of 1990. C. P. Mahoney, *International Enforcement of U.S. Securities Laws* at 895-896.

[312] T. W. Schmidt, 93 Minn. L. Rev. 1120 at 1131.

[313] As one commentator notes, "[w]ary of stricter enforcement, companies increasingly self-report violations and enter into deferred or nonprosecution agreements with U.S. Attorneys to avoid costly litigation and bad press." T. W. Schmidt, 93 Minn. L. Rev. 1120 at 1131.

[314] T. W. Schmidt, 93 Minn. L. Rev. 1120 at 1135 ("France, Italy, and the Netherlands have increased the amount of transnational bribery cases prosecuted").

[315] Witten, 1737 PLI/Corp 527 at 535. Witten states:
  "Specifically, as of mid-2006 there reportedly were as many as forty ongoing bribery investigations being conducted by authorities throughout Europe. According to news reports, BAE Systems plc, for example, reportedly may be facing investigations not only by the U.S. and U.K. governments, but also by authorities in Austria, the Czech Republic, Sweden and Switzerland. Other companies, including Siemens, AB Volvo, and Statoil (a Norwegian oil and gas company), have been involved in anti-bribery investigations involving both the United States and European authorities."
Another sources notes that the US has conducted parallel investigations in foreign jurisdictions including: China, Germany, Greece, Hungary, Indonesia, Israel, Italy, Liechtenstein, Nigeria, Norway, Russia and Switzerland for Siemens; Brazil for Gtech; Costa Rica for Alcatel Lucent; France and Nigeria for Halliburton; France for Total SA; Germany for Bristol Myers and Daimler Chrysler; Italy for Immucor and UDI; and Korea for IBM. D. Newcomb, et. al., 1665 PLI/Corp 367 at 377.
  In Germany, regulators engaged in eighty-eight criminal investigations, just between June 2006 and June 2007. F. C. Razzano & T. P. Nelson, 42 Int'l Lawyer 1259 at 1260-1261.

the increase in multi-national investigations, international regulatory powers are cooperating to enforce anti-bribery laws.[316]

As a result of internationalised and heightened enforcement, a company may face litigation and investigation in multiple countries and from various regulatory authorities within each country.[317] The costs of this more complex litigation may, as Siemens illustrates, be prohibitively high and disrupt a company's operations. A company that violates anti-bribery laws may find itself subject to high penalties, a damaged reputation, high legal fees and the inquiries of both domestic and international parallel investigations. Therefore, a company operating internationally would be well advised to know the contours of the FCPA and to abide by its regulations.

Once the regulatory powers reach an ultimate finding, a company will find itself subject to the prosecutorial discretion of a regulatory authority. The America system provides the most in depth example of this proposition because the US has the most law on point and its prosecutors tend to exercise the broadest discretion in charging crimes.

V. WHAT MAY HAPPEN ONCE THE GOVERNMENT OBTAINS AN ULTIMATE FINDING

Prosecutorial discretion is a hallmark of the American criminal justice system.[318] **8–67**
After the government has begun investigation, but before the government takes final action, the company is vulnerable to prosecutorial discretion.[319] The prosecutor decides whether to charge a company with wrongdoing, decline filing charges or even defer prosecution. This decision-making takes place outside of the court's purview and is thus largely unregulated by the judiciary system.[320] Because corporate liability may result in charges at the corporate and individual levels, prosecutors should carefully weigh the benefits and costs of particular

---

[316] A. W. H. Gourley & C. F. Fletcher, *Combating Corruption*, 6 No. 1 Int'l Government Contractor. Another example beyond Siemens is that of Halliburton. In 2004, a French Magistrate investigated Kellogg Brown and Root's (KBR) payments to a company in Gibraltar, in connection to the development of a gas facility in Nigeria, which were deposited in Swiss bank accounts and passed through a Japanese company. KBR was a subsidiary of Halliburton. The US DOJ relied on cooperation from regulatory authorities in France, Italy, Switzerland and the UK to attain resolution of its investigation. Based on the DOJ's investigations, Halliburton tentatively agreed, in 2008, "to pay the DOJ $362 million in criminal penalties and the SEC $177 million in disgorgement."

[317] Indeed, there has been an increase in cross-border investigations "whether at the behest of a government, jointly or collectively by governments, or by international corporations caught up in multi-country investigations or ensnared by one or more United States laws." 21 Sec. Crimes § 4:57 (2008).

[318] L. Orland, *The Transformation of Corporate Criminal Law*, 1 Brooklyn J. Corp., Financial & Commercial Law 197 at 206 ("Discretionary decision-making permeates the American system of criminal justice").

[319] See B. M. Greenblum, *What Happens to a Prosecution Deferred? Judicial Oversight of Corporate Deferred Prosecution Agreements*, 105 Colum. L. Rev. 1863 at 1886 (2005).

[320] See L. Orland, 1 Brooklyn J. Corp., Financial & Commercial Law 197 at 206.

remedies.[321] The power to fashion remedies grants prosecutors an advantage over wrongdoing corporations and allows prosecutors to attain control over a corporation's internal affairs.[322]

A corporation undergoing a governmental investigation should be aware of the power that the prosecutors possess and of the potential consequences it will face when charged with wrongdoing.[323] The prosecutor may issue a declination, indict the company and seek a plea bargain, criminally charge the company or enter a deferred prosecution agreement with the company. Although the threat of litigation relegates a company to an inferior bargaining position, a company should avoid criminal prosecution. While a declination is not always likely, a deferred prosecution may be a company's best option and allow a company to bypass extinction.[324]

(a) Declinations

8-68   As a result of its prosecutorial discretion, the government may decline prosecution, or opt for a declination, upon procuring an ultimate finding. To effectuate a declination, the government and corporation do not need to effect a formal agreement with the offending company.[325] When the government declines prosecution, a company will not face sanctions.[326]

(b) Plea Bargaining

8-69   Rather than decline prosecution, the government may negotiate with offending companies by means of a plea bargain. Plea bargains are used by both defendants and prosecutors when the outcome of a case is less than certain. The defendant

---

[321] L. Orland, at 207. Orland states:
   "This confluence of criminal and civil regulatory systems thrusts upon the federal prosecutors unusual discretionary powers regarding whether the corporation, as well as corporate individuals, should be prosecuted. This factor imposes onto the federal prosecutors the special responsibility of carefully weighing the adequacy of available non-penal remedies before deciding whether or not to indict the corporation."
The government may wish to convict the person behind the wrongdoing rather than rely on the fictional corporate entity. L. Orland, 1 Brooklyn J. Corp., Financial & Commercial Law 197 at 229.

[322] Note that the decision whether to charge tends to be limited by professional responsibility guidelines. See K. Melilli, *Prosecutorial Discretion in an Adversary System*, 1992 BYU L. Rev. 669 at 683-684 ("Clearly, then, so much responsibility is vested in the hands of the individual prosecutor that much success of the criminal justice system depends upon the quality and integrity of prosecutors").

[323] E. Paulsen, *Imposing Limits on Prosecutorial Discretion in Corporate Prosecution Agreements*, 82 N.Y.U.L. Rev. 1434 at 1454 (2007) (noting that there is a bargaining imbalance between prosecutors and companies, event though the benefits between the pair appear mutual).

[324] See L. Orland, 1 Brooklyn J. Corp., Financial & Commercial Law 197 at 209 ("For a corporation under criminal investigation, the choice of options is potentially the difference between life and death for a corporation. A corporate indictment is a highly publicized event and a corporate plea agreement is subject to public judicial control. In contrast, a declination of prosecution is rarely accompanied by a public announcement from the Judicial Department") (internal quotations omitted).

[325] B. M. Greenblum, 105 Colum. L. Rev. 1863 at 1868.

[326] For example, in 2005, the DOJ decided not to prosecute Royal Dutch/Shell after investigating the company in regard to its recategorization of proved oil and gas reserves. News Release, "Shell Confirms Conclusion of US Department of Justice Reserves Investigation: No Further Action Against Companies" (June 30, 2005), available through *http://www.shell.com* [Accessed July 15, 2010].

effectively pleads guilty and negotiates for a penalty. As a result, "[a] guilty plea results in conviction and collateral consequences"[327] just as if the offender was convicted at trial.[328] The tool allows for judicial economy, avoids the costs of litigation and provides greater certainty to defendants than a criminal prosecution.

(c) Criminal Prosecutions

The consequences of criminal prosecution against a company may be just as **8–70** harmful as, if not more than, those against an individual.[329] The company may face sanctions, including revocation of professional licenses and debarment from government contracting.[330] Depending on the severity of the sanctions, this may cause a company to enter bankruptcy or collapse. Even more, the spectre of litigation may harm a company's reputation, perhaps devastating a company.[331] Thus, a criminal prosecution may be the death of a company.[332]

A company in this position may look to the deferred prosecution as an ideal bargain. The seminal illustration for this proposition is the case of Arthur Andersen.[333] Arthur Andersen was Enron's accounting auditor.[334] Once Enron's scandal became public, Arthur Andersen directed its employees to destroy documents in accordance with its document retention policy.[335] Despite reservations, employees complied.[336] The firm was charged with obstruction of justice as a result of the firm's destruction of documents pertinent to Enron's accounting process.[337] Andersen refused to accept responsibility for its misconduct and declined to fully cooperate with the government.[338]

---

[327] Collateral consequences may include debarment and license forfeiture. B. M. Greenblum, 105 Colum. L. Rev. 1863 at 1885-1886. No further negotiation or discussion was needed and Royal Dutch/Shell faced no criminal penalties.

[328] B. M. Greenblum, 105 Colum. L. Rev. 1863 at 1869.

[329] See B. M. Greenblum, 105 Colum. L. Rev. 1863 at 1885.

[330] B. M. Greenblum, 105 Colum. L. Rev. 1863.

[331] B. M. Greenblum, 105 Colum. L. Rev. 1863 at 1886-1887 ("Adverse publicity is so widely feared that it has ever been proposed as a penalty in and of itself. While a deferral involves indictment, the indictment is accompanied by the government's assurance that the firm is cooperating, making amends, and will be free of criminal liability simultaneously with the corresponding indictments, assuring the public that short of a breach of the deferral agreements, the offenders would not face prosecution").

[332] C. A. Way & R. K. Hur, *Corporate Criminal Prosecution in a Post-Enron World: The Thompson Memo in Theory and Practice*, 43 Am. Crim. L. Rev. 1095 at 1138 (2007) ("For companies facing the possibility of criminal charges, a deferred prosecution may not e the all-out win of a declination, but many companies find the stakes too high to "go for broke" and risk trial and potential ruin").

[333] *Arthur Andersen, LLP v US* 544 US 696 (2005).

[334] 544 US 696 at 698.

[335] 544 US 696.

[336] 544 US 696 at 701 (at this time, there had been a New York Times article and an SEC investigation was underway).

[337] R. S. Gruner, PLI Course Handbook, Advance Corporate Compliance Workshop 2007 (Order No. 11083), 122 (2008).

[338] L. Orland, 1 Brooklyn J. Corp., Financial & Commercial Law 197 at 216.

As a result of these criminal charges, the company collapsed—even though the Supreme Court ultimately overturned Andersen's conviction.[339] The collapse of Arthur Andersen in turn reduced the number of full-service accounting firms, which had a detrimental effect on the entire accounting industry. The devastating consequences of Andersen's criminal indictment may have influenced the government's perceived willingness to enter deferred prosecution agreements and to avoid criminal prosecutions.[340]

8–71   Thus, a company that faces the prospect of litigation would be well-advised to cooperate as much as possible, such that a deferred prosecution agreement is the worst outcome possible. American prosecutors will examine a company's compliance program when they decide whether to criminally charge a company and what penalty to impose.[341] A company's compliance program must be more than a mere sham and must function in a meaningful way.[342] A company must intend to comply and to reform itself. If a company makes a sincere attempt to abide by the law and to eradicate any illegal behaviour, it may avoid the prospect of criminal charges and instead enter a deferred prosecution agreement—at the discretion of the prosecuting authorities.

(d) Deferred Prosecution

8–72   A deferred prosecution affords prosecutors a middle ground between declinations and criminal prosecutions.[343] The tool "allows prosecutors to reform corporate

---

[339] R. S. Gruner, PLI Course Handbook at 122. The Supreme Court overturned the conviction because it determined that the firm's intent to obstruct justice was not sufficiently established. The prosecutor did not retry the case after the firm's demise.

For its role in connection with the Enron scandal, a jury found Arthur Andersen guilty of obstructing justice in violation of 18 USC § 1512(b)(2)(A) and (B). This verdict was upheld on appeal. *US v Arthur Andersen, LLP*, 374 F.3d 281 (5th Cir. 2004). The Supreme Court ruled in 2005, however, that the conviction of Arthur Andersen was tainted by an improper jury instruction and reversed the judgment. *Arthur Andersen*, 544 US 696. The decision came two years too late for the company, which had already dissolved.

[340] KPMG entered into a deferred prosecution agreement with federal prosecutors in order to end a DOJ investigation regarding the company's design, marketing, and implementation of fraudulent tax shelters. See KPMG Deferred Prosecution Agreement (August 26, 2005), available through *http://www.usdoj.gov* [Accessed July 15, 2010]; see also C. Johnson, *KPMG to Admit Role in Tax Shelters; No Criminal Charges Expected, Washington Post* (August 28, 2005), A8 (regarding KPMG, "senior Justice Department officials, concerned about the potentially fatal impact such a move would have on the firm, pushed negotiations"). The government's decision not to prosecute KPMG was reportedly influenced by the fact that such a prosecution would have had a disastrous impact upon what remained of the accounting industry after the demise of Arthur Andersen. See A. Sloan, *KPMG Partners Lucked Out— Thanks to Enron and Arthur Andersen, Business Week* (September 6, 2005).

[341] R. M. Witten, et al., 1737 PLI/Corp 527 at 548. Indeed, this balancing is not unique to the United States. European authorities also prefer that companies have a comprehensive compliance program and consider this to be a mitigating factor when assessing the corresponding sanctions.

[342] R. M. Witten, et al., 1737 PLI/Corp 527 (stating that American authorities "have little regard for compliance "programs" that involve no more than a written policy prohibiting corruption").

[343] E. Paulsen, *Imposing Limits on Prosecutorial Discretion in Corporate Prosecution Agreements*, 82 N.Y.U. L. Rev. 1434 at 1438 (2007); B. M. Greenblum, 105 Colum. L. Rev. 1863 at 1896 ("Deferred prosecution agreements are unique in the way that it punishes offenders outside the purview of the court. When a prosecutor declines to prosecute, any commitment that an offender makes in exchange is unenforceable").

offenders without collaterally damaging the interests of employees, investors, and markets that rely upon these corporations to survive criminal liability."[344] The company receives punishment but avoids the stigma associated with guilt.[345] This mechanism, intended to reduce the negative externalities of criminal prosecution, is authorised by federal statute and the United States Attorneys' Manual.[346]

In essence, a deferred prosecution agreement imposes a term of probation and avoids formal criminal charges.[347] The prosecutor files a criminal charge but then agrees to hold the charge in abeyance for some time, so long as the company does not violate the terms of the agreement entered between the company and the prosecutor.[348] Judicial oversight is absent from this framework. Instead, the prosecutor maintains discretion and the company waives its constitutional right to a speedy trial.[349]

While deferred prosecution agreements may vary, several elements are typical to most agreements.[350] First, deferred prosecution agreements encourage coop-

[344] B. M. Greenblum, 105 Colum. L. Rev. 1863 at 1864. Indeed, this may also avoid the stigma of litigation. A firm can admit its wrongdoing but, at the same time, not plead guilty.

[345] E. Illovsky, *Corporate Deferred Prosecution Agreements*, 21 Crim. Justice 36 (Summer 2006) (characterising deferred prosecution agreements as affording "[a]ll of the punishment, none of the guilt").

[346] 18 USC §§ 3152-54 (2000); USAM §§ 9-22.010 (1997), 105 Colum. L. Rev. 1863 at 1895; L. Orland, 1 Brooklyn J. Corp., Financial & Commercial Law 197 at 211.

[347] See B. M. Greenblum, 105 Colum. L. Rev. 1863 at 36 ("A corporate deferred prosecution agreement is basically a way of imposing a term of probation before a conviction. The government files charges but then agrees to hold them in abeyance pending the company's successful completion of certain terms in the agreement for a period of time"); E. Paulsen, 82 N.Y.U.L. Rev. 1434 at 1438 ("In lieu of criminally prosecuting the entity, the government files some kind of criminal charge–normally a complaint, information, or indictment—but then agrees to hold the charge open as long the corporation successfully fulfills the terms of the agreement. If the prosecutor deems the agreement's terms satisfied, the charges are dismissed"). The term of probation varies and may range from 12 months or over 3 years. E. Illovsky, 21 Crim. Justice at 36 (noting compliance periods that range from 12 months, to 15 months, to 2 years, to 3 years, or even longer).

[348] See fn.348 above. Note, too, that this is not the same as a nonprosecution agreement. In a nonprosecution agreement, the prosecutor does not file any charges. E. Paulsen, 82 N.Y.U.L. Rev. 1434 at 1438. There is no indictment. Also, nonprosecution agreements usually entail lesser levels of culpability, or sanctions. Despite these differences, the nonprosecution agreement is highly similar to the deferred prosecution, with similar terms and enforcement mechanisms. See E. Illovsky, 21 Crim. Justice 36.

[349] B. M. Greenblum, 105 Colum. L. Rev. 1863 at 1864.
"Deferral is a powerful prosecutorial tool because it is negotiated and implemented exclusively by the prosecutor. The prosecutor presents the judge with the fait accompli of a deferral agreement and, at the close of the deferral period, with uncontested assertions of the offender's preparedness to emerge from the shadow of criminal liability."

[350] See E. Illovsky, 21 Crim. Justice 36. Illovsky writes:
"Typical terms come more or less right out of the U.S. Sentencing Guidelines and include an admission of wrongful conduct supported by a detailed factual basis (admissible in a later trial); payment of a fine (which can be quite large—KPMG paid $456 million); cooperation with the government's ongoing investigation (which often obligates the company to make its employees available and includes privilege waivers); the adoption of compliance programs and other reform measures such as changes in corporate governance; personnel actions (e.g., firings, demotions, reassignments); and waivers of speedy trial rights and statutes of limitations defenses."
Stated another way, common terms of a deferred prosecution agreement include: required admissions, immediate disclosures, further investigatory assistance to the government, payments of penalties and/or restitution, institution of required reforms and the adoption of ongoing, independent monitoring. R. S. Gruner, PLI Course Handbook, at 122–123.

eration.[351] Secondly, the company must acknowledge its illicit conduct, by agreeing and admitting to a statement of facts.[352] This agreement is typically made public.[353] Thirdly, the agreements provide for monetary penalties and prosecutors are unlimited in their ability to fashion penalties.[354] Fourthly, a corporation must usually make some changes to its business personnel, whether by disciplining wrongful employees, hiring new management, enacting new compliance programs or creating ethics officers.[355] Finally, the agreements may require the retention of an independent monitor to ensure compliance with the deferred prosecution agreement in place.[356] A company must agree to comply with the agreement.[357]

8-73   Deferred prosecution agreements may also contain some quixotic terms, reminiscent of an individual's prosecutor's quirks or values. For example, in the Bristol-Meyers Squibb Agreement the then US Attorney, Christopher J. Christie, included a provision for the creation of an endowed chair in business

The benefits are not available for those with two or more felony convictions. B. M. Greenblum, 105 Column. L. Rev. 1863 at 1867.

[351] See E. Paulsen, 82 N.Y.U. L. Rev. 1434 at 1439. Paulsen notes that "[c]orporate cooperation has been the most controversial element of prosecution agreements." Commentators are concerned that compelled cooperation provides prosecutors with too much discretion and that this unbridled discretion may infringe upon the attorney client privilege and work product privilege.

[352] Should the company violate the terms of the agreement and face prosecution, the company must agree that the statement of facts will constitute evidence against the company. This, in turn, functions as a corporate admission of guilt. Should the company face criminal charges, it may face a fate similar to that of Arthur Andersen.

This statement of facts, also known as a "noncontradiction provision," functions so that a company admits to the factual basis of its offense. E. Illovsky, 21 Crim. Justice 36 at 38. It is usually attached to the deferred prosecution as an exhibit. Any statements contained in that agreement will provide grounds for impeachment at trial. B. M. Greenblum, 105 Colum. L. Rev. 1863 at 1864. Finally, a company may not make any statement contrary to the agreed statement of facts and any failure to abide by this promise constitutes breach of the agreement. E. Illovsky, 21 Crim. Justice 36 at 38. Employees are bound by the provision as well.

[353] L. Orland, 1 Brooklyn J. Corp., Financial & Commercial Law 197 at 209-210, 230 (stating that the agreements are frequently, but not always, made public). The decision to make the agreement public is subject to the discretion of prosecutors.

[354] See E. Paulsen, 82 N.Y.U. L. Rev. 1434 at 1439. Usually, a corporation will pay restitution or a combination of criminal and civil penalties. Given the discretion present, a corporation may have to pay some unusual penalties.

[355] N.Y.U. L. Rev. 1434 at 1442. Paulsen elaborates that business reforms may be operational or involve personnel. Some of the mechanisms that prosecutors may require include: hiring new board members, provide hotlines for whistleblowers, terminating employees who fail to comply with investigation efforts and enact new personnel hiring policies. Moreover:

"Usually, the company at a minimum must agree to institute a new, or beef up an existing, compliance and ethics program, appoint a compliant officer, and ensure all employees have access to a hotline of some type to allow anonymous reporting of any noncompliance. The government might very well require changes in board of directors composition or the creation of board committees."

E. Illovsky, 21 Crim. Justice 36 at 39.

[356] E Paulsen, 82 N.Y.U. L. Rev. 1434 at 1443. Note that:

"These monitors are normally either compliance specialists or august members of the legal community. The corporation pays the costs of the monitor and his/her staff is expected to give the monitor relatively unfettered access to business operations."

Corporate monitors may have a substantial impact upon a corporation's internal affairs. L. Orland, 1 Brooklyn J. Corp., Financial & Commercial Law at 228.

[357] E. Illovsky, 21 Crim. Justice 36 at 39.

ethics at his alma mater.[358] Other agreements have required a hospital to donate health care worth millions of dollars to the public and for a company to create 1,600 new jobs within a time period of 10 years.[359] The deferred prosecution agreement may include a limitation on a company's public statements as well.[360]

Companies should understand that prosecutors have vast discretion and that a company that violates the law is left at the prosecutor's mercy. A company charged with serious wrongdoing should be ready to encounter a lack of predictability and the possibility of prosecutorial overreaching when negotiating a deferred prosecution agreement.[361] Similarly, a company facing potential government investigation should be aware of some existing deferred prosecution agreements and should understand the implications of entering such agreements.

Deferral has both advantages[362] and disadvantages.[363] Deferred prosecution agreements reduce caseloads, ensure judicial economy and facilitate cooperation for the effective resolution of an investigation.[364] The agreements save individuals and companies from the stigma of criminal convictions, while deterring other companies from similar misconduct.[365] As a cost, however, deferral injects the prosecutor into corporate management and affairs. In deciding whether to indict a company or enter a deferred prosecution agreement, the corporation may be guided by the Thompson, McNulty and Filip Memorandums, issued by the DOJ in response to a surge in corporate crime.[366]

The Thompson Memo, issued in 2003 by then Deputy Attorney General Larry D. Thompson, set forth nine factors for prosecutors to evaluate when determining whether to charge a corporation with wrongdoing.[367] These factors are: 8–74

---

[358] E. Paulsen, 82 N.Y.U. L. Rev. 1434 at 1443; R. S. Gruner, PLI Course Handbook, at 158. Christie's alma mater is Seton Hall Law School, in Newark, NJ.

[359] See E. Illovsky, 21 Crim. Justice 36 at 37.

[360] 21 Crim. Justice at 36.

[361] E. Paulsen, 82 N.Y.U. L. Rev. 1434 at 1459-1461, 1467-1468.

[362] Gruner states that advantages include:

1) Opportunity to avoid corporate fines and probation [,]
2) Lack of conviction triggering further adverse consequences like automatic debarment from government contracting or exclusion from government programs [,]
3) Distinguishing corporation from offender in public perception [,]
4) Specification of adequate future conduct in terms of obligations specified in deferred prosecution agreement.

R. S. Gruner, PLI Course Handbook, at 126.

[363] Gruner states that risks and disadvantages include:

1) Implementation under prosecutorial control [,]
2) Lack of uniform standards [,]
3) Extensive cooperation may be required [,]
4) Evidence revealed may confirm further offenses [,]
5) Admissions and evidence transferred may effectively preclude subsequent criminal defense [,]
6) Disclosures may aid civil claimants [,]
7) Cooperation with prosecutors may undercut employee relations with company.

[364] See, e.g. W. R. LaFave, et al., 4 Crim. Proc. § 13.6(a) (2007-2008).

[365] L. Orland, 1 Brooklyn J. Corp., Financial & Commercial Law 197 at 215 (Society is deterred from the crime because prosecution sends a message to the general community that wrongful conduct will not be tolerated).

[366] E. Paulsen, 82 N.Y.U. L. Rev. 1434 at 1451.

[367] E. Paulsen, 82 N.Y.U. L. Rev. 1434.

1. the nature and seriousness of the offense, including the risk of harm to the public, and applicable policies and priorities, if any, governing the prosecution of corporations for particular categories of crime ... ;

2. the pervasiveness of wrongdoing within the corporation, including the complicity in, or condonation [sic] of, the wrongdoing by corporate management ... ;

3. the corporation's history of similar conduct, including prior criminal, civil, and regulatory enforcement actions against it ... ;

4. the corporation's timely and voluntary disclosure of wrongdoing and its willingness to cooperate in the investigation of its agents, including, if necessary, the waiver of corporate attorney-client and work product protection ... ;

5. the existence and adequacy of the corporation's compliance program ... ;

6. the corporation's remedial actions, including any efforts to implement an effective corporate compliance program or to improve an existing one, to replace responsible management, to discipline or terminate wrongdoers, to pay restitution, and to cooperate with the relevant government agencies ... ;

7. collateral consequences, including disproportionate harm to shareholders, pension holders and employees not proven personally culpable and impact on the public arising from the prosecution ... ;

8. the adequacy of the prosecution of individuals responsible for the corporation's malfeasance; and

9. the adequacy of remedies such as civil or regulatory enforcement actions.[368]

The factors are illustrative and not exhaustive, and thereby preserve prosecutorial discretion.[369] The Memo encourages prosecutors to focus on the sincerity of a corporation's cooperation and on its compliance and governance programs.[370] The Memo encourages alternative forms of sanctions, rather than criminal prosecution.[371] The adoption of this Memo marked the DOJ's endorsement of alternative resolutions and sparked public outcry.[372]

The McNulty Memorandum, issued in 2006 by then Deputy Attorney General Paul McNulty, modified the Thompson Memo in response to the public outcry

---

[368] Memorandum from Larry D. Thompson, Deputy Attorney General, to Heads of Department Components and United States Attorneys (20 Jan 2003), available through *http://www.usdoj.gov*.

[369] E. Paulsen, 82 N.Y.U. L. Rev. 1434 at 1451.

[370] C. A. Wray & R. K. Hur at 1097.

[371] E. Paulsen, 82 N.Y.U. L. Rev. 1434 at 1098.

[372] E. Paulsen, 82 N.Y.U. L. Rev. 1434 .

that resulted from the Thompson Memo.[373] First, the McNulty Memo states that "prosecutors generally may not consider whether a corporation is advancing an employee attorneys' fees in assessing cooperation."[374] Secondly, the Memo restricts waivers of attorney-client privilege so that the waivers are used only when a legitimate need exists, when the waiver of the privilege is the least intrusive waiver provision needed and after vetting by senior DOJ officials.[375]

As noted above, the Filip Memo, issued by Deputy Attorney General Mark R. **8–75**
Filip in 2008, replaces the McNulty Memo. As discussed earlier, this Memo redefines the guidelines for assessing corporate cooperation. The government cannot request that the corporation disclose "non-factual attorney-client privileged materials ... except in extremely limited circumstances."[376] Although some commentators state that the guidelines will provide corporations with greater security against overreaching deferred prosecution agreements, others disagree that the Filip Memo will overhaul the McNulty Memo.[377] The guidelines are non-binding and are limited to the DOJ, not the SEC or other regulatory bodies.[378]

Subsequent to the Thompson and McNulty Memos, and even after the Filip Memo, deferral agreements have become the norm.[379] A company should note that cooperation with the government is highly encouraged, but may come at a price.[380] Despite the limitations imposed by the McNulty Memo, prosecutors retain significant discretion outside the purview of judicial oversight.

As noted earlier, many deferred prosecution agreements include waiver provisions for the attorney-client privilege and/or work product privilege.[381] Although the waiver is non-negotiable, because the prosecutor holds superior bargaining power, a court of law will view the decision as a voluntary waiver of

---

[373] E. Paulsen, 82 N.Y.U. L. Rev. 1434.

[374] E. Paulsen, 82 N.Y.U. L. Rev. 1434 at 1451-1452.

[375] E. Paulsen, 82 N.Y.U. L. Rev. 1434 at 1452.

[376] See C. W. McIntyre, McNulty Memo Out, Filip Memo In: DOJ Makes Revisions to Corporate Charging Guidelines (September 4, 2008), available through *http://www.mcguirewoods.com* [Accessed July 15, 2010].

[377] C. W. McIntyre, McNulty Memo Out; M. J. Stein & J. L. Levine, *The Filip Memorandum: Does It Go Far Enough?*, New York Law Journal (September 8, 2008), available through *http://www.law.com* [Accessed July 15, 2010].

[378] See fn.69 et seq. above.

[379] B. M. Greenblum, 105 Colum. L. Rev. 1863 at 1874 ("Since the dissemination of the Thompson Memo, no corporation has been charged in a major corporate fraud investigation outside of a deferral agreement").

[380] R. S. Gruner, PLI Course Handover, at 175. Gruner states that:
"This price may be paid in many ways, from restrictions on future business activities, to required adoption of extensive compliance and ethics programs, to ongoing monitoring by independent observers chosen by government officials. A corporation's safe passage beyond the immediate threat of corporate criminal liability may also come at a significant cost to the corporation's former business leaders, partners, and associates."

[381] Indeed, "corporate deferral has become a mechanism commonly used to incentivize waiver of the privilege." B. M. Greenblum, 105 Colum. L. Rev. 1863 at 1891.

privilege.[382] A waiver of privilege at the federal level will result in a waiver of privilege at the civil level. Should the stockholders seek to file a lawsuit against the company, then the company will have no recourse to claim attorney-client privilege. Therefore, a company may still face litigation.[383]

8-76   In addition, the prosecutor continues to hold considerable power after a corporation enters a deferred prosecution agreement. He decides whether the corporation has abided by the terms of the agreement and may unilaterally decide to prosecute a company. The prosecutor's power lies outside of the court's regulation. Hence, a company would be well advised to know what the terms of the bargain are and then to abide by that bargain. A company must be ready to face consequences for violating the law and must seek to remedy its noncompliance with the law.

Despite the potential drawbacks presented by deferred prosecution agreements, the agreements do allow companies to avoid criminal liability and stigma.[384] A company that finds itself in this situation would be well advised to remember that the DOJ is willing to avoid criminal prosecution if a company willingly admits its wrongdoing and cooperates with investigators.[385]

In sum, a corporation charged with wrongdoing must accept responsibility for its conduct, discipline its wrongdoers and reform its internal system, cooperate with the government and do so promptly.[386] A corporation must be ready to waive its attorney-client privilege and defend itself in civil actions.[387] The difference between indictment and deferred prosecution agreements may be one between life and death for a corporation. While the use of deferred prosecution agreements is characteristically American, other countries may increasingly follow similar approaches.

(e) Civil Recovery Orders

8-77   The UK's SFO uses the US's deferred prosecution agreements as a model for its Civil Recovery Order (CRO).[388] The CRO is used in the UK's foreign bribery prosecutions. In the words of one commentator, it "allows authorities to recover a

---

[382] Indeed:

"[N]ot only is the imposition of sanctions by deferral beyond the court's reach, so too are curtailments of the attorney-client privilege, extrajudicial processes for adjudicating breach, and, at least in [one case], the use of the deferral mechanism to impose a substantial legal obligation unrelated to the underlying offense."

105 Colum. L. Rev. 1863 at 1883; see also *Upjohn Co v US* 449 US 383.

[383] This has led some commentators to suggest that "waiver can actually harm corporate governance by discouraging consultation with lawyers and making it more difficult to detect and fix wrongdoing early." E. Illovsky, 21 Crim. Justice 36 at 38.

[384] B. M. Greenblum, 105 Colum. L. Rev. 1863 at 1864.

[385] See A. W. H. Gourley & C. F. Fletcher, *Combating Corrupting*, 6 No. 1 Int'l Government Contractor.

[386] L. Orland, 1 Brooklyn J. Corp., Financial & Commercial Law 197 at 26 ("corporations faced with serious wrongdoing by corporate executives must promptly accept full responsibility, discipline wrongdoers, institute serious institutional reform and fully cooperate with the government").

[387] L. Orland, 1 Brooklyn J. Corp., Financial & Commercial Law 197.

[388] Jonathan Cotton, *A New, More American World?* (2009), available through *http://www.slaughterandmay.com* [Accessed July 15, 2010].

monetary penalty without a corresponding criminal prosecution and represents a powerful new tool for U.K. anti-corruption regulators."[389] The CRO also affords prosecutors much discretion, comparable to that of US prosecutors. The United Kingdom is moving closer to the American model of prosecution under the FCPA by reforming its laws to provide prosecutors with more discretion.[390] This is significant, given that British criminal law has traditionally granted UK prosecutors little discretion in prosecuting criminal violation.

In 2008, the SFO received judicial authorisation to attain a CRO against Balfour Beatty Plc, a major construction company.[391] The SFO charged the company with fraud arising from payment irregularities regarding Balfour Beatty's construction of the Bibliotheca Alexandria in Egypt, a project that began in 1996 and ended in 2001.[392] Balfour Beatty conducted its own internal investigation and admitted its wrongdoing.[393] Perhaps due to Balfour Beatty's cooperation, the SFO investigation concluded that there was a failure to keep adequate records, but declined to prosecute Balfour Beatty.[394]

Instead, the SFO imposed sanctions and avoided the expense and time of litigation.[395] As a result of this process, Balfour Beatty has enacted reforms so as to avoid a repeat occurrence and to increase its compliance mechanisms.[396] This was the first CRO issued by the SFO against a major company.[397]

A company operating in this context should be aware that Britain's use of the CRO may increase in the upcoming years. The quintessential nature of American investigation and prosecutorial discretion may soon become the norm across the Atlantic. While it remains to be seen how American jurisprudence will affect global prosecution under the FCPA, a company operating within the jurisdic-

---

[389] J. Cotton, *A New, More American World?* (2009).

[390] A. S. Joshi, *Britain's Fight against the 'Silver Lance,' A Radical Overhaul of the U.K.'s Bribery Laws*, 33 Champion 36 (February, 2009).

[391] A. S. Joshi 33 Champion 36 at 40. See also A. W. H. Gourley & C. F. Fletcher, Combating Corruption.

[392] J. Leitch, ContractJournal.com, *Balfour given £2.5m fine after SFO investigation*, available through *http://www.contractjournal.com* [Accessed July 15, 2010] (October 6, 2008); T. Sharp, *The Herald, Balfour Beatty settles investigation into Egyptian project*, available through *http://www.theherald.co.uk* [Accessed July 15, 2010] (October 7, 2008) (The SFO reported that the case related to "inaccurate accounting records arising from certain payment irregularities. These occurred once the project, which ran from 1996 to 2001, had already begun") (internal citations and quotations omitted).

[393] See fn.393 above.

[394] T. Sharp, *Balfour Beatty settles investigation into Egyptian project*. The SFO concluded that a prosecution would not be warranted under the circumstances of this particular case, although it did conclude that sanctions would be appropriate.

[395] Of note, no action was taken against any individual. See J. Leitch, *Balfour given £2.5 on fine after SFO investigation*.

[396] J. Leitch, above. As the Herald reported, Balfour Beatty's statement on point said:
"This agreement expressly recognises that Balfour Beatty acted promptly and responsibly in connection with the matter, that Balfour Beatty has co-operated with the SFO throughout the investigation, and that appropriate steps have been taken to ensure that no recurrence could take place in the future."
T. Sharp, *Balfour Beatty settles investigation into Egyptian project* (internal quotations omitted).

[397] A. S. Joshi, 33 Champion 36 at 40 (stating that, as of 2008, "[t]he United States has prosecuted 105 foreign bribery cases in the past 11 years, compared with only one in the U.K."). It remains to see how aggressive the UK will be in the upcoming years.

tional reach of American law would be well-advised to heed American law. Therefore, a company that encounters the spectre of litigation should cooperate and seriously consider the possibility of a voluntary disclosure of wrongdoing. By encouraging corporate reform and effective internal mechanisms for prosecution, a company may decrease the likelihood of succumbing to governmental strong-arming and control, as well as avoid violations under the FCPA.

CHAPTER 9

FORENSIC AND ACCOUNTING ISSUES ASSOCIATED WITH INTERNATIONAL CORRUPTION ENQUIRIES

A. INTRODUCTION

With any International Corruption Enquiry it is critical to have a clear strategic **9-01** vision. There are many difficulties arising out of investigating in potentially multiple overseas jurisdictions, and thus dealing with different laws and cultures, which, combined with a high degree of regulatory oversight and public interest, mean that having a clear understanding of what one is trying to achieve is essential.

For example, one may need to convince a regulator that a sufficiently thorough and rigorous investigation has been completed, lessons have been learnt, appropriate remedial actions have and are being taken and the organisation has truly changed. Alternatively, an investor may wish to know whether the organisation's controls and risk management around bribery and corruption are adequate, particularly moving forward. Whatever the purpose (or indeed purposes) of the investigation, they must be clearly articulated at the outset and the required deliverables specified as these will define the overall strategy. Once this is known, the detailed tactics and actions can be carefully planned.

As part of defining the deliverables, one must carefully consider reporting lines and requirements:

- Who is the investigation being carried out for (who is giving the instructions)?
- Who is being reported to?
- Who are the stakeholders?
- Who will be reported to internally?
- Are there any other potential audiences?

Any reports will need to be flexed to the relevant audience, ensuring their needs are addressed. Consideration will also, of course, need to be given on the frequency of reporting: this can range from regular ongoing reporting (perhaps verbal) to one final written report. Whatever the format, carefully documented supporting records must be identified throughout the investigation. For example, current practice in the United States before agencies like the US Department of Justice and the US Securities and Exchange Commission, typically calls for investigative findings to be reported in privileged power point presentation formats, supported by relevant emails, key hard copy documents, and other analyses.

9–02   It is also critical to ensure that the investigation will be thorough enough to give comfort that the entirety of the problem has been addressed and that potential other problems are considered. For example, are there any potential frauds in the business unit or could a similar problem have occurred in another territory? International Corruption Enquiries should not be considered without taking the broader business operations and risks into account.

An investigation of this sort should not be seen as the end of the matter. To gain the maximum value from an enquiry, an organisation should consider what lessons have been learnt, what remedial actions have and must yet be taken and what preventative strategies can be put in place. All of these will then feed into the business's risk management framework, the policy and guideline framework and auditing strategy. They will also be important in setting the appropriate tone from the top and defining corporate culture.

In this chapter we discuss some general points regarding Forensic and Accounting Investigations and apply these in the context of an International Corruption Enquiry, giving relevant examples along the way. We also discuss selected areas of risk and industries which are particularly vulnerable to bribery and corruption. We also look at the specific issues and challenges facing the corruption investigator and various tools and methodologies for tackling these issues.

9–03   In our experience, the most effective investigations typically follow a common course involving five core elements. Of course, an investigation is not necessarily linear and the following steps may run in parallel, in particular data collection and fieldwork are often carried out simultaneously. One is also likely to need to re-plan and re-focus the investigation along the way as various findings are made. Nonetheless, the following elements should typically be completed.

1.   **Planning, Scoping and Orientation**—gathering initial information for the enquiry and conducting initial data gathering interviews in order to plan for resource, logistical and technical requirements and also to prepare an initial work plan and scope for the investigation. As with any investigation, the scope of work will likely evolve as facts and evidence are discovered and the investigating team must therefore be prepared to flex the scope of work accordingly on a real time basis. Liaison and coordination with any "interested" regulators may also need to be taken into account. For example, "real time" interim reporting and base touching is a preferred practice by the US DOJ and SEC in FCPA investigations.

2.   **Data Collection**—undertaking detailed data collection (of both hard

copy and electronic records) which provides a robust and informed platform for field work.

3. **Field Work**—in this element the detailed enquiry takes place, using both the knowledge gained from the first two elements and the investigator's expert judgement and experience to enquire into the relevant events and issues under investigation and draw preliminary conclusions. More detailed interviews will often then have to be conducted and even more data will be analysed.

4. **Follow up and verification**—confirmation of the findings of the field work underpinned by robust evidence (including documentary evidence wherever possible).

5. **Reporting**—reports into each area of investigation for the appropriate stakeholders, such as the Audit Committee, Board, Auditors or relevant Regulators.

We shall look at each of these elements in turn in the context of an International Corruption Enquiry.

B. PLANNING, SCOPING AND ORIENTATION

It is important to consider carefully the nature of the specific problem being   **9–04**
investigated. This will, in turn, also often depend on how the problem has come to light; e.g. was there a whistleblower allegation, has Internal Audit uncovered a discrepancy, has a regulator approached the company indicating it has received notification of or has identified a problem? It is not only important to determine how well the allegation is founded but also to consider the wider implications. An investigative work plan needs to be drawn up that will provide comfort that all of the relevant issues have been identified. This plan may change as the investigation evolves but the objectives and corresponding scope of what the investigation is trying to achieve needs to be clearly established at the outset. For example, consideration needs to be given to whether an individual bribe paid to secure a particular contract in one business unit is likely to have been an isolated occurrence or could potentially be indicative of a wider problem. Of course, at the outset, such is not always known, and thus one often finds one has to approach such investigations in a broader fashion and to "hone" the effort down as one finds out the limits or "ring fencing " of the full issues at hand. If there is a chance that the matter may have occurred at other business units or in other jurisdictions, possibly due to connections with the same individuals, chain of command or lack of controls being present, then the scope of work will doubtless need expanding.

Once it has been determined what the allegation is and what jurisdictions are or may be involved, the next steps are to determine the objectives of the investigation, who will conduct the investigation and what the purpose will be, for example will the matter have to be reported to a regulator or is it likely to lead to an internal disciplinary matter. These questions will guide the planning on what data will need to be obtained and the format of any reporting requirements. It is also best practice to identify recommendations for remedial actions such as internal control enhancements, robust governance structures and anti-bribery and corruption compliance programme advice and hence this needs to be factored in to the scoping to ensure relevant advice and recommendations are collated along the way. Sometimes there is a need to fix things quickly and therefore it can be sensible to consider remediation steps during the investigation, particularly to prevent further recurrence.

At this stage of an International Corruption Enquiry, it is typically necessary to gain an understanding of the workings of the relevant business unit, including its client base, local suppliers (in particularly agents and third parties), employees and IT systems. It makes later work easier if it can be identified how local data is managed, what volume of records is involved or whether it is held on a common IT platform (it may even be reported back to or stored at the Head Office). Interviews with trusted individuals and analysis of relevant business plans and operating manuals can help in this area. A detailed assessment of local legislation should also likely be conducted together with a review of the organisation's relevant operating and employment procedures and rules. It may be that some of this work has to be done in the next phase, i.e. during the site visit, if there is no detailed knowledge within the head office team or the information is not readily available.

9–05   It is important to consider the potential motivations of anyone involved in wrongdoings. Fraud practitioners often point to three factors that are commonly found when fraud occurs (the Fraud Triangle—Figure 9A) and these are equally applicable in International Corruption Enquiries. First, perpetrators of corruption have an incentive or pressure to engage in misconduct. Secondly, there has to be an opportunity to commit fraud and thirdly, perpetrators are often able to rationalise or justify their actions. In a recent survey of economic crime,[1] it was found that 68 per cent of respondents attributed greater risk of fraud to increased "incentives or pressures"; 18 per cent reported that "more opportunities" to commit fraud was the most likely reason for greater risk of fraud; and 14 per cent believed that people's "ability to rationalise" was the main factor contributing to greater risk of fraud.

The most commonly reported factor contributing to these increased pressures and incentives was that "financial targets were more difficult to achieve", covering both individual targets and those for the business as a whole.

It may seem obvious but it is also critically important to take into consideration local culture and custom as well as the practicalities of working in the specific jurisdiction. To do business in China, for example, a company's representatives must have "guanxi", that is, good, strong, one-to-one personal relationships.

[1] Source: *http://www.pwc.com/crimesurvey* [Accessed July 15, 2010].

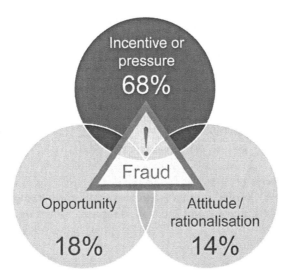

Figure 9A: Fraud Triangle

With the right relationships in place, a company can achieve a high success rate but without those relationships, a company may expend a great deal of effort without achieving success. Methods of overcoming language barriers and other general travel and logistical issues also need to be built in to the plan.

The typical issues which are likely to be faced at this stage are access and availability to both key individuals and documents. It is worth considering whether the investigation will be overt (i.e. the purpose will be declared to those under investigation) or covert (i.e. the true nature will be hidden, for example the investigation could be carried out under the auspices of a regular audit). If overt, some background enquiries and data collection might be best carried out before "going public" about the investigation in order to secure documentation and facilitate planning. More covert styles investigations may enable evidence to be secured quickly, however, they carry significant risks and may not be allowed in certain jurisdictions or circumstances. Legal advice should be taken before conducting any covert enquiries. Obviously this will differ on a jurisdiction by jurisdiction basis, and care must be given to avoid any possible perception of "pretexting", i.e. obtaining information by deception, which would obviously not be part of any forensic accounting investigation. In practice, it is very difficult to investigate effectively if you are operating covertly, particular when you need to speak to people.

Planning whom to interview, when and in what order can be a difficult tactical decision. It may be important to interview witnesses or suspects simultaneously in order to obtain independent accounts. Typically, as well, you will want to "work up the ladder" in terms of interviewees, so as to build your investigative knowledge before taking on in interviews those closest to the allegations. Again, this will depend on the context of the investigation.

9–06

In the conduct of interviews in the United States, however, it is also critical for the investigative accountants to clearly identify the parties for whom they are working and, most importantly, that they are not there representing or providing advice to the interviewees. This kind of an "Upjohn"[2] style warning is a requirement in US investigations and is good practice elsewhere to avoid any misunderstandings later. There would be little value to tremendously well done investigative interviews if they could not be used because of a claim by the miscreants that they believed the interviewers represented them.

9–07   When conducting investigations overseas or under a tight timescale, it often helps to prepare and send an "Information Request List" in advance. This can speed up the process of investigating during the site visit. The investigator must consider, however, whether they have been provided with a full data set as a result of a pre-visit information request and make appropriate enquiries to give themselves comfort that they have seen sufficient original documentation. There is also a risk that a request such as this will provide any miscreants with the opportunity to create a "second set of books", or even worse, to somehow tamper with the existing evidence. Such Requests should be carefully timed and coordinated with counsel to insure that such requests are sent out after distribution of the "document and date hold notices".

Any Information Request must also typically be focussed towards particular highly relevant risk areas. In an International Corruption Enquiry these are likely to include, inter alia, the following:

- Background, Organisation and Environment—organisation charts, board minutes, risk registers, etc.

- Policies, Procedures and Guidance Material—whistleblower policy and procedure, vetting of staff, tendering and contracting, political and charitable donations, sponsorship, facilitation payments, segregation of duties in accounting functions, etc.

- Communication and Training—details of any compliance or anti-bribery and corruption training programmes; training material, intranet sites, codes of conduct, etc.

- Business relationships—joint ventures, third party, agent and other intermediary contracts, major customers, government customers, etc.

- Accounting and Transaction analysis—chart of accounts, trial balance, payroll, supporting documentation for transactions in high risk areas, expense claims, authorisation limits, details on methods of payments, documentation for adjusting and manual entries, list of suppliers, etc.

- Bank accounts and cash balances.

---

[2] *Upjohn Co. v US*, 449 U.S. 383 (1981).

- IT System details—software used, system architecture, key individuals responsible, back up procedures, etc.

- Previous internal or external audit or investigative reports.

- Lists of high risk third parties, such as agents, intermediaries, dealers, distributors, et al.

This is by no means an exhaustive list nor will all this information be required in every investigation. The context of the enquiry will normally guide what information should be sought.

I. WHO IS AT RISK?

In principle, any company operating under legislation, such as the US FCPA or UK Bribery Act 2010, discussed elsewhere in this book, is at risk. Much legislation is focussed on prohibitions regarding potential or actual corruption of foreign officials and, as such, the risk attaches to the interactions or dealings of whatever kind with government entities and officials, the definition of which is wide ranging and usually covers, inter alia: 9–08

- Ministers of state and civil servants.

- Government employees, including doctors, teachers, law enforcement and military personnel.

- Employees of any enterprise majority owned or otherwise controlled by the state.

- Tax authorities.

- Local government officials.

- Officials of any political party and candidates for political office.

- Judges, prosecutors and other court officials.

Some industry sectors face heightened exposure in this way. These include:

- Oil and gas, mining and other extractive industries.

- Energy generation and distribution.

- Construction of roads, buildings and infrastructure.

- Pharmaceuticals and medical devices.

- Freight forwarding entities.

- Aerospace and defence.

- Information and communication technology.

The definition of "a government official" is broadly construed. While who may or may not be a foreign official can often appear obvious, this is often NOT the case under the US FCPA, where previous enforcement actions and settlements may dictate a quite broad definition of who is or isn't a government official under the US FCPA. For example, these can be public hospital systems physicians; state run university professors; members of NGOs such as the IRC (International Red Cross); officials of such entities as the World Bank; or employees of state-owned or state-controlled enterprises.

9–09 Given the variety of legislation and business involved, it is important for companies (both as a preventative measure and to aid detection and investigation) to have a well thought through and frequently updated risk register, covering the key country risks for geographical areas of operational activity and transactional risks for the type of business conducted, and to rigorously and regularly audit these risks. If the worst happens and corruption or fraud is suspected, any investigation can be focussed on these risks in the first instance. Under the US FCPA, there are expectations by US regulators that companies subject to the US FCPA have "rigorous and proactive" compliance programmes designed to "deter and detect" inappropriate payments. US Regulators, for example, regularly point to available guidance, such as US DOJ FCPA opinion releases (particularly 04–02 and others) to describe minimum or threshold levels for such compliance programmes. There is also guidance on this and other relevant matters published by the UK Serious Fraud Office (see Ch.11, section B.III).

II. TYPICAL HIGH RISK ACTIVITIES

9–10 Activities which will generally heighten the risk of legislative violations include:

- Sales to government and government related entities.

- Other dealings with government such as settlement of tax affairs, applications for licences, concessions, planning consent, travel visas, provision of utilities, etc.

- Dealings with customs officials relating to the import or export of goods.

- Provision of gifts, entertainment, reimbursement of travel expenses, etc. to government officials.

- Donations to or sponsorship of government related entities, or even charities and not-for-profit organisations where there is a link to a government entity or official.

- Lobbying of government on policy, legislation, etc.

- Use of intermediaries, such as agents (sales, customs, etc.), representatives, business consultants, lobbyists and anyone else interacting with government officials on the company's behalf.

- Entering into acquisitions of, or joint ventures or consortia with, companies involved in any of the above activities.

The risks attached to these activities are further heightened where they take place in countries with a poor record on corruption, of which there are many. Probably the most comprehensive source of guidance on this point is the annual Corruption Perceptions Index produced by Transparency International, which ranks countries according to perceived levels of corruption. On a scale of 10 (clean) to zero (corrupt), 132 out of 180 countries ranked have a score of 5.0 or less,[3] including all of the major emerging economies, and therefore bear a higher degree of corruption risk. A summary of the result is included at Appendix A.

C. DATA COLLECTION AND PRESERVATION

I. CONTEXT AND FOCUS

It is very easy with any financial investigation to obtain an overwhelming volume of data, both in terms of paper records and electronic data. As with all successful investigations, planning and preparation are essential in bribery and corruption investigations. Focus on key risk areas enables efficient investigations but this must be balanced against a need to preserve evidence, particularly with a mind to disclosure rules and other regulatory requirements.   **9–11**

The first critical step is data preservation: ensuring that paper documents aren't shredded and electronic data isn't deleted or written over. A subset of preserved data can be copied or captured, and a smaller subset analysed. This not only includes paper documents, electronic files and email, but also transactional data from accounting and other enterprise systems. It's necessary to have a good understanding and receive reliable legal advice on data protection and data privacy regulations for all relevant jurisdictions.

Technology can help the investigator. Documents and emails can be de-duplicated so that reviewers only have to read them once. Both electronic information and paper documents can be indexed so they quickly respond to keyword searches. More sophisticated systems provide automatic document grouping and concept clustering to help investigators quickly get a sense of what is contained in the document population. Transactional data can be analysed for anomalous transactions.

Like all aspects of an investigation, data capture can be disruptive to ongoing operational activity. Again, planning can help minimise any detrimental impact on the organisation's day to day business activity.   **9–12**

When planning data capture it is important to be led by the investigative requirements. In particular, if there are, for example, regulatory requirements or

---

[3] Based on 2009 data, source: *http://transparency.org/policy_research/surveys_indices/cpi/2009* [Accessed July 15, 2010].

whistle-blower allegations, these will allow the context for the investigation to be clearly defined. The volume of data involved may necessitate a phased approach to the investigation; this may involve looking at specific time periods separately (for example, looking at most the recent period first before expanding the investigation to earlier periods) or by working through separate stages of the investigation in phases (for example securing evidence and interviewing staff before progressing to a review of the data).

As much use as possible should be made of other reviews and reports, such as relating to internal and external audits, when planning the investigation. Knowledge of what data is held by whom and where it is located can be vital.

II. PAPER AND DOCUMENTARY EVIDENCE

9–13 Identification of relevant material should preferably be carried out at the planning stage. Once this has been done, efforts should be made to secure the necessary documents whilst causing the minimum amount of disruption. Preservation of contemporaneous records will be crucial to the success of an investigation and is normally a legal requirement in criminal investigations.

Consideration should be given to making copies of the key documents which can be left with the business in order to minimise disruption and to enable original documents to be secured. Originals may be important for legal proceedings but if these are not envisaged, copies are likely to be acceptable; this will depend on the context of the enquiry.

It is important to record the location from which documents are taken and who had access to them as this information can be as important as the document itself. Detailed records should be made of precisely where individual documents were taken from. In some circumstances, it may be appropriate to seal documents in evidential bags as used by law enforcement agencies. This will again depend on the context of the enquiry.

9–14 Access to third party data is much more difficult. If there is a formal relationship with the third party, such as an agency agreement, there may be contractual clauses allowing access to their books or even some types of audit rights over third party books and records. Organisations should make sure that rights of inspection and audit are regularly carried out, whether or not there are allegations of corruption, and secure copies of important documents are retained. This is of particular importance in International Corruption Enquiries as bribes or facilitation payments are frequently channelled through third parties in order to mask the true nature of the payment. Bribes can then be disguised as commission payments to sales agents, for example.

Scanning of documents can make review and investigation much easier. Optical character recognition (OCR) tools can make scanned documents searchable. Scanning also facilitates document sharing and production of bundles of evidence for interviews and court.

III. Electronic Data and Media

The forensic technology environment is becoming increasingly complex. Bribery **9–15** and corruption cases, such as those brought under OECD, EU, UK or US anti-corruption and anti-bribery regulations, for example, can demand the capture and analysis of very large volumes of data from many systems across various jurisdictions. More and more corporate data is stored electronically, there are continuous developments in technology, and there is growing understanding and appreciation of electronic information by the courts and regulators. It is important to get the balance right and to minimise cost and disruption.

The nature of electronic evidence makes early planning beneficial because electronic data is harder to manage than paper. Large volumes of data can be stored on very small devices. Early discussion of e-disclosure requirements as part of case management is increasing and highly recommended; it allows parties to focus on proportionality, avoid accidental destruction of data, and manage the costs and disruption.

Many types of electronic storage media can have data recovered after it has been deleted. In addition, most electronic information has associated meta-data (data about the data) such as the time a document was modified or the login name of the person who posted the transaction. The meta-data can be just as revealing as the data itself, so it's important that it is captured correctly.

It is important that specialist equipment is used by trained professionals when **9–16** seizing electronic data to ensure that all the data is correctly captured and is evidentially sound.

Data from networked computers can also often be captured remotely, i.e. the investigator does not necessarily need to have physical access to the specific computer. However, the speed of this process depends on the quality of the network and it may not always be practical to obtain the data in this manner.

Emails and fileservers are obvious sources for important evidential material. In many international bribery and corruption investigations, there are critical pieces of evidence with high investigatory value found in emails, such as "who asked whom for what; what was the quid pro quo". These pieces of electronic evidence are typically quite important to establishing the "mens rea", intent and authorisation/approval aspects of the inappropriate payments or benefits. Other systems should not be overlooked. These will include network access logs, system logs, building access records, system information, financial systems and enterprise systems (such as vendor relations databases, sales management databases, personnel and payroll records, etc.).

Despite the volume, it is often best to secure as much electronic data as possible **9–17** but then to interrogate this data intelligently and in a focussed manner (see section E below).

It is also sensible to secure other sources of electronic data such as back-up tapes and off-site data warehouse contents. This is true whether or not the team will ultimately actually review this source of data. The "locking down" and securing of such data is often a critical element in determining the thoroughness of the investigative effort. For example, failure to "turn off" automatic 60 day tape rotation and "overwriting" of tapes can inadvertently destroy important evidence and create undeserved credibility challenges with regulators.

Again, access to third party data is much more difficult and will depend on contractual clauses.

Once captured, data has to be processed to remove system files, create indexes for searching, remove duplicates and so on. The data is then loaded into a review environment where investigators can look through the data and make case notes on each document, without affecting the underlying evidence. This review is normally conducted on a subset of the data after appropriate searches and filters have been applied to the data (see section E below). There are several issues to consider here, such as data protection and privacy laws which are discussed in more detail below.

IV. Witness Evidence

9–18   It is likely that different types of interview will be necessary at different stages of the investigation. For example, one might interview a witness at an early stage of an investigation in order to identify further lines of enquiry but at that stage it might not be practical to ask probing questions about specific documents and so a follow-up interview may be necessary. This may be particularly true if the email analysis has not yet been finished at the time of the initial interviews.

In order to help with interview planning, the purpose of the interview should be clarified such as:

- to gather information;

- to gather evidence; or

- to differentiate or eliminate suspects and witnesses.

Witnesses of fact are not only necessary if legal proceedings are likely but are also of great assistance in bringing focus to the investigation. Corroboration of witness evidence should be obtained to verify authenticity. In some circumstances and jurisdictions it may be sensible to require a witness to provide a signed statement which may help to ensure they provide an accurate account, as well as providing a written record at a set point in time, which may be of benefit should the investigation take a long time.

Some witnesses may wish to remain anonymous; there may indeed be legislation to protect them in this regard. Nonetheless, their evidence can be of great assistance to the investigator.

9–19   Interview technique is a very broad topic which we will not, in this short chapter, be able to address fully. Suffice it to say, however, that given the considerations necessary and the skills required, it is always best to have appropriately qualified, trained and experienced individuals conduct interviews.

However, the following represent a few of the issues to consider and pitfalls to avoid.

It is better to conduct interviews with witnesses as soon as practically possible, not only because memories fade but also because it may identify key lines of inquiry and prevent wasted investigative time. Witnesses can provide details which will not be found in documents such as customs and practices beyond those set out in internal manuals as well as behavioural information regarding other employees. However, even if interviewing early, it is important to be prepared and have planned thoroughly; one should not rush in to interviewing. It also is quite important to recognise that it is vitally important to have the "right people" doing the interviews. For example, it would not be advisable to conduct interviews of CFOs and other financial types, covering controls and accounting issues without the involvement of accounting "savvy" personnel.

As with all investigative techniques, interviews should be carefully planned setting out the topics to be covered and specific questions if necessary. Where possible, it is of benefit to have documents available to refresh the witness's memory. It is best practice whenever possible to have two interviewers present.

It is worth considering what action would be taken during an interview if the **9–20** interviewee made an admission of a crime or wrongdoing. The value of obtaining an admission is considerable, however, the admissibility as evidence of this admission will depend on the law of the relevant jurisdiction. Consideration must, of course, also be given to the interviewee's legal rights.

If the interview is not being recorded, it is important to take contemporaneous notes which should be written up in full as soon after the interview as possible. If the witness is not prepared to make a statement, it may be possible to at least get their agreement to the accuracy of the note of the interview. It is worth considering the legal implications of recording an interview, for example in most jurisdictions an interviewee must be informed that the interview is being recorded and give consent to such recording; it might well be illegal otherwise as well as rendering the recording inadmissable as evidence.

It is of course important to be sensitive to language or cultural issues when interviewing a witness. Also, organisational manuals and employment terms may set out rules and codes of conduct for interviewing employees.

D. DATA PROTECTION AND PRIVACY LAW CONSIDERATIONS

I. DATA PROTECTION

This is a particularly important area in International Corruption Enquiries as it is **9–21** very likely that access to personal data will be required and this data is likely to be transmitted between jurisdictions. It is sensible to obtain competent legal advice in this area. Every case and situation is different and therefore the specific circumstances must be considered every time in order to adhere to the various rules and regulations surrounding Data Protection and other privacy law enactments.

In the EU, all data protection legislation stems from the EU Directive on Data Protection. As with all EU directives, the directive is implemented by each government, which means they are implemented slightly differently and interpreted differently in each EU country. The directive (and therefore the legislation that follows from it, such as the UK's Data Protection Act 1998) only applies to personal data (not corporate data); personal data is defined as "data which relate to a living individual who can be identified (a) from those data, or (b) from those data and other information which is in the possession of, or is likely to come into the possession of, the data controller". While this might appear to be a fairly narrow definition, any email with a signature line that contains a name and contact information would allow someone to be identified. Care must therefore be taken when reviewing emails of individuals and reference should be made to any terms and conditions in employment contracts and other manuals regarding these matters. In general, for example, UK law is one of the less stringent Data Protection Acts, whereas Germany and France have more stringent requirements; for example in Germany there can be a requirement for the client to discuss the personal data issues with the employees' trade union before transfers/processing of personal data.

Various countries have banking secrecy acts, e.g. Switzerland, which may prevent the transfer of data between jurisdictions. Appropriate advice should be sought before transferring data between any jurisdictions.

Global data protection law could form an entire book in itself. It is therefore recommended that appropriate advice is sought for specific investigations. The overarching principles are that personal data is likely to be protected, banking and financial data is often protected and transmission of data between jurisdictions can be regulated.

II. Further Privacy Considerations

9–22   Other legislation may also be relevant to data protection considerations. For example, the UK Regulation of Investigatory Powers Act 2000 requires authorisation to be given for, inter alia, interception of telecommunications data. This could extend to reviewing previously unopened emails.

Internal manuals and terms and conditions of employments may also have a bearing on investigations and should be taken into account during the planning phase.

Freedom of Information laws might also apply in various jurisdictions but, again, these will need to be considered on a case by case basis.

E. FIELD WORK—DETECTING CORRUPT PAYMENTS IN BOOKS AND RECORDS

When attempting to identify potentially problematic or suspicious transactions, **9–23** one must first consider the context and areas of particular risk in order to define appropriate tests and lines of enquiry. In this section, we will discuss typical risk areas and methods for detecting corrupt payments within these. As stated above, one needs to design tests that will ensure one has identified the full scale of the problem and considered what broader problems might exist. We will look at two methods in more detail: data analytics and corporate intelligence; and we will consider some examples of investigations we have conducted.

It is likely that there will be some form of allegations or suspicions of impropriety and it is obviously sensible to place the initial focus on the specified area and then build out to what other problems might exist. One should attempt to check that there is substance and/or foundation to the allegations and that they have not simply been made out of malice or misinterpretation. Regardless, a thorough investigation should still be conducted to conclusively determine this. One should then consider, for example, whether there are similar types of transactions which are also vulnerable or whether the individuals concerned might be involved in other malfeasance. Further consideration should be given to the vulnerability of other sites/locations/branches to similar malfeasance.

Once the specifics have been bottomed out, one can refer back to the investigation strategy to determine how far further enquiries need to be taken beyond the known boundaries of the problem, for example to justify the extent of the problem to a regulator, has the investigation provided sufficient evidence to demonstrate that the problem is isolated? If not, what will the follow-up investigations be? The strategy and context of the investigation will determine just how far the wider boundary of the problem will extend.

Once the above has been considered and the relevant risks have been identified, **9–24** a focussed investigation plan can be drawn up to target the high risk areas within the books and records of the company. The detailed approach will vary from business to business but the following sections cover the key techniques which can be deployed.

Let us consider, as an illustrative example, a fictitious company in the construction industry. It has been particularly successful in winning contracts in several developing countries to build hospitals. It is headquartered in Europe and listed on both the local and New York stock exchanges. It uses third party agents in each jurisdiction to assist with bid negotiations and planning applications. It also uses local sub-contractors to undertake various parts of the construction. Financial control is decentralised with manual consolidation at group level on a monthly basis. An anonymous email is received by the group FD alleging bribes have been paid by an overseas branch to win a contract. What should the FD do? This is the first he has heard of anything like this. Is it just sour grapes from the competitor at losing the contract? We shall work through this example in the next few sections and consider some of the courses of action might be appropriate. There are many more investigations which would be advisable but which are not discussed here as the purpose of this example is to give some selected illustrations of the topic.

I. WITNESSES, WHISTLEBLOWERS, ALLEGATIONS

9–25 The importance of following up swiftly and effectively on any allegations of malfeasance can not be overstated. Organisations should have an effective plan in place for how to deal with such situations as they arise. Regulators often refer to this as the "playbook". There should be a well documented and well thought out plan of how the company should proceed when and if presented with such allegations. This should include a full investigation to corroborate or dismiss the allegation. Even if the allegations prove to be malicious or simply unfounded, a record of decisions should be made and kept on file in case future allegations arise. It is clearly much easier to focus an investigation if detailed and specific allegations are made.

Organisations should also place a high priority on encouraging whistleblowing and issue reporting. It is all too frequent to hear from employees after a problem has occurred that they thought there was something odd going on but presumed they were mistaken or somebody would already be doing something or that it was not their responsibility to deal with it. Whistleblower processes can take many forms from telephone hotlines through to email and web based forms to paper based postal systems. They can be run internally or through independent advisers. Some companies choose a mixture of all of these in order to meet the local cultural needs of their business. However it is done, it is important to encourage openness both as a means of detection and as a deterrent.

It is also important to consider the potential protection afforded to whistleblowers such as the UK Public Interest Disclosure Act. US protection is more onerous and regulated and includes, for example, SARBOX whistleblower protection and SEC rules encouraging "dropping a dime" on miscreants directly to the SEC/DOJ.[4] An effective whistleblower process can also form part of the "adequate procedures" defence against allegations of failing to prevent bribery under the UK Bribery Act (see para.11–06).

9–26 In our example, the FD has had an allegation made by an anonymous and perhaps internal whistleblower. There may be no substance to the allegations but

---

[4] The Dodd-Frank Wall Street Reform and Consumer Protection Act came into law mid July 2010 and introduced two parallel whistleblower programmes that will provide powerful financial incentives for individuals to report suspected securities or commodities trading violations to the SEC and Commodity Futures Trading Commission. With the mandatory awards to whistleblowers of between 10 and 30% of the monetary sanctions imposed by the SEC or other government agencies, it is suspected that this will lead to a substantial increase in the amount of investigations. A similar whistleblower incentive scheme was introduced in the US False Claims Act which resulted in over $24bn in recoveries and judgments since 1986.

can the FD risk the consequences of not investigating? In this example, there are several red flags to consider:

1. The contract is to build a hospital and in this case, is with the local Ministry for Health. The involvement of foreign officials increases the level of risk associated with the contract in that any illicit payments will be a breach of the FCPA due to the company's dual listing.

2. The construction industry is prone to corruption given the number of sub-contractors involved, planning and other permissions needed, the high incidence of cash transactions, the physical security of building materials, in particular the difficulties associated with tracking assets and stock control, the length of contracts and the high volume of financial transactions to monitor, amongst many other factors.

3. Third party agents have been used to negotiate the contract.

4. The accounting controls seem weak given the decentralisation and manual consolidation.

Wisely, the FD decides to call in a team of investigators. Next we will consider what they will look for and how the will obtain the information they need.

II. Methods and Techniques for Detecting Corrupt Payments

As stated above, if there are allegations of inappropriate payments or benefits provided, these should be the starting place for investigations. However, in order to broaden the investigation from these allegations or in circumstances where there are no specific leads, the investigator should look into particularly high risk types of transaction and look for suspicious patterns of transactions within the accounting process.   **9–27**

Typically high risk transactions include:

- Intercompany transfers.

- Gifts.

- Donations and sponsorships.

- Community development programmes.

- Entertainment.

- Training.

- Marketing.

- Consulting Fees.

- Legal Fees.

- Audit, Tax and other Professional Fees.

- Commissions.

- Travel.

- Customs and Duties.

- Visas, permits and licences.

- Facilitation payments.

- Dealings with anyone in para.9–08.

In our example, the key concern is around the award of the contract and bribe. The investigation should not be limited to this though as third parties have also been used to obtain planning permission and sub-contractors have been used in the build process.

Before identifying the specific detection methods for our example, let us look at some of the typical investigations that might be undertaken in specific areas.

(a) Accounts Based

9–28   Data analytic work, as discussed in section E.III, can be of particular benefit when investigating accounting records and systems as it speeds up the review process. It may be possible to conduct some of this work before on-site investigations commence. Some methods of detecting unusual transactions are as follows:

- Reviewing high risk transactions such as those listed in para.9–27 above.

- Reviewing non-recurring transactions—it is often the case that bribes are found to be related to "one-off" type payments.

- Analysis of payments made to potentially connected parties before tenders are awarded—any significant transactions before such awards will need further investigation to demonstrate that they are not linked to the award.

- Identification of unusual transfers of value other than payment (e.g. credit notes where none would be expected, excessive free samples, training/ travel for clients which would not normally be expected)—payment in kind is a common method of bribery. This may be accompanied by unusual packaging or delivery requests by customers such as removal of customer branding on packaging.

- Matching payroll to supplier list—as well as highlighting conflicts of interest, this may identify supplier companies set up by employees to conceal removal of funds for onward payment of bribes.

- Review of bank accounts for US Dollar account or US bank account connections—this will be important in order to determine whether there is an underlying nexus with FCPA requirements.

- Identification of missing files, dates on records not tallying, lack of original documentation—this may just be poor record keeping (although see FCPA books and records comment below) but it may be indicative of concealment or suspicious activity.

- Review of non-financial information held on sales and accounting databases—for example dates of payments to highlight patterns or unusual dates (e.g. public holidays), sequential number transactions to highlight duplicates or gaps, and unusual addresses such as PO Boxes.

(b) Transaction Based

As a more detailed follow up to the accounts review, specific transactions should be reviewed with tests including:

9–29

- Identification of the number and timing of payments to agents—are these in line with agreements and sales volume and are non-recurring payments supported.

- Reasonableness tests on value of commission payments compared to contract value—it is common for bribes to be paid through agents and these are often included within genuine payments in order to conceal the reality of the transaction.

- Analysis such as Benfield's Law can be applied where statistical analysis is undertaken on the values of transactions; and

- Authorisation limits.

(c) Contract Based

Paperwork and correspondence should be checked to ensure controls have been adhered to and to identify irregularities. Test could include:

9–30

- Checking/reconciling high risk area payments to contracts and supporting documents—it is also important to ensure that the supporting documents are genuine.

- Review of the tender documents and contracts themselves, along with relevant correspondence to identify unusual items.

- Wider conflict of interest checks (see section E.IV below).

- Changes to usual specification of goods—this might suggest a different recipient of the goods to the contracted buyer.

- Review contract modifications and change-control management—this is a common means of including corrupt payments at a local level once scrutiny of the contract is lower.

(d) Policy and Controls Based

9-31   Basic compliance checks can also be conducted at the same time as an investigation to reinforce policy, for example:

- Checks that local management are adhering to policies and procedures on, inter alia, anti-bribery and corruption, whistleblowing, internal audit, review board minutes—poor management is not necessarily an indication of corruption however it may make it easier for corruption to go unidentified or it may indicate management collusion;

- Check communication of anti-bribery and corruption policies to agents, intermediaries and third-parties—it is not acceptable to turn a blind-eye to suppliers' practices.

- Standard checks of, inter alia, segregation of duties, authorisation and sign-off procedures—breaches of normal accounting controls can lead to corruption going unnoticed or indicate deliberate manipulation.

In order to be able to form a view on the accuracy of the recording of transactions in an entity's books and records as required by the FCPA, it is important to evaluate the adequacy and effectiveness of those control procedures designed to address the FCPA provisions as well as those dealing with an entity's overall system of internal accounting controls, such as:

- Reconciliations of intercompany accounts and suspense accounts.

- Support (business rationale and documentation) and authorisation of journal entries.

- Completeness of revenues, especially commissions and rebates.

- Reliability and support for significant estimates and reserves.

- Appropriateness of the methods and tools employed (such as Accounting Manuals) used to comply with relevant GAAP.

- Understanding of key employees of relevant GAAP.

- The experience and expertise of the accounting department.

- Whether operational personnel can make or post journal entries.

- Methods to prevent management override of established controls.

- Procedures to confirm inventory existence.

- Completeness of cash balances and bank accounts.

A similar approach to accounting control effectiveness will also be relevant to "adequate procedures" as referred to in the UK Bribery Act (see para.11–06).

9-32   This is not an exhaustive list of investigations which may be necessary, nor will there be the need to conduct all of the above in all circumstances; the circumstances, context and strategy will dictate what is appropriate. Once these tests are completed, a review of the investigation strategy and plan will confirm whether the allegations are corroborated or not, whether further investigations are needed (in which case more planning will be necessary) and what broader issues are worthy of consideration, i.e. has the investigator found what they were looking for and are they confident that their investigations are complete and that there is nothing else out there.

So in our example, what are the likely first steps that the investigation team will take and what areas will they be interested in? Obtaining the tender and contract details are going to be a high priority, as are contracts and transactional data in connection with third party agents and sub-contractors. These combined with the accounting records are likely to provide the basis for conclusions around the allegations but it is always worth considering what else might be there. It is important to gain a rounded understanding of the allegations and potential other issues. In the next two sections we shall look at some detailed methods of detecting corruption, data analytic techniques and corporate intelligence, which require specialist skills but which can provide invaluable information and insights.

III. DATA ANALYTICS

Organisations hold vast amounts of data spread across financial systems, enterprise resource planning (ERP) systems, procurement systems and so on. The problem is that, given the amount of electronic data stored in today's business environment, even if only part of the system is searched, it is still likely to leave the investigators with an information headache. For example, in 2009, one US attorney working in the oil industry estimated his organisation held nearly 800 terabytes of data; the equivalent of over seven million filing cabinets of documents. In another recent case we were faced with reviewing a data set of over 2.5 million e-mail messages and attachments.   **9–33**

The size of the task is not helped by the fact that, in order to ensure completeness, e-mail and relevant documents are copied from both individual computers and the company's network for analysis, which leads to duplication. It is important to ensure, prior to review, that the data is properly de-duplicated so that the reviewers are not swamped with multiple copies of the same document. This must be done in an environment which preserves the details of where each email was found and where identical copies are located.

Prior to starting the data capture exercise, it is worth putting the technology to one side and investigating what might be relevant through interviews with key individuals rather than simply capturing everything. In other words, ask the patient where it hurts before opening them up and searching round for the injury (assuming, of course, that you trust the patient). It is particularly important to recognise that in most instances, most of the documents and files will prove to be irrelevant. Our own statistics put the average percentage of relevant documents identified from the initial search of all captured data at between three and four per cent.[5] That said, there is also a strong argument for capturing all available data in order to safeguard the evidence, even if you do not use it all; you may also wish to return to it at a later stage if further lines of inquiry open up.

9–34   Once this has been done it is important to start thinking about relevant search terms. Search terms should be adapted to match the terminology used by the individuals under review, as well as including obvious terms such as "fraud" and "bribe". For example, in corruption cases our experience tells us individuals are more likely to use words such as "gift" and "facilitation" or even code words rather than "bribe" and "fraud". In other instances, terms that are local "patois" for inappropriate payments should be used as well, whether that is "mordida" or the "bite" in Central or Latin America; the "red envelope" or "black money" in Asia; the "backhander" in Continental Europe; or the "kola nut" in certain West Africa nations. Data analytic software tools are advancing rapidly and can apply more sophisticated technology to identifying relevant documents. For example, it is possible to combine search terms to provide more focussed results and the latest software allows for "concept searching" where the software will identify similar types of document or unusual patterns. The software will review the data for the investigator and group items together based on a common theme, highlighting potential problem items or allowing large volumes of data to be identified as being unlikely to be relevant. This can speed up the investigator's review of data immensely and, when combined with experienced staff, can lead to more thorough investigations in a shorter time.

In the context of International Corruption Enquiries, consideration must also be given to the ability of any software tools used to cope with foreign language and character sets. This is of particular importance for character recognition or voice recognition software.

In essence, when using technology to search electronic data, it is important to focus less on the review tool and more on the investigation, i.e. remember to apply the investigative mindset to the electronic process, as opposed to being solely reliant on the technology to find the "smoking gun".

9–35   In our example, analysis of the cash book transactions identified three round sum payments to the same bank account used by the agent responsible for negotiating the contract. The payments were on consecutive days immediately before the award of the contract but were allocated against a different vendor account. The analysis also shows that on the last day of the month, four payments are made to a vendor account with only a PO Box address and with sparse details on the vendor database. All of these payments are just under the authorisation limit for a sole-signatory. It seems the allegations may have some substance. The investigation team now need to do some research on the connected parties, which is where Corporate Intelligence can be useful.

It is worth noting that some data analytic software can be used to monitor live

---

[5] Based on unpublished internal analysis of data acquisition and analysis by PwC Forensic Technology Solutions, London.

transactions for unusual practices. This will only be practical if the organisation is running an integrated accounting system across its various operations.

IV. CORPORATE INTELLIGENCE—CONFLICTS OF INTEREST

Corporate reputations are both forged and destroyed by the way in which business is done and the people with whom business is done. In today's global marketplace, commercial and state organisations interact on a daily basis with thousands of third parties from hundreds of different countries. Therefore, when something "goes wrong" in an organisation the number of people who could potentially be involved at one time or another is enormous.

9–36

Corporate Intelligence is the identification, analysis and corroboration of public record data and market intelligence to provide a fuller understanding of the background, management track record, source of funds, attributes, activities and connections of business partners (including agents, distributors, key suppliers and customers, licensees, JV and alliance partners) with whom a business interacts. The results of this type of research enable a company or individual to identify and protect against a variety of business issues and risks. In particular it can prove useful in the investigation of deception, fraud, and corruption (particularly in relation to the FCPA).

For our illustrative example, reviews of vendor account to which the three round sum payments were, identifies that the director of this company is a senior official in the local Ministry of Health. Asset tracing on the payments to the company at the PO Box address are matched to the payroll database and show that the cash has gone to the account of the local financial controller's deputy. A review of the tender documents show that the successful bidder must purchase building materials from a single specified local company. Corporate Intelligence research identifies that this company is owned by the brother of the local Head of Planning. It looks like there will be a lot of follow-up work, interviews, meetings with police and regulators and many changes for the company as it begins remediation.

In a real example, during an investigation at a major electronics and technology company, there were allegations that its agents and consultants had paid bribes to win foreign government contract. As a result, the company faced regulatory investigation and prosecution in the United States, Germany and Italy. The work performed involved working with the company's investigators to identify the third parties involved in suspicious transactions in more than 75 jurisdictions, assessing their background, role and activities in those transactions and seeking to establish links to any government officials.

9–37

F. INVESTIGATING AGENT AND THIRD PARTY PAYMENTS

9–38   Many bribes are paid indirectly, via third party agents, including sales representatives, logistics agents and marketing consultancies, with or without the commissioning organisation's consent and knowledge. It is essential to ensure that risk-based compliance and due diligence checks are carried out on third parties that the organisation plans to employ. Formal contracts with these third parties should require them to behave in an ethical way and in compliance with all relevant legislation, including specifically anti-bribery legislation. Approval and monitoring procedures need to be established to check that payments made to the third party appear reasonable in relation to the service performed (see para.11–25).

When a large organisation engages smaller third parties, it should take steps to support those smaller business partners in achieving compliance with anti-bribery laws and regulations. This support could include, for example, providing training in the organisation's expectations of what constitutes compliant behaviour. Third parties should also be given details of how to make use of whistleblower facilities so that they can report any behaviour that raises suspicions of corruption.

G. FOLLOW-UP AND VERIFICATION

9–39   Follow-up and verification are often conducted either in parallel with the field work element or may be necessary once the report is being drafted, when gaps in evidence can become apparent.

It may be necessary to plan further investigations at other branches of the organisation. If this is the case, the processes detailed in the earlier sections of this chapter should be repeated in the new context.

It may also be appropriate to validate the findings against records held centrally or against public or independent records. Where possible, these should be obtained or requested in parallel to the field work in order to speed up the process.

H. REPORTING

9–40   As stated earlier, the format and timing of reports should be agreed in advance. Attention should be paid to the agreed strategy and terms of reference for the investigation in order that all of the stakeholders' requirements are addressed. These will include inter alia:

- the primary investigation and organisation needs—reports to the instructing business unit, the board, the audit committee, internal and external auditors and other interested internal parties should be considered and tailored as appropriate, clearly setting the findings with support and advising on follow up actions;

- regulatory and law enforcement needs—will the investigator be called to give evidence on their findings and is the report in an appropriate format such as a witness statement; has the impact on the organisation been quantified; are legal and regulatory requirements (discussed elsewhere in this book) addressed in sufficient detail with actions to be taken set out clearly;

- meetings with stakeholders—will face to face meetings be required or will there be an ongoing dialogue such as settlement negotiations with regulators; and

- remediation and organisational learning—what plans are in place to put matters straight and to prevent recurrence of the problem; what messages will be passed on to the wider organisation; what changes will be made to auditing and control programmes and procedures or organisation policies in general.

By way of example, in international bribery and corruption cases under the FCPA, it is often necessary to provide US regulators with the findings of one's investigation under the so called "voluntary disclosure" procedure. Such disclosures, often summarised in a presentation made to the regulators, are typically done in person (with counsel and forensic accountants both present). The key elements of such reporting should include fulsome answers to the following typical questions often raised by US regulators:

- What was the alleged bad conduct? Who participated? Who knew about these payments? Who authorised or approved them? How far "up" does it go?

- Has the alleged bad conduct been stopped and fixed/made better?

- Where did the bad conduct occur? How did it happen?

- What were the preexisting compliance controls in place in this/these countries? How were they "gotten around"?

- Is the company's compliance programme really robust and proactive or a "paper tiger"?

- Is there evidence of other similar behaviour elsewhere? If so how many other places?

- What have you done to test/demonstrate that the bad conduct is limited?

- What are the specifics of the problematic payments or benefits? What business or contracts are involved? How much was made on these? What was the benefit or value obtained by the company as a result of the bad behaviour?

- Have other (non-US) regulators been notified?

CHAPTER 10

ANTI-CORRUPTION CONSIDERATIONS IN INTERNATIONAL MERGERS AND ACQUISITIONS[1]

A. INTRODUCTION

Cross-border investigations happen for a reason. If they seem more frequent than they were in the past—and they are—it may simply be because cross-border activity has increased. This is an inevitable effect (and to some degree a cause) of globalisation.   **10–01**

One of the principal rationales for these investigations is international corruption. And one of the most common ways in which such corruption comes to light is through due diligence in mergers and acquisitions.

The situation normally arises as follows: one company bids to acquire or combine with another. Sometimes the two companies hail from the same country; sometimes they do not. In either event, part of the deal's appeal is that one or both companies have substantial international reach.

As the parties explore the deal further, each reviews details of the other's operations and accounts. This is the process of due diligence. It is the bread-and-butter of lawyers conducting merger and acquisition work. And in the case of companies operating in potentially corrupt environments, it is rife with risk.   **10–02**

The risk is two-fold: for the company doing business in a corrupt environment—and doing it corruptly—there is every chance that the prospective merger partner or acquirer will want to report corrupt activity to regulators. The risk for the company doing the due diligence is that it fails to find out about corrupt payments at the other company, or that it fails to report them to its own regulator(s).

Why does an acquiring or merging company care about what happened in the past at another company? We can answer from the law and from common sense.

From the legal perspective, an acquiring company in many jurisdictions will inherit the legal liability of its acquisition. So if one company buys another company that has been paying bribes to government officials, the acquired company's past behaviour is now the acquirer's problem.   **10–03**

[1] The authors acknowledge the assistance of Jeffrey Miller and Bisha Nurse in preparing this chapter.

From the standpoint of common sense, furthermore, an acquirer needs to be especially careful that a pre-existing culture tolerating corrupt payments does not survive a merger or acquisition.

The risk is unsurprisingly more acute for companies that answer to American regulators. The rigidity of the fearsome Foreign Corrupt Practices Act ensures that acquirers will pay a high price for ignoring corruption, no matter in what posture they come across it.

10–04   It is for this reason that regulators—again often US regulators—come to learn of corruption in the midst of merger activity between companies. Where companies fully and frankly disclose what they have uncovered, regulators tend to be forgiving. Where they do not, regulators are much more draconian.

It is therefore important to understand what regulators expect in relation to alertness to corruption of companies involved in merger and acquisition due diligence, and what companies can do to minimise the risk of adverse exposure.

The issue is of more than academic interest to non-American companies doing international business. First of all, many such companies may find themselves subject to American jurisdiction one way or another—not least because a prospective merger or acquisition partner has an American nexus. Furthermore, as other jurisdictions catch up with the FCPA's enforcement regime, it seems inevitable that they too will eventually focus on corruption risks in mergers and acquisitions. In this respect, the United Kingdom's new Bribery Act bears close watching. As discussed in Ch.1, the Act makes senior officers of companies liable for failure to prevent bribes, unless those companies had "adequate procedures" in place to do so. Although we do not know how this provision will play out, it may be that such "adequate procedures" will include guidelines on appropriate due diligence of acquisitions in higher-risk jurisdictions.

10–05   Paragraphs 10–06–10–17 of this chapter will examine a few of the prominent cases involving anti-bribery compliance issues in connection with mergers and acquisitions. Paragraphs 10–18–10–32 will take a more practical approach, providing a how-to guide for companies engaging in corporate transactions to protect themselves from anti-bribery liability. This entails a description of the best practices from an acquirer's perspective, with a focus on three major areas: due diligence, contractual provisions, and integration of the target into an appropriate compliance programme.

B. CASE STUDIES

I. TITAN

10–06   The failure of a proposed merger between Lockheed Martin ("Lockheed") and Titan, a military intelligence and communications contractor, offers perhaps the best evidence of the growing importance of anti-corruption compliance in the context of M&A transactions. On September 15, 2003, Titan and Lockheed entered into a merger agreement in which Lockheed agreed to acquire Titan for $1.8 billion, or $22 a share, pending certain contingencies.[2] During the course of its pre-acquisition due diligence, Lockheed discovered evidence of multiple FCPA violations, including substantial suspicious payments to agents and foreign officials.[3] Lockheed informed Titan of the findings, and the parties voluntarily disclosed the potential violations to the Department of Justice ("DOJ") and the Securities and Exchange Commission ("SEC").[4]

The resulting internal and government investigations revealed that Titan had provided approximately $2 million in campaign contributions for the re-election of the President of Benin in order to aid the company in developing a tele-communications project and to obtain the Benin government's consent to higher project management fees.[5] Titan falsely invoiced the payments as "consulting services" and paid its Benin agent in cash or by wire transfer to his offshore account.[6] The SEC's complaint also alleged that employees of Titan and its subsidiaries submitted false documents to the US government and to several foreign governments, enabling its agents to under-report commission payments on numerous occasions.[7]

Following the discovery of potential FCPA violations, Lockheed postponed closing the deal twice before finally backing out entirely.[8] On April 7, 2004, Lockheed and Titan amended the merger agreement to reduce the terms of sale to $20 a share.[9] The amended agreement stated that, prior to closing, Titan must either (i) obtain written confirmation from the DOJ that it considered the FCPA issues resolved and does not intend to pursue any claims against the firm or (ii) enter into a plea agreement with the DOJ and complete the sentencing process.[10] The revised agreement also permitted either party to terminate the transaction if the merger was not completed by June 25, 2004.[11] Titan failed to reach an agreement with the DOJ by that date, and Lockheed terminated the merger, refusing Titan's request for another extension.[12]

In March 2005, Titan negotiated a settlement with the DOJ and the SEC for **10-07**

---

[2] See Litigation Release No. 19107, SEC, *SEC Sues the Titan Corporation for Payments to Election Campaign of Benin President* (March 1, 2005); Jonathan Karp, *Lockheed-Titan Deal Appears to Collapse as Deadline Looms*, Wall St. J., June 25, 2004, at A2.

[3] Martin J. Weinstein, *The World of International Compliance: What Transactional Lawyers Need to Know to Perform Ethically and Responsibly*, 29 Hous. J. Int'l L. 311 at 312 (2007).

[4] See fn.2 above.

[5] Litigation Release No. 19107, SEC, *SEC Sues the Titan Corporation for Payments to Election Campaign of Benin President* (March 1, 2005).

[6] Renae Merle, *Titan Admits Bribery In Africa: Contractor Will Pay $28.5 Million to Settle Criminal, SEC Cases, Washington Post*, March 2, 2005, at E1.

[7] Litigation Release No. 19107, SEC, *SEC Sues the Titan Corporation for Payments to Election Campaign of Benin President* (March 1, 2005).

[8] Jonathan Karp, *Lockheed-Titan Deal Appears to Collapse as Deadline Looms*, Wall St. J., June 25, 2004, at A2.

[9] Press Release, Lockheed Martin, *Lockheed Martin and Titan Announce Amended Merger Agreement* (April 7, 2004).

[10] Lockheed Martin, *Lockheed Martin and Titan Announce Amended Merger Agreement*.

[11] Lockheed Martin, *Lockheed Martin and Titan Announce Amended Merger Agreement*.

[12] Jonathan Karp, *Lockheed-Titan Deal Appears to Collapse as Deadline Looms*, Wall St. J., June 25, 2004, at A2.

approximately $28.5 million—the largest FCPA penalty ever paid by a publicly traded company at the time, thought long since dwarfed by later penalties.[13] The SEC complaint indicated that it was not only the improper payments and false documentation that led to the large settlement amount but also the extreme lack of an FCPA compliance protocol:

"Despite utilizing over 120 agents and consultants in over 60 countries, Titan never had a formal company-wide FCPA policy, failed to implement an FCPA compliance program, disregarded or circumvented the limited FCPA policies and procedures in effect, failed to maintain sufficient due diligence files on its foreign agents, and failed to have meaningful oversight over its foreign agents."[14]

The breakdown of the merger and subsequent settlement signalled to companies everywhere that effective FCPA due diligence and compliance are vitally necessary protections from liability when participating in international transactions.

II. Syncor

10–08   Before Titan and Lockheed, health care companies Syncor International ("Syncor") and Cardinal Health provided a much more efficient example of how to deal with anti-bribery issues that arise in the course of a corporate transaction. On June 14, 2002, Cardinal Health announced its proposed acquisition of Syncor, a major firm in the nuclear pharmacy services business.[15] Cardinal Health soon discovered certain suspicious payments in the course of conducting due diligence and conditioned closing on the further investigation and resolution of these concerns.[16] Syncor promptly formed a special committee to investigate the payments and then voluntarily made full disclosure of its findings to the DOJ and the SEC.[17] By the end of the year, on December 10, 2002, Syncor reached a settlement with the government requiring it to pay $2.5 million in response to formal charges that it made at least $600,000 in improper payments to doctors in hospitals controlled by foreign governments to secure business.[18]

Though Syncor paid a significant amount, the SEC praised its handling of the situation:

---

[13]   Renae Merle, *Titan Admits Bribery In Africa: Contractor Will Pay $28.5 Million to Settle Criminal, SEC Cases, Washington Post*, March 2, 2005, at E1.

[14]   Complaint at 3, *SEC v Titan Corp*, No. 05–0411 (JR), 2005 WL 516541 (DDC March 30, 2005).

[15]   Press Release, Cardinal Health, *Cardinal Health Responds To Syncor Announcement* (November 6, 2002).

[16]   Roger M. Witten, et al., *Prescriptions for Compliance with the Foreign Corrupt Practices Act: Identifying Bribery Risks and Implementing Anti-Bribery Controls in Pharmaceutical and Life Sciences Companies*, 64 Bus. Law. 691 at 721 (Section II.D.) (2009).

[17]   Press Release, Cardinal Health, *Cardinal Health Responds To Syncor Announcement* (November 6, 2002).

[18]   Litigation Release No. 17887, SEC, *SEC Obtains $500,000 Penalty Against Syncor International Corporation for Violating the Anti-Bribery Provisions of the Foreign Corrupt Practices Act* (December 10, 2002).

"In determining to accept Syncor's settlement offer, the Commission considered the full cooperation that Syncor provided to the Commission staff during its investigation. The Commission also considered the fact that Syncor—after being alerted to the relevant conduct by another company that was conducting due diligence relating to a previously announced merger with Syncor—promptly brought this matter to the attention of the Commission's staff and the U.S. Department of Justice."[19]

It certainly appears that Syncor's penalty could have been much more severe if it had not been so proactive and cooperative in facing the apparent FCPA violations.

Cardinal Health also helped itself out a great deal through its response to discovering the potential impropriety. Cardinal Health shielded itself from liability not only by conditioning closing on settlement of the FCPA issues but also by later obtaining an advisory opinion from the DOJ stating that the Department did not intend to take action against it for any of Syncor's pre-acquisition conduct.[20] Moreover, after uncovering the suspicious payments, Cardinal Health was able to negotiate a purchase price roughly $90 million lower than that initially agreed upon.[21]

III. InVision

Similarly, General Electric ("GE") effectively limited successor liability for FCPA violations in the context of its acquisition of InVision Technologies ("InVision"), the leading US supplier of airport explosive-detection equipment.[22] The parties entered into a merger agreement on March 15, 2004, with GE agreeing to pay $900 million and an expected closing date in mid-July.[23] After GE uncovered potential FCPA issues in due diligence, InVision conducted an internal investigation in consultation with GE, and the parties then voluntarily disclosed to the DOJ and the SEC "certain possible offers of improper payment by distributors in connection with foreign sales activities."[24] Both GE and InVision retained the right to walk away from the deal if it could not close with regulatory approval and the FCPA issues resolved by certain dates.[25]

    The government investigations revealed evidence that InVision had knowledge of a high probability that its foreign agents or distributors had made improper payments or offered to make improper payments to government officials in China,

10–09

---

[19] Litigation Release No. 17887, SEC, *SEC Obtains $500,000 Penalty Against Syncor International Corporation for Violating the Anti-Bribery Provisions of the Foreign Corrupt Practices Act* (December 10, 2002).

[20] Roger M. Witten, et al., *Prescriptions for Compliance with the Foreign Corrupt Practices Act: Identifying Bribery Risks and Implementing Anti-Bribery Controls in Pharmaceutical and Life Sciences Companies*, 64 Bus. Law. 691 at 721 (Section II.D.) (2009); see FCPA Opinion Procedure Release 2003-01, DOJ (January 15, 2003), available through *http://www.usdoj.gov* [Accessed July 15, 2010].

[21] Press Release, Cardinal Health, *Cardinal Health Responds to Syncor Announcement* (November 6, 2002).

[22] Bob Egelko, *InVision settles SEC suit*, S.F. Chron., February 15, 2005, at D1.

[23] Kathryn Kranhold, *GE Faces Delay on InVision as a U.S. Probe Looms*, Wall St. J., August 2, 2004, at B4.

[24] Kathryn Kranhold, Wall St. J., August 2, 2004.

[25] Kathryn Kranhold, Wall St. J., August 2, 2004.

Thailand, and the Philippines in connection with the sale of airport security screening machines.[26] The SEC also alleged that InVision failed to adequately investigate and train its foreign agents and lacked proper internal controls to monitor FCPA compliance.[27] On December 6, 2004, InVision reached an agreement with the DOJ to pay $800,000 in penalties and to negotiate a settlement in the SEC's parallel investigation.[28] As part of the ultimate resolution with the DOJ, GE completed the acquisition, agreeing to integrate InVision into its FCPA compliance programme, effectuate the performance of InVision's obligations, refrain from contradicting the government allegations, and disclose any other potential FCPA issues it discovered in connection with InVision's pre-acquisition conduct.[29] InVision paid the DOJ settlement and also a settlement reached with the SEC in February 2005 for approximately $1.1 million in disgorgement of profits, interest, and penalties.[30]

In an October 2006 speech at an American Bar Association event, the Assistant Attorney General Alice S. Fisher praised GE while highlighting the importance of FCPA due diligence:

> "[B]ecause the conduct was discovered before the transaction was completed, GE avoided having to potentially accept successor liability for InVision's conduct. Although GE entered into a separate agreement with the Department to ensure InVision's compliance..., think of the potential consequences to GE if they had not performed thorough due diligence in that case."[31]

An acquirer that discovers FCPA compliance issues prior to closing can shield itself from liability for a target's violations. A less vigilant acquirer may be held accountable for the entirety of the pre-acquisition misconduct upon discovery.

IV. Vetco Gray

10–10   Repeat offender Vetco Gray demonstrates that an acquirer's anti-bribery obligations are not limited to due diligence. ABB, a leading power and automation technology company, agreed to sell its upstream oil and gas subsidiaries—ABB Vetco Gray Inc and ABB Vetco Gray (UK) Ltd—to a private equity investment

---

[26] Press Release No. 04-780, DOJ, InVision Technologies, Inc. Enters Into Agreement with the United States (December 6, 2004).

[27] Litigation Release No. 19078, SEC, *SEC Settles Charges Against InVision Technologies for $1.1 Million for Violations of the Foreign Corrupt Practices Act* (February 14, 2005).

[28] Press Release No. 04-780, DOJ, *InVision Technologies, Inc. Enters Into Agreement with the United States* (December 6, 2004).

[29] Press Release No. 04-780, DOJ, *InVision Technologies, Inc. Enters Into Agreement with the United States* (December 6, 2004).

[30] Litigation Release No. 19078, SEC, *SEC Settles Charges Against InVision Technologies for $1.1 Million for Violations of the Foreign Corrupt Practices Act* (February 14, 2005).

[31] Alice S. Fisher, *Prepared Remarks at the American Bar Association National Institute on the Foreign Corrupt Practices Act* (October 16, 2006).

group in October 2003.[32] After discovering certain improper payments, ABB and the investment group jointly conducted an extensive FCPA compliance review and voluntarily disclosed their findings to the DOJ and the SEC.[33] Chief among the Vetco Gray entities' FCPA violations were the payments of cash and gifts to officials of the Nigerian state-owned agency responsible for overseeing investment in petroleum.[34] In return, the company received a highly lucrative contract to provide drilling equipment for Nigeria's offshore Bonga Oil Field.[35]

ABB reached settlements with the US government in July 2004 requiring it to pay $5.9 million in disgorgement of unlawful profits and $10.5 million in criminal fines.[36] The acquirer avoided liability and further shielded itself by seeking and obtaining an advisory opinion that the DOJ did not intend to take additional action against the investment group or the newly acquired entities with respect to the pre-acquisition FCPA violations.[37] In obtaining this favourable outcome, the acquirers represented that they would adopt a "rigorous anti-corruption compliance code ... to detect and deter violations of the FCPA and foreign anti-corruption laws" that they outlined in substantial detail.[38]

Despite devising a suitable FCPA compliance programme, the successor entity failed to follow through with it. The newly formed Vetco International Ltd later voluntarily disclosed that subsidiaries Vetco Gray Controls Inc, Vetco Gray Controls Ltd, and Vetco Gray UK Ltd had continued making improper payments several months after the transaction.[39] According to the DOJ, from at least September 2002 (nearly two years prior to the new company's formation) to April 2005, the Vetco Gray subsidiaries authorised at least 378 corrupt payments totalling $2.1 million to Nigerian government officials.[40] The Vetco Gray subsidiaries agreed to pay criminal fines in the aggregate amount of $26 million, which was the largest FCPA criminal fine to date.[41]

In demanding such a large monetary penalty, the DOJ indicated that the repeat **10–11** nature of the conduct and the failure to abide by the compliance programme outlined in the FCPA Opinion Release contributed to the amount.[42] The DOJ

---

[32] Press Release, ABB, *ABB concludes compliance review of upstream Oil, Gas and Petrochemicals business* (July 7, 2004).

[33] Press Release, ABB, *ABB concludes compliance review of upstream Oil, Gas and Petrochemicals business* (July 7, 2004).

[34] Complaint at 3, *SEC v ABB Ltd*, No. 04-CV-01141 (DDC July 6, 2004).

[35] See fn.34 at 4.

[36] Litigation Release No. 18775, SEC, *SEC Sues ABB Ltd. in Foreign Bribery Case* (July 6, 2004).

[37] FCPA Opinion Procedure Release 04-02, DOJ (July 12, 2004), available through *http://www.usdoj.gov* [Accessed July 15, 2010].

[38] See fn.32 above.

[39] Press Release No. 07-075, DOJ, *Three Vetco International Ltd. Subsidiaries Plead Guilty to Foreign Bribery and Agree to Pay $26 Million in Criminal Fines* (February 6, 2007).

[40] Press Release No. 07-075, DOJ, *Three Vetco International Ltd. Subsidiaries Plead Guilty to Foreign Bribery and Agree to Pay $26 Million in Criminal Fines* (February 6, 2007).

[41] Press Release No. 07-075, DOJ, *Three Vetco International Ltd. Subsidiaries Plead Guilty to Foreign Bribery and Agree to Pay $26 Million in Criminal Fines* (February 6, 2007).

[42] Press Release No. 07-075, DOJ, *Three Vetco International Ltd. Subsidiaries Plead Guilty to Foreign Bribery and Agree to Pay $26 Million in Criminal Fines* (February 6, 2007).

detailed the required conduct under the terms of the Opinion Release before remarking, in calculating the fine:

> "The corrupt payments underlying today's guilty pleas continued unabated from the period prior to the acquisition until at least mid-2005, notwithstanding the acquirer's commitments to the Justice Department under the Opinion Release. The sale to new owners, the prior directives issued by the Department of Justice, and Vetco Gray UK's prior conviction were all taken into account."[43]

This should put acquirers on notice that thorough due diligence does not shelter them from punishment for pre-acquisition conduct if the conduct is permitted to continue. Moreover, if an acquirer chooses to seek an advisory opinion from the DOJ that it does not intend to pursue action against the acquirer on account of a proposed compliance programme, the acquirer must actually follow through with its proposal. Failure to do so may compound the liability for future or continued FCPA violations rather than protecting the company from it.

V. Halliburton

10–12   The case of Halliburton provides a cautionary example of what can happen when an acquirer's FCPA due diligence and FCPA compliance efforts are both unsatisfactory. In September 1998, Halliburton acquired Dresser Industries.[44] The M.W. Kellogg Company, a subsidiary of Dresser Industries, was then combined with Halliburton subsidiary Brown & Root to form Kellogg, Brown & Root ("KBR").[45] According to pleadings, KBR was part of a joint venture which won several contracts worth more than $6 billion to construct liquefied natural gas production facilities on Bonny Island, Nigeria.[46]

In 2003, the DOJ and the SEC began investigating the conduct of the joint venture in response to allegations that it had made improper payments to Nigerian government officials through agents or subcontractors.[47] While the investigations were ongoing, Halliburton sought to separate itself from KBR. To enhance KBR's financial position for a spin-off, Halliburton indemnified KBR for any penalties or monetary damages resulting from violations of the FCPA and other anti-corruption laws in connection with the existing investigations.[48]

KBR and former parent Halliburton settled the US government investigations in February 2009 for a total amount of $579 million, including $177 million in

---

[43] Press Release No. 07-075, DOJ, *Three Vetco International Ltd. Subsidiaries Plead Guilty to Foreign Bribery and Agree to Pay $26 Million in Criminal Fines* (February 6, 2007).

[44] Complaint at 1, *SEC v Halliburton Co and KBR, Inc*, No. 4:09-CV-399, (S.D. Tex. (Houston) February 11, 2009).

[45] Complaint at 1, *SEC v Halliburton Co and KBR, Inc*, No. 4:09-CV-399, (S.D. Tex. (Houston) February 11, 2009).

[46] Complaint at 2.

[47] *Halliburton Announces Settlement of Department of Justice and Securities and Exchange Commission Foreign Corrupt Practices Act Investigations*, Reuters, February 11, 2009, available through http://www.reuters.com [Accessed July 15, 2010].

[48] See fn.47 above.

disgorgement of profits and $402 million in fines.[49] The SEC alleged that beginning in 1994 or 1995, KBR predecessor M.W. Kellogg Company transacted with a UK agent for the purpose of bribing Nigerian officials to secure government construction projects.[50] Over the course of nearly a decade, from a few years before Halliburton's acquisition through the first several years of the combined KBR entity, the UK agent allegedly received more than $100 million that it systematically transferred to the accounts of high-ranking Nigerian government officials.[51] The SEC further alleged that the entities paid a Japanese agent more than $50 million between 1996 and 2004 to bribe lower-level Nigerian officials in connection with the Bonny Island projects.[52]

The SEC justified the imposition of penalties on Halliburton for both pre- **10–13** acquisition and post-acquisition conduct by detailing its failures to conduct adequate due diligence or maintain adequate internal controls. In connection with the 1998 acquisition of Dresser Industries, Halliburton's due diligence investigation "did not seek to determine how the UK Agent would or could carry out his duties" and "did not check all of the references provided by the UK Agent, some of which were false."[53] The SEC continued by claiming that Halliburton conducted no due diligence on the Japanese agent at all.[54] Halliburton's persistent inability to detect or prevent the bribery scheme, resulting falsified documents, and lack of appropriate internal controls all contributed to the record settlement amount.[55]

Halliburton was more mindful of FCPA considerations when recently bidding on public UK company Expro International. Due to legal restrictions on the bidding process, Halliburton lacked the opportunity to conduct appropriate anti-corruption due diligence prior to closing if it prevailed on its bid.[56] In order to insulate itself from potential liability, Halliburton designed a comprehensive post-closing due diligence and compliance plan and submitted its proposal to the DOJ for an advisory opinion.[57] Though Halliburton did not win its bid, the resulting favourable Opinion Release demonstrates that in certain circumstances, an acquirer can shield itself from not only pre-acquisition FCPA violations but also

---

[49] Litigation Release No. 20897A, *SEC, SEC Charges KBR, Inc. with Foreign Bribery; Charges Halliburton Co. and KBR, Inc. with Related Accounting Violations—Companies to Pay Disgorgement of $177 Million; KBR Subsidiary to Pay Criminal Fines of $402 Million; Total Payments to be $579 Million* (February 11, 2009).

[50] Complaint at 6, *SEC v Halliburton Co and KBR, Inc*, No. 4:09-CV-399, (S.D. Tex. (Houston) February 11, 2009).

[51] Complaint at 6–8.

[52] Complaint at 9.

[53] Complaint at 10–11.

[54] Complaint at 11.

[55] Litigation Release No. 20897A, SEC, *SEC Charges KBR, Inc. with Foreign Bribery; Charges Halliburton Co. and KBR, Inc. with Related Accounting Violations—Companies to Pay Disgorgement of $177 Million; KBR Subsidiary to Pay Criminal Fines of $402 Million; Total Payments to be $579 Million* (February 11, 2009).

[56] Paul R. Berger et al., *Avoiding FCPA Anxiety*, Mergers & Acquisitions, April 2009, at 46.

[57] See FCPA Opinion Procedure Release 08-02, DOJ (June 13, 2008), available through *http://www.usdoj.gov* [Accessed July 15, 2010].

post-acquisition violations for a limited time if it adheres to thorough and proper due diligence and compliance procedures.[58]

We discuss the Opinion Release further below. Halliburton's recent experiences illustrate the extremes in potential successor liability for a target's anti-bribery issues.

VI. Monsanto

10-14 Monsanto is an American agricultural company. It acquired Delta & Pine Land Company and a subsidiary; both were also US Corporations. One diligence during the acquisitions process revealed that the target had paid bribes to Turkish government officials.

The Target reported the payments to the SEC. It paid $300,000 in a civil penalty, and agreed to retain an independent monitor.[59]

VII. El Paso

10-15 The merger of El Paso Energy Corporation with Coastal Corporation demonstrated the risks that a hitherto-compliant company can face after it merges. El Paso and Coastal merged in 2001. The SEC alleged that Coastal had paid surcharges to third parties on oil purchases under the UN's oil-for-food programme. The third parties remitted those surcharges to Iraqi government officials. Some of these payments continued after the merger with El Paso.

El Paso paid a $2.2 million civil penalty to the SEC.[60] It also paid $5.5 million in disgorgement of profits to the DOJ.[61]

VIII. Opinion Release 08-02

10-16 Can companies ever fail to do their due diligence before an acquisition and still escape liability if they go ahead with the deal and later discover it? Only if exceptional circumstances exist.

The DOJ's Opinion Release Procedure (See Ch.3) provides one notable example. Ironically, perhaps, the opinion involves Halliburton, a company very familiar with the strictures of the FCPA.

Halliburton's question to the DOJ was as follows: it was interested in acquiring a UK company. The UK company did business in more than 50 countries, many of them generally viewed as corruption-prone. UK listing rules required that

---

[58] See FCPA Opinion Procedure Release 08-02, DOJ (June 13, 2008), available through *http://www.usdoj.gov* [Accessed July 15, 2010].

[59] *SEC v Delta & Pine Land Co* SEC Lit. Ref. No. 20214 (July 26, 2007)

[60] *SEC v El Paso Corp*m Lit. Ref. No. 19991 (February 7, 2007).

[61] *US Announces Oil-for-Food Settlement with El Paso Corporation* available through *http://www.usdoj.gov*.

Halliburton tender a bid for the company before having been able to conduct thorough due diligence.

Halliburton therefore asked the DOJ whether it would be immune from suc- **10–17** cessor liability if it won the bid, acquired the company, conducted an extensive post-acquisition due diligence review, and reported its findings to the DOJ.

The DOJ opined that the circumstances exempted Halliburton from pre-acquisition due diligence and successor liability.[62] In doing so, however, the DOJ relied on Halliburton's explicit undertaking to conduct a post-acquisition due diligence review and to report all its findings to the DOJ.[63]

The Halliburton case represented a special circumstance because UK legal requirements did not give Halliburton the time to conduct due diligence in the ordinary course. It seems unlikely that regulators would take an indulgent view of a company's failure to conduct pre-acquisition due diligence where no such special circumstances existed to prevent it.

C. BEST PRACTICES

I. COMPREHENSIVE DUE DILIGENCE/PROTECTIVE CONTRACTUAL PROVISIONS/ FCPA COMPLIANCE PROGRAM INTEGRATION

Recently, the number of FCPA proceedings and penalty amounts have increased **10–18** dramatically.[64] For example, in 2009 alone, a Halliburton subsidiary settled FCPA charges with the SEC and DOJ for over $570 million.[65] However, the fine or penalty may not be the worst repercussion of a FCPA violation. Collateral consequences of a FCPA violation can include lawsuits by shareholders, loss of government contracts (and the right to seek future government contracts), a decline in a company's share price, and even law suits by competitors.[66]

Towards the end of the first decade of this century and the beginning of the second, non-American regulators have also finally begin to flex their muscles as they exercise their anti-bribery authority.

To avoid negative repercussions, companies must do extensive due diligence within the mergers and acquisition setting. This should consist of a three part

---

[62] DOJ Opinion of Release 08–02.
[63] DOJ Opinion of Release 08–02.
[64] See Joel M. Cohen, Michael P. Holland & Adam P. Wolf, Under the FCPA, *Who is a Foreign Official Anyway?* 63 Bus. Law 1243 at 1247 (2008); Nelson D. Schwartz & Lowell Bergman, *Payload: Taking Aim at the Corporate Bribery*, *New York Times*, November 25, 2007, at 31.
[65] FCPA Opinion Procedure Release 08–02, DOJ (June 13, 2008), available through http://www.usdoj.gov.
[66] Roger M. Witten et al., *Prescriptions for Compliance with the Foreign Corrupt Practices Act: Identifying Bribery Risks and Implementing Anti-Bribery Controls in Pharmaceutical and Life Sciences Companies*, 64 Bus. Law. 691.

programme of: comprehensive due diligence, negotiating protective contractual provisions and anti-bribery compliance programme integration.[67]

10–19   These steps are important not only to assess whether a target's current business dealings violate anti-bribery provisions but also to limit the potential exposure to liability for actions of the acquiring entity. Following these steps *may* sufficiently demonstrate to regulators that an acquirer lacked knowledge of improper behaviours.

Entities should take extreme care. The FCPA can have long arms even when not conducting business in the tradition sense in the United States. The FCPA does not apply to non–US affiliates or subsidiaries *unless* conducting business in the United States that advances a FCPA violation.[68] However, conduct in violation of the Act can be as simple as sending emails, making telephone calls, and wire transfers to or from the United States.

Since the laws of the FCPA are the most stringent and still by far the most frequently invoked of any country, complying with the FCPA will most likely make a company compliant under the laws of a foreign country. Advice for conducting an effective due diligence review, tips on drafting effective contractual provisions and compliance programme integration techniques are discussed in detail below.

II. COMPREHENSIVE DUE DILIGENCE

10–20   A comprehensive due diligence programme should include (1) risk assessment (identifying red flags), (2) a tailored review of red flags and (3) appropriate reaction to the results of the review.[69] Vigilant care must be given to each step.

(a) Risk Assessment—Identifying Red Flags

10–21   The first step in the due diligence process for an acquirer is to identify red flags.

Evaluating the Country

10–22   One of the biggest factors to be considered is the corruptibility of a country's public officials. The most frequently used and commonly accepted gauge of such corruptibility is Transparency International's Corruption Perception Index. The index ranks countries on a scale from 1 to 10, with 1 being the most corrupt.[70] Certain counties have a long history of corruption and extensive due diligence

---

[67] Martin J. Weinstein, *The World of International Compliance: What Transactional Lawyers Need to Know to Perform Ethically and Responsibly*, 29 Hous. J. Int'l L. 311 at 312 (2007).

[68] FCPA § 103(b) codified at 15 U.S.C. § 78ff(c)(2)(A) (2006

[69] J. Weinstein, *The World of International Compliance: What Transactional Lawyers Need to Know to Perform Ethically and Responsibly*, 29 Hous. J. Int'l L. 311 at 312 (2007).

[70] See Transparency International, *Transparency International Corruption Perceptions Index 2008*, available through *http://www.transparency.org* [Accessed July 15, 2010] (The CPI ranks 180 countries by their perceived levels of corruption using expert assessments and opinion surveys. A ranking of 1 being most corrupt with 10 being least corrupt).

should take place when considering doing business in these areas. See map below.[71]

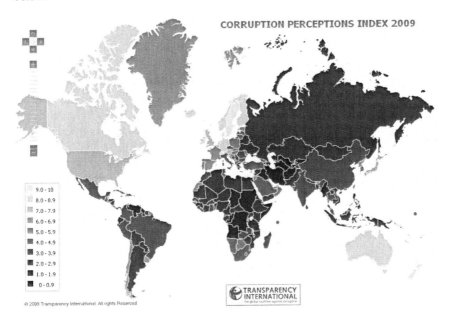

CORRUPTION PERCEPTIONS INDEX 2009

9.0 - 10
8.0 - 8.9
7.0 - 7.9
6.0 - 6.9
5.0 - 5.9
4.0 - 4.9
3.0 - 3.9
2.0 - 2.9
1.0 - 1.9
0 - 0.9

© 2009 Transparency International. All rights Reserved.

TRANSPARENCY INTERNATIONAL

Transparency International's Corruption Perceptions Index measures the perceived level of public sector corruption as seen by business people and country analysts; ranging between 10 (highly clean) and 0 (highly corrupt)

A country's poor reputation regarding corruption is a major red flag. This may put an acquirer on notice that a target company hailing from or doing extensive business I that country may have committed an anti-bribery law violation in the past or may do so in the future.[72] Many unacceptable payment cases have come from the same cluster of countries. Underwriters and acquirers should be familiar with the index above.

Assess the Nature of the Business

The exact level of due diligence review required prior to a merger or acquisition will depend on a range of factors. After evaluating the countries in which a target company does business an acquirer should evaluate the *nature* of the target's business in *every* country in which it operates. At the very least, the following questions should be addressed:

10–23

---

[71] Transparency International, *Transparency International Corruption Perceptions Index 2008.*
[72] Valerie Ford Jacob, *The Foreign Corrupt Practices Act and the Due Diligence Process*, 1545 Prac. L. Inst./Corp. 59 at 64–65 (2006).

What kinds of products does the target company sell?
Some industries have a long history of violations. Red flags are raised when dealing in defence, oil, aviation engineering and construction.[73]

Does the target employ a direct sales force or use third parties?
Improper payments are often funnelled through third parties. Often, "consultants" are paid large sums of money despite little experience and services rendered.[74] The use of agents and consultants may suggest an increased risk for corruption as these third parties are outside the direct control of the target.[75] Thus, it is extremely important to make sure that you have formed a business affiliation with a trustworthy and knowledgeable agent.[76] Some agents in foreign countries are notorious for their illegal conduct. By employing one of these agents, an acquirer may be put on notice that payments may be going to foreign officials, in violation of anti-bribery laws.[77] It is always helpful to ask the following additional questions when dealing with third parties:

- Did the target do due diligence on the third party agent prior to conducting business (was a record check, background check and approval process followed)?

- What is the reputation of the agent with the acquiring company's national consulate, local business, and clients?

- What is the character and quantity of the agent's clients?

- Is the agent's commission above the "going rate"?

- Have there been improper payment audits or government investigations in the recent past?

- Are third parties willing to agree in writing to comply with anti-bribery and certify they have complied fully in the past?

- Has there been public knowledge of commercial bribes or kick-backs to consumers or others?[78]

Questionable answers to any of the above questions should raise red flags.

---

[73] V. Jacob, 1545 Prac. L. Inst./Corp. 59.

[74] V. Jacob, 1545 Prac. L. Inst./Corp. 59.

[75] Martin J. Weinstein, *The World of International Compliance: What Transactional Lawyers Need to Know to Perform Ethically and Responsibly*, 29 Hous. J. Int'l L. 311 at 322 (2007).

[76] Lay Person's Guide to FCPA: Anti-bribery Provisions, DOJ, available through *http://www.usdoj.gov*.

[77] Valerie Ford Jacob, *The Foreign Corrupt Practices Act and Due Diligence Process*, 1545 Prac. L. Inst./Corp. 59 at 66 (2006).

[78] See Martin J. Weinstein, *The World of International Compliance: What Transactional Lawyers Need to Know to Perform Ethically and Responsibly*, 29 Hous. J. Int'l L. 311 at 321–322 (2007); *Lay Person's Guide to FCPA: Anti-bribery Provisions*, DOJ, available through *http://www.usdoj.gov*; Roger M. Witten et al., *Prescriptions for Compliance with the Foreign Corrupt Practices Act: Identifying Bribery Risks and Implementing Anti-Bribery Controls in Pharmaceutical and Life Sciences Companies*, 64 Bus. Law. 691 at 732 (Section III.B); Valerie Ford Jacob, *The Foreign Corrupt Practices Act and Due Diligence Process*, 1545 Prac. L. Inst./Corp. 59 at 64–5 (2006).

Assess The Degree of Government Interaction

The degree to which a company conducts business with foreign officials should be **10-24**
given heavy weight. Doing business with an agent or third party employed by a
company with foreign officials as members, partners or equity owners is a very
high risk violation condition.[79] Moreover, a large number of foreign companies are
entirely or in some measure owned by government entities.[80] Under the FCPA
and other anti-bribery laws, conducting business with some of these entities may
be seen as giving an improper benefit to a government official even if the company
thought it was entering a legitimate transaction.[81] As the ownership of a foreign
target company is not always readily discernible, it is best to ask third parties to
identify their ownership from the onset of any transaction.[82]

Additionally, one must ask if the agent or third party employed has been
recommended by a local government official. An affirmative answer may suggest
an illegal arrangement for kickbacks. Finally, if the target business requires
government licenses, approvals, interaction with customs agents, police or military officials, the risk of anti-bribery law violations may be very high.[83] Questions
used to identify red flags in this area should include:

- What is the overall involvement of government officials in the company's
  business?

- What percentage of business comes from public institutions in each
  international market?

- Which departments need regulatory approvals and registrations?

- What is the relationship of any third party agents to the company?[84]

Assess the Target's Business Intelligence

While hard to define, one should be wary of generally suspicious conduct. If the **10-25**
deal simply seems suspicious, there may be a hidden violation of the anti-bribery
laws. This includes unusual payment patterns, lack of transparency in the

---

[79] Valerie Ford Jacob, *The Foreign Corrupt Practices Act and Due Diligence Process*, 1545 Prac. L.
Inst./Corp. 59 at 65 (2006).
[80] Priya C. Huskins, *FCPA Prosecutions: Liability Trend to Watch*, 60 Stan. L.Rev. 1447 at 1456
(March 2008).
[81] Priya C. Huskins, *FCPA Prosecutions: Liability Trend to Watch*, 60 Stan. L.Rev. 1447 at 1456
(March 2008).
[82] Priya C. Huskins, *FCPA Prosecutions: Liability Trend to Watch*, 60 Stan. L.Rev. 1447 at 1456
(March 2008).
[83] Martin J. Weinstein, *The World of International Compliance: What Transactional Lawyers Need to
Know to Perform Ethically and Responsibly*, 29 Hous. J. Int'l L. 311 at 322 (2007).
[84] Valerie Ford Jacob, *The Foreign Corrupt Practices Act and Due Diligence Process*, 1545 Prac. L.
Inst./Corp. 59 at 65 (2006); Priya C. Huskins, *FCPA Prosecutions: Liability Trend to Watch*, 60 Stan.
L.Rev.1447 at 1455–1456 (March 2008); Roger M. Witten et al., *Prescriptions for Compliance with the
Foreign Corrupt Practices Act: Identifying Bribery Risks and Implementing Anti-Bribery Controls in
Pharmaceutical and Life Sciences Companies*, 64 Bus. Law. 691 at 732.

accounting records, suspicious entries in a target's books and records, advanced payments, significant write- offs, political contributions and unusually loose credit terms.[85] Important questions to ask include:

- Have large or atypical bonuses been paid to managers of foreign operations?

- Have transactions been recorded as "cash" without proper documentation?

- Are there unusual payment patterns or off- shore payments?

- What is the overall "tone at the top"?

- What is the state of the targets books?[86]

Assess the Target's Compliance Programme

10–26   Risk assessment should always include an evaluation of the target company's compliance programme. This must include a review of all policies and procedures designed to make certain a company is compliant with applicable anti-bribery laws and standards.[87] Obviously, a lack of a compliance programme is a red flag unto itself. Conversely, a written policy with no controls or implementation is also a red flag.

It is important to focus compliance training in the areas and countries at highest risk for violation. Additionally, employees in certain positions are more likely to be bribed.[88] Careful review of the conduct of these employees should be undertaken. Questions should include:

- Is there a formal compliance programme?

- Is the program overseen by the appropriate personnel? [89]

- Have all offices and employees received training?

- Is training mandatory and updated regularly?

---

[85] See Priya C. Huskins, *FCPA Prosecutions: Liability Trend to Watch*, 60 Stan. L.Rev.1447 at 1455 (March 2008); Roger M. Witten et al., *Prescriptions for Compliance with the Foreign Corrupt Practices Act: Identifying Bribery Risks and Implementing Anti-Bribery Controls in Pharmaceutical and Life Sciences Companies*, 64 Bus. Law. 691 (Section III.B); Lay Person's Guide to FCPA: Anti-bribery Provisions, DOJ, available through *http://www.usdoj.gov.*

[86] See fn.85 above.

[87] Martin J. Weinstein, *The World of International Compliance: What Transactional Lawyers Need to Know to Perform Ethically and Responsibly*, 29 Hous. J. Int'l L. 311 at 322 (2007).

[88] Priya C. Huskins, *FCPA Prosecutions: Liability Trend to Watch*, 60 Stan. L.Rev.1447 at 1455 (March 2008).

[89] Roger M. Witten et al., *Prescriptions for Compliance with the Foreign Corrupt Practices Act: Identifying Bribery Risks and Implementing Anti-Bribery Controls in Pharmaceutical and Life Sciences Companies*, 64 Bus. Law. 691 at 736.

- Do all employees have access to guidance for bribery related issues?

- Can assistance be given anonymously?[90]

Components of a proper compliance programme are discussed in detail in Ch.11.

(b) Tailored Review

The pre-existing due diligence files of a target's agents should be acquired and reviewed along with the target's files.[91] Once red flags have been identified, a due diligence review workplan tailored to address high risk red flags should be created. Red flags should be organised into high risk, medium risk and low risk categories.[92] This should include a review of applicable documents and emails and conducting interviews with appropriate personnel and third parties.[93] A full examination should be conducted of expense reports (including entertainment and meals), gifts for government officials, correspondence with government officials, licenses obtained and copies of contracts with government officials.[94] Careful attention should be given to any indication of human rights abuse through written records or reports by the media.[95]

    10–27

The work plan should be implemented immediately. If need be, the acquiring entity should enlist the help of outside counsel, third party consultants, forensic accountants, and use proper internal resources to conduct the anti-corruption due diligence review.[96] Periodically, the work plan should be reviewed and revised if necessary as new information is learned.[97] All information gathered should be evaluated and documented in a written due diligence report.[98]

(c) Reacting to Results of the Review

After carrying out the work plan, a company should determine if potential violations are severe enough adversely to affect the proposed transaction.[99] Potential

    10–28

---

[90] Priya C. Huskins, *FCPA Prosecutions: Liability Trend to Watch*, 60 Stan. L.Rev.1447 at 1454–1455 (March 2008).

[91] Martin J. Weinstein, *The World of International Compliance: What Transactional Lawyers Need to Know to Perform Ethically and Responsibly*, 29 Hous. J. Int'l L. 311 at 325 (2007).

[92] See FCPA Opinion Procedure Release 08–02, DOJ (June 13, 2008), available through *http://www.usdoj.gov*.

[93] Martin J. Weinstein, *The World of International Compliance: What Transactional Lawyers Need to Know to Perform Ethically and Responsibly*, 29 Hous. J. Int'l L. 311 at 325 (2007).

[94] Martin J. Weinstein, *The World of International Compliance: What Transactional Lawyers Need to Know to Perform Ethically and Responsibly*, 29 Hous. J. Int'l L. 311 at 325 (2007).

[95] Martin J. Weinstein, *The World of International Compliance: What Transactional Lawyers Need to Know to Perform Ethically and Responsibly*, 29 Hous. J. Int'l L. 311 at 325 (2007).

[96] See FCPA Opinion Procedure Release 08-02, DOJ (June 13, 2008), available through *http://www.usdoj.gov*.

[97] See FCPA Opinion Procedure Release 08-02, DOJ (June 13, 2008), available through *http://www.usdoj.gov*.

[98] Martin J. Weinstein, *The World of International Compliance: What Transactional Lawyers Need to Know to Perform Ethically and Responsibly*, 29 Hous. J. Int'l L. 311 at 325 (2007).

[99] Martin J. Weinstein, *The World of International Compliance: What Transactional Lawyers Need to Know to Perform Ethically and Responsibly*, 29 Hous. J. Int'l L. 311 at 325 (2007).

liability for violations should be weighed against any potential benefit from the transaction. Keep in mind disclosure to the acquirer's government may be required and criminal and civil liability may be pursued.[100] If information is voluntarily disclosed to the US government, for example, full cooperation with the DOJ and SEC should take place.[101] As shown above, the DOJ has been more lenient in determining whether to prosecute FCPA violators when a timely disclosure has been made and a company has shown a willingness to cooperate with authorities.[102] An acquirer may request an opinion from the DOJ based on specific red flags discovered, but time constraints of the merger or acquisition may make this option unrealistic.

If the transaction is to proceed, pre-existing compliance problems should be addressed prior to closing. If this is not possible, corrective measures should be taken as soon as possible. This can include, but is not limited to, disclosures to the investing public (if appropriate), instructions given to employees to cease payments to foreign officials, exporting the acquirer's compliance programme to the target company, penalising employees who have committed violations, requiring follow-up procedures and demanding executed compliance certifications.[103] These safeguards are often memorialised in contractual provisions and the integration of a new compliance programme. These steps will be discussed in further detail below.

III. CONTRACTUAL PROTECTIONS

10–29   In addition to conducting a thorough due diligence review, contractual provisions may help limit anti-bribery violation liability. These two safeguards must go hand-in-hand, representations and warranties alone are usually insufficient to protect an acquiring company from liability and reputation damage.[104] The types of contractual protections sought will depend on the due diligence findings and the types of red flags discovered.[105] At the very least, standard provisions on

---

[100] Martin J. Weinstein, *The World of International Compliance: What Transactional Lawyers Need to Know to Perform Ethically and Responsibly*, 29 Hous. J. Int'l L. 311 at 325 (2007). See also *FCPA Opinion Procedure Release 08-02*, DOJ (June 13, 2008), available through *http://www.usdoj.gov*.

[101] Martin J. Weinstein, *The World of International Compliance: What Transactional Lawyers Need to Know to Perform Ethically and Responsibly*, 29 Hous. J. Int'l L. 311 at 325 (2007). See also *FCPA Opinion Procedure Release 08-02*, DOJ (June 13, 2008), available through *http://www.usdoj.gov*.

[102] *Principals of Federal Prosecution of Business Organizations*, DOJ (January 20, 2003); available through *http://www.usdoj.gov* (The Thompson Memo).

[103] Martin J. Weinstein, *The World of International Compliance: What Transactional Lawyers Need to Know to Perform Ethically and Responsibly*, 29 Hous. J. Int'l L. 311 at 325 (2007); FCPA Opinion Procedure Release 2003-01, DOJ (January 15, 2003), available through *http://www.usdoj.gov*.

[104] Roger M. Witten et al., *Prescriptions for Compliance with the Foreign Corrupt Practices Act: Identifying Bribery Risks and Implementing Anti-Bribery Controls in Pharmaceutical and Life Sciences Companies*, 64 Bus. Law. 691 at 736 (2009).

[105] Roger M. Witten et al., *Prescriptions for Compliance with the Foreign Corrupt Practices Act: Identifying Bribery Risks and Implementing Anti-Bribery Controls in Pharmaceutical and Life Sciences Companies*, 64 Bus. Law. 691 at 736 (2009).

compliance with the acquirer's and local anti-bribery laws should be incorporated into the deal documents.[106]

Furthermore, certain additional provisions may need to be tailored to the transaction, including recusal certifications. These should be used to stop government officials from servicing shareholders, officers, directors or employees of the target company.[107] Acquirers may also require indemnification provisions or condition closing on the resolution of any violations.[108] Counsel should be enlisted in drafting provisions in order to best limit liability.

The acquiring company should also directly enter into new agent agreements with all third parties. The new contracts should use specific and unambiguous language in which both parties agree not to conduct themselves in a way that would violate the anti-bribery laws.[109] At a minimum, the representations and warranties of these contracts should include: confirmation that the parties are aware of the terms of applicable anti-bribery laws; an agreement not to violate them; an agreement not to pay money to foreign officials or unapproved third parties; and a representation that the party is not an agent, employee or officer of a foreign government. [110]

One final but important contractual provision should require an acquirer to **10–30** alter or export the parent company's compliance programme onto the target company.[111]

Sample standard contractual provisions are provided below:

- (FCPA Representation) The Company is in compliance in all material respects with the provisions of the Foreign Corrupt Practices Act of 1977, as amended. Neither the Company nor any of its Subsidiaries nor, to the knowledge of the Company, any director, officer, agent, employee or other Person acting on behalf of the Company or any of its Subsidiaries, has (i) used any corporate or other funds for unlawful contributions, payments, gifts or entertainment, or made any unlawful expenditures relating to

---

[106] Roger M. Witten et al., *Prescriptions for Compliance with the Foreign Corrupt Practices Act: Identifying Bribery Risks and Implementing Anti-Bribery Controls in Pharmaceutical and Life Sciences Companies*, 64 Bus. Law. 691 at 736 (2009).

[107] Roger M. Witten et al., *Prescriptions for Compliance with the Foreign Corrupt Practices Act: Identifying Bribery Risks and Implementing Anti-Bribery Controls in Pharmaceutical and Life Sciences Companies*, 64 Bus. Law. 691 at 736 (2009).

[108] Roger M. Witten et al., *Prescriptions for Compliance with the Foreign Corrupt Practices Act: Identifying Bribery Risks and Implementing Anti-Bribery Controls in Pharmaceutical and Life Sciences Companies*, 64 Bus. Law. 691 at 736 (2009).

[109] Priya C. Huskins, *FCPA Prosecutions: Liability Trend to Watch*, 60 Stan. L.Rev.1447 at 1456 (March 2008).

[110] Valerie Ford Jacob, *The Foreign Corrupt Practices Act and Due Diligence Process*, 1545 Prac. L. Inst./Corp. 59, 64-65; *FCPA Opinion Procedure Release 2001-01*, DOJ (May 24, 2001), available through *http://www.usdoj.gov*.

[111] See FCPA Opinion Procedure Release 08-02, DOJ (June 13, 2008), available through *http:// www.usdoj.gov*.

political activity to government officials or others or established or maintained any unlawful or unrecorded funds in violation of the Foreign Corrupt Practices Act of 1977, as amended.[112]

- (Closing Condition) As of the date of closing, neither the company nor any of its Subsidiaries has received written notice to the effect that a Governmental Authority claimed or alleged that the Company was not in compliance with any Law applicable to the Company.[113]

- (Third Party) Acquirer would take appropriate remedial actions in the event that it discovers any FCPA or corruption-related problems, including suspending or terminating any agents and other third parties and taking relevant remedial action regarding employees.[114]

- (Compliance Program) Upon closing Acquirer will immediately impose its own Code of Business Conduct and specific FCPA and anti-corruption policies and procedures on Target, including effectively communicating the same to all employees. Within 90 days of closing, Acquirer will proved FCPA and anti-corruption training to all Target employees whose positions warrant training on an expedited basis, including employees in management, sales, accounting and financial control positions. Acquirer shall provide training to all other employees within 90 days of closing.[115]

IV. COMPLIANCE PROGRAMME INTEGRATION

10–31   Once a deal has closed, it is important to implement an effective compliance programme immediately.[116] To the extent possible, modifications to the programme should take place prior to closing in order to halt improper practices early on.[117]

Anti-bribery laws generally do not set out specific requirements for an ideal FCPA compliance programme. However, government advisory opinions and the terms of settlement agreements that have resolved enforcement proceedings may serve as guidelines. It should be noted, in the case of advisory opinions from US

---

[112] See *Glazer Capital Management, LP v Sergio Magistri*, 2008 LEXIS 24245 1 at 9 (referring to violations of the Securities and Exchange Act of 1934); Complaint at 3, *SEC v Titan Corp*, No. 05-0411 (JR), 2005 WL 516541 (DDC March 30, 2005).

[113] *Glazer* at 9–10.

[114] See FCPA Opinion Procedure Release 08-02, DOJ (June 13, 2008), available through *http://www.usdoj.gov*.

[115] See FCPA Opinion Procedure Release 08-02, DOJ (June 13, 2008), available through *http://www.usdoj.gov*.

[116] See *FCPA Opinion Procedure Release 03-01*, DOJ (January 15, 2003), available through *http://www.usdoj.gov*.

[117] Roger M. Witten et al., *Prescriptions for Compliance with the Foreign Corrupt Practices Act: Identifying Bribery Risks and Implementing Anti-Bribery Controls in Pharmaceutical and Life Sciences Companies*, 64 Bus. Law. 691 at 736 (2009).

regulators, that the terms of particular opinions can only be enforced by parties to the proceedings and are not legally binding on others.[118] However, these opinions do reflect the US government's approach to compliance programmes and should be used as guides.[119]

An ideal compliance programme should be tailored to specific industries, company size, countries of business, clientele, interaction with government officials, and deal terms.[120] Understanding the organisation and operational aspects of a company is the first step in implementing an effective company-specific compliance programme.[121] Still, all compliance programs should include certain core components. These include:

- (Written compliance code) A clearly articulated compliance code against violations of domestic and foreign anti-bribery laws. The code should include detailed operational policies and procedures that address specific risks. Prohibitions on bribery, guidelines for permissible gifts to government officials and procedures for hiring thirds party agents should be addressed (including background checks). The written code should also clearly articulate disciplinary procedures for non-compliance which should include termination of employees. Conversely, compliance rewards and incentives may be tied to the compensation process. The code should be written practically and simply so that all levels of employees can understand it. Specific examples of acceptable and unacceptable behaviour should be listed in the written policy. The compliance code should be disseminated to all employees, officers and agents and updated periodically. Officers and employees should be required to submit periodic written certifications confirming that they have no knowledge of violations.[122]

- (Tone at the Top) Senior executives should establish a no-nonsense "tone at the top" towards incompliance. Although this is a hard issue to address, it is very important. Even the most comprehensive compliance program will have little weight within the company if it is not take seriously by those in charge. Senior officers must be highly visible in instructing employees and agents on how to comply with anti-bribery regulations.

---

[118] Roger M. Witten et al., *Prescriptions for Compliance with the Foreign Corrupt Practices Act: Identifying Bribery Risks and Implementing Anti-Bribery Controls in Pharmaceutical and Life Sciences Companies*, 64 Bus. Law. 691 at 723 (2009).

[119] Roger M. Witten et al., *Prescriptions for Compliance with the Foreign Corrupt Practices Act: Identifying Bribery Risks and Implementing Anti-Bribery Controls in Pharmaceutical and Life Sciences Companies*, 64 Bus. Law. 691 at 723 (2009).

[120] FCPA Opinion Procedure Release 08-02, DOJ (June 13, 2008), available through *http://www.usdoj.gov*.

[121] FCPA Opinion Procedure Release 08-02, DOJ (June 13, 2008), available through *http://www.usdoj.gov*.

[122] See FCPA Opinion Procedure Release 04-02, DOJ (July 12, 2004), available through *http://www.usdoj.gov*; FCPA Opinion Procedure Release 03-01, DOJ (January 15, 2003), available through *http://www.usdoj.gov*; Priya C. Huskins, *FCPA Prosecutions: Liability Trend to Watch*, 60 Stan. L.Rev. 1447 at 1454 (March 2008).

Compliance officers should include a high profile executive in addition to a legal department employee. In addition to formal trainings, senior officers should inform employees of times when managers refused to violate the anti-bribery laws and/or the company compliance code. Finally, officers must be consistent in the tone that they set.[123]

- (Risk Areas) Additional guidance should be given to employees doing business in countries and industries where local business norms often violate the anti-bribery laws. More effort should be spent training employees in countries with a high on The Corruption Perceptions Index. Employees in a position most likely to be bribed should be identified and monitored closely.[124]

- (Records) Accounting and records systems should be properly maintained and updated regularly. Expenses, government contracts, donations, travel, entertainment and gifts should be documented in detailed reports. Supporting invoices should be maintained electronically. Finance department personnel should be trained in identifying red flags including dealings with government officials, checks made out to "cash", payments to suspicious third parties, payments to off shore accounts, and large charitable contributions. See Section A above for a more detailed description of red flags. Internal and external audits should be conducted periodically.

- (Mandatory Training and Updates) Serious and effective training is critical to the efficacy of the compliance programme. Training should be mandatory (with attendance recorded) and initially conducted in person. Email reminders of training sessions should be sent. Employees should repeat training every couple of years. Periodic compliance newsletters detailing recent anti-bribery updates may be used to keep employees well informed.

- (Accessible Guidance) No matter how extensive, written policies and training cannot account for every situation an employee may encounter during the course of business. It is important for employees to be able to obtain immediate guidance on issues they may be currently facing. Employees also must have a safe place to report conduct by others that may have violated the anti-bribery laws. This can be accomplished through an in-office compliance officer. A central hotline is a key addition in that it can provide assistance on an anonymous basis.

---

[123] See FCPA Opinion Procedure Release 04-02, DOJ (July 12, 2004), available through *http://www.usdoj.gov*; FCPA Opinion Procedure Release 03-01, DOJ (January 15, 2003), available through *http://www.usdoj.gov*; Priya C. Huskins, *FCPA Prosecutions: Liability Trend to Watch*, 60 Stan. L.Rev. 1447 at 1454 (March 2008).

[124] See FCPA Opinion Procedure Release 04-02, DOJ (July 12, 2004), available through *http://www.usdoj.gov*; Priya C. Huskins, *FCPA Prosecutions: Liability Trend to Watch*, 60 Stan. L.Rev. 1447 at 1454 (March 2008).

Companies should regularly assess the effectiveness of their compliance pro-gramme and make adjustments accordingly. The *Vetco Gray* case, discussed in paras 10–10–10–11 above, is a prime example of why compliance both before and after a merger is imperative.[125] Remember that after discovering certain improper payments, ABB and the investment group jointly conducted an extensive FCPA compliance review and voluntarily disclosed their findings to the DOJ and the SEC. ABB reached settlements with the government in July 2004 requiring it to pay $5.9 million in disgorgement of unlawful profits and $10.5 million in criminal fines. Despite creating a compliance programme under advice from the DOJ, the successor entity failed to follow through with its compliance plan. Violations continued. Years later, the DOJ and SEC accepted a settlement from Vetco Gray. Vetco Gray subsidiaries agreed to pay criminal fines in the aggregate amount of $26 million. Fines may have been higher had they not voluntarily disclosed violations a second time. Had the original compliance programme been effectively implemented in the first place, Vetco would have been saved millions.[126]

V. CONCLUSION

Many anti-bribery violations are not innocent mistakes; they are committed by people intentionally engaging in improper behaviour. Acquiring entities must be sure to do extensive due diligence as the acquirer of a company may well inherit any liability of the acquired entity. As noted above, several companies in recent years have paid hefty fines to make amends for the actions of acquired sub-sidiaries. Companies should learn from their mistakes.   **10–32**

---

[125] Press Release No. 07-075, DOJ, *Three Vetco International Ltd. Subsidiaries Plead Guilty to Foreign Bribery and Agree to Pay $26 Million in Criminal Fines* (February 6, 2007)
[126] See FCPA Opinion Procedure Release 04-02, DOJ (July 12, 2004), available through *http://www.usdoj.gov.*

CHAPTER 11

EFFECTIVE ANTI-CORRUPTION PROGRAMMES

A. INTRODUCTION

This chapter considers what are the key elements of an effective anti-corruption **11–01** programme based on the practical experience, knowledge and expertise of working with global organisations in the design, development and implementation of sustainable anti-corruption frameworks that meet (and exceed) regulatory guidelines and legal requirements. Specifically, this chapter will:

- Confirm why an effective anti-corruption programme is required;

- Provide an overview of what "good looks like";

- Highlight some of the key considerations in the design and development of an effective programme; and finally

- Seek to address the question why some anti-corruption programmes fail.

B. WHY DO ORGANISATIONS NEED AN EFFECTIVE ANTI-CORRUPTION PROGRAMME?

For many organisations having an anti-corruption programme in place and being **11–02** able to demonstrate that it is effective is becoming increasingly important. There are numerous drivers which help explain this increased focus:

I. Ensuring the company, its directors and employees are compliant with the law in the jurisdictions that it operates in

There are significant corporate and personal consequences of non-compliance **11–03** within the legal and regulatory framework, both criminal and civil, including unlimited fines, disbarment from government contracts and prison sentences. Can organisations and individuals afford to take the risk of not having an effective anti-corruption programme in place?

II. Retaining market and stakeholder credibility around ethical business
practices and protecting shareholder value

11–04   The non-financial impact of non-compliance with anti-corruption laws should not be underestimated. In particular, damage to shareholder trust and corporate reputation can be significant and long lasting. Companies can be disbarred from tendering for government work or can find, even without an official disbarment, that government tenders become more difficult to obtain. Other effects include an inability to attract and retain the most talented people as well as enduring damage to brand.

III. Providing a defence or mitigating evidence should it be determined
that corruption has occurred

11–05   When an organisation experiences one or more violations of anti-corruption legislation, relevant criminal and regulatory authorities will, in many jurisdictions, wish to consider whether the procedures and processes in place to prevent corruption within the company were adequate. In order for a company to obtain criminal sanctions or a civil settlement that is at the lower end of the range in terms of prosecutorial discretion, it will be incumbent on the company to show that its procedures were adequate (both in terms of effective design and operation).

US sentencing guidelines[1] provide the US federal courts with guidance on the factors that can be taken into account when sentencing a company in relation to a range of criminal charges including, fraud, bribery, anti-trust and other matters. These factors include guidance on the arrangements to prevent corporate crimes including bribery and what is an appropriate response on the part of a company once bribery or other crimes have been detected. While many major fraud trials are not tried in court, the SEC and the DOJ at various times have taken into account a company's compliance with the US federal sentencing guideline in reaching settlements with companies under investigation.

11–06   The new Bribery Act introduces a corporate offence of failing to prevent bribery. A defence to the failure to prevent offence will exist if it can be shown that "adequate procedures" were in place. The UK government will be required to provide guidance on what is meant by "adequate procedures". It is anticipated that guidance will be indicative, setting out principles and illustrative good practice examples rather than prescriptive standards.[2]

---

[1] Federal Sentencing Guidelines (amended 2009), Ch.8, Pt B 2.1.
[2] Pending the introduction of this guidance, a memorandum from the Serious Fraud Office, "Approach of the Serious Fraud Office to dealing with overseas corruption" dated July 21, 2009, provides guidance on regulatory expectations in the UK.

IV. DOING BUSINESS GLOBALLY

Global organisations face significant challenges in complying with the differing   **11–07**
bribery laws of the territories that they operate in, recognising also that the
jurisdiction of those laws will extend beyond national borders. To compete in
global markets and to win new business, employees need to understand what is
acceptable business practice and what is not. People need to understand also the
principles upon which the company's compliance programme is based, have
sufficient knowledge of the detailed rules that affect the business they operate in
and know who and when to consult an appropriate resource with more expertise.

    An anti-corruption framework provides guidance on the ways that a company
can do business. It empowers employees to go forward and compete in global
markets with confidence, in the knowledge that their actions will not threaten a
breach of bribery laws thereby placing the company or the individual at risk of
prosecution.

C. WHAT DOES AN EFFECTIVE ANTI-CORRUPTION COMPLIANCE PROGRAMME LOOK LIKE?

There is no single template solution for an effective anti-corruption compliance   **11–08**
programme which an organisation can implement and be guaranteed success.
There are a number of different sources of guidance both from regulatory bodies,
industry groups and other sources. A company evaluating its compliance programme will often consider first which guidance is most applicable to its circumstances before conducting an assessment of current arrangements. While
most if not all of the guidance is helpful, the key to developing a successful anti-
corruption programme lies in the ability to assess the corruption risks then
develop a programme, combining overarching principles and more detailed guidance which best mitigate these risks.

I. EXISTING GUIDANCE

We have discussed earlier in this chapter the existence of guidance promulgated   **11–09**
by different territories' regulatory and criminal authorities including the US
federal sentencing guidelines and the guidance offered by the Serious Fraud
Office ("SFO") in the UK.

    There are other sources of guidance, each with slightly different content and
points of emphasis, that are available to support companies in the development of
the anti-corruption compliance programme. Other guidance includes UN Global
Compact, OECD Global Business Principles, Transparency International
Guidelines, World Economic Forum, Industry Standards and Ethics Toolkits and
other non-regulatory standards or reviews that may have been proactively commissioned by national organisations.

II. AN EFFECTIVE FRAMEWORK

11-10 We have drawn upon existing guidance to create a framework which companies can use to consider and develop their anti-corruption programmes. In our view an effective framework is founded on three key elements:

- Overarching principles;

- Tailored procedures; and

- Effective implementation.

The approach should be principles led, recognising that an effective compliance programme is not just about processes and controls but must also consider how people in an organisation understand and are influenced by business ethics and company values. A principles based approach should be supported by a robust set of procedures, tailored to the organisation's circumstances, where consistency of actions throughout the organisation is paramount—particularly in high risk areas. Finally, there must be effective implementation over the long term. The inter-relationship between the three key elements is illustrated in figure 11A.

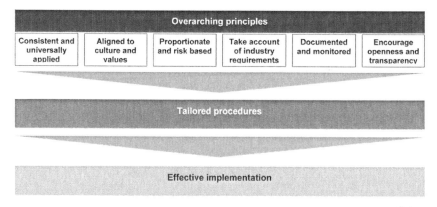

Figure 11A: Illustration of an effective framework

(a) Overarching principles

11-11 The overarching principles form the basis for creating adequate anti-corruption procedures. The over-arching principles upon which an effective anti-corruption programme is founded should:

- **Be consistent and universally applied**—to promote consistent and effective implementation throughout the organisation at all levels.

- **Be aligned to the organisation's culture, values and wider compliance programmes**—to recognise the context in which the company operates and design the anti-corruption programme accordingly and also to recognise that the anti-corruption programme will need to be part of arrangements that address other compliance risks including fraud, anti-trust and other ethical issues.

- **Be proportionate to the organisation's size, resources and risk profile**—to ensure that higher risk areas are prioritised and addressed.

- **Take account of existing and evolving industry requirements or practices**—to ensure that the programme operates at or above the minimum standards already expected and on a sustainable basis.

- **Be documented and monitored**—to evidence that procedures operate in practice, not just in theory.

- **Encourage openness and transparency**—to provide an overriding sense of the "right" behaviour to everyone acting for, or on behalf of, the organisation.

(b) Tailored procedures

There is no "one size fits all" solution. Procedures will need to be tailored to the unique circumstances and risk profile of each organisation and achieve the right balance between preventative and detective anti-corruption measures. There are, however, components which appear in almost all effective anti-corruption programmes, as illustrated in figure 11B.
    Experience has shown us that simply incorporating the components shown in figure 11B without the required change in behaviour from all individuals within the organisation is unlikely to deliver the benefits that should be expected of a comprehensive anti-corruption programme. The key is effective implementation and a significant change in behaviour, leading to sustainable business conduct. Both implementation and sustainability are discussed later in this chapter.

11–12

Leadership Commitment and Oversight—the Board must convey the importance of the programme by committing sufficient time and qualified resources to its development. This may also involve Board members undergoing training on anti-bribery legislation and its implications. The Board will also need to consider how its commitment to ethical business practices is communicated across the organisation.

Ethical Risk Assessment—designed to identify areas of highest risk in terms of potential exposure to bribery and corruption, by carefully assessing a variety of influences. Risk assessments are discussed in more detail in para.11–15 below.

People—through effective use of HR functions an organisation can further embed the ethical values which underpin the anti-corruption framework, hence initiating and later sustaining, cultural change amongst the organisation.

Figure 11B: Elements of good practice within an anti-corruption programme.

Ethics and Compliance Policies and Guidelines—an Ethical Standards and Compliance Code supported by robust anti-corruption policies and guidelines are essential for setting the right "tone at the top", and providing a common and consistent operating framework within which to work across the organisation.

Consultation and Whistleblowing Facilities—a mechanism allowing for anonymity and confidentiality for employees and agents to report improper activity or seek guidance. Consultation and whistleblowing facilities are discussed in more detail in para.11–24 below.

Business Partner Compliance—it is essential for organisations to ensure that risk-based compliance due diligence checks are carried out on business partners and third parties who the organisation plans to engage with, as bribes are often paid indirectly without the commissioning organisation's knowledge.

Internal Investigations and Compliance Reviews—ongoing, independent reviews of regulatory compliance and ethical standards including books and records, and internal control procedures.

Monitor Government Business—ensuring full transparency and visibility of transactions and contracts with the full range of suppliers, vendors, advisers and business partners who are defined as government and government-related entities as per the appropriate regulatory compliance.

Gatekeeper Functions and Networks—contribute to an independent assessment of, and are instrumental to assessing and improving the organisations compliance, whilst ensuring it remains sustainable. Typically such functions include Internal Audit, Legal and Compliance.

Behaviour-based Training and Engagement—educating individuals around the compliance programme by conducting effective training programs and appropriately disseminating information in order to have members of the organisation engaged in the programme.

Monitoring and Reporting—the tracking and reporting of compliance and ethical standards effectiveness and implementation across the organisation. This is central to providing the standard of transparency and visibility required by regulators to ensure the compliance and ethics programme is followed.

Internal Controls—addressing gaps identified through regulatory compliance and business ethics reviews and investigations by having a standard set of controls which can be adapted for specific business units and functions, along side customised controls which address specific issues.

Compliance and Ethical Business Conduct Governance—as part of implementing and embedding compliance and ethical business standards globally across the organisation, the development of a network of Compliance Managers should be deployed locally to champion local business units and functions.

Compliance Embedded in M&A Process—for complex large-scale organisations who are involved in M&A transactions on a regular basis, the process of embedding compliance and business ethics into the M&A processes means minimum standards are defined at the outset and any shortcomings are quickly identified and actively monitored.

Sustainability and Continuous Improvement—allows for the compliance programme to grow and develop as an organisation matures. Sustainability and continuous improvement is discussed in more detail in para.11–38—Why do some anti-corruption programmes succeed while others fail?

Based on our practical experience, some of these components present organisations with greater levels of risk, and significant challenges in design and implementation. Where we believe this to be the case we have explored the component in further in paras 11–17–11–27.

D. HOW TO DESIGN AN EFFECTIVE ANTI-CORRUPTION COMPLIANCE PROGRAMME

11–13   Many organisations will have begun to realise the importance of having an anti-corruption framework in place, however, they will also be considering how to set about designing such a framework. Typically an organisation will look to implement an anti-corruption framework as the result of either a pro-active initiative—involving the initial design and subsequent review on a regular basis, or as a reaction to a crisis situation.

Regardless of whether the situation is proactive or reactive the steps in designing such a framework remain broadly the same, however, there is one distinct difference—a reactive situation is preceded by an investigation. The process is illustrated within figure 11C.

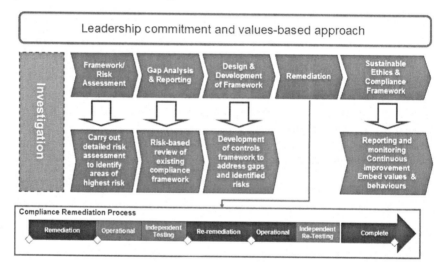

Figure 11C: Overview of the design process for an anti-corruption framework

I. Investigation

11–14   Where an organisation has been subject to an instance of known corruption there is likely to be an investigation, often followed by remedial action which is likely to take a form like that illustrated above. Investigations are discussed in more detail in Ch.9.

II. FRAMEWORK/RISK ASSESSMENT

A framework/risk assessment is an essential step any organisation should **11–15** undertake when improving or designing an effective anti-corruption programme. The assessment should be designed to identify areas of highest risk in terms of potential exposure to bribery and corruption. These are the areas that will need to be addressed first. Note that risk is not necessarily associated with the size of operations in a particular jurisdiction. Small operations in countries with high perceived levels of corruption are likely to be high risk.

The risk assessment should examine a number of factors including: the high risk areas in which the company operates; whether the business model includes large scale projects; tenders or long term contracts; the degree to which intermediaries are used to do business; whether the company has interactions with government officials; if a new business acquisition or joint venture is planned; and the gifts, hospitality and entertainment activities employed. These are some of the most vulnerable areas for businesses which need to be carefully considered and prioritised. It is by no means exhaustive. By completing such a detailed and focused risk assessment organisations will benefit from focusing their resources on key risks, rather than chasing the hot topic of the day.

Following the completion of a risk assessment an organisation can then use this information in a number of ways. First, the information can be used by the organisation to identify where the main corruption and bribery risks exist. Secondly, the information may persuade an organisation to avoid certain markets or partners altogether because the possibilities of becoming involved in corruption are judged too high. Finally, the information can equip an organisation to move with confidence into a challenging environment, where cultural and business practices are unfamiliar, knowing that it has identified the key corruption risks and can design processes to manage these appropriately.

III. GAP ANALYSIS AND REPORTING

Once the risk assessment has identified the underlying risks of bribery and cor- **11–16** ruption within an organisation, the next step is to assess how the existing compliance framework addresses the identified risks, considering any gaps.

An effective gap analysis will incorporate both the **design** of the compliance programme and also how it is **operating in practice**. There are a variety of approaches that can be used to gather data concerning the existing compliance operation. For example, if there are particular concerns about whether employees are sufficiently aware of, or agree with, the values of the organisation, one approach is to conduct an ethical awareness survey. Ethical risk surveys, when effectively designed can help inform a gap analysis which highlights both the areas of risk which the organisation should prioritise when designing the anti-compliance programme and the extent to which culture change and communications needs to be part of the remediation effort.

11–17   Once an organisation has identified both its bribery and corruption risks, and the gaps in its existing compliance framework, the next stage is to develop a controls framework which will fill the compliance gaps and mitigate the identified risks. There are many different methods which an organisation can use to develop this controls framework, all of which have their merits.

Regardless of which approach the organisation chooses to adopt it is important that the anti-corruption programme is set out in sufficient detail to be able to demonstrate to a regulator or court that the organisation is committed to establishing an effective anti-corruption programme.

Documenting in sufficient detail the components of the anti bribery programme in such a way as to enable those charged with governance of the organisation to consider whether those procedures are adequate is a step that we find is often overlooked but is critical to ensuring a company, if challenged, had gone through due process in developing its approach.

11–18   As mentioned in para.11–12 above there are some components which, in our opinion, present organisations with greater levels of risk, and significant challenges in design and implementation. In the sections that follow we have explored these in detail, with the aim of giving some guidance to organisations as to what is meant by "sufficient detail".

(a) Leadership Commitment and Oversight

11–19   A successful anti-corruption programme must begin with a clear commitment from senior management. Not "should" but "must". From our experience failure to get early, sustained and visible senior management support for the anti-corruption programme is almost always fatal to the likely success of the programme.

Senior management must make clear that bribery is not tolerated under any circumstances but also must commit adequate qualified resources, both internal and external, necessary to its development. Board members and other governing body members should also undergo relevant training to ensure they have appropriate knowledge of the anti-bribery legislation and its implications. This allows senior management to have overall responsibility for the anti-corruption framework and helps effectively establish and maintain the "tone from the top".

Establishing the right tone at Board level and within senior management in relation to bribery is important, sustaining that tone and culture over time is even more so. In addition to being knowledgeable about anti-bribery legislation and its implications, best practice shows us that the Board of Directors must also be knowledgeable about the content and operation of the anti-corruption programme whilst exercising reasonable oversight with respect to its implementation and effectiveness. Robust governance and reporting and monitoring procedures, both during the remediation process and after implementation, will be critical to ensuring the Board has adequate line of sight throughout the business and is cognizant of new and emerging risks. Smart metrics and key performance indicators which are measurable and focused on anti-corruption, underpinning the overall balanced scorecard, will enable visibility and transparency of effective risk management.

(b) Case Study—Leadership Commitment and Oversight

The organisation had a strong brand and worldwide reputation which was **11–20** synonymous with good, ethical business practice. However, allegations of widespread bribery emerged with a number of senior management from across the globe being arrested and subject to investigation. This led to a high level of uncertainty at lower levels within the organisation.

The organisation faced significant challenges in communicating and re-emphasising its corporate values to its employees in ways that would be perceived as credible. These challenges were heightened as ongoing investigations and associated press coverage meant that that staff continued to receive inaccurate information concerning alleged wrongdoing.

With external guidance and support, senior board members were engaged from the outset and became directly involved in the compliance programme at every level. Corporate webcasts and presentations were used as a means to deliver key messages and were delivered centrally and then replicated at a local level to ensure maximum engagement from all members of the organisation. A number of other approaches were also used to demonstrate the absolute commitment of senior management to sustained ethical business practices.

Feedback on the success of this anti-corruption programme was monitored through compliance officers and employee feedback at a local level. The leadership team also made public announcements on the anti-corruption programme, which although demonstrating their engagement, also made them directly accountable to the wider public. Finally, evidence to support the success of the anti-corruption programme was also achieved through independent messages in the media.

(c) Ethics and Compliance Policies and Guidelines

An ethical standards and compliance code supported by robust policies and **11–21** guidelines is essential for setting the right "tone at the top" and providing a common and consistent operating framework which can work across the organisation. A good practice framework should include corporate values, code of conduct, code of ethics and policies and guidelines at both corporate and local level. The framework must address local regulatory and compliance laws of countries in which the businesses are operating, as well as that of the Head Office. This can be often be best achieved by using the framework to guide ethical behaviour through underlying principles, rather than a prescriptive set of rules.

If the organisation does not already have a code of ethics or code of conduct, this needs to be created. Such codes should address bribery and corruption, as well as other issues related to business ethics. Existing codes need to be reviewed and enhanced where necessary to ensure that anti-corruption aspects are adequately covered. All codes should have been through a formal board-level approval process and reflect the core values the organisation seeks to operate by.

Codes of conduct are supported by policies which give more detailed guidance to management and staff. There will typically be a number of policies relevant to anti-corruption compliance, including:

- Third party intermediaries and other business partners.

- Gifts, hospitality and entertaining.

- Facilitation payments.

- Political and charitable donations and lobbying activities.

- Conflicts of interest.

- Bank accounts, cash and petty cash.

11-22   In our opinion it is not necessary or effective that codes and policies attempt to address every possible situation in which a potential bribe or corruption could occur. It is preferable to use the policies, combined with effective training and communications, to develop and embed clear values which employees then apply to guide ethical decision-making in any specific situation they may face. Policies should be reviewed regularly and their effectiveness assessed by senior management.

Policies are supported by operating procedures and internal controls. These anti-corruption procedures and controls need to be embedded in the company's existing operational framework, including where applicable the internal controls over financial reporting. Implementing new procedures and controls—and testing their effectiveness—can be time consuming and, in our experience, the resource required to undertake this task is often underestimated in planning the roll out of a revised anti-bribery compliance programme.

(d) Case Study—Ethics and Compliance Policies and Guidelines.

11-23   The organisation was faced with compliance policies and guidelines which were out of date or absent in a number of key areas. Further, a pilot review at a number of entities identified significant gaps and inconsistencies in the interpretation, implementation and demonstration of the existing policies. Finally, guidelines lacked sufficient detail to ensure all relevant staff had a proper understanding of policy requirements.

To remediate the situation, the organisation needed to develop comprehensive policies which could be rolled out worldwide while meeting local legal and compliance requirements and deal with both local languages and business customs.

The organisation overcame these significant challenges to implement a successful anti-corruption programme through reviewing existing policies at a corporate level, updating them to address current requirements and communicating these through a network of compliance officers. Implementation kits were designed to guide local compliance officers and management. Local entities were required to adapt the policies and guidelines to meet their language requirements and train local staff.

In order to fully demonstrate commitment to the anti-corruption programme senior management required entities to demonstrate that they had communicated the policies fully to their employees. Further, the organisation also reviewed centrally all locally adapted policies and guidelines to ensure they were not contravening any anti-corruption legislation which the organisation was legally required to abide by.

(e) Consultation and Whistleblowing Facilities

The US Federal Sentencing Guidelines stipulate that an effective anti-corruption **11–24** programme must have and publicise a mechanism which offers employees and agents both anonymity and confidentiality for reporting improper activity or seeking guidance. This is echoed by current best practice guidelines for countering bribery and corruption which typically require the provision of both consultation and whistleblowing facilities.

Consultation and whistleblowing should be two clearly separate facilities. The consultation line should provide employees with the opportunity to seek clarification on policy and also offer guidance on ethical business dilemmas. The whistleblowing line should operate as a mechanism whereby individuals can report any suspicions of corrupt behaviour confidentially and, if they wish, anonymously. Companies with international operations must ensure both these facilities are available to individuals in appropriate languages and time zones.

Both facilities need to be robust in order to instil employee confidence in them. Specifically, the whistleblowing line should establish how matters should be addressed, including escalation to senior levels, avoidance of actual and perceived conflicts of interest, and follow-up and investigation processes.

Whistleblowing facilities should be recognised as an important source of information for the organisation in its anti-corruption programme, and should inform the assessment of the effectiveness of the programme.

(f) Business Partner Compliance

Bribes can be paid by third party agents, including sales representatives, logistics **11–25** agents, bogus or disreputable law firms and marketing consultancies, with or without the organisation's consent or knowledge. It is essential to ensure that risk-based compliance due diligence checks are carried out on third parties and business partners that the organisation plans to engage with and that due diligence is reperformed from time to time.

Large organisations, engaging with smaller third parties and business partners should take steps to support those smaller business partners in achieving compliance with anti-bribery laws and regulations. This support could include, for example, providing training in the organisation's expectations of what constitutes compliant behaviour. Third parties should also be given details of how to make use of whistleblower facilities, so that they can report any behaviour that raises suspicions of corruption.

In addition to providing support, organisations should also contract with third parties and business partners, to require them to behave in an ethical way and in compliance with organisation standards and relevant legislation, including anti-corruption legislation. Approval and monitoring procedures need to be established to check that payments made to the third party appear reasonable in relation to the service performed.

In many instances an organisation will need to establish a right of access to the books and records of a third party in order to be able to exercise some form of monitoring or audit. It will also be necessary to determine under what circumstances it would be appropriate to exercise such a right and what compliance information it should require from the third party as part of the ongoing business relationship.

(g) Case Study—Business Partner Compliance

11–26   The organisation was subject to an investigation, where bribery and corruption was suspected. Specifically there were suspicions around a number of third party payments given the lack of supporting documentary evidence. The investigation highlighted a gap in the organisation's compliance framework in that there was no reliable record of the third parties with whom the company was doing business with around the world.

In trying to improve their compliance framework, the organisation found adopting a consistent approach to due diligence challenging, particularly where relationships with third parties were cross border. Specifically there were tensions between the need to perform proper due diligence and the need to maintain appropriate commercial business relationships.

The organisation sought to develop a tool which facilitated a consistent due diligence process for all countries and outlined policies and procedures for both the contract and payment stages of a third party relationship. The policies and procedures required the regular review of risks associated with existing third parties and the creation of a central log of blacklisted business partners which was communicated world wide.

To demonstrate to regulators the commitment of the organisation to the anti-corruption programme, senior management required that all due diligence was fully documented. Contract files and logs were required for all third party engagements and were subject to central, senor level review. Further, given the scale of the investigation, and associated fines, the organisation subjected all third parties to independent testing as part of the initial remediation, and on an ongoing basis, and required third parties to take part in the compliance program improvements.

(h) People

People management includes a number of HR related functions such as objectives **11–27** setting and target agreements, disciplinary procedures and sanctions policy, zero-tolerance policy, recruitment and promotion measurements and processes, and performance related pay and incentives. Through effective use of these HR functions an organisation can further embed the ethical values which underpin the anti-corruption framework, hence initiating and later sustaining cultural change. Here we look at the specific HR functions and how an organisation can use these when implementing an anti-corruption framework.

Effective HR processes begin before people join the organisation (or are being considered for promotion to senior or sensitive positions). Background checks should be conducted that look for evidence of involvement in illegal activity or other question marks regarding integrity. As with other elements of a compliance programme, a risk based approach to the design of background checking processes should be applied.

The anti-corruption framework can be supported through the review of performance management systems. In particular, appropriate and specific compliance-related performance targets should be set in management objectives (including the objectives of board members) and then assessed as part of the variable remuneration process.

Finally, organisations also need to ensure they have appropriate disciplinary procedures and processes in place to deal with any policy or guideline breaches. Disciplinary procedures need to be fair, open and transparent and consistently enforced. Employees need to understand how the disciplinary process works and the consequences of breaching policy or guidelines.

V. REMEDIATION

The remediation process addresses the gap between the current and existing **11–28** framework for mitigating bribery risk and the desired end state for the organisation, based on the regulatory and legal framework in place and global good practice. Remediation consists of the design and development of the underpinning mechanisms, tools, policies, processes and controls to build the anti-corruption programme which is then followed by implementation and testing of design and operational effectiveness.

Remediation is complex and, dependent on the scale and scope of the organisation's business geographically and the nature of its business, is not a short term activity. To build an enduring and sustainable anti-corruption compliance programme that is meaningful and relevant globally, is a journey which many organisations find challenging.

E. IMPLEMENTATION OF AN EFFECTIVE ANTI-CORRUPTION COMPLIANCE PROGRAMME

11–29 The world's best-designed anti-corruption programme is not enough by itself. The importance of effective implementation cannot be understated. Too many companies fail when it comes to implementation, says Mr Brooks of Transparency International:

> "They don't do too badly on the policy. And they do understand that it's part of risk management. But then they sit back and say: 'Well, we'll just put it on notice boards, we'll put it on our website, and then everyone inside and outside the company knows about it.'"

Experience shows more effort is needed.

There is some debate as to whether programme implementation should be primarily a top-down affair, or whether employees should be actively involved at all stages of the process. In fact both are important. Senior management need to demonstrate their commitment to the programme through leading by example and deploying adequate resources. Obtaining buy in from staff at an early stage will increase levels of engagement with the programme and shorten the time period to achieve compliance maturity.

We have identified four factors that are critical to the successful implementation of an anti-corruption programme.

1. Leadership

2. Adequate resource

3. Effective project planning

4. Communications and training

I. LEADERSHIP

11–30 We have considered earlier in this chapter the importance of senior management and Board level commitment and leadership. Setting the right tone from the top and securing senior leadership commitment to any anti-corruption compliance programme is a key priority. Without the commitment and direction set by the Board and Executives, the impact of any anti-corruption compliance programme will be diluted and questioned both internally and externally by others. How the Board thinks, feels, talks, and acts on bribery and corruption sets the tone and communicates the standard to which others must also follow and reach. Equipping the leadership to be able to deliver this tone is key—what messages must be given out and how? What are the tools and mechanisms they can use to demonstrate their commitment, such as reward and recognition of good behaviour? How are the leadership measured on their own behaviours and values?

Following up on improper behaviour and responding appropriately to incidents are both key actions by leadership that illustrate their commitment to the compliance programme. In addition, supporting the leadership in their ethical decision-making in business operations and transactions will demonstrate to others the cultural and behavioural values that are embedded in the way the organisation does business.

II. ADEQUATE RESOURCE

A remediation exercise can require significant resource, often drawn from different parts of the business, including "gatekeeper functions" and line business units, to form a project team. A multi-disciplinary team can be important for gaining the support and commitment of the wider organisation but significant strain can be placed on team members who will often need to continue to support other commitments.

11–31

We recommend careful consideration is given to the resource requirements of anti bribery remediation projects and the extent to which core team members will have sufficient time to deliver on project work streams. Implementation of remediation programmes and in particular the successful sequencing of different programme elements is critical to a successful outcome. A failure to implement effectively can be misinterpreted as a lack of commitment on the part of the organisation to sound ethical business practice. Selective use of external advisers can assist in ensuring that the anti-bribery project is delivered effectively and on time.

Resource may be needed to operate ongoing compliance arrangements in the future. There may be a need to formalise responsibilities of existing staff to undertake compliance roles or in some instances to employ further staff. A common mistake we see is the assumption that the internal audit function will have sufficient time, using existing resources, to conduct bribery compliance reviews in order to provide the Board with assurance over the effectiveness of the anti-bribery programme.

III. EFFECTIVE PROJECT PLANNING

In principle, effective project planning for an effective anti-corruption compliance programme should follow the same good practice guidelines and tools as any other programme. However, there are some specific elements to be considered which are key:

11–32

- The compliance remediation programme must be based on a sufficiently detailed risk assessment.

- Identification and management of the interdependencies between different remediation components, often across entities and territories, will be critical.

- Measuring the culture change and responding in a way that is meaningful and relevant at the local level is paramount—a heavy focus on central project planning with little empowerment at business unit level will not encourage ownership and accountability in the territory.

- Ensuring there is adequate project planning resource to manage process, resolve conflicts and deliver the reporting will vary depending on the maturity and complexity of the compliance programme as it develops.

IV. Training and Communications

11–33 Training and Communications are important in developing the compliance mindset and enhancing the success of the Anti-Corruption programme. Communications and training are integral to increasing the understanding and obtaining the commitment of the directors, employees and other related business partners and third parties.

(a) Training

11–34 Most organisations conclude that all their employees need some training to ensure that the values incorporated in the anti-corruption programme are translated into action. Different employee groups will require different amounts and types of training depending on their roles in the business and consequent exposure to bribery risk. The style and content of the training will vary, for example:

- Awareness sessions for all employees.

- Induction and orientation training for new recruits.

- Decision making training for people exposed to areas of greater complexity and/or corruption risk.

- Leadership training for those taking on broader responsibility, e.g. management, local compliance officers.

The training needs to be designed and run in a way that maximises the level of engagement. This includes decisions on the style of training (face to face, computer based, on-the-job, coaching, learning groups), which languages to use to maximise coverage, when and where to run the training and also who will deliver it (professional trainers, HR, local managers).

Training needs to be recorded so that attendance or non-attendance can be monitored and followed up with appropriate actions. Regulators can ask to see evidence of staff training in the course of an investigation. Finally, the training needs to be monitored for effectiveness with updates as appropriate.

Training interventions / Learners	BoM workshop	Executive roadshow	Face to face training course (1 day)	Paper copy of policy with CEO letter	Multi-media communication	Online learning – all topics	Online learning – selected modules	Team briefing by local manager
Board of management	✓			✓	✓			
Executive boards		✓		✓	✓			
Senior management			✓	✓	✓	✓*		
Other staff in high risk territories			✓	✓	✓	✓*		
Other staff in high risk functions			✓	✓	✓	✓*		
All other staff				✓	✓		✓	✓

* = If face to face training is not possible

Figure 11D: An illustration showing an anti-corruption training programme which has recently been successfully implemented at a global organisation

(b) Critical success factors

Factors critical to the effectiveness of training and communications are: 11–35

- Demonstrate visible support of the leadership and key senior sponsors.

- Be part of an integrated and wider programme of Anti-Corruption Policy and guidance—it is not enough in itself to train the employees.

- Messages need to be delivered consistently across the business.

- Focus on areas of highest risk to begin with. These stakeholders need to play a key role in the further roll out of training and communication initiatives.

- Seek to achieve maximum effectiveness while minimising time away from the workplace—enabling participants to see a clear link between the training and the real impact it will have on their jobs.

(c) Communication

Training can help create culture change around ethical values but it needs 11–36
effective communication to support and sustain that change.

The starting point in development of the anti-corruption communication plan is to gain a full understanding of who the businesses stakeholders are. These can be both internal (leaders, management, staff) and external (regulators, government, investors, customers, pressure groups, consumer groups).

Internally, the company needs to promote employee awareness of and compliance with company values, the policies that are in place relating to bribery and corruption, where to go to gain help and support and the sanctions that they face through non-conformity. Externally, communication should be used to demonstrate the transparency of the business and the credibility of its policies and procedures. This in part will help to strengthen corporate reputation and deter attempts to approach the business with corrupt intent.

As with training, the communication needs to use mediums, branding and languages that fits with the business.

(d) Case Study—Training and Communication

11–37   Following the decision to implement a comprehensive compliance framework, this organisation needed to develop an awareness of the benefits of good compliance and the collective and individual responsibility of staff.

To be effective, the training and communications programme needed to respond to significant challenges that were raised by employees about the need for the anti-bribery programme. Sceptical comments from employees included:

"This is the reality of how business is done";

"Our competitors do this—why shouldn't we?"; and

"It's not the sort of thing our people would do".

It was essential that the training and communications programme addressed these concerns fully. By ensuring both that the guidance being issued reflected the nuances of the business and that the associated training (both face to face and eLearning) was rich in practical case studies, senior management was able to gain the commitment and support of employees.

The impact of the compliance programme was monitored through the use of feedback from training programmes, the nature and number of queries being raised to the consultation office, staff surveys which tested the embedding and recognition of key messages. A database of training attendance by employees was used for reporting to the SEC where requested.

F. WHY DO SOME ANTI-CORRUPTION PROGRAMMES SUCCEED WHILE OTHERS FAIL?

11–38   This question is one many organisations ask when the latest corruption headline appears in the media—"why does this keep on happening and how do we ensure that our own anti-corruption programme will stop this happening to us?"

Research and experience shows that the majority of complex change programmes fail primarily because of the lack of appreciation and understanding of the people issues. This is no different for an anti-corruption compliance programme. Understanding and responding to the cultural change and behavioural element of a compliance programme is key to success. Why is this?

- Organisations are now operating globally, with many diverse cultures and values.

- Applying a "one size" fits all approach is not going to work where local ways of working, languages, laws and customs differ from country to country.

- Adopting a rules-based approach can lead to mis-interpretation and confusion amongst different political, legal, social and environmental structures.

- Delivering training and communication that is not relevant and not reflective of the local business will create barriers and build resistance to any corporate-wide compliance programme.

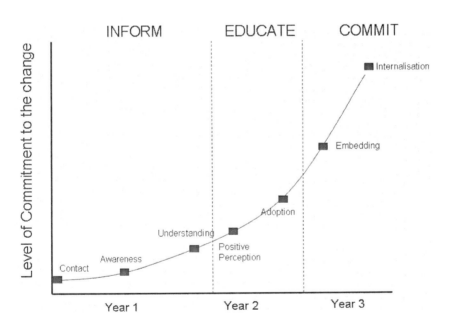

Figure 11E: A maturity model to illustrate the journey upon which the organisation and people will travel in building and embedding a sustainable anti-corruption programme over a period of time.

And last, but by no means least, recognising that the compliance journey is one that is complex and takes time, is fundamental to its success. Understanding the different levels of maturity of compliance as seen in figure 11E, both for the organisation and for the individual, is a key part of building and embedding an anti-corruption programme that is sustainable and effective.

G. CONCLUSION

11–39   Albert Camus, twentieth-century philosopher, author and journalist, said that "integrity has no need of rules". Whilst that may be true for the individual, where people come together to achieve a common purpose, perceptions of what is ethical will differ. In today's fast-moving global market place, employees need help to understand what integrity means to their company and principles-based frameworks within which they can act with certainty, confident that they are doing the right thing.

There is no one right solution to mitigating corruption and bribery; it is bespoke to each organisation and reflective of risks, operating models and cultural make-up. Where those charged with governance show real leadership, in our experience employees will follow. The benefits to those companies that are seen as class leading in their ethical conduct will be significant in terms of brand value, recruitment and retention of talented people, and competing with confidence in global markets. The penalties for getting it wrong however will be substantial.

APPENDIX A

Transparency International's Corruption Perceptions Index measures the perceived level of public sector corruption as seen by business people and country analysts; ranging between 10 (highly clean) and 0 (highly corrupt)

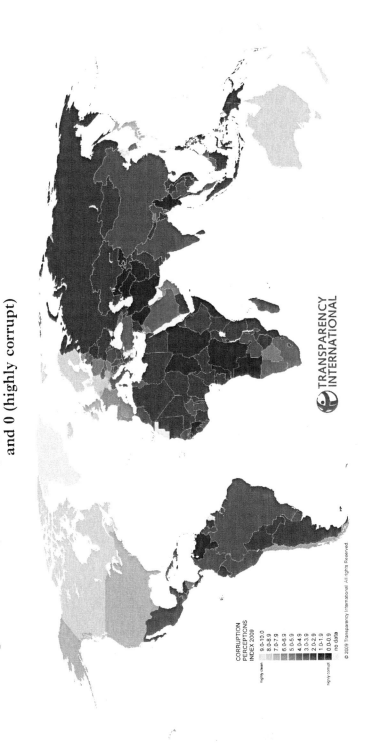

CORRUPTION
PERCEPTIONS
INDEX 2009

highly clean
9.0-10.0
8.0-8.9
7.0-7.9
6.0-6.9
5.0-5.9
4.0-4.9
3.0-3.9
2.0-2.9
1.0-1.9
highly corrupt 0.0-0.9
no data

TRANSPARENCY
INTERNATIONAL

© 2009 Transparency International. All rights reserved.

361

BRIBERY ACT 2010

2010 CHAPTER 23

An Act to make provision about offences relating to bribery; and for connected purposes. [8th April 2010]

B e it enacted by the Queen's most Excellent Majesty, by and with the advice and consent of the Lords Spiritual and Temporal, and Commons, in this present Parliament assembled, and by the authority of the same, as follows:—

General bribery offences

1 Offences of bribing another person

(1) A person ("P") is guilty of an offence if either of the following cases applies.

(2) Case 1 is where—
    (a) P offers, promises or gives a financial or other advantage to another person, and
    (b) P intends the advantage—
        (i) to induce a person to perform improperly a relevant function or activity, or
        (ii) to reward a person for the improper performance of such a function or activity.

(3) Case 2 is where—
    (a) P offers, promises or gives a financial or other advantage to another person, and
    (b) P knows or believes that the acceptance of the advantage would itself constitute the improper performance of a relevant function or activity.

(4) In case 1 it does not matter whether the person to whom the advantage is offered, promised or given is the same person as the person who is to perform, or has performed, the function or activity concerned.

(5) In cases 1 and 2 it does not matter whether the advantage is offered, promised or given by P directly or through a third party.

2 Offences relating to being bribed

(1) A person ("R") is guilty of an offence if any of the following cases applies.

(2) Case 3 is where R requests, agrees to receive or accepts a financial or other advantage intending that, in consequence, a relevant function or activity should be performed improperly (whether by R or another person).

(3) Case 4 is where—

    (a) R requests, agrees to receive or accepts a financial or other advantage, and

    (b) the request, agreement or acceptance itself constitutes the improper performance by R of a relevant function or activity.

(4) Case 5 is where R requests, agrees to receive or accepts a financial or other advantage as a reward for the improper performance (whether by R or another person) of a relevant function or activity.

(5) Case 6 is where, in anticipation of or in consequence of R requesting, agreeing to receive or accepting a financial or other advantage, a relevant function or activity is performed improperly—

    (a) by R, or

    (b) by another person at R's request or with R's assent or acquiescence.

(6) In cases 3 to 6 it does not matter—

    (a) whether R requests, agrees to receive or accepts (or is to request, agree to receive or accept) the advantage directly or through a third party,

    (b) whether the advantage is (or is to be) for the benefit of R or another person.

(7) In cases 4 to 6 it does not matter whether R knows or believes that the performance of the function or activity is improper.

(8) In case 6, where a person other than R is performing the function or activity, it also does not matter whether that person knows or believes that the performance of the function or activity is improper.

3 Function or activity to which bribe relates

(1) For the purposes of this Act a function or activity is a relevant function or activity if—

    (a) it falls within subsection (2), and

    (b) meets one or more of conditions A to C.

(2) The following functions and activities fall within this subsection—

    (a)   any function of a public nature,

    (b)   any activity connected with a business,

    (c)   any activity performed in the course of a person's employment,

    (d)   any activity performed by or on behalf of a body of persons (whether corporate or unincorporate).

(3) Condition A is that a person performing the function or activity is expected to perform it in good faith.

(4) Condition B is that a person performing the function or activity is expected to perform it impartially.

(5) Condition C is that a person performing the function or activity is in a position of trust by virtue of performing it.

(6) A function or activity is a relevant function or activity even if it—

    (a)   has no connection with the United Kingdom, and

    (b)   is performed in a country or territory outside the United Kingdom.

(7) In this section "business" includes trade or profession.

4 Improper performance to which bribe relates

(1) For the purposes of this Act a relevant function or activity—

    (a)   is performed improperly if it is performed in breach of a relevant expectation, and

    (b)   is to be treated as being performed improperly if there is a failure to perform the function or activity and that failure is itself a breach of a relevant expectation.

(2) In subsection (1) "relevant expectation"—

    (a)   in relation to a function or activity which meets condition A or B, means the expectation mentioned in the condition concerned, and

    (b)   in relation to a function or activity which meets condition C, means any expectation as to the manner in which, or the reasons for which, the function or activity will be performed that arises from the position of trust mentioned in that condition.

(3) Anything that a person does (or omits to do) arising from or in connection with that person's past performance of a relevant function or activity is to be treated for the purposes of this Act as being done (or omitted) by that person in the performance of that function or activity.

5 Expectation test

(1) For the purposes of sections 3 and 4, the test of what is expected is a test of what a reasonable person in the United Kingdom would expect in relation to the performance of the type of function or activity concerned.

(2) In deciding what such a person would expect in relation to the performance of a function or activity where the performance is not subject to the law of any part of the United Kingdom, any local custom or practice is to be disregarded unless it is permitted or required by the written law applicable to the country or territory concerned.

(3) In subsection (2) "written law" means law contained in—
    (a) any written constitution, or provision made by or under legislation, applicable to the country or territory concerned, or
    (b) any judicial decision which is so applicable and is evidenced in published written sources.

Bribery of foreign public officials

6 Bribery of foreign public officials

(1) A person ("P") who bribes a foreign public official ("F") is guilty of an offence if P's intention is to influence F in F's capacity as a foreign public official.

(2) P must also intend to obtain or retain—
    (a) business, or
    (b) an advantage in the conduct of business.

(3) P bribes F if, and only if—
    (a) directly or through a third party, P offers, promises or gives any financial or other advantage—
        (i) to F, or
        (ii) to another person at F's request or with F's assent or acquiescence, and
    (b) F is neither permitted nor required by the written law applicable to F to be influenced in F's capacity as a foreign public official by the offer, promise or gift.

(4) References in this section to influencing F in F's capacity as a foreign public official mean influencing F in the performance of F's functions as such an official, which includes—
    (a) any omission to exercise those functions, and
    (b) any use of F's position as such an official, even if not within F's authority.

(5) "Foreign public official" means an individual who—
    (a) holds a legislative, administrative or judicial position of any kind, whether appointed or elected, of a country or territory outside the United Kingdom (or any subdivision of such a country or territory),
    (b) exercises a public function—

(i) for or on behalf of a country or territory outside the United Kingdom (or any subdivision of such a country or territory), or

(ii) for any public agency or public enterprise of that country or territory (or subdivision), or

(c) is an official or agent of a public international organisation.

(6) "Public international organisation" means an organisation whose members are any of the following—

(a) countries or territories,

(b) governments of countries or territories,

(c) other public international organisations,

(d) a mixture of any of the above.

(7) For the purposes of subsection (3)(b), the written law applicable to F is—

(a) where the performance of the functions of F which P intends to influence would be subject to the law of any part of the United Kingdom, the law of that part of the United Kingdom,

(b) where paragraph (a) does not apply and F is an official or agent of a public international organisation, the applicable written rules of that organisation,

(c) where paragraphs (a) and (b) do not apply, the law of the country or territory in relation to which F is a foreign public official so far as that law is contained in—

(i) any written constitution, or provision made by or under legislation, applicable to the country or territory concerned, or

(ii) any judicial decision which is so applicable and is evidenced in published written sources.

(8) For the purposes of this section, a trade or profession is a business.

Failure of commercial organisations to prevent bribery

7 Failure of commercial organisations to prevent bribery

(1) A relevant commercial organisation ("C") is guilty of an offence under this section if a person ("A") associated with C bribes another person intending—

(a) to obtain or retain business for C, or

(b) to obtain or retain an advantage in the conduct of business for C.

(2) But it is a defence for C to prove that C had in place adequate procedures designed to prevent persons associated with C from undertaking such conduct.

(3) For the purposes of this section, A bribes another person if, and only if, A—

    (a) is, or would be, guilty of an offence under section 1 or 6 (whether or not A has been prosecuted for such an offence), or

    (b) would be guilty of such an offence if section 12(2)(c) and (4) were omitted.

(4) See section 8 for the meaning of a person associated with C and see section 9 for a duty on the Secretary of State to publish guidance.

(5) In this section—

"partnership" means—

    (a) a partnership within the Partnership Act 1890, or

    (b) a limited partnership registered under the Limited Partnerships Act 1907,

or a firm or entity of a similar character formed under the law of a country or territory outside the United Kingdom,

"relevant commercial organisation" means—

    (a) a body which is incorporated under the law of any part of the United Kingdom and which carries on a business (whether there or elsewhere),

    (b) any other body corporate (wherever incorporated) which carries on a business, or part of a business, in any part of the United Kingdom,

    (c) a partnership which is formed under the law of any part of the United Kingdom and which carries on a business (whether there or elsewhere), or

    (d) any other partnership (wherever formed) which carries on a business, or part of a business, in any part of the United Kingdom,

and, for the purposes of this section, a trade or profession is a business.

8 Meaning of associated person

(1) For the purposes of section 7, a person ("A") is associated with C if (disregarding any bribe under consideration) A is a person who performs services for or on behalf of C.

(2) The capacity in which A performs services for or on behalf of C does not matter.

(3) Accordingly A may (for example) be C's employee, agent or subsidiary.

(4) Whether or not A is a person who performs services for or on behalf of C is to be determined by reference to all the relevant circumstances and not merely by reference to the nature of the relationship between A and C.

(5) But if A is an employee of C, it is to be presumed unless the contrary is shown that A is a person who performs services for or on behalf of C.

9 Guidance about commercial organisations preventing bribery

(1) The Secretary of State must publish guidance about procedures that relevant commercial organisations can put in place to prevent persons associated with them from bribing as mentioned in section 7(1).

(2) The Secretary of State may, from time to time, publish revisions to guidance under this section or revised guidance.

(3) The Secretary of State must consult the Scottish Ministers before publishing anything under this section.

(4) Publication under this section is to be in such manner as the Secretary of State considers appropriate.

(5) Expressions used in this section have the same meaning as in section 7.

Prosecution and penalties

10 Consent to prosecution

(1) No proceedings for an offence under this Act may be instituted in England and Wales except by or with the consent of—
   (a) the Director of Public Prosecutions,
   (b) the Director of the Serious Fraud Office, or
   (c) the Director of Revenue and Customs Prosecutions.

(2) No proceedings for an offence under this Act may be instituted in Northern Ireland except by or with the consent of—
   (a) the Director of Public Prosecutions for Northern Ireland, or
   (b) the Director of the Serious Fraud Office.

(3) No proceedings for an offence under this Act may be instituted in England and Wales or Northern Ireland by a person—
   (a) who is acting—
      (i) under the direction or instruction of the Director of Public Prosecutions, the Director of the Serious Fraud Office or the Director of Revenue and Customs Prosecutions, or
      (ii) on behalf of such a Director, or
   (b) to whom such a function has been assigned by such a Director,
   except with the consent of the Director concerned to the institution of the proceedings.

(4) The Director of Public Prosecutions, the Director of the Serious Fraud Office and the Director of Revenue and Customs Prosecutions must

exercise personally any function under subsection (1), (2) or (3) of giving consent.

(5) The only exception is if—
    (a) the Director concerned is unavailable, and
    (b) there is another person who is designated in writing by the Director acting personally as the person who is authorised to exercise any such function when the Director is unavailable.

(6) In that case, the other person may exercise the function but must do so personally.

(7) Subsections (4) to (6) apply instead of any other provisions which would otherwise have enabled any function of the Director of Public Prosecutions, the Director of the Serious Fraud Office or the Director of Revenue and Customs Prosecutions under subsection (1), (2) or (3) of giving consent to be exercised by a person other than the Director concerned.

(8) No proceedings for an offence under this Act may be instituted in Northern Ireland by virtue of section 36 of the Justice (Northern Ireland) Act 2002 (delegation of the functions of the Director of Public Prosecutions for Northern Ireland to persons other than the Deputy Director) except with the consent of the Director of Public Prosecutions for Northern Ireland to the institution of the proceedings.

(9) The Director of Public Prosecutions for Northern Ireland must exercise personally any function under subsection (2) or (8) of giving consent unless the function is exercised personally by the Deputy Director of Public Prosecutions for Northern Ireland by virtue of section 30(4) or (7) of the Act of 2002 (powers of Deputy Director to exercise functions of Director).

(10) Subsection (9) applies instead of section 36 of the Act of 2002 in relation to the functions of the Director of Public Prosecutions for Northern Ireland and the Deputy Director of Public Prosecutions for Northern Ireland under, or (as the case may be) by virtue of, subsections (2) and (8) above of giving consent.

11 Penalties

(1) An individual guilty of an offence under section 1, 2 or 6 is liable—
    (a) on summary conviction, to imprisonment for a term not exceeding 12 months, or to a fine not exceeding the statutory maximum, or to both,
    (b) on conviction on indictment, to imprisonment for a term not exceeding 10 years, or to a fine, or to both.

(2) Any other person guilty of an offence under section 1, 2 or 6 is liable—

    (a) on summary conviction, to a fine not exceeding the statutory maximum,

    (b) on conviction on indictment, to a fine.

(3) A person guilty of an offence under section 7 is liable on conviction on indictment to a fine.

(4) The reference in subsection (1)(a) to 12 months is to be read—

    (a) in its application to England and Wales in relation to an offence committed before the commencement of section 154(1) of the Criminal Justice Act 2003, and

    (b) in its application to Northern Ireland,

as a reference to 6 months.

Other provisions about offences

12 Offences under this Act: territorial application

(1) An offence is committed under section 1, 2 or 6 in England and Wales, Scotland or Northern Ireland if any act or omission which forms part of the offence takes place in that part of the United Kingdom.

(2) Subsection (3) applies if—

    (a) no act or omission which forms part of an offence under section 1, 2 or 6 takes place in the United Kingdom,

    (b) a person's acts or omissions done or made outside the United Kingdom would form part of such an offence if done or made in the United Kingdom, and

    (c) that person has a close connection with the United Kingdom.

(3) In such a case—

    (a) the acts or omissions form part of the offence referred to in subsection (2)(a), and

    (b) proceedings for the offence may be taken at any place in the United Kingdom.

(4) For the purposes of subsection (2)(c) a person has a close connection with the United Kingdom if, and only if, the person was one of the following at the time the acts or omissions concerned were done or made—

    (a) a British citizen,

    (b) a British overseas territories citizen,

    (c) a British National (Overseas),

    (d) a British Overseas citizen,

    (e) a person who under the British Nationality Act 1981 was a British subject,

    (f) a British protected person within the meaning of that Act,

    (g) an individual ordinarily resident in the United Kingdom,

> (h) a body incorporated under the law of any part of the United Kingdom,
>
> (i) a Scottish partnership.

(5) An offence is committed under section 7 irrespective of whether the acts or omissions which form part of the offence take place in the United Kingdom or elsewhere.

(6) Where no act or omission which forms part of an offence under section 7 takes place in the United Kingdom, proceedings for the offence may be taken at any place in the United Kingdom.

(7) Subsection (8) applies if, by virtue of this section, proceedings for an offence are to be taken in Scotland against a person.

(8) Such proceedings may be taken—

> (a) in any sheriff court district in which the person is apprehended or in custody, or
>
> (b) in such sheriff court district as the Lord Advocate may determine.

(9) In subsection (8) "sheriff court district" is to be read in accordance with section 307(1) of the Criminal Procedure (Scotland) Act 1995.

13 Defence for certain bribery offences etc.

(1) It is a defence for a person charged with a relevant bribery offence to prove that the person's conduct was necessary for—

> (a) the proper exercise of any function of an intelligence service, or
>
> (b) the proper exercise of any function of the armed forces when engaged on active service.

(2) The head of each intelligence service must ensure that the service has in place arrangements designed to ensure that any conduct of a member of the service which would otherwise be a relevant bribery offence is necessary for a purpose falling within subsection (1)(a).

(3) The Defence Council must ensure that the armed forces have in place arrangements designed to ensure that any conduct of—

> (a) a member of the armed forces who is engaged on active service, or
>
> (b) a civilian subject to service discipline when working in support of any person falling within paragraph (a),

which would otherwise be a relevant bribery offence is necessary for a purpose falling within subsection (1)(b).

(4) The arrangements which are in place by virtue of subsection (2) or (3) must be arrangements which the Secretary of State considers to be satisfactory.

(5) For the purposes of this section, the circumstances in which a person's conduct is necessary for a purpose falling within subsection (1)(a) or (b)

are to be treated as including any circumstances in which the person's conduct—

    (a)   would otherwise be an offence under section 2, and

    (b)   involves conduct by another person which, but for subsection (1)(a) or (b), would be an offence under section 1.

(6)   In this section—

"active service" means service in—

    (a)   an action or operation against an enemy,

    (b)   an operation outside the British Islands for the protection of life or property, or

    (c)   the military occupation of a foreign country or territory,

"armed forces" means Her Majesty's forces (within the meaning of the Armed Forces Act 2006),

"civilian subject to service discipline" and "enemy" have the same meaning as in the Act of 2006,

"GCHQ" has the meaning given by section 3(3) of the Intelligence Services Act 1994,

"head" means—

    (a)   in relation to the Security Service, the Director General of the Security Service,

    (b)   in relation to the Secret Intelligence Service, the Chief of the Secret Intelligence Service, and

    (c)   in relation to GCHQ, the Director of GCHQ,

"intelligence service" means the Security Service, the Secret Intelligence Service or GCHQ,

"relevant bribery offence" means—

    (a)   an offence under section 1 which would not also be an offence under section 6,

    (b)   an offence under section 2,

    (c)   an offence committed by aiding, abetting, counselling or procuring the commission of an offence falling within paragraph (a) or (b),

    (d)   an offence of attempting or conspiring to commit, or of inciting the commission of, an offence falling within paragraph (a) or (b), or

    (e)   an offence under Part 2 of the Serious Crime Act 2007 (encouraging or assisting crime) in relation to an offence falling within paragraph (a) or (b).

14   Offences under sections 1, 2 and 6 by bodies corporate etc.

(1)   This section applies if an offence under section 1, 2 or 6 is committed by a body corporate or a Scottish partnership.

(2) If the offence is proved to have been committed with the consent or connivance of—

(a) a senior officer of the body corporate or Scottish partnership, or

(b) a person purporting to act in such a capacity,

the senior officer or person (as well as the body corporate or partnership) is guilty of the offence and liable to be proceeded against and punished accordingly.

(3) But subsection (2) does not apply, in the case of an offence which is committed under section 1, 2 or 6 by virtue of section 12(2) to (4), to a senior officer or person purporting to act in such a capacity unless the senior officer or person has a close connection with the United Kingdom (within the meaning given by section 12(4)).

(4) In this section—

"director", in relation to a body corporate whose affairs are managed by its members, means a member of the body corporate,

"senior officer" means—

(a) in relation to a body corporate, a director, manager, secretary or other similar officer of the body corporate, and

(b) in relation to a Scottish partnership, a partner in the partnership.

15 Offences under section 7 by partnerships

(1) Proceedings for an offence under section 7 alleged to have been committed by a partnership must be brought in the name of the partnership (and not in that of any of the partners).

(2) For the purposes of such proceedings—

(a) rules of court relating to the service of documents have effect as if the partnership were a body corporate, and

(b) the following provisions apply as they apply in relation to a body corporate—

(i) section 33 of the Criminal Justice Act 1925 and Schedule 3 to the Magistrates' Courts Act 1980,

(ii) section 18 of the Criminal Justice Act (Northern Ireland) 1945 (c. 15 (N.I.)) and Schedule 4 to the Magistrates' Courts (Northern Ireland) Order 1981 (S.I. 1981/1675 (N.I.26)),

(iii) section 70 of the Criminal Procedure (Scotland) Act 1995.

(3) A fine imposed on the partnership on its conviction for an offence under section 7 is to be paid out of the partnership assets.

(4) In this section "partnership" has the same meaning as in section 7.

Supplementary and final provisions

16 Application to Crown

This Act applies to individuals in the public service of the Crown as it applies to other individuals.

17 Consequential provision

(1) The following common law offences are abolished—

    (a) the offences under the law of England and Wales and Northern Ireland of bribery and embracery,

    (b) the offences under the law of Scotland of bribery and accepting a bribe.

(2) Schedule 1 (which contains consequential amendments) has effect.

(3) Schedule 2 (which contains repeals and revocations) has effect.

(4) The relevant national authority may by order make such supplementary, incidental or consequential provision as the relevant national authority considers appropriate for the purposes of this Act or in consequence of this Act.

(5) The power to make an order under this section—

    (a) is exercisable by statutory instrument,

    (b) includes power to make transitional, transitory or saving provision,

    (c) may, in particular, be exercised by amending, repealing, revoking or otherwise modifying any provision made by or under an enactment (including any Act passed in the same Session as this Act).

(6) Subject to subsection (7), a statutory instrument containing an order of the Secretary of State under this section may not be made unless a draft of the instrument has been laid before, and approved by a resolution of, each House of Parliament.

(7) A statutory instrument containing an order of the Secretary of State under this section which does not amend or repeal a provision of a public general Act or of devolved legislation is subject to annulment in pursuance of a resolution of either House of Parliament.

(8) Subject to subsection (9), a statutory instrument containing an order of the Scottish Ministers under this section may not be made unless a draft of the instrument has been laid before, and approved by a resolution of, the Scottish Parliament.

(9) A statutory instrument containing an order of the Scottish Ministers under this section which does not amend or repeal a provision of an Act of

the Scottish Parliament or of a public general Act is subject to annulment in pursuance of a resolution of the Scottish Parliament.

(10) In this section—

"devolved legislation" means an Act of the Scottish Parliament, a Measure of the National Assembly for Wales or an Act of the Northern Ireland Assembly,

"enactment" includes an Act of the Scottish Parliament and Northern Ireland legislation,

"relevant national authority" means—

(a) in the case of provision which would be within the legislative competence of the Scottish Parliament if it were contained in an Act of that Parliament, the Scottish Ministers, and

(b) in any other case, the Secretary of State.

18 Extent

(1) Subject as follows, this Act extends to England and Wales, Scotland and Northern Ireland.

(2) Subject to subsections (3) to (5), any amendment, repeal or revocation made by Schedule 1 or 2 has the same extent as the provision amended, repealed or revoked.

(3) The amendment of, and repeals in, the Armed Forces Act 2006 do not extend to the Channel Islands.

(4) The amendments of the International Criminal Court Act 2001 extend to England and Wales and Northern Ireland only.

(5) Subsection (2) does not apply to the repeal in the Civil Aviation Act 1982.

19 Commencement and transitional provision etc.

(1) Subject to subsection (2), this Act comes into force on such day as the Secretary of State may by order made by statutory instrument appoint.

(2) Sections 16, 17(4) to (10) and 18, this section (other than subsections (5) to (7)) and section 20 come into force on the day on which this Act is passed.

(3) An order under subsection (1) may—

(a) appoint different days for different purposes,

(b) make such transitional, transitory or saving provision as the Secretary of State considers appropriate in connection with the coming into force of any provision of this Act.

(4) The Secretary of State must consult the Scottish Ministers before making an order under this section in connection with any provision of this Act which would be within the legislative competence of the Scottish Parliament if it were contained in an Act of that Parliament.

(5) This Act does not affect any liability, investigation, legal proceeding or penalty for or in respect of—

    (a) a common law offence mentioned in subsection (1) of section 17 which is committed wholly or partly before the coming into force of that subsection in relation to such an offence, or

    (b) an offence under the Public Bodies Corrupt Practices Act 1889 or the Prevention of Corruption Act 1906 committed wholly or partly before the coming into force of the repeal of the Act by Schedule 2 to this Act.

(6) For the purposes of subsection (5) an offence is partly committed before a particular time if any act or omission which forms part of the offence takes place before that time.

(7) Subsections (5) and (6) are without prejudice to section 16 of the Interpretation Act 1978 (general savings on repeal).

20 Short title

This Act may be cited as the Bribery Act 2010.

SCHEDULES

SCHEDULE 1   Section 17(2)

CONSEQUENTIAL AMENDMENTS

Ministry of Defence Police Act 1987 (c. 4)

1   In section 2(3)(ba) of the Ministry of Defence Police Act 1987 (jurisdiction of members of Ministry of Defence Police Force) for "Prevention of Corruption Acts 1889 to 1916" substitute "Bribery Act 2010".

Criminal Justice Act 1987 (c. 38)

2   In section 2A of the Criminal Justice Act 1987 (Director of SFO's pre-investigation powers in relation to bribery and corruption: foreign officers etc.) for subsections (5) and (6) substitute—

"(5) This section applies to any conduct—

    (a) which, as a result of section 3(6) of the Bribery Act 2010, constitutes an offence under section 1 or 2 of that Act under the law of England and Wales or Northern Ireland, or

    (b) which constitutes an offence under section 6 of that Act under the law of England and Wales or Northern Ireland."

International Criminal Court Act 2001 (c. 17)

3   The International Criminal Court Act 2001 is amended as follows.

4   In section 54(3) (offences in relation to the ICC: England and Wales)—
    (a) in paragraph (b) for "or" substitute ", an offence under the Bribery Act 2010 or (as the case may be) an offence", and
    (b) in paragraph (c) after "common law" insert "or (as the case may be) under the Bribery Act 2010".

5   In section 61(3)(b) (offences in relation to the ICC: Northern Ireland) after "common law" insert "or (as the case may be) under the Bribery Act 2010".

International Criminal Court (Scotland) Act 2001 (asp 13)

6   In section 4(2) of the International Criminal Court (Scotland) Act 2001 (offences in relation to the ICC)—
    (a) in paragraph (b) after "common law" insert "or (as the case may be) under the Bribery Act 2010", and
    (b) in paragraph (c) for "section 1 of the Prevention of Corruption Act 1906 (c.34) or at common law" substitute "the Bribery Act 2010".

Serious Organised Crime and Police Act 2005 (c. 15)

7   The Serious Organised Crime and Police Act 2005 is amended as follows.

8   In section 61(1) (offences in respect of which investigatory powers apply) for paragraph (h) substitute—
    "(h) any offence under the Bribery Act 2010."

9   In section 76(3) (financial reporting orders: making) for paragraphs (d) to (f) substitute—
    "(da) an offence under any of the following provisions of the Bribery Act 2010—
        section 1 (offences of bribing another person),
        section 2 (offences relating to being bribed),
        section 6 (bribery of foreign public officials),".

10   In section 77(3) (financial reporting orders: making in Scotland) after paragraph (b) insert—
    "(c) an offence under section 1, 2 or 6 of the Bribery Act 2010."

Armed Forces Act 2006 (c. 52)

11   In Schedule 2 to the Armed Forces Act 2006 (which lists serious offences the possible commission of which, if suspected, must be referred to a service police force), in paragraph 12, at the end insert—
    "(aw) an offence under section 1, 2 or 6 of the Bribery Act 2010."

12   The Serious Crime Act 2007 is amended as follows.

13 (1) Section 53 of that Act (certain extra-territorial offences to be prosecuted only by, or with the consent of, the Attorney General or the Advocate General for Northern Ireland) is amended as follows.

     (2) The existing words in that section become the first subsection of the section.

     (3) After that subsection insert—

> "(2) Subsection (1) does not apply to an offence under this Part to which section 10 of the Bribery Act 2010 applies by virtue of section 54(1) and (2) below (encouraging or assisting bribery)."

14 (1) Schedule 1 to that Act (list of serious offences) is amended as follows.

     (2) For paragraph 9 and the heading before it (corruption and bribery: England and Wales) substitute—

> *"Bribery*
>
> 9   An offence under any of the following provisions of the Bribery Act 2010—
> - (a) section 1 (offences of bribing another person);
> - (b) section 2 (offences relating to being bribed);
> - (c) section 6 (bribery of foreign public officials)."

     (3) For paragraph 25 and the heading before it (corruption and bribery: Northern Ireland) substitute—

> *"Bribery*
>
> 25 An offence under any of the following provisions of the Bribery Act 2010—
> - (a) section 1 (offences of bribing another person);
> - (b) section 2 (offences relating to being bribed);
> - (c) section 6 (bribery of foreign public officials)."

SCHEDULE 2 Section 17(3)

REPEALS AND REVOCATIONS

Short title and chapter	*Extent of repeal or revocation*
Public Bodies Corrupt Practices Act 1889 (c. 69)	The whole Act.
Prevention of Corruption Act 1906 (c. 34)	The whole Act.
Prevention of Corruption Act 1916 (c. 64)	The whole Act.
Criminal Justice Act (Northern Ireland) 1945 (c. 15 (N.I.))	Section 22.
Electoral Law Act (Northern Ireland) 1962 (c. 14 (N.I.))	Section 112(3).
Increase of Fines Act (Northern Ireland) 1967 (c. 29 (N.I.))	Section 1(8)(a) and (b).
Criminal Justice (Miscellaneous Provisions) Act (Northern Ireland) 1968 (c. 28 (N.I.))	In Schedule 2, the entry in the table relating to the Prevention of Corruption Act 1906.
Local Government Act (Northern Ireland) 1972 (c. 9 (N.I.))	In Schedule 8, paragraphs 1 and 3.
Civil Aviation Act 1982 (c. 16)	Section 19(1).
Representation of the People Act 1983 (c. 2)	In section 165(1), paragraph (b) and the word "or" immediately before it.
Housing Associations Act 1985 (c. 69)	In Schedule 6, paragraph 1(2).
Criminal Justice Act 1988 (c. 33)	Section 47.
Criminal Justice (Evidence etc.) (Northern Ireland) Order 1988 (S.I. 1988/1847 (N.I.17))	Article 14.
Enterprise and New Towns (Scotland) Act 1990 (c. 35)	In Schedule 1, paragraph 2.

Short title and chapter	Extent of repeal or revocation
Scotland Act 1998 (c. 46)	Section 43.
Anti-terrorism, Crime and Security Act 2001 (c. 24)	Sections 108 to 110.
Criminal Justice (Scotland) Act 2003 (asp 7)	Sections 68 and 69.
Government of Wales Act 2006 (c. 32)	Section 44.
Armed Forces Act 2006 (c. 52)	In Schedule 2, paragraph 12(l) and (m).
Local Government and Public Involvement in Health Act 2007 (c. 28)	Section 217(1)(a). Section 244(4). In Schedule 14, paragraph 1.
Housing and Regeneration Act 2008 (c. 17)	In Schedule 1, paragraph 16.

CONVENTION ON COMBATING BRIBERY OF FOREIGN PUBLIC OFFICIALS IN INTERNATIONAL BUSINESS TRANSACTIONS

Adopted by the Negotiating Conference on 21 November 1997

Preamble

The Parties,

Considering that bribery is a widespread phenomenon in international business transactions, including trade and investment, which raises serious moral and political concerns, undermines good governance and economic development, and distorts international competitive conditions;

Considering that all countries share a responsibility to combat bribery in international business transactions;

Having regard to the Revised Recommendation on Combating Bribery in International Business Transactions, adopted by the Council of the Organisation for Economic Co-operation and Development (OECD) on 23 May 1997, C(97)123/FINAL, which, *inter alia*, called for effective measures to deter, prevent and combat the bribery of foreign public officials in connection with international business transactions, in particular the prompt criminalisation of such bribery in an effective and co-ordinated manner and in conformity with the agreed common elements set out in that Recommendation and with the jurisdictional and other basic legal principles of each country;

Welcoming other recent developments which further advance international understanding and co-operation in combating bribery of public officials, including actions of the United Nations, the World Bank, the International Monetary Fund, the World Trade Organisation, the Organisation of American States, the Council of Europe and the European Union;

Welcoming the efforts of companies, business organisations and trade unions as well as other non-governmental organisations to combat bribery;

Recognising the role of governments in the prevention of solicitation of bribes from individuals and enterprises in international business transactions;

Recognising that achieving progress in this field requires not only efforts on a national level but also multilateral co-operation, monitoring and follow-up;

Recognising that achieving equivalence among the measures to be taken by the Parties is an essential object and purpose of the Convention, which requires that the Convention be ratified without derogations affecting this equivalence;

HAVE AGREED AS FOLLOWS:

Article 1

The Offence of Bribery of Foreign Public Officials

1. Each Party shall take such measures as may be necessary to establish that it is a criminal offence under its law for any person intentionally to offer, promise or give any undue pecuniary or other advantage, whether directly or through intermediaries, to a foreign public official, for that official or for a third party, in order that the official act or refrain from acting in relation to the performance of official duties, in order to obtain or retain business or other improper advantage in the conduct of international business.

2. Each Party shall take any measures necessary to establish that complicity in, including incitement, aiding and abetting, or authorisation of an act of bribery of a foreign public official shall be a criminal offence. Attempt and conspiracy to bribe a foreign public official shall be criminal offences to the same extent as attempt and conspiracy to bribe a public official of that Party.

3. The offences set out in paragraphs 1 and 2 above are hereinafter referred to as "bribery of a foreign public official".

4. For the purpose of this Convention:

    a) "foreign public official" means any person holding a legislative, administrative or judicial office of a foreign country, whether appointed or elected; any person exercising a public function for a foreign country, including for a public agency or public enterprise; and any official or agent of a public international organisation;

    b) "foreign country" includes all levels and subdivisions of government, from national to local;

    c) "act or refrain from acting in relation to the performance of official duties" includes any use of the public official's position, whether or not within the official's authorised competence.

Article 2

Responsibility of Legal Persons

Each Party shall take such measures as may be necessary, in accordance with its legal principles, to establish the liability of legal persons for the bribery of a foreign public official.

Article 3

Sanctions

1. The bribery of a foreign public official shall be punishable by effective, proportionate and dissuasive criminal penalties. The range of penalties shall be comparable to that applicable to the bribery of the Party's own public officials and shall, in the case of natural persons, include deprivation of liberty sufficient to enable effective mutual legal assistance and extradition.

2. In the event that, under the legal system of a Party, criminal responsibility is not applicable to legal persons, that Party shall ensure that legal persons shall be subject to effective, proportionate and dissuasive non-criminal sanctions, including monetary sanctions, for bribery of foreign public officials.

3. Each Party shall take such measures as may be necessary to provide that the bribe and the proceeds of the bribery of a foreign public official, or property the value of which corresponds to that of such proceeds, are subject to seizure and confiscation or that monetary sanctions of comparable effect are applicable.

4. Each Party shall consider the imposition of additional civil or administrative sanctions upon a person subject to sanctions for the bribery of a foreign public official.

Article 4

Jurisdiction

1. Each Party shall take such measures as may be necessary to establish its jurisdiction over the bribery of a foreign public official when the offence is committed in whole or in part in its territory.

2. Each Party which has jurisdiction to prosecute its nationals for offences committed abroad shall take such measures as may be necessary to establish its jurisdiction to do so in respect of the bribery of a foreign public official, according to the same principles.

3. When more than one Party has jurisdiction over an alleged offence described in this Convention, the Parties involved shall, at the request of

one of them, consult with a view to determining the most appropriate jurisdiction for prosecution.

4. Each Party shall review whether its current basis for jurisdiction is effective in the fight against the bribery of foreign public officials and, if it is not, shall take remedial steps.

Article 5

Enforcement

Investigation and prosecution of the bribery of a foreign public official shall be subject to the applicable rules and principles of each Party. They shall not be influenced by considerations of national economic interest, the potential effect upon relations with another State or the identity of the natural or legal persons involved.

Article 6

Statute of Limitations

Any statute of limitations applicable to the offence of bribery of a foreign public official shall allow an adequate period of time for the investigation and prosecution of this offence.

Article 7

Money Laundering

Each Party which has made bribery of its own public official a predicate offence for the purpose of the application of its money laundering legislation shall do so on the same terms for the bribery of a foreign public official, without regard to the place where the bribery occurred.

Article 8

Accounting

1. In order to combat bribery of foreign public officials effectively, each Party shall take such measures as may be necessary, within the framework of its laws and regulations regarding the maintenance of books and records, financial statement disclosures, and accounting and auditing standards, to prohibit the establishment of off-the-books accounts, the making of off-the-books or inadequately identified transactions, the recording of non-existent expenditures, the entry of liabilities with incorrect identification of their object, as well as the use of false documents, by companies subject to those laws and regulations, for the purpose of bribing foreign public officials or of hiding such bribery.

2. Each Party shall provide effective, proportionate and dissuasive civil,

administrative or criminal penalties for such omissions and falsifications in respect of the books, records, accounts and financial statements of such companies.

Article 9

Mutual Legal Assistance

1. Each Party shall, to the fullest extent possible under its laws and relevant treaties and arrangements, provide prompt and effective legal assistance to another Party for the purpose of criminal investigations and proceedings brought by a Party concerning offences within the scope of this Convention and for non-criminal proceedings within the scope of this Convention brought by a Party against a legal person. The requested Party shall inform the requesting Party, without delay, of any additional information or documents needed to support the request for assistance and, where requested, of the status and outcome of the request for assistance.

2. Where a Party makes mutual legal assistance conditional upon the existence of dual criminality, dual criminality shall be deemed to exist if the offence for which the assistance is sought is within the scope of this Convention.

3. A Party shall not decline to render mutual legal assistance for criminal matters within the scope of this Convention on the ground of bank secrecy.

Article 10

Extradition

1. Bribery of a foreign public official shall be deemed to be included as an extraditable offence under the laws of the Parties and the extradition treaties between them.

2. If a Party which makes extradition conditional on the existence of an extradition treaty receives a request for extradition from another Party with which it has no extradition treaty, it may consider this Convention to be the legal basis for extradition in respect of the offence of bribery of a foreign public official.

3. Each Party shall take any measures necessary to assure either that it can extradite its nationals or that it can prosecute its nationals for the offence of bribery of a foreign public official. A Party which declines a request to extradite a person for bribery of a foreign public official solely on the ground that the person is its national shall submit the case to its competent authorities for the purpose of prosecution.

4. Extradition for bribery of a foreign public official is subject to the conditions set out in the domestic law and applicable treaties and arrangements of each Party. Where a Party makes extradition conditional upon the existence of dual criminality, that condition shall be deemed to be fulfilled if the offence for which extradition is sought is within the scope of Article 1 of this Convention.

Article 11

Responsible Authorities

For the purposes of Article 4, paragraph 3, on consultation, Article 9, on mutual legal assistance and Article 10, on extradition, each Party shall notify to the Secretary-General of the OECD an authority or authorities responsible for making and receiving requests, which shall serve as channel of communication for these matters for that Party, without prejudice to other arrangements between Parties.

Article 12

Monitoring and Follow-up

The Parties shall co-operate in carrying out a programme of systematic follow-up to monitor and promote the full implementation of this Convention. Unless otherwise decided by consensus of the Parties, this shall be done in the framework of the OECD Working Group on Bribery in International Business Transactions and according to its terms of reference, or within the framework and terms of reference of any successor to its functions, and Parties shall bear the costs of the programme in accordance with the rules applicable to that body.

Article 13

Signature and Accession

1. Until its entry into force, this Convention shall be open for signature by OECD Members and by Non-Members which have been invited to become full participants in its Working Group on Bribery in International Business Transactions.

2. Subsequent to its entry into force, this Convention shall be open to accession by any non-signatory which is a member of the OECD or has become a full participant in the Working Group on Bribery in International Business Transactions or any successor to its functions. For each such non-signatory, the Convention shall enter into force on the sixtieth day following the date of deposit of its instrument of accession.

Article 14

Ratification and Depositary

1. This Convention is subject to acceptance, approval or ratification by the Signatories, in accordance with their respective laws.

2. Instruments of acceptance, approval, ratification or accession shall be deposited with the Secretary-General of the OECD, who shall serve as Depositary of this Convention.

Article 15

Entry into Force

1. This Convention shall enter into force on the sixtieth day following the date upon which five of the ten countries which have the ten largest export shares set out in DAFFE/IME/BR(97)18/FINAL (annexed), and which represent by themselves at least sixty per cent of the combined total exports of those ten countries, have deposited their instruments of acceptance, approval, or ratification. For each signatory depositing its instrument after such entry into force, the Convention shall enter into force on the sixtieth day after deposit of its instrument.

2. If, after 31 December 1998, the Convention has not entered into force under paragraph 1 above, any signatory which has deposited its instrument of acceptance, approval or ratification may declare in writing to the Depositary its readiness to accept entry into force of this Convention under this paragraph 2. The Convention shall enter into force for such a signatory on the sixtieth day following the date upon which such declarations have been deposited by at least two signatories. For each signatory depositing its declaration after such entry into force, the Convention shall enter into force on the sixtieth day following the date of deposit.

Article 16

Amendment

Any Party may propose the amendment of this Convention. A proposed amendment shall be submitted to the Depositary which shall communicate it to the other Parties at least sixty days before convening a meeting of the Parties to consider the proposed amendment. An amendment adopted by consensus of the Parties, or by such other means as the Parties may determine by consensus, shall enter into force sixty days after the deposit of an instrument of ratification, acceptance or approval by all of the Parties, or in such other circumstances as may be specified by the Parties at the time of adoption of the amendment.

Article 17

Withdrawal

A Party may withdraw from this Convention by submitting written notification to the Depositary. Such withdrawal shall be effective one year after the date of the receipt of the notification. After withdrawal, co-operation shall continue between the Parties and the Party which has withdrawn on all requests for assistance or extradition made before the effective date of withdrawal which remain pending.

ANTI-BRIBERY AND BOOKS & RECORDS PROVISIONS OF THE FOREIGN CORRUPT PRACTICES ACT
Current through Pub. L. 105-366
(November 10, 1998)
UNITED STATES CODE
TITLE 15. COMMERCE AND TRADE
CHAPTER 2B—SECURITIES EXCHANGES

§ 78m. Periodical and other reports

(a) Reports by issuer of security; contents

Every issuer of a security registered pursuant to section 78l of this title shall file with the Commission, in accordance with such rules and regulations as the Commission may prescribe as necessary or appropriate for the proper protection of investors and to insure fair dealing in the security—

(1) such information and documents (and such copies thereof) as the Commission shall require to keep reasonably current the information and documents required to be included in or filed with an application or registration statement filed pursuant to section 78l of this title, except that the Commission may not require the filing of any material contract wholly executed before July 1, 1962.

(2) such annual reports (and such copies thereof), certified if required by the rules and regulations of the Commission by independent public accountants, and such quarterly reports (and such copies thereof), as the Commission may prescribe.

Every issuer of a security registered on a national securities exchange shall also file a duplicate original of such information, documents, and reports with the exchange.

(b) Form of report; books, records, and internal accounting; directives

* * *

(2) Every issuer which has a class of securities registered pursuant to section 78l of this title and every issuer which is required to file reports pursuant to section 78o(d) of this title shall–

(A) make and keep books, records, and accounts, which, in reasonable detail, accurately and fairly reflect the transactions and dispositions of the assets of the issuer; and

(B) devise and maintain a system of internal accounting controls sufficient to provide reasonable assurances that—

(i) transactions are executed in accordance with management's general or specific authorization;

(ii) transactions are recorded as necessary (I) to permit preparation of financial statements in conformity with generally accepted accounting principles or any other criteria applicable to such statements, and (II) to maintain accountability for assets;

(iii) access to assets is permitted only in accordance with management's general or specific authorization; and

(iv) the recorded accountability for assets is compared with the existing assets at reasonable intervals and appropriate action is taken with respect to any differences.

(3) (A) With respect to matters concerning the national security of the United States, no duty or liability under paragraph (2) of this subsection shall be imposed upon any person acting in cooperation with the head of any Federal department or agency responsible for such matters if such act in cooperation with such head of a department or agency was done upon the specific, written directive of the head of such department or agency pursuant to Presidential authority to issue such directives. Each directive issued under this paragraph shall set forth the specific facts and circumstances with respect to which the provisions of this paragraph are to be invoked. Each such directive shall, unless renewed in writing, expire one year after the date of issuance.

(B) Each head of a Federal department or agency of the United States who issues such a directive pursuant to this paragraph shall maintain a complete file of all such directives and shall, on October 1 of each year, transmit a summary of matters covered by such directives in force at any time during the previous year to the Permanent Select Committee on Intelligence of the House of Representatives and the Select Committee on Intelligence of the Senate.

(4) No criminal liability shall be imposed for failing to comply with the requirements of paragraph (2) of this subsection except as provided in paragraph (5) of this subsection.

(5) No person shall knowingly circumvent or knowingly fail to implement a system of internal accounting controls or knowingly falsify any book, record, or account described in paragraph (2).

(6) Where an issuer which has a class of securities registered pursuant to section

78l of this title or an issuer which is required to file reports pursuant to section 78o(d) of this title holds 50 per centum or less of the voting power with respect to a domestic or foreign firm, the provisions of paragraph (2) require only that the issuer proceed in good faith to use its influence, to the extent reasonable under the issuer's circumstances, to cause such domestic or foreign firm to devise and maintain a system of internal accounting controls consistent with paragraph (2). Such circumstances include the relative degree of the issuer's ownership of the domestic or foreign firm and the laws and practices governing the business operations of the country in which such firm is located. An issuer which demonstrates good faith efforts to use such influence shall be conclusively presumed to have complied with the requirements of paragraph (2).

(7) For the purpose of paragraph (2) of this subsection, the terms "reasonable assurances" and "reasonable detail" mean such level of detail and degree of assurance as would satisfy prudent officials in the conduct of their own affairs.

* * *

§ 78dd-1 [Section 30A of the Securities & Exchange Act of 1934].

Prohibited foreign trade practices by issuers

(a) Prohibition

It shall be unlawful for any issuer which has a class of securities registered pursuant to section 78l of this title or which is required to file reports under section 78o(d) of this title, or for any officer, director, employee, or agent of such issuer or any stockholder thereof acting on behalf of such issuer, to make use of the mails or any means or instrumentality of interstate commerce corruptly in furtherance of an offer, payment, promise to pay, or authorization of the payment of any money, or offer, gift, promise to give, or authorization of the giving of anything of value to–

(1) any foreign official for purposes of—

(A) (i) influencing any act or decision of such foreign official in his official capacity, (ii) inducing such foreign official to do or omit to do any act in violation of the lawful duty of such official, or (iii) securing any improper advantage; or

(B) inducing such foreign official to use his influence with a foreign government or instrumentality thereof to affect or influence any act or decision of such government or instrumentality,

in order to assist such issuer in obtaining or retaining business for or with, or directing business to, any person;

(2) any foreign political party or official thereof or any candidate for foreign political office for purposes of—

(A) (i) influencing any act or decision of such party, official, or candidate in its or his official capacity, (ii) inducing such party, official, or candidate to do or omit to do an act in violation of the lawful duty of such party, official, or candidate, or (iii) securing any improper advantage; or

(B) inducing such party, official, or candidate to use its or his influence with a foreign government or instrumentality thereof to affect or influence any act or decision of such government or instrumentality.

in order to assist such issuer in obtaining or retaining business for or with, or directing business to, any person; or

(3) any person, while knowing that all or a portion of such money or thing of value will be offered, given, or promised, directly or indirectly, to any foreign official, to any foreign political party or official thereof, or to any candidate for foreign political office, for purposes of–

(A) (i) influencing any act or decision of such foreign official, political party, party official, or candidate in his or its official capacity, (ii) inducing such foreign official, political party, party official, or candidate to do or omit to do any act in violation of the lawful duty of such foreign official, political party, party official, or candidate, or (iii) securing any improper advantage; or

(B) inducing such foreign official, political party, party official, or candidate to use his or its influence with a foreign government or instrumentality thereof to affect or influence any act or decision of such government or instrumentality,

in order to assist such issuer in obtaining or retaining business for or with, or directing business to, any person.

(b) Exception for routine governmental action

Subsections (a) and (g) of this section shall not apply to any facilitating or expediting payment to a foreign official, political party, or party official the purpose of which is to expedite or to secure the performance of a routine governmental action by a foreign official, political party, or party official.

(c) Affirmative defenses

It shall be an affirmative defense to actions under subsection (a) or (g) of this section that–

(1) the payment, gift, offer, or promise of anything of value that was made, was lawful under the written laws and regulations of the foreign official's, political party's, party official's, or candidate's country; or

(2) the payment, gift, offer, or promise of anything of value that was made, was a reasonable and bona fide expenditure, such as travel and lodging expenses, incurred by or on behalf of a foreign official, party, party official, or candidate and was directly related to–

(A) the promotion, demonstration, or explanation of products or services; or

(B) the execution or performance of a contract with a foreign government or agency thereof.

(d) Guidelines by Attorney General

Not later than one year after August 23, 1988, the Attorney General, after consultation with the Commission, the Secretary of Commerce, the United States Trade Representative, the Secretary of State, and the Secretary of the Treasury, and after obtaining the views of all interested persons through public notice and comment procedures, shall determine to what extent compliance with this section would be enhanced and the business community would be assisted by further clarification of the preceding provisions of this section and may, based on such determination and to the extent necessary and appropriate, issue–

(1) guidelines describing specific types of conduct, associated with common types of export sales arrangements and business contracts, which for purposes of the Department of Justice's present enforcement policy, the Attorney General determines would be in conformance with the preceding provisions of this section; and

(2) general precautionary procedures which issuers may use on a voluntary basis to conform their conduct to the Department of Justice's present enforcement policy regarding the preceding provisions of this section.

The Attorney General shall issue the guidelines and procedures referred to in the preceding sentence in accordance with the provisions of subchapter II of chapter 5 of Title 5 and those guidelines and procedures shall be subject to the provisions of chapter 7 of that title.

(e) Opinions of Attorney General

(1) The Attorney General, after consultation with appropriate departments and agencies of the United States and after obtaining the views of all interested persons through public notice and comment procedures, shall establish a procedure to provide responses to specific inquiries by issuers concerning conformance of their conduct with the Department of Justice's present enforcement policy regarding the preceding provisions of this section. The Attorney General shall, within 30 days after receiving such a request, issue an opinion in response to that request. The opinion shall state whether or not certain specified prospective conduct would, for purposes of the Department of Justice's present enforcement policy, violate the preceding provisions of this section. Additional requests for opinions may be filed with the Attorney General regarding other specified prospective conduct that is beyond the scope of conduct specified in previous requests. In any action brought under the applicable provisions of this section, there shall be a rebuttable presumption that conduct, which is specified in a request by an issuer and for which the Attorney General has issued an opinion

that such conduct is in conformity with the Department of Justice's present enforcement policy, is in compliance with the preceding provisions of this section. Such a presumption may be rebutted by a preponderance of the evidence. In considering the presumption for purposes of this paragraph, a court shall weight all relevant factors, including but not limited to whether the information submitted to the Attorney General was accurate and complete and whether it was within the scope of the conduct specified in any request received by the Attorney General. The Attorney General shall establish the procedure required by this paragraph in accordance with the provisions of subchapter II of chapter 5 of Title 5 and that procedure shall be subject to the provisions of chapter 7 of that title.

(2) Any document or other material which is provided to, received by, or prepared in the Department of Justice or any other department or agency of the United States in connection with a request by an issuer under the procedure established under paragraph (1), shall be exempt from disclosure under section 552 of Title 5 and shall not, except with the consent of the issuer, be made publicly available, regardless of whether the Attorney General responds to such a request or the issuer withdraws such request before receiving a response.

(3) Any issuer who has made a request to the Attorney General under paragraph (1) may withdraw such request prior to the time the Attorney General issues an opinion in response to such request. Any request so withdrawn shall have no force or effect.

(4) The Attorney General shall, to the maximum extent practicable, provide timely guidance concerning the Department of Justice's present enforcement policy with respect to the preceding provisions of this section to potential exporters and small businesses that are unable to obtain specialized counsel on issues pertaining to such provisions. Such guidance shall be limited to responses to requests under paragraph (1) concerning conformity of specified prospective conduct with the Department of Justice's present enforcement policy regarding the preceding provisions of this section and general explanations of compliance responsibilities and of potential liabilities under the preceding provisions of this section.

(f) Definitions

For purposes of this section:
(1) A) The term "foreign official" means any officer or employee of a foreign government or any department, agency, or instrumentality thereof, or of a public international organization, or any person acting in an official capacity for or on behalf of any such government or department, agency, or instrumentality, or for or on behalf of any such public international organization. (B) For purposes of subparagraph (A), the term "public international organization" means—
    (i)   an organization that is designated by Executive Order pursuant to

section 1 of the International Organizations Immunities Act (22 U.S.C. § 288); or

(ii) any other international organization that is designated by the President by Executive order for the purposes of this section, effective as of the date of publication of such order in the Federal Register.

(2) (A) A person's state of mind is "knowing" with respect to conduct, a circumstance, or a result if—

(i) such person is aware that such person is engaging in such conduct, that such circumstance exists, or that such result is substantially certain to occur; or

(ii) such person has a firm belief that such circumstance exists or that such result is substantially certain to occur.

(B) When knowledge of the existence of a particular circumstance is required for an offense, such knowledge is established if a person is aware of a high probability of the existence of such circumstance, unless the person actually believes that such circumstance does not exist.

(3) (A) The term "routine governmental action" means only an action which is ordinarily and commonly performed by a foreign official in—

(i) obtaining permits, licenses, or other official documents to qualify a person to do business in a foreign country;

(ii) processing governmental papers, such as visas and work orders;

(iii) providing police protection, mail pick-up and delivery, or scheduling inspections associated with contract performance or inspections related to transit of goods across country;

(iv) providing phone service, power and water supply, loading and unloading cargo, or protecting perishable products or commodities from deterioration; or

(v) actions of a similar nature.

(B) The term "routine governmental action" does not include any decision by a foreign official whether, or on what terms, to award new business to or to continue business with a particular party, or any action taken by a foreign official involved in the decision-making process to encourage a decision to award new business to or continue business with a particular party.

(g) Alternative Jurisdiction

(1) It shall also be unlawful for any issuer organized under the laws of the United States, or a State, territory, possession, or commonwealth of the United States or a political subdivision thereof and which has a class of securities registered pursuant to section 12 of this title or which is required to file reports under section 15(d) of this title, or for any United States person that is an officer, director, employee, or agent of such issuer or a stockholder thereof acting on behalf of such issuer, to corruptly do any act outside the United States in fur-

therance of an offer, payment, promise to pay, or authorization of the payment of any money, or offer, gift, promise to give, or authorization of the giving of anything of value to any of the persons or entities set forth in paragraphs (1), (2), and (3) of this subsection (a) of this section for the purposes set forth therein, irrespective of whether such issuer or such officer, director, employee, agent, or stockholder makes use of the mails or any means or instrumentality of interstate commerce in furtherance of such offer, gift, payment, promise, or authorization.

(2) As used in this subsection, the term "United States person" means a national of the United States (as defined in section 101 of the Immigration and Nationality Act (8 U.S.C. § 1101)) or any corporation, partnership, association, joint-stock company, business trust, unincorporated organization, or sole proprietorship organized under the laws of the United States or any State, territory, possession, or commonwealth of the United States, or any political subdivision thereof.

§ 78dd-2. Prohibited foreign trade practices by domestic concerns

(a) Prohibition

It shall be unlawful for any domestic concern, other than an issuer which is subject to section 78dd-1 of this title, or for any officer, director, employee, or agent of such domestic concern or any stockholder thereof acting on behalf of such domestic concern, to make use of the mails or any means or instrumentality of interstate commerce corruptly in furtherance of an offer, payment, promise to pay, or authorization of the payment of any money, or offer, gift, promise to give, or authorization of the giving of anything of value to–

(1) any foreign official for purposes of—

(A) (i) influencing any act or decision of such foreign official in his official capacity, (ii) inducing such foreign official to do or omit to do any act in violation of the lawful duty of such official, or (iii) securing any improper advantage; or

(B) inducing such foreign official to use his influence with a foreign government or instrumentality thereof to affect or influence any act or decision of such government or instrumentality,

in order to assist such domestic concern in obtaining or retaining business for or with, or directing business to, any person;

(2) any foreign political party or official thereof or any candidate for foreign political office for purposes of—

(A) (i) influencing any act or decision of such party, official, or candidate in its or his official capacity, (ii) inducing such party, official, or candidate to do or omit to do an act in violation of the lawful duty of such party, official, or candidate, or (iii) securing any improper advantage; or

(B) inducing such party, official, or candidate to use its or his influence with a foreign government or instrumentality thereof to affect or influence any act or decision of such government or instrumentality,

in order to assist such domestic concern in obtaining or retaining business for or with, or directing business to, any person;

(3) any person, while knowing that all or a portion of such money or thing of value will be offered, given, or promised, directly or indirectly, to any foreign official, to any foreign political party or official thereof, or to any candidate for foreign political office, for purposes of—

(A) (i) influencing any act or decision of such foreign official, political party, party official, or candidate in his or its official capacity, (ii) inducing such foreign official, political party, party official, or candidate to do or omit to do any act in violation of the lawful duty of such foreign official, political party, party official, or candidate, or (iii) securing any improper advantage; or

(B) inducing such foreign official, political party, party official, or candidate to use his or its influence with a foreign government or instrumentality thereof to affect or influence any act or decision of such government or instrumentality,

in order to assist such domestic concern in obtaining or retaining business for or with, or directing business to, any person.

(b) Exception for routine governmental action

Subsections (a) and (i) of this section shall not apply to any facilitating or expediting payment to a foreign official, political party, or party official the purpose of which is to expedite or to secure the performance of a routine governmental action by a foreign official, political party, or party official.

(c) Affirmative defenses

It shall be an affirmative defense to actions under subsection (a) or (i) of this section that—

(1) the payment, gift, offer, or promise of anything of value that was made, was lawful under the written laws and regulations of the foreign official's, political party's, party official's, or candidate's country; or

(2) the payment, gift, offer, or promise of anything of value that was made, was a reasonable and bona fide expenditure, such as travel and lodging expenses, incurred by or on behalf of a foreign official, party, party official, or candidate and was directly related to–

(A) the promotion, demonstration, or explanation of products or services; or

(B) the execution or performance of a contract with a foreign government or agency thereof.

(d) Injunctive relief

(1) When it appears to the Attorney General that any domestic concern to which this section applies, or officer, director, employee, agent, or stockholder thereof, is engaged, or about to engage, in any act or practice constituting a violation of subsection (a) or (i) of this section, the Attorney General may, in his discretion, bring a civil action in an appropriate district court of the United States to enjoin such act or practice, and upon a proper showing, a permanent injunction or a temporary restraining order shall be granted without bond.

(2) For the purpose of any civil investigation which, in the opinion of the Attorney General, is necessary and proper to enforce this section, the Attorney General or his designee are empowered to administer oaths and affirmations, subpoena witnesses, take evidence, and require the production of any books, papers, or other documents which the Attorney General deems relevant or material to such investigation. The attendance of witnesses and the production of documentary evidence may be required from any place in the United States, or any territory, possession, or commonwealth of the United States, at any designated place of hearing.

(3) In case of contumacy by, or refusal to obey a subpoena issued to, any person, the Attorney General may invoke the aid of any court of the United States within the jurisdiction of which such investigation or proceeding is carried on, or where such person resides or carries on business, in requiring the attendance and testimony of witnesses and the production of books, papers, or other documents. Any such court may issue an order requiring such person to appear before the Attorney General or his designee, there to produce records, if so ordered, or to give testimony touching the matter under investigation. Any failure to obey such order of the court may be punished by such court as a contempt thereof.

All process in any such case may be served in the judicial district in which such person resides or may be found. The Attorney General may make such rules relating to civil investigations as may be necessary or appropriate to implement the provisions of this subsection.

(e) Guidelines by Attorney General

Not later than 6 months after August 23, 1988, the Attorney General, after consultation with the Securities and Exchange Commission, the Secretary of Commerce, the United States Trade Representative, the Secretary of State, and the Secretary of the Treasury, and after obtaining the views of all interested persons through public notice and comment procedures, shall determine to what extent compliance with this section would be enhanced and the business community would be assisted by further clarification of the preceding provisions of this section and may, based on such determination and to the extent necessary and appropriate, issue—

(1) guidelines describing specific types of conduct, associated with common types

of export sales arrangements and business contracts, which for purposes of the Department of Justice's present enforcement policy, the Attorney General determines would be in conformance with the preceding provisions of this section; and

(2) general precautionary procedures which domestic concerns may use on a voluntary basis to conform their conduct to the Department of Justice's present enforcement policy regarding the preceding provisions of this section.

The Attorney General shall issue the guidelines and procedures referred to in the preceding sentence in accordance with the provisions of subchapter II of chapter 5 of Title 5 and those guidelines and procedures shall be subject to the provisions of chapter 7 of that title.

(f) Opinions of Attorney General

(1) The Attorney General, after consultation with appropriate departments and agencies of the United States and after obtaining the views of all interested persons through public notice and comment procedures, shall establish a procedure to provide responses to specific inquiries by domestic concerns concerning conformance of their conduct with the Department of Justice's present enforcement policy regarding the preceding provisions of this section. The Attorney General shall, within 30 days after receiving such a request, issue an opinion in response to that request. The opinion shall state whether or not certain specified prospective conduct would, for purposes of the Department of Justice's present enforcement policy, violate the preceding provisions of this section. Additional requests for opinions may be filed with the Attorney General regarding other specified prospective conduct that is beyond the scope of conduct specified in previous requests. In any action brought under the applicable provisions of this section, there shall be a rebuttable presumption that conduct, which is specified in a request by a domestic concern and for which the Attorney General has issued an opinion that such conduct is in conformity with the Department of Justice's present enforcement policy, is in compliance with the preceding provisions of this section. Such a presumption may be rebutted by a preponderance of the evidence. In considering the presumption for purposes of this paragraph, a court shall weigh all relevant factors, including but not limited to whether the information submitted to the Attorney General was accurate and complete and whether it was within the scope of the conduct specified in any request received by the Attorney General. The Attorney General shall establish the procedure required by this paragraph in accordance with the provisions of subchapter II of chapter 5 of Title 5 and that procedure shall be subject to the provisions of chapter 7 of that title.

(2) Any document or other material which is provided to, received by, or prepared in the Department of Justice or any other department or agency of the United States in connection with a request by a domestic concern under the procedure established under paragraph (1), shall be exempt from disclosure under section 552 of Title 5 and shall not, except with the consent of the domestic

concern, by made publicly available, regardless of whether the Attorney General response to such a request or the domestic concern withdraws such request before receiving a response.

(3) Any domestic concern who has made a request to the Attorney General under paragraph (1) may withdraw such request prior to the time the Attorney General issues an opinion in response to such request. Any request so withdrawn shall have no force or effect.

(4) The Attorney General shall, to the maximum extent practicable, provide timely guidance concerning the Department of Justice's present enforcement policy with respect to the preceding provisions of this section to potential exporters and small businesses that are unable to obtain specialized counsel on issues pertaining to such provisions. Such guidance shall be limited to responses to requests under paragraph (1) concerning conformity of specified prospective conduct with the Department of Justice's present enforcement policy regarding the preceding provisions of this section and general explanations of compliance responsibilities and of potential liabilities under the preceding provisions of this section.

(g) Penalties

(1) (A) Any domestic concern that is not a natural person and that violates subsection (a) or (i) of this section shall be fined not more than $2,000,000.
(B) Any domestic concern that is not a natural person and that violates subsection (a) or (i) of this section shall be subject to a civil penalty of not more than $10,000 imposed in an action brought by the Attorney General.

(2) (A) Any natural person that is an officer, director, employee, or agent of a domestic concern, or stockholder acting on behalf of such domestic concern, who willfully violates subsection (a) or (i) of this section shall be fined not more than $100,000 or imprisoned not more than 5 years, or both.
(B) Any natural person that is an officer, director, employee, or agent of a domestic concern, or stockholder acting on behalf of such domestic concern, who violates subsection (a) or (i) of this section shall be subject to a civil penalty of not more than $10,000 imposed in an action brought by the Attorney General.

(3) Whenever a fine is imposed under paragraph (2) upon any officer, director, employee, agent, or stockholder of a domestic concern, such fine may not be paid, directly or indirectly, by such domestic concern.

(h) Definitions

For purposes of this section:

(1) The term "domestic concern" means—
(A) any individual who is a citizen, national, or resident of the United States; and

(B) any corporation, partnership, association, joint-stock company, business trust, unincorporated organization, or sole proprietorship which has its principal place of business in the United States, or which is organized under the laws of a State of the United States or a territory, possession, or commonwealth of the United States.

(2) (A) The term "foreign official" means any officer or employee of a foreign government or any department, agency, or instrumentality thereof, or of a public international organization, or any person acting in an official capacity for or on behalf of any such government or department, agency, or instrumentality, or for or on behalf of any such public international organization.

(B) For purposes of subparagraph (A), the term "public international organization" means–

(i) an organization that has been designated by Executive order pursuant to Section 1 of the International Organizations Immunities Act (22 U.S.C. § 288); or

(ii) any other international organization that is designated by the President by Executive order for the purposes of this section, effective as of the date of publication of such order in the Federal Register.

(3) (A) A person's state of mind is "knowing" with respect to conduct, a circumstance, or a result if—

(i) such person is aware that such person is engaging in such conduct, that such circumstance exists, or that such result is substantially certain to occur; or

(ii) such person has a firm belief that such circumstance exists or that such result is substantially certain to occur.

(B) When knowledge of the existence of a particular circumstance is required for an offense, such knowledge is established if a person is aware of a high probability of the existence of such circumstance, unless the person actually believes that such circumstance does not exist.

(4) (A) The term "routine governmental action" means only an action which is ordinarily and commonly performed by a foreign official in—

(i) obtaining permits, licenses, or other official documents to qualify a person to do business in a foreign country;

(ii) processing governmental papers, such as visas and work orders;

(iii) providing police protection, mail pick-up and delivery, or scheduling inspections associated with contract performance or inspections related to transit of goods across country;

(iv) providing phone service, power and water supply, loading and unloading cargo, or protecting perishable products or commodities from deterioration; or

(v) actions of a similar nature.

(B) The term "routine governmental action" does not include any decision by a foreign official whether, or on what terms, to award new business to or to continue business with a particular party, or any action taken by a foreign official involved in the decision-making process to encourage a decision to award new business to or continue business with a particular party.

(5) The term "interstate commerce" means trade, commerce, transportation, or communication among the several States, or between any foreign country and any State or between any State and any place or ship outside thereof, and such term includes the intrastate use of—

(A) a telephone or other interstate means of communication, or

(B) any other interstate instrumentality.

(i) Alternative Jurisdiction

(1) It shall also be unlawful for any United States person to corruptly do any act outside the United States in furtherance of an offer, payment, promise to pay, or authorization of the payment of any money, or offer, gift, promise to give, or authorization of the giving of anything of value to any of the persons or entities set forth in paragraphs (1), (2), and (3) of subsection (a), for the purposes set forth therein, irrespective of whether such United States person makes use of the mails or any means or instrumentality of interstate commerce in furtherance of such offer, gift, payment, promise, or authorization.

(2) As used in this subsection, a "United States person" means a national of the United States (as defined in section 101 of the Immigration and Nationality Act (8 U.S.C. § 1101)) or any corporation, partnership, association, joint-stock company, business trust, unincorporated organization, or sole pro-prietorship organized under the laws of the United States or any State, territory, possession, or commonwealth of the United States, or any political subdivision thereof.

§ 78dd-3. Prohibited foreign trade practices by persons other than issuers or domestic concerns

(a) Prohibition

It shall be unlawful for any person other than an issuer that is subject to section 30A of the Securities Exchange Act of 1934 or a domestic concern, as defined in section 104 of this Act), or for any officer, director, employee, or agent of such person or any stockholder thereof acting on behalf of such person, while in the territory of the United States, corruptly to make use of the mails or any means or instrumentality of interstate commerce or to do any other act in furtherance of an offer, payment, promise to pay, or authorization of the payment of any money, or offer, gift, promise to give, or authorization of the giving of anything of value to–

(1) any foreign official for purposes of—

(A) (i) influencing any act or decision of such foreign official in his official capacity, (ii) inducing such foreign official to do or omit to do any act in violation of the lawful duty of such official, or (iii) securing any improper advantage; or

(B) inducing such foreign official to use his influence with a foreign government or instrumentality thereof to affect or influence any act or decision of such government or instrumentality,

in order to assist such person in obtaining or retaining business for or with, or directing business to, any person;

(2) any foreign political party or official thereof or any candidate for foreign political office for purposes of—

(A) (i) influencing any act or decision of such party, official, or candidate in its or his official capacity, (ii) inducing such party, official, or candidate to do or omit to do an act in violation of the lawful duty of such party, official, or candidate, or (iii) securing any improper advantage; or

(B) inducing such party, official, or candidate to use its or his influence with a foreign government or instrumentality thereof to affect or influence any act or decision of such government or instrumentality.

in order to assist such person in obtaining or retaining business for or with, or directing business to, any person; or

(3) any person, while knowing that all or a portion of such money or thing of value will be offered, given, or promised, directly or indirectly, to any foreign official, to any foreign political party or official thereof, or to any candidate for foreign political office, for purposes of–

(A) (i) influencing any act or decision of such foreign official, political party, party official, or candidate in his or its official capacity, (ii) inducing such foreign official, political party, party official, or candidate to do or omit to do any act in violation of the lawful duty of such foreign official, political party, party official, or candidate, or (iii) securing any improper advantage; or

(B) inducing such foreign official, political party, party official, or candidate to use his or its influence with a foreign government or instrumentality thereof to affect or influence any act or decision of such government or instrumentality,

in order to assist such person in obtaining or retaining business for or with, or directing business to, any person.

(b) Exception for routine governmental action

Subsection (a) of this section shall not apply to any facilitating or expediting payment to a foreign official, political party, or party official the purpose of which is to expedite or to secure the performance of a routine governmental action by a foreign official, political party, or party official.

(c) Affirmative defenses

It shall be an affirmative defense to actions under subsection (a) of this section that–

(1) the payment, gift, offer, or promise of anything of value that was made, was lawful under the written laws and regulations of the foreign official's, political party's, party official's, or candidate's country; or

(2) the payment, gift, offer, or promise of anything of value that was made, was a reasonable and bona fide expenditure, such as travel and lodging expenses, incurred by or on behalf of a foreign official, party, party official, or candidate and was directly related to—

(A) the promotion, demonstration, or explanation of products or services; or

(B) the execution or performance of a contract with a foreign government or agency thereof.

(d) Injunctive relief

(1) When it appears to the Attorney General that any person to which this section applies, or officer, director, employee, agent, or stockholder thereof, is engaged, or about to engage, in any act or practice constituting a violation of subsection (a) of this section, the Attorney General may, in his discretion, bring a civil action in an appropriate district court of the United States to enjoin such act or practice, and upon a proper showing, a permanent injunction or a temporary restraining order shall be granted without bond.

(2) For the purpose of any civil investigation which, in the opinion of the Attorney General, is necessary and proper to enforce this section, the Attorney General or his designee are empowered to administer oaths and affirmations, subpoena witnesses, take evidence, and require the production of any books, papers, or other documents which the Attorney General deems relevant or material to such investigation. The attendance of witnesses and the production of documentary evidence may be required from any place in the United States, or any territory, possession, or commonwealth of the United States, at any designated place of hearing.

(3) In case of contumacy by, or refusal to obey a subpoena issued to, any person, the Attorney General may invoke the aid of any court of the United States within the jurisdiction of which such investigation or proceeding is carried on, or where such person resides or carries on business, in requiring the attendance and testimony of witnesses and the production of books, papers, or other documents. Any such court may issue an order requiring such person to appear before the Attorney General or his designee, there to produce records, if so ordered, or to give testimony touching the matter under investigation. Any failure to obey such order of the court may be punished by such court as a contempt thereof.

(4) All process in any such case may be served in the judicial district in which such person resides or may be found. The Attorney General may make such rules relating to civil investigations as may be necessary or appropriate to implement the provisions of this subsection.

(e) Penalties

(1) (A) Any juridical person that violates subsection (a) of this section shall be fined not more than $2,000,000.

(B) Any juridical person that violates subsection (a) of this section shall be subject to a civil penalty of not more than $10,000 imposed in an action brought by the Attorney General.

(2) (A) Any natural person who willfully violates subsection (a) of this section shall be fined not more than $100,000 or imprisoned not more than 5 years, or both.

(B) Any natural person who violates subsection (a) of this section shall be subject to a civil penalty of not more than $10,000 imposed in an action brought by the Attorney General.

(3) Whenever a fine is imposed under paragraph (2) upon any officer, director, employee, agent, or stockholder of a person, such fine may not be paid, directly or indirectly, by such person.

(f) Definitions

For purposes of this section:

(1) The term "person," when referring to an offender, means any natural person other than a. national of the United States (as defined in 8 U.S.C. § 1101) or any corporation, partnership, association, joint-stock company, business trust, unincorporated organization, or sole proprietorship organized under the law of a foreign nation or a political subdivision thereof

(2) (A) The term "foreign official" means any officer or employee of a foreign government or any department, agency, or instrumentality thereof, or of a public international organization, or any person acting in an official capacity for or on behalf of any such government or department, agency, or instrumentality, or for or on behalf of any such public international organization. For purposes of subparagraph (A), the term "public international organization" means—

    (i) an organization that has been designated by Executive Order pursuant to Section 1 of the International Organizations Immunities Act (22 U.S.C. § 288); or

    (ii) any other international organization that is designated by the President by Executive order for the purposes of this section, effective as of the date of publication of such order in the Federal Register.

(3) (A) A person's state of mind is "knowing" with respect to conduct, a circumstance, or a result if—

    (i) such person is aware that such person is engaging in such conduct, that such circumstance exists, or that such result is substantially certain to occur; or

      (ii)   such person has a firm belief that such circumstance exists or that such result is substantially certain to occur.

(B) When knowledge of the existence of a particular circumstance is required for an offense, such knowledge is established if a person is aware of a high probability of the existence of such circumstance, unless the person actually believes that such circumstance does not exist.

(4) (A) The term "routine governmental action" means only an action which is ordinarily and commonly performed by a foreign official in—

      (i)   obtaining permits, licenses, or other official documents to qualify a person to do business in a foreign country;

      (ii)   processing governmental papers, such as visas and work orders;

      (iii)   providing police protection, mail pick-up and delivery, or scheduling inspections associated with contract performance or inspections related to transit of goods across country;

      (iv)   providing phone service, power and water supply, loading and unloading cargo, or protecting perishable products or commodities from deterioration; or

      (v)   actions of a similar nature.

(B) The term "routine governmental action" does not include any decision by a foreign official whether, or on what terms, to award new business to or to continue business with a particular party, or any action taken by a foreign official involved in the decision-making process to encourage a decision to award new business to or continue business with a particular party.

(5) The term "interstate commerce" means trade, commerce, transportation, or communication among the several States, or between any foreign country and any State or between any State and any place or ship outside thereof, and such term includes the intrastate use of—

(A) a telephone or other interstate means of communication, or

(B) any other interstate instrumentality.

§ 78ff. Penalties

(a) Willful violations; false and misleading statements

Any person who willfully violates any provision of this chapter (other than section 78dd-1 of this title), or any rule or regulation thereunder the violation of which is made unlawful or the observance of which is required under the terms of this chapter, or any person who willfully and knowingly makes, or causes to be made, any statement in any application, report, or document required to be filed under this chapter or any rule or regulation thereunder or any undertaking contained in a registration statement as provided in subsection (d) of section 78o of this title, or by any self-regulatory organization in connection with an application for membership or participation therein or to become associated with a member thereof, which statement was false or misleading with respect to any material fact, shall upon conviction be fined not more than $5,000,000, or imprisoned not more than 20 years, or both, except that when such person is a person other than a natural person, a fine not exceeding $25,000,000 may be imposed; but no person shall be subject to imprisonment under this section for the violation of any rule or regulation if he proves that he had no knowledge of such rule or regulation.

(b) Failure to file information, documents, or reports

Any issuer which fails to file information, documents, or reports required to be filed under subsection (d) of section 78*o* of this title or any rule or regulation thereunder shall forfeit to the United States the sum of $100 for each and every day such failure to file shall continue. Such forfeiture, which shall be in lieu of any criminal penalty for such failure to file which might be deemed to arise under subsection (a) of this section, shall be payable into the Treasury of the United States and shall be recoverable in a civil suit in the name of the United States.

(c) Violations by issuers, officers, directors, stockholders, employees, or agents of issuers

(1) (A) Any issuer that violates subsection (a) or (g) of section 30A of this title [15 U.S.C. § 78dd-1] shall be fined not more than $2,000,000.
(B) Any issuer that violates subsection (a) or (g) of section 30A of this title [15 U.S.C. § 78dd-1] shall be subject to a civil penalty of not more than $10,000 imposed in an action brought by the Commission.

(2) (A) Any officer, director, employee, or agent of an issuer, or stockholder acting on behalf of such issuer, who willfully violates subsection (a) or (g) of section 30A of this title [15 U.S.C. § 78dd-1] shall be fined not more than $100,000, or imprisoned not more than 5 years, or both.
(B) Any officer, director, employee, or agent of an issuer, or stockholder acting on behalf of such issuer, who violates subsection (a) or (g) of section 30A of this title [15 U.S.C. § 78dd-1] shall be subject to a civil penalty of not more than $10,000 imposed in an action brought by the Commission.

(3) Whenever a fine is imposed under paragraph (2) upon any officer, director, employee, agent, or stockholder of an issuer, such fine may not be paid, directly or indirectly, by such issuer.

FOREIGN CORRUPT PRACTICES ACT REVIEW

Opinion Procedure Release

No .: 04-02
Date: July 12, 2004

The Department has reviewed the FCPA Opinion Procedure request of an investment group consisting of, among others, JPMorgan Partners Global Fund, Candover 2001 Fund, 3i Investments plc, and investment vehicles ["Newcos"], all of which are hereinafter referred to as the "Requestors." The Requestors are acquiring certain companies and assets from ABB Ltd. ["ABB"] relating to ABB's upstream oil, gas, and petrochemical businesses ["OGP Upstream Business"].

On July 6, 2004, the Department announced guilty pleas to violations of the Foreign Corrupt Practices Act ["FCPA"] entered in the United States District Court for the Southern District of Texas by ABB Vetco Gray, Inc. and ABB Vetco Gray (UK) Ltd., two of the entities being acquired by the Requestors. On the same date, the U.S. Securities and Exchange Commission filed a settled enforcement action in the United States District Court for the District of Columbia charging ABB with violating the anti-bribery, books and records, and internal accounting and controls provisions of the FCPA relating to transactions involving business in several foreign countries, including Nigeria.

Previously, after the Requestors and ABB had executed a Preliminary Agreement dated October 16, 2003, relating to the acquisition of the OGP Upstream Business, they agreed to mutually conduct an FCPA compliance review—through separately-engaged counsel—of the OGP Upstream Business for the prior five-year period. ABB and the Requestors separately engaged forensic auditors to assist in the review and analysis of financial information, and ABB provided the Requestors with access to witnesses and records related to its OGP Upstream Business.

Requestors have represented that the review of OGP Upstream Business involved more than 115 lawyers and over 44,700 man-hours. Requestors conducted a manual review of over 1,600 boxes of printed e-mails and other documents, CD-ROMs, and hard drives of electronic records, amounting to more than 4 million pages. Over 165 interviews of current and former employees and agents of the

411

OGP Upstream Business were conducted. In addition, the forensic accountants visited 21 countries, assigning more than 100 staff members to review and analyze hundreds of thousands of transactions. Counsel for the Requestors also produced 22 analytical reports of OGP Upstream Business operations, with supporting evidence. All documents and witness interview memoranda were provided to the Department and the SEC as they were produced.

The requestors represent that they have taken, and will continue to undertake, a number of precautions to avoid, in the future, a knowing violation of the FCPA. The Requestors have represented and undertake, on behalf of their newly acquired entities, to:

1. Continue to cooperate with the Department and the SEC in their respective investigations of the past payments and to cooperate with other interested U.S. government agencies, as well as foreign law enforcement authorities, as may be applicable;

2. Ensure that any employee or officer of the OGP Upstream Business who continues to be employed by Newco and who is found to have made or authorized unlawful or questionable payments to foreign officials is appropriately disciplined;

3. Disclose to the Department any additional pre-acquisition payments to foreign officials relating to the OGP Upstream Business made by ABB that it discovers after the acquisition;

4. Ensure that Newco adopts a system of internal accounting controls and a system designed to ensure the making and keeping of accurate books, records, and accounts; and

5. Cause Newco to adopt a rigorous anti-corruption compliance code ("Compliance Code"), as described further below, that is designed to detect and deter violations of the FCPA and foreign anti-corruption laws. Newco's anti-bribery Compliance Code will consist of the following elements:

    (A) A clearly articulated corporate policy against violations of the FCPA and foreign anti-bribery laws and the establishment of compliance standards and procedures to be followed by all directors, officers, employees, and all business partners, including, but not limited to, agents, consultants, representatives, and joint venture partners and teaming partners, involved in business transactions, representation, or business development or retention in a foreign jurisdiction (respectively, "Agents"; and "Business Partners") that are reasonably capable of reducing the prospect that the FCPA or any applicable foreign anti-corruption law of Newco's Compliance Code will be violated;

    (B) The assignment to one or more independent senior Newco corporate officials, who shall report directly to the Compliance Committee of the Audit Committee of the Board of Directors, of responsibility for the implementation and oversight of compliance with policies, standards, and procedures established in accordance with Newco's Compliance Code;

(C) The effective communication to all shareholders' representatives directly involved in the oversight of Newco ("Shareholders") and to all directors, officers, employees, Agents, and Business Partners of corporate and compliance policies, standards, and procedures regarding the FCPA and applicable foreign anti-corruption laws, by requiring (i) regular training concerning the requirements of the FCPA and applicable foreign anti-corruption laws on a periodic basis to all Shareholders, directors, officers, employees, Agents, and Business Partners and (ii) annual certifications by all Shareholders, directors, officers, employees, including the head of each Newco business or division, Agents, and Business Partners certifying compliance therewith;

(D) A reporting system, including a "Helpline"; for directors, officers, employees, Agents, and Business Partners to report suspected violations of the Compliance Code or suspected criminal conduct;

(E) Appropriate disciplinary procedure to address matters involving violations or suspected violations of the FCPA, foreign anti-corruption laws, or the Compliance Code;

(F) Clearly articulated corporate procedures designed to assure that all necessary and prudent precautions are taken to cause Newco to form business relationships with reputable and qualified Business Partners;

(G) Extensive pre-retention due diligence requirements pertaining to, as well as post-retention oversight of, all Agents and Business Partners, including the maintenance of complete due diligence records at Newco;

(H) Clearly articulated corporate procedures designed to ensure that Newco exercises due care to assure that substantial discretionary authority is not delegated to individuals whom Newco knows, or should know through the exercise of due diligence, have a propensity to engage in illegal or improper activities;

(I) A committee consisting of senior Newco corporate officials to review and to record, in writing, actions relating to (i) the retention of any Agent or subagents thereof, and (ii) all contracts and payments related thereto;

(J) The inclusion in all agreements, contracts, and renewals thereof with all Agents and Business Partners of provisions: (i) setting forth anti-corruption representations and undertakings; (ii) relating to compliance with foreign anti-corruption laws and other relevant laws; (iii) allowing for internal and independent audits of the books and records of the Agent or Business Partner to ensure compliance with the foregoing; and (iv) providing for termination of the Agent or Business Partner as a result of any breach of applicable anti-corruption laws and regulations or representations and undertakings related thereto;

(K) Financial and accounting procedures designed to ensure that Newco maintains a system of internal accounting controls and makes and keeps accurate books, records, and accounts, and;

(L) Independent audits by outside counsel and auditors, at no longer that three-year intervals, to ensure that the Compliance Code, including its anti-corruption provisions, are implemented in an effective manner.

Based upon all the facts and circumstances, as represented by the Requestors, the Department does not presently intend to take an enforcement action against the Requestors or their recently-acquired entities, for violations of the FCPA committed prior to their acquisition from ABB.

This opinion is subject to the following caveats:

1. Although the Department views the Requestors' representations concerning a compliance program to be significant precautions against future violations of the FCPA, the Department's opinion should not be deemed to endorse any specific aspect of the Requestors' program.

2. The Department's opinion does not speak to any prospective conduct by the Requestors or any of the entities acquired from ABB following the acquisition.

The FCPA Opinion Letter referred to herein and this release have no binding application to any party which did not join in the request and can be relied upon by the requesting parties only to the extent that the disclosure of facts and the circumstances in their request is accurate and complete and continues to accurately and completely reflect such facts and circumstances.

FOREIGN CORRUPT PRACTICES ACT REVIEW

No.: 08-02
Date: June 13, 2008

Opinion Procedure Release

The Department has reviewed the Foreign Corrupt Practices Act ("FCPA") Opinion Procedure request of Halliburton Company and its controlled subsidiaries ("Halliburton"), a U.S. issuer, which is currently considering making an additional bid to acquire the entire share capital of a company based in the United Kingdom ("Target"). Target is traded on the London Stock Exchange, has approximately 4,000 employees, and operates in over fifty countries, including throughout Africa, the Middle East, Asia, the former Soviet Union, South America, Europe, and North America. Target is involved in well flow management and provides specialized products and services in the upstream oil and gas industry. Target has a number of national oil companies as customers. A company formed by a consortium of primarily foreign investors ("Competitor") is also bidding to acquire Target. Competitor submitted the first, and more recently the highest, bid, which is unconditional.

Halliburton has submitted a request for an opinion regarding the Department's present intention to take enforcement action under the circumstances here, specifically posing the following three questions: (1) whether the proposed acquisition transaction itself would violate the FCPA; (2) whether through the proposed acquisition of Target, Halliburton would "inherit" any FCPA liabilities of Target for pre-acquisition unlawful conduct; and (3) whether Halliburton would be held criminally liable for any post-acquisition unlawful conduct by Target prior to Halliburton's completion of its FCPA and anti-corruption due diligence, where such conduct is identified and disclosed to the Department within 180 days of closing.

Circumstances of the Request

The circumstances of the request are as follows: Halliburton represents that, as a result of U.K. legal restrictions inherent in the bidding process for a public U.K. company, it has had insufficient time and inadequate access to information to complete appropriate FCPA and anti-corruption due diligence and that it can only complete such due diligence post-closing. Pursuant to the U.K. bidding process, given that Target's board has already recommended to its shareholders the acceptance of Competitor's bid, Target is legally obliged to provide to Halliburton the same information given to Competitor, but it is not required either to (1) provide any additional information to Halliburton, or (2) agree to entertain an offer by Halliburton that is subject to any condition that has not already been imposed upon Competitor.

Thus, if Halliburton wanted to condition the making of its bid on the satisfactory completion of FCPA and anti-corruption diligence or on the pre-closing completion of remediation to its satisfaction, Target would be under no legal obligation to agree to any such terms, and might well reject a conditional, higher bid by Halliburton in favor of the lower, but unconditional bid of Competitor.

While in connection with the bidding process Halliburton has had access to a data room with certain information concerning Target, under the terms of a confidentiality agreement entered into between Halliburton and Target, Halliburton is not permitted to discuss with the Department whether any specific FCPA, corruption, or related internal controls or accounting issues have arisen, and if so, the nature and extent of such issues, except as required by applicable law.[1]

Halliburton represents that, in light of the above restrictions, if it makes an additional bid which is successful and thus acquires Target, it intends to implement the following post-closing plan:

Immediately following the closing, Halliburton will meet with the Department to disclose whether the information made available to Halliburton or otherwise learned by Halliburton pre-closing suggests that any FCPA, corruption, or related internal controls or accounting issues exist or existed at Target and, if so, will disclose such information to the Department.

Within ten business days of the closing, Halliburton will present to the Department a comprehensive, risk-based FCPA and anti-corruption due diligence work plan which will address, among other things, the use of agents and other third parties; commercial dealings with state-owned customers; any joint venture, teaming or consortium arrangements; customs and immigration matters; tax matters; and any government licenses and permits. Such work plan will organize the due diligence effort into high risk, medium risk, and lowest risk elements. Halliburton shall consult with the Department regarding the work plan. Over time, the work plan shall be reviewed and, if necessary, revised as the plan is implemented and more information is learned.

---

[1] While the Department accepts the representation that in order to be a viable bidder for Target, Halliburton had to enter into the confidentiality agreement, the Department discourages companies wishing to receive an FCPA Opinion Release in the future from entering into agreements which limit the information that may be provided to the Department.

Within 90 days of the closing, Halliburton will report to the Department the results to date of its high risk due diligence. Halliburton will provide the Department periodic progress reports over the course of the 90 days, and thereafter as appropriate.

Within 120 days of the closing, Halliburton will report to the Department the results to date of its medium risk due diligence. Halliburton will provide the Department periodic progress reports over the course of the 120 days, and thereafter as appropriate.

Within 180 days of the closing, Halliburton will report to the Department the results to date of its lowest risk due diligence. Halliburton will provide the Department periodic progress reports over the course of the 180 days, and thereafter as appropriate.

To the extent that issues identified during Halliburton's due diligence require further examination beyond the 180-day period, Halliburton will complete such remaining due diligence expeditiously and provide periodic reports thereof to the Department until concluded.

In any event, Halliburton will complete its due diligence and remediation related to Target, including completing its investigation of any issues that are identified within the 180-day period, by no later than one year from the date of closing.

Halliburton will retain external counsel and third-party consultants, including forensic accountants, as well as utilize internal resources, as appropriate, to conduct the FCPA and anti-corruption due diligence. The due diligence process shall include, under all appropriate circumstances and in all appropriate locations, examination of relevant Target records, including e-mail review and review of company financial and accounting records, as well as interviews of relevant Target personnel and other individuals.

All agents and other third parties associated with Target who are expected to continue to work for Target post-closing, and as to whom there are no compliance issues to be resolved, will as soon as commercially reasonable be required to sign new contracts (rather than contract modifications or extensions) with Halliburton that incorporate appropriate FCPA and anti-corruption representations and warranties, anti-corruption provisions, and audit rights, as provided for under Halliburton's Code of Business Conduct and related policies and procedures. Agents and other third parties who will not continue to work for Target post-closing will be terminated as expeditiously as possible. Based on the results of its due diligence efforts, Halliburton will take appropriate remedial action in the event it discovers any FCPA or corruption-related problems, including suspending or terminating any agents and other third parties and taking appropriate remedial action regarding relevant employees.

Upon closing, Halliburton will immediately impose its own Code of Business Conduct and specific FCPA and anti-corruption policies and procedures on

Target, including effectively communicating the same to all Target employees. Within 60 days of the closing, Halliburton will provide FCPA and anti-corruption training to all Target officers and all Target employees whose positions or job responsibilities warrant such training on an expedited basis, including all employees in management, sales, accounting, and financial control positions. Halliburton shall provide all other appropriate Target employees with such training within 90 days of closing.

Halliburton will disclose to the Department all FCPA, corruption, and related internal controls and accounting issues that it uncovers during the course of its 180-day due diligence. Halliburton will complete any additional steps the Department deems necessary to complete the due diligence and remediation plan. Halliburton further represents that post-closing, it will maintain Target as a wholly-owned subsidiary for so long as the Department is investigating any conduct by Target or any of its officers, directors, employees, agents, subsidiaries, and affiliates. Halliburton expressly acknowledges and agrees that Target, and all Target subsidiaries and affiliates, retain their liability for past and future violations of the FCPA, if any.

Analysis and Conclusion

Based upon all the facts and circumstances as represented, and assuming Halliburton satisfactorily completes each of the steps detailed herein, the Department does not presently intend to take any enforcement action against Halliburton for: (1) the acquisition of Target in and of itself; (2) any pre-acquisition unlawful conduct by Target disclosed to the Department within 180 days of the closing; and (3) any post-acquisition conduct by Target disclosed to the Department within 180 days of the closing, and which does not continue beyond the 180-day period or, if in the judgment of the Department the alleged conduct cannot be fully investigated within the 180-day period, which does not continue beyond such time as the conduct can reasonably be stopped. In issuing this Opinion Release, the Department specifically notes the particular circumstances of this transaction, including the foreign legal impediments to robust pre-acquisition due diligence. In the view of the Department, for the reasons set forth below, the issuance of this Opinion Release advances the interests of the Department in enforcing the FCPA and promoting FCPA due diligence in connection with corporate transactions, and permits the Requestor to proceed with an additional bid for Target with the benefit of the protections afforded by the Opinion Release procedure.

First, consistent with precedent, the Department believes that the execution of the transaction here would not, in and of itself, create FCPA liability for Halliburton. In FCPA Opinion Procedure Release 2001-01 (May 24, 2001), the Department addressed whether funds a corporation contributes as part of a corporate combination transaction may be considered a "payment" that is "in furtherance of" a bribe within the meaning of 15 U.S.C. § 78dd-1. The

Department discussed the risk that funds contributed to a joint venture by Corporation A might be used to make payments to an agent under pre-existing unlawful contracts that Corporation B contributed to the joint venture. Those issues, however, do not appear to be present here. Target is a public company listed on a major exchange, and at least 65% of its shares are held by large, institutional investors. Any amounts Halliburton pays to acquire Target will go to shareholders and not to Target itself. It is unlikely that any Target shareholders were corruptly given their shares such that the purchase of Target by Halliburton would improperly enrich such shareholders. Moreover, as a practical matter, it is impossible for any acquirer of a substantial public company to determine the identity of all shareholders and investigate how such shares were acquired.

Second, in light of the facts presented here and the particular restrictions in U.K. law regarding the bidding process, the Department does not presently intend to take any enforcement action with respect to any pre-acquisition conduct by Target disclosed to the Department during the 180-day period following the closing, provided Halliburton satisfactorily proceeds in accordance with the post-closing plan and remediation detailed above.

Third, the Department notes that an acquiring company may be held liable as a matter of law for any unlawful payments made by an acquired company or its personnel after the date of acquisition. In that regard, in a prior Opinion Release, which related to an acquiring corporation's potential FCPA liability based on the target's pre-acquisition conduct, the Department did not provide assurances with respect to unlawful "payments made after the date of acquisition." Release No. 2003-01 (January 15, 2003). Under the circumstances here, however, there is insufficient time and inadequate access to complete appropriate pre-acquisition FCPA due diligence and remediation. As represented by Halliburton, under the application of the U.K. Takeover Code, it has no legal ability to require a specified level of due diligence or to insist upon remedial measures until after the acquisition is completed. As a result, Halliburton's ability to take action to prevent unlawful payments by Target or its personnel during the period immediately after the closing has been severely compromised. Assuming that Halliburton, in the judgment of the Department, satisfactorily implements the post-closing plan and remediation detailed above, and assuming that no Halliburton employee or agent knowingly plays a role in approving or making any improper payment by Target, the Department does not presently intend to take any enforcement action against Halliburton for any post-acquisition violations of the antibribery provisions of the FCPA committed by Target during the 180-day period after closing provided that Halliburton: (a) discloses such conduct to the Department within 180 days of closing; (b) stops and remediates such conduct within 180 days of closing, or, if the alleged conduct, in the judgment of the Department, cannot be fully investigated within the 180-day period, stops and remediates such conduct as soon as it can reasonably be stopped; and (c) completes its due diligence and remediation, including completing its investigation of any issues that are identified within the 180-day period, by no later than one year from the date of closing.

The Department reserves the right, however, to take enforcement action against Halliburton with respect to: (a) any FCPA violations committed by Target during the 180-day period that are not disclosed to the Department during this same time period; (b) any FCPA violations committed by Target at any time where any Halliburton employee or agent knowingly participates in the unlawful conduct; and (c) any issues identified within the 180-day period which are not investigated to conclusion within one year of closing. In no event does this Opinion Release provide any protection for any conduct which occurs after the 180-day period. The Department further reserves the right to prosecute or take enforcement action against Target and any of its subsidiaries and affiliates for any and all violations of the FCPA or any other federal criminal statute either pre- or post-acquisition, whether disclosed to the Department or not. The Department notes, however, that any unlawful conduct by Target disclosed to the Department by Halliburton pursuant to the post-closing plan and this Opinion Request would qualify as a "voluntary disclosure" under the Department's Principles of Federal Prosecution of Business Organizations, Section VII, and such disclosure may be considered by the Department as a factor in any determination whether to charge Target.

This FCPA Opinion Release applies to the Requestor, Halliburton, only, has no binding application to any party which did not join in the request, and can be relied upon by Halliburton only to the extent that the disclosure of facts and circumstances in this request is accurate and complete and continues to accurately and completely reflect such facts and circumstances.

INDEX

Accessories/accomplices
  Brazil, 5–26, 5–28
  Hong Kong, 6–18–6–19
  Spain, 2–38
Accounts
  see also **Forensic and accounting
    issues associated with
    International Corruption
    Enquiries**
  civil recovery orders, 1–33
  compliance programs, 10–31
  false accounting, 1–15
  Foreign Corrupt Practices Act 1977, 3–
    36–3–52
  GAAP (generally accepted accounting
    principles), 3–41
  India, 7–31
  investigations, 9–28
  mergers and acquisitions, 10–31
  Securities and Exchange Commission, 3–
    46
  trivial amounts, 1–04
Acquisitions
  see **Mergers and acquisitions**
Active bribery or corruption
  Brazil, 5–32, 5–42–5–44
  Bribery Act 2010, 1–38
  definition, 1–38
  example, 1–38
  Hong Kong, 6–06
  improper, definition of, 1–38
  Public Bodies Corrupt Practices Act
    1889, 1–06
  public nature, functions or activities of a,
    1–38
Adequate procedures
  compliance programs, 11–06
  definition, 1–38
  foreign public officials (FPOs), bribery
    of, 1–38

  prevent bribery, failure of commercial
    organisations to, 1–38–1–39
  strict liability, 1–38
Administrative misconduct
  Brazil, 5–02, 5–04–5–24
Administrative sanctions
  Australia, 4–13
Agents
  agent/principal concept, 1–03, 1–12, 1–
    17, 6–05
  books and records, 9–41
  contracts, entering into new, 10–29
  defence, consent as, 1–17
  definition of agent, 1–12
  due diligence, 10–27
  Foreign Corrupt Practices Act 1977, 3–
    08, 3–09, 3–14
  foreign public officials, 1–17
  Hong Kong, 6–05
  indemnities, 3–08
  investigations, 9–41
  Law Commission, 1–7
  mergers and acquisitions, 10–27, 10–29
  Prevention of Corruption Act 1906, 1–
    03, 1–12, 1–17
  Public Bodies Corrupt Practices Act
    1889, 1–09
Alkaloids of Australia Pty Ltd
  investigations, 4–27–4–28
Al-Yamamah
  see **BAE Systems and Al-Yamamah**
AMEC Plc
  civil recovery orders, 1–33, 1–63
  Serious Fraud Office, 1–42, 1–63
American Depository Receipts (ADRs)
  Foreign Corrupt Practices Act 1977, 3–
    15
**Americanisation of UK anti-corruption
  efforts**
  deferred prosecution agreements, 1–73

non-prosecution agreements, 1–73
plea agreements, increased use of, 1–72
Amount of bribe
common law, 1–04
facilitation payments, 3–30–3–32
Foreign Corrupt Practices Act 1977, 3–30–3–32
Serious Fraud Office, 1–43, 8–05
trivial amounts, 1–04
Anonymity
data collection and preservation, 9–18
witnesses, 9–18
Anti-corruption compliance programs
see **Compliance programs**
Anti-Terrorism, Crime and Security Act 2002 (United Kingdom)
common law, 1–05
conspiracy, 1–21–1–22
course of conduct, 1–21–1–22
definitions, 1–25
extraterritoriality, 1–21–1–24
foreign public officials, 1–05, 1–21
jurisdiction, 1–20–1–25
OECD Anti-Bribery Convention, 1–20, 1–25
presumption of corruption, 1–24
repeal of Part 12, 2–41
statutory interpretation, 1–21
Aon Ltd
systems and control enforcement, 1–70–1–71
Argentina
Criminal Procedure Code (draft), 2–31
delays, 2–31
OECD Anti-Bribery Convention, report on implementation of, 2–31
Arthur Andersen
collapse, 8–70
Assets Recovery Agency (United Kingdom), 1–32
Attorney-client privilege
deferred prosecution agreements, 8–75–8–76
waiver, 8–76
Attorney General
BAE Systems and Al-Yamamah, 1–51–1–54
Bribery Act 2010, 1–40
civil recovery orders, 1–32
limited role, 2–41
prosecution, consent to, 1–40
Serious Fraud Office, 1–42
Audits and auditors
Australia, 4–19

compliance programs, 11–26
conflicts of interest, 8–39
data collection and preservation, 9–14
India, 7–31
internal investigations, conduct of, 8–40–8–42
Australia
administrative sanctions, 4–13
Alkaloids of Australia Pty Ltd, 4–27–4–28
auditors, 4–19
Australian Federal Police, 4–17–4–19, 8–06
Australian Transaction Reports and Analysis Centre (AUSTRAC), 4–19
Australian Wheat Board Oil for Food Programme, 4–16, 4–22–4–26
awareness, 4–34
blocking statutes, 8–30
bodies corporate, 4–02
Commonwealth Constitution, 4–09
complaints, 4–17
confiscation, 4–15
Corporations Act, breach of, 4–12
Corruption Perception Index, 4–16
Criminal Code, 4–01–4–15
criminal codes of states, 4–08
custom, 4–03–4–04, 4–24
defences, 4–05–4–11, 4–26
disqualification from managing companies, 4–12–4–13
enforcement, 4–16–4–20, 8–06
evidential burden, 4–06
extradition, 4–15
facilitation payments, 4–07–4–09
federal police, 4–17–4–19, 8–06
financial reporting, 4–19
financial service licences, loss of, 4–12
fines, 4–12–4–13
foreign public officials,
defences, 4–05–4–11
offence, 4–02–4–04, 4–11, 8–06
penalties, 4–12–4–15
prosecutions, 4–11
forfeiture, 4–14
government entities and police, cooperation between, 4–17–4–18, 8–06
imprisonment, 4–12–4–13
intention, 4–03
International Trade Integrity Act 2007, 4–06, 4–26
investigations, 4–17–4–19, 4–21–4–31, 8–06

Iraq Oil-For-Food Programme, 4–16, 4–22–4–29
jurisdiction, 4–10–4–11, 4–15
lawful in foreign official's country, defence that conduct is, 4–06, 4–26
media reports, 4–17, 8–06
money laundering, 4–26
mutual assistance, 4–15, 4–32, 8–06
national economic interest, 4–17, 8–06
nationality jurisdiction, 4–10
'not legitimately due' concept 4–24
OECD Anti-Bribery Convention, implementation and ratification of, 4–01
Oil-For-Food Programme, 4–16, 4–22–4–29
omissions, 4–04
penalties, 4–12–4–15
police, 4–17–4–19, 8–06
proceeds of crime, confiscation of, 4–15
prosecutions, 4–11
reporting, 4–17, 8–06
Rhine Ruhr Pty Ltd, 4–29
Rio Tinto Ltd, 4–30–4–31
routine government action, 4–07
searches, 4–15
seizure, 4–15
states, codes of, 4–08
tainted property, forfeiture of, 4–14
territorial jurisdiction, 4–10–4–11, 4–15
Transparency International, 4–16
United Nations,
    Convention against Corruption, 4–32–4–33
    resolutions, 4–21, 4–24
whistleblowing, 4–20

Back-up and off-side data
locking down and securing, 9–17
BAE Systems and Al-Yamamah
Attorney General, 1–51–1–54
investigations, 1–51–1–60
judicial review, 1–55–1–57, 1–60
national security, 1–02, 1–51, 1–53–1–57
OECD Anti-Bribery Convention, 1–52, 1–56
OECD Working Group, 2–42
plea agreement, 1–58–1–60
public interest, 1–51, 1–53–1–54, 1–57
Serious Fraud Office, 1–51–1–53, 1–55–1–60
Shawcross exercise, 1–51

US Department of Justice, agreement with, 1–58–1–60
Balfour Beatty Plc
civil recovery orders, 1–33, 1–61, 8–77
Serious Fraud Office, 1–42, 1–61–1–62
Bank secrecy
data protection, 9–21
employees of banks, 8–16
fines, 8–16
imprisonment, 8–16
internal investigations, conduct of, 8–16–8–29
money laundering, 8–17
mutual legal assistance treaties, 8–19–8–22
non-transparency, 8–18
Siemens, 8–28–8–29
Switzerland, 8–16, 8–23
tax evasion, 8–23–8–25
tax havens, 8–26–8–29
UBS, case of, 8–23–8–25
United Kingdom, mutual legal assistance treaties in, 8–20
United States, 8–19, 8–21, 8–23–8–25
Behaviour modification
compliance programs, 11–12, 11–38
Best practices
compliance program, 10–18–10–31
contractual protections, 10–29–10–30
cooperation following reviews, 10–28
due diligence, 10–18–10–31
Foreign Corrupt Practices Act 1977, 10–18–10–31
human rights abuses, 10–27
intelligence, assessing the target's business, 10–25
internal investigations, conduct of, 8–01
interviews, 10–27
limitation of liability, 10–29–10–30
mergers and acquisitions, 10–18–10–31
program, assessing the target's compliance, 10–26
reviews, 10–27–10–28
risk assessment, 10–21–10–27
tailored review, 10–27
work plans, 10–27–10–28
Bills of rights
Hong Kong, 6–04, 6–23
Blocking statutes
Australia, 8–30
Canada, 8–30
France, 8–30, 8–32
internal investigations, conduct of, 8–30–8–33

South Africa, 8–30
United States, 8–30–8–33
Bofors scandal, 7–40
Bona fide expenditures
defence, 3–09, 3–35
Books and records
account-based investigations, 9–28
agents, 9–41
allegations, 9–25–9–26, 9–32, 9–37
character sets, 9–35
compliance programs, 10–31, 11–12, 11–25–11–26
conflicts of interest, 9–36–9–37
contract–based investigations, 9–27, 9–30, 9–32, 9–37
control-based investigations, 9–31
Corporate Intelligence, 9–36–9–40
data analytics, 9–33–9–35
detection of corrupt payments, 9–23–9–40
electronic data, 9–33–9–35
European Bank example, 9–38–9–39
European Technology Company example, 9–40
facilitation payments, 9–27
falsification, 3–41
field work, 9–23–9–40
follow up, 9–42
Foreign Corrupt Practices Act 1977,
control-based investigations, 9–31
Corporate Intelligence, 9–36
offences, 3–11, 3–13, 3–40–3–41, 3–36–3–52
power point presentations, 9–42
self-reporting, 9–42
typical questions, 9–42
voluntary disclosure, 9–42
forensic and accounting issues, 9–23–9–43
high risk transactions, examining, 9–27
India, 7–18
investigating agents, 9–41
issue reporting, 9–25
language, 9–34
live transactions, software for monitoring, 9–35
methods and techniques for detecting corrupt payments, 9–27–9–32
planning, 9–24
policy-based investigations, 9–31
reporting, 9–25, 9–43
self-reporting, 9–42
software, 9–33–9–35
tender details, 9–32

third party payments, 9–41
transaction-based investigations, 9–27, 9–27
verification, 9–42
whistleblowing, 9–25–9–26, 9–41
witnesses, 9–25–9–26
Brazil
active corruption, 5–32, 5–42–5–44
administrative misconduct, 5–02, 5–04–5–24
aiding and abetting, 5–26, 5–28
Bilac Pinto Law, 5–03
Bill 6826/2010), 5–53–5–54
burden of proof, 5–14
civil liability, 5–02, 5–06, 5–10, 5–17
Code of Criminal Liability, 5–06
companies, liability of, 5–09–5–10, 5–37, 5–50–5–52
confiscation, 5–37
Constitution, 5–01–5–02, 5–04–5–08, 5–15
criminal liability,
civil liability, 5–02
Code of Criminal Liability, 5–06
companies, 5–50–5–52
Law of Administrative Probity, 5–10
Penal Code, 5–06, 5–22–5–24, 5–37, 5–41–5–42, 5–45
strict liability, 5–13
current legislation, 5–04–5–05
customary gratuities, 5–44
economic damage, 5–12
embezzlement, 5–25–5–26
employees of private companies, 5–24
enforcement, 5–40, 5–49, 5–55
fines, 5–17, 5–53
foreign public officials,
definition, 5–03, 5–35, 5–38, 5.41–5–44
international commercial transactions, 5–41–5–48
forfeiture, 5–17
forthcoming legislation, 5–53–5–54
fraud, 5–46
freezing of assets, 5–15, 5–18–5–21
individuals, liability of, 5–09–5–10
influence peddling, 5–45–5–47
Inter-American Convention against Corruption (OAS), 5–34–5–38, 5–40, 5–48–5–49
intermediaries, 5–33, 5–43
jurisdiction, 5–10
Law of Administrative Probity, 5–05–5–21

misfeasance in office, 5–05
misuse of public office, 5–03
money laundering, 5–37, 5–40
multinationals, 5–10
mutual assistance, 5–35, 5–39
negligence, 5–13
OECD Anti-Bribery Convention, 5–34,
    5–36–5–38, 5–40, 5–48–5–49
OECD Working Group, 5–48
passive corruption, 5–27–5–29
Penal Code, 5–06, 5–22–5–24, 5–37, 5–
    41–5–42, 5–45
penalties and sanctions, 5–01, 5–11–5–
    12, 5–15–5–17, 5–24–5–30, 5–33, 5–
    43–5–44, 5–53
Pitombo-Godoy Ilha Law, 5–02–5–03
precautionary measures, 5–19
preventive measures, 5–34
private interests by public officials,
    furthering of, 5–30–5–31
private parties, acts of corruption carried
    out by, 5–32–5–33
provisional remedies, 5–18–5–21
public assets or finance, damage to, 5–12,
    5–17
Public Interest Civil Lawsuit, 5–06–5–
    10, 5–21
public officer, definition of, 5–03
seizure, 5–18–5–21, 5–26
settlements, 5–07
solicitation, 5–27
strict liability, 5–13
Transparency International, 5–48
treaties and conventions, 5–34–5–39
UN Convention against Corruption, 5–
    34, 5–38–5–39, 5–48–5–49
unjust enrichment, 5–19, 5–34
whistleblowing, 5–34
wilful misconduct, 5–13
Bribery Act 2010 (United Kingdom)
active bribery, 1–38
Attorney-General's consent to prosecute,
    1–40
bill, 1–37
compliance programs, 11–05–11–06
drafting, 1–37
entry into force, 1–02
extraterritoriality, 1–40
foreign public official, bribery of, 1–38
intelligence agencies, authorising conduct
    of, 1–40
introduction, 1–02, 1–37, 1–38
Law Commission, 1–37, 2–42
mergers and acquisitions, 10–04

parent companies for acts of subsidiaries,
    liability of, 1–39
passive bribery, 1–38
prevent bribery, failure to, 1–38
safe harbour, 1–38
sentencing, 1–40
transitional provisions, 1–02
Burden of proof
Australia, 4–06
Brazil, 5–14
Hong Kong, 6–20
India, 7–09
Prevention of Corruption Act 1916, 1–
    18–1–19
reversal of burden, 1–18–1–19
Business partner compliance
case study, 11–26
compliance programs, 11–12, 11–25–11–
    26

Case studies
business partner compliance, 11–26
compliance programs, 11–20, 11–22, 11–
    26, 11–37
due diligence, 10–06–10–17
ethics and compliance policies and
    guidelines, 11–22
Foreign Corrupt Practices Act 1977, 10–
    06–10–17
leadership commitment and oversight,
    11–20
mergers and acquisitions, 10–06–10–17
training and communication, 11–37
Canada
blocking statutes, 8–30
Changes in behaviour
compliance programs, 11–12, 11–38
Charges
internal regulatory investigations in
    United States, cooperation with, 8–
    12
list of factors for determining whether to
    bring charges, 8–12
Chile
OECD Anti-Bribery Convention, report
    of implementation of, 2–32
Penal Code, reform of, 2–32
**City of London Police Overseas Anti-
    Corruption Unit (OACU)**
establishment, 1–46
prosecutions, 1–46
Serious Fraud Office, 1–46
website, 1–46

Civil liability and sanctions
Brazil, 5–02, 5–06, 5–10, 5–17
companies, 3–29
Foreign Corrupt Practices Act 1977, 3–
29, 3–43, 8–02
internal regulatory investigations in
United States, cooperation with, 8–
02–8–03
Civil recovery orders (CROs)
accounting requirements, 1–33
AMEC, 1–33, 1–63
Assets Recovery Agency, 1–32
Attorney-General's guidance, 1–32
Balfour Beatty Plc, 1–33,1–61, 8–77
deferred prosecution agreements, 8–77
fines, 8–77
Innospec Ltd, 1–66
internal investigations, conduct of, 6–77
prosecution, avoidance of, 1–33
Serious Fraud Office, 1–32–1–33, 1–42,
8–77
standard of proof, 1–32
Code of Liberalisation of Capital
Movements
OECD, 2–05
Code of Liberalisation of Current
Invisible Operations
OECD, 2–05
Collection of data
see **Data collection and preservation**
Commercial organisations' failure to
prevent bribery
see **Prevent bribery, failure of**
commercial organisations to
Common law
amount of bribe, 1–04
Anti-Terrorism, Crime and Security Act
2002, 1–05
criminalization, 1–03
definition of bribery, 1–04
foreign public officials, bribery of, 1–05
misconduct in public office, 1–04, 6–10
scope of offence, 1–04
trivial amounts, 1–04
Communication
case study, 11–37
compliance programs, 11–33, 11–36–11–
37
stakeholders, 11–36
Companies
civil actions, 3–29
employees or agents, 3–09
foreign companies, 3–15, 3–38

Foreign Corrupt Practices Act 1977, 3–
07–3–09, 3–15, 3–29, 3–38, 3–48
guidance, 3–07
indemnities for officers, directors,
employees, agents or shareholders,
3–08
OECD Anti-Bribery Convention, 2–18
multinationals, 2–15, 5–10, 11–07
parents and subsidiaries, 1–39
stigma, 3–48
subsidiaries, 1–39, 3–38
Tumukunde & Tobiasen, 1–69
Turkey, 2–40
Complaints
see also **Whistleblowing**
Australia, 4–17
India, 7–29–7–31, 7–35
Compliance programs
accessible guidance, need for, 10–31
accounting and records system, 10–31
adequate procedures, 11–06
advisory opinions, 10–31
assessment of target's program, 10–25
audits, 11–26
behaviour-based training and
engagement, 11–12
best practices for, 10–18–10–31
books and records of third parties, 11–26
Bribery Act 2010, 11–05–11–06
business partner compliance, 11–12, 11–
25–11–26
case studies,
business partner compliance, 11–26
ethics and compliance policies and
guidelines, 11–22
leadership commitment and oversight,
11–20
training and communication, 11–37
change in behaviour, 11–12, 11–38
commitment, level of, 11–38
communication, 11–33, 11–36–11–37
consultation facilities, 11–12, 11–24
continuous improvement, 11–12
controls, 11–12, 11–17–11–18, 11–22
core components, 10–31
country, evaluating the, 10–31
criminal charges, defence to, 11–05–11–
06
cultural change, 11–38
defence, providing a, 11–05–11–06
deferred prosecution agreements, 8–71
design, 11–13–11–28
directors, 11–03
disciplinary procedures, 10–31, 11–27

dismissal of employees, 10–31
dissemination, 10–31
documented, procedures must be, 11–10
effectiveness, 11–01–11–39
employees, 11–03, 11–07, 11–24, 11–27, 11–29, 11–36, 11–39
ethics,
code, 11–12, 11–21–11–22
policies and guidelines, 11–21–11–23
risk assessment, 11–12, 11–16
existing and evolving industry requirements or practices, taking into account, 11–10
export of program onto target company, 10–30
format, 11–08
gap analysis and reporting, 11–16
gatekeeper functions and networks, 11–12
globally, doing business, 11–07
governance, 11–12
government business, monitoring, 11–12
guidance,
sentencing, 11–05, 11–09
sources, 11–09
human resources, 11–12, 11–27
implementation, 11–10, 11–12, 11–22, 11–29–11–37
integration, 10–31
internal controls, 11–12, 11–17–11–18, 11–22
internal investigations, 8–10–8–13, 11–12
investigations, 11–12, 11–14
key elements, 11–01–11–39
leadership commitment and oversight, 11–12, 11–19–11–20, 11–30
market credibility, retaining, 11–04
mergers and acquisitions, 10–18–10–31, 11–12
mitigation, 11–05
monitoring, 11–10, 11–12, 11–26
multinationals, 11–07
need for program, 11–02–11–07
operating principles, 11–22
overarching principles, 11–10
oversight, 11–12, 11–19–11–20, 11–30
partners, 11–12, 11–25–11–26
performance management, 11–27
people,
change in behaviour, 11–12, 11–38
directors, 11–03
employees, 11–03, 11–07, 11–24, 11–27, 11–29, 11–36, 11–39
human resources, 11–12, 11–27

leadership commitment and oversight, 11–12, 11–19–11–20
success, reasons for, 11–38
principles-based approach, 11–10
project planning, 11–32
proportionality, 11–10
remediation, 11–29
reporting, 11–12, 11–16
resources, adequacy of, 11–31
reviews, 11–12
risk assessment, 11–08, 11–12, 11–15–11–16
senior management, 10–31, 11–19–11–20
Serious Fraud Office, 11–09
stakeholders,
communication, 11–36
credibility, retaining, 11–04
success
critical factors, 11–35
reasons, 11–38
sustainable business conduct, 11–12, 11–29
tailored principles, 11–10, 11–12
third parties, 11–25–11–26
tone at the top, 10–31
training, 10–31, 11–12, 11–21, 11–33–11–34, 11–37
transparency, 11–10, 11–36
United States, 11–05, 11–09, 11–24
whistleblowing facilities, 11–12, 11–24, 11–25
written codes, 10–31
Compulsion, evidence obtained by Serious Fraud Office, 1–44
Computers
see **Electronic data; Information technology; Software**
Confidentiality
see also **Bank secrecy**
employees, 8–61
Hong Kong, 6–30
internal investigations, conduct of, 8–43, 8–61
Serious Fraud Office, 1–44
Confiscation
Australia, 4–15
Brazil, 5–37
Hong Kong, 6–27
India, 7–17
Mabey & Johnson Ltd, 1–49
Conflicts of interest
auditors, 8–39
books and records, 9–36–9–37
Corporate Intelligence, 9–36–9–37

internal investigations, conduct of, 8–39
Consulting fees
internal investigations, conduct of, 8–46
Conspiracy
Anti-Terrorism, Crime and Security Act 2002, 1–21–1–22
Foreign Corrupt Practices Act 1977, 3–25
Consultation facilities
compliance programs, 11–12, 11–24
Contracts
agents' contracts, entering into new, 10–29
best practices, 10–29–10–30
books and records, 9–27, 9–30, 9–32, 9–37
employees, 8–47
Foreign Corrupt Practices Act 1977, 10–30
investigations, 9–27, 9–30, 9–32, 9–37
limitation of liability, 10–29–10–30
mergers and acquisitions, 10–20–10–30
new contracts, entering into, 10–29
public procurement contracts, debarment from, 1–34, 1–50
sample provisions, 10–30
Controls
books and records, 9–31
compliance programs, 11–12, 11–17–11–18, 11–22
Foreign Corrupt Practices Act 1977, 9–31
investigations, 9–31
systems and control enforcement, 1–70–1–71
Conventions
see **OECD Anti-Bribery Convention; Treaties and conventions; UN Convention against Corruption**
Cooperation
best practices, 19–28
credit, 8–12, 8–14–8–15, 8–36
employees, inducing or compelling, 8–43–8–46
Filip Memo, 8–75
guidance, 8–75
internal investigations, conduct of, 8–10–8–15
mergers and acquisitions, 10–28
OECD Anti-Bribery Convention, 2–22–2–23
police, 4–17–4–18, 8–06
regulators, 8–10–8–15
reviews, 10–28

United States, 8–10–8–15, 8–75
Cooperation with internal regulatory investigations in United States
complaints, 8–11
compliance programmes, 8–12–8–13
credit for cooperation, 8–12, 8–14–8–15
Department of Justice, 8–10–8–13
disciplinary measures, 8–13
disclosure, 8–12
Filip Memorandum, 8–12–8–13
McNulty Memorandum, 8–12
remedial actions, 8–13–8–14
restitution, 8–13
Seaboard Report (SEC), 8–14
Securities and Exchange Commission, 8–10–8–11, 8–14
self-reporting, 8–12, 8–14
triggers for investigations, 8–11
Corporate liability
Brazil, 5–09–5–10, 5–37, 5–50–5–52
criminal liability, 1–26
directing mind and will, 1–26
failure to prevent bribery, 1–26
identification principle, 1–26
Law Commission, 1–26
mens rea, 1–26
Corporate Intelligence
books and records, 9–36–9–40
conflicts of interest, 9–36–9–37
European Bank example, 9–38–9–39
European Technology Company example, 9–40
examples, 9–37–9–40
mergers and acquisitions, 10–25
Corroboration
data collection and preservation, 9–18
Hong Kong, 6–18
Corruption Perception Index (Transparency International)
Australia, 4–16
forensic and accounting issues, 9–10
Hong Kong, 6–40
India, 7–01
mergers and acquisitions, 10–22
Corruptly, definition of
Foreign Corrupt Practices Act 1977, 3–08, 3–17–3–21
Prevention of Corruption Act 1906, 1–14
Public Bodies Corrupt Practices Act 1889, 1–10
Counsel
see **Legal advisers**
Country, evaluating the
mergers and acquisitions, 10–22, 10–31

Credit for cooperation
internal investigations, conduct of, 8–36
internal regulatory investigations in
United States, cooperation with, 8–
12, 8–14–8–15
CROs
see Civil recovery orders (CROs)
Crown servants
Public Bodies Corrupt Practices Act
1889, 1–09
Culture
compliance programs, 11–38
India, 7–44
Custodial sentences
see Imprisonment
Custom
Australia, 4–03–4–4, 4–24
Brazil, 5–44
India, 7–01
OECD Anti-Bribery Convention, 2–17

Data analytics
books and records, 9–33–9–35
character sets, 9–35
electronic data, 9–33–9–35
interviews, 9–33
language, 9–34
search terms, 9–34
software, 9–33–9–35
Data collection and preservation
admissions, 9–20
anonymity, 9–18
audits, 9–14
context, 9–11–9–12
corroboration, 9–18
documentary evidence, 9–13–9–14
electronic data and media, 9–15–9–17
emails, 9–11, 9–16
employees, interviewing, 9–20
focus, 9–11–9–12
forensic and accounting issues, 9–03, 9–
06, 9–11–9–20
inspection, 9–14
internal investigations, conduct of, 8–55–
8–57
interviews,
employees, 9–20
planning, 9–18
techniques, 9–19–9–20
locking down and securing of back-up
and off-side data, 9–17
optical character recognition, 9–14
paper evidence, 9–13–9–14

remote capture of electronic data, 9–16
scanning of documents, 9–14
seizure, 9–16
third party data, 9–14
United States, 8–56
witnesses, 9–18–9–20
Data protection
banking secrecy, 9–21
Data Protection Directive, 9–21
employee emails, reviewing, 9–21
forensic and accounting issues, 9–21
legal advice, access to, 9–21
personal data, access to, 9–21
Defences
affirmative defences, 3–09, 3–30–3–35
agent/principal concept, 1–17
Australia, 4–05–4–11, 4–26
compliance programs, 11–05–11–06
consent, 1–17, 2–41
criminal charges, 11–05–11–06
Foreign Corrupt Practices Act 1977, 3–
09, 3–30–3–35
foreign public officials, bribery of, 4–05–
4–11
joint defence agreements, 8–53–8–54
lawful in foreign official's country,
defence that conduct is, 3–09, 3–33–
3–34, 4–06, 4–26
reasonable and bona fide expenditures, 3–
09, 3–35
routine government action, 3–09, 3–30–
3–32
Deferred prosecution agreements
Americanisation of UK anti-corruption
efforts, 1–73
Arthur Andersen, 8–70
attorney-client privilege, 8–75–8–76
Balfour Beatty Plc, 1–62
civil recovery orders, 8–77
compliance programs, 8–71
definition, 1–73
discipline, 8–76
factors, 8–74
Filip Memo, 8–75
fines, 8–72
internal regulatory investigations in
United States, cooperation with, 8–
08, 8–70–8–76
McNulty Memo, 8–75
publicity, 8–72
Serious Fraud Office, 1–62
stigma, 8–72, 8–76
Thompson Memo, 8–73–8–74
typical elements, 8–72

US Attorneys' Manual, 8–72
waiver, 8–75
work conduct privilege, 8–75
Definition of bribery
common law, 1–04
Department of Justice (DOJ) (United States)
BAE Systems and Al-Yamamah, 1–58–1–60
composition, 8–02
Criminal Division, 8–03
Foreign Corrupt Practices Act 1977, 3–05, 3–44–3–52, 8–02–8–03, 8–08, 8–66
Fraud Section, 8–03
Innospec Ltd, 1–64–1–65
internal regulatory investigations, cooperation with, 8–02–8–04, 8–08, 8–10–8–11, 8–64–8–66
KBR & Nigeria LNG, 1–67–1–68
multi-jurisdictional investigations, coordinating responses to, 8–64–8–66
Siemens, 8–64–8–66
parallel investigations, 8–08
prosecutions, 8–03, 8–08
Securities and Exchange Commission, 8–08
US Attorneys, 8–03
Developing countries
Foreign Corrupt Practices Act 1977, 3–25
international organisations, 3–25
OECD Anti-Bribery Convention, 2–10–2–11, 2–15
Directors and officers
false statements, 3–41
Foreign Corrupt Practices Act 1977, 3–08, 3–14, 3–41
Hong Kong, 6–28
indemnities, 3–08, 8–61–8–52
internal investigations, conduct of, 8–51–8–52
Discipline
compliance programs, 11–27
deferred prosecution agreements, 8–76
internal regulatory investigations in United States, cooperation with, 8–13
mergers and acquisitions, 10–31
Disclosure
abusive discovery, 8–31
conviction rate, 1–72

Foreign Corrupt Practices Act 1977, 3–04, 3–47, 9–42
France, 8–32
Hong Kong, 6–12–6–15, 6–23
India, 7–29, 7–32
internal investigations, conduct of, 8–12, 8–62–8–63
United States, 3–04, 3–47, 8–12, 8–31, 9–42
waiver, 8–62–8–63
Discovery
see **Disclosure**
Dismissal of employees
immunity, 8–46
internal investigations, conduct of, 8–46–8–47
mergers and acquisitions, 10–31
Disqualification
Australia, 4–12–4–13
Hong Kong, 6–28
Documentary evidence
data collection and preservation, 9–13–9–14
DOJ
see **Department of Justice (DOJ) (United States)**
Double jeopardy
foreign public officials, bribery of, 1–40
Innospec Ltd, 1–66
main bribery offence, 1–40
Due diligence
agents, 10–27
best practices, 10–18–10–31
case studies, 10–06–10–17
contractual protections, 10–29–10–30
Foreign Corrupt Practices Act 1977, 10–07–10–31
mergers and acquisitions, 10–18–10–31
recusal certificates, 10–29
reports, 10–02, 10–27
reputation damage, 10–29
reviews, 10–27–10–28
risk assessment, 10–02, 10–04, 10–21–10–26
successor liability, 10–32
tailored review, 10–27

Eckhardt Amendment
Foreign Corrupt Practices Act 1977, 3–09
Education
see **Public awareness and education**

El Paso and Coastal Corporation
mergers and acquisitions, 10–15
Electronic data
books and records, 9–33–9–34
collection and preservation, 9–15–9–17
data analytics, 9–33–9–35
data protection, 9–21
emails, 8–57, 8–61, 9–11, 9–16, 9–21
internal investigations, conduct of, 8–57,
8–60–8–61
optical character recognition, 9–14
remote capture, 9–16
scanning, 9–14
search terms, 9–34
Emails
data collection and preservation, 9–11, 9–
16
data protection, 9–21
internal investigations, conduct of, 8–58,
8–61
Employees
see also **Training**
at will employees, 8–47
bank secrecy, 8–16
Brazil, 5–24
compliance programs, 11–03, 11–07, 11–
24, 11–27, 11–29, 11–36, 11–39
confidentiality, 8–61
consulting fees, 8–46
contract, 8–47
cooperation, inducing or compelling, 8–
44
counsel, providing, 8–40–8–42, 8–49–8–
50
data protection, 9–21
discipline, 8–13, 8–76, 10–31, 11–27
dismissal, 8–46–8–47, 10–31
documents, securing, 8–58–8–61
emails, 9–21
Foreign Corrupt Practices Act 1977, 3–
08, 3–09, 3–14, 3–23–3–24, 3–39
Hong Kong, 6–05, 6–28
human resources, 11–12, 11–27
immunity from sanctions or dismissal, 8–
46
indemnities, 3–08, 8–51–8–52
inducing or compelling cooperation, 8–
43–8–46
internal investigations, conduct of, 8–07,
8–43–8–54, 8–58–8–61
interviews, 9–20
joint defence agreements, 8–53–8–54
legal fees, indemnification for and
advancement of, 8–51–8–52

mergers and acquisitions, 10–31
non-cooperation, protection against
company action for, 8–47–8–48
personal communications, 8–61
Prevention of Corruption Act 1906, 1–13
self-incrimination, privilege against, 8–44
United States 3–08, 3–09, 3–14, 3–23–3–
24, 3–39, 8–44
whistleblowing, 8–07, 8–48
work conduct privilege, 8–75
Enforcement
Australia, 4–16–4–20, 8–06
Brazil, 5–40, 5–49, 5–55
Foreign Corrupt Practices Act 1977, 3–
05, 3–43–3–52, 8–02–8–04
India, 7–01–7–02, 7–34–7–37, 7–44
internal regulatory investigations in
United States, cooperation with, 8–
02
OECD Anti-Bribery Convention, 2–20–
2–22
Securities and Exchange Commission, 8–
04
Serious Fraud Office, 8–05
systems and control enforcement, 1–70–
1–71
UN Convention against Corruption, 5–
40
Enquiries
see **Forensic and accounting issues
associated with International
Corruption Enquiries**
Enron scandal
internal regulatory investigations in
United States, cooperation with, 8–
70
Ethics
case study, 11–22
code, 11–12, 11–21–11–22
compliance programs, 11–12, 11–16, 11–
21–11–23
parents and subsidiaries, 1–39
policies and guidelines, 11–21–11–23
risk assessment, 11–12, 11–16
Evidence
see also **Witnesses**
compulsion, evidence obtained by, 1–44
corroboration, 6–18, 9–18
documentary evidence, 9–13–9–14
Hague Evidence Convention, 8–31
Hong Kong, 6–17–6–21, 6–35
India, 7–09
Serious Fraud Office, 1–44
Extradition

Australia, 4–15
KBR & Nigeria LNG, 1–67–1–68
Extraterritoriality
  Anti-Terrorism, Crime and Security Act
    2002, 1–21–1–24
  Bribery Act 2010, 1–40
  India, 7–14, 7–18
  OECD Anti-Bribery Convention, 1–36,
    2–10
  United Kingdom, 1–21–1–24, 1–40, 2–41

Facilitation payments
  amount, 3–30–3–32
  Australia, 4–07–4–09
  books and records, 9–27
  definition, 3–07
  Foreign Corrupt Practices Act 1977, 3–
    07, 3–09, 3–30–3–32, 3–39
  guidance, 3–07
  OECD Anti-Bribery Convention, 2–17
  reporting, 3–39
  routine governmental action, 3–09, 3–30–
    3–32
  safeguards, 3–32
Failure of commercial organisations to
  prevent bribery
  see **Prevent bribery, failure of**
    commercial organisations to
Fair hearing, right to a
  Prevention of Corruption Act 1916, 1–18
False statements
  directors or officers, 3–41
  false accounting, 1–15
  Foreign Corrupt Practices Act 1977, 3–
    41
  Hong Kong, 6–15
  Prevention of Corruption Act 1906, 1–15
  Serious Fraud Office, 1–44
Falsification of books and records
  Foreign Corrupt Practices Act 1977, 3–
    41
FCPA
  see **Foreign Corrupt Practices Act**
    1977 (United States)
Federal Bureau of Investigation (FBI)
  Foreign Corrupt Practices Act 1977, 8–
    66
Fees
  consulting fees, 8–46
  indemnification for and advancement of
    legal fees to employees, 8–51–8–52
  internal investigations, conduct of, 8–46
Field work

books and records, 9–23–9–40
forensic and accounting issues, 9–03, 9–
  23–9–40
Filip Memorandum
  cooperation, guidelines for assessing
    corporate, 8–75
  deferred prosecution agreements, 8–75
  internal regulatory investigations in
    United States, cooperation with, 8–
    12–8–13
Financial services
  see also **Bank secrecy**
  Australia, 4–12
  Financial Services Authority, 1–70–1–74
  India, 7–18
  licences, loss of, 4–12
  money laundering, 1–28
Financial Services Authority (FSA)
  (United Kingdom)
  Serious Fraud Office, 1–74
  systems and control enforcement, 1–70–
    1–74
Fines
  Australia, 4–12–4–13
  bank secrecy, 8–16
  Brazil, 5–17, 5–53
  civil recovery orders, 8–77
  deferred prosecution agreements, 8–72
  employees, 8–16
  Foreign Corrupt Practices Act 1977, 3–
    05, 3–29, 3–48, 10–07, 10–10–10–
    11, 10–18, 10–31
  Hong Kong, 6–15, 6–26–6–28
  India, 7–10, 7–12–7–14
  Innospec Ltd, 1–65
  Mabey & Johnson Ltd, 1–49
  mergers and acquisitions, 10–07, 10–10–
    10–11, 10–18, 10–31
  systems and control enforcement, 1–71
Foreign companies
  Foreign Corrupt Practices Act 1977, 2–
    15, 3–38
Foreign Corrupt Practices Act 1977
  (United States)
  accounting, 3–36–3–52
  affirmative defences, 3–09, 3–30–3–35
  agents, 3–08, 3–09, 3–14
  Alternative Jurisdiction amendments, 3–
    16
  American Depository Receipts (ADRs),
    3–15
  amount, 3–30–3–32
  anti-bribery provisions, 3–05, 3–11, 3–
    12–3–30, 3–44–3–46, 8–04

background, 3–02–3–04
best practices for compliance program, 10–18–10–31
bookkeeping, 3–05–3–06
books and records offences, 3–11, 3–13, 3–40–3–41, 9–31, 9–36, 9–42
case studies, 10–06–10–17
civil actions, 3–29, 3–43, 8–02
companies,
    civil actions, 3–29
    employees or agents, 3–09
    foreign companies, 3–15, 3–38
    guidance, 3–07
    indemnities for officers, directors, employees, agents or shareholders, 3–08
    stigma, 3–48
conspiracy, 3–25
contractual provisions, 10–30
control-based investigations, 9–31
Corporate Intelligence, 9–36
corruptly, definition of, 3–08, 3–17–3–21
Criminal Division, 8–03
criminalisation approach, 3–04, 3–06
defences, 3–09, 3–30–3–35
Department of Justice, 3–05, 3–44–3–52, 8–02–8–03, 8–08
developing countries, 3–25
directors, 3–08, 3–14, 3–41
disclosure, 3–04, 3–47, 9–42
domestic concern, definition of, 3–14
due diligence, 10–07–10–31
Eckhardt Amendment, 3–09
El Paso and Coastal Corporation, 10–15
employees, 3–08, 3–09, 3–14, 3–23–3–24, 3–39
enforcement, 3–05, 3–43–3–52, 8–02–8–04
exceptions, 3–30–3–35
facilitation payments, 3–07, 3–09, 3–30–3–32, 3–39
false statements by directors or officers, 3–41
falsification of books and records, 3–41
FBI (Federal Bureau of Investigation), 8–66
fines, 3–05, 3–29, 3–48, 10–07, 10–10–10–11, 10–18, 10–31
foreign companies, 3–15, 3–38
foreign subsidiaries, 3–38
foreign public officials, 1–38, 2–08, 3–23–3–25
forensic and accounting issues, 9–08–9–09

Fraud Section, 8–03
GAAP (generally accepted accounting principles), 3–41
government interaction, assessing the degree of, 10–24
guidance, 3–08, 3–35, 3–48
Halliburton, 10–12–10–13, 10–16–10–18
history of legislation, 3–02–3–08
Hong Kong, 6–33
improper advantage, 3–10
imprisonment, 3–05, 3–29, 3–48
indemnities for officers, directors, employees, agents or shareholders, 3–08
informants, 3–47
injunctions, 3–29
intention, 3–18–3–21, 3–26
internal accounting controls, 3–05–3–06, 3–42
internal regulatory investigations in United States, cooperation with, 8–07, 8–34, 8–66
International Anti-Bribery and Fair Competition Act 1998, 3–10
international organisations, 3–24–3–25
interpretation, 3–01
interstate instrumentality, 3–16
investigations, 8–03–8–04, 8–08
InVision and General Electric, 10–09
issuers, 3–12–3–13, 3–26
jurisdiction, 3–10, 3–13, 3–37, 10–04
knowledge, 3–18–3–21, 3–26
lawful under written laws of country, defence that payments are, 3–09
limitation periods, 3–52
lodging, payments for, 3–35
mail, making use of the, 3–12, 3–14, 3–15–3–16
mergers and acquisitions, 10–18–10–31
Monsanto and Delta & Pine Land Company, 10–14
obtaining or retaining business, 3–27–3–28
OECD Anti-Bribery Convention, 2–08–2–10
officers, 3–08, 3–14, 3–41
Omnibus Trade and Competitiveness Act 1988, 3–09, 3–49
Opinion Procedure, 3–49–3–51
parallel investigations, 8–08
penalties, 3–05, 3–29, 3–43, 3–48
political parties or candidates, 3–25
power point presentations, 9–42
promises to pay, 3–22

prosecutions, 8–03
public international organisations, 3–24–3–25
reasonable and bona fide expenditures, defence of, 3–09, 3–35
record-keeping, 3–36–3–52
recipients, 3–25
reporting, 3–39
Review Procedure, 3–49–3–51
revisions, 3–09–3–11, 3–15–3–16
risk, 10–03
routine governmental actions, 3–09, 3–30–3–32
Securities and Exchange Commission, 3–02–3–05, 3–14–3–15, 3–37, 3–44–3–52, 8–02, 8–04, 8–08
Securities Exchange Act 1934, 3–05, 3–37, 3–46
securities trading, 3–13, 3–15
self–reporting, 8–08, 9–42, 10–28
slush funds, 3–02–3–03
stigma, 3–48
subsidiaries, 3–38
Syncor and Cardinal Health, 10–08
Titan and Lockheed, 10–06–10–07
travel, payments for, 3–35
UN Convention against Corruption, 3–10
US Attorneys, 8–03
value, payment or anything of, 3–22
Vetco Gray and ABB, 10–10–10–11, 10–31
Watergate scandal, 3–02
wilfulness, 3–20
written laws of country, payments are lawful, 3–09, 3–33—3–34
Foreign exchange
India, 7–18
Foreign public officials (FPOs), bribery of
see also **Foreign Corrupt Practices Act 1977 (United States); OECD Anti-Bribery Convention**
adequate procedures, 1–38
agent/principal concept, 1–13
Anti-Terrorism, Crime and Security Act 2001, 1–05, 1–21
Australia, 4–02–4–15, 8–06
Brazil, 5–35, 5–38, 5.41–5–44
Bribery Act 2010, 1–38
common law, 1–05
defences, 4–05–4–11
definitions, 1–38, 2–15, 3–23–3–25, 5–35, 5–38, 5–41–5–44

double jeopardy, 1–40
Foreign Corrupt Practices Act 1977, 1–38, 2–08, 3–23–3–25
international organisations, 1–38
Law Commission, 1–38
OECD Anti-Bribery Convention, 1–38
OECD Working Group, 1–36, 2–12
penalties and sanctions, 4–12–4–15
Prevention of Corruption Act 1906, 1–13
private interests by public officials, furthering of, 5–30–5–31
prosecutions, 4–11
safe harbour, 1–38
Serious Fraud Office, 2–42
strict liability, 1–38
UN Convention against Corruption, 5–38
United Kingdom, 1–05, 1–13, 1–21, 1–38, 2–42
United States, 1–38, 2–08, 3–23–3–25
Forensic and accounting issues associated with International Corruption Enquiries
books and records, detecting, 9–23–9–43
Corruption Perceptions Index, 9–10
data collection and preservation, 9–03, 9–06, 9–11–9–20
data protection, 9–21
field work, 9–03, 9–23–9–40
follow up, 9–03
Foreign Corrupt Practices Act 1977, 9–08–9–09
fraud, 9–05
government official, definition of, 9–08
high risk activities, 9–10
industry sectors at risk, 9–08
Information Request List, 9–07
information technology, 9–04
interviews, 9–06
motivations, 9–05
objectives of investigations, 9–04
orientation, 9–03, 9–04–9–10
planning, 9–03, 9–04–9–10, 9–43
preservation of data, 9–11–9–20
privacy, 9–22
reporting,
  lines, 9–01
  types, 9–03
risk, 9–08–9–10
scoping, 9–03, 9–04–9–10
site visits, 9–07
Transparency International, 9–10
United States,

Foreign Corrupt Practices Act 1977, 9–08–9–09
  interviews, 9–06
  UPJOHN style warnings, 9–06
UPJOHN style warnings, 9–06
verification, 9–03
whistleblowing, 9–04
Forfeiture
  Australia, 4–14
  Brazil, 5–17
  India, 7–04
FPOs
  see **Foreign public officials (FPOs), bribery of**
France
  blocking statutes, 8–30, 8–32
  discovery, 8–32
  OECD Anti-Bribery Convention, 2–12
  Tax Recommendation (OECD), 2–12
Fraud
  see also **Serious Fraud Office (SFO) (United Kingdom)**
  Brazil, 5–46
  Department of Justice, 8–03
  Foreign Corrupt Practices Act 1977, 8–03
  forensic and accounting issues, 9–05
  India, 7–33
Freedom of information
  privacy, 9–22
Freezing assets
  Brazil, 5–15, 5–18–5–21
  India, 7–17

GAAP (generally accepted accounting principles)
  Foreign Corrupt Practices Act 1977, 3–41
Gap analysis and reporting
  compliance programs, 11–16
Gatekeeper functions and networks
  compliance programs, 11–12
Germany
  OECD Anti-Bribery Convention, 2–12
  Siemens, 8–28–8–29, 8–63–8–66
  Tax Recommendation (OECD), 2–12
Globalization
  internal investigations, conduct of, 8–64
Governments
  Australia, 4–17–4–18, 8–06
  bodies, 4–17–4–18, 8–06
  compliance programs, 11–12
  departments, definition of, 7–06

Foreign Corrupt Practices Act 1977, 10–24
India, 7–06, 7–43
internal investigations, conduct of, 8–08
mergers and acquisitions, 10–24
ministers, scandals involving, 7–43
monitoring government business, 11–12
officials, definition of, 9–08
police, cooperation with, 4–17–4–18, 8–06
routine government action, 3–09, 3–30–3–32, 4–07
Gratification
  definition, 7–07, 7–22
  India, 7–07, 7–09–7–10, 7–22
Grease payments
  see **Facilitation payments**
Guidance
  accessible guidance, need for, 10–24
  case study, 11–22
  companies, 3–07
  compliance programs, 10–31, 11–05, 11–09
  ethics, 11–21–11–23
  facilitation payments, 3–07
  Foreign Corrupt Practices Act 1977, 3–08, 3–35, 3–48
  internal regulatory investigations in United States, cooperation with, 8–11–8–14
  mergers and acquisitions, 10–24
  plea agreements, 1–49–1–50
  sentencing, 11–05, 11–09
  sources, 11–09

Habitual commission of offence
  India, 7–12
Hague Evidence Convention
  United States, 8–31
Halliburton
  mergers and acquisitions, 10–12–10–13, 10–16–10–18
Harassment
  India, 7–36
High risk transactions
  examination of transactions, 9–27
  forensic and accounting issues, 9–10
Hong Kong
  accomplices, 6–18–6–19
  active bribery, 6–06
  advantage 6–05–6–07
  agencies, relationship between ICAC and other, 6–37

arrest, 6–25
background, 6–01–6–04
bill of rights, 6–04, 6–23
burden of proof, 6–20
confidentiality, 6–30
confiscation, 6–27
conspiracy, 6–19
corroboration, 6–18
Corruption Perception Index, 6–40
Director of Public Prosecutions, 6–34–6–35
directors, 6–28
disclosure, 6–12–6–15, 6–23
disqualification from being election or appointed to public bodies, 6–28
employees, 6–05, 6–28
enforcement, 6–01–6–02, 6–29–6–33, 6–37
evidence, 6–17–6–21, 6–35
false statements, 6–15
fines, 6–15, 6–26–6–28
Foreign Corrupt Practices Act 1977, 6–33
imprisonment, 6–26–6–28
Independent Commission against Corruption 6–02–6–03, 6–11, 6–29–6–34, 6–37–6–40
informants,
    protection of, 6–22–6–25, 6–30–6–31
    public awareness, 6–29
    witnesses, 6–30
information, powers to obtain, 6–12–6–15
Inland Revenue, material held by, 6–13, 6–15
interception of communications, 6–16
investigations, 6–02, 6–11–6–15, 6–34–6–40
limitation periods, 6–24
mens rea, 6–05
misconduct in public office, common law offence of, 6–10
mutual legal assistance, 6–39
OECD Anti-Bribery Convention, 6–33
official emoluments to be proved by certificate, 6–18
passive bribery, 6–06
penalties, 6–19, 6–26–6–29
police, 6–02, 6–37
press gag law, 6–23
prevention, 6–37
Prevention of Bribery Ordinance, 6–04–6–33
principals/agents, 6–05

private sector, 6–09, 6–38
procedure, 6–17–6–21
prosecutions,
    consent, 6–25, 6–36
    Director of Public Prosecutions, 6–34
    procedural and evidential provisions enhanced to improve prospects of successful, 6–17–6–21
public awareness, 6–29, 6–32, 6–37
public interest, 6–36
public relations, 6–32
reporting, encouraging, 6–29, 6–32
reports, 6–03, 6–34
seizure, 6–11
standard of living, 6–08, 6–18
statutory offences, 6–05–6–40
Transparency International, 6–40
UN Convention against Corruption, 6–39
unexplained property, offence of possession of, 6–07–6–08, 6–17–6–18, 6–26
witnesses,
    informants, 6–30–6–31
    protection, 6–22–6–25, 6–31
    statements or declarations, 6–17
Human resources
compliance programs, 11–12, 11–127
Human rights
best practices, 10–27
fair hearing, right to a, 1–18
Hong Kong, 6–04, 6–23
mergers and acquisitions, 10–27
privacy, 9–22

Identification principle
corporate criminal liability, 1–26
Illicit enrichment
bank secrecy, 8–17
Immunity
dismissal, 8–46
internal investigations, conduct of, 8–46
penalties or sanctions 8–46
Imprisonment
Australia, 4–12–4–13
bank secrecy, 8–16
employees, 8–16
Foreign Corrupt Practices Act 1977, 3–05, 3–29, 3–48
Hong Kong, 6–26–6–28
India, 7–10, 7–12–7–14
money laundering, 8–17
Improper advantage

definition, 1–38, 2–16
 Foreign Corrupt Practices Act 1977, 3–
  10
 OECD Anti-Bribery Convention, 2–16,
  3–10
Improper performance, concept of
 passive bribery, 1–38
Indemnities
 agents, 3–08
 directors and officers, 3–08, 8–51–8–52
 employees, 3–08
 Foreign Corrupt Practices Act 1977, 3–
  08
 internal investigations, conduct of, 8–51–
  8–52
 mergers and acquisitions, 10–29
 shareholders, 3–08
India
 abetment, 7–11
 accountability, 7–20
 accounts, 7–31
 ADM-OECD Anti-Corruption Action
  Plan, 7–16
 Administrative Reforms Commission, 7–
  03
 Anti-Corruption Laws (Amendment) Act
  1964, 7–02
 appeals, 7–21
 audits, 7–31
 background, 7–01–7–04
 banking, 7–18
 Bofors scandal, 7–40
 burden of proof, 7–09
 Central Bureau of Investigation, 7–01, 7–
  02, 7–24, 7–30, 7–37, 7–42
 Central Government Corruption
  Division, 7–30
 Central Vigilance Commission, 7–01, 7–
  03–7–04, 7–28–7–29, 7–34–7–37, 7–
  40
 Chief Information Commission, 7–32
 codes of conduct, 7–23
 Companies Bill, 7–33
 complaints, 7–29–7–31, 7–35
 Comptroller and Auditor General, Office
  of, 7–31–7–32
 confiscation, 7–17
 Constitution, 7–03, 7–24, 7–31
 Corruption Perception Index, 7–01
 corruption scandals, 7–38–7–43
 criminal offences, 7–02, 7–13, 7–15
 culture, 7–44
 custom, 7–01
 delay, 7–03

 Delegation of Financial Power Rules, 7–
  24
 disclosure, 7–29, 7–32
 elections, 7–22
 enforcement, 7–01–7–02, 7–34–7–37, 7–
  44
 equal treatment, 7–35
 evidence, 7–09
 extraterritoriality, 7–14, 7–18
 financial services, 7–18
 fines, 7–10, 7–12–7–14
 First Information Report, 7–30
 foreign exchange, 7–18
 foreign public officials, liability of, 7–26
 forfeiture, 7–04
 fraud, 7–33
 freezing assets, 7–17
 General Financial Rules, 7–24
 government departments, definition, 7–
  06
 gratification,
  definition of, 7–07, 7–22
  taking, 7–09–7–10
 habitual commission of offence, 7–12
 harassment, 7–36
 imprisonment, 7–10, 7–12–7–14
 individuals, liability of private, 7–25
 influence,
  means of, 7–10
  personal, 7–10
 information, right to, 7–01, 7–20–7–21
 informers, protection of, 7–29
 institutional framework, 7–27–7–37
 investigations, 7–33, 7–35
 Jharkhand Mukti Morcha MPs, 7–41
 judiciary scandals, 7–42
 Law Commission, 7–04
 legislation,
  amendments, 7–17
  anti-corruption laws, 7–05–7–13
  history, 7–02–7–04
  money laundering, 7–18–7–19
  service rules, 7–23
  subordinate legislation, 7–23
 LIC-Mundra deals, 7–39
 limitation periods, 7–03
 ministers, scandals involving, 7–43
 money laundering, 7–18–7–19
 Naresh Chandra Committee, 7–33
 Office of the Comptroller and Auditor
  General, 7–31–7–32
 official acts, public servants taking
  gratification other than legal

remuneration in respect of, 7–07, 7–09
Penal Code, 7–02, 7–13, 7–15
penalties, 7–10, 7–12–7–14
personal influence, 7–10
presumption, 7–09
Prevention of Corruption Act 1947, 7–02–7–03
Prevention of Corruption Act 1988, 7–05–7–14
preventive measures, 7–17
public duty, definition of, 7–05
Public Interest Disclosure (Protection of Informers) Bill, 7–01, 7–04
public official definition of, 7–05
public procurement, 7–24–7–26
record-keeping, 7–18
reports, 7–30, 7–31
Right to Information Act 2007, 7–01, 7–20–7–21
Santhanam Committee, 7–02–7–03, 7–28, 7–35
scandals, 7–38–7–43
seizure, 7–17
Serious Fraud Investigation Office, 7–33
service rules, 7–23
Single Directive, 7–35–7–36
Special Police Establishment, 7–02
subordinate legislation, 7–23
territorial jurisdiction, 7–13, 7–14, 7–18
transparency, 7–20
Transparency International, 7–01, 7–17
treaties and conventions, 7–16–7–23
UN Convention against Corruption, 7–01, 7–16–7–17, 7–26
UN Convention against Transnational Organised Crime, 7–16
valuable thing without consideration, public servant obtaining, 7–08
Vineet Narain Case, 7–35
VK Krishna Menon Scandal, 7–38
whistleblowers, 7–04, 7–20, 7–29
Industry sectors at risk
forensic and accounting issues, 9–08
Influence peddling
Brazil, 5–45–5–47
India, 7–10
personal influence, 7–10
Informants
Foreign Corrupt Practices Act 1977, 3–47
Hong Kong, 6–22–6–25, 6–30–6–31
India, 7–29

protection of, 6–22–6–25, 6–30–6–31, 7–29
public awareness, 6–29
witnesses, 6–30
Information, obtaining
freedom of information, 9–22
Hong Kong, 6–12–6–15
India, 7–01, 7–20–7–21
OECD Working Group, 2–28
Information technology
see also Electronic data
books and records, 9–33–9–35
forensic and accounting issues, 9–04
live transactions, software for monitoring, 9–35
power point presentations, 9–42
Injunctions
Foreign Corrupt Practices Act 1977, 3–29
internal regulatory investigations in United States, cooperation with, 8–03
Innospec Ltd
civil recovery orders, 1–66
double jeopardy, 1–66
fine, level of, 1–65
investigations, 1–64–1–66
public interest, 1–66
Serious Fraud Office, 1–64–1–66
settlement, 1–64–1–65
US Department of Justice, 1–64–1–65
Inquiries
see Forensic and accounting issues associated with International Corruption Enquiries
Inspection
data collection and preservation, 9–14
Institutionalized corruption
Siemens, 8–28–8–29
Intelligence
see Corporate Intelligence; Intelligence agencies
Intelligence agencies
authorising conduct, 1–40
Bribery Act 2010, 1–40
Inter-American Convention against Corruption (OAS)
Brazil, 5–34–5–38, 5–40, 5–48–5–49
Interception of communications
Hong Kong, 6–16
Intermediaries
see also Agents
Brazil, 5–33, 5–43
Prevention of Corruption Act 1906, 1–13

Internal controls
 compliance programs, 11–12, 11–17–11–
  18, 11–22
Internal investigations, conduct of
 see also **Internal investigations in**
  United States, conduct of
 attorney-client privilege, 8–53
 attorney-client relationship, 8–37–8–39
 auditors, 8–39–8–42
 Australian Federal Police, 8–06
 bank secrecy, 8–16–8–29
 best practices, 8–01
 blocking statutes, 8–30–8–33
 civil recovery orders, 6–77
 compliance programs, 11–12
 confidentiality, 8–43, 8–61
 conflicts of interest, 8–39
 consulting fees, 8–46
 cooperation with regulatory
  investigations, 8–10–8–15
 counsel,
  audit committees, 8–40–8–42
  employees, 8–49–8–50
  hiring outside, 8–38–8–42
  indemnification for and advancement
   of legal fees, 8–51–8–52
 credit, 8–36
 directors and officers, indemnities for, 8–
  51–8–52
 dismissal, 8–46–8–47
 documents,
  electronic documents, 8–57, 8–61
  email, 8–57
  employees, securing documents from,
   8–58–8–61
  preservation, 8–55–8–57
  waiver of privileges and protections
   from disclosure, 8–62–8–63
 electronic documents, 8–57, 8–60–8–61
 email, 8–57, 8–61
 employees,
  at will employees, 8–47
  confidentiality, 8–61
  consulting fees, 8–46
  contract, 8–47
  counsel, providing, 8–49–8–50
  dismissal, 8–46–8–47
  documents, securing, 8–58–8–61
  immunity from sanctions or dismissal,
   8–46
  indemnification for and advancement
   of legal fees, 8–51–8–52
  inducing or compelling cooperation,
   8–43–8–46

 joint defence agreements, 8–53–8–54
 non-cooperation, protection against
  company action for, 8–47–8–48
 personal communications, 8–61
 self-incrimination, privilege against, 8–
  44
 whistleblowing, 8–07, 8–48
globalization, 8–64
government actions, 8–08
immunity from sanctions or dismissal, 8–
 46
impediments to investigations, 8–16–8–
 33
indemnities, 8–51–8–52
independence, 8–37
inquiries, 8–07
joint defence agreements, 8–53–8–54
legal fees, indemnification for and
 advancement of, 8–51–8–52
media stories, 8–07
multi-jurisdictional investigations,
 coordinating responses to, 8–64–8–
 66
preservation of documents, 8–55–8–57
regulatory authorities, 8–01–8–16
regulatory investigations, in conjunction
 with, 8–36–8–37
self-incrimination, privilege against, 8–44
self-regulatory authorities, 8–09
Serious Fraud Office (UK), 8–05, 8–77
ultimate findings, responses by
 government to, 8–67–8–77
waiver of privileges and protections from
 disclosure, 8–62–8–63
whistleblowing, 8–07, 8–48
witnesses, 8–43–8–46
Internal investigations in United
 States, conduct of
Arthur Andersen, 8–70
centralisation, 8–03
charges, list of factors for determining to
 bring, 8–12
civil enforcement, 8–02–8–03
compliance programs, 8–13, 8–71
cooperation with regulatory
 investigations, 8–10–8–15
counsel, hiring outside, 8–41
deferring prosecution, 8–08, 8–70–8–76
Department of Justice, 8–02–8–04, 8–08,
 8–10–8–11, 8–64–8–66
discretion on prosecution, 8–67–8–77
document preservation, 8–56
employees, 8–44
enforcement, 8–02

Enron scandal, 8–70
Filip Memorandum, 8–12
Foreign Corrupt Practices Act 1977, 8–07, 8–34, 8–66
guidelines on cooperation, 8–11–8–14
injunctions, 8–03
McNulty Memorandum, 8–12
multi-jurisdictional investigations, coordinating responses to, 8–64–8–66
parallel investigations, 8–08
penalties, 8–11, 8–70
plea bargaining, 8–67, 8–69
prosecutions, 8–03, 8–08, 8–12, 8–67–8–77
Seaboard Report (SEC), 8–14
Securities and Exchange Commission, 8–02, 8–04, 8–08, 8–10–8–11, 8–35, 8–63–8–66
self-incrimination, privilege against, 8–44
self-reporting, 8–08, 8–12, 8–14, 8–35
Siemens, 8–64–8–66
triggers for internal investigation, 8–11
ultimate findings, responses by government to, 8–67–8–76
US Attorneys, 8–03
waiver of privileges and protections from disclosure, 8–63
Watergate scandal, 8–34
International Corruption Enquiries
see **Forensic and accounting issues associated with International Corruption Enquiries**
International mergers and acquisitions
see **Mergers and acquisitions**
International organisations
definition of public international organisations, 3–25
developing countries, 3–25
Foreign Corrupt Practices Act 1977, 3–24–3–25
foreign public officials (FPOs), bribery of, 1–38
OECD, 2–06
public international organisations, 3–24–3–25
public officials, definition of, 3–24–3–25
Interviews
best practices, 10–27
cautions, 1–44
data analytics, 9–33
data collection and preservation, 9–18–9–20
employees, 9–20

forensic and accounting issues, 9–06
mergers and acquisitions, 10–27
planning, 9–06, 9–18
Serious Fraud Office, 1–44
techniques, 9–19–9–20
United States, 9–06
Investigations
see also **Forensic and accounting issues associates with International Corruption Enquiries; Internal investigations, conduct of; Internal investigations in United States, conduct of**
accounts, 9–28
agents, 9–41
Alkaloids of Australia Pty Ltd, 4–27–4–28
AMEC, 1–63
Attorneys' Manual, 8–03
Australia, 4–17–4–19, 4–21–4–31, 8–06
Australian Wheat Board Oil for Food Programme, 4–16, 4–22–4–26
BAE Systems and Al-Yamamah, 1–51–1–60
Balfour Beatty Plc, 1–61–1–62
compliance programs, 11–12, 11–14
contract-based investigations, 9–27, 9–30, 9–32, 9–37
control-based investigations, 9–31
criteria, 8–05
cross-border investigations, 10–01
FBI (Federal Bureau of Investigation), 8–66
Foreign Corrupt Practices Act 1977, 8–03–8–04, 8–08
Hong Kong, 6–02, 6–11–6–15, 6–34–6–40
India, 7–33, 7–35
Innospec Ltd, 1–64–1–66
investigations, 9–27, 9–29–9–32, 9–37
Iraq Oil for Food Programme, 4–16, 4–22–4–26
Japan, 2–35–2–36
KBR & Nigeria LNG, 1–67–1–68
Mabey & Johnson Ltd, 1–49–1–50
OECD Anti-Bribery Convention, 2–22
parallel investigations, 8–08
policy-based investigations, 9–31
Securities and Exchange Commission, 8–04, 8–08
Serious Fraud Office, 1–41, 1–44, 1–74, 8–05
transaction-based investigations, 9–29

triggers for investigations, 8–11
Tumukunde & Tobiasen, 1–69
United Kingdom, 1–01, 1–41, 1–44, 1–74, 2–41, 8–05
United States, 8–03–8–04, 8–08, 8–10–8–15, 8–66
InVision and General Electric
mergers and acquisitions, 10–09
Iraq Oil for Food Programme
Australian Wheat Board Oil for Food Programme, 4–16, 4–22–4–26
Mabey & Johnson Ltd, 1–49
Turkey, 2–39–2–40
Ireland
Criminal Justice (Theft and Fraud Offences) Act 2001, 2–34
foreign bribery offences, consolidation of, 2–34
OECD Anti-Bribery Convention, report of implementation of, 2–33–2–34
Phase II obligations, 2–33
Prevention of Corruption (Amendment) Act 2001, 2–34
Prevention of Corruption (Amendment) Bill 2008, 2–34
Issue reporting
books and records, 9–25
Issuers
Foreign Corrupt Practices Act 1977, 3–12–3–13, 3–26

Japan
investigations, impediments to, 2–35–2–36
nationality jurisdiction, 2–35
OECD Anti-Bribery Convention, report of implementation of, 2–35–2–36
Phase II obligations, 2–35
prosecution, impediments to, 2–36
self-assessment, 2–36
territorial jurisdiction, 2–36
Jharkhand Mukti Morcha MPs
India, 7–41
Joint defence agreements
internal investigations, conduct of, 8–53–8–54
Judiciary scandals
India, 7–42
Jurisdiction
Anti-Terrorism, Crime and Security Act 2002, 1–20–1–25
Australia, 4–10–4–11, 4–15
Brazil, 5–10

Foreign Corrupt Practices Act 1977, 3–10, 3–13, 3–37, 10–04
India, 7–13, 7–14, 7–18
Japan, 2–35–2–36
internal regulatory investigations in United States, cooperation with, 8–64–8–66
multi-jurisdictional investigations, coordinating responses to, 8–64–8–66
nationality, 2–198, 2–35, 4–10
OECD Anti-Bribery Convention, 2–19
territorial,
Australia, 4–10–4–11, 4–15
India, 7–13, 7–14, 7–18
Japan, 2–36
OECD Anti-Bribery Convention, 2–19
United Kingdom, 2–41
United Kingdom, 1–20–1–25, 2–41

KBR & Nigeria LNG
extradition, 1–67–1–68
investigations, 1–67–1–68
mutual assistance, 1–67–1–68
Serious Fraud Office, 1–67–1–68
US Department of Justice, 1–67–1–68
Knowledge
Foreign Corrupt Practices Act 1977, 3–18–3–21, 3–26

Language
books and records, 9–34
Law Commission
agent/principal concept, 1–17
Bribery Act 2010, 1–37, 2–42
corporate criminal liability, 1–26
foreign public officials (FPOs), bribery of, 1–38
Prevention of Corruption Act 1906, 1–13, 1–17
Public Bodies Corrupt Practices Act 1889, 1–09
Lawful in foreign official's country, defence that conduct is
Australia, 4–06, 4–26
Foreign Corrupt Practices Act 1977, 3–09
written laws, 3–09
Leadership commitment and oversight
case study, 11–20
compliance programs, 11–12, 11–19–11–20, 11–30
Legal advisers

access, 9–21
attorney-client privilege, 8–53, 8–75–8–76
attorney-client relationship, 8–37–8–39
audit committees, 8–40–8–42
data protection, 9–21
employees, 8–49–8–50
fees, indemnification for and advancement of, 8–51–8–52
hiring outside counsel, 8–38–8–42
indemnification for and advancement of legal fees, 8–51–8–52
internal investigations, conduct of, 8–37–8–42, 8–49–8–50, 8–53
US Attorneys, 8–03, 8–72
Legal persons, liability of
Luxembourg, 2–37
LIC-Mundra deals
India, 7–39
Limitation periods
Foreign Corrupt Practices Act 1977, 3–52
Hong Kong, 6–24
India, 7–03
OECD Anti-Bribery Convention, 2–21
Live transactions
software for monitoring, 9–27
Local authorities
local public bodies, definition of, 1–08
Prevention of Corruption Act 1916, 1–18
Public Bodies Corrupt Practices Act 1889, 1–08
Locking down and securing of back-up and off-side data
data collection and preservation, 9–17
Luxembourg
legal persons, liability of, 2–37
OECD Anti-Bribery Convention, report of implementation of, 2–37
Phase II obligations, 2–37

Mabey & Johnson Ltd
confiscation orders, 1–49
fines, 1–49
investigation, 1–49–1–50
Iraq oil-for-food program, 1–49
plea bargaining, 1–49–1–50, 1–72
procurement, debarment from, 1–50
self-reporting, 1–50
Serious Fraud Office, 1–49–1–50
settlements, 1–50
Main bribery offence
double or triple jeopardy, 1–40

foreign public officials, 1–40
Market credibility
retention, 11–04
Marshall Plan
OECD, 2–02
McNulty Memorandum
deferred prosecution agreements, 8–75
internal regulatory investigations in United States, cooperation with, 8–12
Media
Australia, 4–17, 8–06
deferred prosecution agreements, 8–72
Hong Kong, 6–23
internal investigations, conduct of, 8–07
Serious Fraud Office, 1–43, 8–05
Mergers and acquisitions
accounting and records system, 10–31
advisory opinions, 10–31
agents,
  contracts, entering into new, 10–29
  due diligence, 10–27
best practices,
  compliance program, 10–18–10–31
  contractual protections, 10–29–10–30
  cooperation following reviews, 10–28
  due diligence, 10–18–10–31
  human rights abuses, 10–27
  intelligence, assessing the target's business, 10–25
  interviews, 10–27
  limitation of liability, 10–29–10–30
  program, assessing the target's compliance, 10–26
  reviews, 10–27–10–28
  risk assessment, 10–21–10–27
  tailored review, 10–27
  work plans, 10–27–10–28
Bribery Act 2010 (United Kingdom), 10–04
case studies, 10–06–10–17
compliance program,
  accessible guidance, need for, 10–31
  accounting and records system, 10–31
  advisory opinions, 10–31
  best practices for, 10–18–10–31
  core components, 10–31
  country, evaluating the, 10–31
  discipline and dismissal of employees, 10–31
  dissemination, 10–31
  effectiveness, 11–12
  export of program onto target company, 10–30

integration, 10–31
senior executives, tone of, 10–31
tone at the top, 10–31
training and updates, 10–31
written codes, 10–31
contractual protections,
  agents' contracts, entering into new,
    10–29
  limitation of liability, 10–29–10–30
  sample provisions, 10–30
cooperation following reviews, 10–28
Corruption Perception Index, 10–22
country, evaluating the, 10–22, 10–31
cross-border investigations, 10–01
discipline and dismissal of employees,
  10–31
due diligence,
  agents, 10–27
  best practices, 10–18–10–31
  case studies, 10–06–10–17
  contractual protections, 10–29–10–30
  recusal certificates, 10–29
  reports, 10–02, 10–27
  reputation damage, 10–29
  reviews, 10–27–10–28
  risk assessment, 10–02, 10–04, 10–21–
    10–26
  successor liability, 10–32
  tailored review, 10–27
El Paso and Coastal Corporation, 10–15
employees, discipline and dismissal of,
  10–31
export of compliance program onto target
  company, 10–30
fines, 10–07, 10–10–10–11, 10–18, 10–31
Foreign Corrupt Practices Act 1977,
  best practices for compliance program,
    10–18–10–31
  case studies, 10–06–10–17
  contractual provisions, 10–30
  due diligence, 10–07–10–31
  El Paso and Coastal Corporation, 10–
    15
  fines, 10–07, 10–10–10–11, 10–18, 10–
    31
  government interaction, assessing the
    degree of, 10–24
  Halliburton, 10–12–10–13, 10–16–10–
    18
  InVision and General Electric, 10–09
  jurisdiction, 10–04
  Monsanto and Delta & Pine Land
    Company, 10–14
  risk, 10–03

self-reporting, 10–28
Syncor and Cardinal Health, 10–08
Titan and Lockheed, 10–06–10–07
Vetco Gray and ABB, 10–10–10–11,
  10–31
government interaction, assessing the
  degree of, 10–24
guidance, need for accessible, 10–31
Halliburton, 10–12–10–13, 10–16–10–18
human rights abuses, 10–27
indemnities, 10–29
intelligence, assessing the target's
  business, 10–25
interviews, 10–27
InVision and General Electric, 10–09
liability of acquiring company, 10–03
limitation of liability, 10–29–10–30
Monsanto and Delta & Pine Land
  Company, 10–14
nature of business, assessing the, 10–24
recusal certificates, 10–29
red flags, identifying, 10–21–10–27, 10–
  29
reporting, 10–02, 10–27
reputation damage, 10–29
reviews,
  cooperation following reviews, 10–28
  due diligence, 10–27–10–28
  reacting to results, 10–28
risk assessment,
  best practices, 10–21–10–27
  compliance program, assessing the
    target's, 10–26
  country, evaluating the, 10–22, 10–31
  due diligence, 10–02, 10–04, 10–21–
    10–27
  government interaction, assessing
    degree of, 10–24
  intelligence, assessing the target's
    business, 10–25
  nature of business, assessing the, 10–
    24
  red flags, identifying, 10–21–10–27,
    10–29
  tailored review, 10–27
self-reporting, 10–28
senior executives, tone of, 10–31
successor liability, 10–03, 10–09, 10–17,
  10–32
Syncor and Cardinal Health, 10–08
tailored review, 10–27
Titan and Lockheed, 10–06–10–07
tone at the top, 10–31
training and updates, 10–31

Transparency International, 10–22
Vetco Gray and ABB, 10–10–10–11, 10–31
work plans, 10–27–10–28
written codes, 10–31
Mens rea
corporate criminal liability, 1–26
Hong Kong, 6–05
money laundering, 1–27
Public Bodies Corrupt Practices Act 1889, 2–10
Ministers, scandals involving
India, 7–43
Misconduct in public office
common law, 1–04, 6–10
Misfeasance in office
Brazil, 5–05
Misuse of public office
Brazil, 5–03
Mitigation
compliance programs, 11–05
Money laundering
Australia, 4–26
bank secrecy, 8–17
Brazil, 5–37, 5–40
Financial Intelligence Unit, reporting to, 1–28
illicit enrichment, 8–17
India, 7–18–7–19
mens rea, 1–27
Proceeds of Crime Act 2002, 1–27–1–29
regulated financial sector, obligations on, 1–28
reporting suspicions, 1–28
Serious Organised Crime Agency, 1–28
tax havens, 8–17
Monitoring and oversight
case study, 11–20
compliance programs, 11–10, 11–12, 11–19–11–20, 11–26, 11–30
leadership commitment and oversight, 11–12, 11–19–11–20, 11–30
live transactions, software for monitoring, 9–35
OECD Anti-Bribery Convention, 2–24
OECD Working Group, 2–24–2–27
Monsanto and Delta & Pine Land Company
mergers and acquisitions, 10–14
Motivations
forensic and accounting issues, 9–05
Multi-jurisdictional investigations
coordinating responses, 8–64–8–66
Multinationals

Brazil, 5–10
compliance programs, 11–07
OECD Anti-Bribery Convention, 2–15
Mutual assistance
Australia, 4–15, 4–32, 8–06
bank secrecy, 8–18–8–22
Brazil, 5–35, 5–39
categories of country, 1–48
Crime (International Co-operation) Act 2003, 1–47–1–48
definition, 2–22
dual criminality principle, 8–19
Home Office Mutual Assistance Unit, 1–47
Hong Kong, 6–39
investigations, 2–22
KBR & Nigeria LNG, 1–67–1–68
Mutual Legal Assistance Treaties, arrangements under, 1–47
OECD Anti-Bribery Convention, 2–22
Serious Fraud Office, 1–47, 1–74
treaties and conventions, 8–18–8–22
United Kingdom, 1–47–1–48, 1–74, 8–20–8–21
United States, 8–19, 8–21

Naresh Chandra Committee
India, 7–33
National economic interest
Australia, 4–17, 8–06
National security
BAE Systems and Al-Yamamah, 1–02, 1–51, 1–53–1–57
Nationality discrimination
OECD, 2–05
Nationality jurisdiction
Australia, 4–10
Japan, 2–35
OECD Anti-Bribery Convention, 2–19
Natural persons, liability of
OECD Anti-Bribery Convention, 2–18
Negligence
Brazil, 5–13
Non-prosecution agreements (NPAs)
Americanisation of UK anti-corruption efforts, 1–73
Balfour Beatty Plc, 1–62
definition, 1–73
'Not legitimately due' concept
Australia, 4–24

OECD
see Organisation for European

Economic Co-operation
(OECD); OECD Anti-Bribery
Convention; OECD Working
Group
OECD Anti-Bribery Convention
accession, 1–35
Anti-Terrorism, Crime and Security Act
2001, 1–20, 1–25
applicability, 2–18
Argentina, 2–31
Australia, 4–01
BAE Systems, 1–52, 1–56
Brazil, 5–34, 5–36–5–38, 5–40, 5–48–5–
49
Bribery in International Business
Transactions Recommendation, 2–
11–2–12
Chile, 2–32
Commentaries, 2–17
companies, liability of, 2–18
custom, 2–17
definition of a public foreign official, 2–
15
developing countries, 2–10–2–11, 2–15
enforcement, 2–20–2–22
entry into force, 2–13
extraterritoriality, 1–36, 2–10
facilitation payments, 2–17
Foreign Public Corrupt Practices Act
1977, 2–08–2–10, 3–10
France, 2–12
Germany, 2–12
history, 2–08–2–12
Hong Kong, 6–33
implementation, 1–01, 2–24, 2–26–2–42
improper advantage, 2–16, 3–10
international cooperation, 2–22–2–23
investigations, cooperation with, 2–22
Ireland, 2–33–2–34
jurisdiction, 2–19
limitation periods, 2–21
local custom, 2–17
Luxembourg, 2–37
monitoring, 2–24
multinational enterprises, 2–15
mutual legal assistance, 2–22
nationality jurisdiction, 2–19
natural persons, liability of, 2–18
official duties, 2–16
peer review, 2–24
penalties, 2–18
prosecutorial discretion, abuse of, 2–20
public function, definition of, 2–16

foreign public officials (FPOs), bribery
of, 1–38
ratification, 1–35, 2–13
recommendations, 2–11–2–12
Revised Bribery in International Business
Transactions Recommendation, 2–
12–2–13
Spain, 2–38
Tax Recommendation, 2–12
territorial jurisdiction, 2–19
Turkey, 2–39–2–40
United Kingdom, 1–01, 2–41–2–42
United States, 2–08–2–11, 3–10
OECD Working Group
BAE Systems and Al-Yamamah, 2–42
Brazil, 5–48
creation, 2–12, 2–24
education, 2–28–2–29
effectiveness of legislation, examining, 2–
27
foreign public officials, bribery of, 1–36,
2–12
implementation of OECD Anti-Bribery
Convention, 2–24–2–42
information, dissemination of, 2–28
interviews, 2–27
Investment Committee, 2–25
lenient penalties, 2–28
mandate, 2–25
monitoring, 2–24–2–27
mutual assistance, 2–25
penalties, 2–28–2–29
Phase I, 2–26, 2–28, 2–41
Phase II, 2–27, 2–28–2–29, 2–35, 2–37,
2–39
questionnaires, 2–26, 2–27
reports, 2–26–2–28, 2–30–2–42
resource, allocation, 2–28
Revised Recommendation, 2–26
self-evaluation, 2–24
whistleblowers, protection of, 2–29
Officers
see **Directors and officers**
Officials, bribery of
see **Foreign public officials (FPOs),
bribery of**
Oil for Food Programme
see **Iraq Oil for Food Programme**
Optical character recognition
data collection and preservation, 9–14
**Organisation for European Economic
Co-operation (OECD)**
see also **OECD Anti-Bribery**

Convention; OECD Working Group
accession, 2–05–2–06
background, 2–01
Code of Liberalisation of Capital Movements, 2–05
Code of Liberalisation of Current Invisible Operations, 2–05
Committees, 2–04, 2–05
Council, 2–04
functions, 2–01, 2–07
global partners, 2–06
governing bodies, 2–04
history, 2–02
international organisations, agreements with, 2–06
Investment Committee, 2–06
legal instruments, 2–07
Marshall Plan, 2–02
membership, 2–05–2–06
monitoring, 2–07
nationality discrimination, 2–05
Organisation for European Economic Co-operation (OEEC), 2–02
origins, 2–01
peer review process, 2–07
purpose, 2–03
Secretariat, 2–04, 2–07
staff, 2–04
standards, 2–07
structure, 2–04
tax havens, black list of, 8–17
Organised crime
UN Convention against Transnational Organised Crime, 7–16
Oversight
see Monitoring and oversight

Parents and subsidiaries
ethics policies, 1–39
liability, 1–39
Partners
compliance programs, 11 11–12, 11–25–11–26
Passive bribery or corruption
Brazil, 5–27–5–29
Bribery Act 2010, 1–38
Hong Kong, 6–06
improper performance, concept of, 1–38
Public Bodies Corrupt Practices Act 1889, 1–06
Peer review
OECD, 2–07, 2–24

Penalties and sanctions
see also Civil liability and sanctions; Civil recovery orders (CROs); Fines; Imprisonment; Sentencing
administrative sanctions, 4–13
Australia, 4–12–4–15
Brazil, 5–01, 5–11–5–12, 5–15–5–17, 5–24–5–30, 5–33, 5–43–5–44, 5–53
Foreign Corrupt Practices Act 1977, 3–05, 3–29, 3–43, 3–48
foreign public officials, bribery of, 4–12–4–15
Hong Kong, 6–19, 6–26–6–29
immunity, 8–46
India, 7–10, 7–12–7–14
internal regulatory investigations in United States, cooperation with, 8–11, 8–70
legal persons, 2–38
mitigation, 8–11
OECD Anti-Bribery Convention, 2–18
OECD Working Group, 2–28–2–29
Public Bodies Corrupt Practices Act 1889, 1–11
severity, 8–70
Performance management
compliance programs, 11–27
Phase I obligations under OECD Anti-Bribery Convention
OECD Working Group, 2–26, 2–28, 2–41
United Kingdom, 2–41
Phase II obligations under OECD Anti-Bribery Convention
Japan, 2–35
Luxembourg, 2–37
OECD Working Group, 2–27, 2–28–2–29
Turkey, 2–39
Plans
best practices, 10–27–10–28
books and records, 9–24
forensic and accounting issues, 9–03, 9–04–9–10, 9–43
interviews, 9–06, 9–18
mergers and acquisitions, 10–27–10–28
project planning, 11–32
Plea agreements
Americanisation of UK anti-corruption efforts, 1–72
BAE Systems and Al-Yamamah, 1–58–1–60
guidance, 1–49–1–50

internal regulatory investigations in
  United States, cooperation with, 8–
  67, 8–69
Mabey & Johnson Ltd, 1–49–1–50, 1–72
Serious Fraud Office, 1–49–1–50, 1–72,
  2–42
Police
Australia, 4–17–4–19, 8–06
City of London Police Overseas Anti-
  Corruption Unit, 1–46
government entities, cooperation with,
  4–17–4–18, 8–06
Hong Kong, 6–02, 6–37
India, 7–02
Political parties or candidates
Foreign Corrupt Practices Act 1977, 3–
  25
Hong Kong, 6–28
India, 7–22
Power point presentations
Foreign Corrupt Practices Act 1977, 9–
  42
Preservation of data
see **Data collection and preservation**
Presumption of corruption
Anti-Terrorism, Crime and Security Act
  2002, 1–24
**Prevent bribery, failure of commercial
  organisations to**
adequate procedures, defence of, 1–38–
  1–39
associated persons, 1–38
Bribery Act 2010, 1–38
corporate criminal liability, 1–26
guidance, 1–38
jurisdiction, 1–38
safe harbour, 1–38
vicarious liability, 1–38
**Prevention of Corruption Act 1906
  (United Kingdom)**
agent/principal concept, 1–03, 1–12, 1–
  13, 1–17
corruptly, meaning of, 1–14
employees, 1–13
false statements, 1–15
foreign public officials, 1–13
intermediaries, 1–13
Law Commission, 1–13, 1–17
scope, 1–13
sentencing, 1–16
**Prevention of Corruption Act 1916
  (United Kingdom)**
burden of proof, reversal of, 1–18–1–19
fair hearing, right to a, 1–18

local authorities, 1–18
public body, definition of, 1–18
public bodies, 1–19
scope, 1–18
Principles-based approach
compliance programs, 11–10
Privacy
forensic and accounting issues, 9–22
freedom of information, 9–22
Regulation of Investigatory Powers Act
  2000 (United States), 9–22
surveillance, authorisation of, 9–22
**Private interests by public officials,
  furthering of**
Brazil, 5–30–5–31
**Private parties, acts of corruption
  carried out by**
Brazil, 5–32–5–33
Private sector
see also **Companies**
Hong Kong, 6–09, 6–38
Public Bodies Corrupt Practices Act
  1889, 1–09
Privilege against self-incrimination
internal investigations, conduct of, 8–44
Serious Fraud Office, 1–44
Procurement
see **Public procurement contracts,
  debarment from**
Programs
see **Compliance programs**
Project planning
compliance programs, 11–32
Promises to pay
Foreign Corrupt Practices Act 1977, 3–
  22
Proportionality
compliance programs, 11–10
Prosecutions
see also **Deferred prosecution
  agreements**
Americanisation of UK anti-corruption
  efforts, 1–73
Attorney General's consent, 1–40
centralisation, 8–03
City of London Police Overseas Anti-
  Corruption Unit, 1–46
civil recovery orders, 1–33
consent, 6–25, 6–36
criteria, 8–12
declination, 8–08, 8–68, 8–70–8–71
Department of Justice, 8–03, 8–08
discretion, 2–20, 8–67–8–77

Foreign Corrupt Practices Act 1977, 8–03

foreign public officials, bribery of, 4–11

Hong Kong, 6–17–6–21, 6–25, 6–34, 6–36

internal regulatory investigations in United States, cooperation with, 8–03, 8–08, 8–12, 8–67–8–78

Japan, 2–36

non-prosecution agreements, 1–62, 1–73

OECD Anti-Bribery Convention, 2–20

Serious Fraud Office, 1–41, 8–05

United Kingdom, 1–01, 1–40, 1–46, 1–73, 2–41, 8–05

Public awareness and education

Hong Kong, 6–29, 6–32, 6–37

informants, 6–29

OECD Working Group, 2–28–2–29

Turkey, 2–39

Public Bodies Corrupt Practices Act 1889 (United Kingdom)

active bribery, 1–06

agents, 1–09

corruptly, meaning of, 1–10

criminalization, 1–03

Crown servants, 1–09

inducement or reward, 1–07

Law Commission, 1–09

local public bodies, definition of, 1–08

mens rea, 1–10

passive bribery, 1–06

penalties, 1–11

private sector, 1–09

public body, definition of, 1–08

public office, definition of, 1–08

scope, 1–09

sentencing, 1–11

Public interest

BAE Systems and Al-Yamamah, 1–51, 1–53–1–54, 1–57

Hong Kong, 6–36

Innospec Ltd, 1–66

Public officials, bribery of

see also **Foreign public officials (FPOs), bribery of**

definition of public official, 1–08, 3–24–3–25, 5–03, 5–38, 7–05

international organisations, 3–24–3–25

misconduct in public office, 1–04, 6–10

misfeasance in office, 5–05

misuse of public office, 5–03

private interests by public officials, furthering of, 5–30–5–31

Public procurement contracts, debarment from

discretion, 1–34

economic operators, 1–34

Mabey & Johnson Ltd, 1–50

Public Procurement Directive, 1–34

self-reporting, 1–34, 1–50

Public relations

Hong Kong, 6–32

Publicity

see also **Public awareness and education**

deferred prosecution agreements, 8–72

Questionnaires

OECD Working Group, 2–26, 2–27

Reasonable and bona fide expenditures

defence, 3–09, 3–35

Records

see **Books and records**

Recusal certificates

mergers and acquisitions, 10–29

Red flags, identifying

mergers and acquisitions, 10–21–10–27, 10–29

Regulators

see also **particular regulators (eg Financial Services Authority (FSA)(United Kingdom))**

cooperation, 8–10–8–15

internal investigations, conduct of, 8–01–8–16, 8–36–8–37

self-regulatory authorities, 8–09

Remote capture

electronic data, 9–16

Reporting

see also **Self-reporting**

Australia, 4–17, 8–06

books and records, 9–25, 9–43

compliance programs, 11–12, 11–16

deterrence, sentencing as a, 1–31

due diligence, 10–02, 10–27

facilitation payments, 3–39

Financial Intelligence Unit, reporting to, 1–28

Foreign Corrupt Practices Act 1977, 3–39

forensic and accounting issues, 9–01, 9–03

gas analysis and reporting, 11–16

Hong Kong, 6–29, 6–32

issue reporting, 9–25

mergers and acquisitions, 10–02, 10–27
money laundering, 1–28
OECD Working Group, 2–28
sentencing, 1–31
Reputation damage
mergers and acquisitions, 10–29
stigma, 3–48, 8–72, 8–76
Resources
adequacy, 11–31
compliance programs, 11–31
OECD Working Group, 2–28
Serious Fraud Office, 1–74
Restitution
internal regulatory investigations in
    United States, cooperation with, 8–
    13
Reviews
best practices, 10–27–10–28
compliance programs, 11–12
cooperation, 10–28
due diligence, 10–27–10–28
Foreign Corrupt Practices Act 1977, 3–
    49–3–51
mergers and acquisitions, 10–27–10–28
peer review, 2–07, 2–24
reacting to results, 10–28
Rhine Ruhr Pty Ltd
Australia, 4–29
Rio Tinto Ltd
Australia, 4–30–4–31
Risk
see also **Risk assessment**
compliance programs, 11–08, 11–12, 11–
    15–11–16
Foreign Corrupt Practices Act 1977, 10–
    03
forensic and accounting issues, 9–08–9–
    10
high risk transactions, 9–10, 9–27
industry sectors at risk, 9–08
who is at risk, 9–08–9–09
Risk assessment
best practices, 10–21–10–27
compliance programs, 10–02, 10–04, 10–
    21–10–26, 11–08, 11–12, 11–15–11–
    16
country, evaluating the, 10–22, 10–31
due diligence, 10–02, 10–04, 10–21–10–
    27
ethics, 11–12, 11–16
government interaction, assessing the
    degree of, 10–24
intelligence, assessing the target's
    business, 10–25

mergers and acquisitions, 10–02, 10–04,
    10–21–10–27, 10–29
nature of business, assessing the, 10–24
red flags, identifying, 10–21–10–27, 10–
    29
tailored review, 10–27
Routine government action
Australia, 4–07
definition, 3–30
facilitation payments, 3–09, 3–30–3–32
Foreign Corrupt Practices Act 1977, 3–
    09, 3–30–3–32

Safe harbour
Bribery Act 2010, 1–38
foreign public officials (FPOs), bribery
    of, 1–38
prevent bribery, failure of commercial
    organisations to, 1–38
Scanning
data collection and preservation, 9–14
Seaboard Report
internal regulatory investigations in
    United States, cooperation with, 8–
    14
Searches
Australia, 4–15
search terms for electronic data, 9–34
Serious Fraud Office, 1–45
warrants, 1–45
SEC
see **Securities and Exchange
    Commission (SEC) (United
    States)**
Secrecy
see **Bank secrecy**
**Securities and Exchange Commission
    (SEC) (United States)**
accounting, 3–46
Department of Justice, referrals to, 8–08,
    8–66
enforcement, 8–04
Foreign Corrupt Practices Act 1977, 3–
    02–3–05, 3–14–3–15, 3–37, 3–44–3–
    52, 8–02, 8–04, 8–08
internal regulatory investigations,
    cooperation with, 8–02, 8–04, 8–10–
    8–11, 8–14, 8–35, 8–63, 8–66
investigations, 8–04, 8–08
Seaboard Report (SEC), 8–14
Siemens, 8–64–8–66
waiver of privileges and protections from
    disclosure, 8–63

whistleblowing, 9–25
Securities trading
  Foreign Corrupt Practices Act 1977, 3–13, 3–15
Seizure
  Australia, 4–15
  Brazil, 5–18–5–21, 5–26
  data collection and preservation, 9–17
  Hong Kong, 6–11
  India, 7–17
Self-incrimination, privilege against
  internal investigations, conduct of, 8–44
  Serious Fraud Office, 1–44
Self-regulatory authorities
  internal investigations, conduct of, 8–09
Self-reporting
  AMEC, 1–63
  Balfour Beatty Plc, 1–61–1–62
  books and records, 9–42
  Foreign Corrupt Practices Act 1977, 8–08, 9–42, 10–28
  internal regulatory investigations in United States, cooperation with, 8–08, 8–12, 8–14, 8–35
  Mabey & Johnson Ltd, 1–50
  mergers and acquisitions, 10–29
  OECD Working Group, 2–24
  power point presentations, 9–42
  procurement, debarment from, 1–34, 1–50
  Serious Fraud Office, 1–42
Senior management
  compliance programs, 10–31, 11–19–11–20
  leadership commitment and oversight, 11–12, 11–19–11–20, 11–30
  mergers and acquisitions, 10–31
  tone at the top, 10–31
Sentencing
  see also **Fines; Imprisonment; Penalties and sanctions**
  Bribery Act 2010, 1–40
  guidance, 11–05, 11–09
  Prevention of Corruption Act 1906, 1–16
  Public Bodies Corrupt Practices Act 1889, 1–11
  reporting, deterrent to, 1–31
  United States, 11–05, 11–09, 11–24
Serious Fraud Office (SFO) (United Kingdom)
  acceptance of cases, aims and criteria for, 1–43
  AMEC, 1–42, 1–63
  amount of money involved, 1–43, 8–05

Anti-Corruption Domain, 1–42
Attorney-General, 1–42
BAE Systems and Al-Yamamah, 1–51–1–53, 1–55–1–60
Balfour Beatty Plc, 1–42, 1–61–1–62
City of London Police Overseas Anti-Corruption Unit, 1–46
civil recovery orders, 1–32–1–33, 1–42, 8–77
compliance programs, 11–09
compulsion, evidence obtained by, 1–44
confidentiality, 1–44
control systems, 1–70–1–71
deferred prosecution agreements, 1–62
Director, 1–42
enforcement, 1–70–1–71, 8–05
evidence,
  compulsion, evidence obtained by, 1–44
  powers, 1–44
falsifying, cancelling or destroying documents, 1–44
Financial Services Authority, 1–74
foreign public officials, 2–42
Innospec Ltd, 1–64–1–66
internal investigations, conduct of, 8 8–05, 8–77
international dimension, cases with, 1–43
interviews under caution, 1–44
investigations, 1–41, 1–44, 1–61–1–62, 1–74, 8–05
KBR & Nigeria LNG, 1–67–1–68
Mabey & Johnson Ltd, 1–49–1–50
mutual assistance, 1–74
national publicity, 1–43
non-prosecution agreements, 1–62
plea bargaining, 1–49–1–50, 1–72, 2–42
prosecutions, 1–41, 8–05
public concern, 1–43, 8–05
publicity, 1–43, 8–05
reasonableness, 1–42
resources, increase in, 1–74
search warrants, 1–45
section 2 powers, 1–44–1–45, 8–05
self-incrimination, privilege against, 1–44
self-reporting, 1–42
serious or complex fraud, 1–44–1–45, 8–05
staff, 1–42, 1–74
strategy, change in, 1–62
systems and control enforcement, 1–70–1–71
Tumukunde & Tobiasen, 1–69

Serious Organised Crime Agency (SOCA)
money laundering, 1–28

Settlements
AMEC, 1–63
Balfour Beatty Plc, 1–62
Brazil, 5–07
Innospec Ltd, 1–64–1–66
Mabey & Johnson Ltd, 1–49–1–50

SFO
see **Serious Fraud Office (SFO) (United Kingdom)**

Shawcross exercise
BAE Systems and Al-Yamamah, 1–51

Siemens
bank secrecy, 8–28–8–29
Department of Justice, 8–64–8–66
Germany, 8–28–8–29, 8–64–8–66
institutionalized corruption, 8–28–8–29
internal regulatory investigations, cooperation with, 8–64–8–66

Site visits
forensic and accounting issues, 9–07

Slush funds
Foreign Corrupt Practices Act 1977, 3–02–3–03

Software
books and records, 9–33–9–35
live transactions, monitoring, 9–35

Solicitation
Brazil, 5–27

South Africa
blocking statutes, 8–30

Spain
accessorial sanctions, 2–38
legal persons, sanctions for, 2–38
OECD Anti-Bribery Convention, report of implementation of, 2–38

Stakeholders
communication, 11–36
compliance programs, 11–04, 11–36
credibility, retaining, 11–04

Standard of living
Hong Kong, 6–08, 6–18

Stigma
deferred prosecution agreements, 8–72, 8–76
Foreign Corrupt Practices Act 1977, 3–48

Strict liability
adequate procedures, 1–38
Brazil, 5–13
foreign public officials (FPOs), bribery of, 1–38

Subsidiaries
Foreign Corrupt Practices Act 1977, 3–38
foreign subsidiaries, 3–39
parents and subsidiaries, 1–39

Successor liability
due diligence, 10–32
mergers and acquisitions, 10–03, 10–09, 10–17, 10–32

Surveillance
Hong Kong, 6–16
Regulation of Investigatory Powers Act 2000, 9–22

Sustainable business conduct
compliance programs, 11–12, 11–29

Switzerland
bank secrecy, 8–16, 8–23

Syncor and Cardinal Health
mergers and acquisitions, 10–08

Systems and control enforcement
Aon Ltd, 1–70–1–71
fines, 1–71
Serious Fraud Office, 1–70–1–71

Tailored principles
best practices, 10–27
compliance programs, 11–10, 11–12
due diligence, 10–27
mergers and acquisitions, 10–27

Tax
bank secrecy, 8–23–8–25
evasion, 8–23–8–25
France 2–12
Germany, 2–12
havens, 8–17, 8–26–8–29
Hong Kong, 6–13, 6–15
OECD black list, 8–27
OECD Anti-Bribery Convention, 2–12
UN General Assembly resolutions, 8–27

Tenders
books and records, 9–32

Territorial jurisdiction
Australia, 4–10–4–11, 4–15
India, 7–13, 7–14, 7–18
Japan, 2–36
OECD Anti-Bribery Convention, 2–19
United Kingdom, 2–41

Third parties
books and records, 9–41
compliance programs, 11–25–11–26
data collection and preservation, 9–14
whistleblowing, 9–41

Thompson Memo
  deferred prosecution agreements, 8–73–
    8–74
Time limits
  see Limitation periods
Titan and Lockheed
  mergers and acquisitions, 10–06–10–07
Tone at the top
  mergers and acquisitions, 10–31
Training
  behaviour modification, 11–12
  case study, 11–37
  compliance programs, 10–31, 11–12, 11–
    21, 11–33–11–34, 11–37
  mergers and acquisitions, 10–31
Transactions
  books and records, 9–29
  high risk transactions, examining, 9–27
Transparency
  bank secrecy, 8–18
  compliance programs, 11–10, 11–26
  India, 7–20
Transparency International
  see Corruption Perception Index
    (Transparency International)
Travel, payments for
  Foreign Corrupt Practices Act 1977, 3–
    35
Treaties and conventions
  see also OECD Anti-Bribery
    Convention; UN Convention
    against Corruption
  Brazil, 5–34–5–39
  Hague Evidence Convention, 8–31
  India, 7–16–7–23
  Inter-American Convention against
    Corruption (OAS), 5–34–5–38, 5–
    40, 5–48–5–49
  mutual assistance, 8–19–8–22
  UN Convention against Transnational
    Organised Crime, 7–16
Trivial amounts
  common law, 1–04
Tumukunde & Tobiasen
  investigations, 1–69
  Overseas Anti-Corruption Unit, 1–69
  Serious Fraud Office, 1–69
Turkey
  awareness raising, 2–39
  corporate liability, 2–40
  Iraq Oil-for-Food Programme, 2–39–2–
    40
  OECD Anti-Bribery Convention, report
    of implementation of, 2–39–2–40

Phase II obligations, 2–39

UBS
  bank secrecy, 8–23–8–25
UN Convention against Corruption
  Australia, 4–32–4–33
  Brazil, 5–34, 5–38–5–39, 5–48–5–49
  enforcement, 5–40
  Foreign Corrupt Practices Act 1977, 3–
    10
  foreign public official, definition of, 5–38
  Hong Kong, 6–39
  public official, definition of, 5–38
Unexplained property, offence of
  possession of
  Hong Kong, 6–07–6–08, 6–17–6–18, 6–
    26
United Kingdom
  see also Bribery Act 2010 (United
    Kingdom); Civil recovery
    orders; Serious Fraud Office
    (SFO) (United Kingdom)
  Americanisation of UK anti-corruption
    efforts, 1–72–1–73
  anti-corruption law,
  Anti-Terrorism, Crime and Security Act
    2002, 1–05, 1–20–1–25, 2–41
  Attorney General, 1–32, 1–40, 1–42, 1–
    51–1–54, 2–41
  bank secrecy, 8–20
  City of London Police Overseas Anti-
    Corruption Unit, 1–46
  common law, 1–03–1–05
  corporate criminal liability, 1–26
  Crime (International Co-operation) Act
    2003, 1–47–1–48
  criminalization, 1–03
  current state of law, 1–01–1–02
  definition of bribery, 1–04
  extraterritoriality, 2–41
  Financial Services Authority, 1–70–1–74
  foreign public officials, bribery of, 1–05,
    1–38
  investigations, unsatisfactory record of,
    1–01, 2–41
  Law Commission, 1–09, 1–13, 1–17, 1–
    38, 2–42
  misconduct in public office, 1–04
  mutual assistance treaties, 8–20–8–21
  OECD Anti-Bribery Convention,
    implementation, 1–01, 2–41–2–42
  Phase I obligations, 2–41
  report on implementation, 2–41–2–42

Phase I obligations, 2–41
Prevention of Corruption Act 1906, 1–03, 1–12–1–17
Prevention of Corruption Act 1916, 1–17–1–19
principal consent as defence, 2–41
Public Bodies Corrupt Practices Act 1889, 1–03, 1–06–1–11
public procurement contracts, debarment from, 1–34, 1–50
prosecutions, unsatisfactory record of, 1–01, 2–41
Regulation of Investigatory Powers Act 2000, 9–22
Serious Organised Crime Agency, 1–28
surveillance, authorisation of, 9–22
territorial jurisdiction, 2–41
trivial amounts, 1–04
whistleblowing, 9–25
United Nations (UN)
see also **UN Convention against Corruption**
Australia, 4–21, 4–24
Convention against Transnational Organised Crime, 7–16
resolutions, 4–21, 4–24, 8–27
tax havens, resolution on, 8–27
United States
see also **Department of Justice (United States); Foreign Corrupt Practices Act 1977 (United States); Internal investigations in United States, conduct of; Securities and Exchange Commission (SEC) (United States)**
abusive discovery, 8–31
Americanisation of UK anti-corruption efforts, 1–72–1–73
Attorneys, 8–03, 8–72
bank secrecy, 8–19, 8–21, 8–23–8–25
blocking statutes, 8–30, 8–32
complaints, 8–11
compliance programs, 8–12–8–13, 11–05, 11–09, 11–24
conviction rate, 1–72
credit for cooperation, 8–12, 8–14–8–15
disciplinary measures, 8–13
disclosure, 8–12, 8–31–8–33
Filip Memorandum, 8–12–8–13
forensic and accounting issues, 9–06
Hague Evidence Convention, 8–31
hardship, 8–33
international discovery, 8–32–8–33
interviews, 9–06
McNulty Memorandum, 8–12
mutual legal assistance treaties, 8–19, 8–21
foreign public officials (FPOs), bribery of, 1–38
remedial actions, 8–13–8–14
restitution, 8–13
SARBOX protection, 9–25
Seaboard Report (SEC), 8–14
Securities and Exchange Commission, 8–10–8–11, 8–14
self-reporting, 8–12, 8–14
sentencing guidelines, 11–05, 11–09, 11–24
triggers for investigations, 8–11
UBS, 8–23–8–25
United Kingdom, 1–72–1–73, 8–21
UA Attorneys, 8–03, 8–72
UPJOHN style warnings, 9–06
whistleblowing, 9–25, 11–24
Unjust enrichment
Brazil, 5–19, 5–34
money laundering, 8–17
UPJOHN style warnings
forensic and accounting issues, 9–06

Value, payment of anything
Foreign Corrupt Practices Act 1977, 3–22
India, 7–08
valuable thing without consideration, public servant obtaining, 7–08
Vetco Gray and ABB
mergers and acquisitions, 10–10–10–11, 10–31
Verification
books and records, 9–42
forensic and accounting issues, 9–03
Vicarious liability
prevent bribery, failure of commercial organisations to, 1–38
Vineet Narain Case
India, 7–35
VK Krishna Menon Scandal
India, 7–38

Watergate scandal
Foreign Corrupt Practices Act 1977, 3–02
internal regulatory investigations, cooperation with, 8–34

Whistleblowing
Australia, 4–20
books and records, 9–25–9–26, 9–41
Brazil, 5–34
compliance programs, 11–05, 11–09, 11–24
employees, 8–07, 8–48
forensic and accounting issues, 9–04
India, 7–04, 7–20, 7–29
internal investigations, conduct of, 8–07, 8–48
OECD Working Group, 2–29
protection, 9–25
Securities and Exchange Commission, 9–25
third parties, 9–41
United Kingdom, 9–25
United States, 9–25, 11–24
Wilful misconduct
Brazil, 5–13

Witnesses
anonymity, 9–18
books and records, 9–25–9–26
corroboration, 9–18
data collection and preservation, 9–18–9–20
evidence, 9–18–9–20
Hong Kong, 6–17, 6–22–6–25, 6–31
informants, 6–30–6–31
internal investigations, conduct of, 8–43–8–46
interview planning, 9–18
protection, 6–22–6–25, 6–31
statements, 6–17, 9–18
Work conduct privilege
deferred prosecution agreements, 8–75
Written laws of country, payments are lawful under
Australia, 4–06, 4–26
Foreign Corrupt Practices Act 1977, 3–09, 3–33—3–34